Milles. *Europa and the Bull.* (Bronze study) 1926. Worcester Art Museum, Worcester, Mass.

THE LANGUAGE
OF ART

PHILIP C. BEAM

Bowdoin College

The Ronald Press Company · New York

Library of Congress Catalog Card Number: 58–6055

PRINTED IN THE UNITED STATES OF AMERICA

To

CHANDLER RATHFON POST

and

PAUL JOSEPH SACHS

great teachers and staunch friends

Preface

Art books in a specialized age are generally written with emphasis on one of three main approaches—philosophical, historical, or technical—and allow only passing notice of the other two.

For the reader beginning a study of the whole of art, sudden immersion into one of these—say, philosophy—without a leavening of historical information and some treatment of technique is likely to be more confusing than helpful or exciting. And there is so much material to be covered by a strictly historical approach to man's art that no single chronological volume can do much more than scratch the surface.

On the other hand, the *principles* discoverable in all works of art are more manageable in a single work. They are relatively few. They can be set down and discussed, and they can be illustrated by the juxtaposition of works from many locations in the long gallery of human artistic production. Being few enough to be remembered easily and understood, principles can be transferred to new experiences in art.

The nonartist who has been smothered in an avalanche of facts without understanding of the fundamental, universal principles can parrot stereotyped criticism when he is confronted with a thoroughly familiar painting or piece of sculpture in a museum. But, faced with an unfamiliar work, he is likely to be helpless—unable to interpret coherently even to himself the impact the work may have on him. One can test the sad validity of this point by watching and listening to viewers he meets in the Museum of Modern Art in New York or even in the Uffizi, the Louvre, or the Rijksmuseum.

This book, then, gives the reader an opportunity to survey the field of art as comprehensively as possible by studying some of the main principles that have underlain artistic expression for centuries and note some current theories about them.

Part I treats and illustrates the nature of art; Part II deals with its methods and content; Part III sketches these subjects in some perspective on the canvas of history and geography and discusses the factor of the individual as artist. The appendix furnishes an outline of art history which supplements both the text and the extensive bibliography.

Throughout this book it has been necessary to illustrate each broad idea or general principle with only a few reproductions. No one of these is to be construed as the only possible example in existence, or even the greatest. Each is meant primarily to illustrate a type or an idea. Numerous other examples could be cited. If the reader remembers this, he can supplement these introductory examples with others from his own experience almost indefinitely, without confusion.

I am indebted to many people in a way that has bearing on this book. To my teachers in the Department of Fine Arts of Harvard—in and out of class—I owe much. My debt to Arthur Pope, professor emeritus, is inestimable, and the point of view expressed here reflects much of his teaching.

From countless discussions of the nature of art with my students and colleagues, and from innumerable visits to museums and exhibitions with friends, I have learned things about works of art that I should not have seen on my own.

Encouragement is no small factor in the long task of writing a book, and it was offered abundantly by Chandler R. Post, Alston H. Chase, Thomas C. Means, Carl N. Schmalz, Jr., Albert S. Roe, James W. Fowle, Thomas A. Riley, Samuel A. Ladd, Jr., and my wife Frances M. Beam. For their constancy of interest I am grateful. The Librarian of Bowdoin College, Kenneth Boyer, helped me in many valuable ways, as did the President of the College, James S. Coles, who aided me both officially and personally.

Four friends assisted me in a way that can never be fully measured or repaid. Alfred H. Fenton read and helped me virtually to rewrite the first fourteen chapters. Professor Arthur LeRoy Greason and Stephen E. Merrill, a distinguished lecturer and photographer, read the manuscript in its entirety and generously showed me many ways to improve it. Both left their mark on style and clarification of ideas throughout. Miss Gertrude Plaisted did much more than type the manuscript in both draft and final forms; she worked tirelessly to make it as free of errors as possible.

PHILIP C. BEAM

Brunswick, Maine
   February, 1958

Acknowledgments

Acknowledgment is hereby made to the persons and institutions listed below for permission to reproduce material in the figures indicated:

Albright Art Gallery, Buffalo: Figure 275.

Alinari, Florence, and Art Reference Bureau, New York: Figures 46, 47, 51, 62, 64, 66, 75, 79, 85b, 87, 88, 101, 102a, 108, 109, 110, 121, 125, 126, 133, 134, 166, 167, 175, 181, 188, 207, 214, 224, 225, 244, 254, 255, 256, 259a, 263, 271, 272, 273, 282, 291, 295, 300, 306, 310, 312, 315, 321, 324, 325, 326, 329, 331, 332, 344, 354, 357, 358, 363, 382, 392, 394, 397, 398, 403, 406, 410, 416, 419, 426, 427.

Anderson, Rome: Figures 59, 85a, 85c, 94, 99, 104, 105, 106, 128, 136, 165, 168, 177, 183, 197, 245, 253, 257, 264, 270, 305, 351, 352, 359, 371, 380, 393, 399, 400, 411, 413, 414, 417, 422, 431, 434.

Archives Centrales Iconographiques d'Art National, Brussels: Figure 231.

Archives Photographiques d'Art et d'Histoire, Paris: Figures 31, 311.

Art Institute of Chicago: Figures 13, 15, 40, 96, 123, 141, 226, 302, 328, 345, 346, 362, 368.

Athene Magazine, Chicago: Figure 50.

The Barnes Foundation, Merion, Pa.: Figures 42, 43. Reproduced by courtesy of The Barnes Foundation.

Hedrich Blessing Studio, Chicago: Figure 213.

Bowdoin College Museum of Fine Arts, Brunswick, Me.: Figures 72, 84, 113, 186, 198, 204, 241, 265, 294, 309, 336, 361.

Braun & Cie., Paris, and Erich S. Herrmann, Inc., New York: Figures 28, 30, 38, 41, 44, 56, 93, 98, 129, 130, 147, 179, 192, 196, 211, 216, 242, 262, 274a, 279, 284, 293, 298, 299, 308, 319, 335, 378, 408.

The British Museum, London: Figures 58, 67, 111, 267, 286, 356, 370. Reproduced by courtesy of the Trustees of the British Museum, London.

Brooklyn Museum: Figures 137, 155.

F. Bruckmann Verlag, Munich: Figures 32, 353.

Carnegie Institute, Department of Fine Arts, Pittsburgh: Figure 227.

Cleveland Museum of Art: Figures 77, 117, 278, 421.

Compagnie des Arts Photomécaniques, Paris: Figures 180, 206, 339, 435.

Detroit Institute of Arts: Figure 232.

Duell, Sloane & Pierce, Inc., New York: Figure 249. From *In the Nature of Materials.* Copyright 1942 by Frank Lloyd Wright and Henry-Russell Hitchcock.

Dumbarton Oaks Research Library and Collection, Harvard University (Washington, D. C.): Figure 313.

Egyptian National Museum, Cairo: Figure 296.

Essex Institute, Salem, Mass.: Figures 387, 388.

Fogg Museum of Art, Harvard University: Figures 145, 153, 194.

Foto-Marburg: Figures 135, 157, 182, 184, 208, 209, 260, 333, 366a, 405, 407, 409, 412, 415, 418, 423, 433.

The Frick Collection, New York: Figures 266, 287. Copyright, the Frick Collection, New York.

The Isabella Stewart Gardner Museum, Boston: Figures 100, 132, 190, 195, 237.

Mrs. Charles R. Henschel, New York: Figure 119.

The John Herron Art Institute, Indianapolis: Figure 80.
Mrs. Charles L. Homer, Scarborough, Maine: Figures 20, 60.
S. C. Johnson & Son, Inc., Racine, Wisconsin: Figures 86a, 86b.
William Taylor McKeown, New York: Figure 26.
The Macmillan Co., New York: Figure 430. From Roos, *Illustrated Handbook of Art History* (1954), p. 57A.
Stephen Merrill, Brunswick, Maine: Figures 14, 37, 186.
Metropolitan Museum of Art, New York: Figures 6, 18, 19, 27, 36, 39, 103, 116, 120, 124, 164, 169, 189, 217, 219, 277, 280, 303, 304, 307, 314, 342, 343, 355, 367, 404.
William P. Morgan, Lynn, Massachusetts: Figure 48.
The Pierpont Morgan Library, New York: Figure 49.
William H. Muir, Stonington, Maine: Figures 185, 186.
Musée Guimet, Paris: Figure 172.
Museum of Fine Arts, Boston: Figures 2, 4, 11, 22, 25, 34, 52, 61, 68, 69, 97, 114, 115, 118, 139, 144, 146, 148, 149, 152, 154, 160, 163, 215, 221, 238, 243, 276, 281, 288, 322, 334, 340, 341, 350, 360, 364, 372, 373, 374, 375, 377.
Museum of Modern Art, New York: Figures 1, 5, 29, 45, 53, 54, 55, 140, 173, 212, 269, 289.
The National Gallery, London: Figures 57, 82, 83, 89, 90, 95, 131, 138, 193, 228, 233, 246, 258a, 301, 318, 320, 327, 349, 365, 396. Reproduced by courtesy of the Trustees, The National Gallery, London.
National Gallery of Art, Washington, D. C.: Figures 127, 151, 158, 191, 199, 200, 297.
National Museum of Art (Ny-Carlsberg Glyptothek), Copenhagen: Figure 65.
Nelson Gallery and Atkins Museum, Kansas City, Missouri: Figures 3, 171, 187, 218, 220, 236, 337.
New Mexico State Tourist Bureau: Figure 389.
Dr. J. Robert Oppenheimer, Princeton, New Jersey: Figure 140.
Pennsylvania Academy of the Fine Arts, Philadelphia: Figure 285.
Philadelphia Museum of Art: Figures 63, 78, 150, 159, 317.
The Phillips Gallery, Washington, D. C.: Figures 9, 70, 76, 316.
Photographie Giraudon, Paris: Figure 402.
Frederick A. Praeger, Inc.: Figures 33, 142. From Maringer and Bandi, *Art in the Ice Age* (1952), figure 82.
G. P. Putnam's Sons, New York: Figure 170. From Meier-Graefe, *The Development of Modern Art* (1908), p. 32.
Rhode Island School of Design, Providence: Figures 107, 283.
Rockefeller Institute for Medical Research, New York: Figure 292.
Santa Barbara (California) Chamber of Commerce: Figure 391.
Walter Scott, Ltd., Bradford, England: Figure 432.
Renée Sintenis, Berlin, Germany: Figure 162.
Skidmore, Owings and Merrill, New York: Figures 71, 178, 251.
Smithsonian Institution, Freer Gallery of Art, Washington, D. C.: Figures 112, 252.
Mr. and Mrs. Alfred Stern: Figure 261.
Mr. and Mrs. Justin K. Thannhauser, New York: Figure 45.
James Thurber and *The New Yorker:* Figure 143. Copyright 1932, James Thurber. Originally published in *The New Yorker.*
University Prints, Cambridge, Mass.: Figures 388, 483, 484.
Mies van der Rohe: Figure 250.
Victoria and Albert Museum, London: Figures 348, 376.
Wadsworth Atheneum, Hartford, Connecticut: Figure 122.
The Walters Art Gallery, Baltimore: Figures 161, 420.
Wallace Collection, London: Figures 290, 347. Reproduced by permission of the Trustees of the Wallace Collection.
George Wittenborn, Inc., New York: Figure 229. From Giedion-Welcker, *Contemporary Sculpture (Documents of Modern Art,* volume 12), p. 101.
Worcester Art Museum, Worcester, Massachusetts: Frontispiece, Figure 379.

Contents

PART I: THE NATURE OF ART

PART II: THE METHODS OF ART

20 THE CONDITIONS OF MAN 592
    The Sex Urge, 593; Romantic Love, 596; Marital Love,
    597; Maternal Love, 600; Benevolence, 602; Confidence,
    602; Modesty, 605; Mental Vitality, 605; Alcoholic Ani-
    mation, 608; Joie de Vivre, 609; Physical Strength, 611;
    Physical Grace, 612; Nervous Vitality, 615; The Repre-
    sentation of Physical, Mental, and Spiritual Illness, 617;
    The Hierarchy of Values, 634.

21 ORGANIZATION OF IDEAS 642
    Finitude and Infinitude of Ideas, 643; Harmony of Ideas,
    649; Sequence of Ideas, 653; Balance of Ideas, 658; Qual-
    ity of Ideas, 661; Disruption of Ideas, 669.

22 COORDINATION OF IDEA AND SPATIAL DESIGN 682
    Harmony of Attitude, 683; Harmony of Measure, 688;
    Harmony of Shape, 695; Harmony of Surface, 699; Se-
    quence of Continuity, Gradation, Alternation, 708; Axial
    and Occult Balance, 712.

23 COORDINATION OF IDEA AND COLOR DESIGN 721
    Harmony of Hues, 722; Harmony of Values, 724; Har-
    mony of Intensities, 726; Sequence of Color: Alteration
    and Gradation, 730; Balance of Color, 733.

24 THE PRINCIPLE OF FITNESS 737

PART III: THE HISTORICAL FACTORS IN ART

25 AN INTRODUCTION TO THE HISTORICAL FACTORS IN ART . . 747
    The Worlds of East and West, 749; Region, 767; Nation-
    ality, 789.

26 PERIOD 801

27 INDIVIDUALITY 843
    The Nature of Individuality, 843; The Universal Signs
    of Individuality, 844; The Specific Signs of Individuality,
    845; The Measure of Individuality, 847; The Historical
    Proofs of Individuality, 851; The Justification of Indi-
    viduality, 854.

    APPENDIX: AN OUTLINE OF ART HISTORY 857

    BIBLIOGRAPHY 907

    INDEX 917

PART I

The Nature of Art

Introduction

The purpose of examining art, as it is conceived here, is to "interpret, clarify, and intensify" our experiences with art and through them our experiences in life. These words of Irwin Edman imply that through art we can gain an aggregate of intellectual, emotional, and spiritual experiences far stronger, clearer, and more sensitive than our own. But we can do this only on one condition. We must be able to *read* the language in which those experiences are expressed.

In the case of the arts studied here, the language is silent and visual. It is, nevertheless, a language in the sense that it is a vehicle contrived by men for two purposes: to express themselves in some more or less permanent medium, and to communicate with other men through signs. As in the case of all languages, an understanding of it must be acquired.

We can easily put this to a test by looking at Fig. 1, an oil painting by Pablo Picasso, *Guernica*. I think we would grant that Picasso probably expressed himself to his own satisfaction; he had had years of professional experience when he painted the picture, and he consented to its public exhibition. Still, those without any previous training in the language of the visual arts fail to understand what he is trying to say. In other words, expression and communication are by no means synonymous and automatic. An artist expresses and we interpret. He sometimes may seem to be speaking an unknown tongue, but that does not mean that he is saying nothing. It merely means that we have not yet learned his language. In the long run we shall see that expression and communication are closely connected, but we shall not be able to understand either without a good deal of study.

3

FIG. 1. Picasso. *Guernica*. May–June, 1937. Collection of the artist.

FIG. 2. *Seated Statue of Khum-Ba-F. ca.* 2725 B.C., V Dynasty. Museum of Fine Arts, Boston.

FIG. 3. *A Lohan.* 10th-11th centuries, Sung Dynasty. Nelson Gallery and Atkins Museum, Kansas City, Mo.

There is an encouraging side to the problem, however. Almost anyone, looking at Fig. 2, can feel at once the dignity, poise, and human warmth of the ancient Egyptian scribe represented. Similarly, we can feel the aloofness of the Chinese *Lohan,* a kind of Buddhist saint, in Fig. 3. We can compare and contrast the two figures intelligently, noting the similarities of posture and the differences in other respects. We can perceive the sturdy massiveness of the one and the elegant linear quality of the other, and we can connect the treatment [or form] of each statue with its content. Moreover, we can do this immediately, or after a relatively short period of training. This is not because anyone can understand the visual arts without effort, but because that effort is facilitated by their immediacy and directness of appeal. The reason for this is not hard to find. It lies in the fact that we have to learn only one universal alphabet and its elements: the lines, masses, textures, and colors which make up the form of pictures, statues, and buildings everywhere are few in number, whereas if we were dealing with written languages the number of alphabets which have come and gone could hardly be counted.

Furthermore, the task is not so formidable as it may have seemed at first, because each of us brings to it a considerable amount of visual experience in life, of the sort that the artist himself draws upon. What is difficult and strange for us in the beginning is the language in which this experience is phrased in works of art. With intelligent application the gap between these two kinds of experience —the common and universal but nonartistic and the artistically expressed—can be narrowed.

CHAPTER 1

The Role of Reality

Man has lived intimately with art from the beginning. Through it he has attempted to capture beauty and to create it, and to express his emotional reactions to the world about him.

On one fact we can all agree: we are surrounded by a vast world that we can neither fully understand nor control. But for centuries human beings have tried to do both: we have tried on our own, and we have sought and given help. This common plight and practice is our strongest social bond.

Not the least cause of our confusion is the character of the visible world, which comes to us through the senses of sight and touch in two ways: directly as sensations and indirectly as potential ideas. In either case the effect is, for the majority of us, only partly clear. More often it is confused, blurred, or meaningless.

In every century a few men have been able to see through the confusion of the natural world and human life more clearly than the rest, and they have created the valid works of art.

So when we ask *What can art do for us?* the answer is *clarify, intensify, and interpret the meaning of reality.* This "reality" actually comprises two worlds: one the spiritual, subjective reality of human consciousness; the other the external world made up of the cosmos and our planet with its mountains, rivers, and trees, the lower animals and physical man; and also all that man has made, including works of art. Since our minds, blank at birth, are only gradually filled by experience, our contact with reality is the objective source of all art. A study of it cannot help shedding some light on the character of art itself. In this chapter we shall concentrate on the nature of the outer world.

Works of art have been described as the products of the reaction

6

of inner reality to the outer world, but the role assigned to art in the interplay of the two realities has been very differently conceived.

THE PROBLEM OF VISUAL CONTROL

The layman usually believes that the function of art is limited to the recording of a ready-made natural beauty or the imitation of natural appearances as accurately as manual skill permits.

The critic, who opposes this view, is also concerned with realism, but a different kind. He is interested in the underlying importance, rather than the surface appearances, of reality, and in the validity of human experience. He holds that the value of a work of art lies in the difference between it and its worldly model. Goethe said, "Art is art because it is not nature," and Paul G. Konody has written, "Art begins where the artist departs from strict imitation of nature, imposing upon her a rhythm [or order] of his own creation, according to his own sense of fitness," [1] a statement so basic that understanding it will carry us far toward the comprehension of all artistic expression. We shall allude to this many times.

When the nature-loving realist asks "What is wrong with copying the outer world as it is when there are moonlit nights, glowing sunsets, and autumn scenes in which all men rejoice?" the critic rejoins that the province of art includes the whole of a reality in which these scenes of natural beauty are exceptional, adding that the layman's view of nature is indiscriminate. Without turning his back upon nature, the critic insists upon the need for artistic transformation. This difference of opinion hinges upon the question of *why* the artist "departs from strict imitation of nature." To answer that we must analyze the character of the visible world and consider honestly its effect upon us.

If we stand upon a mountain peak and survey a panorama of the Swiss Alps at Rigi Kulm (Fig. 7), the first characteristic of nature which strikes us is vastness. Gigantic mountains are lost in the expanse and nothing is outstanding. Yet we are seeing only a fraction of the range. Our whole experience with reality is always fragmentary and piecemeal, a mentally constructed patchwork of what we witness directly, see indirectly through pictures, read or hear about. Even the small part that we know about is difficult to understand in any relation to the whole.

The vastness of the visible world which we attempt to control and understand with limited perceptual means puts us at a disadvantage

1 "Art," *Encyclopædia Britannica*, 16th ed. (1948), II, 441.

from the very beginning. So we tend to move closer to scenes in order to see them in clearer focus. But when we do this we are put at an even greater disadvantage by two other characteristics of the natural scene: profusion and diversity, a superabundance of numbers and kinds.

Two illustrations of this are to be found in Figs. 10 and 12. The first, a photograph of a deep Alpine ravine, shows the effect that different extents of distance have upon the human point of view. Whereas the mountain range at Rigi Kulm was too far away, the inability of our eyes to focus clearly making us want to move closer, here in the ravine we are too close. We can see too much. The vastness of nature has been reduced, but another problem, the amount of detail that we can see clearly, has been enormously increased. To the romantic mind such a jungle growth might symbolize the fertility of nature, and thus have a positive value, but it is visually a perfect example of chaos.

Fig. 12, a photograph of wild tropical ferns, demonstrates the overpowering effect of profusion and diversity on the human eye when we move still closer to the natural scene. A hundred such examples are to be met on any hike through a densely growing wood. They give us an insight into Somerset Maugham's assertion that the jungle forests of the tropical East repel the human soul. Between us and rampant nature there is a profound antipathy, a point we overlook when, among parks and lawns, we forget what wild nature is really like.

Philosophers of art have added to the three descriptive terms *vastness, profusion,* and *diversity,* another set, based upon the observation of dual characteristics in every perceivable universal in reality. The terms, which are grouped in pairs, are *universality* and *individuality, simplicity* and *complexity, continuity* and *change.* All are illustrated by the photograph of waves and rocks (Fig. 16). Both rocks and waves exemplify universality because they are world-wide. Yet they also illustrate individuality, in that no two of the waves or rocks are exactly alike.

Similarly, the ocean is both simple and complex, depending upon the point of view. One may see it as a great plane stretching to the horizon or as a broken, complex surface. The same distinction applies to the rocks, which one can see either as masses and general outlines or rough surfaces and irregular silhouettes.

Both rocks and waves likewise illustrate continuity and change. Through calm and storm the water remains water and the rocks remain rocks, never appearing quite the same yet never changing into something else. This is their continuous character. In visual experience each symbolizes contrasting qualities of continuity and change.

The point to observe here is that pairs of attributes pose the problem of choice. When these pairs of attributes are considered together, individuality, complexity, and change emerge as the ones most likely to cause confusion. Like profusion and diversity, they force themselves upon our attention while obscuring universality, simplicity, and continuity. The complex, rapidly changing waves in the foreground of Fig. 16 undoubtedly catch our eye more quickly than the ocean's simpler and more continuous plane, but they are, for that very reason, the cause of our visual difficulties. It is the old problem of not seeing the forest for the trees.

There is a third way of viewing the interplay of the two realities. A kind of order underlies nature's larger characteristics of time, space, and movement. Any of us can sense a universal orderliness in the cycle of the seasons, the alternation of day and night, and the processional breaking of waves upon a shore. We sense a certain simplicity under the endless complexity. We sense continuity amid all the change. We sense under the individuality of every tree universal characteristics which make its uniqueness within the family of trees only a matter of degree. There is in each of us a philosophic strain which the thinking artist can appeal to, aid, and exploit.

Nature also appears orderly in many of her minute forms—in the smooth roundness of a pebble, in the spiral shell of a snail, or the symmetry of a leaf. Who has not admired one of these, or wondered at the form of a pine cone? Thus at her two extremes, her largest and smallest aspects, nature is orderly to our eyes.

Our difficulty lies in the fact that nature is also chaotic and confusing both in the quantity and arrangement of its details. They are too profuse and diverse, and presented on too vast a scale. From our limited point of view there is too much of nature; there are too many details and too many kinds; and in the natural setting they are jumbled together in a mixture of sizes, shapes, directions, textures, and colors.

Our limited minds and sensory apparatus cannot cope with this quantity and variety in its natural state. The reason is not hard to find: psychologists tell us that our *attention span* can only embrace a few objects at one time. They point to the almost magic appeal of the number three to the universal human mind. That number, of course, can be exceeded indefinitely in art, through organization, but the important fact here is that nature does not so organize its details for our benefit. Following no law of visual harmony that we can discern, it tends to confuse us with excess, like an overdecorated

Christmas tree. To bring order out of chaos, the artist eliminates this troubling confusion by a process of selection.

In the relationship between the two realities, the external world is an inexhaustible source of inspiration for the human imagination, but in its natural state it is only the raw material of art. To imitate it directly on the assumption that one thereby creates a work of art is as illogical as believing that one creates a finished product in steel merely by moving iron ore from one place to another. There is in the raw material of nature no categorical beauty, ugliness, or confusion. These are products of the human mind. Beauty and order, rhythm and unity are, as Konody points out, qualities which the artistic imagination must discover or invent amid the superabundance of artistic raw material.

When the character of reality is thus squarely faced, the critic's emphasis upon the intensification and clarification of visual experience, which is summed up in the word *control*, becomes apparent and the imitative theory of representation fades away.

THE PROBLEM OF UNDERSTANDING

The problem of understanding the meaning of visual experience for human life is, like the problem of control, complicated by popular misconceptions. These obscure and limit the meaning of art and must be cleared away. Their common denominator is wishful thinking.

Lodged deep in the troubled human mind there has always been a yearning to believe that the world was intended to be a beautiful, benign, and orderly environment for mankind. Placed originally in a paradise, man was expelled because of sin. Such wishful thinking, rationalization, and moral penance has been tempered in the course of time, but it still persists in all beliefs in the existence of a consistently and completely acceptable natural beauty. A lingering sense of guilt makes us place the blame for our intellectual shortcomings upon the moral sins of man instead of upon the unavoidable disparity between the tremendously complex outer world and our limited powers of understanding. What is called for is an acceptance of facts; but this is difficult when, at the same time, we wish to believe that God made man in his own image and created the world primarily for man's benefit. When we cannot understand why some natural catastrophe inflicts disaster upon apparently blameless people, we have throughout history blamed hidden sins, Original Sin, or the wrath of the gods, and actually no more convincing explanation has been forthcoming. In our uncertainty we have tried as often to escape natural consequences as we have sought to face them squarely. The history of the human race has been characterized by a simultaneous pursuit after, and flight from, truth. In fleeing truth, people have come to regard art as a refuge in which they might recapture the original beauty of life. Conceiving art as an escape, they have demanded that it limit itself to the representation of that part of experience which is pleasant.

In direct opposition to this retreat into an artistic paradise stand the modern philosopher and scientist. There may be, they assert, a Supreme Intelligence which can see perfect order in the cosmos and perceive that even its apparent faults were introduced for the good of man, but that order and purpose are as yet beyond the range of objective proof or limited human comprehension and can only be presumed on faith. Despite the most strenuous efforts, science has been able to prove only that nature is independent of man and follows its own laws with sublime indifference to the spiritual needs of human life. These laws, which are basically simple, may be reduced in every case to this rule: nature's one and only concern is the procreation and preservation of the species. It is a limited and strictly physical program which is carried out undeviatingly. Inevitably it separates nature and the lower animals from man, for the latter has never been willing to submit entirely to such a lowly role.

The consequences of this difference are inestimable, for out of the desire to live rationally and freely, and to control and understand the world around, as well as to exist, arise the human motivations of art.

The historical origins of the misconceptions of realism and beauty in art are clear. Both had large popular followings in the nineteenth century. Despite the materialism of that century, which manifested itself in an insistence upon visual "realism," critical literature was full of praise for "the ideal," "the noble," "the beautiful," and "the sublime." Each of these visual and conceptual attitudes has a legitimate use, but they are as incompatible as oil and water. Joined together, they produced some of the worst paintings in history when, for instance, the Goddess of Justice was represented with a realism more appropriate to the depiction of a washerwoman. Whatever symbolism was intended was destroyed by the all-too-real flesh of the commonplace girl who was used as a model. At the same time, people who held to this idealistic-realistic contradiction did not hesitate to malign the honest and appropriate realism of Winslow Homer because he represented fishermen, hunters, and other supposedly nonbeautiful themes.

It is this contradiction in terms that our own laity has inherited.

Every teacher of beginners in the subject knows the initial depth of their bias in favor of photographic realism in all artistic representation. Nor can any reader of our major journals miss the numerous letters to the editors which ridicule contemporary art on the premise that art should not only be beautiful but should portray "the beautiful," whatever that may be. Perhaps most ominous is the significance of an incident which combined the realistic-idealistic assumptions. A few years ago a large number of educated men condemned a series of pictures by a passionately expressive and hard-hitting modern painter, and demanded that they be removed from sight. Their most common reasons were that inasmuch as the (or *a*) dictionary stated that art should represent or create beauty, and these pictures were not beautiful, they were, *ipso facto,* not art; they were full of socialist propaganda; they did not look "real" and they represented a hard and ugly side of life. Fortunately, the head of the institution which owned them stood his ground and the pictures were not destroyed. Today they rank high among modern paintings, and hundreds of people go to see them every year.

Much of this confusion is due to shortsightedness. For the art-must-depict-the-beautiful theory excludes too much of the admittedly great. A large proportion of all art has treated grim and tragic themes, the Crucifixion being represented far more often than Paradise or the Garden of Eden. A celebrated series of pictures which is far removed from "the beautiful" is Goya's almost sickening brutal etchings called *The Disasters of War* (Fig. 4). In them war-maddened men behave worse than animals. But few would argue that Goya's *Disasters of War* are not art.

Some other attitudes relating to this problem of "the beautiful" versus "the ugly" can be illustrated with a comparative test. When a class of students was shown Maillol's *Female Torso* (Fig. 5) and Rodin's *Aged Courtesan* (Fig. 6), the immediate response was unanimously in favor of the Maillol. There was general agreement that it is beautiful in both form and content. Everything about it connotes health, strength, youth, and confidence, all that is agreeable in life. Rodin's *Aged Courtesan* was described as being ugly in form and evil and depressing in idea. But as the discussion progressed, a change in tenor developed. It was admitted that an unlimited diet of sweetness and light produces a diminishing return, until the beautiful statue appears almost cloying. The longer the class looked at the *Aged Courtesan,* the more it was impressed by its uncompromising revelation of a side of life which cannot be ignored. Did this mean, the class was asked, that Rodin's statue was truer to life than Maillol's? The answer was the sensible one that they are comple-

FIG. 4. Goya. *With Reason, or Without.* From "The Disasters of War," 1810-1813. Museum of Fine Arts, Boston.

FIG. 5. Maillol. *Female Torso.* 1910. Museum of Modern Art, New York.

FIG. 6. Rodin. *The Aged Courtesan. ca.* 1880. Metropolitan Museum of Art, New York.

mentary; life cannot be fully represented by either, but only by the two together. This is the kind of answer that critics hope for.

It is against narrow and limiting conceptions of art that philosophers and critics stand opposed, not to inveigh against realism per se, but against the belief that any one kind of representation can do justice to a complex visible work or satisfy the human psyche. They demand for the artist the privilege of attempting to interpret every side of life, the harsh and cruel, tragic and sordid, as well as the pleasant and benign.

Of further importance, they point out the practical gains when freedom is allowed. So plentiful, for instance, are the subjects to be found in the natural world that Turner alone painted more than 19,000 landscapes and marines without repeating himself. If he had limited himself to idyllic natural scenes, he could not have contrived a tenth so many or made them half so convincing. His career is an excellent argument for a free-ranging study of the objective world.

Thus the role of outer reality is a double one. It confuses us by its variety and profusion; it is also an unlimited source of stimulation and interest to the human imagination.

THE METHODS OF VISUAL CONTROL

Having examined the need for the control and understanding of visual experience, let us consider in a preliminary way some of the methods by which they have been achieved.

The illustrations which follow have been divided for comparative purposes into two parallel series: the first, consisting of photographs of actual scenes such as anyone might encounter, was selected to show the character of physical reality. This is the raw material upon which the artistic consciousness works. In most instances the need for selection, emphasis, and elimination of excessive variety will be apparent. The second group is meant to reveal how the artistic mind realizes the artistic potentialities of nature in actual works of art, separating the wheat from the chaff.

The illustrations are arranged to demonstrate the foregoing principles by allowing the reader to observe three things: the actual visual characteristics of external reality; the resemblances and differences between roughly similar natural scenes and artistic interpretations; and the difference between paintings that possess to a marked degree the rhythm of which Konody spoke and those that lack it.

The first universal characteristic of nature which forces every artist to select, limit, and reduce, as he interprets, is vastness. When anyone stands on top of a mountain and looks toward a distant range,

FIG. 7. Panorama of the Alps at Rigi Kulm.

FIG. 8. Peaks in the Swiss Alps. Wengern-alp: Mounts Eiger and Mönch.

FIG. 9. Kokoschka, *Courmayeur. ca.* 1920. Phillips Collection, Washington, D.C.

as in Fig. 7, the prospect before him includes many peaks and valleys. His view will include only an infinitesimal fragment of reality; yet he cannot possibly include in any representation all that his own eyes can survey. He must reduce the panorama to a limited view. Some kind of limitation is always the first artistic step.

Secondly, nature is not orderly. It offers the materials for composition on every hand, but the arrangement itself has to be made by the human mind. Limitation alone is not enough. The observer who wishes to record nature in some visual medium must take a second step. After he selects a limited part of the visible whole, he rearranges the several parts of the scene into what is called a composition.

The photographer who recorded the mountain valley in the Swiss Alps shown in Fig. 8 both selected and centered the image on the ground glass of his camera. By contrasting Fig. 7 with Fig. 8, we can observe the difference between ordinary, roving perception and a deliberately selected view; between unlimited nature and artistic limitation. In this case the difference is due largely to a close, as distinct from a distant, view. Angle of view and distance are thus crucial to composition, and, taken together, offer unlimited possibilities to human intelligence.

Comparison of Figs. 7 and 8, plus a simple analogy, will also demonstrate what is meant by *intensification* and *clarification*. In chemistry it is common to distil large quantities of liquids. As the quantity is reduced and superfluous elements are eliminated, the liquids become purer and more concentrated; *refined* is the word most generally used to describe them. An instance of such a gain in quality through reduction in quantity occurs in the making of perfume. Starting with thousands of flowers, the manufacturer produces finally a few ounces of concentrated liquid. He calls this residue the *essence*. Its value is as great as its quantity is small. Something of the same transformation occurs in the visual arts which we call *fine;* there, too, quality is more important than quantity. As we look out over a range of mountains, such as that in Fig. 7, the general effect of the vast expanse is diffuse; no one or two mountains stand out emphatically because of the distracting effect of their surroundings. All compete for attention. By contrast, the two mountains in Fig. 8 stand out more than they would in actuality. Thus the reduction, selection, and limitation resulting here from a closer view have distilled or concentrated the visual image. The result is a gain in both clarification and intensification of effect.

Nature's vastness must be reduced in order to produce any kind of clarity or intensity of effect. Vastness itself is not entirely a fault, as we shall see when we consider landscape painting. A feeling of spaciousness has often been deliberately sought; it merely creates a problem. Owing to the diversity of the human mind, vastness may elicit two opposite reactions. The anthropocentric Greeks who believed that man is the measure of all things resented both mountains and inanimate nature generally, and excluded them from competition with man in their arts. The peoples of the mountainous regions of northern Europe viewed the Alpine peaks with a contrasting philosophy. Although mountains may dwarf man, man can scale the highest peaks. Looking at mountains in that way, they saw them as something physically greater but spiritually less than man, a measure and symbol of his ability to live with and to conquer the forces and masses of nature.

The natural characteristics of profusion and diversity, universality and individuality similarly force every artist to choose as he interprets. Like all other natural forms, the mountains in Fig. 8 present three sets of characteristics. Any may be emphasized, but selection must be made first. The first set of characteristics is discernible in the main masses of the twin peaks. Under their surface variations are two great conical or pyramidal masses which resemble the main outlines of all mountains. These simple, static bases are their universal characteristics. Overlaying them are the individual surface features which distinguish one peak from another. Thus the mountains may be said to have an inner and outer reality; a simple, universal, highly regular core, and a complex, individual, highly irregular exterior: the former discernible only to interpretation, the latter immediately apparent. This principle of duality may be applied by extension to the interpretation of every animate and inanimate form in universal reality.

The photographer overcomes nature's vastness and achieves a degree of clarification and intensification by reducing and composing the visual image within a frame of his own choosing. But this is not enough to satisfy our psychological needs for interpretation. A comparison of Fig. 8 with a painting of a mountain scene entitled *Courmayeur* (Fig. 9) by the modern Austrian expressionist Oskar Kokoschka, shows how much further the painter can carry the process of interpretation and personal expression. The photographer can limit and compose the natural image with undeniable skill and judgment, but the painter can express much more forcibly his own nervous energy and personal traits of vision. By comparison with Kokoschka's highly personal, vigorous manner of painting, as unique and identifiable as his signature, the photograph appears impersonal and anonymous.

Through his representation of Courmayeur Kokoschka has expressed something identifiable as his personal vision of reality, or, if you will, his personality; but he has also interpreted a significant aspect of the mountain town and valley with a sense of fitness, with an appreciation of something inherent in the nature of the scene. A good northerner who grew up among mountains, he has intensified their natural wildness. Yet he has done this artistically. He has reduced the mixed-up diversity of nature—the broken, craggy surfaces and jagged outlines of the snow-covered peaks—to a unified picture by the consistently sketchy character of his brush strokes and a rhythmic repetition of angular outlines. As a consequence, the painting has a dynamic quality which makes the photograph appear static. To give life in this way to an inert natural scene serves the double purpose of expressing the artist's personality and unifying nature in a rhythmic manner.

Fig. 10, a photograph of the famous Via Mala gorge in the Swiss Alps, has already been mentioned as an example of natural chaos, of extreme profusion and diversity. It would impose on any artist a heavy burden of selection and elimination. Yet the early nineteenth-century English master Turner has accepted precisely such a challenge and shown what can be done in his mezzotint of an Alpine ravine (Fig. 11). Although called romantic because his lively imagination thrived on scenes of natural action and the wilder haunts of the earth's surface, Turner made his composition as orderly as its natural counterpart is chaotic. He simplified the scene into a pattern of broad areas of light, dark, and middle gray values; he further simplified these main areas by suppressing the clutter of detail within them. Thus separated and subdued, the bold masses of rocks, the trees, and the bridge can be easily observed, as they cannot be in the natural scene, and the whole effect is clarified.

Fig. 12, a photograph of wild tropical ferns, was likewise cited as an example of the profusion and diversity which confuses the human eye and mind when we observe wild nature close at hand. Yet it was from such jungle profusion that the organizing eye of Henri Rousseau, the foremost of the so-called modern primitives, extracted his boldly simple, decorative patterns. As a young man he had seen military service in Central America, and he later drew upon his recollections of the luxuriant forests to paint *The Waterfall* (Fig. 13) and similar pictures. How much he clarified, intensified, and interpreted his impressions in the process will be made obvious by a comparison of his composition with Fig. 12.

The salutary effect of numerical limitation is vividly shown by

FIG. 10. Alpine Ravine. Bridge II over the Via Mala,
Switzerland.

FIG. 11. Turner. *Little Devils Bridge over the Russ Above
Altdorf Switzerland*. From "The Liber Studiorum." 1809.
Museum of Fine Arts, Boston.

19

FIG. 13. Henri Rousseau. *The Waterfall.* 1910.
Art Institute of Chicago.

FIG. 12. Wild Ferns. California.

FIG. 14. Stephen E. Merrill.
Irises. 1948.

FIG. 15. Cézanne. *Vase of Tulips.* 1890-1894.
Art Institute of Chicago.

Fig. 14, a picture of three irises removed from their beds, carefully rearranged and photographed in isolation from their normally complex surroundings. Thus segregated, they are simple enough for anyone to appreciate their delicate shapes and colors. The same principle of limitation can be applied to the wild ferns in Fig. 12, which are individually symmetrical and orderly. Indeed, the principle can be extended indefinitely. One of the finest modern American painters, Georgia O'Keeffe, has based her art on the clarifying and vivifying effects that are to be gained by isolating forms, a practice as time honored as the ancient art of painting still life in small groups. The modern French master Paul Cézanne employed this principle when he painted his *Vase of Tulips* (Fig. 15.) Like Fig. 14, it consists of so few elements that the eye can embrace and enjoy them with ease.

Fig. 16 presents nature in a dynamic mood, with a heavy surf battering the rocks along the coast of California. It has the intrinsic appeal of movement with an underlying rhythmic surge. It also dramatizes the eternal and universal conflict between the dynamic and the static, the irresistible force and the immovable object. Here is the raw material for powerful art. The two marine paintings of a similar character which appear in Figs. 17 and 18 show how it may be used.

Frederick Waugh's *Roaring Forties* (Fig.17) depicts a storm-lashed ocean the idea of which, quite apart from artistic considerations, is bound to impress us. His visual presentation, however, offers no observable reduction of the complexity of the natural scene. One has the feeling that he loved the scene so much that he could not bring himself to leave out a single detail. Satisfying as this may be for the naturalist, it places a heavy burden upon the observer who is seeking some measure of artistic interpretation. Every minor wave, ripple, and fleck of foam is forced upon our attention, as though we were looking at the actual scene from the deck of an ocean liner. The eye, lacking any focus of interest or any place to rest, is pulled everywhere and nowhere at once. As a result, the burden of selection and organization is placed almost entirely upon the spectator.

When Waugh's paintings of the sea were shown at the Carnegie International Exhibitions in the 1930s they were enormously popular with the public, which found in them its ideal of something "real" in painting. This should surprise no one; the same thing could happen today. But time has shown the matter in a different light to critics and philosophers and a growing number of students of art.

FIG. 16. Waves and rocks. Coast of California.

FIG. 17. Waugh. *The Roaring Forties. ca.* 1930. Metropolitan Museum of Art, New York.

FIG. 18. Homer. *The Northeaster*. 1895. Metropolitan Museum of Art, New York.

If such an excess of detail confuses the eye in static scenes, such as Fig. 10 and Fig. 12, in a scene of action it is even less logical, for the human eye cannot see a moving object with the precision of a camera. The net effect of this contradiction between movement and detail is to make the waves seem frozen. Thus the scene which appears at first glance so "real" comes in time to appear psychologically and visually quite unreal. Let us remember that it is human experience that the master artist clarifies and interprets; a perfect record of turbulent nature is a record of chaos, a hindrance rather than an aid to visual understanding.

By contrast, Winslow Homer's *The Northeaster* (Fig. 18) appears simple because Homer intelligently limited the image to approximately what the human eye could actually see of a moving form. He has contented himself with one burst of spray, one compactly massed rock formation, and one huge wave instead of a dozen. And he has arranged these into a pattern of three main, easily perceived light and dark areas, as Turner did in his Alpine mezzotint (Fig. 11). Owing to this simplification, the design gains greatly in clarity and the meaning of the picture is intensified. It is a powerful interpretation of change *versus* continuity, symbolized by the universal conflict between waves and massive rocks.

Fig. 19, a photograph of San Francisco Bay, illustrates the ordering effect of concentrated light and widespread shadow. It may give us a clue to the reason why, with the possible exception of a glowing sunset, we regard a full moon over an expanse of water as nature's most brilliant spectacle. Analyzing the picture's visual aspects, we can see that only in the relatively small reflection of the moonlight is the broken surface of the water apparent; and even there the dancing light delights our eyes. Throughout most of the picture nature's profusion and diversity of detail is softened or completely obscured by darkness, distance, or a veil of atmosphere. Owing to the limitations of human eyesight, the same phenomenon applies to our observation of nature in general. Details which are confusing at ten feet, as in Fig. 12, become less confusing as they recede into the distance. With darkness they disappear completely. Common sense has recognized this transformation in the axiom *distance lends enchantment*. In scientific and artistic terms this means that, although physical chaos remains fixed, the human point of view changes; it is from this that art evolves.

Because of its peacefulness and spaciousness, its brilliant effect of light and its minimum of details, Fig. 19 presents nature in something very close to an artistically acceptable form. Artistry in this case lies largely in recognizing the opportunity, as Winslow Homer

FIG. 19. Schooner in moonlight. San Francisco Bay.

FIG. 20. Homer. *Schooners in Moonlight, Saco Bay.* 1885. Collection of Mrs. Charles L. Homer, Prout's Neck, Me.

did in his strikingly similar watercolor painting of *Schooners in the Moonlight, Saco Bay* (Fig. 20).

Despite the close resemblance of Homer's watercolor and the photograph of the schooner on San Francisco Bay, there is an important difference between the painted and the natural image. Homer has taken advantage of the fact that there are no brush strokes in nature to exploit the unique quality of his watercolor technique. We have already met this difference between art and nature in our comparison of Kokoschka's *Courmayeur* and an Alpine valley. A similar comparison of Cézanne's *Vase of Tulips* with the irises in Fig. 14 will confirm the difference that the artistic medium introduces. Few other resources of the artist enable him better to express his own vitality and, at the same time, unify his picture surface. The factor of medium establishes a crucial difference between art and nature.

The several illustrations which we have now considered reveal how much the visible character of nature varies, from the extreme chaos of the Alpine ravine (Fig. 10) to the almost complete orderliness of the photograph of San Francisco Bay (Fig. 19). Many other natural conditions are at the opposite pole from the jungle. Recall, for instance, any smooth drift of new snow, an expanse of wind-blown desert, a long beach of tide-washed sand, a foggy night, or the mirror-like surface of a millpond at dawn. All of these offer the eye a maximum of simplicity and a minimum of confusing details. When these conditions are added to the detail-surpressing effects of distance, an artist possesses a wide choice of opportunities. Consequently, the problem of bringing nature within the attention span and making it esthetically pleasing is not based on a fixed or absolute condition but varies with the material at hand.

Figs. 21 and 23 show that nature is not the only villain or hero in the drama of the eye. Fig. 23, a superb Renaissance château in the Loire Valley of central France, is an illustration of man-made order, an architectural masterpiece surrounded by well-groomed lawns.

Because much of our civilized environment has been retrieved from nature by art in varying degrees, we profit greatly from gardens, parks, and all cultivated areas which are at least as artistic as they are natural. Every time a man mows his lawn he is contributing to the ceaseless struggle against natural wildness. There is hardly a person in the world who does not express a sense of order in some way, modest though it may be, from decorating a Christmas tree to selecting a tie or combing his hair, none of which is an absolute necessity.

There are also lapses from the sense of order, as there are from every other commendable human trait. Then man-made chaos appears. For example, the port of Marseilles (Fig. 21) seems to have

FIG. 21. The Port of Marseilles.

FIG. 22. Utrillo.
Church of Sacré Coeur de Montmartre.
ca. 1931. Museum of Fine Arts, Boston.

FIG. 23. Château d'Ussé. 15th and 16th centuries. Loire Valley, France.

26

FIG. 24. A ruined medieval donjon.

FIG. 25. Turner. *Norham Castle on the Tweed.* From "The Liber Studiorum." 1809. Museum of Fine Arts, Boston.

FIG. 26. William T. McKeown. Maine farmhouse in winter. 1943.

FIG. 27. Burchfield. *November Evening.* 1932. Metropolitan Museum of Art, New York.

grown like some sprawling jungle plant. The narrow streets twist and wander, the buildings which line them are a jumble of styles, sizes, and shapes. Here man has been his own worst enemy. What happens when he ceases his vigilance against the smothering encroachment of growing natural forms is graphically illustrated by the ruin of a medieval donjon (Fig. 24). This is how the walls and towers of the Château d'Ussé (Fig. 23) would probably appear today if it had not been continually cared for. These are the two extremes of man-made chaos—the planless city and the deserted ruin. Between them exist innumerable other examples: the slums of any city, the back alleys of almost any town, the local dump heap of either, and the farms of poorer rural areas. Fig. 26 illustrates grimly the latter type, a farmhouse in the dead of northern winter. Bleak, desolate, windswept, it would seem to offer unpromising material for any serious artist. It is a far cry from the touching sentiments of poems such as "Snowbound" or calendar pictures entitled *Home for Christmas*.

In our common visual experience we are constantly confronted with a mixture of chaos and order: the fashionable New York apartment building within a stone's throw of a tenement; a clearing in a jungle; a bridge over an Alpine gorge; a park next to the city dump. Over a period of years we evolve from our experience with the natural, artistic, and social juxtapositions of order and chaos a common esthetic measure, a simple, probably subconscious conception of the meaning of order: that in ninety-nine cases out of a hundred it is compounded of both unity and variety.

When variety is so included in our mental formula of order, and latitude allowed in the interpretation of ideological meanings, the raw material of art that exists in the world around us is greatly extended. Seen in that light, the twisting back streets of a port such as Marseilles become colorful or picturesque; the slums teem with vitality; the ruin plays upon the romantic in our imagination; the mountain peaks, ravines, and woods offer new artistic possibilities. A Utrillo finds artistic material in the narrowest side streets of Paris (Fig. 22); a Bellows turns the cliff-dwellers of Manhattan into striking subject matter; a Sloan discovers untouched themes in Union Square; a Turner reveals the tragic quality in a once-mighty English fortress (Fig. 25); and a Burchfield underscores the dull and gloomy side of life in Western American farmlands (Fig. 27). This conversion of apparently ugly and unpromising raw material into moving and esthetically stirring works of art is an achievement which no art-must-depict-the-beautiful theory can ignore or explain out of existence.

The artist who represents external reality has, in addition to a choice of subject, wide latitude in treatment which tests whether he possesses that sense of fitness and rhythm of his own of which Konody spoke. Choice of treatment is, in fact, forced upon him because any part of reality presents many possibilities for interpretation. In literary practice an author may describe individual qualities by giving a catalog account of such things as height, weight, color of hair and eyes, dress; the universal qualities he will convey through action, speech, and thought. It is the *universal* which is considered indispensable in making a literary character vital and alive, and so ranks high in the professional critic's scale of values. An instance of a fictional character who lives in this sense is Fielding's Tom Jones; we neither remember nor care whether his hair was black or brown.

Something of the same scale of values applies to the critical appraisal of the visual arts. In his *1814* (Fig. 28) Meissonier has depicted, with fidelity to detail and impeccable craftsmanship, Napoleon's army on the march during one of his last campaigns. The artist has given a complete catalog of the visual appearance of the scene. If these physical characteristics combined with the intrinsically impressive subject were enough to create great art, Meissonier's picture would rank among the masterpieces of oil painting. Instead, its reputation has declined from the exalted position it enjoyed when first exhibited in 1865. The representation, as we now see with clearer eyes, does not depart from nature, as Konody maintains it should. For Meissonier valued truth to appearance above every inner quality and copied the chaotic condition of the rutted snow at the expense of any artistic simplification or order. In this and other pictures he was trapped by his own insistence upon transferring every detail of external reality to canvas. Manet is reported to have said of his pictures, "Everything in them looks like steel except the swords."

Rosa Bonheur's *Lion and Lioness Resting* (Fig. 30), painted in the same manner, has, in my opinion, the same defects. There is no apparent departure from nature; every detail that the eye could possibly see has been included without regard to selection, simplification, or pictorial unity. There is not the slightest suggestion of rhythmic life. Bonheur, like Meissonier, has given a complete catalog of the physical appearance of these two captive lions which she observed at the Paris Zoo, but she has not endowed them imaginatively with any of the inner power that makes us call the lion the king of beasts.

A comparison of these two faithful imitations of external reality with Orozco's *Zapatistas* (Fig. 29) demonstrates the value of artistic interpretation. More than that, it shows the difference between two

FIG. 28. Meissonier. *1814*. 1864. Louvre, Paris.

FIG. 29. Orozco. *Zapatistas*. 1931. Museum of Modern Art, New York.

FIG. 30. Bonheur. *Lion and Lioness Resting.* 1894. Louvre, Paris.

FIG. 31. Barye. *The Black Panther.* ca. 1850. Louvre, Paris.

artists who were coldly mechanical and one who felt and communicated a sense of life. The Mexican artist imposed on the scene a rhythm or unity of his own creation, consisting of sharp outlines, uniform brush strokes which have a swift and sweeping quality, and vivid, deliberately harsh contrasts of light, shadow, and color. The rendering is as hard and raw-boned as the subject. As a result, the picture has life; the marching soldiers swing along, and the horsemen tower against the abstractly suggested Mexican mountains, giving meaning to the theme according to Orozco's sense of fitness.

With similar intelligence, Barye has interpreted the meaning of two animals in his *Black Panther* (Fig. 31). He has bothered little with superficial appearance, including for instance only the suggestion of a setting. Instead of getting lost in the clutter of finicky details which makes Bonheur's lions appear static and lifeless, he has concentrated upon an artistic unity suitable to the essential nature of his subject, the feline capacity for stealthy, gliding movement. He has served both nature and art by employing soft textures and outlines and a curvilinear pattern throughout his composition, conveying simultaneously a life-giving artistic rhythm and the dynamic quality of the big cats.

If the illustrations of this chapter are now reviewed, all except the Waugh, Meissonier, and Bonheur will be seen to possess this quality of artistic unity. Each offers a different rhythm which the artist deemed appropriate to his particular subject, yet each exemplifies in its own way the nature of fine art.

Two final illustrations will show how little that nature has changed in thousands of years. Franz Marc's *Two Deer* (Fig. 32) represents the modern tendency to carry Barye's rhythmic design to its logical conclusion by placing a minimum of stress upon external reality and a maximum of emphasis upon the inner attributes. Marc departed completely from the path of Meissonier and Bonheur to follow his own sense of fitness. A brilliant young German who was killed in the Battle of Verdun, Marc loved animals and made them his principal subjects. He had a deep feeling for their characteristic movements, in this case the exquisitely light-footed grace of the deer, and he was artist enough to bring this out by the soft textures, bright colors, and sweeping curves of his design. When Marc abandoned the surface realism of his immediate predecessor, Bonheur, to join hands with Barye, he subscribed to a conception of art which actually dates from the earliest efforts of man to clarify, intensify, and interpret his visual experiences with reality and impose upon them a vital rhythm and pictorial unity.

This is the company of true artists, men who have given us the

FIG. 32. Marc. *Two Deer.* *ca.* 1911. Neue Staatsgalerie. Haus der Kunst, Munich.

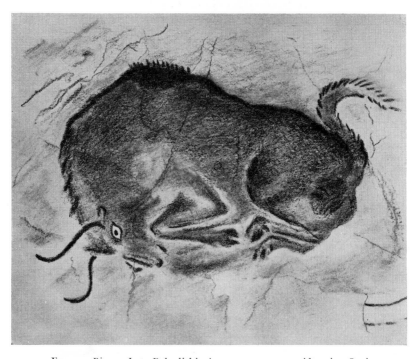

FIG. 33. *Bison.* Late Paleolithic Age, *ca.* 20,000 B.C. Altamira, Spain.

benefit of their sharp eyes and alert senses, and even more, of their feelings and creative imaginations. Barye, like Bonheur, was only able to study the corpses of animals or the tired, captive creatures that dozed in the Paris Zoo, but he used his imagination to conceive what they would be like in their natural freedom. Where Bonheur surrendered to the limitations of the immediate situation, Barye, like all great artists, transcended them.

Another member of this company who makes one forget the element of time is an unknown artist who observed and then painted a bison (Fig. 33) on the wall of a cave. Some 19,000 or more years have elapsed since he painted his picture, but the life and unity he gave his design make it seem eternally modern.

We need not labor the stylistic similarities between the prehistoric artist's *Bison* and Franz Marc's *Two Deer*. The works of the ancient hunter-painter and the modern artist illustrate clearly the kinship of their conceptions. The lesson is simple and clear; true art never was and never will be merely an imitation of nature's externals but an interpretation of physical and spiritual essentials, conceived to bridge the gap between nature and man's psychological needs.

CHAPTER 2

The Role of Perception

In the previous chapter we came to a conclusion that is now taken for granted by critics but is seldom obvious to beginners—that art aims at and should be valued as an interpretation rather than an imitation of external reality. The reason for this may be traced to two causes: one, the nature of reality that we have already considered, the other, the character of human perception. Our next task, then, is to determine why this is so and observe its bearing on art.

As an example of the diversity of human perception, imagine an art critic and an inexperienced layman standing before a realistic painting such as Léon Gérôme's *L'Éminence Grise* (Fig. 34). They will almost certainly view it with different eyes. The critic will be unimpressed by the picture, while the layman will admire it; it has been a popular favorite in the Museum of Fine Arts, Boston, for many years. If they were standing before Picasso's *Guernica* (Fig. 1) in the Museum of Modern Art in New York, their attitudes would be reversed. The layman who greatly admired Gérôme's imitative skill and careful craftsmanship will think Picasso's more abstract picture unintelligible. The critic, on the other hand, will recognize its expressive power and praise its abstract means. Our objective is to resolve such misunderstandings by showing the universal nature of perception.

Defined simply, *perception is the process by which we become aware of the world and form our opinions of it.* Psychologists, working to be more exact, explain the fundamentals of visual perception by distinguishing between the physical image which the eye's lens projects upon the retina and the mental image which this sensory impression induces. The first stage is sometimes called *physical seeing* to separate it from *mental seeing*. The important thing for us

FIG. 34. Gérôme. *L'Éminence Grise. ca.* 1865. Museum of Fine Arts, Boston.

FIG. 35. Cannon Rock. Prout's Neck, Me.

FIG. 36. Homer. *Cannon Rock.* 1895. Metropolitan Museum of Art, New York.

to notice is that it is a two-part process in every case. In this process the physical image is transformed into a personal image by one's accumulated experience in life, under innumerable influences of environment and inheritance. Since these experiences cannot have been identical for any two human beings, no two people view the world exactly alike.

The instant the optic nerves relay a sensory image to the brain, the mind begins to reconstruct it into a personal image. If that image were then projected onto a screen, the difference between the original physical image and the revised mental image could be observed. Something very close to this happens when an artist observes some fragment of the world, such as a landscape or a city street, and then projects his mental image of it onto a canvas. This principle of transformation applies even to Gérôme's *L'Éminence Grise*. That is why the critic maintains that a wholly impersonal, objective vision is psychologically impossible; photographic realism is therefore an illusion.

Later on we shall wish to refer to the two stages of perception as *seeing* and *knowing*. The French, as a matter of fact, have long indicated this distinction by using *voir* for physical seeing (looking) and *savoir* for mental perception (understanding or perceiving). The Bible also differentiates repeatedly between those who see with their eyes but do not have understanding hearts.

On one point there can be no doubt: *savoir* is more important for art and human life than *voir* because our brains differ far more than our eyes. The main difference between us and animals is not in eyesight, in which they often excel, but in understanding. Opticians, who deal daily with radical variations in eyesight from 20–20 vision to astigmatism and near-blindness, will challenge the statement that the retinal images of twenty artists who are painting a single landscape will be nearly alike. But differences between these images are nothing compared to those between the mental images which result. As a general rule there will be similarity at the initial sensory stage and diversity at the interpretive. That is why the critic says the layman values the two aspects of perception in reverse order of importance by praising Gérôme's imitative skill.

In the history of art a relatively objective approach and a highly subjective point of view have both been pursued vigorously, as in the work of Rosa Bonheur and Franz Marc, respectively; each has enjoyed its day of favor. Nevertheless, what an artist expresses cannot help being a personal interpretation of reality. Bonheur's appearance of 100 per cent objectivity is deceptive; her painting is not wholly devoid of the subjective element, for anyone familiar with her style can always recognize it and distinguish it from the similar style of Meissonier. Personality was merely weak or repressed in both cases, creating the illusion of complete objectivity. Hence the critic asserts that the layman's admiration for Gérôme, Bonheur, and Meissonier is based on a misconception.

By considering our own everyday experiences, we can easily realize why it is more natural for several artists to interpret the same scene in several different ways than it is for all to imitate it exactly. For example, climbing a mountain trail some years ago, I pointed out a particularly massive and colorful boulder to two companions. One, a geologist, was indifferent to my interests, but discussed the rock's probable history. The other, a student of German literature, remarked that Goethe had been keenly interested in rock formations. Each had carried his conception of boulders up the mountain with him and had it ready and waiting for use. These conceptions, moreover, were offshoots of a larger and continuing point of view. Throughout our ascent the geologist unconsciously described whatever he saw in geological terms, while the scholar of literature continued to see the mountains and valleys through the eyes of poets and writers. For one, nature was illustrating science; for the other, it was illustrating literature.

This phenomenon of appreciation follows a universal pattern which has a direct bearing upon creative activity. If we substitute an artist for the geologist or scholar, he will paint partly what he observes in the rocks before him; the rest of his vision will come from long-standing interests and attitudes. To paraphrase Konody once more, the painter will not only depart from a strict imitation of nature but will impose on it a rhythm of his own creation which has been developing throughout his life.

THE CONTRIBUTION OF PSYCHOLOGY

The contribution of psychology has been to reduce these common experiences to general principles. By a series of tests applied to many subjects, psychologists have arrived at an understanding of human perceptual habits. In doing this they have confirmed the critic's insistence upon the importance of individuality. Among the findings which shed the most light upon art are those of Professor Hermann F. Brandt, who has measured the reading of pages of print and works of art by means of ocular photography.

Dr. Brandt's studies permitted only one conclusion: perception is not a passive absorption of impressions but is a selective process guided by intelligence, the chief determinant being the brain which guides the eye. He discovered in the observation of pictures that the untrained viewer did not know what to look for in, for instance, a reproduction of Leonardo da Vinci's *Last Supper,* whereas an artist was able to analyze the main lines of the design and pick out the important personages quickly and systematically, proving the value of training in perception.

These principles can easily be applied to the creation of works of art. Summing up, Brandt says,

there is no one-to-one relationship between the neural response and the physical events that produce them. The eyes are too often looked upon as cameras photographing whatever is exposed to them. Quite to the contrary, the retina, which is the photographic plate of the eye, suppresses certain portions of the sensitive cell area and enhances others. To illustrate the above phenomenon would be to imagine a picture painted on a large plastic. Due to the selective process of attention, interest, and interpretation, certain areas of the observed field would rise and others would recede, presenting a relief map in motion. [1]

If we were to add to this selective process the ability to regroup forms, alter their shapes, textures, outlines, and colors, and suppress and emphasize in a variety of other ways, we should have an excellent description of an artist's mental reaction to nature. It is, as Brandt observed, far from a one-to-one relationship.

Psychological studies have also demonstrated that we project concepts mentally upon any object we observe and judge it accordingly. For example, in viewing Rosa Bonheur's *Lion and Lioness Resting* (Fig. 30) we measured her lions against a concept of the lion as the king of beasts and found them wanting. Researchers have also explained why the artist with an insight into what is essential has the greatest chance of achieving lasting appreciation. Barye's art has survived while Bonheur's has not, because she became lost among the unimportant details, whereas he generalized his *Black Panther* (Fig. 31) in a way that brings out the universal characteristics of the feline family. Barye was not the superior artist because he was the better copying machine, but because he fully understood what he saw.

THE CONTRIBUTION OF ART HISTORY

In the study of perception art historians have played no less important a role than the psychologists. Where the scientists, using controlled experiments to gain verifiable evidence, have outlined

[1] *The Psychology of Seeing* (New York: Philosophical Library, Inc., 1945), p. 200,

the basic principles which underlie the perceptual process, the historians have recorded the story of human perception as it has been revealed through the fine arts. They have amassed evidence which allows us to understand when, where, how, and why specific artists revealed their inner worlds and depicted their environments as they have.

Notable among the studies made by art historians in recent years are those of John Rewald, who has utilized the camera to record the natural motifs that Monet, Cézanne, Van Gogh, and others used as points of departure for their paintings. Thanks to these photographs, we can observe specifically and concretely the significant difference between these natural sources and artistic perception. Rewald's photographic evidence confirms, as do psychological studies, the three general observations made above: that photographic record and human perception differ importantly, that so-called objective or realistic vision is merely relative, and that no two people perceive the outer world, or even a single scene, exactly alike.

Rewald's photographs prove, for example, that whereas Van Gogh took great liberties with the appearance of any scene (which will surprise no one) Monet, who had among his contemporaries a reputation for unusually acute eyesight, preserved the greatest respect for his natural subjects. He scrutinized them minutely, and painted directly from them. Yet no one would confuse Monet's paintings with the photographs of the places which inspired them. No less enlightening are several photographic juxtapositions by which Rewald allows us to compare the results of the following known situations. Cézanne, Renoir, and Pissarro were close friends and often painted the same scene side by side, but their several paintings exhibited more differences of conception than similarity of subject.

THE CONTRIBUTION OF CREATIVE ART

In the work of creative artists we find evidence which, though predating it by centuries, positively confirms the modern idea of the nature of perception. Let us juxtapose a series of pictures which ought to look alike, but for various reasons do not, and deduce what we can from what we can see directly and explain historically, using the *seeing* and *knowing* phases of perception.

Figs. 35 and 36 enable us to compare a well-known painting and the natural motif on which it was based. The photograph shows a formation, called Cannon Rock because of its shape, which is located at Prout's Neck, Maine. It was there that Winslow Homer lived from 1883 until his death in 1910 and found a dozen or more natural

formations which are clearly recognizable in his major marine paintings.

Fig. 36 is the painting of Cannon Rock which Homer completed
in 1895. It is now in the Metropolitan Museum of Art. Significant
differences between the artist's composition and the photograph will
be apparent. Homer has viewed Cannon Rock from a point considerably above the formation; he has bracketed it by a V-shaped cleft
which sets off the rock parenthetically and cuts the lower corners of
the picture diagonally; and he has pointed the rock seaward toward
an incoming wave, which balances the upper and lower halves of the
composition. He has also divided the composition into two major
fields, the dark silhouette of the rocks below and the light planes of
water and sky above. Within these two areas he has reduced details
to a minimum. Compared to the broken surfaces of rocks and waves
in the natural scene, Homer's interpretation is a simple, selective,
and emphatic clarification and intensification of the visual image.

These differences were not achieved accidentally. Commenting
on them, Charles L. Homer, the artist's nephew and a lifelong student of his work, said, "The actual outline of Cannon Rock is so
small and insignificant that newcomers to Prout's have to hunt for it.
Hundreds of people pass by it without a second glance. Seeing its
artistic possibilities, Homer put a frame around it for us. Thanks to
him, anyone can now find the formation along the cliff front and
recognize it as the subject of his painting, but the similarity ends
there. I have tried many times to find the exact point of view that
Homer used. No such view exists. His picture is a composite of the
scene taken from many angles, some of them humanly impossible to
duplicate; no one can stand high enough to see Cannon Rock itself
as he has seen it. The crevice forms no such convenient V-design as he
has used; it is square and boxlike. Also, the water only comes into
the opening at high tide, but his single breaker, caused by a sub-
merged shelf, occurs only at low tide. Using artistic license, he
combined them. In fact, the picture is full of licenses. Nobody ever
actually saw Cannon Rock as my uncle painted it." [2]

The significance of Mr. Homer's statement is this: great artists
paint more than they talk. They rarely leave verbal guides to what
they had in mind when they painted specific pictures. Rembrandt
left hardly a word about his art, and Matisse's comments are typically
general and theoretical. But Homer had a hard and fast credo for
his own painting—the credo of an avowed photographic realist.
When a young artist came from nearby Portland to seek his advice, he

2 Conversation, 1939, with the late Charles L. Homer, Prout's Neck, Maine.

said, "Try to paint exactly what you see before your eyes. Whatever else you have to offer will come out of its own accord." [3] Homer undoubtedly realized how much this applied to his own art; nevertheless he took great pains to procure proper physical accessories for his illustrative paintings—a ship's bell for his *The Look-out, "All's Well"* and a genuine net (still in his old studio at Prout's) for the *Fisher Girl*. He would wait for months to check a natural lighting effect, as he did for his *Fog Warning* (Fig. 61). When he could not paint on the spot, he repeatedly carried his canvas to the waterfront to compare it with its natural counterpart. His was a painstaking and practical point of view.

John W. Beatty, a long-time friend, recorded an exchange he had with the artist:

Once when we were picking our way along the shore, over the shelving rocks he painted so often, I suddenly said, "Homer, do you ever take the liberty, in painting nature, of modifying the color of any part?" I recall his manner and expression perfectly. Arresting his steps for an instant, he firmly clenched his hand, and bringing it down with a quick action, exclaimed: "Never! Never! When I have selected the thing carefully, I paint it exactly as it appears." [4]

Although Homer made this assertion when he was a mature artist, it is perfectly clear from the internal evidence in Figs. 35 and 36 that he did not practice what he preached. If his statement were literally true, he would be the layman's perfect realist. Instead, his work exemplifies Konody's definition, "Art begins where the artist departs from strict imitation of nature and imposes on her a rhythm of his own creation." For an artist's own sake he must be judged by what he does, not by what he says. The human perceptual process is often subconscious and as a consequence the finest art often conceals its art, even from its own creator.

Figs. 38 and 39 are two landscapes which were painted by nineteenth-century French masters, Théodore Rousseau and Paul Cézanne, in the same general locale, the Forest of Fontainebleau. Rousseau, who lived from 1812 to 1867, painted in and around Fontainebleau for many years after 1835 and was associated with the loosely defined school named after the town of Barbizon. Cézanne did not visit the forest region until 1872 and later, after Rousseau's death, so their activities there did not actually overlap, but the forest itself had presumably changed little. The specific differences between their paintings must therefore have arisen from different outlooks in the mental half of perception.

[3] Conversation, 1943, with Alexander Bower, N.A., who quoted Walter Gilchrist.
[4] "Recollections by John W. Beatty," appended to Lloyd Goodrich, *Winslow Homer* (New York: The Macmillan Co., 1944), p. 220.

FIG. 37. Stephen E.
Merrill. In a Maine
wood. 1950.

FIG. 38. Théodore
Rousseau. *The Old
Swamp of Bas-Bréau.*
ca. 1850. Louvre, Paris.

FIG. 39. Cézanne. *Forest of
Fontainebleau.* 1894-1898.
Metropolitan Museum of Art,
New York.

44

The photograph in Fig. 37 was taken in a Maine wood which, though not identical with the Forest of Fontainebleau, is similar enough to provide a means of comparing the two paintings. The photograph offers four salient characteristics: the wood, taken as a whole, bears universal resemblances to all woods, but also possesses individual characteristics. Each element in the scene, each tree, rock, waterfall, exemplifies the duality of all perceptual universals and their attributes. The scene may also be conceived as comprised of two major components. Omitting the water for the moment, these are the rocks and trees. Each of these two groups also has specific subordinate attributes. The important thing for us to notice is that the existence of four sets of characteristics (the universal and individual and the geological and floral) offers opportunities for personal selection and emphasis. The differences between Rousseau's painting and Cézanne's lie largely in the way each has responded to this opportunity.

In his interpretation Rousseau has stressed the luxuriant fertility of wild nature as manifested by millions of leaves and the rampant growth of other floral forms. Details crowd upon the eye from every portion of the picture. The effect, although rich and tapestry-like, is serene and static. Looking at the forest, he emphasized the leafy quality of the trees and played down the solidity of tree trunks and rocks. His view was specific and individual. This, definitely, is the Old Swamp of Bas-Bréau.

From the same woods Cézanne extracted quite different elements. His picture is called, simply, *Forest of Fontainebleau;* it might be typical of any corner of the Forest or, for that matter, of many woods in many lands. Emphasizing only the universal aspects of woods, and generalizing rocks and trees consistently, Cézanne was content to suggest the essential characteristics of both woodland components wherever they may be found, underscoring the massive density, weight, and immobility of the rocks and the airy, dancing quality of the leaves. Avoiding particular description deliberately, he summarized the appearance of the leaves with quick strokes of the brush. Nowhere are single leaves defined exactly; instead they are implied by a kind of shorthand formula. In contrast rocks are made heavy, definite, and solid by means of clearly defined outlines. Thus the major characteristics of Cézanne's rocks and leaves enhance and complement each other. Similarly, the actual colors of the scene were translated into universal woodland colors—violet for the deep, cool-warm forest shadow, interlaced with touches of yellow, green, and blue. Together they represent the kind of colored light which we associate with forest glades everywhere. By paying tribute to

FIG. 40. Toulouse-Lautrec. *At the Moulin de la Galette.* 1890.
Art Institute of Chicago.

FIG. 41. Renoir. *Dance at the Moulin de la Galette.* 1876. Louvre, Paris.

46

typical leafy and rocky qualities, by avoiding minute description, Cézanne achieved an interpretation of all nature. Moreover, his freedom from strictly local details allowed him to give his design a restless, dynamic, rhythmic life through skilfully used artistic devices— the oppositely tilted planes of rocks, and brush strokes which vibrate and yet unify the picture surface.

Cézanne brought to his task an organizing perception, an insight into essentials, and an artistic ingenuity of the first order. So, when the photograph, the Rousseau, and the Cézanne are compared, marked variations emerge. Our problem of the moment however, is not to determine whether one is superior, but to note for our study of perception that they *are* different.

Although a sprawling area such as a forest presents many prospects for interpretation, a room and the people in it can also produce differences in perception. This problem can be tested in another way by considering Figs. 40 and 41, which represent the Moulin de la Galette in Paris as it appeared to Henri de Toulouse-Lautrec and to August Renoir. Renoir's painting was executed in 1876, Lautrec's in 1889. Since the noted entertainment center might have changed in that time, the comparison cannot be exact. Yet we may assume that it retained some continuity of character. The greater differences must be explained by the fact that Renoir and Lautrec projected highly personal points of view upon everything they saw. More pertinent questions are, *how* and *why?*

To Lautrec the Moulin de la Galette was a study in contrasts. Located at the crossroads of Parisian night life, it was a meeting point of slumming upper-crust roués and denizens of the underworld. Hard, hawked-faced men in bowler hats, like the one seated at the table in the foreground (actually here the artist Joseph Albert) rubbed elbows with gentlemen in silk top hats. Like any place which teems with life and suggests evil, the Moulin de la Galette had its fascinating side. Lautrec thrived on it. Never a sentimentalist, he conveys the impression through his painting that the habitués of the famous old wineshop and outdoor dance hall were, under their cosmetics and hair dye, cheap, sordid, tough, and rather dull, their gaiety always threatened by boredom. Lautrec observed the subject as impartially as anyone could, but his execution, which inevitably conveys his attitude, is harsh and angular.

It is difficult to believe that Renoir's *Dance at the 'Moulin de la Galette'* represents the same subject. Where Lautrec's dancers suggest the rowdy cancan then in vogue, Renoir's seem to be executing a waltz. His whole conception has the atmosphere of a genteel lawn party under Japanese lanterns. The women appear gracious and beautiful, the men immaculately dressed and gallant. In keeping with this interpretation, Renoir's brush strokes are deft and feathery, making forms seem like colored cotton and light softly glamorous.

The obvious question is, which of these two artists is telling the truth? Oddly enough, both are. For reality is never singular, and may actually present two distinct faces quite apart from any interpretation. In his biography of Toulouse-Lautrec, Gerstle Mack writes:

> The Moulin de la Galette led a sort of double life and catered to two entirely separate groups of clients. On Monday nights it was invaded by an exceedingly noisy, rowdy public. The men, for the most part, were of the type known as *apaches*—the forerunners of our modern gangsters—brutal and swaggering, well launched upon careers of petty crime; while nearly all of the women, if they were not already professional prostitutes, were destined to end their lives in brothels, the prison of Saint-Lazare, or the river.
>
> On Sunday afternoons and evenings, however, from three o'clock to midnight, the Moulin took on a much less sinister complexion. An admission fee of one franc fifty centimes for "cavaliers" and twenty-five centimes for "ladies" was charged, and these gatherings were immensely popular, especially in the summer months, when the management provided the additional attraction of a *Grande Kermesse* in the Garden. The Sunday crowds, though still noisy and boisterous, maintained a certain bourgeois formality. A few of the younger girls were still carefully chaperoned by watchful mothers; and even those who had already strayed had not yet lost their freshness. Most of the men who attended the Sunday dances were honestly employed as clerks or artisans during the week. [5]

There can be little doubt as to which of the two kinds of *galas* held at the Moulin de la Galette each artist intended to portray. So different were the ways in which they saw life that what was real to Lautrec appeared sordid to Renoir, and, conversely, what the latter regarded as normal and healthy the former considered merely bourgeois. Like most of us, each managed to see what he preferred and to avoid what he disliked. What is equally to the point for our study, they continued to do this as long as they lived. This continuity of attitude is clearly evident in Figs. 42 and 43.

Lautrec's painting is called by its present owners *The Laundress.* It has also been entitled variously *The Singer, The Harlot, Rosa La-Rouge,* and *Carmen*: the latter, a girl who posed at the studio of Lautrec's one-time master, Cormon. She was probably not a harlot, and another painting of the same girl suggests that she was a laundress. In any case, she is represented as a girl of the lower classes. Her clothes are mean, her hair unkempt; she is scrawny and flat-chested. Her pose suggests defiance, and her appearance proclaims that if she

5 *Toulouse-Lautrec* (New York: Alfred A. Knopf, Inc., 1938), pp. 121-22.

FIG. 42. Toulouse-Lautrec. *The Laundress*. *ca.* 1889. Barnes Foundation, Merion, Pa.

FIG. 43. Renoir. *Nude in a Brook*. 1895. Barnes Foundation, Merion, Pa.

49

were not actually ill-used by life, she was a member of the under-
privileged classes which survived by a wiry toughness. The form of
the picture, like its theme, is rough, angular, and harsh.

Compared to *The Laundress*, the young girl in Renoir's *Nude in
Brook* (Fig. 43) lived in an idyllic, pastoral world full of sunlight and
color. Young and well fed, she is a picture of unselfconscious innocence and blooming health. Renoir painted this picture in 1895,
nearly twenty years later than his *Dance at the 'Moulin de la Galette,'*
but his attitude had not changed. Everything that came from his
brush was still soft and round, light-hearted and colorful.

The reasons behind this continuity of outlook are best found in
the lives of the two men. Lautrec's life was tragic and contradictory.
Born into one of the oldest and noblest families of Southern France,
the Counts of Toulouse, he inherited every advantage in life that
wealth and prestige can confer. Then a double tragedy struck him.
At the age of thirteen he broke his legs in a series of accidents. Owing to a natural brittleness and his frail health, their growth was
permanently arrested. In adulthood he had the mature mind and
torso of a man, but the grotesque limbs of a dwarf. Naturally small
and never handsome, when dressed up in his expensive, tailor-made
gentleman's attire, he was a tragicomic figure. A second blow, which
struck at his spiritual development, fell when his robust, ultramascu-
line father, a huntsman and devoted falconer, lost interest in the
nonathletic son. Although he continued to support him, he could
not bring himself to regard the weak cripple as a worthy son and heir.
In spite of some generously worded letters, the boy was a disappointment. Thus Henri, though wealthy and aristocratic by birth, was
barred from the life of his own class. He sought to compensate for
his position by losing himself among those multitudes of Paris who,
if not crippled physically, were handicapped in other ways. With
prostitutes, theatrical performers, laundresses, and the poor he was
not at such a disadvantage. Indeed, in the amoral demimonde Montmartre, he found some friendship and solace. Generous and magnanimous in disposition himself, he repaid this live-and-let-live acceptance by immortalizing the Quarter in an artistic record which, if not
sympathetic, is at least dispassionate and never self-pitying. Given
these circumstances in life, Lautrec could hardly have painted his
Laundress any other way. In the end, life among the streetwalkers
was poor fare for a sensitive and intelligent nobleman. He died an
incurable drunkard in a sanatorium at Malromé in 1901, two months
before his thirty-seventh birthday.

Renoir, like Lautrec, never painted a religious, literary, or intellectual picture, and took his subjects from the familiar and near-at-

hand. But if he and Lautrec visited the Moulin de la Galette during the same years, they went there, so to speak, on different nights. In every other respect they followed divergent mental paths. The bulk of Renoir's subjects represents the simple, wholesome, everyday things he loved—members of his family, servants in his harmonious household, children, buxom mothers, smiling meadows, lush flowers, and young girls such as the bather in Fig. 43. He was extraordinarily natural, frankly sensual and, if you will, a sentimentalist who saw the world through rose-colored glasses. Yet, ironically, Renoir had more to embitter him than Lautrec. Extremely poor in his youth and always hardworking, he was so crippled by arthritis in his old age that he could only paint from a wheelchair with a brush strapped to his hand. Yet none of this suffering ever appears in his pictures. He loved the sensuous qualities of oil paint and color, rose petals and human flesh as few men ever have, and painted to the very end. He died famous and at peace with the world at the age of seventy-nine.

During the years between 1884 and 1901, when Lautrec occupied a studio in the Rue Tourlaque in Montmartre, another artist, Edgar Degas, living in the same building, proved again that individuality can have an impact on environment as well as the other way around, and also that Paris had a thousand sides, each of which drew subtly different responses from men who went forth each day from the same door. Thirty years older than Lautrec and already famous, Degas was extravagantly admired by the younger man, though their paths seldom crossed. Degas, a bachelor who lived more and more to himself as the years went by, was shy and unapproachable. Despite his aloofness, however, Degas had something in common with Lautrec. Thin-skinned, hypersensitive, and highly intelligent, he took a dim view of life for reasons that he kept to himself. An unfortunate early love affair is supposed to have affected him, but he never talked about it.

Where Renoir had been born on the poor side of the railroad track, Degas, like Lautrec, had grown up on the favored side, in an old and well-to-do family. But for him too life turned sour and he also chose to bury himself in Montmartre. There he painted, with a great feeling for formal design, people of the lower classes laboring at their daily tasks, like the *Laundresses* in Fig. 44.

Degas' work differs from Lautrec's as the two men differed, but it is relatively similar when contrasted with Renoir's buoyant optimism. The two occupants of the Rue Tourlaque studio were at one mental pole and Renoir was at the other. No one would describe either Lautrec's or Degas' life work as a "hymn in praise of the goodness of life." There is little joy in Degas' work (his sense of design and

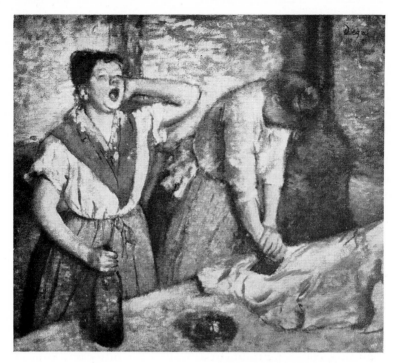

FIG. 44. Degas. *Laundresses. ca.* 1884. Louvre, Paris.

FIG. 45. Picasso. *Woman Ironing.*
1904. Collection of Mr. and Mrs.
Justin K. Thannhauser, New York.

color are different matters) and, for all the activity in his many scenes of ballet girls practicing and jockeys exercising their mounts, nobody in them seems to be having a good time.

In the *Laundresses,* one of the women bends the full weight of her powerful body over an iron; the other pauses and yawns from fatigue or boredom. Neither would be mistaken for a Gainsborough duchess. Husky and strong, they are physically equal to their occupations; but no pretense is made that they like their hard work. Through these two figures Degas is expressing his social philosophy, that one lives as one can and works because one must, and on the whole life is filled with much labor and much boredom. His was a neutral, detached view because he could not help it; he was too intelligent to be bitter and too frail physically to be enthusiastic or light-hearted.

How powerfully circumstances can color a man's outlook is even more eloquently illustrated by Fig. 45, *Woman Ironing,* by Pablo Picasso. In it a bony, emaciated laundress leans over a steaming iron. She is putting her whole weight into the task, but, unlike Degas' broad-shouldered women, she has hardly the strength or will to continue. As her head sags, one shoulder is pushed up almost out of joint. Despair is written on her face and in every angle of her body. Life is killing her physically, as it has already killed her spiritually. It makes one weary just to look at the picture, yet the subject is only indirectly important. What Picasso is telling us through this painting is not, like Degas' *Laundresses,* something about ironing as a hard occupation, but his own desperate frame of mind during his first years in Paris.

He had come to the art capital of the world in 1900, at the age of nineteen, and though destined to be the most celebrated painter of the first half of the twentieth century, he was then unknown and poor. His fortunes changed for the better about 1905 when Gertrude Stein recognized his talent and bought some of his pictures, and he reflected this improvement by launching the so-called "Rose Period" of his work (1905-1906). But from 1900 to 1905 he was hungry, friendless, and virtually unemployable because he could speak only a few words of French. His chief artistic idols at that time were Toulouse-Lautrec and Degas; hence the similarity of subject in Figs. 44 and 45. Otherwise, the two pictures could hardly be more unlike: Degas' conception was based on a close study of actual women at work, Picasso's was imaginary and subjective. Any other back-breaking work would have served as well. To re-enforce his mood, he devised a color scheme that is as symbolic as his conception of the subject. Cold blues, grays, and neutral greens predominate to convey a feeling of personal depression. When this color scheme appeared in everything he painted at that time, the name "Blue Period" was applied. Seldom has artistic style been used more effectively to reveal a perception that had retreated into inner reality.

One final test suggests itself for our study of the role of perception in art. To take a more limited subject than women ironing or the Moulin de la Galette on different nights, let us consider two illustrations of the same episode in the New Testament, the Annunciation. St. Luke described the event in these words:

And in the sixth month the angel Gabriel was sent from God unto a city of Galilee, named Nazareth, to a virgin espoused to a man named Joseph, of the house of David; and the virgin's name was Mary. And the angel came in unto her, and said, Hail, thou that art highly favoured, the Lord is with thee: blessed art thou among women. And when she saw him, she was troubled at his saying, and cast in her mind what manner of salutation this should be.

Here is something specific. It is hard to imagine two artists doing justice to the theme and at the same time departing from it to any marked degree. Furthermore, the whole weight and authority of the Catholic Church would have held any artists who worked for it to the Church's traditional interpretation of the subject; they were not free to the extent that Degas, Cézanne, Renoir, and Lautrec were. Yet witness the different interpretations of the Annunciation which appear in Figs. 46 and 47.

In the mural painting by Fra Angelico, the Virgin is seated serenely in a garden-enclosed cloister when Gabriel arrives with his message. Although the Bible says "She was troubled at his saying," Fra Angelico's Mary simply folds her hands and leans forward slightly to hear better. The even lighting and still atmosphere of the garden remain undisturbed; the cloister is hushed and peaceful.

What a contrast is Tintoretto's *Annunciation*! His Gabriel swoops almost threateningly through the door of a ruin, accompanied by a swarm of cherubs and preceded by the luminous dove of the Holy Spirit. The darkness of Mary's room is rent as though by a flash of lightning, and she is violently startled. Outside, Joseph works at his carpentry amid a clutter of planks. The total effect of the painting is almost melodramatic. Tintoretto not only took the word *troubled* seriously, he magnified its implications several fold. Yet we suspect that more lies behind these contrasting interpretations than a play on words. Radically different personalities must have been at work.

Fra Angelico lived quietly in the Dominican monastery of St. Mark at Florence, dividing his time between prayer and painting.

FIG. 46. Fra Angelico. *Annunciation*. 1439-1445. San Marco Museum, Florence.

FIG. 47. Tintoretto. *Annunciation*. 1583-1587. Scuola di S. Rocco, Venice.

The cloister in his *Annunciation* was carefully studied from one then being built in the monastery after the design of the famous architect Michelozzo, and includes both the newly popular classical capitals and the iron tie rods which held the arches together. But Fra Angelico, though observant, was not primarily a realist. His love of pretty girls, beautiful angels, joyous colors, and a peaceful, flower-filled world suggests that temperamentally he was rather like Renoir. His view of life was lyrical. His friends and fellow monks called him *Il Beato*—pure of spirit.

Tintoretto, who lived in Venice somewhat later, although devout, was not consecrated to holy orders. Rather, he was a prodigiously active professional painter, one of the most prolific the world has known. Everything he created was filled with energy. His name means *Little Dyer*, but those who knew him described him in stronger terms. When he sought the commission to decorate the School of San Rocco in Venice in 1564, one member insisted that the work should not be done by that unorthodox painter, the "furious" Tintoretto. The presence of the *Annunciation* in San Rocco shows that the member could not in the end resist Tintoretto's design. The School is a shrine of his art, as St. Mark's is of Fra Angelico's.

As with personality, a difference in time asserts itself through these two *Annunciations*. Fra Angelico's was painted in the early fifteenth century. Florence was looking forward to the best years of the Renaissance, and faith in the Church and its doctrines was still unchallenged. Tintoretto's *Annunciation* of 1564 followed a disastrous change in the fortunes of Italy and a direct challenge to the authority of the Church. Between 1494 and 1527 northern Italy had been overrun by the French army and Rome sacked by troops of the Holy Roman Emperor. Within the same period of time Martin Luther had set off the Protestant movement. As a result of these events, restlessness, fear, and uncertainty infected the air of Italy, coloring the outlook of every artist who, like Tintoretto, was alert to the spirit of the times.

Through a series of comparisons we have observed the role of the artist in demonstrating the nature of human perception. We have seen him reaffirming the conclusions of historians, psychologists, and common observers about the nature of that perception. We must conclude that no matter how similar the points of departure may be in nature, perception will always transform them into individual conceptions according to the cumulative effects of inheritance, environment, time, place, native ability, personal temperament, and a dozen other diversifying influences. As a consequence there can be no one correct way of copying what we see. There can only be interpretations, for, owing to the nature of perception, nothing else is humanly possible. If this is so, our emphasis in judging works of art should be placed primarily on the quality of the mind and spirit behind the interpretation and on the significance for human life at large of the subjects interpreted, and only incidentally on an assumed one-to-one physical resemblance to the outer world.

CHAPTER 3

The Orientation of Perception

A work of art does not reflect a mirror image of external reality, but expresses a perception which is individual. We must not, however, exaggerate the individuality of perception, lest we overlook its universal side.

For example, even though Renoir and Cézanne, working within three feet of each other on the same afternoon, painted different versions of Mont Sainte Victoire, their pictures have common characteristics which identify them with the art of nineteenth-century France and set them apart from anything painted in other countries or at other times. We can account for this only by recognizing certain factors which influence expression above and beyond either momentary or individual perception.

We have already touched upon one of these factors in observing the continuity of individual perception. An artist spends his whole life preferring a few kinds of content and form out of numerous possibilities, his long-range preferences emerging as a personal style. But there is another side to the same coin. An artist like Cézanne is also influenced by the ideas which affect him from without, causing him to express not only his own thoughts but those common to nineteenth-century France. The particular direction taken by the form and content of an artist's work we call the *orientation of perception,* a process determined by the prevailing attitudes in the artist's environment. No man is entirely free or wholly enslaved, but some circumstances make freedom more difficult than others. In cultural terms the determinants are the political, economic, and social attitudes which prevail at a given time and create the environment in which an artist works. At one time the prevailing social climate will favor individual freedom, as it has since the beginning of the Renaissance. At another it will suppress liberty in the same country and impose conformity and collective thinking on all who are not in positions of authority, as it did during the Dark Ages. Time, however, is not the only factor. No citizens in history should be better equipped than we are to observe how, at one and the same moment, freedom and collectivism may be separated only by a political "Iron Curtain." In our case, place is the crucial factor.

As the pendulum of history has swung between polar opposites, individuality has never been wholly killed, but strong pressures have been exerted on the directions it might take. Thus free, individual perception, like objective observation, is always relative. Consequently, the history of art may be viewed broadly by noting the collective orientations of perception which have influenced even the most rugged individualists. They account for those artistic period-styles which form the main chapter headings of the history of art. The major orientations of artistic perception may be listed as naturalistic, religious, humanistic, social, introspective, architectural, abstract, and artistic.

THE NATURALISTIC ORIENTATION

The naturalistic orientation of perception is one of the oldest in human history, as well it might be, for nothing surrounds us so completely as nature or affects us more profoundly. The earliest prehistoric artists whose work we know represented scores of animals, such as the bison in Fig. 33. They might have done this partly because the animals they hunted had a life-or-death meaning for them, or partly for religious reasons. But one cannot look at the *Bison* without feeling that the artist also observed this animal for its own sake.

The careful study of natural forms has hardly ever been wholly absent from art. But the interest has been expressed in different ways from time to time; sometimes incidentally in a floral border or bit of still life, at other times prominently in an outburst of landscape painting. The whole period from the beginning of the Renaissance to the end of the nineteenth century has been described as a "Discovery of Reality," meaning especially natural reality. Most of the famous masters of that period studied nature assiduously. This interest reached its peak during the nineteenth century, when some of the leading artists of the time were primarily landscape painters.

An excellent example is Joseph Mallord William Turner, whose *Seascape with a Squall Coming Up* is illustrated in Fig. 48. Here is a painting based on a penetrating study of natural phenomena. The

Fig. 48. Turner. *Seascape with a Squall Coming Up. ca.* 1803. Public Library, Malden, Mass.

Fig. 49. *Virgin Enthroned.* From the "Four Gospels." 12th century. Pierpont Morgan Library, New York.

60

tilt of the boat which has tacked across the wind and the luff of the sail on the boat which has come about are sure signs of a practiced and watchful eye, as are the scudding clouds and the feeling of wind which fills the picture. The flecks of foam blown from whitecaps and the translucent wave crests are touches rendered with perfect understanding. To be sure, Turner has taken arbitrary liberties with the pattern of light and shadow for the sake of the design, as he did in his mezzotint of an Alpine ravine (Fig. 11), but on the whole his picture is a convincing and natural-looking representation of the weather-beaten coast of England.

Behind this achievement lay four hundred years of study and observation of nature by some of the masters of Western painting, Pieter Bruegel, Rubens, Ruysdael, and Claude Lorrain, to name only a few. Turner, however, added to his inheritance. A large catalog would be required to list the natural forms and phenomena that he painted from close up and far away. No shell, bird, or pebble was too small for his scrutiny. Note, for instance, the perfection of the tiny sea gulls as they light on the water (Fig. 48), as well as the spaciousness of the distance. In order to stock his mind with what he needed for his art, he would stand by the edge of the Thames for hours, watching the effect of the tide's action on the sand or studying the rhythmic lapping of the water's edge.

Once, sailing with the North Sea fishing fleet, he had himself lashed to a mast during a storm so that he might observe it without being washed overboard. The knowledge he gained in this way accounts for much of the character of pictures like this seascape. In fact, his knowledge was so accurate and comprehensive that his paintings still amaze and delight the most exacting scientists. He never forgot, however, to be an artist and a poet. His range of interests embraced not only the appearance of nature on a universal scale, but its many moods perceived through feeling, from turbulent storms to the serene sunset in his *Norham Castle* (Fig. 25).

Turner's long and active life of seventy-eight years was devoted to the study of nature. Few men in history have traveled farther—twenty-five miles a day by foot and carriage from one end of Europe to the other and into every corner of England—in pursuit of a favorite theme. A human encyclopedia of natural information, he was academically illiterate. He occasionally painted such pictures as *The Destruction of Sodom, The Tenth Plague of Egypt,* and *Dido and Aeneas Leaving Carthage,* but the bulk of his 19,000 pictures is devoted to nature, not to the Bible or classical literature.

Turner is therefore an outstanding example of a painter whose perception was naturalistically oriented. Yet he is of the company of landscape artists who number into the hundreds. Greater than most, he is still representative.

THE RELIGIOUS ORIENTATION

Turner wandered over the earth and seas at will. Sometimes he seemed to his friends as close to nature as a wild animal. He painted whatever he wanted to and sold enough of his work to maintain a mansion in Queen Anne Street in London and travel widely. He was as free as any man could be.

There was another time in history when men were not free, but were constrained in movement and thought. This was the period called the Middle Ages, that is, from A.D. 400 to roughly 1400. During the first part of this thousand-year period, the Dark Ages, liberty was most suppressed and human thought was directed collectively by the few people in authority in the universal Catholic Church, a situation representing an extreme reaction from the materialistic and individualistic Roman conception of life to an orientation toward God and the needs of the spirit.

As historians now recognize, the Roman Empire did not collapse because it was conquered by barbarians from without or weakened by Christian meekness within (as Gibbon maintained). It failed by default, because its slave-ridden, dog-eat-dog, every-man-for-himself philosophy ceased to provide a tolerable way of life for the majority of human beings within its system. Instead, it bred cynicism even among the favored. By overemphasizing materialism, it starved another side of man's nature and caused the pendulum to swing violently in the other direction.

Nevertheless, when Rome collapsed, its virtues as well as its faults went with it. Within a short time the solid material foundation on which Rome's Empire stood was allowed to deteriorate into uselessness. One eye-witness says that the population of the city of Rome shrank from a million to thirty thousand—mostly thieves. Roads fell into disrepair, cutting the Roman universal state into thousands of political islands, each ruled by a local strong man. Agriculture declined to such a primitive level that farmers scratched out furrows in their tiny fields with sticks. As late as the fifteenth century the children who appeared in Flemish paintings obviously suffered from malnutrition. The great Roman aqueducts which provided water for cities and farms went unrepaired, for the Christians of the Dark Ages had neglected the Roman applied sciences of engineering, road-building, architecture, and medicine. In the course of time plagues broke out as a result of unsanitary conditions and decimated a population already weakened by malnutrition. It took a very long time, well into the eleventh century, before the peoples of Europe knew again the barest minimum of comfort, enlightenment, and security.

If, in turning from materialism and naturalism to an extreme orientation of perception toward religion, the afterlife, and God, the medieval peoples saved their souls from one kind of misery, they paid a heavy penalty in another direction. The fall of the hated Roman Empire was not all gain, even from the Christian point of view.

The twelfth-century manuscript illumination of the *Virgin Enthroned* (Fig. 49) is a typical example of the kind of painting created under the conditions described above. It is diametrically opposed to the painting of Turner or any other naturalistically oriented artist. Taking its elements singly, we find an over-all shallowness of design contrasting with Turner's representation of deep space; the figures and setting are either in a single plane or compressed forward. No attempt was made to relate the sizes of the figures correctly according to any naturalistic criterion. Rather, the Virgin looms twice life-size. Similarly, the color was applied arbitrarily and symbolically in flat, shadowless areas, without regard for natural modeling.

In keeping with the shallow space and flat color, the people appear thin and weightless. Their bodies have no bulk; neither do they stand firmly on the ground nor sit solidly on any seat. Instead, the seated Virgin seems to hang in mid-air. Finally, perspective as we know it is ignored; in fact, the church above the Virgin's throne is rendered in reverse perspective and resembles a toy house.

Since great strides had been made in ancient Greek sculpture and Roman wall painting in the study of human proportions, action, and weight relationships, and in the representation of space, the only explanation of this *Virgin Enthroned* lies in an orientation of perception away from naturalistic observation. The medieval artists painted in this way not because they lacked a tradition, but because they deliberately turned their backs on everything connected with Roman materialism and their own misery during the early days of Christianity. Having abandoned Roman civilization and its arts at the beginning of the Middle Ages, artists eventually lost the requisite knowledge to paint naturalistically.

The characteristics of the *Virgin Enthroned* are therefore due partly to ignorance (the loss of one tradition) and partly to intention (the development of another tradition). Let us insist only that each age has the right to express itself in its own manner. Two divergent ways of doing this are to emphasize what one sees with one's eyes, or to stress what one knows or believes in one's mind. Turner's way, like most naturalistic perception, was to favor the former; the *Virgin Enthroned* is an example of the latter. When studied carefully it reflects a profound indifference to the world of appearances. Its artist was as unobservant of visual facts as Turner was aware of them. Working from the mind, or ideologically, the medieval master was concerned mainly with the relative importance of ideas.

If the Virgin was ideologically more important to him than the worshippers at her feet, he expressed this evaluation by making her twice as large. It never occurred to him that he should not do this. From his point of view he had every right and reason, for his kind of painting was following a logic which was consistent with his purposes and just as valid as any other kind. It was the logic of a religious orientation of perception, of which the *Virgin Enthroned* is an excellent and typical example.

In the course of time the medieval orientation of perception ceased in its turn to provide a satisfactory way of life. Constrained by its emphasis on religion and the afterlife, people began to crave again some of the pleasures of everyday existence. When this desire was strengthened by the revival of commerce and by crusades which showed men a larger world, the medieval counterpart of a first world war ditty, "How are you going to keep 'em down on the farm after they've seen Paree?" went into effect. The dawn of a new day was only a matter of time.

One minor episode, unnoticed at the time, brings the old and new into sharp contrast. The great Italian writer Petrarch, traveling through southern France in the early fourteenth century, wanted to climb Mont Ventoux for no other reason than to obtain a good view of the countryside and admire an imminent sunset. In a letter to his tutor he told how he asked a peasant about a possible path to the summit. The peasant, a perfect incarnation of the medieval mind, was horrified at the idea of anyone entering a forest path with darkness in the offing. If wild animals did not destroy him, demons and evil spirits would. As for admiring a natural landscape and phenomena for their own sakes, that was incomprehensible. Nobody had done that for a thousand years. So Petrarch, orienting perception once more toward nature, stood alone on the peak and joined hands with Horace in the remote past and Turner in the future.

THE HUMANISTIC ORIENTATION

During the long medieval period, when man's attention was directed toward religion, the afterlife, and God, it was proportionately directed away from himself. The craving for individual fame, which makes an artist sign his work and want personal credit for it, was not tolerated. For the same reason, portraits of nonclerical personages virtually disappeared. Sensuous pleasure or carnal desire was taboo. Forbidden above all were references to sex or the human body in which sensuous pleasure and carnal desires are centered. So long as the Church's authority reigned supreme, the study of man and his physical appearance, the workings of his mind and body, his daily activities, interests, and material needs were scarcely touched upon in art. Man's soul and salvation were paramount.

The nude human body, far from being a thing of beauty, was considered a loathsome and evil reminder of Original Sin. When not excluded from art, it was represented for negative reasons to show the shame of Adam and Eve or the unprotected nakedness of sinners in Hell. Demons, too, were naked, but good people or saints never. The exclusion of nude man from medieval art tells us much about the era.

Conversely, the frequent representation of the male and female nude in art, with an obvious enjoyment of fine proportions and strong or graceful movements, denotes a wholly different point of view and civilization. Fig 50 compared with Fig. 49 illustrates this point strikingly. No mere difference in medium between painting and sculpture could account for the contrast between the two works. It must stem from widely different orientations of perception in society at large.

Comparing the two works point by point, we can see where the medieval painting is shallow and its figures paper-thin, the statue is three-dimensional. It rests solidly on the ground, but could move freely and easily over it, as the human body does in actuality. Throughout the body the sculptor has revealed his close attention to the proportions of limbs and external appearance in general, and also to what Elie Faure called aptly the life of the muscles. It was the Greek artist's knowledge of the inner working of the body, as well as its external appearances, that makes the implied movement of his figure so convincing.

On the other hand, there is not the slightest hint of a sexual or lascivious interest. Rather, the sculptor concentrated upon the co-ordination of a moving body without a thought for shame of Original Sin. He accepted the natural body, which he had probably seen a thousand times, as unself-consciously as he would have an undecorated tree. From that we may deduce that he was a man of the south, where, to the present day, nudity is taken as a matter of course. Apart from a few periods when a moralistic attitude prevailed, the southerner has accepted the unclad body without any puritanical

FIG. 50. *Zeus from Artemisium*. Transitional period, 480-450 B.C. National Museum, Athens.

FIG. 51. Giotto. *Presentation of the Virgin in the Temple. ca.* 1305. Arena Chapel, Padua.

qualms. Even today, boys swim in the nude beneath the bridges of Florence without arousing comment.

The superb male statue in Fig 50 was found at Artemisium in Euboea under circumstances which indicated to archaeologists that it is an original Greek statue. Moreover, it dates from one of the finest moments of Greek history, the so-called Transitional Period (480–450 B.C.) which came between the victorious repulsion of the Persians and the Golden Age of Pericles. Greece knew no better time and this figure represents its balanced, prosperous, and optimistic frame of mind.

Although called the *Zeus from Artemisium,* ostensibly representing a religious figure of the chief of the gods poised to hurl a thunderbolt, it is really a tribute to a perfectly developed human being. If it did not derive from an actual athlete practicing with the javelin on the playing field, it shows significantly that the Greek sculptors could imagine human beings in such terms. That is, if no single mortal posed for this figure, human physical beauty at least inspired it. For, where the medieval artist sang *Glory to God in the highest,* the Greek sculptors proclaimed *Man is the measure of all things.* And where the Old Testament Hebrews said *God created man in His own image,* the Greeks rejoined by reversing the process. They created deities who, though larger and more beautiful than life, were passionately human in behavior. Their gods were human, and their best men godlike. So true was this similarity that some of their early statues of young athletes were called Apollos. We cannot be sure today which they were meant to be.

The *Zeus from Artemisium* might have been cast in bronze before or after the Middle Ages (possibly during the Renaissance "Revival of Antiquity"), but it is significant that it could never have been conceived during the Middle Ages. Not only would the religious orientation of the time have forbidden it, but the knowledge of anatomy so evident in Fig. 50 did not exist. It had been discarded with Roman paganism. As a consequence, the medieval artist could not have modeled this figure even if he had wanted to. It could only have come from a time when men looked long and carefully at the human body at rest and in action; when, as a result of study, they knew its construction and articulation and handed their knowledge down from generation to generation. The figure of Zeus, like Turner's *Seascape with a Squall Coming Up,* came midway in a long period of study, not at its beginning. Finally, the *Zeus* could only have come from a time when both artists and laymen admired man's appearance and extended their interest to all of his activities. When such an attitude is widespread, we call it a humanistic orientation of perception. Seldom in history has it existed to a greater degree or borne finer fruit than in Ancient Greece.

THE SOCIAL ORIENTATION

If the humanistically oriented Greeks gave the world a new understanding of the reality which is man, and the religiously oriented peoples of medieval Christendom exalted his spiritual side, both left unexploited another side of human personality—that group *esprit* and emotional relationship which is expressed by the behavior of human beings toward each other.

The social impulse derives from man's sense of incompleteness, and from the fact that he finds his greatest opportunity for mutual understanding and fulfilment in other beings like himself. Being cut off from society by ostracism, exile, solitary confinement, or shipwreck is a dreadful fate. Just imagining ourselves in the plight of Robinson Crusoe is appalling. Crusoe's discovery of one savage footprint and his rescue are tremendously meaningful. Nothing in life interests human beings more than other human beings, a fact which has been given expression in countless works of art.

If, bearing this in mind, we now compare Figs. 49 and 50, we cannot help seeing that they differ on at least one score. The *Zeus from Artemisium* presents man by placing him on a pedestal. The *Virgin Enthroned* contains, by contrast, four figures, but their relationship with each other is not responsive or sympathetic in any usual sense. Rather, it is oriented by the respect of the worshippers for the religious significance of the Madonna and Child and Her orientation toward God. Any warm human relation between Christ and Mary is incidental. Certainly it is not stressed.

In Fig. 51, the *Presentation of the Virgin in the Temple* by Giotto, we find a very different conception. Although as humanistic as the sculptor of the *Zeus from Artemisium*, Giotto's concern was social. The meaning of his picture is centered in the behavior of the Biblical characters toward one another. Unlike the *Virgin Enthroned*, who stares into space, Giotto's Anna ushers her child, the Virgin Mary, up the stairs of the temple with all the pride of a real-life parent, and the priest receives Her with grave solicitude. The spectators to left and right are not wooden symbols, but true witnesses who exchange meaningful glances of interest and understanding. One feels in this social orientation of the figures an emotional focus, a ripple of excitement which binds the group. An interplay of social concern emanates from the event, expressing itself through gestures, glances, alert attention. To all of this interest the young Mary responds socially, comporting herself with a childish dignity befitting the occasion.

We are told in the Apocrypha how Mary, the future mother of Christ, was taken to the temple at the age of three and presented to the priest by her parents, Joachim and Anna, and how she charmed all the beholders by dancing on the steps of the altar. Giotto did not elect to depict her dancing, but he captured the spirit of the sacred legend in every other respect. The questions for us to ask are, why did he represent the story at all, and how does his representation convey a different conception of religion from that expressed through the *Virgin Enthroned?*

The answer can only be that some great change in the conditions under which artists worked permitted Giotto to forego for the time being the religious concern for God and the afterlife in Paradise or Hell, and to underscore the social implications of Christ's teachings. Giotto was only re-emphasizing a major aspect of Christianity. Moreover, his attitude toward religion was evolutionary rather than revolutionary. Like Luther, who originally had no intention of breaking with the Mother Church, Giotto wished only to revitalize the symbols of medieval religious art with the quality of daily life. The soundness of his instincts was demonstrated by those who, following his example, created the great religious paintings of the Renaissance.

Giotto's example rested only partly upon religious content. In great measure it was due to his sincere interest in people. Long before he undertook to decorate the Arena Chapel at Padua, he forearmed himself by studying the behavior of his fellow Florentines. During violent outbreaks of civil war he saw mothers and wives grieving over their men, who had been killed in the streets. In happier times he observed a husband bidding his wife goodby, a mother fondling a newborn child or presenting a daughter for confirmation. Thus, when commissioned to tell the equally human Biblical stories, he was prepared to paint an *Entombment*, a *Nativity*, or a *Presentation in the Temple* that carried the conviction of real life.

Where Turner's observation was directed toward nature, Giotto's turned toward social behavior; both represented long and zealous discipline. They spoke in comprehensive terms—Turner's naturalistic and northern, Giotto's humanistic and southern. For if Giotto reacted against medieval religious austerity, another older Italian tradition was in his blood. In an effort to give the sacred episodes the appearance and impact of real life, he joined hands with the ancients and endowed his figures with that modeled bulk and weight that we found in the *Zeus from Artemisium* but missed in the *Virgin*

Enthroned; his people stand firmly on the ground. He also introduced depth into his composition, a sense of space around and between the figures. And his architectural settings, though toylike to
modern eyes, marked a great advance over the background of the
Virgin Enthroned.

Giotto, a good son of the Mediterranean, also insisted that man is
the measure of all things. Though he painted a vivid blue sky above
the Temple in place of the flat gold background of the Middle Ages,
and provided a natural setting for his *Flight into Egypt,* his cardboard
mountains and miniature trees are never so convincing as his human
figures. He may have inspired hundreds of socially minded artists
in the centuries that followed, but he was not the forerunner of
Turner or any landscape school. His interests did not lie in that
direction.

By concentrating his attention, Giotto set an example of social
orientation. His strong, optimistic interest in human emotions struck
a responsive chord in the minds of his contemporaries. They delighted in his heart-warming, storytelling pictures, and thousands of
art lovers since have echoed this delight.

THE INTROSPECTIVE ORIENTATION

"Man is set in a world of beauty diversified with terror. His spirit
goes out to explore it. He is ever seeking to come to terms with the
world outside himself, to attain some sort of harmony with the living
and vast energies which pervade it, or at least some understanding
of them. He may return upon himself, persuaded that all the varied
beauty of the material world is an illusion, and that only within the
mind is secure reality to be sought."

When Laurence Binyon wrote these words for the *Spirit of Man
in Asian Art,*[1] he was speaking primarily of the Orient, but he also
described the universal characteristics of the introspective orientation
of perception. Indeed, he might have alluded with equal truth to
two western paintings, Figs. 52 and 53.

By introspection we do not mean ordinary self-consciousness, nor
the occasional meditations of any normal person. We mean a habitual emphasis upon internal reality. This withdrawal occurs usually
at the expense of the outer world and signifies confusion and trouble
in that world. Introspection is often, in a word, retreat. It may
identify the confirmed dreamer who is to be found in any society,
or it may be a sign of widespread historical conditions.

[1] Cambridge: Harvard University Press, 1936; p. 74.

FIG. 52. El Greco. *St. Dom-inic. ca.* 1595. Museum of Fine Arts, Boston.

FIG. 53. Dali. *The Persistence of Memory.* 1931. Museum of Modern Art, New York.

Fig. 52, which looks almost as though it were designed to illustrate Binyon's statement, is a painting of St. Dominic by El Greco. It is basically a study of the external manifestations of an introspective state of mind. The saint kneels in prayer with his attention focused on the Crucifix and the feeling of reverence it inspires. Because of his intense awareness of the Crucifix and all it symbolizes to his mind he is, as we say, lost to the world. A cataclysm could occur without his notice. El Greco has implied this complete withdrawal by treating the sky dynamically, its turbulence suggesting turmoil in the soul of the saint. The sky also suggests by its weird, unnatural quality that an adherence to normal appearances is unnecessary. To the religious mind, which is best when least materialistic, the outer world is insignificant, a thing to be used freely for some higher spiritual purpose.

This vibrant background expresses something typical of El Greco's point of view. We shall see it again in his *View of Toledo,* where he takes even greater liberties with external reality. Free rearrangement of the outer world and frequent distortions of shape and proportion are, to generalize for a moment, common signs of an introspective orientation. They are prominent in El Greco's work. His Dominic is, like all of his other figures, lean, bemused, and hypersensitive.

Behind this kind of painting lay the overwrought religious fanaticism of the Counter-Reformation. El Greco had arrived in Italy from Crete after the optimism and pagan delight in the physical world of the early Renaissance masters such as Giotto and Fra Angelico had begun to deteriorate under the impact of political catastrophes and soul-searching religious doubts. His awareness of psychological trends was always acute, and when he moved to Spain he reflected the turmoil of the times in his painting. His pictures are still, however, external revelations of inner states.

With Dali's *The Persistence of Memory* (Fig. 53) we come to a different treatment of introspection. Something new in the history of art, it is an attempt to convey visually the actual character of the inner world. To state the case simply, it is as though Dali, instead of portraying what a man looks like when lost in prayer or thought, attempted to enter his mind and explore his thoughts. *The Persistence of Memory* has only this in common with *St. Dominic:* it shows an indifference toward the ordinary relations of objective reality, toward which neither artist feels any binding obligation. Dali uses only what supports his attempt to express the importance and character of the introspective world and alters all else to suit his purpose.

Although rearranging forms, proportions, and relationships as arbitrarily as he pleased, not even Dali could avoid representing the physical properties which exist only in the outer world. In order to express or communicate anything, he had to convert the intangible into the tangible. His method was to conceive his paintings as though he were projecting images from the mind's eye, or the subconscious world of dreams, upon a visible screen. Granted that the images originated in external reality, they have been transformed by introspection.

Dali's painting has caused such confusion that some notice should be paid to what he is *not* attempting to do. For one thing, he is not pretending to reveal any image that ever existed literally, even in the most vivid imagination. He is trying to convey certain general characteristics of the subconscious world, to make us more aware of that realm, and to shed some light on its behavior. But he is not painting a specific dream. One of the chief characteristics of dreams is that their sharpness disappears rapidly as we awake. Anyone who has tried to describe a dream clearly to another person will recall that it lingers only as a vague feeling of a once intense experience. And, since an artist cannot paint while he is asleep, whatever of the subconscious realm he conveys must be conveyed through the devices of conscious artistry, like El Greco's angular shapes, distorted forms, and vibrant brushstrokes.

Because of the impossibility of catching a dream during the only time it is sharp, Dali has used artistic license to represent the dreamworld clearly, sharply, and vividly. In fact, he has represented it more precisely than we would ever see the outer world. He was probably influenced in this respect by his admiration for the quite undreamlike, highly realistic perception of the early Renaissance Flemish painters, like Jan Van Eyck, who scrutinized every detail of natural reality as though they were viewing the world through a telescope.

Although Dali transfers this ultra-sharp perception from the outer to the inner world in a way which may seem contrary to experience, he is not being merely perverse. He is not asserting that anyone dreamed this particular dream, or that anyone's dreams were ever in such sharp focus. Least of all is he asking us to judge his scene by any particular scene in the objective world. Instead, dealing with the general character of introspection, he is asserting that the mind plays tricks on us. When we are asleep or off guard, when we are released momentarily from our habitual inhibitions and social brakes, the subconscious mind inverts the normal relationships of outer reality. That the unrepressed mind does this, any honest adult will agree. Laughingly we say "I can dream, can't I?" And, dreaming, we create imaginary contexts which better our lot in life, making the

everyday world more tolerable. Thus, kept within bounds, introspection acts as a safety valve.

Dali has sought to convey the way the mind plays tricks on us by
making his *Persistence of Memory* exactly the reverse of ordinary
reality. Every form in the "landscape," both near and far, appears
super-sharp and clear to a degree that it never is in our daily experience. His treatment implies that we can rise in our dreams above
the physical limitations of eyesight. Indeed, he consistently made
everything in the picture the exact opposite of ordinary circumstances
and associations. A leafless tree grows unnaturally out of a blocklike
mass; over its lone branch a watch droops like a soggy pancake. A
fly wanders across another watch while ants swarm over a third.
Everything is out of its usual context, yet the picture flirts with
credibility. It suggests poignantly through visual means a weird,
disturbed feeling, like the distorted emotional residue of our own
dreams. It brings into clear focus what is normally vague and elusive.
Therein lies its fascination.

Confronted with paintings like *The Persistence of Memory,* laymen scoff. They doubt both the seriousness and the sanity of the
artist. Undoubtedly the modern Dadaists, surrealists, and fantastic
artists have indulged in a certain amount of leg-pulling and irrational
antics, such as the *Fur-lined Teacup* and the *Love Machine.* What
the layman overlooks is the long history of so-called "surrealistic"
painting. It has been a continuing artistic interest for centuries.
This in itself suggests something deeper than mere fun-making or
charlatanism. Furthermore, although the modern surrealist movement was intensified by the tensions of the First World War, it originated in the clear-eyed, purposeful scientific studies of Freudian psychoanalysis. These, too, were scoffed at originally. Nevertheless,
they revealed hitherto unsuspected regions of internal reality. The
subjective world which is the province of introspection is without
doubt a perfectly legitimate field of artistic exploration.

Whether the subjective world is a fruitful field for most painters
is another question. It seems clear that introspective perception
worked at a disadvantage in the visual arts. These static media lend
themselves less well than the sequential media—literature, music, the
drama, and the cinema—to the expression of the "stream of con-
sciouness" or the flowing character of our mental life. One may even
doubt whether such penetrating introspective painting as Dali's will
ever appeal to more than a few people or be commonly understood.

One great obstacle stands in the way of surrealist introspection:
lacking an external means of verification, such as we have in naturalistic, humanistic, and social perception, we can never prove or dis-

prove anyone else's dreams. We must accept them on faith. And faith, like mental telepathy, is not a satisfactory basis for artistic communication. Considering, also, that a trained psychoanalyst must devote many hours to drawing out and interpreting the complex inner life of a single patient, the difficulty of expressing our deeper thoughts becomes apparent. One suspects that sheer lack of time and energy preclude any profound communication of subjective reality except among a few unusually introspective artists and observers. The mental life of each human being is the most real, but also the most private and individual, aspect of total reality. By that token it is also the least universal, the farthest removed from common understanding.

Notwithstanding inherent limitations, some introspective painting has demonstrated remarkable insight into the innermost workings of the mind. At its best it has shed more light upon the function of the mind than any other kind of painting and justified itself by revealing universal patterns in internal reality. Finally, there is little doubt about the sensitivity or seriousness of its best practitioners. Thus, if Dali's kind of introspection has limitations as a basis of universal expression, and El Greco's represents man driven to the wall by adverse conditions, each is nevertheless an important key to the nature and history of man.

THE ARCHITECTURAL ORIENTATION

Fig. 54 is a picture painted in 1930 by the American artist Charles Sheeler and entitled *American Landscape*. If we ask which orientation of perception it expresses, we find that it suggests none that we have already studied. Although sky and water are represented, no stress has been laid on the natural character of either. The quietly unobtrusive sky is a mere backdrop, and the water has been channeled artificially between the straight, rigid walls of a canal. Furthermore, the lone human figure present is scarcely noticeable. In sum, the composition does not express any strongly marked naturalistic, religious, humanistic, social, or introspective orientation. So we shall have to seek in another direction: namely, among the many signs that Sheeler has given of his interest in what man has built. For want of a better term we shall define that predilection as an architectural orientation of perception.

A not uncommon kind of interest, the architectural orientation derives from the following facts. In adjusting himself to nature, man has created cushions against both the elements and psychological confusion, thus satisfying his need for protection and orderly sur-

FIG. 54. Sheeler. *American Landscape.* 1930. Museum of Modern Art, New York.

FIG. 55. Mondrian.
*Composition in White,
Black, and Red.* 1936.
Museum of Modern
Art, New York.

76

roundings. From the beginning of civilized life he has built build-ings to such an extent that shelter is called one of the three essential requirements of human life, and some architectural or esthetic order has been deemed to be almost as essential. Therefore, the architec-tural orientation expresses psychological values as well as practical, and in our study the psychological are the more important. Finally, this orientation may be extended to include other kinds of human products—machines, furniture, or pots and pans; but the world of buildings is its largest province.

Human beings have not only shown their ability to create a man-made, man-ordered reality; they have been fascinated by it. One of the first men to rise above the anonymous herd in ancient Egypt was the architect Imhotep, who built a great pyramid for the Pharaoh Zoser nearly 3000 years before the birth of Christ. And such prod-ucts of his professional descendants as the Pyramids, the Parthenon, the Colosseum, Chartres Cathedral, St. Peter's, the Taj Mahal, Ver-sailles Palace, and the Empire State Building have loomed large ever since in the imagination and history of man. Man the builder has gradually transformed our environment. What is more, the impor-tance accorded building has created an architectural orientation of life. In our time a city-dweller can go his way for days without set-ting foot on raw earth or a blade of grass. His only reminder of natural reality may be a potted plant.

The architect, of all artists, augments and expresses this archi-tectural orientation most directly. Our concern here, however, is with man's attitude toward architecture, and that has been expressed more accurately through paintings and relief sculpture; hence our use of Sheeler's *American Landscape* instead of a building as a point of departure. Moreover, an architectural interest has hardly ever been absent from painting for very long.

Among the paintings we have observed in this study, the following illustrate at least some recognition of man-made architectural reality: Kokoschka's *Courmayeur,* Utrillo's *Church of Sacré Coeur,* Turner's *Norham Castle,* Burchfield's *November Evening,* Lautrec's *At the "Moulin de la Galette,"* Fra Angelico's *Annunciation,* Tintoretto's *Annunciation,* the medieval *Virgin Enthroned,* and Giotto's *Pres-entation of the Virgin.*

To these specific examples one may add many illustrations from ancient Assyrian relief sculpture; Roman painting and sculpture; Persian, Mughal, Indian, Chinese, and Japanese painting in the Orient; and innumerable examples of Western art from the Renais-sance to the present day. In short, recognition of the role of man's architectural environment has a long and universal history. Significance lies, therefore, in the character of its representation and the degree of prominence given to it at different times.

Considered in this light, the architectural illustrations of this book fall into four main groups:

1. Those which emphasize nature, but include architecture incidentally like Kokoschka's *Courmayeur*.
2. Those which reverse this order and make nature secondary to an architectural center of interest, like Turner's *Norham Castle*.
3. Pictures whose settings are exclusively architectural, but secondary to some other interest, such as the religious or social activities of man. Giotto's *Presentation* is an example.
4. Compositions in which architecture is the primary and most prominent feature, as in Utrillo's *Sacré Coeur*.

If the history of art is considered as a whole, the majority of paintings will fall, not surprisingly, in the first three groups; for human beings have generally given nature and man precedence over any architectural environment. Yet the fourth group includes numerous examples, and what is particularly significant about them are the historical conditions which an outright architectural orientation expresses.

Broadly speaking, man's structural environment has been given the greatest prominence in art under two conditions. First, when a highly active school of painters has been closely associated with some city which had a strongly defined architectural character and tradition in which it took pride, notable instances being the schools associated with Pompeii, Florence, Rome, Venice, Paris, and New York. Utrillo's paintings, for instance, can be fairly described as a series of portraits of the streets of Paris. Second, when the environment in which these artists worked was in the highest degree urban and the least rural. In most cases, that degree of development has occurred when societies were well advanced in their histories and tending progressively toward an emphasis on metropolitan life.

No great insight is required to see that in such times the city becomes a primary focus of attention, an end in itself. Rome, Paris, New York are entities in their own right. More than that, they dominate human beings to the point where many older values and orientations are inverted. Humanistic, naturalistic, and religious interests are pushed down the scale.

In great urban centers people tend, moreover, to stress the material and utilitarian sides of life. These were little thought of in the Middle Ages, but are prominent in our own day, when radio and television have projected an industrialized concept of life into the most rural areas. Thinking in the remotest farms is influenced by what man-made devices can do to lighten the burden of labor.

Is it strange, then, that Sheeler should have given expression to a universal orientation of our time through a whole series of pictures? His *Upper Deck*, a vivid representation of a corner of an ocean liner, and his *Steam Turbine* speak the language of our day. The technique of his *American Landscape* has the precision of a machine. Nor is its title without significance, for the true landscape of our time probably should depict a city street or a factory. In all of these respects Sheeler's painting is a timely and apt representative of an architectural orientation of perception.

THE ABSTRACT ORIENTATION

Since physical and mental limitations make all human perception selective, every work of art is abstract to some extent. We can distinguish, however, between unintentional and deliberate abstraction. When the zealous realist Gérôme painted his *L'Éminence Grise* (Fig. 34), he tried to push representation as far as it can be pushed through the medium of paint. His attitude was as inclusive and nonabstract as he could make it. In this discussion we are dealing with the opposite of his point of view.

The term *abstract* has come in our time to have a special meaning. According to the dictionary, when abstract applies to works of art it means "presenting or characterized by nonrepresentational designs depicting no recognizable thing, only geometric figures, or abstruse diagrams, or mechanical or amorphous shapes." It is in that sense that we are using the term.

In the Museum of Modern Art in New York there is a painting by Mondrian whose sole title is *Composition in White, Black, and Red* (Fig. 55). It is a perfect illustration of Webster's definition of the abstract orientation of human perception. When we compare it with the other illustrations in this chapter, certain distinguishing characteristics emerge strongly. By a process of elimination we can discern that Mondrian has excluded the naturalistic, religious, humanistic, social, introspective, and architectural orientations. His composition reflects nothing in reality except itself. It is the most self-sufficient work of art we have studied. It is also the one most likely to be misunderstood.

When laymen see Mondrian's *Composition* in the Museum of Modern Art they are prone to scoff that it is "nothing but a linoleum design from one of those tin-can and shoe-box modernistic houses." They are more right than they realize on one count, for abstract painting, modern architecture, contemporary interior decoration, and industrial design have all influenced each other to the point of creating a comprehensive artistic style. But they are wrong on the other count; abstract painting is a good deal more than a linoleum pattern framed and hung on a wall.

In order to correct this error and avoid a furor which has divided modern painters and laymen into opposite camps, we must try to relate abstract painting to certain fundamental facts of art, history, and human perception. To take the second first, modern abstract painting was started on its course by Paul Cézanne sometime in the late nineteenth century. Vollard writes that a young artist made a pilgrimage to Aix to see the master. Cézanne, a socially shy person, was caught off guard at church, but presently he clutched a button on the young man's jacket and said earnestly, "Listen! Everything in Nature is a cylinder or a cube." [2]

This statement contained the germ of abstract art. Cézanne's eyes saw cubes, cones, spheres, and cylinders in rocks, trees, apples, and mountains. But habits of perception give way slowly in human history, and Cézanne was too close to the naturalism of the nineteenth century to sacrifice nature entirely for his abstract interests, so he blended both. However, he saw the trend that his art would start and called himself the primitive of a new movement.

Once set in motion, any fruitful movement, any new way of understanding our world, tends to be explored and exploited until it is exhausted. Artists carry it to a dead end or, to vary the metaphor, drain it dry. Then they start on another tack or begin all over again. The artists of the Renaissance did this with the innovations of another pioneer of a new movement, Giotto. It is an old pattern in the history of art. So it should not surprise us to see that Mondrian has fulfilled Cézanne's prophecy. His *Composition* simply carries to a logical conclusion the ideas which Cézanne laid on the table. Picasso's analytical cubism of about 1909 was but a step on the way.

The layman who laughs at Mondrian's *Composition* or Dali's *Persistence of Memory* does not connect either with man's age-old attempts to understand the creative process that is centered in the way human beings think. Abstraction is a common fact in human thought and represents an old and widespread orientation. It has cropped out repeatedly in the decorative arts from Egyptian times to the present day. Without it there would be no mathematics, no science, and little music. Mondrian's *Composition* expresses not

---

[2] Ambroise Vollard, *Paul Cézanne, His Life and Art* (New York: Frank-Maurice, Inc., 1926), p. 161.

only a kind of thought consciously set in motion by Cézanne, but one always latent in human perception. All we ourselves need to understand his *Composition* is sufficient flexibility of mind to carry abstraction to its logical conclusion.

If Mondrian's kind of abstraction goes against the grain because it is patently antinaturalistic, let us recognize that he has had much company in the history of man's contact with his environment. From the beginning of time human beings have longed to free themselves from the trials and tribulations forced upon them by nature, from the quarrels of society, and the gropings and confusions of mental life. They have craved peace and order around them and clarity of thought within. Mondrian's *Composition* is his answer to these deficiencies and the need of man for order. It says, further, that when we cannot satisfy that need by compromising with nature, we have every right to create it in a reality made by man solely for man.

Quite apart from whether we like Mondrian's *Composition*, or whether we ourselves are prepared to go with him to such an extreme, we must not forbid him his own right to do so. That he has created a man-made reality is a plain fact, and its orderliness, which is directed exclusively to the human mind, without circumlocutions through nature, may exert a powerful appeal. Being direct, its effect is immediate, intense, and clear. And if clarity, intensity, and vividness of effect are desirable in works of art, Mondrian's *Composition* cannot be dismissed with a laugh merely because we do not understand it. No other picture in this book is its superior in visual impact.

The abstract orientation, being the least naturalistic, is the most artificial expressed through painting. In the layman's opinion this is bad. The abstract painter replies that the objection is based on habit. He points out that musicians long ago won the privilege of abstracting the world of sound in etudes, compositions, symphonies, and sonatas which justify themselves musically without any reference to babbling brooks, waterfalls, thunder and lightning, or hummingbirds in the spring. Any suggestion of these natural sounds is purely coincidental. Beethoven's *Fifth Symphony* has an ideological theme, but no one needs to know the "story" to love the music. The man-made musical reality is a self-justifying, independent end in itself.

The abstract painter points, also, to the architect's privilege of designing supports without any obligation to make columns suggest trees. He refers, further, to the avowed aim of scientists to reduce natural phenomena to laws and principles which depart to the utmost degree from their original objects of study and at their best are reducible to purely mathematic symbols. Nature is nothing but the raw material for a more important objective, an understanding of the universal, timeless, and fundamental aspects of reality.

The abstractionist can cite many other examples of man's desire and ability to free himself from natural limitations. He cites these examples to challenge the fixed idea that painting must represent something identifiable in the external world, that it must be merely a means, instead of a reality in its own right. And he challenges the older thinking in order to gain for the painter the same privileges of abstraction that are freely accorded music, architecture, mathematics, and science.

For the artist to push ahead and the public to try to hold him to its slower pace is an old story. It inevitably creates conflicts which are increased by the originality of the artist. But most of these conflicts must be taken in stride. Time alone will reveal whether or not the abstract movement in painting has expressed a fundamental orientation of perception. If it has, its place is assured.

THE ARTISTIC ORIENTATION

In February, 1835, Turner first exhibited publicly a spectacular painting, the *Burning of the House of Lords and Commons,* and in the same year the British government commissioned two architects, Sir Charles Barry and Augustus Welby Pugin, to design a new building to replace the structure which had been destroyed the year before. The result was the Houses of Parliament which stand beside the Thames. Fig. 56 shows them as they appear today, mellowed by time and London fog. For our purpose they exemplify perfectly the eighth and final attitude toward reality that we shall study, the artistic orientation of perception. They illustrate its weaknesses and strengths, blind spots and justifications. For everything conspired to make the new Houses of Parliament reflect strongly the building artistry of the past.

The conservative Victorian British insisted upon a style which would express the continuity of their national institutions, especially those which harked back to the days of the first trials by jury and the signing of the Magna Carta. Indeed, the English, high and low, had, as they still have, a special place in their affections for the Middle Ages and the great castles, cathedrals, and universities which arose during them.

In addition, both of the architects were wedded to the past. Barry was a classicist and Pugin a romanticist. The latter not only shared the revivalist beliefs of most nineteenth-century architects, but believed fervently that the machine age had to recapture the medieval

Fig. 56. Barry and Pugin. Houses of Parliament. 1840-1860. London.

religious and artistic spirit (i. e., the pride of craftsmanship instilled by the guilds) for its moral salvation. He steeped himself in both the forms and spirit of Gothic architecture.

Other factors oriented the minds of the public, architects, and government officials strongly toward the artistic past. Westminster Hall, the undamaged nucleus around which the new buildings were to be built, was a center and symbol of English political history. There some of the earliest parliaments had been held, Charles I had been condemned to death, and Cromwell had presided over the Rump Parliament. It was rich in memories of the fight for freedom and constitutional government. Since the Hall was truly medieval, dating from the eleventh to the fourteenth centuries, the Gothic style was virtually preordained. The architects accepted their mandate wholeheartedly. It was their execution of it which met with mixed success.

There is no doubt that the Houses of Parliament expressed what the English people wanted expressed at that time, and the majority love them still. The buildings express, too, the historical continuity which Englishmen prize, and are reasonably harmonious with their famous neighbor, Westminster Abbey, which appears in the left background of Fig. 56. The Big Ben and Victoria Towers, their two most prominent features, have come to be sentimentally revered around the world. In these several respects the buildings have been successful.

It is the architectural character of the Houses of Parliament which is now challenged in a debate applying to the whole question of an artistic orientation of perception. At a distance, the massive structure is impressive, its silhouette bold and striking. It occupies a superb site where it can be seen properly. But on closer inspection the impossibility of imitating in an industrial age any religiously inspired, handicraft style like Gothic becomes apparent. Despite Pugin's fervor and his knowledge of Gothic architectural decoration, there were some obstacles he could not overcome. He could not make Victorian laborers think and feel like Gothic sculptors in the face of all the training and practices of their own times. Speaking broadly, he could not run against the tide of the Industrial Revolution or turn back the clock. Modernists say that no one else can either.

The British, placing associations, continuity, and symbolic values above efficiency and modernity, have loved the venerable buildings in spite of mediocre plans and other functional inconveniences. But architects in other lands—Germany, France, America, Sweden, Switzerland—have taken a different view of the Houses of Parliament.

They have belittled the buildings which carried the day for Romanticism in the mid-nineteenth century for their poor design and worse example. The battle rages around the following points.

Progressive architects maintain that architecture should express the spirit of our time, which is an industrial era and not the Middle Ages. They apply this argument especially to buildings which express modern, rather than medieval, ideals of government, like the United Nations Building in New York. They point out how the prestige of the Houses of Parliament caused the Gothic style to be applied indiscriminately in scores of cases where there was not the excuse of historical continuity—to "Gothic" factories, warehouses, water towers, railroad stations, and other children of the machine age.

Most of all, forward-looking builders regret the lack of creativity signified by widespread copying. They challenge the implication that the time-honored past had a monopoly on beauty and dignity. If, they say, the builders of the classical Parthenon and Gothic cathedrals were able to design buildings that expressed their own days and societies, we should have the originality to do the same. And so the battle rages.

Painting and sculpture are another matter. They differ especially from architecture in the matters of practical function and construction. Not having been badly limited by practical considerations or benefited by revolutionary advances in materials or techniques, artists have been freer to use or discard the lessons of the past without arousing violent opposition. In painting and sculpture the words *influenced by* have no such red flag connotations as *revivalism* in architecture. However, two opposite attitudes seem to have existed. One is illustrated by the art of Picasso, who has learned everything he could from the old masters; the other by Winslow Homer, who early in his career said, "If a man wants to be an artist, he should never look at pictures." Of the two points of view, Homer's adamant independence is exceptional. The majority of artists have eagerly studied the work of their colleagues, both living and dead.

Many of these artistic orientations can only be determined indirectly by a study of internal evidence. Giorgione and Rembrandt, for instance, left no written tributes to their sources of inspiration. But there are more cases where we do not have to guess. Ingres so worshipped Raphael's art that he stood guard before the *St. Michael* in the Louvre during a revolutionary uprising and vowed to kill anyone who harmed it. Tintoretto wrote this artistic credo on his studio wall: *the form of Michelangelo and the color of Titian.* Van Gogh praised the Japanese print-makers and other artists in scores of letters to his brother Theo. Rubens and Rembrandt owned large collections of the art of other men. Cézanne said, "I wish to remake Poussin after nature," and "The Louvre is the book in which we learn to read." Toulouse-Lautrec never lost an opportunity to laud the art of Degas. Turner modeled his noted mezzotint series, *The Liber Studiorum,* on Claude Lorrain's *Liber Veritatis* and specified in his will that one of his landscapes should always hang beside one of Lorrain's masterpieces in the National Gallery in London. Turner was in turn called "master" by a group of Impressionists, including Monet, Sisley, and Pissarro, who acknowledged their debt to him in an open letter.

The artistic orientation of perception in painting and sculpture is an established fact. The only questions concern its character, usefulness, and historical role. The charge most commonly heard against an artistic orientation concerns copying. Students who are set to copying old paintings usually fear that their originality will be hurt. Vollard, noting this fear, wrote, "Pissarro, who was also working at Auvers, cautioned Cézanne not to let himself be dominated by the masters." [3] Daumier, mindful of the copyists in the Louvre, caricatured the practice, and said, "One must be of one's own time." And the outspoken realist Courbet, angered by the worship of the past by Ingres and his followers, cried that all art museums should be destroyed.

Yet Cézanne was not dominated by the old masters. Daumier learned invaluable lessons from the works of Rembrandt and Michelangelo in the Louvre. Courbet worked there as well as outdoors, and absorbed more from the old Dutch painters than he admitted. The Louvre was, in fact, a training ground for the outstanding French artists of the nineteenth century. One of the most original of all modern masters, Henri Matisse, copied masterpieces there for ten years, earning a living and learning to paint. Before him Manet had trained himself in the same way; his copy of Titian's *Madonna of the Rabbit* now hangs beside the original in the Louvre. No one, however, mistakes Manet's painting for Titian's, because any original artist impresses his own personality upon anything he copies.

For those who would learn from the old but create anew, Renoir showed the way. He said that he got his material from nature, but learned how to paint from masterpieces in the museums. By using both, he avoided the danger of adhering slavishly to either. His advice had been anticipated long before. Five hundred years before Christ, Confucius said, "When nature exceeds art, you have a rustic. When art exceeds nature you have a clerk. When nature and art are

[3] *Ibid.,* p. 47.

blended harmoniously, you have a superior man." And if Hsieh Ho's third rule was "conformity with nature," his sixth was the "copying of classical masterpieces." Turner is an example of a westerner who created art by doing both.

Thus the evidence strongly suggests that an artistic orientation is not ruinous; it merely creates a problem—the problem of being inspired without being dominated.

THE INTERRELATION OF THE ORIENTATIONS

Although we have studied the orientations of perception separately, they are not mutually exclusive. Often they overlap. The *Zeus from Artemisium* is humanistic but also religious. Similarly, Turner's *Seascape* contains human figures and man-made objects as well as sea and sky, and its naturalistic orientation is tempered by reminiscences of the artistic influence of Ruysdael. Giotto's *Presentation* is highly social, but religiously so, and not without an architectural interest. El Greco's *St. Dominic* is also religious as well as introspective, and it is humanistic in that it shows us a significant side of human life. Dali's *Persistence of Memory* deals with introspection, but it is also artistically inclined toward the painting of the fifteenth-century Flemish masters. The medieval *Virgin Enthroned* could not easily be called naturalistic, but its religiosity did not exclude some observation of human behavior or a passing notice of architecture. These overlappings merely express the fact that at no time in history have people preferred only one aspect of reality to the exclusion of all others. Neither have they been intensely interested in all eight aspects of reality at once. As we have seen, their interests are selective. At one time they are most interested in two or three aspects of reality, at another time they prefer others. As their interests vary, so does their history, and the changes are reflected in works of art. Dominant interests are evident in almost every case. Thus a work of art usually expresses a combination of orientations whose meaning lies in the make-up of the combination and in the main impression that it conveys.

CHAPTER 4

The Human Equation

The artist expresses an individual interpretation of the world tempered by the orientations of thought in his own time and place. In addition, and quite without recognizing it, he expresses universal traits of human nature every time he picks up a pencil, chisel, or brush. The purpose of this chapter is to determine what these traits may be and the role they have played in art.

We often refer to this side of creativity in sweeping fashion by saying that *art expresses the human spirit,* but we cannot define or appreciate anything so comprehensive as a spirit. Reason is not enough to explain it. Inspiration, emotion, and imagination are also distinctively human attributes that set men above the level of animals and machines. But these elements of personality, differing widely among men, do not appear as a single, uniform whole in any work of art, allowing us to say that a specific picture or statue is imbued with *the* human spirit. The human spirit in art is, instead, a reflection of the variability of personality and outstanding attributes of individual character. It will appear in the imaginative quality of one work of art, in the logic of design of another, and in the exalted inspiration of a third. But no one work is expected to express the entire possibilities of the human spirit at their highest level.

We can best discover the human spirit in art by reducing it to certain agreed-upon emotional and intellectual components of a varying equation, examining them first separately and then together. We can thereby gain some impression of the part played by human nature in art without losing sight of its individuality. Eight human qualities important in artistic expression will suffice: curiosity, memory, logic, imagination, sympathy, empathy, vitality, and will. Each affects the others, but the first four are mainly intellectual, the last four predominantly emotional.

CURIOSITY

Curiosity is the desire to know more. It is shared by both animals and man, but with a significant difference. Animal curiosity is dominated by two instincts—hunger and sex. In man curiosity has a greater range: all human learning develops from it.

In the fine arts, curiosity does not itself create. It gathers the raw materials upon which the rest of the mind works. Like all the other spiritual attributes, curiosity's role has varied through the various periods of history. When it was suppressed, art has been conventional and conformist with a minimum of originality and diversity. The early Middle Ages was such a period.

From the beginning of the Renaissance, which overthrew medieval taboos, all the individual artists we now call "old masters" exhibited exceptional curiosity. Many exhibited it at an early age; most maintained their enthusiasm for their art and for visual experience to the end of their lives.

Few artists have shown greater curiosity about every aspect of reality than did Leonardo da Vinci. Living in the Renaissance, when the versatile, many-sided genius was esteemed, he surpassed his time. A modern admirer has described him as having specialized in omniscience. Volumes have been written about his search for knowledge. Every orientation described in the previous chapter except the abstract can be illustrated by examples from his studio. The whole realm of subjective reality fascinated him: he was a master psychologist. There was little that did not arouse Leonardo's interest. In addition to a religious masterpiece, *The Last Supper,* he painted a penetrating psychological portrait of La Gioconda, the "Mona Lisa." There are pictures inspired by pagan mythology, such as *Leda and the Swan,* studies of social behavior, and illustrations of his humanistic interests. Extant, too, are incidental but fine drawings of architecture and other man-made contrivances. His drawings alone reveal an encyclopedic range of interests. In them we find beautiful young women and children, and scrawny, beetlebrowed old men. Ugliness fascinated him as much as beauty, as did facial expressions and bodily postures. Among his drawings are the *Hanging of Bernardo di Bandini, Heads of Warriors for the "Battle of Anghiari,"* a *Tuscan Landscape, Stratified Rocks,* sketches of *Water Passing Obstacles,* a *Mountain Deluge, Studies of Male Shoulder Muscles,* a

FIG. 57. Da Vinci. Detail, *Virgin of the Rocks. ca.* 1483-1486. National Gallery, London.

FIG. 58. Michelangelo. *Adam.* 1508-1512. Preparatory drawing for the *Creation of Adam* in the Sistine ceiling decorations. British Museum, London.

FIG. 59. Raphael. *The Mass of Bolsena.* 1512. Stanza d'Eliodoro. Vatican, Rome.

Section of Female Internal Organs, An Embryo in a Womb, and a *Median Section of a Skull.*

What did Leonardo *do* with the vast knowledge his curiosity caused him to accumulate? How did it contribute to his art? The artistic quality of his most scientific drawings leaves little to be desired. Yet, by themselves they are only fragments. They leave us expecting from such a mind more than the proofs of a restless curiosity. We want to see the gatherings of this curiosity synthesized into works of art of a more complex and higher order.

Leonardo does not disappoint us. He drew largely for his own enlightenment, appending notes in a private cipher. It was his paintings that he submitted to the world as works of art. The relationship between his drawings and paintings is important: the observation which went into his drawings made his paintings possible. A case in point is Fig. 57, a detail of flowers from his *Virgin of the Rocks,* now in the National Gallery, London. Although they seem to have been done directly from nature, they were probably painted from knowledge and drawings after years of preparation. Leonardo exemplified the Renaissance attitude toward nature as something to be studied eagerly but carefully. He never painted momentary impressions of any passing scene. Even his sketches of mountain storms imply universal characteristics. When he painted one of his few pictures over a long period of time (*The Last Supper* required three years; "Mona Lisa" was, in his opinion, never finished), he meant to incorporate into it a lifetime of knowledge. By comparing his painted flowers with his original drawings, we can see how Leonardo prepared himself. When the time came to paint, he was ready.

In the *Virgin of the Rocks,* the flowers are small. They are likely to go unnoticed, but to Leonardo, the perfectionist, they were important. He painted them with the care born of years of thought behind which lay his intense curiosity.

So, if curiosity did not create the flowers in the *Virgin of the Rocks,* it provided the initial impulse that eventually brought them into being and made them real. This order is typical of curiosity's initiative role in the creative process. Although contributory, it is a vital spur to great and original art.

MEMORY

Memory makes mental continuity, perception, and development possible, preserving what we learn for future use. Its importance is apparent in the way it overcomes the physical limitations of visual perception. Since the human eye can focus on only one limited area

at a time in reading a page of print or viewing a landscape, memory
retains in the mind a series of impressions until they can be synthesized into ideas or concepts. Through memory the new experiences
are also related to the past. In painting a picture, for example, an
artist reverses the perceptual process through a series of steps which
evolve from years of training. That is what Whistler meant when he
maintained, in a famous lawsuit instigated by John Ruskin, that he
was not asking two hundred guineas for a picture painted in a few
hours but for the experience of a lifetime. Memory relates, continues, and unifies our whole lives. It is important to artists because
without it there would be no development or continuity in their
work.

Among the several kinds of memory, the artist emphasizes the
visual. At the technical level he deliberately cultivates habit. Both
characteristics are well illustrated by the work of Renoir and Michelangelo. Renoir, painting almost every day during his seventy-eight
years, trained his hand to perform technical chores quickly. He could
set his palette and mix paints with a minimum of effort. By repetition he gained muscular coordination. Habit of this sort is both
necessary and good; when the hand can paint in a relaxed, almost
self-guided manner, the artist's mind is free to deal with more original problems of composition. The result is a spontaneity of execution that is free of tension and awkwardness. By picking up two
or three colors on his brush and letting them mix themselves in the
stroke, he achieved effects which appear miraculous. Neither a copy-
ist nor Renoir himself could duplicate them exactly. Nevertheless,
they were not pure luck—if Renoir could not duplicate a Renoir, he
could paint another.

Michelangelo's work shows how an artist may specialize his memory. During his youth he studied anatomy zealously. A sexton
provided him corpses, for a fee, and Michelangelo dissected them
secretly at night. The revolting chore turned his stomach for the
rest of his life, but the knowledge he gained made his later art possible. That Michelangelo knew the difference between an anatomical study and a work of art is clear from a comparison of any of his
preparatory drawings with the final paintings, such as his drawing of
Adam (Fig. 58) in the British Museum and his *Creation of Adam*
(Fig. 126) on the Sistine ceiling. The latter owes its accuracy to the
former. Having once mastered human anatomy, Michelangelo was
able to construct the superhuman figures in the Sistine ceiling from
memory and make each of them articulate perfectly. Without this
knowledge, the Sistine ceiling could not have been painted by one

man in four years or a dozen. Though used in a different way, memory was as great an aid to Michelangelo as it was to Renoir.

The art of Turner, too, shows us the relationship between memory and imagination, for Turner retained a firm hold on the tangible world, even though in his final period he dissolved it in a haze of atmosphere and sunlight. The point is illustrated by Alexander J. Finberg, Turner's biographer, who says of a small watercolor signed and dated by Turner in 1818 (more than halfway through his career) and entitled *A First-Rater Taking in Stores:*

This is the drawing Turner is said to have begun and finished one morning at Farnley, between breakfast and lunch. There had been some talk at breakfast between Mr. Fawkes and Turner about the relative sizes of small sailing-craft and men-of-war. After breakfast, Turner said to young Hawksworth Fawkes that he would make a drawing to illustrate what they had been talking about. The boy sat beside him for three hours while the drawing was being made, the artist, says Thornhill, "tearing up the sea with the eagle claw of his thumbnail, and working like a madman; yet the detail is full and delicate, betraying no sign of hurry." [1]

Finberg questions the time element in the story, but not the accuracy of Turner's memory or the esthetic unity and vitality of his picture.

Like most creative artists, Turner was working from a memory that was accurate and comprehensive. When he took liberties with nature, he did so deliberately, not from vagueness of recollection. If, at the end, he sought artistic unity in an imaginary world, it was only after he had acquainted himself thoroughly with the world as it is. He progressed from observation to dreams, not the other way round. Most apparently imaginative paintings, for example, the landscapes of the Sung dynasty painters in China, usually owe their reality to a long and close study of nature. The path followed by Renoir, Michelangelo, and Turner was a well-worn path.

LOGIC

Logic is reason, distinct from instinct or impulse. It allows us to connect cause and effect, to explain *why* something happened, and is our principal means of understanding. Plato likened reason and impulse to a chariot driver and a team of wild horses. To him reason was the highest human virtue.

In art, logical power is specialized. It is devoted to visual relationship in design, to social and other practical relationships in the

[1] *Turner's Water-Colours at Farnley Hall* (London: Crowell [Studio], 1910), description of Plate VIII.

content of a picture, and to a fresh and logical fusion of the two. Creating a work of art is a selective process. An artist must make many decisions, hinging upon what goes together and what should be omitted. Winslow Homer's hardest decision was knowing when to stop. All are logical questions; the chances for errors of judgment are unlimited and account for the wide range between great and poor painting. The logical process of thought that an artist employs is thus specialized, but it resembles all other forms of logic in dealing basically with relationships of cause and effect.

The history of art shows two contrasting modes of thought, each with its own form of logical consistency. One is the vital but elusive creativity popularly attributed to inspiration and usually identified with the romantic point of view. Renoir's art demonstrates this type of apparently uncontrived creativity. The other kind of logic is the calculating, analytical type which we more normally think of as reason. For proof that the Age of Intuition proved its point as well as the Age of Reason, we have only to observe the results in the cathedrals of Chartres, Reims, and Amiens. Unfortunately, inspiration which appears to come to an artist in a flash seems too easy. We underrate the process, overlooking the work and thought behind it. We tend to forget that behind Renoir's facility lay years of continuous practice. In art there are no unearned masterpieces; nothing is solely the product of a moment's inspiration, however intense. We must also acquire respect for the logical power shown by artists in deliberate planning, and for the mode of thought by which a picture is carefully studied out, developed through numerous preparatory drawings, and built up step by step.

The two periods of history which have accorded the greatest prestige to conscious logical power are antiquity—with a culmination at Athens in the fifth century before Christ—and the Renaissance in Italy, with Raphael epitomizing its intellectual qualities. A poised and controlled person, Raphael was a fresco painter and an organizer of the first rank, as is shown among other places in his painting of the *Mass of Bolsena* (Fig. 59). The incident depicted is based on the legend of a miracle which took place in the church of Santa Cristina at Bolsena, a town between Florence and Rome. There a young German priest was torn by doubts about the literal truth of Transubstantiation. Celebrating Mass one day in 1263, he saw the wafer of the Host in his hands dripping with the blood of the Saviour at the moment of consecration. The stained corporal, still preserved in the cathedral of Orvieto (where Julius II saw it in 1506) gave rise to the Feast of Corpus Domini and a holy legend still popular in Italy.

Pope Julius II commissioned Raphael to represent it and specified that he be included with his suite; the Pope is the massive figure kneeling before the altar.

Raphael found his material prescribed to a considerable extent. Julius II, a positive man, dictated to his artists without hesitation. Also, the space was prescribed. The main area created by the overhead arch was semicircular. The shape itself offered no great difficulty; Raphael had successfully filled many similar areas before. But this particular space presented a new and unusual problem because it contained an off-center window. So he faced a dual problem in representation and design; to tell the story and balance the area at the same time. His method was to combine a symmetrical architectural setting with an asymmetrical but balanced distribution of figures. In the process he played the active and irregular human figures against the static architecture in a way that enhances both.

Success hinged on balancing the architectural setting. Here Raphael dealt his best stroke. He prolonged the top of the window toward the right, making the altar steps on either side appear to be equidistant from the frame. Once the steps were centered, he could forget the off-center window. He accented the central axis further by placing the altar squarely upon it, instead of over the axis of the window. He likewise centered the heavy balustrade of the altar platform and the other background architectural members upon the picture axis, and underscored his point by stressing the dark arch over the altar.

With the architecture stabilized, Raphael was able to give life and variety to his dramatic actors within a freer balance. In the larger space on the right he placed a group of the Vatican's Swiss Guards. Calm and dignified, as are the Pope and cardinals, they attract attention because of their colorful costumes. In order to offset them within the small space on the left, Raphael introduced action among the spectators who were excited by the miracle. Thus he satisfied a representational need and overcame a difficulty in design at the same time.

Faced with a problem, Raphael showed his gift for composing intelligently by turning an obstacle to brilliant account. His final result is more impressive than if he had started with a perfectly regular space; his solution is ingenious in its simplicity.

Ironic as it may seem, logic such as Raphael's is not an unmixed blessing. Combined with temperate social interests and restrained feelings, with moderation, habitual refinement, and natural grace, it allowed his head to rule his heart. Raphael matured early and died

young, famous and rich. He seemed to have been favored by the
gods; his contemporaries called him "divine." In his art he approached perfection. Perfection, however, is a heavy burden to carry
and a dangerous one to imitate. Raphael is said to have been the
ruin of his followers and of weaker men in succeeding centuries who
copied his methods of composition—triangles, pyramids, cones—without observing his shrewd, practical solutions of unique problems.
They turned his direct art into a manner.

It takes all kinds to make a world, and art is richest when it is
many-sided. Since sufficient stress is placed on feeling in art, it is well
to have a Raphael demonstrate the role conscious intellect can play.

IMAGINATION

Imagination permits the mind to conceive without relying on direct sensory experience. It can be used in several ways. It allows us
to invent a scene which does not actually exist, or to imagine one we
have only heard about. It also allows us to improve upon experience.

An illustration of logical, controlled imagination is to be found in
Raphael's creation of the same *Mass of Bolsena* that we have been
discussing. Raphael, who lived in the sixteenth century, did not witness the miracle, but reconstructed it imaginatively from hearsay information. He blended elements which were, like his own relation
to the miracle, widely separated in time. Pope Julius II, who kneels
before the altar during the Mass, was contemporary with the painter,
not with the miracle. Indeed, the original miracle must have appeared very different from Raphael's painting. Yet the painting
demonstrates a remarkable characteristic of the imagination—its
power to create scenes which, though highly synthetic, are credible.
So persuasive is the imagination that the result is often more vivid
than actuality itself. Giotto's Biblical illustrations which separated
themes from the distractions of daily life are in sharper focus than
most actual incidents.

In fact, people who have witnessed historical events through the
imaginative eye of art are often disappointed by actual counterparts.
Warfare, for instance, is exciting to read about, but notoriously burdensome to practice. The Second World War furnished an example in
a group of soldiers who had fought their way onto an island near
Japan. One evening, while watching a movie of submarine warfare
in the North Atlantic, an air raid sent them flying to cover. Here
was real war, real danger, but their attitude toward it was only annoyance; they could hardly wait to get back to the excitement of
the cinematic war. Similarly, in the *Mass of Bolsena,* art steals the

FIG. 60. Homer. *Halibut Fishing.* 1884. From a signed photograph in the collection of Mrs. Charles L. Homer, Prout's Neck, Me.

FIG. 61. Homer. *The Fog Warning.* 1885. Museum of Fine Arts, Boston.

show from life. The painting is substance, the actual event of 1263 only a shadow.

When imagination endows a work of art with such credibility that it seems more real than life, as in Raphael's painting or a motion picture, that credibility points to a fusion of imagination and logic. Raphael joined both when he included only elements which were appropriate to the kind of story he was depicting and excluded all others. He included Pope Julius because Julius was a religious symbol and acted his part accordingly. The difference in time became unimportant.

It would be easy to illustrate imagination by some fantasy which has no counterpart in direct human experience, such as Albrecht Dürer's *Four Horsemen of the Apocalypse* or Hieronymous Bosch's lurid *Temptation of St. Anthony*. But Winslow Homer's *Fog Warning* (Fig. 61) is a better example, for a seemingly contradictory reason: it looks as though it were painted directly from actuality. We are tempted, as a consequence, to give the artist little credit for invention. Oddly enough, he would have regarded that as a sign of success and encouraged that point of view by insisting to his friend John W. Beatty that he painted as directly and accurately from nature as he could.

For a long time the realism of the picture convinced critics that Homer must have studied a fishing fleet off the Grand Banks of Newfoundland. But residents of Prout's Neck, Maine, who knew the artist intimately in the 1880's—Mrs. Annie J. Munroe, Roswell Googins, and Leonard Libby—maintained that he neither took nor needed such a trip; the sight of dorymen rowing daily along the coast could easily have given him his initial idea. Moreover, they agreed with Alexander Bower's description of the way Homer set out to execute his conception.

One day the artist, who used genuine accessories and visual aids whenever he could find them, propped a dory against a sand bank on the beach between Checkley Point and the present Yacht Club, at an angle simulating the pitch of a boat on a wave. Into the dory he put Henry Lee, a local handyman with a dark spade beard who was a good model for a deep-sea fisherman. Then he set to work.

Beginners may be encouraged to learn that after an afternoon of painting, Homer had used up a whole block of Winsor and Newton water color paper without being able to realize his conception. He tossed Henry Lee a five-dollar gold piece and went home.

Only the germ of an idea was now lodged in his imagination. The following year he executed a vigorous oil study which he named

Halibut Fishing (Fig. 60). But after having a photograph made which he signed and hung on his studio wall, he gave the picture to an acquaintance in Portland. The conception lacked dramatic interest; a man fishing from a dory was not enough.

A year later, the solution he was seeking crystallized in his imagination and he painted his final version, *The Fog Warning* (Fig. 61), which is now in the Museum of Fine Arts, Boston. The change in title marked a significant change in conception. The halibut fisherman still rides his dory, but his situation carries more dramatic impact because he is in danger. A fog bank has appeared on the horizon and is drifting ominously toward the schooner. The captain has sounded a warning to the fisherman who, hearing it, has started to row to safety, racing the fog. Less melodramatic than his tempestuous *Life-Line* of the year before, Homer's *Fog Warning* is more effective for its understatement. Death stalks the fisherman silently: we do not know whether the rower won his race or not, we can only guess.

A comparison of Figs. 60 and 61 will show that as Homer's design improved so did his dramatic idea. He made his boat larger and the schooner smaller, increasing significantly the distance the doryman must row. He also moved the schooner to the right side of the horizon and turned the fisherman's head, as well as the halibut's tail, toward it, linking the left and right sides of the composition. The level oars emphasize the flat expanse of the sea, while the angle of the dory is echoed by streamers from the bank of fog. Horizontals and diagonals, foreground and distance, are played against each other. The colors are appropriately cold and somber. Idea and form are united.

The demonstrable imaginative content of a realistic picture like *The Fog Warning* points a lesson. Imagination may be present where we least expect it and is constantly employed even by the avowed realist.

We must distinguish between the two kinds of imagination which affect the quality of art—dramatic imagination and formal imagination. Gérôme and Meissonier were endowed with both technical skill and dramatic imagination; what they lacked was formal imagination. Mondrian, on the other hand, had the ability to invent designs and compositions to a high degree, but left no evidence of any dramatic imagination. Raphael's imagination combined both kinds. His was the pattern followed by most of the masters, the one we shall refer to most often. The imaginative union of form and idea has been the aim of artists throughout the history of art.

SYMPATHY

Sympathy makes us understand the feelings and interests of others. It gives life and art a warmth without which the most logical intelligence is cold. Sympathy is measured by sincerity and depth of feeling, but the motivations are complicated and—in relation to art—can best be discussed in connection with an actual painting, the *Entombment* (Fig. 62), now in the Louvre, which the Venetian artist Titian painted in 1525 for his patron, Federigo of Mantua.

The story of the Entombment is told with simple eloquence in chapter 23 of the Gospel of St. Luke:

And, behold there was a man named Joseph, a counsellor; and he was a good man, and a just: (The same had not consented to the counsel and deed of them;) he was of Arimathaea, a city of the Jews: who also himself waited for the kingdom of God. This man went unto Pilate, and begged the body of Jesus. And he took it down, and wrapped it in linen, and laid it in a sepulchre that was hewn in stone, wherein never man before was laid.

In Titian's picture the crucified Christ is being carried on the linen cloth toward the sepulchre which Joseph of Arimathaea provided. The crown of thorns has been removed and lies on the ground. Christ's body is supported by Joseph, probably the swarthy man on the left, the disciple John, and Nicodemus, a wealthy Jewish nobleman. Mary the Mother of Christ follows, supported in her grief by the younger Mary Magdalene. Behind the upturned head of John is a sunset, signifying the end of the terrible day. Lengthening shadows indicate the approach of night and a sleep from which the Master may never awake. All that His followers can comprehend at the moment is that the bravest and noblest man they have ever known is dead, and the manner of His going has moved them to pity. They are strong men, but they carry His body tenderly.

By the sixteenth century the *Entombment* had been painted many times—by Giotto, Fra Angelico, Botticelli, and others; it was a thoroughly familiar story. Yet Titian was able to raise the theme to a new level by his interpretation and artistry. Behind this achievement lies a simple fact: the story moved him deeply. He treated it later in life (in 1559) in a picture now in the Prado at Madrid, and again at the end of his long career in the *Pietà* that hangs in the Academy at Venice.

Somerset Maugham gives an insight into the Louvre *Entombment* when he writes that the picture does not convey to him the chill of death but the love of life written on the faces of the followers. It is true that nothing increases our appreciation of life so much as an awareness of death. Knowing this, Titian built his composition

FIG. 62. Titian. *Entombment. ca.* 1525. Louvre, Paris.

FIG. 63. Daumier. *The Drinking Song. ca.* 1850. Philadelphia Museum of Art.

around a contrast of the two extremes. Christ's large and heavy body intensifies the dead weight of His limp form; the shaded head contrasts with the lighted torso, the coldly naked limbs, and the drooping hand. The men, who are dressed in warm and handsome clothes, appear strong and healthy. And though the Madonna is grief-stricken, her bowed head emphasizes the youthful beauty of Mary Magdalene.

The colors of the picture present the same contrasts; the lividness of Christ's body and the shadows of the shining garment of Nicodemus, the deep blue of the Madonna's robe, the auburn hair of Mary Magdalene, the radiant face of John. The final touch is the juxtaposition of the limp arm of Christ and the scarf of Nicodemus, the scarf curled on the ground in an echo of the dead Christ's fingers. In conceiving his picture, Titian, a man of great vitality, surely identified himself with the followers of Christ rather than with His broken body, and imbued the followers both with pity for Christ and with his own love of life.

Part of the poignance of the *Entombment* comes from the puzzled, half-believing expression of the faces. The Resurrection, the Supper at Emmaus, the Miraculous Draught of Fishes, and other proofs of His divinity have not yet occurred. At the time of the *Entombment* the followers know only that Christ has achieved an incredible triumph over pain. Yet they seem to have the first inkling of a divinity whose meaning will grow upon them as the story unfolds.

The date of the *Entombment*, 1525, is significant. It reminds us that a profound expression of sympathy in art rarely comes from a young man. Usually it is the mark of feeling deepened by mature thought. Titian was forty-eight in 1525. He showed remarkable skill at an early age, but the enrichment of content in his work had to await his middle and later years.

Sympathy is not limited to tragedy. It is one of the best means we have of understanding any emotional condition. For example, the nineteenth-century French artist Honoré Daumier identified himself in his art with feelings of many sorts, ranging from despair to uninhibited gaiety.

In creating one of his most delightful pictures, a pen and wash drawing entitled *The Drinking Song* (Fig. 63), Daumier projected himself imaginatively into a group of nocturnal celebrants who have gotten drunk and are having a gay time. Daumier was not being censorious. Knowing the hardships of life firsthand, he understood that the poor and all other "creatures of circumstance," as Maugham describes us, must steal what fun they can from life. In the *Drinking*

Song he is telling us with sympathy and approval what a carefree time these men are having. It is a fine example of self-identification in art. One can almost see Daumier grinning while he worked; his pen must have danced over the paper as he threw himself into the mood of the scene. Nothing is defined too carefully; this gaiety, snatched from the cares of life, will be gone with the morrow; nothing in the picture implies that it has any permanence. In a sense, Daumier was expressing his own recognition of the fleetingness of fun amid worries and work. Throughout his own career, which ended in poverty and blindness, he had to wrest from existence what pleasure he could, and he often did this by living vicariously with the people of his imagination.

A final word may be said for the part sympathetic understanding has played in Western art. The Christian tradition has conditioned us to believe that there is more to art than design and technique. When we compare an "artist's artist" with the company of those who were also great human beings—Giotto, Michelangelo, Titian, Bruegel, Rubens, Rembrandt, Goya, and Daumier—we do not withhold admiration from the former, but we feel a closer comradeship with the latter.

EMPATHY

Empathy is also a kind of identification. The Greeks, who invented the term, conceived it to mean mainly identification with the physical sensations of others, especially pain. Modern psychologists and estheticians have given empathy a much broader meaning, but we shall confine ourselves here to the Greek interpretation. According to them empathy meant projecting one's self mentally into the physical situation of another animate being by reacting to the outward signs of muscular and nervous tension and relaxation. Within these limits it is a valuable key to an understanding of art.

It is improbable that any appeal to sympathy could be made representationally without the employment of empathy. Titian's *Entombment* (Fig. 62) depends to a high degree upon an empathic response for the communication of its meaning. Much of the tug and pull of the design is lost unless we identify ourselves with the followers of Christ and feel the mixture of strength and gentleness with which they carry His body to the tomb. Similarly, we must feel physically the dead weight of His limp form in order to comprehend the interplay of inertia and energy in the picture as a whole. In the *Entombment* empathy is allied to sympathy because, as Titian knew, sentiments translate themselves into outward signs of tension

FIG. 64. Pollaiuolo. *Hercules Strangling Antaeus.* *ca.* 1470. National Museum, Florence.

FIG. 65. Van Gogh. *Mountainous Landscape.* June, 1889. Ny-Carlsberg Glyptothek, Copenhagen.

and relaxation and are interpreted accordingly. An excellent example here is the figure of Mary the Mother of Christ, who expresses her grief through her clutched hands. In this particular case empathy and sympathy are inseparable. Sympathy of this sort has been felt or expressed by only a fraction of the world's artists. Empathy is virtually universal. Being primarily physical, it has been present with everyone from the cradle on.

In the arts, empathic expression has varied greatly according to time, place, and individuality, indicating many possible degrees of development. Empathy was valued the least in those periods when men's minds were directed collectively away from an observation and enjoyment of human life. The low ebb came with the art of the Byzantine Empire and persisted through most of the Middle Ages. It is negligible in the Romanesque *Virgin Enthroned* shown in Fig. 49.

Empathy was accorded the highest value in those periods which loved to observe the free human animal at work or play. The highest development of this attitude in ancient times coincided with the art of the humanistic, sports-loving Greeks of the fifth century B.C.; a fine example is the *Zeus from Artemisium* (Fig. 50). A revival of empathic enjoyment came with the Renaissance and has lasted to the present. The paintings of Michelangelo, Titian, Tintoretto, Bruegel, Rubens, and many other Western masters of the Renaissance and post-Renaissance periods are full of empathic appeal.

So it is not strange that one of the vivid representations of action in art is a bronze group of *Hercules Strangling Antaeus* (Fig. 64) by a Florentine sculptor of the fifteenth century, Antonio Pollaiuolo. Trained as a goldsmith, Pollaiuolo loved to demonstrate his skilful technique in metal figures which he filled with such energy that they seem much larger than they actually are. Like many Florentine contemporaries who combined the ideals of the classical revival with a searching study of human anatomy, he was an artist, a humanist, and a scientist, a spiritual cousin of Leonardo da Vinci and a precursor of Michelangelo. Whenever possible he joined his interest in pagan mythology to his love for the human nude body in violent action. It is not surprising that he should have elected to represent *Hercules Strangling Antaeus,* or that the result should be generally regarded as his masterpiece.

We shall understand the group better if we know something of the ancient Greek myth which it represents as recorded in Bulfinch:

A celebrated exploit of Hercules was his victory over Antaeus. Antaeus, the son of Terra, was a mighty giant and wrestler, whose strength was invincible so long as he remained in contact with his mother Earth. He compelled all

strangers who came to his country to wrestle him, on condition that if conquered (as they all were) they should be put to death. Hercules encountered
him, and finding that it was of no avail to throw him, for he always rose
with renewed strength from every fall, he lifted him up from the earth and
strangled him in the air.

The latter moment is the one depicted here, and it is done so effectively that we can almost hear the scream Antaeus emits as Hercules crushes him. That effectiveness was no accident. It derived
from Pollaiuolo's careful training, from his penetrating study of
anatomy, and from his love of the pagan myths, especially those pertaining to the heroic exploits of Hercules. It derived from his capacity to identify himself so thoroughly with the ancient antagonists
that he could feel the strain of their struggle in every nerve and
muscle of his own body.

Pollaiuolo's skill lay in translating his empathic feeling to a mass
of bronze so that the viewer might feel it too. He did this by par-
ticularizing the signs of tension throughout the bodies of both figures.
Reading these signs, we are able to observe exactly the amount of
strain exerted by every limb, toe, arm, or finger. We can feel the
tautness of the tendons in Hercules' legs, the grip of his toes upon
the ground, the strain of his back as he lifts Antaeus bodily into the
air, and the power in his viselike hold. We can perceive the frantic
downward thrust of Antaeus' arms as he struggles to free himself from
the death grip, and note the careful distinction between Antaeus'
tense, upraised leg and the relatively slack leg which dangles in mid-
air. We grasp this life-and-death combat in every particular because
Pollaiuolo has given us all of the relevant signs. Consistent throughout, he has even shaped the feet of his pedestal to echo the firm plant
of Hercules' feet on the ground.

We need not labor the point that the *Hercules Strangling Antaeus,*
compared to Titian's *Entombment,* appeals to us in a different way
and on a lower spiritual plane. Its appeal is empathic but not sympathetic. There is little in either the character or the story of Antaeus
that makes us care what happens to him. And Hercules, as usual,
does not need our sympathy. Hence our vicarious enjoyment of the
contest, while physically keen, is emotionally almost neutral. Working within these limitations Pollaiuolo gave us examples of empathic
expression which are still authoritative.

Compared to this group, the *Zeus of Artemisium* is simplified and
generalized; for that reason it is superbly graceful. Each in its own
way expresses a different conception of energetic action, one controlled and the other vehement. If it is vehemence that one seeks,
Pollaiuolo's small but heroic group is a classic example.

VITALITY

Vitality is the motive power of both the mind and the emotions. Its most prominent characteristic in the artist is its capacity for renewal; the masters have all been endowed with deep reserves of energy. Critics place vitality high in any scale of values. They will forgive many ineptitudes in a work which possesses force, but regard dimly the most polished form if it is lifeless.

The life and work of the modern Dutch painter Vincent Van Gogh illustrate both the benefits and burdens of vitality. Vitality burned so hot within him that it was a curse as well as a blessing. In the end it shattered his body, burned out his nerves, and destroyed his mental balance. During his lifetime Van Gogh was a misunderstood man. The vicissitudes of his troubled life have been widely publicized and will not be dwelt upon here except to demonstrate his creative vitality.[2]

Van Gogh's productivity was amazing. J. B. De La Faille, his cataloger and chief authority, reproduces 816 paintings alone, not including his many drawings. At first glance this number may not seem large, but it becomes so when one notes the character of Van Gogh's paintings and the short span of his career. Each of his pictures contains hundreds of brush strokes, his work as a whole hundreds of thousands. Solely in terms of mechanical effort, this sum represents a tremendous expenditure of energy.

In Van Gogh's career it is the element of time which makes his productivity impressive. He was born in 1853 and died in 1890. He did not start painting until 1881, after misadventures as an art dealer and missionary, by which time he was nearly thirty, relatively old for a beginning painter. During his first few years he had to train himself without professional instruction, companionship, or sympathy. In a sense, then, his career did not start until he was thirty-three years of age. In February of that year, 1886, he moved to Paris and discovered the brilliantly colored paintings of the Impressionists and the sharp, clear designs of the Japanese print-makers. Up to that time he had painted some 258 pictures; they were boldly conceived but dark and crudely executed. His real career, his magnificent color and dashing style, all lay ahead.

The facts of the next few years testify to a remarkable acceleration

[2] The reader who desires a clearer picture of Van Gogh can gain one from: Julius Meier-Graefe, *Vincent Van Gogh, A Biographical Study,* trans. J. H. Reece (New York: Payson & Clarke, Ltd., 1928); *The Letters of Vincent Van Gogh to His Brother, 1872–1886* (Boston: Houghton Mifflin Co., 1927); *Further Letters of Vincent Van Gogh to His Brother, 1886–1889* (Boston: Houghton Mifflin Co., 1929); and *Vincent Van Gogh's Letters to Émile Bernard* (New York: Museum of Modern Art, 1938).

of activity. In Paris he lived with his brother Theo, an art dealer who was in the thick of the new movements. Theo not only introduced him to Japanese prints and Impressionist paintings, but to the living men who were revolutionizing painting—Degas, Seurat, Pissarro, Toulouse-Lautrec, Gauguin, and Émile Bernard. The excitement of these meetings in the artistic capital of the world stimulated Van Gogh to a new level of productivity. In the two years at Paris he completed 203 paintings—one nearly every third day.

In February of 1888 Van Gogh made an important move. Seeking quieter surroundings, he settled at Arles in southern France. The effect on him was exactly opposite to what was intended. The invigorating color and sunlight of Provence drove him to even more frenzied activity. During fifteen months at Arles, Van Gogh completed 183 paintings. In the following twelve months at St. Rémy, he finished another 141 canvases, or one every third day. A machine could hardly have worked faster. In the sixty days that he spent at Auvers, he executed 61 finished designs—a phenomenal average. He seems to have had a premonition of his own death by suicide and engaged in a frantic race against it.

Dramatic as was Van Gogh's home-stretch surge, the statistics speak for themselves. Only four and a half years elapsed between his arrival in Paris and his death at Auvers. Allowing only two days in seven for the ordinary needs of life, but nothing for his unmeasurable illnesses, those fifty months contained not more than 1400 painting days. During that time Van Gogh finished 585 designs in oil on canvas—an average of one complete painting every other day. None is a mere sketch and many are acknowledged masterpieces whose impact on modern art has been second only to that of Cézanne.

The vigor which characterized Van Gogh's life and art shows also in the variety of his interests. Too often he is thought of as a specialist in a few limited subjects—sunflowers, cypress trees, and still-life groups. His curiosity actually took a myriad directions. His letters are full of interest in everything around him and in everything he heard or read.

In Van Gogh's pictures there is abundant evidence of his variety of interests. "Expressionistic" though he might have been, his technical knowledge of color theory or anything else pertaining to painting was thorough and his observation acute. Among the subjects he observed these are typical examples: *Chestnut Trees in Flower; The Garden of St. Paul's Hospital; The Pietà, After a Drawing by Delacroix; The First Step, After Millet; Still Life with Lemons; Prisoners in a Courtyard; A Starry Night; Young Girls Walking Along the Fields; The Town Hall at Auvers; On the Threshold of Eternity* (a study of introspection which reflected his final, tormented state of mind). Through these various subjects Van Gogh expressed all of the major orientations of perception except the nonrepresentational abstract, and within most of the categories he created scores of variations. His art reveals a searching, restless mind.

There have been artists who were more prolific or various than Van Gogh—the universally ranging Pieter Bruegel, for example. Others, such as Pollaiuolo, were perhaps his superiors at expressing vitality through scenes of action. But Van Gogh went further and expressed vitality through every passage of the internal structure of his pictures. In his *Mountainous Landscape* (Fig. 65), a typical example of his last, highly productive year, his means are several. Every square inch of the canvas has been covered by numerous brush strokes which are nervous and rapid. Strong in color, they twist and writhe; there is hardly a straight line in the entire picture. The effect of this execution is a landscape alive with movement. Not only do the clouds roll and tumble, but the normally static mountains seem to heave as though moved by an earthquake. This is nature conceived dynamically to the *nth* degree.

This stress on activity was consistent with Van Gogh's way of thinking. He worshipped the sun as a source of energy and painted it repeatedly, making it as much his trade-mark as the butterfly was Whistler's. Everything that signified fertility, growth, movement, and life stimulated his creative energies. More than that, he rendered dynamic those objects which normally comprise the substantial aspects of nature, lending them, as in the fields of his *Mountainous Landscape,* the power of movement from his own abundance of energy. Crucial from an artistic point of view was Van Gogh's ability to channel his driving force along intelligible stylistic lines. Lacking control and direction, his energy might have amounted to no more than a blast of steam in the open air. It is to his credit that he avoided many of the pitfalls of pyrotechnics. His style is a lucidly conceived means of uniting energy and ideas in painting.

Among Van Gogh's devices, the most important was his rhythmic organization of lines in space, without which the effect of his brush technique could have resembled an explosion of firecrackers. As it is, the pattern of lines which weaves through his *Mountainous Landscape* has the double effect of expressing his own vitality and giving life and unity to his representation. Because of these characteristics, the *Mountainous Landscape* may remind us of pictures we have studied in another context—the rhythmic designs of Barye, Orozco, Marc, and the prehistoric painting of a bison, all of which expressed vitality through swinging, cadenced movements.

WILL

Will gives continuity to human effort. It keeps us from being pulled hither and yon by our own imagination and energy, and allows us to complete tasks in the face of discouragements and obstacles. The distractions that will must overcome are both internal and external. Artists, being imaginative men, are often their own worst enemies. Confronted with external difficulties, they require great will power to overcome conflicting characteristics. Will must then be to their vitality and imagination what a gyroscope is to a ship at sea.

In a man dedicated to art, will is a driving force. Few have expressed this idea with more succinct insight than Somerset Maugham. In *The Moon and Sixpence* Strickland (a character modeled on Gauguin) is asked why he deserted his family and a respectable, well-paid position for a Paris garret; he replies, "I've got to paint." Here was will, strength with a purpose, able to endure privation, even a miserable death in the South Seas, in order to paint. In Strickland this urge was an obsession—but with a purpose.

The variations on this theme, the will to art at any price, are countless. Michelangelo's painting of the ceiling of the Sistine Chapel was one of the hardest tasks any painter ever faced, and everyone seemed bent upon blocking his way. Even the beginning of the assignment was ill-omened. Vasari tells that it started as a scheme in the mind of Bramante. That architect, who was then laying the foundations of the new St. Peter's for Pope Julius II, had quarreled with Michelangelo over the hasty destruction of the ancient basilica of St. Peter, and had plotted revenge. Bramante was also the uncle of Raphael and hoped to instal him in Michelangelo's place as the papal favorite. It did not occur to him that there was room for both men in the grandiose plans of the Pope. Instead, he took steps to oust or discredit Michelangelo entirely.

At that time Michelangelo was engaged on the sepulchre of Julius II, a monument which he hoped to make the greatest of his career. So Bramante first persuaded Julius II that it was a mistake for a man to erect his own tomb. The Pope listened and agreed, ordering Michelangelo to abandon his work. Thus began the "tragedy of the tomb" into which Michelangelo had poured his energy and dreams. Even in its abbreviated form, it is, with the *Moses* as its centerpiece, one of the mountain peaks of art history. But Michelangelo could hardly have known that at the time. He left Rome in a fury.

Still the devil's advocate, Bramante next induced the Pope to recall Michelangelo and commission him to decorate the vault of the

Sistine Chapel with a cycle of frescoes. The side walls of the chapel
had already been decorated by the leading Italian painters of the
fifteenth century and were a museum of early Renaissance art, but
the vast ceiling had remained bare. Michelangelo, Bramante said,
was the man to complete the job. Actually, he hoped to ruin his
nephew's rival by a task in which he would surely fail.

Michelangelo, as Bramante knew, had done little painting in
tempera up to this time (his thirty-third year) and none in fresco
painting since he had helped his master, Ghirlandaio, at the age of
thirteen. Moreover, Michelangelo disliked painting; he called it a
woman's art. Dedicated to the ancient and virile art of sculpture, he
wanted only to finish his marble tomb for Julius II. Ordered by the
Pope to design the decoration for the ceiling and begin work
promptly, Michelangelo was forced to work on the largest single area
any man has ever been asked to paint. Its actual dimensions are 132
feet by 44, a total area of 5,808 square feet. The vault is located 68
feet above the floor, and would have to be painted from a supine
position.

From the first, troubles multiplied. As if he had not done enough,
Bramante, at the Pope's request, designed a scaffold which proved to
be useless. Suspended from the ceiling by ropes, it would have left
holes to be filled after it had been removed. Angered but helpless,
Michelangelo had to design his own scaffold. Nothing comparable
to the Sistine ceiling decorations had ever been attempted before.
Thus harassed, he began his unwanted chore.

Hoping to finish the work as soon as possible, he made "a design
for twelve apostles in the lunettes, and for the rest of the ceiling certain compartments filled with ornaments of the usual sort." But
when he showed it to the Pope his conscience rebelled.

"It is a poor thing," he said. "I will make another."

Even with his heart in the problem, the design would have taxed
his skill. He had not only to cover the vast area with decorated
plaster, but to organize his design into a unity. The new composition, much more complex than the first, called for 343 human figures;
no two were alike, and 225 of them ranged from 10 to 18 feet in
height. Michelangelo's imagination had so exceeded his practical
sense that an army of expert assistants would have hesitated before
his plan. The five Florentine artists he hired fared poorly and in-
furiated Michelangelo with their timid efforts. Never an easy man
to please, he locked the door against them and carried on alone.
That is to say, he hired plasterers, color-grinders, stencilers, and
scaffold-movers, but painted nearly every inch of the vault with his
own hand.

It is to his credit that as the work progressed the magnitude of the problem challenged his imagination. Like other great men, he set his standards by his own conscience and would not do a shabby job. In fact, he must have come to realize that painting offered certain unforeseen advantages. If his principal interest was in exploring the expressive postures of the human nude, he could explore more of them with a brush in four years than he could in a lifetime with a chisel. The danger of interruptions to the long, drawn-out process of carving stone must have been brought home to him by the fate of the Julius tomb. In any event, something made him see that he had been granted an opportunity. His response to it is a matter of history.

Yet every step of the way was hard. For four years the Pope kept him a prisoner, hounding him to finish the work but refusing to pay him. At the same time his father and brothers in Florence wrote him constantly for money. He replied, "It is now a year since I had a penny from the Pope," and later, "I live here in the utmost bodily fatigue, without money and with no one to look after me. I have no friends and seek none. I have not even time to eat what I require. Therefore let no additional burdens be put upon me." When his work went badly, or it was too cold in the chapel to plaster and paint, he fell prey to depression.

Technical difficulties arose because of "this not being my art. And so I waste my time without results. God help me!" "He had hardly finished the picture of the *Deluge,*" Condivi writes, "when the work began to throw out mould to such an extent that the figures could not be distinguished through it." Michelangelo hoped to use this as an excuse to get out of the commission, but the Pope had the problem solved and ordered him to continue.

What happens to a man when he lies on his back for four years Michelangelo tells in a sonnet that he wrote to a friend (translated by Symonds):

> I've grown a goitre by dwelling in this den—
> As cats from stagnant streams in Lombardy,
> Or in what other land they hap to be—
> Which drives the belly close beneath the chin:
> My beard turns up to heaven; my nape falls in,
> Fixed on my spine: my breast bone visibly
> Grows like a harp: a rich embroidery
> Bedews my face from brush-drops thick and thin.

At times melancholy nearly overwhelmed Michelangelo, but in the end his resolution won. One day in 1512, after four years of work, he sent his father this simple message, "Today I finished the Chapel I was painting. The Pope is very well satisfied."

There is a general belief that art is usually a product of leisure. After witnessing Michelangelo's ordeal, one wonders. The magnitude of his task demanded a perseverance that tried his soul and body. Yet it was exceptional only in degree. Although many works of art have been created under better circumstances, few of any worth have ever been done without great exercise of will.

THE EQUATION AS A WHOLE

The key to the human equation is development, which sets us above the lower animals, as it separates men from boys and one man from another. At birth we are a set of potentials. In the course of time these potentials of curiosity, memory, logic, and so forth, are so developed that their relative strength varies radically from one adult to another: a man, his wife, and his brother will all differ markedly in their reasoning power, sympathy, and will. A work of art expresses this personal development for all the world to see. Indeed, an artist bares his soul when he creates a work of art, for it will reveal both his spiritual strength and his weakness.

We read the development of an artist through his works on two counts. One is his general development. If this is on such a plane as to be like a plateau above the level of other men, we call him a master. Michelangelo, Shakespeare, and Beethoven were such men. In the company of masters there is room, however, for men who were highly developed in special characteristics. Outstanding among men in general, they represent more irregular peaks of human ability, as Van Gogh did through his intense expression of vitality.

We also read in works of art the effects of historical contexts upon each human personality. Here the crucial factor is the degree of encouragement or suppression which environment exerts upon development. Over the centuries the seeds of potentiality have fallen, like those in the parable, now upon stony ground and now upon fertile; and each condition is reflected in the signs of art. Thus the human spirit is best conceived in terms of an equation whose general, specialized, and historical development has varied with the individual artist and his time.

CHAPTER 5

The Nature of Art

Although all men share in the human spirit, only a few are artists. What, then, is the essential nature of art which only a creative minority has realized successfully?

Many attempts have been made to explain it. By merging their ideas, philosophers of art have gradually brought the aims and methods of art—as distinct, say, from chemistry and coal mining—into clear focus. Most helpful, I think, is Curt J. Ducasse's definition, the gist of which is: *Art is the controlled objectification of feeling.*[1]

This statement is not to be taken as a one-sentence definition of art, but as a springboard for discussion. Only by considering the key words can we fully understand its meaning. For example, art is not just *control* or *objectification* or *feeling*, but a fusion of all three in a special relationship. That is, control, objectification, and feeling may each be employed nonartistically. They are artistic only when they are used together. The first five words of our definition assert that *art is (the) controlled objectification.* This is another way of saying that art is skill, or that skill is indispensable in art.

THE MEANING AND IMPORTANCE OF CONTROL

We understand control as the opposite of accident or wildness, and perceive the necessity for it in hundreds of human activities. A good everyday example is found in baseball, where the terms "control" and

[1] This is not a perfect paraphrasing of Professor Ducasse's ideas on a complicated and extensive subject. For his own full explanation of the meaning of art the reader is urged to consult *The Philosophy of Art* (New York: Dial Press, Inc., 1929), still one of the best books on the subject, and *Art, the Critics, and You* (New York: Piest, 1944), a more recent small volume in which Ducasse summarizes his opinions succinctly.

FIG. 66. Michelangelo. *A Captive. ca.* 1519. Academy, Florence.

FIG. 67. *Governor of Lagash. ca.* 2400 B.C. British Museum, London.

FIG. 68. Hiroshige. *Shower on Ohashi Bridge. ca.* 1850. Museum of Fine Arts, Boston.

FIG. 69. *Hunter and Dog.* Attributed to the "Pan Painter." Active 500-475 B.C. Museum of Fine Arts, Boston.

"wildness" are applied to pitching with easily understood significance. *Control* does not mean intention but something completed successfully, for it is always recognized after it has been achieved. A tennis player, figure skater, and high jumper are awarded points only for what they actually accomplish. Although philosophers are not clear on this point, we judge Rembrandt in the same way. Since he has been dead for nearly three hundred years and left no written explanation of his intentions, we must consider his skill solely through his paintings and hope that we do not misjudge it.

An artist knows when he has achieved control over a conception; and knowledge of something completed is one of the pleasures of artistry, as being thwarted is frustrating. The life of Rembrandt, serene at the end in spite of poverty, is an instance of the former. A contrasting illustration of the blocking of tremendous creative powers at every turn is the life of Michelangelo. His large figure of a captive (Fig. 66) is a symbol of his own career. One of many statues designed for the tomb of Pope Julius II, it was, for many reasons, never completed as originally conceived. Failure to complete other magnificent projects embittered Michelangelo's life.

Yet there is another way of looking at these powerful figures. They were incomplete only from Michelangelo's point of view. From our point of view they may be more expressive than if they had been given a complete "finish." It might even be claimed that some instinct forced Michelangelo to stop at this point. In any case, we must judge these statues as they stand and be grateful even for a distracted Michelangelo.

Deciding when to stop is one of the hardest problems of artistic control, because there are no absolute criteria and the artist must set his own standards. As we might expect, perfectionists suffer the most dissatisfaction. Unable to realize some conception, a chagrined Cézanne often hurled his canvas into the nearest tree. What we regard today as excellent appeared to him unfinished. Michelangelo, in a similar moment of despair, smashed the great *Pietà* now in the Cathedral of Florence. There is often a gap between the artist's ideal and our conception of fulfilment.

In the visual arts, control is realized through technique or craftsmanship. The term *fine* in "the fine arts" implies control of a high order, but it does not favor complexity or virtuosity as a special mark of quality. A small and relatively simple Greek vase (Fig. 69) may exhibit more refinement or subtlety of treatment than a large and elaborate historical painting. What *fine* implies especially is the excellence of ability and training required to achieve control and a high level of control sustained throughout the period of execution. The

Greek vase, though painted quickly, shows long training, and any example of great architecture which was necessarily built over an extended period of time, such as the Parthenon at Athens or the Great Pyramid at Gizeh, illustrates sustained artistry. The fine arts are called fine because they express the maximum development of sensitivity, discipline, and will.

THE MEANING AND IMPORTANCE OF OBJECTIFICATION

By objectification we mean an application of skill, noting that there are two kinds. Perhaps the nearest substitute is expression. The kind of expression illustrated by the performance of a singer is incorporated in the person of the performer. When the concert is over, the objectification ceases also, except as a memory in the minds of the audience. Its life is short, unless the performance was recorded in some way. In that case the objectification is centered in the recording material—wax, film, or whatever it may be—instead of in the person of the artist. Only people who lived during Enrico Caruso's lifetime had the opportunity to hear him display his great control directly. Anyone who owns a recording of Caruso's voice can hear that recording over and over again today. The extension of life that was given to literature by the invention of the printing press can hardly be calculated. The same applies today to the recording of music, the printing of musical scores, or the process of reproducing works of art. But in every instance an artist of some sort had initially to objectify his idea. The melody in a composer's head or the image in a painter's mind are useless to us as such. Once an artist has objectified an idea in a picture, a statue, or a building, it becomes independent of him. It takes on a life of its own which may well exceed his by a thousand years. Some kind of tangible objectification is thus essential to artistic immortality.

There is no expression without objectification, but skilful objectification alone is not enough to explain the nature of art. If an inventor carries out an idea in a new machine, he exemplifies controlled objectification, but he does not create a work of fine art in the accepted sense. In order to create a work of art or practice art in the sense here intended an artist must shape or design his material in such a way as to give it expressive characteristics which stone, canvas, or paper, as such, do not possess. In a work of art he achieves this expressiveness through two characteristics of the object which are dependent upon but superior to either its tangibility or durability. They are the formal elements and the dramatic elements.

THE FORMAL ELEMENTS. In the visual arts the formal elements
are such physical components of a design as lines, planes, masses,
colors, and their specific characteristics. Each of these has expressive potentialities and limitations which are to the visual arts what
words are to speech and literature. For illustrations we shall turn
to an ancient Sumerian statue, an ancient Greek vase, a relatively
modern Japanese print by Hiroshige, a nineteenth-century painting
by Daumier, and a very modern American medical center.

The stone statue of a governor of Lagash (Fig. 67) exemplifies a
solid, round, three-dimensional mass. The medical center (Fig. 71),
though three-dimensional, is rectangular and implies interior space
or volume. Both the statue and the building have boundaries and
within these, lines created by shadows and edges. Actual drawn lines,
as distinct from these apparent lines, are illustrated by the hunter and
dog (Fig. 69) whose figures were skilfully drawn on the Greek vase
with a pointed brush. An equally apt illustration of drawn lines is
provided by *Shower on Ohashi Bridge* (Fig. 68). The lines have also
been given different lengths, widths, and directions and are arranged
in a pattern of areas which have further characteristics of size, shape,
and proportion. By contrast with the sharp lines and edges of the
vase, print, statue, and building, Daumier's *Two Sculptors* (Fig. 70)
appears soft and blurred. Its merit lies rather in the strong play of
light which Daumier has achieved by playing one characteristic of
color—darkness—against another—lightness. The original painting is
no less an example of texture, owing to the manipulation of the pigment. Compare it, for instance, with the smooth surface of the
Governor of Lagash.

In these five illustrations we can see why space, though not one of
the formal elements, cannot be ignored in any consideration of design. Space, which Stephen Pepper defines as "pure emptiness," becomes artistically important as a result of the other formal elements.
So, for that matter, do the intangible lights and shadows in Daumier's painting when they define the outlines and bulk of masses. In
each case invisible space is made appreciable by the formal elements,
and affects them in turn. Neither can be discussed without reference
to the other. Therefore, any visual arrangement is conceived as a
spatial design—an organization of the formal elements in space, not in
a conceptual vacuum.

Part of the sculptural character of the *Governor of Lagash* is due
to the relationship of the surrounding space, and specifically to the
way the compact figure, with hands clasped tightly in front of the
chest, excludes space. Conversely, the Greek lekythos, with its variations of mass from the flat base through the swelling body to the

FIG. 70. Daumier. *Two Sculptors. ca.* 1860. Phillips Collection, Washington, D.C.

FIG. 71. Skidmore, Owings, and Merrill. Model of the New York University–Bellevue Medical Center. 1949. New York.

FIG. 72. Hogarth. *The Enraged Musician.* 1741. Bowdoin College Museum of Fine Arts, Brunswick, Me.

119

slender neck and wide lip, alternately pushes into space and recedes
from it. Space also plays an important part in the free-standing buildings of the medical center. The space between the buildings immediately catches the eye. This may be appreciated by imagining how
the effect of depth would be altered if the buildings were crowded
together within a cluster of larger buildings. Instead of looming up
before us, they would be hemmed in and the depth lessened. Another demonstration of the role of space may be found in a comparison of the Daumier painting and the Hiroshige print. In the painting the figures appear large, close, and enclosed in a room; in the
print the figures appear small, distant, and out-of-doors. The different conception of space which each creates in our minds is not due
to the actual sizes of the pictures (both are small), but to the relationship of the formal elements within the frames.

Together, the formal elements make up the specific design of any
work of art and contribute importantly to its visual expressiveness.
It is through the creation and arrangement of lines, masses, textures,
areas, colors, and other formal elements that the artist expresses himself. He does this as a rule by employing a second means of expression, the dramatic elements.

THE DRAMATIC ELEMENTS. One of the fascinating things about
works of art is that the formal elements—lines, colors, masses, and the
like—can do double or triple duty. We do not let a line remain only
a line. Grouped with other lines in a pattern, or combined with
certain textures and colors, it assumes a recognizable form. It is still
only a line, but in a certain context or arrangement it causes us to
recall a house, a tree, or a human being. Anyone can understand the
simple principle involved here by noting how many different shapes,
like those in Fig. 73, can be made with a piece of string or a few
pieces of wire.

In this group of figures the line a does double duty by demonstrating the specific characteristics of the formal element line, and by
expressing a certain degree of energy and control. Proof of this can
be had by arranging the line in other ways without representing any
recognizable image, as in b. In the remaining figures the line does
triple duty. In addition to fulfilling the functions mentioned, it
brings into play associations with identifiable shapes. It is surprising
how easily these associations can be aroused in our minds by rear-
rangements of the merest stick figures, such as e and f. In the hands
of great artists the formal elements provide the means for remarkably controlled expression.

When the formal elements play this third role they are called the

FIG. 73a–f. Schematic illustrations of the formal and dramatic elements.

FIG. 74a–d. Schematic illustrations of the visual and tactile sensations.

dramatic elements. Hence, a dramatic element is an arrangement of formal elements which conveys an idea. The Sumerian statue, a *Governor of Lagash,* is a single dramatic element. This may tax our conception of the dramatic, but it should not overstrain it if we can imagine this governor in some role in life more active than merely posing for his portrait. Something dramatic is at least implied in the posture of the hunter and dog; in Hiroshige's *Shower on Ohashi Bridge* something close to our usual conception of the dramatic—a storm—is represented. If the dramatic implications of these situations are understood, it will not be difficult to identify the dramatic elements in a storytelling picture where something dramatic is actually happening.

By employing formal elements as dramatic elements the artist adds to his expressive repertory. Through the dramatic elements he can direct our thoughts to a whole world of specific ideas. This the formal entities, as such, can never do. We have now only to see how the entrance of the dramatic elements differentiates all works of visual art into two great groups: works of art which are composed only of formal elements and those in which the formal elements are also dramatic elements. Among our illustrations the first is exemplified by the medical center, the second by the *Shower on Ohashi Bridge.* The same differences would distinguish most examples of the world's architecture from most paintings and statues in the history of art.

THE MEANING AND IMPORTANCE OF FEELING

We have now arrived at the final key word in our definition. Art is the controlled objectification of *feeling.* It can hardly be said strongly enough that the expression of feeling is the end to which all control over objectification, all attempts to express not only externally but permanently, and all manipulations of the formal and dramatic elements are directed. Without control and objectification the artistic expression of feeling could never be achieved, but unless feeling is expressed, control and objectification are stillborn. They may create a pleasant wall decoration or an efficient machine, but their product will not achieve the status of a work of fine art.

The feeling that the artist expresses is of two kinds. One we shall call *sensation,* the other *sentiment.* The artist employs them simultaneously, and we apprehend them together; but we can understand them more clearly by discussing them separately.

SENSATION. Sensation is the response aroused in the human mind by the stimulation of the sense organs or nervous system. We feel heat or cold, redness, heaviness, density, loudness, bitterness, hardness, smoothness, and react to these *sense* impressions with enjoyment or discomfort. This is the physical half of perception. If we are looking at works of visual art, their lines, colors, shapes, textures, and other physical qualities stimulate sensations in us directly. Their arrangement in space stimulates us in an additional way. Together they produce what is called an *esthetic response,* which has at least this much in common with other sensations: it is measured by a sense of pleasure.

In everyday experience the character of sensation is highly complex. Stimuli come to us from every direction, bombarding simultaneously our sense of taste, smell, sight, touch, and hearing. Each stimulus clamors for attention, putting us under constant pressure to select, sort, and order our sensations mentally and practically—to ignore, for instance, distracting sounds while we try to read a book or write a letter. We suffer from an excess of unwanted sensations. The result is that our mental focus of sensations is neither wholly distorted nor entirely sharp. Even under the best of circumstances we can rarely say that the hum of sounds around us is "music to our ears"; we are more likely to sum it up as *noise.* That at least is the way Hogarth felt about the din of London streets, a din conveyed with a pungent mixture of raucous humor and sharply observed truth in his *The Enraged Musician* (Fig. 72), an engraving based on an actual incident.

The artist, like everybody else, is attacked in force by stimuli from the physical world. But he responds to these claims upon his attention in a different manner. The visual artist reacts strongly to the stimuli of color, mass, outlines, textures, and other physical properties. Owing to the very strength of his reactions he is, like Hogarth's hapless musician, disturbed by the excess of sensation and the discord and confusion it causes. Finally, he solves this dilemma positively by creating a work of art.

His aim in objectifying his sensations is to preserve or increase their intensity by a process of controlled clarification. He achieves this dual intention by selecting and emphasizing, for as he clarifies his sense impressions he increases their intensity. For example, the Greek vase painter drew sharp outlines around his hunter and dog and omitted almost everything else. Hiroshige likewise stressed sharp edges, except in the moisture-laden distance. In his highly selective representation no textures are distinguished. The same observation applies to the Sumerian sculptor's treatment in the *Governor of Lagash,* whose carved surface is uniformly smooth. He concentrated upon the mass of the figure and added only the few outlines needed

to suggest limbs, features and clothing. Daumier has emphasized
only the play of strong light which pours through a window into a
relatively dark room and illuminates the figures of the two sculptors.
The architects of the medical center have, of course, represented nothing in nature, but have expressed their own preference for simple
forms which convey an intense sensation of cleanness, smoothness, and
sharpness. Each artist, in his own way, has clarified and intensified
his sensations by selection and emphasis. This is an underlying
principle as old as art.

Visual and Tactile Sensations. Even before selecting and emphasizing his sensations, the artist must initially reduce the welter of
sense impressions to those that are visual and tactile. A visual sensation is any sensation which is conveyed to the mind solely through
sight; it is a strictly optical phenomenon. When we observe a sunset, the colored rays of light fall directly upon the retinas of our eyes.
A parallel experience would be our perception of the effect of light
in Daumier's *Two Sculptors.* Our impressions of atmosphere, color,
and shadow (lack of light) are similarly visual. At least half of our
impressions of the world around us are gained in this direct manner.

There is another half of the physical world which we cannot fully
understand through sight alone, or through touch as it is ordinarily
defined. An additional sense is required which we call *tactile.* It is
a muscular or motor type of response which functions in conjunction
with sight and touch. The perceptual process connected with it may
be described about as follows: when we see a large boulder, we first
observe with our eyes that it is round in shape and greyish brown in
color. But we also observe that it is smooth, dense, and heavy. How
do we know? From past experience of two sorts. At some time or
other we have touched a boulder and discovered that it was round
and smooth. If we tried to lift it or move it in any way (as in Fig.
74b–d) we found that it affected not only the nerves in our fingers
but the muscles in our arms, back, and legs. It resisted, and to the
extent that it resisted we learned that it was dense and heavy. We
probably gained at the same time a respect for boulders and similar
objects. Our memories stored this knowledge for future reference,
enabling us to recall it when we appraise the characteristics of another boulder. It is in this way that we know that a solid object is
heavy, dense, and rough (or smooth) without actually touching it.
The tactile sense, then, is partly visual, partly touch, partly muscular
—a complex, half direct, half indirect sensation. Without it we
could apprehend only half of the physical world. It is consequently
important to artistic expression and appreciation.

The tactile sense was developed to a high degree in the Sumerian sculptor. When we appreciate the sense of mass in the *Governor of Lagash,* it is not far-fetched to say that we measure it much as we do a boulder. Our sensation may be described as a kind of seeing, touching, and lifting with our eyes. It is also worth noting its connection with our empathic capacity for identifying ourselves muscularly with any activity involving tension, strain, and effort. It would be hard to draw a line between the tactile sense and empathic identification, so closely are they related.

The simple sketches (Fig. 74) are intended to show the difference between the visual and tactile sensations as we have described them, Fig. 74*a* standing for the direct appeal to the sense of sight and suggesting the feeling one has upon seeing Daumier's *Two Sculptors.* Figs. 74*b, c,* and *d* refer to the tactile sense, and Fig. 74*d* is likely to recall the *Captive* by Michelangelo (Fig. 66). The great Florentine had an acutely developed tactile sense or empathic capacity. The *Captive,* outstanding in both respects, gives us a combined effect of enormous weight and tremendous struggle.

Throughout the history of art, changes in preference have favored sometimes the tactile and sometimes the visual. A vigorous debate has risen over the merits of the opposing types, one side exalting the tactile virtues of Giotto and Michelangelo, the other the visual merits of Rembrandt and Titian. This debate need not be continued here. Our sensory enjoyment of light, color, and texture is relatively concentrated compared to those sensations of density and mass which bring our whole bodies into play. Yet we must be prepared to respond to all kinds of stimuli if we are to understand both Giotto and Titian, or Daumier's painting and the statue of the governor of Lagash.

SENTIMENT. Through the formal elements an artist induces in us such sensations as lightness, darkness, redness, shape, weight, roughness, or smoothness. Sentiment is something else. By representing, for example, the Virgin, her mother, the priest, the spectators, and the interior of the Temple (Fig. 51), Giotto directed our thoughts to a familiar scene. This brings into play the mental half of perception. But we do not stop here. Remembering similar situations, we identify ourselves with the scene empathically and sympathetically. Our attitude toward the Virgin, her mother, the priest, and the spectators is then colored by nuances of feeling derived from our own experience in life. In short, we have a sentiment. Ducasse calls it an *emotional attitude*—a complex thought colored by feeling.

Sensation and sentiment have different names and may be studied

separately. But unless we are content with half of the artist's expression, we should regard them as Siamese twins. The lines in
Hiroshige's *Shower on Ohashi Bridge* (Fig. 68) are formal elements
which arouse sensations of lines: but the same lines are the dramatic
elements of a rainstorm. In a similar way the suggestion of a beating
rainstorm which drives everyone to cover takes on meaning for us
when we recall our own reactions under similar circumstances. In
both instances one form of perception grows out of the other, so
that the resulting sentiment is neither pure thought nor pure feeling
but a fusion of sensation and past experience.

Although the medical center (Fig. 71) symbolizes a general idea
rather than a specific incident, something of the same transition from
a sense of planes, lines, and masses to a sentiment occurs when we
remember our own experiences with hospitals. This is typical of
our appreciation of all types of buildings. In a similar way sentiment
grows out of sensation when we view the *Governor of Lagash* (Fig.
67). His figure evokes a sentiment by reminding us of officials we
have known who behaved with dignity and composure. There may
appear to be little connection between a Sumerian dignitary who
died more than four thousand years ago and someone we ourselves
know, but our sentiments of the one provide meaning for the other.

It is also important to perceive that strong, clear sentiments like
those expressed by Hiroshige and the Sumerian sculptor not only derive from strong sensations but make the difference between the
clarity of works of art and the blur of common experience. In our
daily lives there is a close parallel between the way our sense impressions are dulled and our ideas are blunted by excessive demands upon
our powers of interpretation. Yet it is in this very excess, confusion,
and indifference that the artist's opportunities lie.

The artist at his best reacts to ideas as he does to sense impressions
—strongly, but with a desire to clarify, intensify, and interpret them.
He accomplishes this by reducing the excess of ideas to manageable
proportions, through selection and emphasis and by cutting through
the mass of current news to something of lasting importance like the
human dignity symbolized by the *Governor of Lagash*. In carrying
out the first approach, Hiroshige has asked us to consider only the
idea of a rainstorm, which we can easily do. The Sumerian sculptor
has presented us a single figure. Even the hospital, though more
complex, is so emphatically a hospital that our problem of understanding is lessened. This principle of clarification and intensification of sentiment by selection and emphasis could be illustrated repeatedly; it follows a universal pattern.

As an interpreter of relative values in life, the artist performs a valuable service. He awakens our interest in the ordinary objects around us—as Van Gogh does in a painting of old shoes or a chair, Chardin through bits of kitchenware and vegetables, Cézanne through a few apples, Renoir through a vase of flowers. The great artists have never needed to travel far to find the meaning of life in our social and elementary experiences with birth, marriage, and death; or rainstorms, sunsets, and moonlit nights. These are the stuff of Giotto's and Turner's art. But the master most likely to come to mind is Rembrandt, who, living quietly in Amsterdam, interpreted human nature in a way that people everywhere can understand.

Because of the quantity of potential dramatic elements which await a perceptive eye, the number and variety of sentiments which artists have drawn from ordinary experience, stored mentally, and expressed through works of art are nearly unlimited. There are, however, two important types which we can study briefly to aid our comprehension; one, *narrative sentiment,* is the easiest to understand; the other, *mood sentiment,* the hardest. The former expresses the thunderclaps of feelings—anger, love, hate, joy, fear, lust, and other strong emotions. The latter speaks in whispers.

Narrative Sentiment. Narrative sentiment has been expressed universally in the always popular storytelling (or narrative) work of art. Characteristically, such a work presents for our attention a limited number of dramatic elements arranged in a clear-cut cause-and-effect relationship. One situation out of a sequence of events is singled out and the idea underlying it stressed.

Few artists have expressed sentiment in the narrative form more directly or clearly than the first great modern pictorial storyteller, Giotto. A lucid example is his *Meeting of Joachim and Anna* (Fig. 75). It is one of a cycle of frescoes in the Arena Chapel at Padua, which Giotto painted in his prime to depict the life of the Virgin, and is related to *The Presentation of the Virgin in the Temple,* which we have already studied (Fig. 51).

This particular scene concerns the story of Mary's parents, who were still childless after twenty years of marriage. To the ancient Hebrews such sterility was a social stigma, a cause for remorse. So when Joachim was expelled from the Temple he retreated into the wilderness to fast and grieve. After twenty days a divine messenger informed both him and Anna that a child would bless their marriage, so he hastened toward Jerusalem while Anna hurried to meet him. The Apocrypha tells how they met at the Golden Gate of the city and embraced before Anna's beaming maids and the one black-cloaked servant who had chided her barren mistress.

FIG. 75. Giotto. *Meeting of Joachim and Anna. ca.* 1305.
Arena Chapel, Padua.

FIG. 76. Sloan. *The Wake of the Ferry.* 1907. Phillips Collection,
Washington, D.C.

128

Giotto has selected the climactic moment of the story so tellingly and presented it with such grace that little comment needs to be added. The picture delighted the people of Giotto's day, as it has people ever since.

Mood Sentiment. Mood sentiment has been expressed through works of art which differ markedly from the storytelling kind. They bring no one idea into sharp focus, but imply a good many associated with some general theme. They channel the mind more by suggestion than by pointed direction, and so give freer play to the imagination. A further difference between the two types is that mood sentiment invariably appears simple at first glance, when in fact it is usually more complex in its implications than narrative sentiment. In a work of art devoted to the expression of mood sentiment nothing singular seems to be happening. Nothing so clear cut as a story with a beginning, middle, and end is evolving; there is no plot or climax. Although the situation represented may have moved the artist strongly, his sentiments about it are necessarily long-range, cumulative, complex, and proportionately indefinite.

John Sloan, the twentieth-century American artist and "Ash-Can" confrere of Bellows, has painted such a situation in *The Wake of the Ferry* (Fig. 76). It depicts nothing more exact than New York Harbor on a mist-shrouded day, probably at twilight. A solitary figure looks out over this scene in which nothing unusual or exciting is occurring. The tugs which ply back and forth have crisscrossed the harbor countless times. But the very familiarity of their route allows the lone spectator to surrender to the impression made upon the senses by the misty day, the dim light, and the subdued colors, and induces us to do the same. The physical characteristics of such a spacious and quiet scene relax our nerves and minds by their vagueness. With nothing in the external scene to fix our attention, our thoughts become reverie and linger over an infinity of associations with the great city and its harbor and human aloneness.

So, though *The Wake of the Ferry* does not depict any one event which spelled New York to John Sloan during his long residence there, it tells us much about his emotional attitude toward the port and city. There is also a compelling logic to his interpretation. When we consult our own feelings about different cities, we find that our memory of New Orleans, Paris, or San Francisco is not crystallized in a few adventures, nor is it a sum of statistics about population, bus service, miles of boulevards, amusement parks, or public buildings. It is all of these and something more, an indefinable sentiment of the tempo, the rhythm, and general character of each metropolis, a recollection of exhilaration or relaxation or some feeling in between. Though hard to define, there is a consensus of the impressions created by different cities. We feel this difference when we travel from Boston to New York, and on to Philadelphia, Washington, and Atlanta. It is a feeling that has impressed itself strongly upon artists. We find it expressed in the representations of Venice by Guardi, Canaletto, Bonington, Turner, Renoir, and Monet; in pictures of Paris by Monet, Pissarro, Sisley, Renoir, Manet, Seurat, and Utrillo. Each artist has felt something different; but all have agreed that any subject as complex as a city can only be suggested, as Sloan has done, by the expression of the mood sentiment induced by long association.

This principle may be applied to all subjects which symbolize in greater or lesser degree many associated sentiments rather than one particular event. This extension brings into the realm of mood sentiment a surprisingly large portion of the world's works of art. It includes almost all of architecture, all examples of abstract painting and sculpture which were suggested, however indirectly, by physical reality, and most of the minor arts. It covers that vast number of drawings, paintings, and statues depicting still life, portraits, landscapes, and a number of other subjects in which nothing climactic is happening. Different though these many categories may be, they have this common characteristic: they endure in works of art according to their capacity to express, either strongly or subtly, some kind of sentiment. Sensation alone is seldom enough to satisfy the human mind.

When all of the works of art which fall into the above groups are added together, they appear to comprise at least 80 per cent of all the works of art in the world. Therefore the person who likes his art not only to appear "real" but to tell a story cuts himself off from most of the art which might give him enjoyment. The commonness of this attitude points out the major problem before us; the need to become alert to the character and value of mood sentiment in works of art. An excellent way to do this is to compare and contrast it with narrative sentiment to determine the exact part that each plays.

THE COMPARATIVE MERITS OF NARRATIVE AND MOOD SENTIMENTS. It is easy to see why narrative expression has always enjoyed such popular favor. At first glance it seems to enjoy every advantage. In Giotto's fresco, as distinct from a still life, something is happening, and where there is action there is life. Furthermore, the event is climactic, which gives it an added psychological impact. The central emotion expressed ranks high in the scale of civilized human values.

The artist has included every dramatic element needed to tell the story fully, but not one element more. Unerring selection and emphasis are evident.

By the exercise of control and judgment Giotto interpreted a significant aspect of life with clarity and intensity. He brought both art and the Biblical story within the comprehension of people of every class and degree of education. To anyone who wished to narrate a story directly and forcefully he pointed the way. And his reward was immediate gratitude, followed by immortality.

To say, then, that narrative sentiment produces only an inferior kind of popular art is foolish, as the Renaissance masters proved. No other sentiment expresses certain aspects of life so well. Yet to add that it leaves most of life unexpressed is only to state a fact. Most of existence lies in the intervals between singular events and consists of the familiar and apparently dull routine of everyday life. It does not reverberate in emotional thunderclaps but speaks in whispers (the phrases are Ducasse's). The whispers are full of overtones, nuances, subtle shades of meaning, all of which can lend excitement to the commonest objects or events, providing we are sensitive to them.

It is this sort of quiet excitement that is expressed in John Sloan's *Wake of the Ferry*. Compared with Giotto's painting, it clearly expresses a range of sentiment that is untouched by the fresco. The appreciation of that sentiment, however, is largely up to the viewer. If we are attuned only to the more obvious thunderclaps of narrative sentiment, we shall not only miss the majority of sentiments that art has expressed but its subtlest, richest, and most enduring. We shall never have to worry much about our ability to understand the sentiments in a narrative picture; it will be the mood emotions that elude interpretation to our great loss.

We have now drawn a few conclusions about the nature and language of the visual arts. A special kind of human activity, unlike the blind phenomena of nature, it is employed for human expression and communication. A primary requirement for practice of these arts is skill or control, a control which is devoted to the objectification of feeling. Between the two, control and feeling, there is no choice; a work of art must incorporate both.

The feeling expressed is generated by experience with reality, either *inner* or *outer,* but most often an interplay of both in the following process: what is objectively real becomes subjectively real in the mind of the artist, and this conception is in turn communicated through the work of art.

The feeling expressed through a work of art is of two interpenetrating or reciprocal kinds; sensation and sentiment. These are objectified through signs which are called the formal and dramatic elements. They are controlled or designed to stimulate in us something of the feeling which the artist felt in himself, his assumption being that his reactions will find some universally responsive strings in us. The language of art is therefore based on certain universal assumptions which transcend the fluctuations of taste and time. Above all, it is a language of feeling. That is its essence.

The definition thus arrived at allows us to see the common aims which underlie and unite the efforts of such diverse artistic personalities as Rembrandt, Michelangelo, Daumier, Hiroshige, Franz Marc, an ancient Sumerian sculptor, and an even more ancient prehistoric artist. However different each was from the other, all demonstrated the essential and unchanging nature of art—control over the objectification of feeling.

CHAPTER 6

The Universals in Art

In our definition of art we stressed the importance of feeling, but we must not leave the impression that feeling takes precedence over thought. Only intellectual power coupled with emotional sensitivity can create a work of art.

In relating the mental processes of artistry to the objectification of emotional reactions we must determine those qualities in art fundamental to a universal language of expression and communication. We cannot do this without considering the qualitative side of art, for we should not only be interested in art and its universality, but in *fine* art and the reasons for its fineness. The two qualities—universality and excellence—are closely connected. We must also appreciate that they derive their importance entirely from human attitudes. They have no natural or absolute validity, but are the expression of the qualities man values most in art.

Why does one man's work endure while another succeeds only for a few years? Plainly, art which endures is built upon those characteristics of nature and human life which remain important to every generation. This is the fact of the matter, but the exact mental processes of selection and organization by which the recognized masters achieved this timelessness and universality are difficult to analyze. We shall do better to examine the history of actual works of art in search of more objective clues.

For example, every work of art has two lives, one short, the other long. The short life is born in the immediate issues, interests, and fashions of the artist's time and place, and passes into history with them; the other is as immortal and universal as the artist's mind and sympathies can make it. There are those who believe that the specific spirit of a period dies forever with those who live through it, that only an actual veteran of Napoleon's final campaigns could really understand Meissonier's *1814* (Fig. 28). But any of us can feel and understand its timeless mood of gloom. The same division applies to a "jazz age" night club scene or an American bread line in the early 1930s. These are fully meaningful only to those who felt the emotions of those days directly and knew the social and economic issues at first hand. The rest of us can only perceive the quality of gaiety in the one and the despair and hunger in the other. These are not limited to any one time or place.

Any picture like the Meissonier which is strongly committed to a particular period or event may be an excellent illustration, but it is a self-limiting work of art. Older readers will remember Sir Lawrence Alma-Tadema's paintings of ancient Roman life which were realistic and archaeologically accurate in every detail. Enormously popular in their classical-minded time, they are now forgotten because their timeless content was buried under a mass of historical costumes, settings, and accessories.

Burchfield's moody *November Evening* (Fig. 27) and Sloan's nostalgic *Wake of the Ferry* (Fig. 76) are consistently moving works because they are not so bound. Their specific narrative content is low; they are scenes which could have been painted almost anywhere. Similarly, Giotto and Goya showed their wisdom in commenting on human life and warfare by avoiding the telltale costumes peculiar to the first century B.C. or the French invasion of Spain (Figs. 4 and 75). With human behavior put first their work is not "dated," but expresses ideas valid for any century.

Another example of a work of art's dual life is Pollaiuolo's story-telling *Hercules Strangling Antaeus* (Fig. 64). The interest in such classical myths was an engrossing one in the Renaissance, but it is not today. A love of power is, however, common to every age. If that power were removed from Pollaiuolo's figures we would quickly feel the loss; they would then be no better than other Renaissance representations of ancient myths to which we scarcely give a second look today. Vigor, not illustration, is what has made Pollaiuolo's figures live.

The qualities which retain their life after the historical or illustrative content of a work of art has become merely academic are often called its *residual content*. In this volume we have called them its universal and timeless properties.

Granted that nature and human life present attributes both universal and individual, both timeless and transitory to every artist, the differences between the survival powers of works of art must stem from varying powers of recognition among the artists themselves. In short, the source of enduring artistic quality lies in the creative and interpretive capacities of the mind.

It is a truism to say that every artist is trying to discover what is significant and lasting, that none of them—Alma-Tadema and Meissonier included—is deliberately trivial or ephemeral. But the odds against communicating something of enduring value appear to be tremendous. The contrast between a Théodore Rousseau's fascination with details and a Cézanne's deeper insight into essentials only illustrates the psychological axiom that it is easy to see, hard to know, and harder still to understand profoundly. What great art offers, therefore, is access to the value judgments of men of penetrating insight and far-reaching understanding.

The properties of nature and human experience which both the ancient Chinese and modern Frenchmen would call fundamental are few. But, although the field is narrow, universal and timeless values must exist, else any artistic communication between a prehistoric artist and ourselves would be impossible. The universally expressed preferences, which vary only in degree of emphasis, reduce to six qualities: vitality and repose, finiteness and infinity, order and variety.

VITALITY

Vitality is life itself. In this instance we have only to observe how artists have valued it for many centuries. The first of Ho Hsieh's six canons for Chinese painting, written fifteen centuries ago, was "rhythmic vitality." Long before Ho Hsieh, the unknown artist of the prehistoric *Bison* (Fig. 33) had responded to the energy of his wild model and captured it in paint.

No great artist since that time has ignored the importance of vitality, but artists have varied in the stress placed upon it. An instance of strong emphasis on vitality is George Bellows' *Stag at Sharkey's* (Fig. 77), a scene of brutal power in which two young and muscular men try to batter each other senseless, one of those club fights staged in small, densely packed, smoke-filled arenas where blood and action are more important than skill. The fighters are like animals in a death struggle. Their raw power has ripped away the audience's veneer of civilization and aroused its killer instincts.

By what he represented Bellows conveys an almost primitive worship of vitality. His picture transports us back to the jungle. At the same time, his artistic skill exemplifies ultimate control. Throwing himself into the mood of the scene, he applied his paint in vigorous strokes, contrasted the gleaming bodies of the boxers with the inky blackness of the background, played the head-long angularity of

FIG. 77. Bellows. *Stag at Sharkey's.* 1907.
Cleveland Museum of Art.

FIG. 78. Eakins. *Between Rounds.*
1899. Philadelphia Museum of Art.

FIG. 79. Giorgione. *Sleeping Venus. ca.* 1505. Royal Painting
Gallery, Dresden.

the fighters against hard, taut ropes, and gave his colors a garish raw-
ness that suggests the acrid odors of sweat and smoke. Like Pollaiuolo, he plays upon our emphatic responses to powerful action.
This is not a pretty picture, but it is notable for its presentation of
vitality.

REPOSE

The human appreciation of repose matches the delight in vitality.
Indeed, vitality in unlimited quantities creates a craving for repose.
So important is repose that it can be found side by side with vitality
even in a melee like Bellows' *Stag at Sharkey's*. Sometimes valued
equally with, or even above, vitality, it is the complement to vitality
which gives it its sharpest meaning.

Throughout the history of art, painters, sculptors, and architects
have introduced repose to express personal preferences for tranquility. It goes without saying that the man to whom quiet is natural
will most effectively speak for its virtues. Corot was, according to
all who knew him, as serene as the pictures he painted. Two other
examples of artists who were equipped by nature to speak for both
the personal and universal merits of repose were Thomas Eakins and
Giorgione.

Fig. 78 is a painting by Eakins, *Between Rounds*. Juxtaposed
with Bellows' *Stag at Sharkey's* it shows how a single activity may be
interpreted from two opposite points of view. Taken together, they
illustrate the difference between the roles played by vitality and
repose. Bellows, a member of the so-called "Ash-Can" school, reveled
in the teeming vulgarity of twentieth-century Manhattan slums, back
alleys, and byways, in its night clubs, theatrical haunts, Turkish
baths, crowded bars, and sports arenas. His *Stag at Sharkey's* is a
personal statement of his own love of the excitement, even the brutality, of metropolitan life. It is an excitement that many have felt
and others, like Damon Runyon and O. Henry, have captured in
various ways. Its essence is a vitality which compensates for dirt and
poverty. Bellows craved this sense of energy.

Thomas Eakins was a different sort of man. He haunted no Great
White Way and rarely rubbed elbows with the millions. Instead, he
lived quietly in Philadelphia, where he studied, practiced, and taught
his art with great seriousness. Devoted to his family and the friend
and equal of many professional men, he was reflective and studious,
an able scientist and anatomist. At the same time he was a virile
man who loved the out-of-doors and was expert in several sports.
His *Between Rounds* reflects these characteristics—his preference for

poised and controlled action and his analytical attitude toward the skilful side of boxing.

Eakins portrayed the moment between rounds which alternates rhythmically with the two or three minutes of intense activity represented by Bellows. Of the two interpretations of the ring, Eakins' is quieter, but it is by no means static. A devotee of boxing will appreciate the air of expectancy which characterizes the ticking off of the seconds between rounds when contestants rest before squaring off again. In their way, the moments between rounds are as dramatic as the moments of furious action. They play upon the imagination of the crowd and stimulate a hum of anticipation.

Eakins, a cool, penetrating observer of any activity that interested him, has brought out the significant points of this respite between rounds, underscoring exactly the aspects which give it meaning—the alert timekeeper in the foreground, the busy solicitous seconds, and the determinedly relaxed fighter. Subtly contrasting various degrees of alertness and repose in a single picture, Eakins has achieved a double effect of intensity within an atmosphere of suspense. It is an illustration of deliberate understatement. It shows, also, the dual relationship of vitality and repose, revealing how they may exist concurrently and implying how they are related in the fight–rest pattern of boxing.

Another master of repose was Giorgione. So well does his *Sleeping Venus* (Fig. 79) sum up our ideas of rest that it is regarded as a classic example. It has earned its fame by the consistency of the idea expressed. A sleeping figure could hardly appear more relaxed in mind or body, more goddess-like in physique, or more innocent in character. She is nude, critics have pointed out; Titian's similarly posed but wide-awake *Venus of Urbino* (Fig. 264) is naked.

The *Sleeping Venus* expresses the temperament of Giorgione, a brilliant Venetian painter who died young, as we have come to know him through the few impeccable paintings he left. Among them this is the best spokesman for his restrained sensuousness and idealistic conception of behavior, his own blend of classical serenity and a romantic nostalgia for a world as peaceful as the one in which his Venus sleeps.

The *Sleeping Venus* illustrates another point which is important for our evaluation of repose. The picture is effective because it makes repose seem so desirable. It presents rest as something positively attractive, rather than a neutral state or a necessary antidote to an excess of activity. In our ordinary thoughts vitality has some advantage over repose. But who would say that Giorgione's offer of calm has less appeal than Bellows' offer of energy? The two are not actually competitors; in life they are partners, each with its special contribution to make.

One final word about repose. It suffers by comparison with vitality because, while activity is the opposite of death, rest approximates its characteristics. But repose is not the sleep of death, nor is it to be confused with weariness or fatigue. It is a pause in activity and may be, as in Eakins' conception of the prize ring, shot through with alertness and suspense. Giorgione accepted the risks of deadness when he put his Venus to sleep; but she only rests, and will awake.

FINITENESS

Finiteness, for all practical artistic purposes, is the defining characteristic of those aspects of the visible world that appear clear and definite to human perception. It is a quality which has long had strong appeal for the human mind and elicited the interest of many artists, with Cézanne prominent among them. Although he did not say so in words, Cézanne proved through his paintings that he loved that portion of the visible world which is stable and disliked those elements which are vague and changeable. He felt strongly the sense of security and pleasure that the former gave him. Observing the natural world according to the strength of the sensations it aroused in him, he subconsciously divided its attributes into two groups and spent his life praising the merits of one of them—that which stands for finiteness in the human mind. In so doing he showed us what constitutes the finite world and outlined and underscored its characteristics.

How he did this we can best observe in an actual painting, the landscape called *House in Provence* (Fig. 80). Basically, the picture consists of a house, a few trees, and a sheer and barren cliff—elements we can take in at a glance. Examining the picture, we see how Cézanne gained clarity and emphasis by selection and exclusion. He included in his painting only tangible objects, especially those which lend themselves to clear and easy sense perception. They are physically solid, weighty, and stable. They are neither minute nor vast, microscopic nor cosmic. They are simple and massive rather than delicate and complex. Dynamically speaking, they are utterly static. Each falls within the optimum range of ordinary human perception, and being highly observable, gives a sense of fulfilment.

For Cézanne, visually comfortable scale, distance, size, and simplicity were only a start. Striving for the utmost clarity of form, he strengthened the outlines of houses, trees, and cliff so that every mass and plane is separated left and right, front and back; nothing is

FIG. 80. Cézanne. *House in Provence.* 1885-1886. John Herron Art Institute, Indianapolis.

FIG. 81. San Francisco Bay.

FIG. 82. Turner. *Rain, Steam and Speed.* 1844. National Gallery, London.

blended, merged, or lost. So treated, his whole world—trees as well as house and cliff—takes on solidity. It is a world with the consistently massive durability of poured concrete: certain, stable, dependable.

In order to achieve his kind of finiteness, Cézanne excluded all of those elements in the natural scene which were inimical to his personal concept and artistic methods. His light is his own, not nature's. It has no identifiable single source. It does not change but is permanent, strong, uniform. There are no deep shadows and no atmosphere—both elements which, in nature, change and shift and obscure the world of forms. In this dependable, well-lighted setting the cliff looms large and near, the sky is as hard and substantial as a plaster wall.

Cézanne's conception is one-sided, but it is a consistent interpretation of the finite half of the physical world. An inventory of what he painted best and most often is tantamount to a definition of the finite. His art is an exploration of shapes and masses—the heavier and denser the better. Specifically, they are fruits, furniture, pottery, the human body, sturdy houses, the earth and its weightier constituents: tree trunks, boulders, cliffs, and promontories. Of all his natural subjects, Mont Sainte Victoire was, significantly, his favorite. Taken together, the objects of his keenest observation and strongest response make up a fixed and solid world.

Sometimes Cézanne had to include in his pictures such fragile or variable elements as water, sky, flowers, and leaves of trees. In every instance he endowed them with an unnatural substantiality or used their softness as a foil to the massiveness of boulders and solid ground or table top, as in his *Vase of Tulips* (Fig. 15) and *Forest of Fontainebleau* (Fig. 39). He showed little interest in the superficial aspects of solids, their petty details or surface textures. Depicting the kind of finiteness which appeals to our tactile senses, he also conveyed his own pleasure in the solid world. He pleaded the case of finiteness eloquently.

INFINITY

If the finite world is that portion of the visible world which falls readily within the limits of clear human perception, the infinite lies, by implication, between the fringes of clear perception and the vanishing point. That such a region exists is a matter of common experience, for we are surrounded by things we can dimly sense but only partially understand. The bulk of the cosmos still lies beyond our mental reach, mysterious, uncertain, unknown. Yet that is not to say that it can have no meaning for us. The infinite has its positive value for human thought, but in view of our dislike of vagueness and unreliability, it will require some explanation.

The least embarrassing way to reverse our field and justify the worth of infinity is to note that if the whole of nature were as finite as Cézanne's *House in Provence,* our world would seem as static and arid as the face of the moon, lifeless and uninteresting. We need to feel the solid earth beneath us, but we need equally the feeling of life around us; and the essence of life is growth, movement, and change.

In studying the presentation of finiteness in art we found an example in Cézanne's *House in Provence.* We could do worse in studying the nature of infinity than to examine a photograph of San Francisco Bay taken about 1890 (Fig. 81). It summarizes the appearance of a naturally infinite scene well for the simple reason that it stands for almost everything that Cézanne disavowed. This is a vast and deep panorama in which the nearest solid objects are on the far horizon. We can barely identify them as square-riggers; many of them are nearly lost in misty shadow. The water has been churned into a seething wake by the steamer that carried the photographer, and the remainder of the surface is broken into minute waves and dancing high lights. The whole sky is in a state of flux, with rapidly changing light playing over moving, billowing clouds. These characteristics provide us with a catalog of the components of infinity: objects which are small or greatly distant; planes which are broken into many details; moving water, atmosphere, vapors, mists, fog, clouds, natural light, and deep shadows. All of these are infinite because they are difficult to perceive.

In his *Creative Evolution,* Henri Bergson suggests why this is so: "Of immobility alone does the intellect form a clear idea." Movement puts us at a disadvantage, as do extremes of minuteness, vastness, remoteness, or obscurity of outline. Atmosphere, distance, shadows, and rapid change are likewise enemies of clear perception. Thus the general character of a scene influences our way of perceiving it. A scene composed predominantly of static solids lends itself to a relatively conscious logical analysis. An infinite scene stimulates our senses only vaguely, and being only half sensed, can only be half guessed at by any direct method of observation. However, it stimulates the imagination to supply what is not visible.

Turner was as devoted to the infinite world as Cézanne was to the finite. In temperament he was opposite to the master of Provence. Cézanne was conservative and sedentary in his habits, Turner an amoral vagabond. Restless as a sandpiper, he traveled from one end of Europe to the other. Cézanne was a product of the sunlit Mediterranean and took the sun for granted; Turner was reared in northern mists and fogs. The southerner eliminated the natural sun from his painted skies without a qualm, while the light-hungry northerner worshipped it. Cézanne was sufficiently logical to form an abstract concept of reality—that all of its solids can be reduced to geometric shapes. Turner was a child of the elements, who loved and painted them intuitively but could never explain them. His lectures at the Royal Academy, when he was its most illustrious member, were beautifully illustrated but verbally unintelligible.

Cézanne's Provençal environment looked more or less as he painted it. He did no violence to it but intensified the natural finiteness which he loved in a happy union of concept and locale. In his own way Turner did the same thing for his part of the world. Living under the cloud-filled skies and ever-changing lights of London, the Channel Coast, and the North Sea, Turner dwelt in a region not unlike the scene of San Francisco Bay; active and imaginative himself, he rejoiced in its transitory, variable character.

Only a glance at his noted *Rain, Steam and Speed* (Fig. 82) is needed to show that he not only accepted the infinite world, but even accentuated its attributes. Neither blinding rain nor intangible steam was anathema to him, as they would have been to Cézanne; he loved them. The idea of speed, symbolized by the new, noisy, smoke-belching iron horse, excited his imagination. True to his own kind of logic, the intuitive apprehension of rapid movement, Turner sacrificed every clear outline and solid form in favor of bare suggestion: everything is vague and ill-defined, as it should be when it is dynamic. If the photograph of San Francisco Bay is predominantly dynamic, Turner's *Rain, Steam and Speed* is even more so.

Turner's view of the world stands at the far pole from Cézanne's. Each was true to his own temperament and native environment. But most important, each perceived a fundamental quality of the world and thus cast a significant light upon it.

ORDER AND VARIETY

Artists have always considered the creation of order one of the primary functions of art. The methods by which this is achieved will be treated fully in a later section. We need consider here only this psychological fact: pure order produces a monotony as disturbing as chaos. The antidote to that condition is *variety*.

The artist's challenge is to recognize its importance without becoming its victim. He must see its complementary relationship to order. Avoiding extremes, he must play one against the other and achieve a kind of flexible balance which will suit his several purposes.

Cézanne cherished order. In his *House in Provence* he stressed it as strongly as he could in the main outlines and masses of his composition. Yet he found room for variety in the free manipulation of his brush, in subtle contractions and expansions of lines, in gradations and contrasts of color. These variations should not be exaggerated; they are the sauce on the meat, not the meat itself; but they give sparkle and life to his picture. Eakins was likewise a man who valued order, thought, and control above any impulsiveness. The quality of order in his *Between Rounds* strikes one immediately; everything is under control. Yet it is a flexible order, with a variety of poses characterizing the juxtaposition of relaxation and hustle in the moment between the rounds—a variety exactly in keeping with the idea at hand.

Turner and Bellows, on the other hand, were men to whom variety, movement, and change were indeed the "spice of life," and their pictures reflect that evaluation. Variety is implicit in the names they selected: *Stag at Sharkey's* and *Rain, Steam and Speed.* The themes were treated accordingly. Turner's picture is one of dynamic force, although a study of its consistently soft outlines will show it is not without order. And Bellows, for all his love of violent action, did not forget the importance of order, achieving it in his own way through the balance of his moving figures, the referee and the two contestants.

Inasmuch as there are scenes which are essentially dynamic, an artist must adapt his means and satisfy order's need for variety or variety's need for order accordingly. Emphasis without excess is his means of avoiding the reactions induced by extremes.

THE INTERRELATION OF THE UNIVERSAL VALUES

In summing up the meaning of the universal values we have studied we must strive for flexibility and scope. We have considered these characteristics separately as a matter of convenience, but at the same time we have seen how naturally each suggests its opposite. Let us now consider these pairs in one group, and assume that if they really arise from universal and timeless human evaluations, no work of art will entirely lack any of them. Bellows' *Stag at Sharkey's* will not utterly lack repose, for all its violence. It must also contain in some degree both order and variety, finiteness and infinity. Its emphasis may favor one of each pair, but the composition must not wholly lack any of their opposites.

These six major characteristics are opposites, but they are not polar extremes. They lie within other characteristics which represent excess:

Uncontrolled	Controlled		Controlled	Uncontrolled
wildness	VITALITY	*versus*	REPOSE	deadness
obviousness	FINITENESS	*versus*	INFINITY	nebulousness
monotony	ORDER	*versus*	VARIETY	chaos

Wildness is vitality so excessive that it obliterates every sign of repose. Deadness is repose utterly lacking in life. Monotony is absolute order from which all variety has been excluded. Chaos is variety without any semblance of order. Situations which appear to us to be characterized by chaos, monotony, wildness, or deadness are common in human experience. The presence of words, invented after the fact to describe them, confirms their existence.

The esthetic quality of a work of art is thus a dynamic equilibrium of characteristics lying within these extremes. Combined in a limitless number of ways, their chief effect is always a kind of tension. A great work of art expresses this tension in high degree, a poor work of art expresses it feebly. For our purposes we must sense its presence and try to explain it coherently. When we are able to do this, we have perceived the meaning of vitality in artistic expression. For an example we can turn to Turner's search for a mean between obviousness and nebulousness in *Rain, Steam and Speed* and note that his choice falls in the region between finiteness and infinity but is much closer to the latter. In this way we not only describe one of the most noticeable characteristics of the picture, but evaluate Turner's judgment and sense of artistry. Cézanne's *House in Provence* may be described in nearly opposite terms, its equation favoring the finite. It is important to observe that if the mean were a fixed point, both would be disbarred. A flexible critical mean discovers greatness in each picture.

With practice, we can go further and relate all six universal qualities. In Bellows' *Stag at Sharkey's* the most prominent characteristic is vitality. But close behind that feature is orderliness; the design is an outstanding example of a type known as occult axial balance. Finiteness and infinity, however, are so balanced that neither is especially noticeable. Properly, the *Stag at Sharkey's* is a classic example of the use of vitality and order in that order of importance, and criticisms of the picture almost invariably refer to those qualities. In another picture infinity and repose may be the dominant characteristics. This variability of emphasis is a reminder of a point made in the previous chapter, that the human spirit is not expressed as a whole in any work of art but through one or two outstanding attributes. Similarly, one or two universal qualities will usually be the most memorable in any work of art.

We must avoid above all a cut-and-dried approach. Any acceptable critical system must be helpful but not dogmatic. It must help us to sense the "life of forms in art," as Henri Focillon has put it, without attempting to reduce a work of art to a mathematical formula. Art expresses *feeling* and must be apprehended to some extent intuitively. So we guide best when we do not dogmatize. Secondly, the system must call our attention to the characteristics which express universal and timeless qualities and yet it must accept the existence of individual preferences, biases, and capacities peculiar to every personality and period. No country or century, for example, has had a monopoly on vitality, and yet none has ever completely lacked it. That quality has clearly varied from time to time and place to place in societies as it has in individuals. Our problem is to use this system to read the signs of these variations and evaluate their meanings. In such variations lies the significance of the history of art.

CHAPTER 7

The Visual Arts

The definition of art as *the controlled objectification of feeling* applies to all of the arts, but there are important differences between the arts which arise from their individual means and capacities. Our concern here is with the special characteristics of the visual arts.

The visual arts began when men lived in caves, when writing did not exist, and spoken language was a matter of grunts. Appearing in response to certain human needs which could be satisfied in no other way, the visual arts have persisted for the same reason. They cannot, of course, express all that man wishes to say, so in the course of time they were joined by literature, music, the drama, the dance. Not even painting and sculpture could satisfy all of man's needs for visual expression, so after he emerged from caves, architecture was added. Each of these arts gave expression in its special way to different sides of man's nature and his experiences with the surrounding world. The purpose of this chapter is to clarify the specific differences between these arts and the causes behind them.

THE MEDIA OF THE ARTS

When the arts are compared, reference is almost bound to be made to the parts played by their media, especially to their effects upon freedom of expression, difficulty of control, and length of artistic life. The question whether Abraham Lincoln wrote his Gettysburg Address on an old envelope, a piece of wrapping paper, or official stationery is merely interesting. The idea alone counts: it would have been great written on parchment or on foolscap.

This is not true of the visual arts. Rubens' genius is embodied in the actual pigment he used and fares as the pigment fares. If it has cracked or faded, grown dark or unbalanced in color composition, to that extent it no longer expresses his original conception. That these changes occur has been frequently and painfully shown. Artists of the nineteenth-century Munich and Düsseldorf schools used bitumen, a coal product, in underpaintings which have now turned shadows into areas of pure black. Renoir had the experience of seeing one of his own pictures change. Observing it in a dealer's window some years after he painted it, he was appalled to note how much a passage of red had faded and thrown the composition out of balance.

For these several reasons, a knowledge of the chemical and other properties of pigments, inks, canvases, papers, brushes, and the like has always been a major concern of the visual arts. In a fifteenth-century treatise by Cennino Cennini on the art of painting, at least half the pages are devoted to the technical problems of tempera and fresco painting. Looking backward, critics and historians give credit for the fine condition of most fifteenth-century Flemish paintings to the standards of craftsmanship enforced by the late medieval guilds. The old masters distilled their oils until they were crystal clear, ground their own colors, and allowed them ample time to dry in application. A picture was constructed as painstakingly as a monastery. While talking much about a "lost medium" of the Van Eycks, modern critics recognize that the real secret of the old Flemings was probably patience and pride of workmanship.

In the pictorial arts, expression is inseparably bound up with the physical objectification which bears the artist's personal touch. There can be no perfect substitute. As a consequence, personality is expressed through the physical medium of a specific and unique work of visual art autographically, and in a way which is irrelevant or impossible in literature. No one can look at a painting by Renoir without being conscious of his personal handling of the brush and paint. By the same token, Renoir spent years training his hand to coordinate with and express his mind. When arthritis afflicted him, it imposed a serious if not disastrous artistic handicap. Without manual control, an otherwise gifted painter or sculptor will never be great.

An architect is less concerned with manual skill, for others do the muscular work of erecting buildings. But he is very much interested in durability. His buildings must stand up. He has to worry about stresses and strains, snowloads and wind resistance, about weatherproof qualities of materials in a way that never troubles the writer or composer, and from which even the painter is comparatively free.

In some parts of the world, anticipating tornadoes, earthquakes, tidal waves, hurricanes, and floods is a normal part of his problem.

It is alleged that one famous modern architect who was consulted about the leaking pipes in a house of his design replied grandly, "Call a plumber." He was claiming an exceptional freedom from responsibility. Frank Lloyd Wright, in contrast, relates in his autobiography how deeply impressed he was by the failure of a large public building to fulfil its basic function of standing intact. The central piers of the building collapsed because of criminally negligent construction, killing and injuring many people. That day Wright resolved that a knowledge of engineering would be the foundation of his art. He later proved a mastery that amounted to genius when he designed the Imperial Hotel in Tokyo. Anticipating the hazards of earthquake and fire, he constructed it so well that it survived the earthquake which devastated the city in 1923. Considering what would have happened if the Imperial Hotel had failed to stand, it is not melodramatic to say that a mastery of materials may sometimes mean the difference between architectural fame and ruin.

If the physical media of the visual arts are compared, it may be justly said that the architect must have a versatile and expert knowledge of materials and an understanding of innumerable structural techniques, engineering principles, and building crafts. He must work hard with mind and hands at his drafting board and in the field. Out of the material difficulties of his art arise labor and diplomatic problems involving many men and conflicting personalities. He is forced to be a persuader, leader, and coordinator; he is temperamental at his peril. But his reward is an artistic vehicle which by its durability insures as great an immortality of ideas as matter can attain.

In his own way the sculptor must struggle just as hard. Working more often alone, he does a larger proportion of the manual labor than the architect. The sculptor who follows a preliminary sketch still cannot turn over anything comparable to a blueprint to others for execution. Assistance he may have, as the ancient Egyptian studio masters did. He may even use such pliable materials as wax or clay, turning over to the founder the problem of casting his figures in bronze. But his task is still a demanding one; it is a virile art which assistance only renders less burdensome.

The reason for this is that the dedicated sculptor holds to two attitudes which do not enter into an architect's attitude toward his material media. The sculptor takes a sensuous delight in personal contact with his materials and in shaping them to his wishes. We feel this sense of challenge and conflict, this relish of direct control, in every chisel mark of Michelangelo's unfinished *Captive;* we learn without surprise that Rodin would twist and pull and compress the malleable clay for hours, obviously loving the feeling of the soft material under his hands; we know that Bernini reveled in giving marble the highest polish it would take. In addition the sculptor holds that, however much assistance he may employ, the final shape and finish are his personal trade-marks. After the cast figure returns from the foundry or the marble statue emerges from the pointing machine, he may spend hours applying a patina to the bronze or refining the carving of marble. It is by these marks that he conveys the final imprint of his personality upon his work. In spite of broken heads and limbs, his reward over the centuries has been beauty and durability. For every ruined Egyptian temple there are twenty Egyptian statues which are just as old. In fact, there are sculptured figures which are thousands of years older than the Pyramids.

Although painting can be back-breaking work, as Michelangelo discovered on the scaffold beneath the Sistine ceiling, it is generally less arduous than either the building or sculptural arts. Painters do not need the strength and stamina of sculptors, who have counted few women among their number; on the other hand, they do not gain through pigment the durability of stone. Their medium is a comparatively fragile one which, unlike the substance of a building or statue, is affixed to another surface and is subject to fading, cracking, and discoloration. Thus the upkeep of a picture is great. For every dollar spent upon the care of statues in a museum, a hundred goes into the preservation of canvases and panels.

The lesser durability of paintings has been offset by other virtues. The more modest costs of the pictorial media have permitted painting to be practiced widely. Forty sculptors could not match the numerical output of Rubens and Turner alone; sheer numbers have aided survival. The practice of painting, less demanding physically, frees the energies of an artist for other equally valuable expressions of nervous energy and sensitivity. Painting is as sensitive as a seismograph in these respects, and without a superior as a vehicle of color. More important still, in the presence of its lighter and less ponderous matter, the viewer is less conscious of matter and more conscious of spirit. Paintings run their risks in the contest for survival, but they gain commensurately in the expression of ideas.

This fact has impressed itself upon civilized peoples everywhere. Noting the physical weakness but the esthetic and spiritual appeal of paintings, they have protected them, much as they would protect a flower while giving no thought to a rock. The practical effect has been to give paintings an additional power of endurance; they now survive nearly as well as their brothers in stone.

Remember that the practical side of art should be neither ignored nor exaggerated. In the visual arts the media must be given their due. But in these arts media and treatment stand in the same relation as matter and mind in life as a whole; the one is dependent upon the other but is superior to it. For the qualitative side of artistic expression we shall have to seek in other directions.

THE TEMPORAL AND SPATIAL MODES OF EXPRESSION

Because a picture or building occupies *space,* while sounds or words occupy *time,* critics differentiate the arts as temporal or spatial, depending upon whether they are directed to our hearing or our sight. Under the heading of temporal they have combined literature, rhetoric, music, the dance, and the theatrical arts; under spatial, the silent arts of architecture, sculpture, painting, drawing, and photography. A third group is often introduced as the mixed arts. It includes the dance and the theatrical arts, such as opera, cinema, and plays. The classification implies that both visible and audible expression are about equally important.

In the spatial group, too, a fourth category is sometimes added. Termed the *mixed visual arts,* it signifies that a new relationship arises when the visual arts are combined, as when sculpture is made a part of an architectural design or a picture is conceived as a mural painting. Famous examples of such mixtures readily come to mind; one can hardly think of the Parthenon sculptures apart from the structure in Athens for which they were designed; one invariably connects Byzantine mosaic pictures with the churches they adorned; one cannot remember the Cathedral of Chartres without recalling its portal statues and stained glass windows; one always remembers the Palace of Versailles as an ensemble of buildings, statues, paintings, parks, and gardens. In each case the designers intended so to channel and control our conceptions. They joined the several arts in a total organization whose whole, esthetically as well as physically, is greater than the sum of its parts. In such a relationship the parts condition each other so much that we cannot think of them separately. The significance of these temporal and spatial conceptions revolves around the control that the creative mind exercises over time and space. This can best be shown by considering the extent to which an artist can predetermine how others will respond to his work. Compared to a composer, a playwright, or an author, the visual artist has only a limited control over the time sequence in which his work may be viewed. In a few instances he can demand a progressive viewing of his composition. The Parthenon frieze illustrates such a prescription. Another instance is Rubens' *Autumn, the Château de Steen* (Fig. 83), whose deep space one is almost bound to read from front to back, as though walking through a period of time into the distance. A better example still is St. Peter's at Rome (Fig. 85) which one perceives as a piazza and colonnade, façade and entrance foyer, nave, side aisles, transept, and apse. One could, of course, enter from the rear or side, as one can skip to the final chapter of a novel, but normally the visitor to St. Peter's follows a predetermined architectural guided tour in which his appreciation of the building's spatial relationship evolves in a sequence, with the grand climax, the altar, coming last. That is one of the reasons why it is a noted example of architectural art. The same may be said of most of the medieval cathedrals of France. Their fronts, middles, and rears are, in a sense, temporal beginnings, middles, and endings; the apse of a well-planned church is like the climax of a great novel. One is especially conscious of time in architecture because one has to walk through a period of time in order to observe a building.

An even better example of control over temporal appreciation of a work of visual art is William Zorach's *The Spirit of the Dance* (Fig. 84). The sculptor was aware of temporal as well as spatial order here for several reasons: the figure was commissioned for a particular place, in which it was to be viewed in a specified manner. It was to be placed near the bottom of a long stairway leading down to the lounge of the Radio City Music Hall in New York City. Since spectators would see the statue from several points of view as they descended, the design had to be equally effective from every angle. Zorach's solution was to conceive his figure within the balanced outlines of a pyramid, with the head of the dancer at the apex. Legs and arms are arranged around a central vertical axis which echoes the axis of the stairway. To emphasize the harmony between statue and stairway, he rotated the torso of the dancer in a spiral.

In spite of such efforts, the fact remains that control over temporal appreciation in the visual arts is relatively limited when compared to the temporal control possible in such arts as poetry and music. The main opportunities for the visual arts lie, instead, in the field of spatial organization, especially in architecture. St. Peter's (Fig. 85a) is literally three-dimensional, both inside and out, giving it six major dimensions and their interrelationships through which expression can be achieved. This hollow three-dimensionality of architecture is borne out by three kinds of drawings which never apply to painting

FIG. 83. Rubens. *Autumn, the Château de Steen.* 1636. National Gallery, London.

153

a

b

d

FIG. 84a–d. Zorach. *The Spirit of the Dance.* 1932. Replica of the statue in Radio City Music Hall, Rockefeller Center, New York. Bowdoin Museum of Fine Arts, Brunswick, Me.

c

or sculpture: the ground plan, elevation, and cross section. Since space elicits emotional and psychological responses of an important kind, as we noted in studying repose, its expressive possibilities in this respect are great. One needs only to glance down the nave of St. Peter's (Fig. 85c) to appreciate how space can be dramatized in architecture.

The observer of architecture walks about, changing his angle of observation constantly. Approaching the building from a distance, and then closer, he savors the quality of the exterior slowly; as he wanders in and out among the arches and side aisles of the interior, he views it in many ways. If he pauses at the crossing and looks up into Michelangelo's dome, he will have a memorable experience. The perception of architecture in this way adds much to its interest, a fact the wise architect anticipates and exploits.

The opportunities for controlled spatial design in the structural arts do not end here, for considerations are involved in architecture which rarely enter into any other of the visual arts. The architects of St. Peter's had to consider, for example, the problem of site, the orientation of the building, and its relation to its numerous older neighbors. How well they chose is brought home many times a day as one travels about Rome. The great edifice looms above its natural rise like a mountain above a plain, dominating the city physically and spiritually. The dome, silhouetted against a sunset, is a sight one never forgets.

Nothing was left to accident in relating St Peter's to its neighbors. Bernini, the architect in charge from 1643 to 1656, designed a colonnade (Fig. 85b) which excludes the jumble of older buildings from sight and prepares the visitor for something on a heroic scale. Shaped like a gigantic keyhole, the Colonnade reaches out and around visitors as they enter the spacious Piazza and draws them toward the entrance, imposing the will of the architect upon all who approach.

In no other visual art is the relation of form to site so full of possibilities as it is in architecture. When that relationship is thoroughly developed, a building's placement becomes a part of its effect. The Parthenon on the Acropolis and Mont Saint Michel on its famous rock are examples of buildings which gained greatly from an imaginative utilization of site.

A second feature of architecture is hardly less important. The hollow character of buildings, as contrasted with solid sculptural figures, poses both opportunities and pitfalls, for the problem of harmony between interior and exterior cannot be ignored. The architects of St. Peter's made the most of their chance by creating an

FIG. 85a. Bramante,
Raphael, Peruzzi,
Michelangelo, Bernini,
Maderna, and others.
Piazza and Church,
St. Peter's. 1506-1663.
Rome.

FIG. 85b. Bernini.
Colonnade and Piazza
of St. Peter's. 1656-
1663. Rome.

FIG. 85c. Nave, St.
Peter's. 1506-1626.
Rome.

exterior in grand and heroic terms which prepares the visitor mentally for the spectacle within. In a similar way, the builders of the French medieval cathedrals coordinated interiors and exteriors: the flaring triple portals of the façade reflect the nave and aisles of the interior, while the external verticality matches the soaring arches of the inner vaults. In particular, the psychological impressiveness of the façade is no greater or less than that of the interior. Neither disappointment nor surprise ensues as one goes from one to the other; a crescendo of feeling is more likely to occur as one enters the building and approaches the altar.

Sculpture is, like architecture, three-dimensional in the round, less so when in relief. The difference is illustrated by Zorach's *The Spirit of the Dance* (Fig. 84); one can walk around it. A relief is, compositionally speaking, no different from a painting: the sculptor assumes that the observer will adopt a frontal and more or less singular point of view. When the Greeks discovered the many-sidedness of sculpture in the round, an important advance was made.

Relief sculpture may even be said to be less three-dimensional in effect than most painting because, while three-dimensionality is actual in relief sculpture, deep space cannot be represented so well sculpturally as it can pictorially. A study of the best efforts of Ghiberti will illustrate that limitation. Relief sculpture has the finest spatial merits neither of painting nor of fully rounded sculpture. Its chief claim to usefulness lies in its adaptability to the decoration of architecture, where it is as durable and weatherproof as the building itself, a fact that the Egyptians, Asiatic Indians, and Greeks exploited.

Painting achieves only an illusion of three-dimensionality through representation, creating the appearance of depth beyond the picture plane. How great and convincing this sense of depth may be is shown by Rubens' panoramic landscape *Autumn, the Château de Steen* (Fig. 83). Another characteristic distinguishing most paintings from all architectural and sculptural works of art is the spectator's point of view. It is permanently fixed by a painting as it can never be by objects which are subject to mobile observation. In addition, the color, intensity, and direction of the light that Rubens wished to depict are established in the design of this *Autumn*. Over these two considerations—of point of view and lighting effect—he had complete artistic control.

Buildings and statues are, by contrast, dependent to some extent upon the position that the viewer chooses to assume; and they are at the mercy of constantly changing and unpredictable lighting; sculpture is notoriously dependent for effective presentation upon lighting, over which the sculptor can have little control. Architecture at least has this advantage: it deals with permanent sites with general climatic and lighting conditions which designers can anticipate. Conversely, paintings and statues are often miles, even oceans, away from their original settings. The finest of them are dependent upon museums for proper presentation. Mural paintings, frescoes, mosaics, stained glass windows, and relief carvings which were conceived as part of architectural ensembles have, of course, largely escaped this fate. But removal to foreign ground has been the lot of statues in the round and easel paintings from the day those two forms were born. Witness the location of Rubens' *Autumn, the Château de Steen* in the National Gallery, London, and the ancient Egyptian *Seated Statue of Khum-Ba-F* (Fig. 2) in the Museum of Fine Arts, Boston. Of the paintings thus far illustrated, a majority of forty-seven are now in places and under ownership which their creators could neither have predicted nor controlled. As a general rule, what applies in these respects to painting and sculpture applies equally to drawing, the graphic arts, and photography.

THE ABSTRACT-SYMBOLIC MODES OF EXPRESSION

In addition to being divided into the temporal and spatial arts, the arts may be thought of as abstract-symbolic or representational, depending upon the means they use for expressive communication. The symbolic arts use abstract signs while the representational depend upon the meanings aroused by images. Reduced to practical examples, the differences are these: a building's design is basically a composition of strictly formal elements. The columns of the Colonnade of St. Peter's (Fig. 85b) do not depend upon comparison with trees for their esthetic meaning. Their cylindrical shapes have at most only a distant connection with natural forms, and appeal most directly to a capacity for abstract thinking. The dome of St. Peter's (Fig. 85a) and the oval plan of the piazza in front of the cathedral (Fig. 85b) are other abstract, geometric shapes. That a harmony between architectural and natural forms can be discerned will be discussed later; all abstract forms in the visual arts derive their ultimate validity from certain universal attributes of natural reality (Cézanne's cubes, cones, and spheres). For present purposes the statement that architecture is an abstract art is less confusing and substantially true.

Architectural forms are abstractly symbolic in this further respect: they possess no inherent meaning, but depend, as do all abstract sym-

bols, upon associations for most of their meaning. There are in the
world a number of famous illustrations. At Nashville, Tennessee,
there stands a modern copy of the Parthenon which is, inch for inch,
as exact a duplicate of the ancient building as twentieth-century
techniques could make it, to say nothing of being in far better condition than the original. Yet no one could possibly look at the two
edifices with the same eye. In the course of twenty-five centuries the
Parthenon at Athens has acquired certain values in people's minds
which no duplication of its physical measurements can transfer. It
hardly needs to be added that an American and a Greek look at the
original Parthenon from two different points of view, just as they
would hold different attitudes toward the Capitol Building at Washington.

The symbolic meaning of architecture is also illustrated by the
influence of national consciousness upon artistic meaning. A case in
point is illustrated in Fig. 85b. In the center of the Piazza of St.
Peter's is a geometric shape which may be recognized as an Egyptian
obelisk. Far removed from its original context, it has lost its ancient
significance and become almost entirely decorative. When the same
geometric shape rises from the Mall in Washington, D. C., and is
called the Washington Monument, we endow it with an entirely new
and un-Egyptian meaning. Similarly, a pyramid which connotes
nothing on a geometry teacher's desk becomes a most meaningful
symbol when it is a Pharaoh's tomb on the banks of the Nile.

The stones, mortar, and shapes of an architectural composition
possess in every case as much symbolical meaning as human associations confer upon them. This principle pertains alike to the Taj
Mahal, the Lincoln Memorial, and the ancient Mausoleum at Halicarnassus. As if to prove the point once and for all, the Mausoleum
summed up the concept of a tomb so well that men have applied its
name to mortuaries ever since.

The depth of our associations requires a word of warning, for
symbolic meaning and artistic worth are by no means identical. Our
respect for a symbol may even blind us to lamentable artistic deficiencies, with the result that a whole nation may erect, condone, and love
public buildings which have little or no esthetic merit in the eyes of
the rest of the world. In that sense a new house may be superior to
a well-loved but commonplace home, and a well-designed factory may
excel, esthetically, the picturesque but mediocre local church. Symbolic meaning has added much to the meaning of the world's artistically great buildings, but no amount of it can make an artistically
poor building great.

Architectural expression is the most collective, as well as the most abstract and symbolic, of all the visual arts. Where a painting expresses the immediate interests of one or two people, architecture almost always involves the work and will of many. A painter may work alone, without anyone else in mind, if he so chooses. His materials are relatively cheap and he can usually buy them on his own. If he is willing to go hungry in a garret and trust to future appreciation, he can attain nearly complete independence of expression. Not so the architect. The materials of a building are costly and unwieldy; its site is permanent and expensive; and the cooperation of many workers is required for its construction. At every turn an architect is dependent upon other people's money. This means that in almost every instance a work of architecture expresses either a compromise or skilful persuasion. Since the architect's work depends upon and speaks for many, collective expression may be one of its greatest merits. The larger the building, the truer this will be. A house, for instance, stands for agreement between the architect and a single client; but the great Gothic cathedrals of France speak, as no painting or statue possibly could, for thousands of people, and for many generations who contributed their time, money, and energy.

Undoubtedly, the collective expression of a great building presents a mighty problem in cooperation. The construction of St. Peter's illustrates this problem well. Erected under the aegis of twenty-two different Popes, who employed eight successive architects-in-chief, it was begun in 1506 by Julius II and not substantially completed until the papacy of Alexander VII, 1655-1667. During the hundred and fifty years that elapsed, radical changes in conceptual emphasis appeared, owing partly to the changes in taste that occur with time. In the early stages of development Bramante, Peruzzi, Raphael, and Michelangelo placed their stress upon a vertical axis, with all lines leading up to the great dome. In the course of time Maderna and Bernini altered this arrangement in favor of a longer nave and larger façade which, though impressively deep and high, hide the dome from any close view. Coming later, their will prevailed while Michelangelo lay in his grave. When this conflict of ideas is considered, the total homogeneity of St. Peter's is doubly remarkable. Its minor conflicts in design make us appreciate anew how the Pyramids of Egypt express the absolute power and consistency that the ancient Pharaohs maintained during the many years required for their completion.

Although architectural expression is collective, abstract, and symbolic, it can produce an intense effect, preparing us to appreciate the building's function. In great architecture this control over our mood is surprisingly reliable. An outstanding example is the Cathedral of

Notre Dame of Paris. Notre Dame does not rise from a quiet town. It is set in the midst of a bustling city. But the minute one enters the cathedral a transformation occurs, as if one had entered another world. The quiet of the interior, the shadowy recesses of aisles and choir, and the color of the stained glass windows create an effect which can be observed in other people. All about one they walk as if on tiptoe and speak in whispers, making the honking of the taxis seem far away. This is architectural control at its best.

The outstanding examples of the world's architecture illustrate its expressive possibilities and establish the criteria by which architecture should be judged. They show that durability, efficiency, even esthetic appeal are not enough unless these factors combine to make a building express its social function and induce an appropriate frame of mind. They also demonstrate that the emotional and psychological climate which they provide must have more than a utilitarian significance for human life, a significance grounded not merely in comfort or convenience but in our hopes and fears. Thus is may be said that the symbolical arts reflect our values: granted equal beauty, the finest garage cannot equal the cathedral where we are baptised, taught, confirmed, married, and mourned.

Architecture alone fulfils one of the basic physical needs of life— shelter. At the same time, it gives expression to the highest aspirations of the largest number of people. It is aptly called "the mother of the arts." Between its physical basis and its spiritual peak it affects our lives more than any other art because it literally surrounds us all of the time. We do not have to read books, listen to music, or watch a play, but we cannot escape our architectural environment. Whether we are aware of it or not, it affects us constantly, creating a feeling of harmony and peace or of irritation and fatigue.

We can easily observe the adverse effects of man-made environment on the inhabitants of slums, prisons, and backwoods towns; or the inspiring effect of St. Peter's or the interior of Notre Dame. It has taken us somewhat longer to heed the effects of architectural design upon the worker in factory and office. But in our time a revolution has occurred in this field which shows a new appreciation of the affective power of architecture. For this revolution we owe much to Frank Lloyd Wright.

Wright began to show industry the way about 1904 in the design for the home office of the Larkin Soap Company (later a victim of the Depression) in Buffalo. But he took his longest stride forward in 1936 with his design for the Administration Building of the S. C. Johnson Wax Company in Racine, Wisconsin (Fig. 86). That the building has fulfilled its minimum architectural function of provid-

Fig. 86a. Wright. Main entrance, administration building, S. C. Johnson & Son, Inc. 1936-1939. Racine, Wis.

Fig. 86b. Wright. Interior, administration building, S. C. Johnson & Son, Inc. 1936-1939. Racine, Wis.

ing shelter and efficient working quarters has never been doubted. But it is more than a utilitarian structure; it is a work of art in which psychological factors were taken into account.

The exterior of the building is composed of flowing geometric shapes which have the clean-cut simplicity of an ocean liner. Like the liner, it expresses the dynamic spirit of the time. It also expresses its social function frankly and honestly for, unlike our pseudo-Roman banks and railroad stations, it is plainly a place in which people carry on the business of modern commerce. No one would mistake it for anything else. In the interior (Fig. 86b) the same curvilinear lines and smooth planes are repeated; vertical and horizontal are played against each other. A harmony between interior and exterior is thus established, one echoing the other.

Such coordination of interior and exterior is not to be taken for granted; it is the mark of fine architecture. It gives individual distinction to a building. To understand this practically, imagine how unthinkable it would be to exchange the façade of St. Peter's with Wright's entrance or, for that matter, with any other fine building whose interior and exterior designs are of a piece.

In the interior of the Administration Building Wright introduced certain new forms and materials with striking effect. One is the so-called dendriform column, which flares from a tiny base and spindly shaft to a traylike top: light and unobtrusive at the bottom, expansive and energetic at the top. For another effect he used tubes of glass to create a beautiful skylight which is more than a source of reading light, even though it is diffused, luminous, and easy on the eyes. In all of these respects his building expresses an understanding of the nature of architecture; it is an excellent building in which to work, according to those who use it daily.

We can sum up the main differences between the abstract and representational arts with a few general observations. Architecture is the most abstract of the visual arts; painting and sculpture are traditionally representational. They are commonly individualistic, while architecture is usually collective. From the point of view of the architect, who must wheedle and coax to preserve his ideas, this collective characteristic must often seem frustrating and burdensome. It has, however, this merit: historically, architecture has been an index of the degree of cooperation which existed within societies at a given time, even revealing whether that cooperation was enforced or voluntary. No other art has given us a better picture of history.

It is no surprise that the great periods of architecture coincided with those ancient and medieval epochs when architecturally minded leaders like Khufu, Justinian, and Abbot Suger were able to command large supplies of labor. Therefore, when we think of the Middle Ages we remember first their great churches, monasteries, cathedrals, and castles. The representational arts of stained glass, mosaic, tapestry, and sculpture played at that time only a decorative role. But our thoughts of the Renaissance and post-Renaissance periods center around the singular geniuses of Michelangelo, Rembrandt, Raphael, and Velasquez. That was the time, *par excellence,* of the individual masters. Collective and individualistic societies thus produce their different fruits. In the long run the soil of collectivism is the most fertile for architecture, the soil of freedom for painting and sculpture.

THE EXPRESSIVE POTENTIALITIES OF THE VISUAL ARTS

In his classic *The Arts and the Art of Criticism,* Theodore Meyer Greene refers to the expressive potentialities and limitations of the several arts. He avoids dogmas which guarantee merit to any subject or medium, stressing instead the necessity of an exploitive treatment. In conjunction with these terms Greene uses two others, *exaggeration* and *suppression.* Together they provide a useful set of critical terms. As a final consideration, let us relate this chapter to the previous one and compare the potentialities of the visual arts for the expression of the universal qualities of order and variety, finiteness and infinity, vitality and repose.

The first may be dismissed summarily. Each of the arts has produced masterpieces of order. If any one of the arts has a slight advantage, it is probably the abstract art of architecture in which no representational element competes with the formal design.

The physical media, on the other hand, have given rise to outstanding differences in the expression of finiteness and infinity. The actual tangibility of architecture and sculpture gives them a running start in underscoring our conception of the static and durable material world. We can confirm this in the massive piers of St. Peter's Church and in the unavoidably metallic character of Zorach's *The Spirit of the Dance.* This feeling of permanent massiveness was exploited to its ultimate by the ancient Egyptians in their statues and in the Pyramids.

The same inherent substantiality hinders the expression of infinity in sculpture and building as lead weights would hinder a bird. There have been sculptural expressions of the sense of infinite movement, such as Pollaiuolo's *Hercules Strangling Antaeus* (Fig. 64), and suggestions of space and atmosphere in Ghiberti's East Doors of the

Florence Baptistry, which Michelangelo likened to the Gates of Paradise. But none of these can compare with the kind of infinity attained with ease in Rubens' *Autumn, the Château de Steen* or Turner's *Rain, Steam and Speed*. In the expression of infinity painting has excelled.

The same distinction holds for the expression of vitality and repose. The relative intangibility of painting, and its capacity for representing atmosphere and movement, make it potentially the best vehicle for the expression of vitality. No architect or sculptor has realized this capacity so fully as Vincent Van Gogh realized it in paint. His *Mountainous Landscape* (Fig. 65) writhes as a building neither could nor should.

Sculpture's capacity for expressing vitality seems to lie somewhere between that of painting and architecture. Its tangibility, which favors static finiteness and continuity, works against the expression of nervous energy and rapid change. In the expression of these qualities the inherent lightness of pen and wash on paper gives a Daumier sketch like *The Drinking Song* (Fig. 63) an advantage over any work in a sculptural medium. But where vitality manifests itself in brute power, desperate struggle, or towering wrath, sculpture is a superior instrument of expression. In the presence of Michelangelo's *Captive* (Fig. 66) or Pollaiuolo's *Hercules Strangling Antaeus*, no other statement seems possible.

One reservation must be added. In relief sculpture, such as Ghiberti's and Donatello's, which attempted effects of atmosphere and deep space, the normal massiveness of sculpture is suppressed or sacrificed. A lightness of appearance results that narrows the differences between sculpture, painting, and drawing. These manners of treatment have been referred to as *pictorial sculpture*. Conversely, sculpture in the round has exploited most fully the inherent static massiveness of the sculptor's materials. Two examples which come to mind immediately are Egyptian sculpture in the round, like the *Seated Statue of Khum-Ba-F* (Fig. 2), and the statues of Michelangelo, in which the weight and massiveness of the material give a feeling of force, as though the figure were engaged in a struggle to free itself from its stony prison (Fig. 66).

A second reservation must be applied to all visual arts. Compared to the temporal arts, the visual arts are static. Movement in them can never be more than implied and is thus quite dependent upon appreciative cooperation. The skyscraper or Gothic vault which is said to "soar" does so only in the spectator's mind. Within this limitation visual artists have achieved remarkably expressive results, such as Bellows' *Stag at Sharkey's* (Fig. 77). But the visual arts have been perfect vehicles for the expression of repose. The Egyptians understood this potentiality thoroughly and exploited it. Early in the history of art they expressed a sense of repose in architecture and sculpture that has rarely been excelled. The Pyramids are justly famous for the impression they convey of sheer inert mass and physical repose. Their statues are hardly less effective, emanating an inner poise and control which is the essence of repose. With these examples before them, artists in every subsequent age have repeatedly proved the aptitude of architecture and sculpture for the embodiment of physical and spiritual repose. William Zorach's *The Spirit of the Dance* continues the tradition for modern times by its unhurried grace and coordination.

Since no one art form possesses all possible virtues, the physically lighter medium of painting, which has been ideal for the representation of the infinite qualities of light and atmosphere, has been somewhat less successful in expressing the repose associated with the tangible masses of architecture and sculpture. But it has been second to neither in capturing the infinite nuances of mood that attend psychological repose. It can express peace of mind without apologies to any other art. Rembrandt's last great portraits prove this point beyond a doubt.

Thus each of the visual arts has capacities for which it is especially suited. Greatness of expression has usually lain in the recognition of each capacity, followed by exploitation. Our task has been to determine in a general way the capacities of each medium, in order to see specifically in the following chapters how they have been realized through the methods of the visual arts.

PART II

The Methods of Art

CHAPTER 8

Introduction

In Part I we defined art as *the controlled objectification of feeling,* but only touched upon the methods which an artist may employ to attain that end. In considering the methods more fully we shall repeatedly use three terms, *representation, design,* and *expression.*

An artist's purpose is to objectify his reaction to the world. His two main means of accomplishing this purpose are representation and design; expression is the effect they create. By representation we mean the employment in objectification of some degree of imitation—the translation of the visual aspect of some subject in actuality into the terms of the medium employed. In this process the artist's aim is to arouse in the beholder the same sentiments and sensations which the original subject aroused in him. To do this he must employ likeness to at least a recognizable extent. Interpretation through imitation is the basic function of representation; the arousing of emotions through association is its ultimate end.

Design is the artist's means of giving his work an abstract rhythm which clarifies and intensifies its effect and endows it with a sense of order. It is the esthetic side of objectification which most clearly expresses his capacity for control. It begins, as Konody says, at the point where he departs from strict imitation and imposes on his work a rhythm of his own creation. Depending less on imitation and more on invention, it is the truly creative side of artistry.

Construed broadly, design includes every aspect of objectification which conveys the artist's creativity and sense of order, and gives his work *form* or *style* in their most inclusive sense. In this study of artistic methods I shall attempt to show how design is achieved in two ways: by a systematic manipulation of the representational means, called here *modes of representation,* and by what the layman ordinarily thinks of as *composition*. When speaking of design I shall mean primarily spatial and color composition. This subdivision of design into modes of representation and composition is, I realize, an arbitrary division. It is done to simplify a complex problem.

The different, almost antithetical, functions of representation and design tend to pull an artist in opposite directions, the one toward naturalism, the other toward formalism. In each work of art he must resolve this polarity by balancing the two interests or committing himself to an emphasis of one or the other. The decision that he expresses characterizes and differentiates his work. Exemplifying a unique ratio of the imitative to the abstract, it is an essential part of his artistic style. We can describe one work of art as adhering closely to natural appearances, a second as containing many departures from strict imitation, and a third as being completely nonobjective. The three possibilities can be discerned in the paintings of Gérôme, Van Gogh, and Mondrian.

But we do not stop here. We ask ourselves *why* one artist leans toward literal imitation and another takes liberties with natural appearances for the sake of a more abstract interpretation. For neither imitation nor abstraction is the ultimate end of artistry. The real goal is the expression of sentiments and sensations; imitation and abstraction are but the means. But since we perceive expression through these means, we must pay close attention to the relationship of representation and design in interpreting each work of art. Representation, design, and expression are so closely bound that each must be considered with the others in mind.

If an artist were a wholly free agent, our appreciation of his work would be less difficult than it is. But in most instances in the history of art he has expressed more than his own inclinations and personality. He has frequently had to respect the wishes of his patrons. He has been influenced by the practical purpose for which his work was intended, by the medium he employed, and by the broad environmental and artistic influences that bore upon him. These are also reflected in his treatment of the representational and esthetic elements of art. They remind us how many different things a work of art expresses at one time. The truth of this we shall understand better by relating these three terms—representation, design, and expression—to the purpose and meaning of four actual works of art, noting, as we do, how expression varies as representation and design change. As with a set of gears, one cannot vary without altering the others.

One glance at David's *Oath of the Horatii* (Fig. 88) tells us that his approach to representation was highly literal. Lighting, back-

FIG. 88. David. *Oath of the Horatii*. 1784.
Louvre, Paris.

FIG. 87. *Crucifixion*. 1082-1105.
Church, Daphni.

FIG. 89. Titian. *Meeting of Bacchus and Ariadne*.
1523. National Gallery, London.

FIG. 90. El Greco. *Agony
in the Garden. ca.* 1608-
1614. National Gallery,
London.

171

ground, and anatomy all seem as correct as though they were photographed. Notwithstanding this painstaking exactness, the actors are frozen in the poses they were told to assume. The design, though adequate, is obvious and ordinary. Its one virtue is consistency. There is nothing out of place, but the general effect is as cold as it is precise. As a result of the stiff representation and the mechanical design, the expression suffers. There is none of the vitality which the artist presumably sought. David's literalness in telling his story has been self-defeating, as it nearly always is when representation is heavily stressed.

El Greco's *Agony in the Garden* (Fig. 90) is quite a different matter. Where David emphasized direct representation, El Greco leans heavily on symbolism. Conceiving the biblical scene with more concern for its meaning than its physical appearance, he has achieved a maximum of mysticism, agony, and drama by deliberately distorting color, forms, postures, and lighting. The design is baroque, fluid, carrying the eye upward and backward along the high lights. The dynamic asymmetrical balance contributes to the dramatic mood of the story. What appears at first highly distorted has a logical basis. El Greco, dealing with one of the momentous episodes of human history, depicts the *Agony in the Garden* in an extraordinary manner and thus lifts it above the commonplace. In his art the emphasis is on spiritual expression, not on literal representation.

In the mosaic picture of the Crucifixion from Daphni (Fig. 87), representation is sacrificed or subordinated even further. It tells no story; it is purely symbolic. Apart from the general ideological meaning of this *Crucifixion,* the chief purpose of the mosaic is decorative. As such it is excellent. The picture fits in well with the lines and color scheme of the building. Mosaic, which is composed of small cubes of glass and stone set into wet plaster, is a tedious and exacting medium. Modeling is difficult, color must follow the architectural design, and forms settle into decorative but unreal patterns. Space and light are almost impossible to render accurately, so the result is flat like the wall. However, these representational disadvantages become virtues when the work is accepted as a decoration. The brilliant colors of the mosaic more than make up for its rigidity. Since dynamic design must be minimized in a mosaic picture, the over-all effect of the composition is austere and static. It has the coldness of symbolism. In this instance design dominates.

Titian's *Meeting of Bacchus and Ariadne* (Fig. 89) is yet another kind of picture. It illustrates a story in an effective manner. This representation of a credible scene is built around the characters of an ancient tale. There is little obvious or objectionable distortion, yet no one would mistake it for a photograph; it is clearly a work of imaginative art. The story is a Greek myth (which Titian may have read in a book by Philostratus) popular during the Renaissance, but the graphic conception is largely Titian's own. The conception is a dramatic one. The scene is alive. Behind it we feel the personal vitality and individual point of view of the artist—Titian's great vigor, health, and love of life.

The design of this picture aids at every point in making the story convincingly alive. The lines of the composition have an abstract rhythm, but they are also employed to enhance the action, as in the contrast of the postures of Bacchus and Ariadne. The colors, too, are dramatic. Even the ring of stars—Ariadne's symbol—fits into the design. Every element is tied into a rich formal organization.

The handling of the material, oil pigment on canvas, is quite successful, the effect both tapestry-like and sensuously appropriate to the pagan theme. Titian respected the decorative purpose of the picture, which was commissioned as one of a pair to be placed in an ornate Renaissance palace. They were designed for a particular space in a large room, so he made the color scheme suitably brilliant for its gilded surroundings and the pattern appropriately bold and sumptuous.

In this picture, representation and design are both directed toward a unified expression. Each is successful, full of complex but clear thought, yet neither overdominates: there is a synthesis of all these aspects. As in Titian's own personality, the component elements are highly developed but balanced.

Unfortunately, the synthesis found in Titian's painting is exceptional, because strong but balanced minds are rare. In most works of art one of the three elements dominates. This is often not bad; it gives unlimited variety to art and enormously extends its expressive range. A wise principle of criticism here will be to see these four pictures as not so much good or bad as different, unique, and nonexchangeable. Since each was conceived with a different purpose, the expressive methods and results had to vary accordingly. Even this brief comparison makes us recognize the inevitably pluralistic character of art and warns us to avoid single standards of artistic appreciation.

CHAPTER 9

Representation in Painting
The Realistic Mode and the Modes of Projection

An artist who employs representation rather than more nearly abstract means of expression does so for several reasons. By representing he can express ideas more exactly than is possible in strictly abstract art. There would, for example, be no way of expressing the specific idea of Titian's *Bacchus and Ariadne* through abstract means alone.

There is no one kind of representation that has always served all purposes. Nor is this a matter of technical deficiencies at earlier dates. Human beings have had different interests and many ways of interpreting their views of the world, and they have devised different methods of expressing themselves through representational means. Carried to its conclusion this would mean learning a unique style for each of thousands of artists; in the long run a serious critic must approach that goal. A beginner, however, cannot cope with such minute distinctions. Scholars such as Arthur Pope have grouped works of art according to common denominators of interest and methods. Pope referred to each group as an illustration of a mode of representation, deliberately distinguishing the mode of painting used for representational purposes from either the compositional side of design or the more inclusive *style*. But he was careful to point out that each mode has a kind of orderly consistency which contributes to the esthetic order of painting. Its function is not solely representational.

Artists who share common historical environments tend to speak a similar artistic language, a fact that makes this kind of study both possible and beneficial. It reduces the impossible welter of individual styles to a few, easily understood modes and saves us from an artistic Tower of Babel. These modes have the further advantage of being identified with well-known chapters in history. As we study them, we learn something of both the history and the principles of art.

There are five major modes: *realistic, line and local color, sculpturesque, pictorial, impressionist.* We shall begin with the realistic. It is the most complex of the modes, especially in its relationships of color. When we understand it, the other modes will be easier to comprehend. We are aided in our study of the realistic mode by familiarity. The average person of today has become acquainted with its general characteristics through photography and through paintings by the many followers of Gérôme, Meissonier, and Bonheur.

THE REALISTIC MODE

Realistic painting is easy to identify because, more than any other kind, it resembles modern color photography. While it departs from a strict imitation of nature in ways which conceal much craftsmanship, it aims at likenesses which come very close to a process of holding a mirror up to nature.

There has been a great deal of realistic painting in the main stream of art, but two artists who have given us unusually consistent or complete examples are the seventeenth-century masters Vermeer and Velasquez. Anyone could be forgiven for mistaking their paintings of *The Cook* (Fig. 93) and the *Maids of Honor* (Fig. 94) for photographs.[1]

Recognizing realistic painting is one matter; understanding it is another. The starting point of any attempt to understand the special character of realistic painting is usually *the visual image.* This is the purely physical image which, striking the retina, gives the artist his first report of the visual components of any scene. The elements of this report are always more or less alike. They are such representable data as outlines, forms, textures, colors, and light—the typical attributes of any portion of the physical world. Their significance lies not in their presence but in the use that is made of them.

Because of variations in the human equation and in the historical orientations of perception, the mind will select and reject these data

---

[1] The reader is reminded of the fact that general principles and broad ideas are illustrated with a few reproductions. No one of these is to be construed as the only possible example. So long as he remembers this, any reader can supplement these introductory examples with others from his own experience almost indefinitely, without confusion.

according to the artist's mental interpretation and the way his era looks at things, so that the resulting works of art present a wide range of departures from and resemblances to their original starting point— the visual image. In the terms we have been using, each mode is characterized by the number of visual elements it includes and the artist's attitude toward them.

Vermeer's *Cook* and Velasquez's *Maids of Honor* include all the elements. No outline, contour, texture, color, or light-and-shadow pattern that would appear in the actual scene has been omitted. This all-inclusive respect for the scene is typical of realistic painting. However, we can refine our characterization by considering the attitude of a realist like Vermeer toward the colors in the visual image as distinct from other possible attitudes. Let us remember that any artist may view color in three valid but quite different ways: symbolically, esthetically, and realistically. If his purpose is symbolic, he may use colors to express religious ideas in the medieval fashion; if esthetic, he may place a red tree against a green sky—as Gauguin often did. Neither tree nor sky will be true to nature, but the effect is, in his opinion, more pleasing esthetically. A realistic painter keeps such liberties within the bounds of credibility. Choosing to adhere to natural appearances, he will paint trees green and skies blue or whatever colors are true to the objective subject matter.

Vermeer painted in this way. He colored the apron which the cook wears blue because he wished the color in his painting to resemble the color in actuality. Although this cook's blue apron is related to her yellow shirt in an esthetically pleasing way, it has no symbolical meaning; nor was it a product of his imagination. The shirt, we may be sure, was actually yellow. This is characteristic of his treatment of each of the color areas in the visual image.

We badly underrate Vermeer's accomplishment, however, if we imagine that he had merely to copy each area of color correctly in order to produce a unified work of art like the *Cook*. Unity is not so easily come by. It requires a clear conception of the unifying principle which underlies the particular mode of representation the artist is employing, and it is not objectified in paint without a considerable capacity for organization.

A painter who wishes to represent the visual image on canvas as Vermeer or Velasquez did must become aware of the relationship of forms in space and the behavior of color in nature as these are recorded by the eye. In this study we shall attack these problems separately, taking the last first. But before we can do even that intelligently we must acquire some knowledge of the vocabulary of color.

THE TERMS OF COLOR.   A hundred years ago the scientific understanding of color was in its infancy.   Criticism was largely subjective
and expressed in such terms as *wonderful, beautiful,* or *ugly,* according to the personal preferences of the beholders.   Since they described nothing objectively, these opinions had no general validity.
Such color terms as were used were no more helpful.   They numbered into the hundreds, yet were based on no common standards.
Consequently, any woman who bought five samples of cloth in five
different stores by using such a picturesque name as "Lincoln" green
usually acquired five different shades.   If order was to replace this
confusion, some way had to be found to enable us to do two things—
first, to talk about the same things when we discussed a given color,
and, second, to discuss color relationships with a reasonable degree
of consistency and objectivity.   Short of this, no analytical discussion
of realistic or any other kind of painting was possible.

In our century a number of physicists and scientific students of
the visual arts began to clarify and systematize our knowledge of color.
The system which was eventually adopted most widely by students
of art grew out of the practical experience of two painters.   It was
originated by Dr. Denman Ross and perfected by Professor Arthur
Pope, both of Harvard.

Basically, the Pope system aimed at correcting our former oversimplified and inadequate conceptions of colors and their relationships.   Too often a man who identified a color as *blue* thought he had
described it completely.   In order to correct this error, Pope pointed
out that every example of color has three universal characteristics
which must all be described before the color is accurately identified—
hue, value, and *intensity.*

Hue refers to the quality of redness or blueness or greenness in a
color.   The complete possibilities of this characteristic of color are
indicated by the so-called "color circle" or "scale of hues" in Fig. 91a.

Value refers to the lightness or darkness of a color, a property it
has in addition to its particular hue.   Blue, for instance, may be
either light or dark, as can orange.   The possible variations in value
between white and black which blue and orange can have are suggested by Fig. 92a.

Intensity refers to the brilliance or dullness of a color.   There are
other terms which describe the same property, such as *purity* or
saturation, but we can probably understand the difference between
high and low intensity by using the ordinary terms *strong* or *weak.*
In Fig. 92a the outside columns of colors are high in intensity, the
central column neutral or without intensity, and the intermediate
columns at half intensity.

a

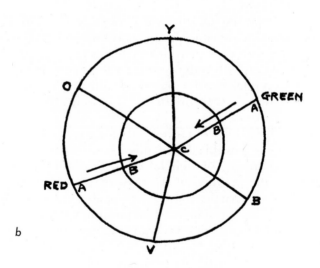

b

FIG. 91a–b. Schematic illustration of changes in color as forms recede into the distance.

178

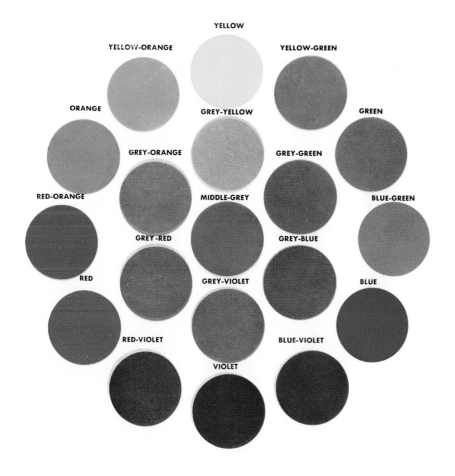

THE COLOR CIRCLE
OR
SCALE OF HUES
FULL INTENSITY AND GREYED HUES

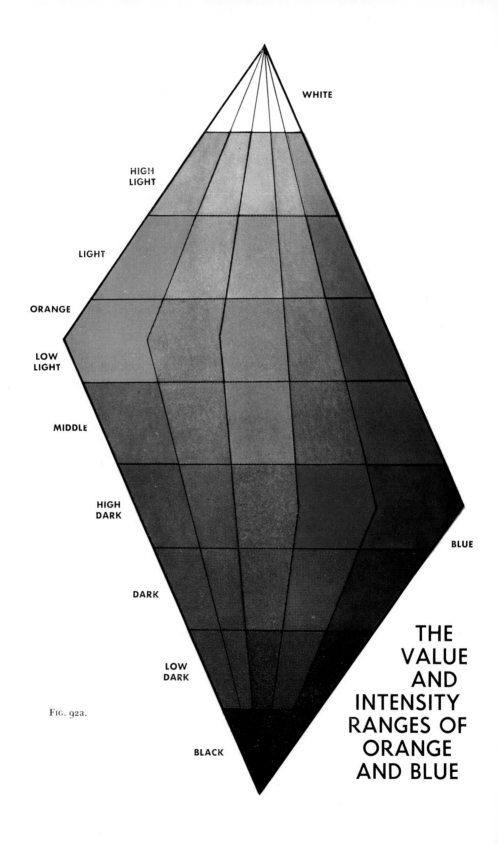

WHITE

HIGH
LIGHT

LIGHT

ORANGE

LOW
LIGHT

MIDDLE

HIGH
DARK

BLUE

DARK

LOW
DARK

BLACK

FIG. 92a.

THE
VALUE
AND
INTENSITY
RANGES OF
ORANGE
AND BLUE

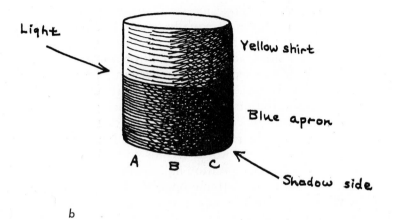

Light

Yellow shirt

Blue apron

A   B   C

Shadow side

b

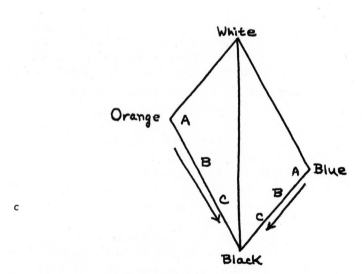

White

Orange

A

B

C

A   Blue

B

C

c

Black

FIG. 92b–c. Schematic illustrations of the principle underlying the modeling of forms in cross-lighting.

The crowning merit of Pope's system is that it is based on the fact that the significance of all color properties is a matter of relationships. Any color is light or dark, intense or dull, red or orange in relation to other colors. Pope measures these relationships exactly by providing us with scales of equally spaced hues, values, and intensities. These set the standards of measure without which we cannot describe anything accurately. *Tall* or *short,* for instance, is meaningful only in two senses, by comparison with a neighboring object or with a universal standard of measure; hence 6'7" means "tall" in comparison to ourselves and human beings generally. The same relativity is true of colors. The Pope system embraces both types of measurement: the relationship of neighboring colors and the position of every color in the world of color possibilities. Red-orange derives significance from its position halfway between red and orange and also in relation to its extreme opposite, blue-green. Any color at middle value is so called because it lies halfway between white and black; but it is also one step darker than its neighbors at low light and two steps lighter than the value of dark. Similarly, a color which is at half intensity can be measured exactly against one that is at full intensity or one-quarter intensity. It is exactly half as strong as the one and twice as strong as the other.

The significance of any and all color characteristics thus depends upon relationships, and the realistic artist must master these relationships within the framework of his particular conception of unity. With this terminology as a background we can now turn to the problem of the artist's conception of the role and behavior of color.

THE BEHAVIOR OF COLOR. There are two opposite possible conceptions of color behavior, both based on perceptual experience and hence containing a measure of truth. To one view, color is what the eye reports; to the other, color is what the mind knows it to be regardless of what the eye reports at the moment. The former stresses change, the latter continuity.

A practical example will illustrate this distinction. If we buy a red tie we recognize that it has dyed into it a more or less permanent color which is known technically as its local color. But we also come to perceive that under certain conditions this local color will appear to change. If, for example, it is cast into shadow, it may appear to lose its color altogether; if it is carried far away from us, its color will fade from sight; finally, if a violet light is played over it, it may appear to change color entirely. This behavior of color may be called illusory, for no matter what the color seems to be, our minds tell us that the tie has not changed its color. Its red dye is neither lighter nor darker, weaker nor more violet than it ever was.

FIG. 93. Vermeer. *The Cook. ca.* 1660. Rijksmuseum, Amsterdam.

FIG. 94. Velasquez. *Maids of Honor.* "Las Meniñas." 1656. Prado, Madrid.

Two contradictory interpretations of color behavior—one actual, the other apparent—are thus thrown into opposition; yet it does not matter to which an artist subscribes. So long as he is consistent, he can achieve pictorial unity. Realistic artists have proved this by adhering strictly to the belief that apparent color is true color and that its only permanent characteristic is constant but consistent change. They have become authorities on the causes and patterns of changes in colors and especially on the effects of light and shadow, atmosphere and distance upon them.

Vermeer's *Cook* is a consistent and authoritative report on such color phenomena. Consider, for instance, his observation of the way the local colors of a round, three-dimensional form (like the cook) are modified as they model from light into shadow in a crosslight. Since the principal light enters the room from the window on the left, the colors of all three-dimensional forms are most intense on the sides toward the source of light and at their lowest intensity on the sides away from the light. Moreover, the colors, while retaining their hues in ordinary white light, become not only gradually duller but also darker as they retreat from the source of light. By recording this gradual change Vermeer achieved the illusion of realness because his representation accords with visual experience. He did not do it only in part of the picture; he achieved unity throughout the painting by adhering to a conception of color behavior which can be reduced to a universal principle with the aid of Fig. 92a. An arrow drawn from the word *blue* downward and inward toward *black* will indicate how all local colors change as they are modeled from light into shadow; the modification is always characterized by a dual loss of value and intensity. Figs. 92b and 92c have been inserted to illustrate this principle graphically; Fig. 92b is an abstraction of the cook's shirt and apron and Fig. 92c its diagramatic equivalent. Whether Vermeer perceived this law intuitively or consciously is incidental to the fact that he achieved pictorial unity by adhering to it.

If the modification of local colors by light and shadow had been the only problem confronting realistic artists, their progress would have been rapid. As it was, there were six other major causes of change which they had to understand and control before the repertory of realistic representation could be considered reliable and complete. More complicated still, four of these ran counter to or disrupted the normal progression of modeling described above. Realistic painters must often have felt that nature was trying to confound them at every turn, but they gradually learned that even the disruptive changes consistently followed certain laws. This complicated the painter's problem, but indicated an underlying orderliness among the natural phenomena.

The principal causes of variations in local colors in the visual image which realistic painters had to master were:

1.   Modeling from light into shadow
2.   Indirect lighting reflected from surface to surface
3.   Reflections from highly reflective surfaces
4.   Cast shadows
5.   Variations in the hues of the principal light sources
6.   Back lighting—coming directly toward the spectator
7.   Changes in local colors as they recede into the distance

There is not space here to discuss these variations fully, but enough attention should be paid to them to make us appreciate the consistency of such artists as Vermeer and Velasquez and the penetrating observation of the better realistic painters. While more arbitrary painters ignored these phenomena, realists had to learn to represent them accurately, and in so doing they opened our eyes to many elusive characteristics of the visible world.

If, for example, the principle underlying modeling from light into shadow was the only one that obtained, the wall around the window in Vermeer's *Cook* would be in deep shadow. He observed, however, that light reflected from the adjacent wall illuminated this surface indirectly. Moreover, he recorded this phenomenon wherever it occurred throughout the scene before him, using it to unify his picture. We see such reflections on the cook's left cheek, on the folds of her dress, and on the underside of the basket on the table. Indirect illumination from reflected light makes all of them higher in value than their positions on the shadow sides would otherwise warrant. Vermeer also noted that these reflections tend to change the hue of any surface they strike. Some of the green hue of the table cloth is reflected up onto the side of the straw-colored basket, modifying the appearance of its local color to the eye.

Highly reflected surfaces of all kinds similarly disrupt the usual modeling of colors because they reflect the color of the light that strikes them instead of transmitting their own local color. A mirror does this completely, as does water to some degree. Satin, polished woods, metals, and glass all disrupt the normal course of modeled color, so that the most intense colors are found adjacent to the highlights instead of in them. This fact did not escape Vermeer, who caught it in his painting of the polished brass vessel which hangs on the wall.

There are several illustrations of cast shadows in the *Cook,* such as the one cast by the small box on the floor. The effect of a cast shadow is to lower both the value and intensity of any color in its path by robbing it of its light. Since, however, some light is always reflected into shaded areas by adjacent surfaces and general diffusion, neither cast shadows nor the shadow sides of modeled forms are ever reduced completely to black, as Vermeer has accurately noted.

Velasquez' eye was no less sensitive. In the *Maids of Honor* he attacked and solved two of the major problems which stood in the way of realistic color representation: the changes which occur in local colors as they recede into the distance and the radical effect of back lighting on human eyesight. The first of these is a problem for all artists who wish to create the illusion of deep space in the representation of landscapes or interior scenes; the second is a more specialized problem. A remarkable characteristic of the *Maids of Honor* is this illusion of space. Velasquez was able to create this effect because he understood the changes which occur when local colors recede into the distance.

Here, in principle, is what happens. We receive the full impact of colors only when they are near our eyes. As they retreat into the distance they progressively lose both their color intensity and their distinction by contrast until they seem to fade into the pale blue-gray color of the distance. All of us have noticed that the foreground colors of a landscape are the strongest, while the distance is a blurred and hazy bluish grey, but we may have overlooked the progressive character of this change. It can be illustrated simply if we will imagine two hunters walking along a road which leads into the far distance (Fig. 91b). One of the men has on a brilliant red coat, the other a bright green. When they are nearby the red and green are clearly distinguishable; they contrast strongly. But as they walk away from us the differences in hue and intensity will grow less every few hundred yards until, when they are far away, all distinctions of hue and intensity have approached the vanishing point. They fade almost from visibility. There is, however, one important difference between this apparent change in local colors and modeling in a crosslight; receding colors lose their strength of hue and intensity, but not their value. Instead of changing in the direction of black (shadow), they converge toward a middle-value bluish gray.

Pope has described this principle as the diminution of contrasts as local colors recede into the distance; it is diagrammed in Fig. 91c. *A* represents the green and red coats when they are in the foreground, *B* when they are in the middle distance, and *C* at the vanishing point. The arrows show the lines of progression toward that point.

Several physical facts underlie this phenomenon. One is the limitation of human eyesight; we cannot perceive distinguishing outlines or colors with any distinctness at a distance. The second is the effect of atmosphere upon light rays and hence upon our perception of them. The atmosphere contains millions of particles of dust and moisture which impede our perception of distant colors by blocking, reflecting back, and warping the light rays which attempt to carry the colors of the green and red coats back to us. The atmosphere is thus poetically but aptly described as a veil. Since it is relatively uniform in character, it distorts or obscures colors in proportion to distance. The farther away an object is from us, the weaker its colors appear to our eyes, hence the principle of the progressive diminution of color contrasts. The third fact—of convergence toward bluish gray instead of a neutral middle-value gray—is due to the greater carrying power of the so-called "cool" or bluish light rays. Distant mountains are not actually blue, as we know well enough, but more of their blue rays reach our eyes.

Velasquez was able to create the illusion of a large three-dimensional interior realistically because he observed and illustrated this principle accurately. The far wall of his room looks distant because he has blurred all of its delineating outlines, such as those of the various pictures hanging on it, and reduced all of the intensities to the exact degree befitting their position in space. Hence the foreground figures stand out sharply, while the studio walls fall in behind. The result creates an illusion of three-dimensionality because it accords with our own visual perception.

Velasquez included in the *Maids of Honor* a *tour de force* which is a kind of capsule illustration of the principle of diminution of color contrasts. In a mirror on the rear wall he represented the reflected images of King Philip IV and his queen, who witnessed the scene portrayed in the picture. Although they presumably stood about where we stand as spectators, their images had to travel some forty feet or more to the glass and back to us. We know this because Velasquez reduced their sizes, blurred the definition of outlines, and diminished the color contrasts. In short, he made them appear exactly as small and indefinite as we ourselves would see them in a mirror.

Velasquez noted one more cause of variation in local colors when he painted the *Maids of Honor:* the effect of back lighting upon human vision. By back lighting is meant illumination coming directly toward the spectator, as when we face the source of light. The effect of such illumination is to blind us partially since the pupil of the eye cannot adjust to areas of strong light and deep shadow simultaneously. As our eyes respond to the intense light the lens openings narrow and we lose our ability to distinguish detail, three-dimensionality, and color in adjacent areas. Any objects which are in or near the path of back light will appear blurred, flat, and shadowy. Leonardo da Vinci mentioned this phenomenon in his *Notebooks*, calling attention to the way trees make flat, fuzzy-edged silhouettes when seen against a sunset. The Dutch painter De Hooch recorded this condition when he painted sunlight flooding into a dark room in his *Mother by a Cradle* (Fig. 98), and George Inness when he painted his *Peace and Plenty*. Velasquez included the same variation in the *Maids of Honor* by introducing an open door in the rear wall and placing the figure of Don Juan of Austria in it. The strong light which comes through the door has the triple effect of reducing his figure to a flat silhouette, depressing the shadowy depths of the studio, and pulling our eye into the distance. It contributes greatly to the picture's luminous, atmospheric, three-dimensional effect. Velasquez used this variation with rare skill as an integral part of the picture which enhances its total effect.

Observant as Vermeer and Velasquez were, they left a good deal of visual research to be done by later generations. They tended, for instance, to use a uniformally white or neutral light. Later artists, especially landscape painters, heeded the fact that hues of light vary through the day and from day to day. The principle which applies is simple: under special lighting conditions all local colors in the visual image will appear to assume the hue of the general illumination. During a brilliant sunset everything will be tinged with red-orange hues; at night the same colors will appear to have turned a shadowy blue; under a green or violet spotlight they will seem green or violet themselves. It matters not what actual hues we know they possess; if seeing is believing, all local colors can be made chameleon-like by changing hues of light. Influenced by this visible fact the realist concludes that there is no such thing as a permanent local color; coloristically, the visible world is always in the process of change. This conception of color leans, consequently, toward the concept of a predominately infinite external world.

A large number of European and American artists explored this field and expressed this point of view during the period from the seventeenth through the nineteenth century, when realistic painting was in high favor. The landscape painters of the nineteenth century explored it especially. A few illustrations will suffice. Claude Lorrain not only "put the sun in the sky" during the seventeenth century in France but allowed its rays to suffuse whole pictures with golden light as well. Rubens painted a number of Netherlandish sunsets which show his cognizance of their transforming effect, while Rembrandt, his great Dutch contemporary, seems to have seen the whole world bathed by a golden spotlight. This interest was an international one at that time.

In the nineteenth century it was pursued even more widely and searchingly under the influence of an accelerating scientific study of natural phenomena. Physicists began to explain why the sun appears red-orange at sunset and the moon orange as it rises, while painters paralleled their efforts with expert representations of the same spectacles. It is not a coincidence that Turner painted his many sunsets and Whistler his nocturnes during the nineteenth century. Other examples of the prevalent interest in colored illumination are Frederick Church's treatment of the chromatic splendor of a volcano, *Cotopaxi,* erupting at sundown, and Winslow Homer's *Moonlight, Wood's Island Light.*

The painters of the period from the seventeenth through the nineteenth century delved into effects of colored illumination for two reasons. The Western world seemed fascinated by optical phenomena; but insofar as these men were also artists, they perceived the possibilities of achieving pictorial unity simultaneously. Realists had much to gain if they could satisfy their desire to be true to appearance and at the same time be esthetically effective. Once they had discovered how moonlight can glamorize even the chaos of a junk-yard they exploited the unifying effects of colored lighting fully. This was the last, but by no means the least, of the causes of variations in local colors in the visual image which realistic artists brought under representational control during the last six hundred years.

THE HISTORY OF REALISTIC PAINTING. The history of realistic painting was not marked by uniformly successful performance. Like every other artistic movement, wish preceded technical mastery. The two can be related so as to trace the movement's history in an evolutionary fashion. The wish to scrutinize reality with a new accuracy and to paint it more as we see it optically began to reveal itself in late Gothic painting. It then made great strides in the fifteenth century in Flanders. When Jan Van Eyck painted his *Marriage of Giovanni Arnolfini and Giovanna Cenami* (Fig. 95) he took a long stride beyond his predecessors. His small panel, which would have been remarkable in any period, must have seemed phenomenal to his contemporaries. It was made possible by the fact that nature endowed Van Eyck with an unbiased mind and a sharp eye. His whole art testifies to an extraordinarily neutral but acute observation. The *Marriage of Giovanni Arnolfini* exemplifies this in every passage. It is an accurate study of the behavior of light and color where they model forms or reflect from various surfaces, and a careful treat-

FIG. 95. Jan Van Eyck. *Marriage of Giovanni Arnolfini and Giovanna Cenami.* 1434. National Gallery, London.

FIG. 96. Wood. *American Gothic.* 1930. Art Institute of Chicago.

FIG. 97. Van der Weyden. *St. Luke Painting the Virgin. ca.* 1455. Museum of Fine Arts, Boston.

FIG. 98. De Hooch. *Mother by a Cradle.* 1651-1660. Kaiser Friedrich Museum, Berlin.

ment of textural distinctions and other major phases of realistic representation. When we compare it with a medieval painting like the *Crucifixion* from Daphni (Fig. 87) we recognize its modernity at once. It speaks a pictorial language which has persisted into our own century and whose continuity is shown by the similarity between Van Eyck's point of view and that of Grant Wood when he painted his *American Gothic* (Fig. 96) in 1930.

Van Eyck's painting shows us, too, that no single artist or generation ever solves all of its problems. In realistic painting the two most critical problems were accurate representation of color behavior based on a criterion of appearances, and a similarly based representation of the spatial relationship of forms. Each of these problems was complex, and Van Eyck solved some aspects of them better than others. The naturalness of his modeling and textural renderings amounts to genius. So too does his observation of outline and minute detail. No wart, hair, or reflection escaped his eye, and his mastery of value and intensity relationships was complete. Nevertheless, one can sense the awkwardness of some of his spatial relationships. For instance, the canopied bed appears to extend up to the ceiling and back to the rear wall, yet a chair is represented beyond the bed—a physical impossibility under the circumstances. Similarly, the shoes which rest on the floor beyond the figures are too small in scale for their position in space. His basic error was in perspective; there are at least four different vanishing points in the picture.

The meaning of these few ineptitudes is this: Van Eyck could cope brilliantly with any color or spatial problems which he could solve by a close-up use of his eyes, but he slipped or failed when he had to devise in a more intellectual fashion a system for relating forms in deep space, especially in the out-of-doors. Optical sensitivity was his forte; analytical thinking was not. The solution of the comprehensive spatial problems fell to the more intellectual Italians.

Van Eyck's strengths and limitations were typical of his northern brethren of the fifteenth century. A case in point is Rogier van der Weyden's *St. Luke Painting the Virgin* (Fig. 97). A handsome and sensitively conceived painting in many respects, it contains inconsistencies which were typical of the beginnings of realistic painting. The most noticeable of these was a result of the weather, which forced the northern artists to work indoors through much of the year. They painted their indoor figures under studio lighting at one time and their landscape backgrounds under different lighting conditions at another time or from imagination. Two different lighting conditions apply with little or no relationship between them. This is clearly the case in the Van der Weyden panel. Not only are the figures of the Virgin and St. Luke lighted from the front, but no illumination at all strikes them from the large door. In fact, the side of St. Luke's face which is toward the door is in shadow.

The second inconsistency derives from this same practice of painting indoors. Although Van der Weyden had studied nature closely, he undoubtedly painted his landscape background from memory. In so doing, he remembered one observable fact but forgot another: he remembered that forms appear progressively smaller as they recede into the distance, but forgot that they grow progressively blurred in outline and details. The technical description is "loss of definition." Van der Weyden either failed to observe this fact or rejected it. His distant forms are small in scale but perfectly defined. In short, they ignore the effects of atmosphere and give the impression of forms viewed through a telescope in an airless world. It is a picture painted from several unrelated kinds of experience and does not "hang together" realistically. It serves, however, to make us appreciate the consistency which Vermeer and Velasquez achieved between figures and settings and interior and exterior illumination.

Realistic observation was not truly synthesized in European painting until the seventeenth century. At that time wish and fulfilment finally coincided. We have proof of this in the separate achievements of Velasquez and Vermeer, one working in Spain, the other in Holland. The minor Dutch masters of the same period proved abundantly that anyone who wished to paint realistically had by then the requisite knowledge at his disposal. A glance at De Hooch's *Mother by a Cradle* (Fig. 98) tells us that it is an accurate representation of an interior scene and that it contains none of the awkward or inconsistent relationships which mark Van Eyck's or Van der Weyden's pioneer efforts at realism.

The conjunction of purpose and technique did not occur until the seventeenth century because it was only then that the Italian mastery of spatial relationships which had penetrated north of the Alps during the sixteenth century was fully assimilated with the northern mastery of color, light, and textures. Utilized together, they made completely realistic painting possible. If Van Eyck had lived in the seventeenth century, he would have been able to represent the visual image as easily and convincingly as De Hooch. His few shortcomings were due to the fact that he was a pioneer, rather than a beneficiary, of an evolutionary development.

The development of any mode of representation is the work of many. Realistic painting was no exception. This is illustrated by Van Eyck's contribution which, though great, left much to be done. It is also illustrated in a somewhat different way by De Hooch's general style. His *Mother by a Cradle* is characteristic of his specialization in one of several problems of color behavior: the way in which strong direct illumination blinds the eyes to details in shadows, blurs outlines, and reduces any solid form in its path to a more or less flat silhouette. By studying the characteristics of this particular optical problem thoroughly, De Hooch solved it for future generations.

Other artists attacked different but related problems. Terborch, another seventeenth-century Dutch artist, specialized in the representation of shiny textiles. He particularly loved to paint the satin and silk garments worn by the middle-class women of his day and mastered the special pattern of high lights created by reflective materials. He did not devote the same attention to other optical phenomena. Sacrificing the total unity of his pictures for the sake of brilliant passages of clothing, he made colors "jump out" from arbitrarily darkened backgrounds. The individual landscape artists of the nineteenth century tended similarly to concentrate their attention upon favorite aspects of the visual image. Turner was attracted to the problem of representing sunsets; Constable delighted in the representation of cloud formations and other atmospheric effects; Monet studied reflections on water; Winslow Homer recorded the play of moonlight over ocean waves; and the Impressionists analyzed the difficult problem of human visual perception of rapidly moving objects. Owing to the efforts of this group very little remained to be discovered about realistic painting by the end of the nineteenth century; as a historical problem it was largely solved. This fact by itself was likely to sound its death knell. When scores of artists with mediocre minds, coarse natures, and little feeling could take realistic representation for granted, it degenerated into a vehicle for mere technical display—feeble in content and expressing little more than manual dexterity or plodding diligence. That is what finally happened to it in the hands of the Meissoniers and Bonheurs, and its prestige was ruined.

Because the complexity of the visible world forced most artists to master it only partly, few paintings by artists like Terborch, Turner, Monet, and Homer portray the total visual effect with comprehensive realism. Their pictures are more likely to be realistic only in limited respects. Consequently, we may view the history of realistic painting in two ways: one as the history of a step-by-step mastery of realistic painting by many specialists, the other as the history of the synthesis of these many bits of knowledge by men with a genius for visual unity. The former contributed to the achievement of realistic painting without being whole-hearted realists themselves, the latter exploited their findings in the truly realistic representation of the total visual effect. The visible difference between the two approaches may be seen in the works of Terborch on the one hand and Vermeer on the other.

The foregoing discussion is meant to bring home this lesson: No one artist ever mastered all of the problems of realistic representation. The facile realism of nineteenth century painters like Gérôme was made possible by centuries of accumulated knowledge. Overlooking this background, the public often thinks of realistic painting as a direct imitation of some actual scene in which success will depend upon immediate skill rather than past knowledge. We cannot stress too strongly that no painter ever has been able to depict the visual image realistically solely by setting up an easel before a scene and duplicating only what his eyes saw, for what he sees is conditioned by accumulated perceptual experience tracing back through centuries of time. To miss this fact is to underrate and misunderstand the realistic mode. Jan Van Eyck probably came as close to an independent mastery of realistic representation as any artist in history. With little realistic painting to guide him, he painted the *Marriage of Giovanni Arnolfini* in a way that still inspires awe among visitors to the National Gallery who have long since been surfeited with realistic art and satiated with photography. But not even Van Eyck could master the whole of realism at one stroke.

THE MERITS AND LIMITATIONS OF REALISTIC PAINTING. The various modes of representation survive and flourish periodically because each possesses certain special merits. There are several modes instead of one because each mode also has limitations.

We can easily determine the merits and limitations of realistic painting by measuring against Konody's definition of art the actual evidence contained in the history of art. Konody said, "Art begins where the artist departs from strict imitation of nature, imposing on her a rhythm of his own creation." If an artist conceived realistic painting only in terms of a strict imitation of nature, his work would not be artistic at all, according to Konody's definition. The masters of realism did not forget this. Two examples of artists who—although seeming to capture the appearance of actuality perfectly—impose on it an extranatural rhythm of their own creation are Velasquez and Vermeer.

How Velasquez and Vermeer served two masters, nature and art, simultaneously and with exquisite subtlety can be seen by studying such details as Figs. 99 and 100. Our immediate impression of their work, especially when viewed at a slight distance, is one of a perfect illusion of actuality. But on closer inspection we see that beneath

FIG. 99. Velasquez. Detail, *Maids of Honor*. 1656. Prado, Madrid.

FIG. 100. Vermeer. Detail, *The Concert*. *ca*. 1670.
Isabella Stewart Gardner Museum, Boston.

this illusion lies an artistry which we usually only sense, for the departure from strict imitation must be slight, lest the painting cease to be realistic. In the case of Vermeer the departure consists of a uniform softening of all the outlines and forms. Photographers get the same effect by photographing a scene through a fine silk screen. Vermeer intensifies the small highlights so that they gleam among the softly modeled forms and furnish variety in minute but telling quantities. He also blocks out the areas of light and shadow, modeling the forms in clear-cut patterns and giving them a distinctly abstract quality. These areas clarify and intensify natural effects without imitating them strictly.

Velasquez also uses melting strokes to unify his picture and convey a sense of atmosphere and transparent shadows, but tends to model his illuminated areas with crisp brush strokes which define forms impressionistically and act as a kind of signature. The combination of melting and crisp brush strokes in the *Maids of Honor* (Fig. 99) is pure Velasquez, not pure nature.

In these ways Vermeer and Velasquez gave their pictures both an order and a variety which they could never have achieved by imitating the profusion and diversity of nature directly. The artistry which goes into great realistic painting of this sort is deceptive and easily overlooked. The art in it lies, as Ovid said centuries ago, in the concealment of art.

Realistic painting can be understood in another way by noting what sensations and sentiments it can handle well, and which poorly or not at all. First of all it reflects a materialistically oriented perception, or what Sorokin terms a sensate point of view. Its favorite province is the physical world and it is at its best within that province. Realistic artists seem to be saying that any aspect of the material world merits attention merely because it exists. But they turn this seemingly uncritical attitude into a merit by their obvious pleasure in the physical attributes of any object—the color and texture of hair, face, and clothing or the light that plays over a wall or gleams on a polished surface. It is these properties which they intensify pictorially.

Yet it is only fair to say that colors and textures are the superficial aspects of any form. Textures appeal to the sense of touch but, by keeping our eyes directed to the surface of things, they neglect somewhat our deeper and even more intense tactile sensations of mass and weight. Moreover, while rendering light and shadow well, realistic paintings often convey a weak perception of outlines. In short, this mode which presents both the finite and infinite aspects of reality in about the same proportions that they are found in natural scenes ends up by presenting few of them with the maximum possible clarity and intensity. If one wishes the sharpest sensations of clear outlines and dense masses, one must turn to another mode. Because realistic painting is so comprehensive, it gives the least concentrated sensations, with the possible exception of textures, of any of the modes.

When we turn to the field of sentiments this fact is apparent: the finest realistic paintings keep our feet on the ground. They are pictures which capture vividly the look of everyday life, like Velasquez's *Maids of Honor* and Vermeer's *Cook*. When depicting down-to-earth, day-by-day actuality, realistic painting is probably unexcelled in the conviction it carries. Even a cursory study will show that most of the masterpieces of realism fall under the heading of genre painting (i.e., scenes from everyday life). The whole school of Dutch little masters combined realism and the genre subject.

Portraiture, which is most often excellent when it is individual and exact, is a kindred field in which realism has scored many triumphs. It is not by accident that Jan Van Eyck's *Marriage of Giovanni Arnolfini* is both an outstanding example of realism and a noted example of portraiture. Grant Wood proved the efficacy of the same incisive realism in portraiture in our time when he painted his *American Gothic*.

But the realistic mode is a poor vehicle for the expression of historical ideas, symbolical idealism, or any highly imaginative subject. There is a great deal of realistic historical painting, but little of it rises above the level of illustration. It pays so much attention to accuracy of appearance that it loses the spirit and vital qualities of the theme. The more archeologically correct David, Meissonier, and Gérôme were, the more they froze the life from their subjects, especially in scenes of action. David's finest historical painting, the *Death of Marat*, is, significantly, a perfectly static scene. Conversely, the spearman in the center of his violent *Battle of the Sabines* looks as though he has held the pose for eternity. The perceptual reason for this is that precise details render any scene static. Rubens and Goya, who loved both action and history, made no such mistake; no matter how grimly realistic their content may be it is always rendered with a freely flowing brush.

A much worse misapplication of realism is found in symbolical idealism. The nineteenth-century French academicians loved to paint high-sounding allegories of Justice and Liberty and Truth but succeeded only in revealing their fundamental materialism. No amount of scales, swords, and classical garments could overcome the all-too-real flesh and blood of their commonplace studio models, and the contradiction in terms is ludicrous.

The foolishness of trying to express any highly imaginative or primarily spiritual idea in realistic terms was proved by none other than Velasquez himself. While Vermeer's practical Dutch instincts steered him away from religious and mythical content, Velasquez, painter to the devout and aristocratic court of Spain, could not resist them. A man who could paint anything beautifully that he could see, he had little or no imagination. His painting *Mars* does not convey the slightest idea of war or power. All one can see in its presence is the flabby rolls of flesh on the nude model's abdomen. He looks like a tired old man posing in a borrowed helmet.

Realistic painting places a premium on visual perception and conveys well those sensations within that experience which can be apprehended directly. It leaves for other modes the selective intensification of special sensations which must be achieved by more limited but concentrated means. Similarly, there is a limit to the ideas which it can express successfully. It is better at presentation than at interpretation or imagination. Its masterpieces are those paintings which were conceived within these dual limitations, its failures those in which idea and representation are ill-suited or contradictory.

THE MODES OF PROJECTION

In order to complete our understanding of the realistic mode, we must now consider projection, a means as important to its methods as color. The knowledge gained from a brief study of the modes of projection will serve, too, as a useful background for our study of the other modes of representation in painting. *Projection is the representational means or mode by which the sense of a third dimension is created.* If, for example, a man walks into a building or around a statue, he has a sense of three-dimensional forms existing in real space. But if he observes a painting, any sense of three-dimensional forms in space beyond the flat picture surface is due to an illusionary or conventional representation of space. All examples of projection can be described as either illusionary or conventional in point of view. The illusionary is a view of the world based primarily on what we *see* with our eyes; the conventional is based upon a system of agreed-upon signs derived from what we *know*.

Painters from the beginning have felt the urge to convey some sense of depth, for projection of one sort or another is universal in painting. The reason for this may lie in the relation of projection to artistic control. Through projection an artist can achieve a high degree of control over spatial relationships. He can fix them for all time and create a clear and intense impression of the exact kind of spatial relationships that he has in mind. Although the illusionary and the conventional are often contradictory, each is a valid reflection of the world. At different places and times in history artists have emphasized one conception or the other and have modified them in various ways. For a practical study of art we must divide the two basic conceptions into four subdivisions: perspective projection, geometric projection, diagonal projection, aerial projection.

The first and last of these are illusionary; the middle two, though different in their individual ways, are essentially conventional. Geometric and diagonal projection, being highly ideological in conception, have been largely used in the Orient and account in no small measure for the strangeness of Oriental art to Western eyes. Perspective and aerial projection are, by contrast, familiar to us from life-long acquaintance; they are a part of our tradition.

We have already alluded indirectly to aerial projection by describing the behavior of color in forms that recede into the distance as part of a realistic artist's intellectual equipment. However, perspective projection is no less essential to the kind of realistic or illusionary painting we have been discussing. Perspective projection had to be developed before realistic painting could be perfected and it preceded aerial projection historically. So it may be helpful to study it before attacking either aerial projection or the strange modes of the Orient.

PERSPECTIVE PROJECTION. Perspective projection can be conceived as a system of imaginary lines which converge on a center or vanishing point, like a spider web. The point is usually located on the horizon or at theoretical infinity in a landscape painting and in or near the center of the picture. The theory of this system is illustrated diagrammatically by Fig. 102b. Almost anyone will remember how the same principle was demonstrated to him during his school days by a view of receding railroad tracks, usually adjoined by rows of telegraph posts and wires. Objects arranged along the lines of convergence in Fig. 102b diminish in size as they approach the vanishing point. Such a system of spatial projection forms the basis of an illusionary or realistic representation of deep space in painting because it corresponds to one type of perceptual experience. Objects appear to the eye to grow progressively smaller as they recede into the distance, and any system of representation which, like the realistic, is based on appearances will adhere to that visual phenomenon.

Perspective projection came into prominence in the Renaissance and has continued to be identified with that period. A noted example is Perugino's fresco painting of *Christ Delivering the Keys of*

FIG. 101. Martini and Memmi. *Annunciation.* 1333. Uffizi Gallery, Florence.

FIG. 102a. Perugino. *Christ Delivering the Keys of Heaven to St. Peter.* 1481. Sistine
Chapel. Vatican, Rome.

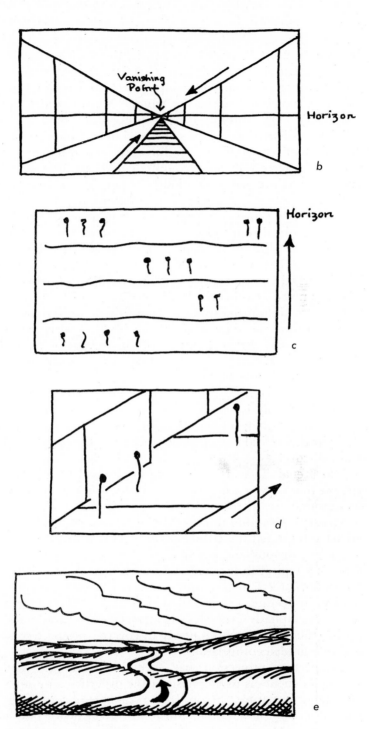

FIG. 102b–e. Schematic illustrations of the modes of projection.

Heaven to Saint Peter (Fig. 102a), in the Sistine Chapel at Rome. To appreciate the sense of deep space it creates by using perspective projection, one has only to compare it with a typical late medieval painting, the *Annunciation* by Simone Martini and Lippo Memmi (Fig. 101). The *Annunciation* expresses not only an exclusively religious orientation of perception but a complete indifference toward man's natural and architectural environment. Perugino's painting reflects the more comprehensive attitude of the Renaissance; though equally religious, it portrays a spacious outdoor setting.

Perspective projection came into prominence in the Renaissance as the combined result of orderly mathematical studies and a desire to create an illusion of depth. Scientifically minded Renaissance masters like Paolo Uccello, Piero della Francesca, and Leonardo da Vinci worked out the mathematics involved with finality. Francesca, who was noted as a theorist in his own time as he now is as an artist, wrote a treatise on the subject which is still authoritative. Perspective projection was thus originally an intellectual refinement of sensory experience. It has been part of the heritage of Western art ever since. In the seventeenth century it was used for purposes of naturalistic illusionism and became inseparable from the realistic mode of painting. Afterward, it was used in modified and more flexible forms. Today it is so well understood that young artists take it almost for granted; Thomas Eakins was the last modern painter to study its theoretical basis with anything like the passion of its Renaissance discoverers.

The Renaissance artists became so obsessed with perspective projection that they repeatedly included architecture in their pictorial backgrounds to intensify its effects; buildings made the otherwise imaginary converging lines vividly apparent. But subsequent painters have respected the reduction in scale as a matter of course without such obvious architectural reinforcement. Perugino's masterpiece is a typical instance of the way Renaissance artists introduced buildings, streets, plazas, and pavement designs extensively to intensify the feeling of space in their pictures. To modern eyes this arbitrary emphasis seems slightly artificial, but it was not so regarded during the days when the newly discovered perspective system elicited unbounded enthusiasm.

Perspective projection has several virtues and faults. Chief among its virtues is its emphasis of the orderliness in our perception of distance in nature. Secondly, it is capable of conveying a sense of natural spaciousness and an illusion of great depth beyond the picture plane. However, this may be a serious fault when a painting that purports to be decorative competes with the architectural plane it is supposed to enhance by puncturing an imaginary hole in the wall. For all their stiffness and coldness, the Byzantine artists who designed such mosaics as the *Crucifixion* at Daphni (Fig. 87) never mistook representation for decoration when embellishing a wall: by keeping their spatial designs shallow they preserved the building's mural qualities. Perugino's *Christ Delivering the Keys of Heaven to Saint Peter* shows the converse tendency of the Renaissance. It is a mural decoration only in that it was painted on a wall; actually it is an example of representation for representation's sake.

The conflict between architectural and representational aims is most noticeable when depth is not projected to the same distance in a series of adjacent pictures. Raphael committed this error when he painted the frescoes on the walls of the Sala della Segnatura in the Vatican. The represented distance in the *Parnassus*, the *Disputa*, and the *School of Athens* differs in each picture. Representational needs rather than a desire for decorative unity governed; though this discrepancy is alleviated somewhat by the use of planes that are parallel to the picture surfaces. Less consistent later painters made this fault of varied recession glaring. By the beginning of the nineteenth century, representation had taken command to such an extent that artists had entirely forgotten how to unite a painting and a wall. Mural decoration, despite many attempts at it by the French academicians, declined to the lowest point in its history; the gains in realistic representation made possible by perspective projection were thus ruinous to the mural arts.

For representation other than mural decoration, perspective projection provides the deepest stage upon which the painter's actors can portray his ideas. It has been notably satisfactory in easel pictures which do not compete with architecture. The full development of landscape painting, in which a sense of spaciousness is very important, would be inconceivable without it. Indeed, if we view Perugino's *Christ Delivering the Keys of Heaven to Saint Peter* apart from its decorative function, its spaciousness is impressive.

This spaciousness was not won overnight. The early Renaissance artists who opened their eyes to the world about them and noted intuitively that objects grow smaller as they recede into the distance were still not able to represent space convincingly. They were not able to do this until they had grasped the principle underlying the phenomenon and reduced it to a system based on a vanishing point; observation alone was not enough. This accounts for the awkward, toylike character of the architectural settings in many early Renaissance paintings. It is not surprising to find that the odd-looking temple step in Giotto's *Presentation in the Temple* (Fig. 51) appears strange the minute we view it because, being painted more intuitively than systematically, it contains half a dozen vanishing points. The same fault is present for the same reason in Giovanni di Paolo's *Presentation in the Temple* (Fig. 103).

By Perugino's time, the latter half of the fifteenth century, the theory and observed facts underlying perspective projection had been brought under control, hence the feeling of consistency which his picture conveys. But he and his contemporaries were so fascinated by the novelty of perspective projection that they often made it an end in itself, frequently allowing buildings and colonnades to dominate their pictures at the expense of the nominal theme. In one drawing of the *Annunciation* by Jacopo Bellini it is almost impossible to find the diminutive figures of the Virgin and Gabriel amid the forest of receding colonnades.

Perugino's picture suffers from another fault. Forgetting how strongly the eye is attracted to the vanishing point in perspective projection, he placed a building rather than his central figures upon it. Amid conflict of interests the eye is drawn away from the human drama and into the distance, thus sacrificing the human elements for the sake of spaciousness.

Raphael, a more skilful artist than his master Perugino, avoided this contradiction. He turned the powerful attraction of the vanishing point to excellent account in his *School of Athens* (Fig. 104). In it the central figures of Plato and Aristotle are placed in front of the vanishing point, so that all converging lines direct the eye toward them. In this way spatial design and idea are united.

Three other aspects of perspective projection are worth attention. First, though it grew from a desire to represent reality as it appears to the eye, it developed into an arbitrary artistic system whose chief merit is orderliness rather than illusion. We do not actually see the world with our mobile eyes in terms of a fixed vanishing point. Such a system is artificial; its virtue is not naturalness but a simplicity which clarifies and intensifies our feeling for spatial relationships in painting and drawing.

Secondly, the comparatively simple Renaissance system was developed in later centuries into an extremely complex system of multiple-vanishing point projection. This is more realistic because it reflects with greater accuracy the way our roving eyes view the world. But it is a question whether the gain in complex truthfulness was not made at the expense of artistic clarity and vividness. After we have looked at one of Bonington's views of Venice which contain diverging vistas, we are likely to return to Perugino's *Christ*

FIG. 103. Di Paolo. *Presentation in the Temple. ca.* 1445.
Metropolitan Museum of Art, New York.

FIG. 104. Raphael. *School of Athens.* 1509-1511. Camera della Segnatura.
Vatican, Rome.

Delivering the Keys of Heaven to Saint Peter with renewed appreciation.

Thirdly, the development of perspective projection was attended by several tangential studies in spatial relationships. These were significant because they extended perspectual studies beyond the time in the Renaissance when frontal perspective projection like that found in Raphael's *School of Athens* was a completed story.

The Renaissance artists apparently anticipated their success with perspective projection, for they soon turned to studies of variations of that system. Mantegna, remarkable for his inventiveness, painted about 1480 a *Dead Christ* (Fig. 105) which advanced the study of what we now call foreshortening. While most of his contemporaries were content with painting figures in normal frontal or profile positions, he depicted the *Dead Christ* from an eye-catching, feet-first point of view. He clearly did not master what he started, for his figure does not diminish in size as it recedes, but he opened up a fertile field of study which added new interest to perspective projection.

In several of his larger pictures, like the *St. James Led to Execution* (Fig. 106), Mantegna used a simple but effective method of capturing attention. Instead of placing his vanishing point near the center of his picture, he put it near the bottom. This makes us seem to view the scene as though it were above us. It is an angle of view such as we would have of a stage play if we were sitting in the orchestra pit. It is, to say the least, an unusual point of view, and its effect was to give new life to the field of spatial design. In fact, it opened up possibilities which were explored well into the nineteenth century.

Degas, for example, gave variety and interest to his compositions by varying Mantegna's principle. Instead of painting his many scenes of ballet dancers practicing or performing on the stage of the Paris Opera House from a frontal point of view, he looked at them from many different angles. Sometimes, like Mantegna, he looked at the stage from the orchestra pit. At another time he saw it from the balcony or an upper box. His *Dancer with a Bouquet* (Fig. 107) is a typical illustration of his practice. By shifting his own position from one part of the theater to another Degas both avoided the monotony of a fixed position and added to the reality of his pictures, for his varying angles and candid-camera-like compositions correspond to our own varying angles of view. We seem actually to be looking over the shoulder of a real spectator and upon a real theatrical performance.

Mantegna was a pioneer in another kind of spatial representation which was destined to enjoy great popularity long after his time: the

FIG. 105. Mantegna. *Dead Christ. ca.* 1480.
Brera Gallery, Milan.

FIG. 106. Mantegna. *St. James Led to Execution.* 1456. Formerly Church of the Eremitani, Padua. Destroyed during World War II. Now being restored.

FIG. 107. Degas. *Dancer with a Bouquet.* 1878. Rhode Island School of Design, Providence.

painting of ceilings so that they appear to open upon the sky. In the Marriage Chamber of the Ducal Palace at Mantua (Fig. 108), Mantegna created the illusion of a "hole" in the ceiling through which a number of spectators look down upon the occupants of the room. He used the basic principles of perspective projection, which were by then well known, to achieve this effect.

Mantegna's ceiling decoration gives the impression that it was conceived as a good-humored *tour de force*. If that was the original intention, the skill with which it was carried out inspired other artists to repeat his performance seriously and on a far grander scale. A tradition of illusionary ceiling decoration developed which was so successful that the vaults of whole rooms were painted out of existence. The spectator is made to feel that he not only is looking out upon the sky but is projected almost bodily up into infinite space. The best of these designs are extraordinarily dynamic in their effect upon us.

One of the outstanding links in this tradition is Correggio's decoration of the cupola of the Cathedral at Parma. It represents the *Assumption of the Virgin* (Fig. 109). So skilfully is the diminution of scale managed among the hordes of celebrants that the Virgin seems literally to fly heavenward. The illusion is the more remarkable because the cupola is actually rather shallow.

Correggio is often described as a precursor of the Baroque because of his dynamic conception of spatial relationships. One might wonder how any artist could go beyond his painting of the cupola, yet the Baroque masters of the seventeenth century greatly extended his feeling for deep space and dynamic arrangements of figures in it. A notable example is Andrea Pozzo's ceiling decoration in the Church of St. Ignatius at Rome, the *Glorification of the Company of Jesus* (Fig. 110). Words can hardly describe the emotional impression it is capable of making upon one. A relatively shallow vault is so painted that the whole roof of the building seems to have opened suddenly upon a drama of celestial proportions. Architectural lines create a powerful sense of convergence and ascension. The columns seem almost to be projecting the flying figures upward as if shot from cannons. In its presence one can easily understand why grand opera as we know it was born in Italy during the same time.

Numerous artists of the eighteenth century continued to paint in the tradition of Mantegna, Correggio, and Pozzo. The Venetian master Tiepolo played innumerable melodies on the same instrument with great skill. After the seventeenth century, artists could handle such designs with facility. But few ever excelled the brilliance and daring of Pozzo's accomplishment.

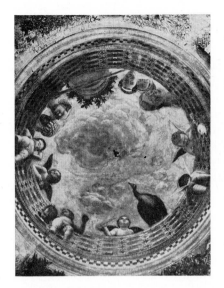 

FIG. 108.   Mantegna. Ceiling decoration,
Marriage Chamber. 1474. Ducal Palace,
Mantua.

FIG. 109. Correggio. *Assumption of the
Virgin.* 1518. Cupola of the Cathedral,
Parma.

FIG. 110.   Pozzo. *Glorification of the Company of Jesus.* 1691-1694. S. Ignazio, Rome.

GEOMETRIC PROJECTION. The perspective mode of projection expresses a relatively late and strictly Western conception of spatial relationships. It does not speak for the artists of either antiquity or the Orient. They employed, instead, a system which is now called *geometric.* It differs from perspective projection in several respects but most fundamentally in being conventional as opposed to illusionary. That is, it was based upon a number of conventions acceptable to both the artists and spectators of antiquity and the Orient. If it appears strange to our eyes, this is because of our lack of familiarity with the conventions. Some of this strangeness can be overcome by an explanation of the kind of thinking which lay behind geometric projection.

A comparatively simple system, it was conceived as a series of bands which are parallel to the bottom of the picture and rise in rows from the bottom to the top. By agreement the bottom row was accepted as the spatial plane closest to the spectator, and the higher rows as successively distant planes. In short, these bands represented a continuous progression from the foreground to the background of the scene.

This idea is expressed diagrammatically by Fig. 102c. Compared to the perspective mode of projection, it shows both simplicity and clarity. Few would assert that it is meaningless. When we remember that the geometric system was devised when the human race was very young—no one knows how ancient the system actually is—it is little less than ingenious. It seems to have sprung spontaneously from a way of thinking which is basic in the human mind; it is the method that untutored children almost invariably use to represent spatial progression. Indeed, because of its combination of simplicity, clarity, and convenience, it retained its popularity for centuries after the Oriental peoples became sophisticated.

This system is illustrated by actual works of art in Figs. 111 and 112. The first of these is an ancient Assyrian relief which depicts the moving of a colossal guardian figure toward the palace of the Assyrian monarch Sennacherib. Figures of this sort were commonly hauled into place by hordes of slaves to ward off evil spirits. In this particular scene the row of trees across the bottom of the relief represents the foreground; then, reading upward, we find a row of slaves who carry the rollers over which the sled bearing the colossal statue is to pass. Next we see another row of soldiers and slaves bearing tools. Four planes are represented in all. At one place in the relief —the second plane—a band is literally created by a line; in other areas the band is only implied. Both methods were used throughout the geometric mode according to the preferences of the designer.

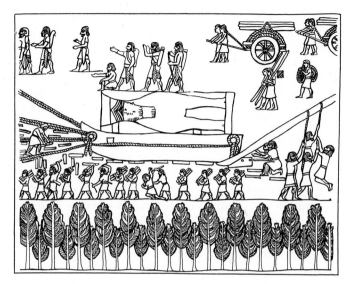

FIG. 111. *Moving a Colossus*. Reign of Sennacherib, 705-681 B.C. Original relief in the British Museum, London.

FIG. 112. *A Polo Game*. 1564. Tabriz school, Safavid period. Smithsonian Institution, Freer Gallery of Art, Washington, D.C.

A typical Egyptian tomb painting could have been substituted for this relief with equal appropriateness, because the geometric system was used throughout the Mediterranean world and the Near East during most of the ancient epoch. Furthermore, the inclusion of a relief instead of a painting here is inconsequential; the same conventions were employed by sculptors and painters.

Fig. 112, a Persian miniature dating from 1546, illustrates the continuance of this mode over a period exceeding two thousand years, for although the bands are treated in this polo game in a freer, more undulating fashion in keeping with a scene of action, it is clearly in the same tradition. Typical of thousands of Near Eastern and Far Eastern paintings in its spatial arrangement, it tells us that the geometric mode had a long and widespread history in Asia.

The Assyrian relief and Persian miniature painting have, in addition to a system based on a series of bands, one other characteristic which identifies them as geometric and sets them apart from any example of perspective projection. There is no diminution of scale as forms recede into the distance. A glance will reveal that the supposedly distant figures at the top of the relief are as large as those in the so-called foreground at the bottom. In some cases they are even larger. The same characteristic can be observed in the Persian painting; it is common to the geometric mode of projection.

We are apt to regard any conventional system which seems to our eyes contrary to the most easily observable facts as false, childishly simple, or an easy way out—as something which, like the art of children, precedes grown-up or maturely civilized art. Actually, geometric projection is based on a perfectly logical way of conceiving the relationships of form in space. If, for example, we watch two men walk away from us, they appear to grow smaller. Perspective projection is based on this perceptual fact, emphasizing what we see. But seeing is not always believing. Geometric projection is based on the fact that our minds tell us the men do not actually become smaller; their diminution in scale is only an illusion and a temporary one at that. If the Oriental artist elects to depict what his mind knows to be permanently true, he has a reasonable right to ignore the apparent reduction of measures in distant objects and make them as large as any in the foreground. Hence the uniformity of scale from top to bottom in the geometric mode. The main fault that we might find with this system is that it does not conform to our point of view. Yet we must admit that it is both consistent and logical.

Geometric projection is an ideological system, for it is based upon ideas projected upon reality. Such a way of thinking has been common in history, as a reading of Sorokin's *Social Dynamics* will readily show. Artists who hold to that conception of perception usually place more importance upon the symbolic values of objects than upon appearances. If they are portraying a group of figures containing a king and slaves, or sacred and secular personages, they will unhesitatingly represent the king larger than the slaves. This practice may be seen in scores of examples of Egyptian and Asiatic art. It occurs in the *Moving a Colossus*. It does not occur in the polo game miniature because the players were equally important. Thus when we understand something of the premises behind unfamiliar art forms, some of their strangeness disappears. Almost all of them have a logical basis, if we can find it.

Briefly stated, geometric projection typifies most primitive painting, art in most of the Mediterranean basin during antiquity, and the art of the Near and Far East from prehistoric times until the present day; its continuity in that half of the world has been remarkable. Furthermore, though it lost favor temporarily in antiquity with the spread of naturalism through late Greek and Roman art, it reappeared with the beginning of the religious and ideologically-minded Middle Ages and held sway for another thousand years in western Europe. It can be seen over and over again in medieval manuscript illuminations, mural paintings, altarpieces, and stained glass windows. All told, its examples probably outnumber those of perspective projection by ten to one.

The geometric mode has certain easily seen virtues. When addressed to an ideologically conditioned audience, it indicates relative economic, political, and social values simply and clearly by greater or lesser size. Generally speaking, it is at its best when representing human activities because it presents all of the participants as though they were in the foreground. Note how easily we can see the figures in the Assyrian relief and the *Polo Game*.

Suitable as this mode is for representing human action, it is inadequate for depicting deep space or natural environment. As a result, the parts of a picture which employ geometric projection will vary in quality to our eyes. In the Assyrian relief the emphasis is plainly upon the human drama, while the natural setting is barely indicated. Such natural elements as are included show the effect of this indifference and limitation; they are quite unconvincing. Witness the row of extremely stylized trees across the bottom of the relief. This discrepancy in skill of representation is even more noticeable in the *Polo Game*. The human actors, though doll-like, are at least alive; the setting is contrastingly artificial. The reason for this is that geometric projection cannot represent more than four or five planes between the bottom and top of a composition and still preserve the largeness and clarity—the sense of nearness—of figures, while perspective projection implies an infinitude of planes stretching into distant space.

The geometric projection of the Assyrian relief cannot do justice to the innumerable planes with the basic plane of trees. When the two modes are contrasted, shallowness is seen to be a limitation that the users of geometric projection had to accept. A finite and orderly mode, it lacks infinity and variety. It is more likely to give the impression of stiffness than of vitality, which is not strange because it has most often been the mode of authoritarian societies. Through the long history of art it has played a prominent part, but it by no means expresses man's highest artistic potentialities.

DIAGONAL PROJECTION. The other mode of spatial representation developed in the Orient is called *diagonal projection*. Like the geometric mode, it is a conventional system. A good example is Masanobu's *Playing Cards* (Fig. 113). Its most noticeable feature is a series of diagonal lines which are meant to be read from the bottom of the picture upward. Translated into spatial terms this means that the foreground is at the bottom of the picture and the horizon at the top but outside of the frame. In looking from the foreground to the horizon the eyes move obliquely, as distinct from the convergent or vertical progression of the perspective and geometric modes, hence the name diagonal projection. In perspective projection the converging lines are also diagonal with respect to the picture frame, but in diagonal projection the lines are parallel. In some instances they even diverge slightly. Since, being parallel, they would never meet, there is no vanishing point in the diagonal system.

Just as the parallel lines never converge in diagonal projection so as to suggest a contraction of space like that represented by the perspective system, neither do the forms or figures diminish in scale. It is similar in this respect to its Asiatic partner in conventional projection, the geometric mode.

A third characteristic is its representation of scenes so that they always appear to be viewed from above. For this reason it is said to give a bird's-eye view. It follows that the space which is represented by this method is always shallow, for we cannot look downward upon a scene and off into the far distance at the same time. This is one of the obvious limitations of the diagonal mode.

The bird's-eye view has, however, a compensating fascination. It is so different from our normal earthbound view of the world that it is at once novel and striking. We are made to feel like unobserved but all-seeing witnesses of scenes which are normally hidden from

FIG. 113. Masanobu. *Playing Cards. ca.* 1730. Bowdoin College Museum of Fine Arts, Brunswick, Me.

FIG. 114. Masanobu. *Playing the Game of Sugo-suku in a Restaurant. ca.* 1750. Museum of Fine Arts, Boston.

FIG. 115. Hiroshige. *Otsu Village, A Traveller Buying an Otsu-E Picture. ca.* 1840. Museum of Fine Arts, Boston.

view by walls and roofs. As a consequence, there is an intimate but detached eye-witness quality to most pictures in which diagonal projection is employed. In order to make this possible the artists commonly eliminate the roofs and walls which might obstruct our view.

The impression one gains from such an arrangement can be likened to what we might see in a large Hollywood studio where scores of different sets can be found side by side. They have walls but no ceilings or roofs, so that one can look into them from above. Fig. 115, Hiroshige's woodblock print of *A Traveller Buying an Otsu-E Picture* suggests strongly what we might see from the catwalks over such a group of sets, or from one of the giant cranes which swing the movie cameramen and their heavy equipment through the air with ease.

Fig. 115 also illustrates a refinement of diagonal projection, namely the use of a system of criss-crossing diagonals. We call this a refinement because it appeared relatively late in history under the pressure of a trend toward realism which not even Asia could withstand during the nineteenth century. It undoubtedly added a measure of realism to the conventions of the system but was exceptional. Masanobu's *Playing Cards* (Fig. 113), in which one set of lines recedes diagonally, while a second set recedes parallel to the bottom of the picture, is more representative of the mode as it was conceived for many centuries.

The diagonal mode of projection appeared somewhat later than the ancient geometric mode, but competed with it in popularity from the sixteenth century on. It may be called the modern mode of the Orient. Its greatest popularity was gained in the Far East, especially in later Japanese paintings and prints like Figs. 113 and 115. It is now widely associated with the Japanese prints which carried Eastern perception as far along the path of realism as it was destined to go. Arthur Pope, looking at such prints as Hiroshige's *Traveller Buying an Otsu-E Picture* as a Westerner but with a sincere admiration for Oriental art, often pointed out how little adjustment is needed to observe examples of diagonal projection without a feeling of strangeness. After one has looked at Fig. 115 for only a little while it seems perfectly normal. We must consciously notice that the lines do not converge but actually diverge.

The comfortable feeling that such an arrangement gives us may be regarded as one of its principal virtues. Unlike the extremely conventional geometric mode, it approximates our direct experience with reality. This in itself suggests something essential in the character and history of the diagonal mode. It is a compromise between "seeing" and "knowing," half conventional and half illusionary, a compound of observed fact and system. And, contrary to common opinion, a compromise can be highly satisfactory. A better term for it in such a case is probably a *balance*.

The historical development of the diagonal mode has not yet been traced with any scholarly thoroughness. One can only deduce certain things about its probable evolution from its character and the periods of its main popularity. Fully developed examples of it appear in the paintings of Ku K'ai Chih, an artist of the fourth century, who probably drew upon an even older tradition. But the largest number of examples appeared between the beginning of the seventeenth and the middle of the nineteenth century in Japan in conjunction with the best periods of Japanese woodblock printmaking. The designers of these prints studied everyday life with a directness and freedom from traditional conventions which was new and refreshing in the Orient and made them highly popular in the West. Being observant, they undoubtedly noticed that lines in reality appear to recede diagonally. But they did not associate these receding lines with a common vanishing point and so never pushed their system to its logical conclusion, perspective projection. There is, moreover, no evidence that they reduced their system to a mathematical formula in any way resembling the scientific, theoretical researches of the artists of the European Renaissance. We might construe this to mean that the Japanese painters simply fell short of a goal which occidental artists reached. More likely, they were simply being true to their own way of thinking. The Japanese were not entirely ignorant of Western perspective projection. A print by the same Masanobu who designed the *Playing Cards* shows that they were acquainted with it. Called *Playing the Game of Sugosuku in a Restaurant* (Fig. 114), it is admittedly an unsatisfactory example of perspective projection because the artist shifts in the background to diagonal projection without warning or logic: note especially the bridge on the left and the uphill slope of the ground plane. The significance of this awkward combination of modes is that the oriental mind was never willing to base its art wholly upon the world of appearances. It supported a traditional and conventional view of reality for centuries because it preferred what the mind says is eternally true to what the eye says is true temporarily. By grafting the visually observed sloping lines of the physical world upon the conventions of the geometric mode, the oriental artists struck a compromise between "seeing" and "knowing," but that was as far as they were willing to go. To find the full exploitation of realism based on an illusionary bias we shall have to return to the West and the development of aerial projection.

AERIAL PROJECTION. During the seventeenth century the artists of Western Europe developed the most complete system yet devised for the representation of deep space within a picture frame. It finally permitted them to paint in either a completely realistic manner or in the arbitrary but sweeping terms of Baroque art. Called the *aerial mode* because it combined a new appreciation of the influence of color, light, and atmosphere with perspective projection, it appeared during an important period of change in European art and life. The cultural leadership of Europe was shifting from Italy to the North, where a weather-ridden climate made artists more conscious of atmospheric effects and changing patterns of light and shadow. At the same time, mural paintings were declining in favor of easel paintings which were independent ends in themselves. In these pictures landscape painting was coming into its own, for if the northerners were not less religious or humanistic, they were more naturalistically inclined.

When these changes occurred, aerial projection followed. The system that the northern landscape painters developed is illustrated diagrammatically by Fig. 102e and pictorially by Figs. 116 and 118. The first of these pictures is *The Wheatfields* by the Dutch master Jacob Ruysdael. It can probably be understood best by comparing it with Perugino's *Christ Delivering the Keys of Heaven to Saint Peter,* a definitive example of the Italian Renaissance perspective mode.

The two pictures are similar in one respect. Both employ a progressive diminution of size to achieve an appearance of recession toward the horizon, and both achieve, as a result, a feeling of great spaciousness. In other respects they are fundamentally different. Whereas Perugino created a system of lines which draws our eye to the vanishing point at the center of the picture, Ruysdael's composition does the opposite. We are hardly conscious of the vanishing point. Indeed, Ruysdael seems to have avoided it deliberately by placing a screen of trees before it. The effect of this screen is to direct our eyes away from the center and to the left, where the greatest depth is to be found. The difference between the two pictures is much like looking into a tunnel as compared to a panorama. Technically one system is convergent, the other divergent. Behind the differences lie certain radical changes in attitude toward our perception of space in- and out-of-doors.

It is probable that Ruysdael and many other seventeenth-century masters were dissatisfied with the perspective system exemplified by Perugino's painting. To their eyes it must have seemed rigid, artificial, and contrary to visual experience. In truth our roving vision does not see nature in terms of a single, arbitrarily fixed vanishing

FIG. 116. Ruysdael. *The Wheatfields.* *ca.* 1670. Metropolitan Museum of Art, New York.

FIG. 117. Lorrain. *Landscape with Cattle.* *ca.* 1650. Cleveland Museum of Art.

point. Our actual experience with nature is more mobile and panoramic. So when the seventeenth-century artists wished to adhere more closely to visual experience, they abandoned the too-perfect straight-lined architectural settings of the Italians in favor of the rolling, meandering hills and fields of nature. This difference is illustrated plainly by the Perugino and Ruysdael paintings. In the one our eyes are led from any point in the forefront or perimeter of the picture directly inward toward the center by guiding lines which are as straight and irresistible as a pair of receding railroad tracks. In the Ruysdael landscape our eyes start their journey in the lower right-hand corner of the picture and wander along a meandering path to the distant horizon on the far left. It is a more leisurely trip that Ruysdael takes us on, but one which gives us a feeling of the sweeping vastness of the out-of-doors. It is panoramic in the largest sense.

An examination of four more examples of aerial projection will illustrate a similar linear recession. In Fig. 119 the recession is oblique; in Figs. 117 and 118 it meanders toward the distant center. But in all cases it proceeds along an indirect path, avoiding the direct-to-the-target obviousness of Renaissance perspective projection. It not only suggests vividly our normal observation of space, but is a subtle system of spatial representation. For, although the seventeenth-century masters were less rigid than those of the Renaissance, they were no less skilful in controlling our visual perception of their pictures. Ruysdael guides our reading of his landscape in one way already described; Claude Lorrain achieves the same result in another typical way. In his *Landscape with Cattle* (Fig. 117) he leads our eyes from the trees on the right foreground to the cliff in the left middle distance, and from there to the centrally located mountain on the horizon. Trees and cliffs thus serve as a frame for the distance, channeling our attention toward it. Within this frame our eyes follow the zigzag or meandering path typical of the aerial mode of projection.

When the seventeenth-century painters shifted their attention from the city to the country, they gave up the architectural settings which the Renaissance masters exploited so conveniently in perspective painting. But, needing some framework of linear recession, they adopted the winding country roads and meandering rivers of rural nature. These became to their pictures what buildings had been to the fifteenth-century paintings. They are a common denominator in all four pictures illustrated in Figs. 116 to 119.

When the seventeenth-century artists turned to marine painting, as Ruysdael did in such pictures as his *Troubled Sea* (in Berlin), they had no buildings, roads, or streams to follow; nothing but the flat plane of the sea. Here they showed their ingenuity by arranging sail boats and ships in a receding zigzag sequence and by inventing a new system of lighting. The latter is the more important, for it could be applied equally well to the development of landscape painting and became, in fact, an outstanding feature of both Ruysdael's and Lorrain's rural scenes.

The system may be described as an arbitrary arrangement of light and shadow in a sequence of bands in which dark and light alternate. In Ruysdael's *Wheatfields,* for example, the foreground has been darkened arbitrarily. The same is true of Lorrain's *Landscape with Cattle.* Because our eyes are attracted to light, this arbitrary darkening of the foreground directs our eyes to the illuminated second plane or back into the distance. Once this rhythm of recession takes hold, our eyes follow it until we have gone by a series of steps to the horizon.

Because of its character and the time of its appearance, Pope has referred to the arbitrary darkening of the foreground as the *Baroque canopy.* It resembles the effect that would be created if a gigantic canopy or awning suspended in the sky cast a great shadow over the foreground. An apt term, it may help us to remember this important feature of the aerial mode of projection.

In addition to the Baroque canopy, the seventeenth-century masters of aerial projection skilfully utilized clouds and luminosity to attract our attention to the distance. Ruysdael, an expert with this device, filled the sky of his *Wheatfields* with billowing clouds which reinforce the lateral direction of his main directional lines and attract our attention to the horizon. They give us a feeling of the vastness of the outdoors which contributes much to his picture's total effect. Remove them and it would be a different picture indeed.

Claude Lorrain used a different but no less effective method of creating a feeling of deep space. He, as the saying goes, put the sun in the sky. Even in his drawing of a landscape with cattle, in which the sun does not appear directly, the luminosity of the sky attracts and holds our attention.

Once established, these two means of creating depth in paintings were repeated either separately or in combination by artists for the next two hundred years. Winslow Homer used them together in his spectacular painting of a coming storm (Fig. 119), which dates from the beginning of our century. The storm-laden clouds are the most dramatic part of the picture, while the sky is visually the most luminous.

The history of aerial projection is well known. Hints of it

FIG. 118. Hirschvogel. *Landscape with a Curved Wooden Bridge.* *ca.* 1545. Museum of Fine Arts, Boston.

FIG. 119. Homer. *The Coming Storm.* 1901. Collection of Mrs. Charles R. Henschel, New York.

appeared in the paintings of Masolino and Masaccio at the beginning of the Renaissance and clear signs of it appeared in the landscape backgrounds of Giorgione and Titian during the High Renaissance. On the whole, though, they were ahead of their times in this field of interest. Most of the painting of the Italian Renaissance is atmosphere-less or nonaerial.

The full development of aerial projection took place within the landscape tradition of the North, starting in the sixteenth century and reaching its first peak in the seventeenth. The time span of the mode can be illustrated by a *Landscape with a Curved Wooden Bridge* (Fig. 118) by the German Hirschvogel and the *Coming Storm* by the New Englander Winslow Homer (Fig. 119). Both were Northern artists. All of the linear and many of the atmospheric elements of the mode are present in Hirschvogel's sixteenth-century design; only the Baroque canopy evolved in the seventeenth century is lacking. His picture anticipates Homer's method to a remarkable extent. While Homer, working at the other end of a tradition that had been handed down for two hundred years, profited by the facility that comes from long experience.

Innumerable painters used the aerial mode between the time of Ruysdael and the death of Homer, making it one of the most popular methods ever invented. So impressive is its record that it is easy to count its merits and difficult to find any serious limitations. Its capacity to convey a sense of far-reaching spaciousness and exploit the psychological appeal of such a quality has been proven many times. Though not so finite as the perspective mode, it has no superior in the suggestion of infinity. In paintings of the out-of-doors this would seem to be an unquestionable virtue. It is an orderly mode, and yet its system of meandering recessional lines and alternative lights and shadows provides a rhythmic variety. Finally, depending upon the temperament of the artist, it can express the reposeful spirit of a Claude Lorrain, the somber moodiness of a Ruysdael, or the vitality of a Homer with equal clarity and intensity.

The modes of projection are both closely allied to and distinguishable from the modes of representation. In this chapter we have considered them separately for the sake of simplicity, clarity, and as a background for our further study of the modes of representation. But in the following chapter we shall see the close connection between the modes of projection and the other modes of representation, as we have already noted the alliance between perspective projection and realistic painting.

CHAPTER 10

Representation in Painting
The Other Modes

Although realistic painting is the most complete and complex of all the modes of representation, it was not fully developed until late in the history of art, and even when perfected it left unexpressed many aspects of man's experience with reality. Searching for broader expression, artists began long ago to invent other methods of representation. Now called the mode of line and local color, the sculpturesque mode, the pictorial mode, the impressionist mode, and, for the time being, the modern modes, they appeared in history in about that order.

THE MODE OF LINE AND LOCAL COLOR

The first of these modes, the mode of line and local color, carries us into far places and back into the earliest history of man; it is the way he began to paint. It has remained the universal mode of primitive peoples up to the present time and is almost without exception the way in which children record their impressions of the world, whether they live in modern New York City or among the aborigines of Australia. It has therefore probably had the greatest number of practitioners of any mode in history. One reason for this is plain: it is the simplest of all the modes thus far developed. Consequently, wherever the mode of line and local color is found it denotes a simple and clear but undeveloped point of view. Like the children and adult artists who employ it, it is uncomplicated and unsophisticated. There are, as we shall see later in the case of the Impressionists and Modernists, two exceptions to this rule; nevertheless it is generally true.

We have already seen an excellent example of this mode in the

Bison at Altamira (Fig. 33), which dates from the prehistoric child-hood of human history. An equally good example takes us back to ancient Egypt and the tomb of Nakht at Thebes (Fig. 120). A detail of the wall paintings which decorate that tomb, it is typical not only of ancient Egypt, but of the whole Mediterranean area for most of the centuries before Christ. It gives us an excellent chance to analyze the general characteristics of the mode of line and local color.

Any mode of representation can be defined by noting what it omits and what it includes of the visual image. Of all the modes the realistic is the most inclusive and complex and is frequently termed the mode of "total visual effect." Quite the opposite method is used in the mode of line and local color. When, for instance, the painter of *Nakht Watching Plowing* expressed his view of the world, he chose to give a highly selective report. He included only the outlines and local colors of each object in his scene, and omitted any reference to specific light sources, shadows, reflections, modeling, atmosphere, and distinctions of texture. Ignoring the whole complicated problem of spatial and color relationships with which the realistic artists of later centuries struggled, he concentrated his attention upon two aspects of the visible world—outline and local color.

In selecting these aspects, he was ideological and conventional. He was ideological because, like other Egyptian artists, he used paintings to convey general ideas rather than momentary appearances, in this case the idea of Nakht watching plowing, but not at any specific time of year or hour of the day. Continuity, not change, was his criterion; hence he gave no hint of such varying aspects of nature as weather, natural light, and shadow. In keeping with this ideological reporting, the artist indicated Nakht's greater importance by making him extra large—a method of the geometric mode he used for projection and a sure sign of an outlook which places conceptual value above visual truth. Having agreed upon a set of conventions, the ancient artists adhered to them for centuries, giving their paintings a timeless air which disregards every sign of change. Once accepted, this system served as a language of communication which conveyed ideas nearly as clearly as words and was, in fact, commonly used in conjunction with them.

Clarity and convenience of statement, not truth of appearance, governed these artists. For example, they combined the profiles of heads and limbs with a frontal rendering of eyes and torsos, because such treatment imparted the maximum information about the shape of each part of the figure. Their reasoning was logical, but based on a logic of ideas instead of normal appearances. Therefore, to com-

FIG. 120. *Nakht Watching Plowing.* Tomb of Nakht, Thebes. XVIII Dynasty, 1580-1350 B.C. Metropolitan Museum of Art, New York.

FIG. 121. *Justinian and Courtiers.* A.D. 526. S. Vitale. Ravenna.

pare the painting of *Nakht Watching Plowing* with Velasquez's *Maids of Honor* (Fig. 94) is to witness the difference between conceptual thinking and visual perception, or the contrast between *knowing* and *seeing*. Artistically the two points of view could hardly be farther apart.

Yet there is an element of truth in the ancient Egyptian's point of view. Consider, for instance, his handling of color. Desiring to convey certain long-range ideas, he painted the bodies of men a deep red-orange and those of the women a lighter tone, probably to show that the one spent more time under the hot Egyptian sun than the other. The cattle are painted their normal hues, while water is a turquoise blue, trees are green, and the earth a neutral sandy color. These colors reveal an observation of physical facts, but an observation which seeks out permanent facts and long-range truths, hence its preference for actual colors over apparent colors. If an ancient Egyptian artist were to paint a man wearing a red coat, he would paint its dyed-in, continuous hue and disregard all temporary effects of lighting.

The Orientals have long agreed with this ancient conception of what is important in visual experience, insisting that Western artists have been addicted since the Renaissance to a temporary and accidental world of appearances. So it is not surprising to find that the mode of line and local color has been the prevailing mode of representation in Asia from prehistoric times to the present. It could be illustrated equally well by an ancient Chinese painting or a Japanese print of only a century ago.

The mode of line and local color is the one generally found in all examples of geometric projection, as it is in *Nakht Watching Plowing*. Not only are they alike in their histories and conventional systems; they have similar limitations. Both have appeared and thrived in history when an ideological, authoritarian, and collective system governed men politically, socially, and religiously, or whenever there was a strong tendency toward uniformity of thought. And since the centuries of totalitarian rule have outnumbered those of free individual expression by at least ten to one, the mode of line and local color which reflects the collective point of view has played a powerful role in history.

There was a time at the end of antiquity when artists, in the Roman school especially, tended strongly toward a more naturalistic orientation and a comparable realism in painting. The painters at such centers as Alexandria and Rome had, it now appears, a remarkably thorough knowledge of both perspective and aerial projection, and even anticipated the Impressionism of modern times. But this trend was cut short when its foundation, Roman factualism and materialism, declined. In the West this brief departure from the mode of line and local color was followed by the long period of medieval art which adhered to it again. It became the principal system of representation employed in Byzantine mosaic and hence appears in the famous mosaic of *Justinian and Courtiers* at Ravenna (Fig. 121) and in the *Crucifixion* at Daphni (Fig. 87). Moreover, it is the manner of rendering used in most illuminated manuscripts of the medieval period, such as the twelfth-century Austrian *Virgin Enthroned* (Fig. 49), in the finest of the stained glass windows which embellish the Gothic cathedrals, and in most medieval tapestries. All of these examples depict the world in terms of a predetermined concept. It was not until the High Gothic decades of the thirteenth century that artists once again accepted the normal character and idiosyncrasies of nature as a rule of art and shifted from collective convention to individual observation. Meanwhile, though we forget what a length of time was involved, a thousand years of history had passed before the first signs of the Renaissance appeared in Gothic art.

In the nineteenth century the mode of line and local color reappeared and gained considerable favor. The reason for that is not hard to discern. It was a reaction against the kind of post-Renaissance realism which became overcomplex. The myriad details of Rosa Bonheur's *Lion and Lioness Resting* (Fig. 30) illustrate the kind of academic painting common in the nineteenth century, though we see little of it today. Such artists as Manet and Degas reacted against this confusing and esthetically ruinous complexity and sought to regain some simplicity. They might have done this by discarding the more cumbersome paraphernalia of latter-day realism; Manet, in fact, did suppress modeling and discarded many of the intricacies of interrelated reflected lights and colors. But these artists had at hand the newly appreciated prints of the Japanese. Following their lead, they regained the lost simplicity by returning, in effect, to the mode of line and local color. Toulouse-Lautrec carried this trend so far by the end of the nineteenth century that his most serious paintings, like the *Jane Avril Leaving the Moulin Rouge* (Fig. 122), though obviously different from any Egyptian fresco or Byzantine mosaic, have more in common with them than with the nineteenth-century academic realism of Meissonier, Bonheur, or Gérôme. Like the early ancient pictures, Lautrec's mode of painting contains neither atmosphere nor any detectable illumination or shadows. It is highly linear, and the colors are applied in flat, independent areas. This

FIG. 122. Toulouse-Lautrec. *Jane Avril Leaving the Moulin Rouge.* *ca.* 1892. Wadsworth Athenaeum, Hartford.

FIG. 123. Matisse. *Odalisque with Raised Arms.* *ca.* 1920. Art Institute of Chicago.

kind of pattern-like painting, used in numerous theatrical posters, justly earned him the title of father of the modern poster.

Lautrec's painting differs from any example of ancient art in its conscious striving for simplification, something no primitive or ancient artist had to do. His art grew out of a reaction, theirs did not. This reaction has continued and deepened in our time, for the increasing complexity of our present civilization has impelled artists toward an even greater simplification. The results of this tendency are apparent in the art of three leading painters of our day, Rouault, Picasso, and Matisse. Whether we recognize the fact or not on first acquaintance, Picasso's *Guernica* (Fig. 1) marks a return to the mode of line and local color. So, too, does Matisse's *Odalisque with Raised Arms* (Fig. 123).

Like the nineteenth-century masters, these contemporary painters have sought guidance and confirmation for their views through an artistic orientation. Picasso turned to primitive art, Rouault to stained glass windows of the Middle Ages, and Matisse to Persian art. Each was expressing his own temperament in this respect. But all were reflecting a common phenomenon in modern art—the return to the simple kinds of painting employed by relatively uncomplicated artists and societies of the past.

Awareness of the art of Picasso and Matisse should guard us against a mistake of naïveté when we sum up the general merits and limitations of the mode of line and local color. It is easy to conceive it only as a start toward something better, as the primitive tribe precedes a civilized society or the boy precedes the man. But the mode of line and local color is not a mere precursor of a better historical development; it is a complete system with a logic of its own. There was a loss as well as a gain when artists abandoned the mode of line and local color for more highly developed and complex modes.

The chief merit of the mode of line and local color is the clarity which goes with its simplicity. Attending this is an intensity of visual effect and an impact of image which is unexcelled. No other mode communicates ideas so quickly or surely. Making the fewest demands on the eye by employing the fewest visual elements, it is the easiest of all the modes to read. This must account in part for its universal popularity in expressing collective ideologies. It has been employed all over the world in posters and on billboards, in eighteenth-century Japan as well as in twentieth-century Europe, whenever artists wished to gain the maximum effect with the minimum of means. The designer of the *Crucifixion* at Daphni (Fig. 87) knew this virtue when he used the mode of line and local color; he was using art not only for architectural decoration but to propagandize the faith.

The mode of line and local color can be described as the most finite of all the modes, so long as we qualify this statement carefully. It provides without a doubt the most exact record of actual local colors. It also provides a record of the outlines of forms which is second to none in definiteness. Nevertheless, it must share its pre-eminence in finiteness with another mode because of an outstanding deficiency or self-imposed limitation: it does not begin to exploit the sense of three-dimensional mass. A flat, shallow mode, it stimulates our tactile sensations only mildly. Both the Egyptians and Matisse overcame this difficulty to some extent by implying mass subtly. But they appear to have restrained themselves deliberately from any full description of three-dimensionality. Generally speaking, we neither find nor expect this quality in pictures executed in this mode. Flatness and a neglect of the tactile sensations are accepted as its limitations, which means that it leaves unexploited that part of finite reality which we refer to as the world of solids.

If the mode of line and local color is a finite mode, especially in its treatment of the silhouettes of forms, it follows that it is a poor mode for the representation of the infinite aspects of reality. Not only is it a poor mode for the representation of rapid movement, but it deliberately omits any suggestion of changing lights and shadows, atmosphere or deep space. Consequently, it lacks mystery or the imaginative appeal to infinite shades of meaning. Both physically and mentally it stands at the far pole from that kind of subtle thought and feeling. Owing to these deficiencies, it left room for other modes of representation. Indeed, it made them obligatory.

THE SCULPTURESQUE MODE

The sculpturesque mode is the mode of line and local color in relief. By adding the appearance of three-dimensionality through the modeling of forms, the users of this mode overcame the chief defect of the mode of line and local color, its shallow flatness and general lack of solidity, while preserving most of its clarity of outlines.

The typical characteristics of the mode can be observed in four illustrations which span its long history. The *Portrait of a Boy* (Fig. 124) represents its beginning in late antiquity when even Egyptian painting became strongly modeled under the influence of Roman naturalism. This beginning was cut short by the decline of Rome and the rise of ideological art in the Middle Ages. Thus

FIG. 124. *Portrait of a Boy.*
Fayum, 2d century A.D. Metro-
politan Museum of Art, New
York.

FIG. 125. Filippino Lippi. *Portrait of a Man. ca.*
1495. Uffizi Gallery, Florence.

FIG. 126. Michelangelo. *The Creation of
Adam.* 1508-1512. Sistine Chapel, Vatican,
Rome.

FIG. 127. Cézanne. *Louis Guillaume.*
1879-1882. National Gallery of Art,
Washington, D.C.

the main development of sculpturesque painting was delayed until after the Middle Ages. Giotto was the leader of this resurgence and Filippino Lippi, whose *Portrait of a Man* is seen in Fig. 125, was a typical follower. The movement culminated in the early sixteenth century in the art of Michelangelo, whose *Creation of Adam* (Fig. 126) is a fully developed example of the sculpturesque mode. Although Michelangelo's name is synonymous with the ultimate perfection of sculpturesque painting, he had a great descendant in Cézanne who, at the end of the nineteenth century, reacted against a later movement, Impressionism, and sought to restore the qualities of classical art. Cézanne's portrait of Louis Guillaume (Fig. 127) is different in certain respects from Lippi's *Portrait of a Man* or the ancient *Portrait of a Boy*, but a strong family resemblance unites them and joins them with the art of Michelangelo. They are all links in a recognizable and distinguished tradition, the most prominent trait of which was an intense feeling for the solid properties of forms.

The disciples of Giotto did this wisely, too, adding to the mode of line and local color exactly what was lacking, yet avoiding the addition of elements which would have defeated their purpose. Since their aim was to make the strongest possible appeal to our tactile sensations, they stressed the weight and density of forms and avoided the superficial appeal of texture.

In its avoidance of the superficial and temporary, the sculpturesque mode shows its kinship with the mode of line and local color. Both favor and stress the finite aspects of reality and eschew the infinite. In neither is there any distinguishable source of light; rather, a strong and uniform illumination of every figure. There is an avoidance of anything which, like atmosphere and deep shadows, would obscure the clear outlines and shapes of forms. Where some shading is necessary for the modeling of forms, reflections are played into the shadow areas to lift them out of obscurity. Thus every contour is clearly defined. Such reflections are found along the jowls of the Egyptian boy, Lippi's man, and Cézanne's Guillaume, and under the arm of Michelangelo's Jehovah; they are typical of finite painting in the sculpturesque mode. The treatment of color reveals, too, an intense desire for finiteness; it is applied in separate areas, each independent of the other and with little or no interplay save participation in the general tonality and lighting. All of these signs point to finiteness as the guiding principle.

Although the sculpturesque mode dates from ancient times, it is associated mainly with the Early and High Renaissance periods in Florence and Central Italy. Characteristic of this period was the

revival of interest in antiquity and a study of objective reality whose
scope and intensity made it a new phenomenon in history. One
consequence of the revival of antiquity was to restore to art something of the sculptor's feeling for three-dimensional masses, for most
of the artistic remains of antiquity then known were statues or buildings. Michelangelo, for example, studied passionately every ancient
relief or statue that he could find. This predilection for sculpture
was deepened by a special characteristic of Renaissance society: it
prized versatility above specialization. Consequently, a large proportion of the artists of the Italian Renaissance practiced sculpture and
architecture as well as painting. Giotto and Michelangelo were
masters of all three arts; Verrocchio and his pupil Leonardo da Vinci
were both sculptors and painters; Raphael was a painter and an
architect; and many others followed their examples. Michelangelo,
in fact, thought of himself primarily as a sculptor. Such a tradition
gave the Renaissance artists the best possible training in thinking
three-dimensionally. And this historical fact probably tempted us
in turn to call their method of painting sculpturesque. It has often
been pointed out that the best way to understand it is to imagine it
in the form of painted relief sculpture.

The rediscovery of objective reality at the time of the Renaissance
gave artists a second reason for developing modeling as a means of
representing the world of solids. For the outburst of interest in the
tangible world created a demand for a greater tactile sense in painting and placed a higher premium on visual experience.

Under the pressure of this change in outlook there was a marked
shift from a collective, ideological conception of reality to one based
on a more individual and direct observation. The flat patterns of
the mode of line and local color would no longer do. What had
sufficed to convey ideas through conventional signs would not satisfy
a people who had responded enthusiastically to the world of appearances. They now demanded three-dimensionality in representation.

Art, like society, moved steadily during the Renaissance from an
ideological and conventional point of view to one based on objective
experience. Such a trend could not help developing full-fledged
realism in the course of time. At this moment in history, however,
the realism was not impartial or complete. To the selective view of
the Renaissance painters, the world of finite solids was more real and
important than the intangible world of atmosphere and changing
lights and shadows. This conception was their classical heritage;
it had prevailed for centuries in the ancient Mediterranean basin,
and the Renaissance artists did everything in their power to perpetuate it. In this respect Raphael and Michelangelo, though

temperamental opposites, were artistic brothers. Raphael's *School of Athens* (Fig. 104) is, like Michelangelo's *Creation of Adam*, a superb illustration of the sculpturesque mode. It also suggests another important point.

One of the devices which the Renaissance artists developed to express their new appreciation of reality was the perspective mode of projection illustrated so well by Raphael's *School of Athens*. By the use of this mode they captured the sense of space in the physical world and made their pictures appear to be as deep as those in the mode of line and local color are shallow. Nevertheless, their conception of space was realistic only in a limited form. Though deep and spacious, it was always airless and finite. Because of this characteristic, perspective projection was the perfect partner for sculpturesque painting. The two modes grew out of the same conception of reality at the same time and are to be thought of together. The sculpturesque mode thus presents a special view of the world which falls visually as it did historically somewhere between the very simple interpretation of the mode of line and local color and the nearly complete record of the realistic mode.

The principal merit of the sculpturesque mode lies in its capacity to represent the quality of mass and so appeal profoundly to the tactile sense. No other kind of painting stimulates sensations of that sort more intensely. Two masters, Giotto and Michelangelo, are prominent in that field and a common characteristic of their art noteworthy. Both painted large figures and kept them well to the front, where, seeming to be almost on top of us, they bulk large; we cannot escape the impression of their massiveness. Consistent with the practice, they avoided the representation of any deep space which might have diluted or detracted from the impact of their human figures. They left the problem of deep space to other artists, like Perugino and his pupil Raphael.

Therefore, the finiteness of Renaissance sculpturesque painting is of two sorts: one a finiteness of mass, the other a finiteness of space. In Perugino's *Christ Delivering the Keys of Heaven to Saint Peter* (Fig. 102a) both space and the forms within it are prescribed exactly, but the impact of the comparatively small figures is weak beside that of Giotto's massive madonnas or Michelangelo's giants, while the latter's compositions are relatively shallow. The merits and limitations are apportioned accordingly.

We have said that the sculpturesque mode added a new sense of mass to the mode of line and local color without any loss of clarity of outline. It is fair to add that the sculpturesque painters, by thinking in terms of varying three-dimensional forms, brought a new richness and variety to outlines and, consequently, a greater flexibility and naturalness. A comparison of *Nakht Watching Plowing* with Michelangelo's *Creation of Adam* will make clear how much less stiff and rigid-looking are the good examples of sculpturesque painting.

From this variety came a greater vitality. It was possible to convey a greater sense of movement, as is clear again from the *Creation of Adam*. However, the vitality implied by movement must be qualified. It is of a special kind of sculpturesque painting—the kind of power which is associated with heavy bodies in motion. Michelangelo was a master of this type of power. But it would be stretching a point to assert that his Jehovah could travel through space with the rapidity of a sprinter or ballet dancer. Lightness and speed of movement are, as a rule, beyond the reach of sculpturesque painting; Botticelli, the one Florentine who suggested light and graceful movement, did so by reverting to an emphasis of lines. However, no mode is its superior at suggesting the repose which we associate with heavy objects at rest. To the extent that the sculpturesque mode excelled in the representation of finiteness, it sacrificed the infinite aspects of reality. This shortcoming forces us to seek further and pass on to a later stage in the development of art.

THE PICTORIAL MODE

During the post-Renaissance periods of European history, a profound change occurred in the mode of representation employed in painting. The term *pictorial* as applied to one stage of this development implies that artists were thinking in terms of the possibilities inherent in their own medium, instead of imitating the qualities of sculpture. The late development of the full possibilities of painting compared to the ancient eminence of sculpture accounts for the belatedness of this mode. Two other concepts parallel this change. One was a movement from a finite to an infinite conception of reality; the other was a shifting of emphasis from tactile to visual sensations in all the creative and appreciative activities. This reorientation of the artistic outlook was so rapid and far-reaching that a brilliant comparative analysis of the art of the short period between 1450 and 1650 by Heinrich Wölfflin entitled *Principles of Art History* presents far more contrasts than similarities and shows how they extended consistently through all the visual arts.

Part of this realignment was due to historic upheavals which drastically altered the environment of artists. The Reformation and Counter-Reformation which followed in quick succession in the sixteenth century produced some of the bitterest wars that man has fought; they ravaged Europe for a hundred years, disrupting its life as badly as two world wars have affected ours. As a result, Europe went through a period of soul-searching in which a new emphasis was placed upon spiritual values. Since the sculpturesque mode of the Renaissance, with its primary emphasis upon the mass and shape of forms, was as physical as it was finite, it was inadequate for the expression of these new attitudes and a new mode had to be devised.

The redirection of Western art during the periods between the early sixteenth century and the late nineteenth, though continuous, made its greatest advances in three stages. The first came during the sixteenth century in Italy. The leadership of the movement was assumed by the school of Venice when the Florentine school, committed predominantly to a sculpturesque and finite point of view, could not respond promptly enough to the new needs of the times.

The *Presentation of the Virgin* (Fig. 128) by the Venetian master Tintoretto shows graphically some of the changes that were occurring. He is said to have written on his studio wall the motto: "The form of Michelangelo and the color of Titian." Legendary or not, this ideal expressed the aims of the Venetians during the transitional period. They wished to enrich the spiritual expression of painting by giving to light, color, and atmosphere a new emphasis without sacrificing the appeal of form. In short, they were striving for a balance of the best in both. Their degree of success is evident in the fame of their school—the first great dedicated colorists in post-medieval Western art.

In the *Presentation of the Virgin*, Tintoretto shows his reluctance to abandon the world of solid forms and his ambition to enhance it. He models every figure firmly; the mother and child in the central foreground stand out in especially bold relief. He does this, moreover, without any loss of outline by distributing areas of light and shadow along the boundaries of forms. He uses the same device to separate forms in recession, intensifying not only the three-dimensional quality of each figure but the depth of the picture as a whole. This method of modeling forms, by playing them against each other in space within a pattern employing light areas against dark and dark against light, was a radical departure from the old method of modeling figures individually and uniformly (as in the sculpturesque mode). It was one of the most ingenious innovations in the history of the visual arts.

Yet Tintoretto's unwillingness to abandon the sculpturesque mode entirely is plain to see. He loved outlines and masses quite as much as he did colors and shadows, though he had only a moderate feeling for atmosphere. This he left to his successors. What he did

FIG. 128. Tintoretto. *Presentation of the Virgin.* 1551-1556. Sta. Maria dell'Orto, Venice.

FIG. 129. Titian. *Madonna of the Cherries.* *ca.* 1515. Imperial Gallery, Vienna.

FIG. 130. Titian. *Christ Crowned with Thorns.* *ca.* 1570. Alte Pinakothek, Munich.

238

do was handle light and shadow in a new manner. Compare his *Presentation* with Giotto's. The illumination of Giotto is uniformly strong; Tintoretto's is selective. The central characters are bathed in light, the minor cast into shadow. The beggars on the left-hand side of the stairs are much more obscure than they would ever have been in the earlier sculpturesque mode.

Although Tintoretto accomplished much, it was another Venetian master, Titian, who took the longest stride forward during this transitional stage. And well he might, for he lived in vigorous health for ninety-nine years and made the most of them, anticipating pictorial developments that were not fully realized until several centuries later. He was to post-Renaissance painting what Giotto had been to Renaissance; masters of the eminence of El Greco, Velasquez, Rubens, Watteau, and Van Dyck followed his leadership, and Delacroix and Renoir were among his artistic descendants. How much he progressed can be seen by comparing one of his relatively early works, the *Madonna of the Cherries* (Fig. 129), with a masterpiece of his later years, *Christ Crowned with Thorns* (Fig. 130).

Because Titian was born in the fifteenth century and learned his first lessons under an older master, Giovanni Bellini, his early *Madonna of the Cherries* retains many characteristics of fifteenth-century sculpturesque painting. The grouping is formal, almost symmetrical, the outlines and masses boldly described. Yet there is a sign of the future in his distribution of light and shadow. The two men flanking the Madonna are arbitrarily cast into shadow, which concentrates our attention on the central group and makes the saints recede into space. Light and shadow play a new dual role. They emphasize the most important figures and areas of the picture selectively, and create an interplay of receding planes by tonal rather than linear means. At the same time, Titian's modeling of forms is softer and less assertive than any treatment found in sculpturesque painting, conveying more the quality of living flesh and less the hard appearance of painted stone.

These advances were only the beginning of Titian's contribution. Through a series of pictures like the Louvre *Entombment* and the *Meeting of Bacchus and Ariadne,* he progressed pictorially and spiritually to the *Christ Crowned with Thorns.* A brutally tragic picture, it calls on new pictorial means to underscore its message. Compared to any fifteenth-century painting, it contains a large amount of shadow. To appreciate what a difference this makes in meaning one need only look at Signorelli's strongly lighted *Flagellation.*

Titian's extensive use of shadows created a new psychology in art.

Where the earlier artists had avoided deep shadows, he cultivated them. He thereby opened up a new way to convey the tragic and mysterious, appeal to the imagination, and suggest the infinite. This could not be done without altering the old relationship of lines, masses, and shadows. In his paintings lines begin to play a progressively lesser role and shadows a greater one. In many areas of the *Christ Crowned with Thorns* the outlines of forms disappear into obscurity, as in the case of the legs of the soldier in the foreground. Titian did not feel any obligation to describe all contours equally. Instead, he uses a selective understatement, knowing that if he illuminates a portion of any body, our imagination will deduce the rest.

His treatment of color departs, too, from any fifteenth-century precedent and looks to the future. It marks an advance even over his own *Madonna of the Cherries*. In that early picture color is treated in a manner typical of fifteenth-century sculpturesque painting: one color is applied to each clearly outlined and more or less independent area, the net effect being piecemeal, subdivided, and nonatmospheric. As Titian suppressed outlines in his later work, sharp boundaries between colors disappeared and neighboring hues blended one into another. The atmospheric content of the picture was thereby greatly increased. More important still, there was a marked gain in pictorial unity.

Before his long life ended, Titian made other contributions to the future of art. Two of these can be illustrated by details from his paintings *Noli Me Tangere* (Fig. 131) and the *Rape of Europa* (Fig. 132). The first illustrates the system that Titian and another brilliant Venetian, Giorgione, perfected to achieve simultaneously a varied pattern of lights and shadows and a clear separation of forms in space. Essential in the system is a gradation of values within each plane, as on the walls and roofs of the several farm buildings. These are so arranged that a light area always borders upon a dark area. The over-all effect is one of a continuous alternation of light and dark areas which our eyes read as a series of superimposed planes and solids. Their fellow-Venetian Tintoretto used the same scheme in his *Presentation of the Virgin;* it is characteristic of the school.

Since this is the system of description which prevailed in Western painting for the next three hundred years, its invention was of far-reaching significance. It is a common denominator in the art of such diverse artists as El Greco, Rubens, and Delacroix; it was continued by Cézanne, who grafted it upon his sculpturesque style; and it lasted into our century, being the basis of Picasso's cubistic style. More masterpieces have been painted in this mode than in any other

FIG. 131. Titian. Detail, *Noli Me Tangere*. *ca.* 1510.
National Gallery, London.

FIG. 132. Titian. Detail, *Rape of Europa*. 1559. Isabella Stewart Gardner
Museum, Boston.

241

in history, probably for this reason: whereas most modes emphasize one visual element at the expense of others, the Venetian pictorial mode achieved at one and the same time a strong effect of outline, mass, and color, a brilliant effect of light and shadow, and a pronounced indication of atmosphere. It came as near as any mode ever has to the perfect, balanced synthesis of all the formal entities in a clear and vivid style. It is therefore little wonder that it remained popular throughout Europe for over three hundred years.

The second detail illustrated here (Fig. 132) is a segment of the distant landscape background of Titian's *Rape of Europa*. It is hardly less prophetic of the future, for in it Titian created such a sense of distant atmosphere that he anticipated the French Impressionist manner which appeared three centuries later. Here he was far ahead of his time.

How much painting had changed by the end of Titian's life can be observed by comparing Giotto's *Death of St. Francis* (Fig. 133), which helped to launch the sculpturesque style of the Early Renaissance, with Caravaggio's *Death of the Virgin* (Fig. 134), a picture painted soon after Titian's death. The older painting is formal and stately, with a classic gravity and dignity. It is highly sculpturesque in style, uniformly lighted, and composed in planes parallel to the picture surface. The later picture is tragic, but with an earthly, unposed, and natural informality. Light and shadow play a far more selective and important role, shadow especially being more prominent than ever before. Only small portions of the figures are illuminated; the rest of the bodies are enveloped in an obscurity which creates a tragic air of mystery.

A new arrangement of forms in space is also employed in Caravaggio's *Death of the Virgin*. Instead of being arranged parallel to the picture plane, the figures recede obliquely. The foremost figure, that of a weeping woman, is placed in the right corner. From her the eye is led to the diagonally placed Virgin and thence to the disciples at the left and rear, a spatial design which contributes much to the natural and informal appearance of the group. It should remind us of another trend in the history of art—the change during the seventeenth century from the Renaissance mode of perspective projection to the Baroque aerial mode in which the spatial composition recedes along a meandering diagonal route. Caravaggio's *Death of the Virgin* is consistent with a general movement away from the formality of the classical Renaissance and toward a greater informality and naturalism.

The second stage in the history of the post-Renaissance pictorial mode came with the seventeenth century, commonly called the

FIG. 133. Giotto. *Death of Saint Francis.* 1325.
Bardi Chapel. S. Croce, Florence.

FIG. 134. Caravaggio. *Death of the
Virgin. ca. 1600.* Louvre, Paris.

FIG. 135. Rembrandt. *Nicholas
Bruyningh.* 1652. Painting Gallery,
Cassel.

FIG. 136. Goya. *Execution of the Madrileños,
May 3, 1808.* Prado, Madrid.

Baroque period. It was a time which, for all its turmoil, wars, and spiritual conflicts, produced as many outstanding artists as any century in history. Indeed, it is possible that the conflicts generated the vitality which is necessary for great art; but two other conditions contributed importantly, too. The seventeenth-century masters were fortunate in having inherited from the Venetians a mode of painting which was not only nearly perfect in itself, but, owing to its versatility, was suited to their times. By slight adjustments in one direction or another, it could be made to express the solidity and form of the finite or the movement, change, and mood of the infinite. Its nuances and overtones were the perfect complement to the realistic painting which was brought to full development at the same time. Between the two modes the seventeenth-century painters had both of the means needed to express the most obvious contradiction of their complex times—its contrasting materialism and passionate, often ecstatic, spirituality; Velasquez on the one side and El Greco on the other.

The second condition which contributed to the high development of seventeenth-century painting was a historical one. During this crucial period the cultural leadership of Europe shifted from Italy to the West and North; Madrid, Paris, Antwerp, and Amsterdam played a larger part in art than ever before. This meant that more of Europe's painting was created in northern environments, where the greater influence of weather, atmosphere, and changing lights and shadows had long since established a tradition in which the infinite takes a leading role. Only when this happened could the tendency toward the infinite be developed fully, for classical Italy was committed to a more finite art. Not even the Venetians could wholly forget this heritage. The full exploitation of the pictorial mode had to take place on new and northern ground.

The artist who took the fullest advantage of the pictorial mode, and so became the greatest and most representative master of his time, was Rembrandt. He was to the Baroque century what Michelangelo had been to the Renaissance, the consummate synthesizer of all the major contemporary trends. His style is as pictorial as Michelangelo's is sculpturesque.

A splendid example from his maturity is the *Portrait of Nicholas Bruyningh* (Fig. 135). If it is compared with any of the three sculpturesque pictures in Figs. 124, 125, and 127, certain important distinguishing characteristics will be apparent. While Rembrandt has not ignored the quality of mass, he has treated it selectively by his special handling of illumination and outline. Arbitrarily playing a strong light over the head, he casts the rest of the figure into shadow; hence the bulk of the head is strongly realized but that of the body only implied. The only outlines with any clarity are those which bound the face and features, and they are not drawn lines in the older sense, but rather are narrow shadows. Throughout the rest of the picture outlines are so softened as to be, in many places, almost indistinguishable. The picture as a whole is predominantly dark.

In these several ways Rembrandt continued the beginnings made by Titian and Caravaggio, but went much further than the latter; for Caravaggio, like a good Italian, could not bring himself to sacrifice sculpturesque form and outlines. His *Death of the Virgin* retains, for all its shadows, some of the old hardness and clarity in such passages as the body of the Virgin and the bald heads of the disciples. Rembrandt's painting is, by comparison, ineffably soft, luminous, and glowing, for to him light was the master key to expression.

The quality of Rembrandt's lighting has been variously described. Some students have aptly contrasted it with the sculpturesque mode's uniform illumination by likening it to the effect created by a spotlight. But a further distinction must be made, for spotlighting would apply equally to Caravaggio's relatively harsh illumination. Probably a truer observation is that Rembrandt's lighting seems to glow from within his figures. Certainly it is not the kind of light one finds in normal experience, but is one which was created by Rembrandt primarily to express spiritual values. It gave him as great a mastery over luminosity as Michelangelo possessed over forms.

Rembrandt sought in every way possible to stress the spiritual and infinite and minimize the finite and physical. For him Nicholas Bruyningh's personality and inner life were more important than his body. To show this, Rembrandt suppressed the tangible aspects of the scene before him and emphasized the intangible—light, shadow, atmosphere, and color. Consequently, he illustrated the artistic connection between the use of the infinite and intangible aspects of reality and the expression of the spiritual attributes of vitality and intelligence. There is little action but great life in the Bruyningh portrait; alert and poised, as though listening to some conversation, he seems almost ready to speak. This lifelike quality is due to the means and the methods that Rembrandt used; it is inherent in his mode of representation.

By the end of the post-Renaissance period the pictorial mode was the universal method of representation in Europe. In fact, the pendulum had swung so far away from the Renaissance sculpturesque mode that Goya, the foremost European master of the late eighteenth and early nineteenth centuries, questioned the validity of painted outlines as a legitimate means of representation. Speaking purely from the bias of the pictorial tradition he exclaimed, "In nature color exists no more than line; there is only light and shade." And though he wielded a mighty line in his etchings of the *Disasters of War* (Fig. 4), he practiced this doctrine consistently in his painting. A noted example is his *Execution of the Madrileños, May 3, 1808* (Fig. 136). In this ghastly scene depicting the murder of the Spanish citizens by Napoleon's militarized automatons, Goya has made illumination his principal visual means, even including the source of his light within the picture. He also elected to portray a nighttime scene, something few Renaissance artists ever did. By combining the two—the blackness of night and the harsh brilliance of the firing squad's lamp—he achieved a stark and grisly vitality. The arbitrary lighting common to the pictorial mode is much to the point here, because it is perfect for the statement that Goya wished to make. In fact, that statement could hardly have been made in the sculpturesque or any other mode.

Goya has often been called the great transitional master between the post-Renaissance period and the development of modern art in the nineteenth century because he applied a pictorial tradition which had begun in the time of Titian to themes which seem vividly modern to our own troubled times. Central in the hard-hitting and dramatic art that he bequeathed to the nineteenth century are light and shadow. These were carried by the nineteenth-century masters into new fields of reality and new areas of subject matter, extending the horizons of pictorial painting into the limitless field of light and shadow, color and atmosphere. In this way they prolonged the life of the pictorial mode for another hundred years of intense activity and discovery.

Both the continuity and newness of this development can be illustrated by calling attention to the kinds of pictures the nineteenth-century artists painted and the special interests which their paintings reveal. Constable, for instance, devoted himself over a period of years to the study of clouds, and especially to their illumination. Turner worshipped the sun, making natural or man-made forms share the stage with it in scores of pictures. A glowing sunset is the most spectacular element in his famous *Fighting Téméraire*. Moreover, he was conscious of his pictorial heritage, for he requested that one of his paintings be perpetually hung in the National Gallery beside a composition from the hand of Claude Lorrain, his seventeenth-century precursor in the study of natural luminosity. Winslow Homer, another ardent student of illumination, worshipped moonlight, making it the subject of numerous paintings, like the *Schooners in the Moonlight, Saco Bay* (Fig. 20), and one of his masterpieces, the *Moonlight, Wood's Island Light*, now in the Metropolitan Museum of Art. Meanwhile, he pursued the study of other conditions of lighting and atmosphere, painting among other subjects the *Houses of Parliament at Sunset* and *The Artist's Studio in an Afternoon Fog*. These were the visual problems which united the outlooks of scores of nineteenth-century artists, linked them with the pictorial tradition, and provided the basis of Impressionism.

THE IMPRESSIONIST MODE

The impressionist mode which arose in the mid-nineteenth century could be regarded as the last stage of the pictorial mode. But it has been given a name of its own because it developed the later tendencies of the pictorial mode with finality into a distinctive style. The difference between the modes is more than one of degree. Throughout its long history the practitioners of the pictorial mode never entirely sacrificed the finite for the sake of the infinite, form for color, or the tactile for visual sensations and often struck eminently satisfactory balances between these elements. They used their mode to create profound interpretations of life and brought the humanistic tradition to one of its highest levels.

The Impressionists departed from this tradition and mode in radical ways. Stylistically, they emphasized their preoccupation with color, light, and atmosphere, with visual rather than tactile sensations and with the infinite, intangible, and transitory aspects of the world instead of the more permanent and substantial. Their work echoed the ancient words of Heraclitus, "Nothing is permanent except change," and attested that momentary impressions of the changing world comprise our truest perceptions—hence the name "Impressionism" that was given to their art by their contemporaries. All their technical means were directed toward the intense expression of these interests and this conception of man's experience with the world, for which they developed a novel and striking manner of painting. In the field of content their predominant interest was in nature; their attitude toward human life and its more serious problems was one of neutrality or indifference. Thus in style, technique, content, and outlook Impressionism was a recognizably different mode of painting.

The principal masters of this movement were French. The movement has therefore been commonly credited to the French Impres-

sionist school. It spread, however, to international proportions.
The French master who exemplifies the impressionist mode and
point of view most consistently is Monet, the painter of *Marée
Montante à Pourville* (Fig. 137). His friends recognized his complete and able commitment to a visual point of view when they said
of him "He is only an eye—but what an eye!"

But Monet's eye was selective. He saw only color, movement,
and light. He had little or no interest in the contours, masses, and
surface textures of forms. Judging by his paintings, his impressions
had small room for the solid world. We can only deduce that his
tactile sense was as weak as his visual sense was acute. He is that
rare historical phenomenon, an artist who was perfectly attuned to
the major outlook of his time.

Monet's devotion to transitory lights and colors at the expense of
forms is illustrated by his well-known paintings of haystacks. Caring
nothing whatever about the form or meaning of haystacks as such,
he regarded them only as reflectors of colored light. As far as he was
concerned, they were as neutral as mirrors, so he did nothing to
represent any of their lasting characteristics. His secondary interest
was in the veil of atmosphere which surrounded the haystacks. The
haystacks themselves were nothing more than objects which blocked
the colored light passing through that veil and had, in fact, no
permanent hues or local colors of their own. The noonday sun or
sunset which glowed on their surfaces was all that mattered. This,
obviously, is the worship of appearances carried to the limit.

Monet was interested in ideas of a subtle kind—the all-pervading
character of light as distinct from the specific meaning of single
forms. His impressionist eye deduced a comprehensive meaning in
the world-wide life of the atmospheric veil where light and weather,
the days and nights, and the seasons act out their endless drama. To
him this stirring play of light was full of a vitality which he conveys
unmistakably through his paintings. If Monet was devoted to the
impermanent and superficial, he was also devoted to the universal.
The only reasonable charge against him is extremism. Lacking the
balance that is found in the greatest artists, he pushed his interests
too far. Consistent he was, but in an excessive way.

Typical impressionist paintings can be found in Figs. 137-139, an
analysis of which will help us understand Impressionism better.
They fall into two distinct types, in keeping with two interests of
Impressionism which cannot always be represented at the same time—
the love of both the reposeful and the dynamic aspects of the infinite
world. Turner gave us an excellent example of the dynamic in his
Rain, Steam and Speed; and Monet, who became acquainted with

FIG. 137. Monet. *Marée Montante à Pourville. ca.* 1882. Brooklyn Museum.

FIG. 138. Renoir. Detail, *Umbrellas.* 1883. National Gallery, London.

FIG. 139. Whistler. *The Lagoon, Venice: Nocturne in Blue and Silver.* 1880. Museum of Fine Arts, Boston.

Turner's art during a visit to London in 1870, continued the same tradition in the full-fledged impressionist manner. In Whistler (Fig. 139) we find an artist using Impressionism to suggest a more reposeful infinity.

Every portion of Monet's *Marée Montante à Pourville* expresses the infinite world in motion through a love of the indefinite carried to extreme. The scene represents a storm-lashed ocean viewed from a promontory. It conveys little sense of the solid earth, but a sharp impression of space and of a sea extending to a faintly indicated horizon. The tangible is neglected, the intangible and active stressed. Outlines in the older sense are merely implied by the sketchiest of strokes. Form is even more vaguely defined. With no boundaries and little modeling to detain it, the eye moves continuously from area to area. This is what Monet intended, for by it he gains a sense of movement throughout the picture. We may not feel any solidity in the cliff, but we have a vivid impression of wind and racing waves, of salt air, spray, and whitecaps. We are convinced that the boats are not where they were a minute ago or will be a moment hence, that the waves are constantly changing their shapes, that the tall grass on the cliff's edge is bowing and bending before the wind. Such action cannot help playing strongly upon our imaginations.

Monet achieves this effect by means which are logical for his purpose. Knowing that anyone in the presence of a similar scene would have an impression of a powerfully pervasive movement but would see few details, he paints accordingly, describing nothing carefully, but creating a unified effect of color, light, and atmosphere in motion.

Just as he employed broken outlines and sketchy modeling in his avoidance of the definite and static, Monet also handled color in a broken and indefinite fashion. He applied strokes of pure color directly to the canvas and relied on the eye to mix them optically. No form has anything resembling its permanent local color, nor has any form a color within boundaries of its own. The colors are shot through with strokes which represent light. The darkest shadows glow with many hues. In this unbounded scene there is a continuous movement of color from one area into another, unifying the picture as threads unify a tapestry or textile.

John Ives Sewall has wisely called the impressionist mode the most realistic in history, because it comes the closest to normal vision. Most of our observations in life are only blurred impressions; rarely do we examine anything in minute detail. The microscopic inspection of every hair on a head by a Van Eyck is therefore super-realistic, while Monet's general impressions reflect a more usual human experience. The danger, as Sewall adds, is that they will be that and nothing more, the premise being that artistic vision should clarify and intensify experience, not merely duplicate it. Monet avoided this danger.

To do so he used broken color in a highly arbitrary way, his purpose being to achieve a consistent type of color vibration which creates pictorial unity on the one hand and captures the vitality of nature on the other. He juxtaposed strokes of yellow and blue to represent green grass, but also introduced hundreds of red strokes in a passage of green, because red, being the complementary of green, creates by contrast a high degree of color vibration. Since this color vibration is psychologically stimulating, it signifies vitality to the human mind and is not primarily representational. Rather, it is an arbitrary artistic device. The *Marée Montante à Pourville* contains scores of such color vibrations. They are far more important than any use of broken color which aims merely at capturing the greenness of grass, for they give the picture its life and sparkle, as well as being stimulating. This use of broken color has representational merits: it is an excellent means of representing such natural phenomena as brilliant light, intense color, transparent shadows, mirror-like reflections, luxuriant foliage, water, snow, clouds, atmosphere, deep space, and moving forms; artistically it permits a high degree of continuity and pictorial unity while being, by its nature, a technique of great variety.

Because of its emphasis upon a comprehensive impression, the impressionist mode does not linger over details. It usually presents the world from a distance, only rarely from close up. Generalization of forms is therefore one of its recognized characteristics. A typical picture in the impressionist mode does not lend itself to close inspection and is best seen at a distance. A small section of a painting of *Umbrellas* (Fig. 138) by Renoir illustrates this common characteristic. Rendered with an incessantly moving brush, its soft and hazy forms may remind us of the painting of Velasquez, but are far removed from anything by the super-realistic Van Eyck. Whereas the Fleming's paintings always tempt us to get as close as we can, those of Renoir and Monet induce us to back away for the best appreciation.

While Monet was demonstrating the capacity of the impressionist mode to represent the infinite dynamically, a contemporary American of keen mind but calmer spirit was measuring its range in the opposite direction. In a series of nocturnes Whistler used the impressionistic mode to represent the infinite in repose. A good example of his work in this vein is the *Lagoon, Venice; Nocturne, Blue and Silver* (Fig. 139). It is as placid and still as Monet's *Marée Montante à Pourville* is dynamic. The hush of night has descended over everything; the water of the lagoon is unruffled; outlines are blurred, details indistinguishable, and forms as soft as velvet. The psychological effect is soothing.

To get this effect Whistler used melting brush strokes instead of the sketchy technique of the more excitable Monet. Yet Whistler's *Nocturne* is impressionist in its indefiniteness; the indefiniteness is only due to a different cause. The indefiniteness of Monet's marine is due to the combined effect of rapid movement and deep space, that of Whistler's *Nocturne* to the obscuring effect of night and space.

In these two paintings Monet and Whistler showed their daring, the French artist by making the static art of painting alive with movement, the American by painting a subject which had hitherto seemed unpaintable. For centuries artists had avoided the representation of unmitigated nighttime. When they did paint it, as Correggio did in his *Holy Night* and Goya in his *Execution of the Madrileños,* they used it as a foil for brilliant illumination.

By deliberately painting the three conditions which put human vision at the greatest disadvantage—rapid movement, lack of light, and deep space—and favoring the intangible at every turn, Monet, Whistler, and the other Impressionists pursued the infinite nearly to the vanishing point and brought the history of pictorial painting, of which Impressionism was the final stage, to its conclusion. After Impressionism there was nothing more to be exploited in its field of study. Like realism, it had served its historical purpose. So, daring and successful as the impressionist mode was, it inevitably gave way before other modes as new times and new artistic needs arose.

Today, if one visits a large exhibition of French impressionist paintings by Monet and his colleagues, he is likely to be impressed by their air of spontaneous vitality. The spontaneity is due to the prevalent sketchiness of the impressionist technique; the gaiety to their general colorfulness. Bright and cheerful colors are the norm in impressionist art. On this score few modes have ever been more visually delightful; they are commonly a feast for the eyes. The esthetic pleasure that this mode gives is, however, specialized; it favors the visual sense at the expense of the tactile. So, too, does its interpretation of reality. The infinite is stressed to the extreme neglect of the finite. Yet we must admit that it fulfils its own purposes well.

Because they favor general impressions rather than close observations, the paintings at an impressionist exhibition will present few examples of narrative illustration; this manner of painting is not specific enough to tell stories well. On the other hand, it is ideal for the expression of moods. Monet's *Marée Montante* and Whistler's *Nocturne* are excellent illustrations of Impressionism's capacity for stimulating our senses to awe and excitement or soothing them into rest.

At an impressionist exhibition we will be struck by the emphasis upon landscapes, marines, and other natural scenes and by the large number of scenes from everyday life. The mode lent itself to that kind of painting. Conversely, we note an absence of religious art and all other philosophical quests into man's troubles and problems. Since it is unreasonable to expect human beings to be serious and gay at the same time, we can admit the philosophical shallowness of most impressionist painting without condemning it. Instead, let us be glad that for about three decades in the nineteenth century artists felt carefree and painted with joy. Such respites from care have been brief in human history. The following decades saw to it that artists returned to a more sober conception of our world. With this change in times the modern modes appeared.

THE MODERN MODES

Western painting has been marked by four radical changes in style during the past two thousand years. The first came at the beginning of the Middle Ages; the second with the Renaissance; the third with the post-Renaissance baroque, with Impressionism as an outgrowth; and the fourth came with modern art. History may record that the last-named brought the most radical changes of all.

It would be premature to speak now of a single modern mode. Far from being sterile, our time has been tremendously productive and has given artists an unprecedented freedom of individuality. Often there seems to be a different style for every artist, numbering into the thousands. One could easily believe that individual expression has come to be the only thing that counts. Lacking the benefit of historical perspective, we cannot know absolutely which artists and stylistic common denominators future generations will deem to be the most important and representative. What we can now do easily for the Renaissance is extremely difficult to do for our own day. Of only one thing can we be certain: future appraisals will probably differ from our own.

Yet there is much that we can safely say. Our century has been one of the most self-conscious in history and one of the most articulate. It has devoted millions of words to self-analysis. By the law of averages many of them must have found the mark.

A consensus has gradually emerged which outlines the common denominators of the modern modes and their history. This is as much as we can expect when a movement is still at an indeterminable point in its history. Since so much has been written on this subject, the following will only attempt to present the points on which there is general agreement.

First, there is agreement about the origin of the modern modes. They were born out of a reaction against two expressive forms of the Renaissance and post-Renaissance periods—the realistic mode and the impressionist mode—which had reached the end of their useful lives. They can therefore be regarded as reacting against certain stylistic excesses of the nineteenth century and against a trend which had reigned in Europe for nearly four hundred years. The latter interpretation conveys something of the magnitude of the revolution.

There is also agreement about the dating of the movement. Although Impressionism enjoyed international popularity as late as 1920, the reaction against it began in the 1880s and continued to overlap it to the present day. Two main subdivisions coincide roughly with the two centuries which modern art has embraced, and several subdivisions have been created by two world wars and the decades between them. In short, though Impressionism and modern art have continued to live side by side, the former has come to be taken for granted, while the latter has inspired all the battle cries and creative vitality of the younger artists.

We cannot know the ultimate masters of the modern modes or whether some genius yet unborn will synthesize the many modes into a single mode with the assurance of a Michelangelo or a Raphael. But there is already agreement about the leadership of the modern movement up to the present. The pioneers of the reaction were three French masters, Seurat, Cézanne, and Gauguin, and a Dutch artist, Van Gogh, who worked mainly during the last two decades of the nineteenth century. Then, in the first decade of the twentieth century, their leadership was confirmed and their gospels spread by a second wave of younger men who are also identified with the French school—Matisse, Rouault, and Picasso, the latter an incredibly gifted Spaniard. Following in their train has come an army of artists who make one point clear: the modern movement started by Cézanne and a few of his contemporaries has carried the day, beyond the slightest doubt.

There is no mystery, either, about the general stylistic direction that representation has taken since the inception of the movement. Born as a reaction against the excesses of latter-day realism and Impressionism, it has been antimaterialistic in attitude and anti-infinite in form. The return to the finite has been one of its most prominent characteristics. In practical terms this has meant a revival of something close to the mode of line and local color and the sculpturesque mode of the Renaissance and earlier times. While reacting against the recent past, the modern leaders found reassuring precedents in the art of the distant past. We found this resemblance to an older point of view in Cézanne's portrait of *Louis Guillaume* (Fig. 127) and in Matisse's *Odalisque with Raised Arms* (Fig. 123). A similar respect for clarity of outline or definite modeling or both is apparent in the paintings of Rouault, who was influenced by medieval stained glass windows, of Dali *(The Persistence of Memory,* Fig. 53), and of the noted Mexican, Diego Rivera, who early gravitated toward the art of Giotto. Picasso's art has shifted back and forth between both modes, his *Woman Ironing* (Fig. 45) being sculpturesque and his *Guernica* (Fig. 1) an example of the mode of line and local color.

Another striking instance of the return to the finite is found in the art of Van Gogh and Gauguin. When the two men attempted to live and paint together at Arles in 1889, Gauguin soon discovered that their temperaments were completely incompatible; he was seeking balance and repose, while Van Gogh seemed uncontrollably dynamic. Gauguin's *Mahana No Atua* (Fig. 141) and Van Gogh's *Sunset over a Plowed Field* (Fig. 140) appear to confirm this conflict. Yet the two artists had more in common than Gauguin realized. Both had a profound respect for the descriptive value of outlines and the appeal of decorative patterns. Each was a composer who designed with clear-cut parts. Each employed a uniform illumination which denotes an appreciation of nature's long-range attributes. In spite of Van Gogh's representation of a sunset, his conception of sunlight has little in common with Monet's; he is concerned with the sun as a symbol of energy, not with its fleeting visual aspects. In Gauguin's picture the exact hour of the day is inconsequential. This joint concern with long-range values makes the art of Van Gogh and Gauguin resemble the Renaissance point of view more than the impressionist.

Without discarding the merits of the visual sense—Van Gogh retained the broken-color technique and became famous as a colorist in his own right—the modern pioneers re-established the claims of the tactile sense and restored some of the balance that Impressionism had lost. The human figures in Gauguin's *Mahana No Atua* suggest three-dimensionality subtly but unmistakably. It remained, how-

FIG. 140. Van Gogh. *Sunset over a Plowed Field*. 1889. Collection of Dr. Robert Oppenheimer, Princeton.

FIG. 141. Gauguin. *Mahana No Atua*. "The Day of the God." 1894. Art Institute of Chicago.

ever, for Cézanne to retrieve the position of the tactile values with an irresistible power, for he was by nature as highly endowed in that sense as Giotto and Michelangelo. When Cézanne revived the art of composing with three-dimensional forms, and Gauguin with beautifully decorative pattern-like figures, they turned modern art away from the impressionist conception of pictorial unity and set it on a path which is at once new and mindful of the classical past.

Gauguin, Van Gogh, and Cézanne had other attitudes in common which were obscured by momentary personal conflicts. They were religious in their own ways. Van Gogh's almost literal exemplification of Christianity is well known; Gauguin's religious outlook is less so. His sophisticated, cynical, hard-boiled exterior concealed a craving for human decency, naturalness, and the simple verities which drove him from Paris to the South Seas. Each man was seeking an affirmation of the importance of inner qualities which he could not find in the impressionist or realistic painting of his day. To each the spiritual values were paramount.

Cézanne was no less antimaterialistic in his own way. Though not conventionally religious or spiritually minded, he scorned the superficial materialism of his time. He had no interest whatever in the play of temporary light effects on the surface textures and peculiarities of detail in any scene or still-life group he was painting, but only in their basic forms and compositional relationships. If his interest was mainly formal, it was like Gauguin's and Van Gogh's devoted to the finite and permanent, the universal and continuous.

Our unprecedented freedom permits artists to paint only to please themselves; there are no patrons like the Renaissance popes and princes or the post-Renaissance monarchs to give them a common direction. Varied personal interests have given rise to hundreds of hybrid styles, one emphasizing outlines, another sculpturesque form, and a third mixing the two. It is a wonder that there is any unity of style whatever. And yet there is. The return to the finite is too universal to be missed—in Dali's *Persistence of Memory*, Sheeler's *American Landscape,* Mondrian's abstractions, and scores of other typical modern paintings.

The underlying unity of outlook expressed through the modern modes derives from a cultural environment whose main characteristics are agreed upon despite its extreme complexity. There is, for example, agreement upon the tremendous role the artistic orientation has played in modern art, accounting for much of its old-new character. This was hardly avoidable. No artists in history have had the past spread out before them and explained so completely as those of our own day. Museums, books, scholarly research, and color reproductions have made it almost impossible for an artist to be ignorant of the past. Matisse, Picasso, and their colleagues can roam the worlds of space and time. Under these circumstances it is little wonder that the work of almost every modern artist reminds us not so much of an immediate predecessor, as Rubens reminds us of Titian, but of some ancient or far-away source of inspiration. To limit one's horizons to the recent past is now considered provincial. If this historical consciousness is not new—witness the Renaissance's revival of antiquity—our time has carried it to an unprecedented extreme. But this does not make us characterless, because the historical consciousness of art merely reflects a similar consciousness in ourselves. Thanks to the increase in knowledge and in its dissemination, we are a historically conscious people.

In our fascination with the past we have been selective, revealing ourselves by our choices. Unlike the citizens of the Renaissance, we care little for classical mythology; the rebellion against the classical learning of our Victorian fathers has carried into the studio as well as the classroom. Neither do we share the Baroque period's fervent interest in Christianity; religious subjects are rare in painting today. Yet we are not without a religious outlook. The social compassion, the feeling for the dignity and brotherhood of man, and the wrath against injustice which run throughout the work of Orozco and Rivera are essentially religious. In fact, they transcend anything the late nineteenth century created in that field.

Self-consciousness has made our artists devote themselves to the contemporary as zealously as to the past. Two world wars have shaken our faith in material progress as the original way to happiness and brought much soul-searching. A grave time of troubles has made the twentieth century more introspective than the nineteenth; at the same time psychoanalysis has given us new techniques of precise inquiry. The psychological elements loom large in twentieth-century art, and the largest element in that inner life seems to be a combination of guilt and despair. The so-called "cult of miserablism" is not the figment of a critic's imagination. Sin and misery permeate the art of one of our most powerful modern painters, Rouault, outweighing the exceptional hedonism of that rare and happy master Matisse. Thus if any considerable group of twentieth-century paintings is set beside a number of impressionist pictures, the Impressionists will seem complacent, naïve, and carefree; the moderns introverted and serious to the point of grimness.

The best known artistic product of this introspective orientation has been surrealism. And the most striking characteristic of that movement has been the use of finite modes of painting. The extreme clarity of outline and form and the complete lack of atmosphere in Dali's *Persistence of Memory* illustrate this desire for finiteness. Offhand it seems strange to delineate dreams and subconscious thoughts sharply, but it is understandable if we remember the universal desire of science to make the infinite as clear as day. Surrealism merely reflects the aims of psychoanalysis.

Paralleling this search for precision in understanding the workings of the human mind is one of the contradictions of our age—an attraction to the wild, morbid, and sadistic. Our time is in rebellion against two characteristics of the Victorian era which came to be regarded as hypocritical under the impact of the First World War: faith in man's rationality and in social sweetness and light. Freud and his followers laid bare the mental jungle at which Stevenson hinted in *Dr. Jekyll and Mr. Hyde,* revealing its monstrosity in detail; and the First World War exposed hidden cruelties on a universal scale. The effect has been to infect the vitality of our time with nervous agitation, making it a high-strung age. Music has reflected this rebellion in two ways, through the cultivation of dissonances and the universal adoption of the high emotional pitch and pulsating rhythms of African music in jazz. No century in history has courted nervous tension and irrationality more assiduously than ours. We are both fascinated and repelled by it. Picasso's *Guernica,* Dali's surrealistic paintings, Rouault's religious pictures, and the whole school of Dadaism are but typical examples of the hypnotic spell that has been cast over us by the bestial, neurotic, and psychopathic in man.

Another point on which there is general agreement is the need for simplicity in our complex and overwrought time. This craving for streamlining can be seen in the way we have turned to the past in the arts of primitive and Asiatic peoples. African masks, South Sea idols, and Japanese prints served the double purpose of providing models with exotic backgrounds and simple but excellent formal values. Most artists have discovered the weird fascination of primitive idols in museums, far from their original contexts; Gauguin, however, sought them out in their native settings before he included them in such canvases as his *Mahana No Atua.* He was one of the first of modern artists to do this, but his followers have been numerous.

Beside the simplicity of primitive art, modern artists liked the novelty of its mysterious religious ideas and its sure esthetic sense in design. The latter appeased an appetite that had been starved by the indiscriminate complexity of nineteenth-century realism and the excessive softness of Impressionism. The clean forms and bold rhythms of primitive art filled a hunger among modern artists for virility and clarity of design and representation. And, once again, these qualities were regained through a return to the finite, for primitive art is universally phrased in terms of lines and local colors or sculpturesque forms.

The impact of the primitive modes upon modern art reinforced a trend that had been gathering momentum through the 1880's and 1890's—the form for form's sake, or the art for art's sake movement. What this means in everyday terms is a heavy emphasis on design, almost to the exclusion of other interests. The pioneers of the modern modes—Cézanne, Gauguin, Seurat, and Van Gogh—all had in common a keen interest in formal organization. The manipulation of outlines, colors, textures, and forms was never for them merely a means of representing some physical object or scene imitatively.

Indeed, one of the cardinal tenets of modern art has been the cry for freedom from any sacred obligation to nature, probably as a reaction against the nineteenth century's subservience to nature. According to the modernists there is no reason except habit why art should not be governed by its own esthetic laws. Their premise is that man creates art for man alone.

In fact, modern art has shown in its reaction against the nineteenth century a hostility toward the naturalistic orientation of that time. While highly conscious of humanistic problems, it has displayed a noticeable indifference toward the natural scene. Though Van Gogh, Seurat, and Cézanne continued the naturalistic interests of their generation, the principal subsequent masters have not. Matisse, Rouault, Picasso, Braque, Rivera, Mondrian, Sheeler, and Dali could not be called landscape painters by any stretch of the imagination.

It is therefore not strange that the signs of a naturalistic orientation of perception have disappeared from the main stream of modern art. No major artists of our time have been interested in the natural effects of luminosity and atmosphere that enthralled Monet. They have concentrated on man, as a tangible, finite, physical object. For this purpose outline, color, and modeling have been sufficient and appropriate.

A movement which has felt little obligation toward the natural landscape, but a great deal toward the integrity of art, it has also felt free to pursue nonrepresentational modes. Hence abstraction has been carried further in our day than at any previous time. This freedom from any apparent connection with nature would seem to carry us outside the limits of representation, were it not for the fact that it had its conscious beginning in the art of Cézanne and was advanced by the art for art's sake movement within the representational framework. Mondrian's paintings are but the end results of a tendency to give design precedence over representation until all natural sources are distilled from the picture. What remains, in the opinion of the modern abstractionists, is the pure essence of reality. We need hardly point out the role that the prestige and example of science has played in furthering this tendency toward analysis to the nth degree. The principal danger is that art will not only lose its natural roots but its emotional basis too. It is safe enough for science to be purely intellectual; but one suspects that something precious is lost when art becomes that way too.

When twentieth-century artists have not "gone abstract" they have often departed from nature in another way by returning to an ideological symbolism. While Cézanne and Matisse were more interested in design than ideas, the majority of modernists have been profoundly concerned with meaning. Van Gogh, Gauguin, Rouault, Rivera, Orozco, and Dali are examples of artists who thought long about the significance of content. Whether their interest was due to a reaction against the hedonistic philosophical poverty of Impressionism or not, they at least wrestled seriously with the problems of their age. Picasso's *Guernica* is a prime example; it is an elaborate ideological analysis of the effect of war and tyranny on human life, presented in allegorical form.

For the spectator the problem posed by modern ideological art lies in the modes of representation used. If this art reminds us of certain ideological art forms of the past, such as those of Egypt and the Middle Ages, it differs from them in one important respect. The older ideological expression was based on collectively recognized conventions which guaranteed communications. By contrast, the individual artists of our free Western societies employ no common conventions. Each contrives, instead, a private set of signs and symbols. Since laymen cannot or will not learn the separate languages of a dozen artists, communication often fails. In fact, frustration on the one hand and bewilderment on the other has been a mountainous obstacle to fulfilling the potentiality of modern art. Seldom in history has there been a greater gulf between many talented artists and a multitude of sincere but bewildered laymen.

No one can place the blame, but the question is crucial to the whole problem of artistic communication. If art is to be a language at all, it must have a reciprocal basis. And reciprocity always means a sacrificing of some individuality for the sake of common understanding. Our basic trouble is that we have abandoned the old conventions, meaning our Classical-Hebraic heritage of Junos and Josephs, without having yet agreed upon any ideas which will be universally meaningful.

But since the whole of Western society has joined in this rebellion in every walk of life, and two wars have created more social, religious, political, and moral conflicts than we have solved, we cannot fairly make artists the scapegoats for unintelligibility. Our world is in a state of ideological flux and ferment. Not until it makes up its own mind about its basic ideas and standards can any artists learn and employ them. Thus artists merely reflect the lack of accepted formulae which marks our period. Up to the present time we have traded agreement for individuality, and no leader has yet appeared who is strong enough to persuade us in any other direction or show us the way out of our dilemma.

One consequence of our freedom is easy to see. Owing to the uninhibited freedom demanded by artists and all the rest of us in our day, explorations have proceeded at a dizzy rate in hitherto uncharted fields. One of them, the field of inner reality, we have mentioned; another is the subvisible field of external reality. By using scientific aids to vision, like microscopes and stroboscopes, artists have revealed fascinating infinitesimal forms and equally interesting aspects of motion. One picture by Marcel Duchamp of a *Nude Descending the Staircase* anticipated stroboscopic photography and has become one of the most noted pictures of the twentieth century. These explorations have proved how far free artists can advance the content of art.

A wartime convoy at sea proceeds at the rate of the slowest ship. Its progress represents the orderly and safe but slow advance of collective art. If, suddenly, all the ships of the convoy were given leave to push forward at their own speeds, some would outstrip the group by many leagues, others would lag far behind.

Something like this has happened in our free society; the men of genius have been allowed to set their own pace. Consequently, many of them have gone so far beyond the crowd that the rest of us have temporarily lost sight of them altogether. Whether they will pause long enough for our appreciation to catch up with them remains to be seen.

Up to the present time modern artists, heady with freedom, have been more concerned with advancing at their utmost speed than with finding a common past. Their individualistic method has been, like that of science, to divide and conquer. Artists like Picasso have shifted gears and turned in new directions faster than a taxi in Manhattan traffic. As a result, they have accumulated a greater stockpile of ideas and representational modes than we can assimilate for many years to come. Like science, they must now pause to synthesize some of these discoveries if we are not to be lost in a chronic state of change.

The time for a coordinating pause arises in the history of every dynamic movement. A perfect precedent is the evolution of Renaissance art. The fifteenth-century masters were no less free, individualistic, active, and specialized than our own. And they would have produced a similar confusion had not men of the stature of Da Vinci, Michelangelo, Raphael, and Titian appeared in the early sixteenth century to tie the many loose ends together. That synthesis has not yet been achieved in the twentieth century, but the need for coordination is plain. The future of the modern modes will depend upon whether the synthesis is accomplished.

Yet, without having arrived at a uniform style, the modern modes have shown prominent characteristics. Representationally the majority of artists have committed themselves to one or another finite mode. They have shown a searching interest in lines and forms and an equal interest in color. While retaining the broken-color technique of the Impressionists, they have contained it within finite boundaries. Conversely, their interest in realistic atmosphere, illumination, and textures has been secondary. As a result, their mode of composition resembles the Renaissance outlook more often than it does the Baroque pictorial; it is a composition of definite parts rather than a continuous unity.

In their concern with content large numbers of modern artists have returned to ideological and symbolical means of expression; but whereas all previous ideological and conventional systems have been socially collective, ours are individual and personal. Second, a significantly large number of artists has turned to the field of human psychology for subject matter, while neglecting the natural landscape. Nor have they shown any greater disposition to continue the time-honored classical and religious themes. Yet, if Aphrodite and the Apostles are conspicuous for their absence, a powerful strain of human compassion is evident. In the third place, a very large number of modern artists has turned to purely abstract painting and has pursued it to a degree that is unprecedented in history. This is perhaps the most unusual feature of all modern painting. Finally, regardless of form or content, modern artists as a body have been in rebellion against the more conventional concepts of beauty handed down from antiquity. They want to be free of Praxiteles and Raphael. Often their impatience suggests revolt for revolt's sake. Nevertheless, only the completely hidebound can miss the beauty that modern artists have created, whether or not we have the critical norms to explain it.

It is too early to assess the long-range merits and limitations of the modern modes. Yet we can already be sure of certain accomplishments. The modern movement has produced a galaxy of brilliant colorists. Van Gogh, Gauguin, Cézanne, Matisse, Rouault, and Picasso can surely vie with any of the old masters in the pleasure their colors give us. The movement has also given us some of the outstanding linear artists of all time. Picasso's mastery of line, to mention only one example, is second to none. Cézanne is, without the slightest doubt, one of the most distinguised composers who has ever manipulated forms and colors within a picture frame; and Gauguin, Van Gogh, and Matisse rank among the great inventors of decorative patterns.

These accolades are not merely subjective acclaims, but are based on a clearly recognizable characteristic of modern art—its capacity for giving new vitality, intensity, and clarity to old forms. We can see this concretely in Van Gogh's *Sunset over a Plowed Field* (Fig. 140) and Gauguin's *Mahana No Atua* (Fig. 141). Each has the old-new look of most modern pictures save the abstractions. The Van Gogh reminds us of Japanese prints and the Gauguin of ancient primitive art. Yet no one would confuse them with either, and few would deny that they are somehow more exciting. For all of its resemblance to the ancient mode of line and local color, Gauguin's painting contains just enough modeling to give contrast to the flatness of the general design. It is a hybrid mode, but an effective one. A more important characteristic still is the rhythmic quality of the linear design; the curves which wind through the picture give it a life of its own. Beside it an ancient Egyptian painting like *Nakht Watching Plowing* appears flat and static.

An intense vitality runs through modern art which is consonant with, and does justice to, our dynamic age. Van Gogh simply intensified the old forms in a different way. His method was to combine perspective projection with the Impressionists' broken colors. That is, he hurtles us back into space while Gauguin guides us from side to side and backward in easy stages, much like the swinging of a slow-moving elephant's trunk. His recession is languidly graceful, as is proper for a scene of the South Seas. Van Gogh's, by contrast, is dynamic in the extreme. If one compares it to any previous example of projection, like Perugino's *Christ Delivering the Keys of Heaven to Saint Peter* (Fig. 102a) or Ruysdael's *Wheatfields* (Fig. 116), the increase in intensity which Van Gogh achieved by a new application of the impressionist mode can be fully appreciated. Certainly, it is a use of broken color that Monet never dreamt of. Only Baroque masters like Pozzo anticipated it at all, and to a lesser degree.

The effect the picture creates has been likened to a group of rifles firing tracer bullets into the distance at night. Such is the impression of speed that the dashlike strokes convey. By inventing such audacious methods Van Gogh raised both color vibration and perspective projection to a new high pitch. The intensification of old forms in keeping with the spirit of a more high-strung age has been one of the singular achievements of modern art, for meeting that emotional need required not only more emotion, but an even more precise artistic control. If the masters of the modern modes show ability along no other line than this they will have earned their place in history. In fact, there are many devotees who believe they have already earned it.

CHAPTER 11

Representation in Drawing

Our study of painting should enable us to understand the organization of representation in drawing without difficulty, because much of what we learned about painting applies to drawing. There are, however, three important differences in drawing. There is less emphasis upon color or, to be more exact, hues. Lines and values are the strong point of pencils, pens, and etching needles. Secondly, drawing utensils are generally hard and pointed, whereas the brushes of the painter are frequently broad and soft. Consequently, one gets a different feeling from using them, and this difference is felt by anyone who is technically sensitive. Finally, drawing cannot capture either the textural or substantial qualities of forms to the same extent as painting. Nor does its common foundation, paper, have the body of canvas, panel, or fresco. By comparison drawings are light and fragile. This lesser materiality reduces its appeal to the tactile sense, as its lesser command of hues reduces its appeal to the visual. Nevertheless, some of the most rewarding works of art in the world are in the form of drawings.

As for similarities, drawing and painting are closer to each other than either is to sculpture or architecture. Thinking alike, the painter and the draftsman have employed kindred modes of representation under similar historical conditions down through the centuries. The principal ones, which we shall designate with an inevitable arbitrariness, are the following modes: *linear, sculpturesque, realistic, pictorial, impressionist,* and *modern.*

The coincidence of these modes with those employed in painting will be apparent. The linear mode, like the mode of line and local color, appeared first. The rest have histories approximating roughly their namesakes in painting.

Our analysis of painting will help us in other ways too. A painter who thinks in terms of one kind of organization when standing before his easel will think in similar terms when he is at his drawing-board. So true is this that we expect Michelangelo to draw much as he painted. If he is interested in massive human figures in the one, he will not shift to a love of light and shadow in the other. His media may change, but his personality does not. Similarly, a baroque artist who unites the pictorial mode with aerial projection on canvas would hardly employ geometric projection when he works on paper. This consistency is a great convenience for us. It allows us to see the patterns and common denominators, the trends and similarities, in an always complex history.

Finally, the modes of drawing have approximately the same representational merits and limitations as their counterparts in painting. These determine their expressive capacities, because a painter who conceives the world in finite terms will also conceive it finitely when he turns to drawing. The media change, but the personality and outlook expressed through them remain constant.

THE LINEAR MODE

Like its counterpart in painting, the linear mode is the oldest method of drawing. It has been used by the same people who used the mode of line and local color and at the same places and times throughout history. Children begin their drawing with it today, as the cave artists did in ancient times. The passage of centuries, the infinite enrichment of art, and even the many excellent new drawing media have not advanced the child's position in art; he still starts where the cavemen did.

The artist who employs the linear mode achieves his ends mainly by drawing the outlines of figures and their parts, and omitting all other descriptive data. He gives us the bare minimum of visual information about the object he has in mind; nevertheless he can do this in a perfectly consistent and orderly fashion. Indeed, unity of method is one of the merits of the linear mode.

This unity of method was well within the capacity of the cave artists, who drew surprisingly well. They possessed what children often lack, a just sense of proportional relationships. Mere outlines, in short, are not enough. A classic example of the prehistoric drafts-man's art is a *Mammoth* (Fig. 142) on the walls of a cave in France. The artist who drew this figure may have done so from a desire for success in the hunt or a need for religious protection from harm; his reasons do not concern us but his representation of an animal which

Fig. 142. *Mammoth*. Late Paleolithic Age, before 12,000 B.C. Combarelles Cave, Dordogne, France.

"Touché!"

Fig. 143. Thurber. *"Touché!"* Copyright, 1932, by James Thurber. Originally published in *The New Yorker*.

we can connect with a modern elephant does. For this artist conveyed visually the fact that, quite apart from all considerations of religion, magic, or hunger, he *saw a mammoth*. He drew a picture of it to communicate his experience to his fellow cave men, and his experience is still intelligible because we too can stand in awe before the spectacle of a huge beast which has a long trunk, ivory tusks, and a funny tail. Our elephants do not have the shaggy hair of the prehistoric mammoths, but they symbolize now, as then, the same kind of lumbering power. The cave artist imbued this drawing with his initial curiosity or fear when he first saw a mammoth, and his later awe or respect when he came to know its power. He indicated all of these reactions by a system of visual description. And that, in essence, is the purpose and merit of all representation in art; only the means change.

The means employed by the cave artist are of the simplest. Yet it is wonderful how much meaning they can convey, owing to our faculty for responding to their implications imaginatively. Being simple, this mode avoids the pitfalls of excessive complexity. Compared to some modes, it may seem to lack variety, but it possesses a high degree of unity and, more than this, clarity. So great is this clarity that it amounts to a vital intensification of sensation. In brief, the linear mode achieves a maximum effect with a minimum of means. No other mode is its superior in economy.

Any mode of drawing with these strong points would deserve the long life that the linear mode has had. It has remained in use from the beginning of art to the present day, hardly any century having failed to produce some outstanding practitioners, especially when men wished to express an idea which required succinct and economical statement, like the modern poster or cartoon. A delightful example of the latter is James Thurber's noted cartoon for the *New Yorker* magazine, *"Touché!"* (Fig. 143). A masterpiece of humorous understatement, the idea expressed must, if its wit is to be preserved, be stated with a few strokes, and this Thurber has done to perfection.

Thurber's subject was, of course, very different from that of the paleolithic artist who drew the mammoth, but the similarity of methods they employed is apparent, as are the merits which accrued to both. We can sum up these merits by asking one question: Would either of these drawings be any better if the descriptive data were more complete?

There is a second kind of drawing within the linear mode that implies more subtly three-dimensional forms. Although only a refinement of the original mode, it is an important refinement, for it permitted many centuries of growth and improvement within the mode. We find it first among the ancient Greeks, whose artists developed the decoration of vases and other pottery vessels with human figures to a high point. The Museum of Fine Arts, Boston, owns a typical but excellent example which depicts a youth and maiden on two sides of a white lekythos (Fig.144). The treatment of both figures implies a three-dimensional quality which was new in ancient drawing and was conveyed by outlines alone without any recourse to modeling.

This suggestion of a third dimension was achieved by varying the character of the lines in several ways. The delineation of the maiden will show how this is accomplished. The artist wished to imply that the arm toward the spectator, the torso, and the arm holding the vase existed in three separate, receding planes. He therefore darkened the outline of the closer forearm and softened the outline of the abdomen, especially where it appears to go behind the arm. Finally, he dropped off the lines of the farther arm before they met the line of the abdomen. Because dark lines and continuous lines seem to our eyes to be closer than weak or discontinued lines, the forms they describe appear separated in space into three planes. This is a system which can be applied to the representation of any objects in space; the Greeks discovered it at an early date and used it to marked advantage in the decoration of their vases. Their skill will seem all the more remarkable to anyone who has struggled and fumbled in an effort to draw one clean, simple line. It is one of the hardest things in the world to do, yet the Greeks made it harder still by drawing with a finely pointed brush—a mark of extraordinary manual coordination and steadiness.

Having devised a way of separating forms in space by the use of lines alone, the Greeks added a method for giving a sense of the volume and varying dimensions of single forms within a composition. Let us consider, for instance, the torso of the maiden. Instead of outlining it with a perfectly uniform line, the Greek artist varied the width of his line as he described the contour of the back. As the form swells and narrows the lines grow wider and thinner, meaning, in effect, darker and lighter. Their flowing, variable quality is thus made to suggest the similar qualities of a three-dimensional body. It is a remarkably simple but efficient method of capturing the undulating quality of a mass.

The efficiency of this system assured it a long and honorable history. The Orientals especially have made it a telling part of all their drawing and painting from ancient times to the present day. Since they committed themselves long ago to a continuous refinement of the mode of line and local color in painting, they have probably had

Fig. 144. *Youth and Maiden.* 4th century B.C. Greek white lekythos. Museum of Fine Arts, Boston.

Fig. 145. *Dwarf of Murad II.* Late 16th century. Fogg Museum of Art, Harvard University.

Fig. 146. Turner. *Martello Towers near Bexhill, Sussex.* June 1, 1811. Museum of Fine Arts, Boston.

271

as great an experience with delineation as any people in the world. The perfection which comes with practice can be clearly seen in a Persian drawing, the *Dwarf of Murad II* (Fig. 145), which dates from the sixteenth century. The lines which describe the figure are extremely precise and sharp, and they do their work well, owing to a perfect application of the system for implying form. The outlines which flow around the dwarf's rotund form grow thick with a protruding belly or an overstuffed pair of shoulders, but taper into nothingness as they define drapery folds which merge with the body of the cloth. The net effect is richly varied and three-dimensional.

The artists of the West have employed essentially the same method. Turner's drawing of *Martello Towers* (Fig. 146) illustrates the extent to which the Greek system of varied outlines can be used to represent forms in deep space, even suggesting the presence of atmosphere. His method was to darken the foreground lines quite heavily and then soften the lines progressively as he carries our eyes into the distance. He also dropped off lines where one plane recedes behind another, and reduced the outlines of the distant hills to a string of dots. In this way Turner carried the old Greek system for suggesting the three-dimensionality of forms and relating them in deep space to its ultimate development.

Judging by these typical examples, the linear mode has certain merits: the ability to create an intense and vitalizing sense of clarity and to do it with a great economy of means. It also has both unity and variety in ample measure.

Its limitations are like those of the mode of line and local color in painting; both, being highly finite, hardly touch the expression of the infinite. Turner's *Martello Towers* makes a beginning in this direction but little more. When he wished to create a truly infinite impression, he felt obliged to add to these etched lines a whole gamut of atmospheric and luminous values by means of mezzotint, a technique whereby tones are superimposed on an etching plate. The linear mode also fails to convey a strong sense of weight and mass. It does not stimulate tactile sensations. Nor is it, despite Thurber's delightful cartoon, the best possible means of representing rapid movement. In spite of its merits, the linear mode left the door open for other modes to enter and make up for its deficiencies.

THE SCULPTURESQUE MODE

The sculpturesque mode of drawing may be described as the linear mode in relief. In adding the property of relief, or three-dimensionality, it resembles the sculpturesque mode of painting. Its history is also similar. Motivated by the same desire for greater realism, it is largely identified with the art of the Renaissance, and especially with the years between 1400 and 1550. The Central Italian schools used it widely during that time and produced the largest body of outstanding practitioners of the mode that we have ever had. Consequently, the sculpturesque mode as practiced by the great Florentines of the fifteenth century has been accepted as the ideal of draftsmanship.

At the apex of this group there stands, not strangely, the same solitary giant who carried the sculpturesque mode of painting to its ultimate development in painting the Sistine ceiling. To study Michelangelo's many drawings for that heroic decorative project is to see the sculpturesque mode of drawing at its finest both technically and imaginatively. His drawings abound with that ingredient which gives life to any method—vitalizing inspiration. Nevertheless, inspiration must have its methods.

One of Michelangelo's drawings, a *Study of the Back of a Nude Male* (Fig. 147), is illustrated here as an object lesson in inspired method. The inspiration is hard to define, the method is not. Michelangelo set himself the task of describing the contours of a muscular male nude body as thoroughly as could be done with the resources of drawing. In so doing he defined the outer boundaries carefully, using all of the devices of the linear mode—flowing lines of varying widths which convey the undulating profile or silhouette. These lines alone would have suggested much of the body's mass. But unlike the strictly linear artists, who prize economy and rely upon implication, Michelangelo was not content with hints. He wanted to describe the figure's three-dimensional properties as finitely and completely as possible. Therefore, he searched out every rise and fall of muscle and flesh within the outer boundaries and described them by means of modeling—a method of rendering which, by grading from light to dark, creates an effect of rounded contours.

Michelangelo thus showed us so perfectly how to describe the main attributes of any form (i.e., the outlines and inner contours of a three-dimensional mass) that Pope has called his kind of drawing Form Drawing. We have chosen to call it sculpturesque in order to avoid the use of too many different terms and to call attention to its connection with the sculpturesque mode of painting.

The parallels between the two are worth attention. For example, Michelangelo employed modeling in a special way both in painting and drawing. He was interested in it solely as a means of capturing a feeling of massiveness. With him it is the round, tangible solid that counts in a strictly finite emphasis. He had little interest in any

FIG. 147. Michelangelo.
*Study of the Back of a
Nude Male.* For the
"Battle of Cascina." 1504-
1506. Albertina Collec-
tion, Vienna.

FIG. 148. Dürer. *Flight Into
Egypt.* 1503. Museum of Fine
Arts, Boston.

illumination or source of light that was external to the figure. In fact, none of the infinite intangibles held any appeal for him.

In his drawing, as in his painting, Michelangelo chose to concentrate on the human figure as the vehicle of his sentiments and sensations of reality. He stressed the tactile sense and empathic reactions. If he had been concerned only with the tactile sense, he might have continued to paint and draw in the manner of Giotto, whose draped human figures have the smooth and massive solidity of boulders. Michelangelo, a more emotional person, was aiming at a dynamic art. Like the Greeks, he loved the "life of the muscles." He therefore bent his energies to arousing in us a tactile response to masses per se and an emphatic reaction to straining muscles. By appealing to both sensations in high degree, he created an effect of great power which shows us the capacity of the sculpturesque mode for representing that particular kind of vitality.

Michelangelo's love of the nude was more than an unreasoning addiction; it showed the sureness of his artistic instincts in a way which carries a general lesson. By drawing the human figure he exploited its principal merit, the capacity for representing the finite. Concentrating his attention on human figures which, being close to our eyes, seem large and impressive, Michelangelo left the representation of nature and forms in deep space to others.

The universality of the sculpturesque mode during the Renaissance is illustrated by the work of the leading German artist of the sixteenth century, Albrecht Dürer. A northerner by birth and background, this contemporary of Michelangelo should have been most interested in nature and its infinite properties, for his was a Gothic heritage. But during the reign of the classical Renaissance to the south, the northerners followed Italy's lead. They compromised their interest in nature with the finite sculpturesque mode of representation, and concentrated for the time being on the representation of tangible forms.

A woodcut of the *Flight into Egypt* (Fig. 148) by Dürer illustrates this temporary subservience to the South. A picture of the out-of-doors, it depicts every natural detail with wire-sharp outlines. The effect is hard but intensely clear. It may properly be called sculpturesque because we can liken it to a relief carving with this qualification—it resembles the kind of wood sculpture that the Teutonic peoples have carved for centuries. Sharp-edged and highly complex, it is made up of many planes and minute details.

Obviously, this conception of the sculpturesque weakens the impression of mass and increases the sense of lines, just as if we were to decorate a perfectly plain sphere with many lines and patterns.

Though three-dimensional and sculpturesque, the work of Dürer is a linear version of the mode. In that respect he was well within his tradition, for whenever northern artists have subscribed to a finite conception of reality under some powerful historical influence, they have tended to express it in a fashion more linear than massive, thus adapting it to the northern point of view. Nevertheless, their method was finite and sculpturesque in point of view. Dürer showed how forms can be modeled expertly with linear means within the sculpturesque mode. Instead of modeling his forms by shading from light to dark with a soft crayon as Leonardo did, or cross-hatching with a pen as Michelangelo did (Fig. 147), Dürer made all of his descriptive lines flow in and out with the rise and fall of contours. If a series of parallel lines describes a concave surface, they loop in a downward curve; if a convex surface, they rise upward in concentric arches. The treatment of the undulating foreground in the *Flight into Egypt* provides a clear example of this method of describing form.

This method stands somewhere between the strictly linear mode of the Greek vase decorators and the sculpturesque drawing of Michelangelo. It must be heeded as the typical northern contribution to the Renaissance way of drawing, but it has neither the simple clarity of the ancient method nor the concentrated massiveness of the Italian. In any event, it was as specialized and finite a manner as Michelangelo's and so left room for the future development of other modes.

THE REALISTIC MODE

The post-medieval rediscovery of physical reality by the artists of the Renaissance created in the course of time a demand for completely realistic art, for the addition of three-dimensionality represented only one aspect of nature's characteristics. The achievement of fully realistic painting occurred in the seventeenth century. The development of a comparable realism in drawing took place almost inevitably at the same time.

The realistic mode of drawing, like its equivalent in painting, is based on a comprehensive appreciation of all physical properties equally. A drawing in this mode will therefore contain no apparent distortions of proportions and no obvious instances of arbitrary lighting. Rather, it will reflect the character of reality as accurately as can be done in drawing. Whereas textures are uniform or ignored in the linear and sculpturesque modes, distinctions of texture are carefully recorded in the realistic mode, attention being paid to make hair appear soft and metal hard. Respect for appearances is thus the guiding principle of the mode. Consequently, its examples include both the finite and the infinite components of any scene in the same proportion as they appear in actuality, but stress neither. It is the most inclusive but least selective of the modes, which means a high degree of variety but a weakened unity. By accepting natural diversity, the realistic draftsman runs the risk of including a confusing amount of detail.

The most serious limitation of the realistic mode is its lack of vitality of form. A complex method, it has little of the vivid clarity and impact of line, form, or illumination found in the other modes. It depends, instead, on content to stimulate vitality. Thus in this mode the artists deprived themselves of the vitalizing effect of treatment.

Nevertheless, the realistic mode has played a creditable role in art. An example of the mode which shows the high level of competence attained in the seventeenth century is the portrait of Louis XIV by Robert Nanteuil (Fig. 149). Closely resembling a photograph, it served much the same function in the days before the camera. Louis XIV, the most powerful monarch of his day, had innumerable political ties throughout Europe which required the support of duplicates of his image. Hence, a record of his appearance was needed for distribution, and Nanteuil, portraitist to the French Court, filled the need by engraving the likeness of Louis XIV and the more important personages at his court. The engraved plate could then be used to reproduce as many copies as were needed. There is no question about Nanteuil's ability to fulfil his intentions within these limitations. Hundreds of engravers have applied his method to the embellishment of various forms of paper money since his time, but few have ever surpassed him. If one wishes to draw realistically, this is the way to do it.

Realism of outlook and realism of expression have always gone hand in hand. The latter seems to thrive when people pride themselves on "facing the facts of life"—usually meaning its disagreeable and ugly sides. Consequently, realistic art is more often serious than gay. A certain morbidity in the troubled Baroque mentality favored the development of realism. Realism then slackened temporarily during the eighteenth century when the aristocratic patrons of art in France and England, the two most active nations of the time, sought more grace in living and thinking. Hogarth, as a consequence, had a difficult time selling his satirical pictures, while the elegant Sir Joshua Reynolds prospered.

The realistic mode came back into prominence in the nineteenth century with the return of a materialistic temper. Side by side with

FIG. 149. Nanteuil.
Louis XIV. 1670. Museum of Fine Arts,
Boston.

FIG. 150. Eakins. *Masked Nude Woman*. *ca.* 1882. Philadelphia Museum of Art.

the realistic painting taught at the French Academy it spread throughout Europe and America. Fig. 150, a drawing of a masked nude woman by Thomas Eakins, exemplifies the American version. Similar to scores of charcoal drawings executed by the young academicians at Paris, it is different only in its utter lack of grace. This is realism of both outlook and treatment with a vengeance. Eakins, a Philadelphian who studied under Gérôme at Paris, had a literal mind that refused to concede to beauty or alleviate ugliness in the slightest degree. If the model was gross and flabby, that is the way he depicted her.

There is a story associated with this drawing. Owing to his European training, Eakins naturally wished to give his own students at the Pennsylvania Academy of Fine Arts in Philadelphia some instruction in drawing from the live nude model. But because of the lingering puritanism of the Victorian period he was allowed to do this only if the model were masked!

The general similarity between Nanteuil's treatment and Eakins's need not be stressed, although the common denominator may be emphasized. Both artists, in keeping with most realists, expressed a keen interest in textures. Taken alone this is not a limiting interest, but, comparatively speaking, textures are the most superficial attributes of any tangible form. They fix our attention on the surface and prevent us from apprehending the form profoundly. Appealing to the finger-tip sense of touch, they obscure the deeper tactile values which affect our whole muscular systems. The realistic mode skims the surface of matter without penetrating it.

Nevertheless, so long as visual experience of the most ordinary kind gives pleasure to men, the realistic mode will not die, for it provides us with opportunities for recognition—a not-to-be-discounted pleasure among men—and at its best fulfils the call of art by intensifying our sensations of the world of textures.

THE PICTORIAL MODE

The realistic mode was an admirable method for materialists, but it did not satisfy the needs of men who prized spiritual values and ideas above physical characteristics. Similarly, the linear and sculpturesque modes suffered from certain limitations. Though the latter represented the essentials of the finite world superbly, it neglected the infinite side of nature and the human mind.

The pictorial mode was the answer to these deficiencies. A complement of, not a substitute for, the other modes, it placed as much stress on light, shadow, and atmosphere as the older modes had upon tangible outlines and forms. It did this, however, in a manner different from that of the seventeenth-century realists. Because illumination, shadows, and atmosphere were conceived to be expressive means rather than predominantly physical elements, they were placed at the service of the logical and imaginative creative faculties instead of the imitative. The artist altered them as he wished, darkening shadows and strengthening lights arbitrarily if, by doing so, he could express a thought or feeling more clearly and intensely.

The development of this attitude coincided with the trend toward pictorial painting in the sixteenth century and reached its culmination in the art of Rembrandt, who was to both pictorial drawing and painting what Michelangelo had been to the sculpturesque art of the Renaissance.

Rembrandt is now nearly as famous for his etchings as for his paintings; the most noted example of his skill in drawing is his *Christ Healing the Sick* (Fig. 151). It is also known as the "Hundred Guilder Print" because of the price it brought in later times. Rembrandt created this etching about 1650, when he was approaching the height of his own personal maturity after a number of misfortunes, and was obviously more concerned with conveying the meaning of Christ's message and his ministration to the poor, ill, and oppressed than he was with the imitation of physical appearances. An accurate record of light and shadow and textures would have been pointless compared to an imaginative interpretation. What was called for was intelligence, not a recording eye. This is not to belittle Nanteuil or Eakins, but it does say that neither, judging by their art, could have done what Rembrandt did.

Rembrandt's problem was to translate his conception of *Christ Healing the Sick* into visual terms. He did this partly by means of his treatment of forms, giving "the lame, the halt, and the blind" decrepit, broken bodies and bent-over postures. But he achieved his ends mainly by skilfully manipulating the intensities and distribution of light and shadow. A large portion of the picture is cast into shadow, with all that it connotes of ill-health and broken spirits. Many of the sick are almost lost in the gloom; the others emerge gradually into the light as they near the presence of Christ. The central figure of Christ is a symbol of healing power. Rembrandt stressed this idea by making Him glow with light as He stands against the shadowy background. A kind of halo radiates from His person. In this way Rembrandt made physical light stand for life and health, and shadow for disease. Played against each other in the design—the darkest shadows are near the brilliant figure of Christ—they enhance each other both visually and symbolically.

To the left of Christ and the horde of poor stands a small group of well-dressed skeptics who watch the scene. Christ seems to be

FIG. 151. Rembrandt. *Christ Healing the Sick.* "The Hundred Guilder Print."
ca. 1650. National Gallery of Art, Washington, D.C.

FIG. 152. Daumier. *Women Gossiping.* From "Actualités."
ca. 1839. Museum of Fine Arts, Boston.

turning in their direction and acting at least partially for their benefit. These men stand in the sunshine of good fortune, but are otherwise mentally ill, for their faces are mean, cynical, and malicious.

Because of this balance between form and illumination, episode and universal meaning, the *Christ Healing the Sick* is rich in content. One might say that it has a double significance, for it can be used to illustrate either the narrative or mood emotions. It presents a complex idea in a clear and balanced fashion. One can hardly overstress the advantage of this versatility in the pictorial mode.

Neither Rembrandt's specific idea nor his particular means were shared by all artists of the complex, individualistic Baroque period. Rubens painted and drew in another manner, as did Caravaggio, Van Dyck, Hals, Ruysdael, and El Greco; no one would confuse their paintings or drawings. Yet all worked within the framework of the pictorial mode. The framework was flexible; variety was its strong point. It permitted the realistic Caravaggio, the sensuously pagan Rubens, the infinitely subtle Rembrandt, the earthy Hals, the elegant Van Dyck, and the nervously imaginative El Greco to stress spirit or substance or strike a balance between the two according to their personal preferences and still stay within the bounds of the pictorial mode. As a result, Baroque art possesses a great variety of manners within an impressive unity of mode. Simply on its record of achievements, the pictorial mode is one of the finest we have ever had.

The many uses of the pictorial mode extended its popularity into the nineteenth century. The similarity between Daumier's lithograph *Women Gossiping* (Fig. 152) and Rembrandt's work is not accidental, for Daumier not only followed the pictorial tradition, but admired the art of Rembrandt, which he saw in the Louvre. Moreover, he employed the pictorial mode because of a similarity of aims. Like Rembrandt, he was more interested in the spirit of his idea than in the substance of his actresses. Wishing to capture the malevolence of these women who gather in the hall at night to gossip, he attained his end in two ways: by giving them vicious faces and illuminating these from below with candlelight which spreads weirdly upward over their features and casts eerie shadows on the wall behind. Three witches scheming at midnight could hardly be more evil-looking.

THE IMPRESSIONIST MODE

During the middle years of the nineteenth century European drawing, in unison with painting, steadily shifted its emphasis to the infinite until a climax was reached in the work of the Impressionists. Although this represented the logical outcome of a four-hundred-year-old tradition, it brought with it a point beyond which there could only be diminishing returns.

The life span of this final chapter was brief, the end quick. The first signs can be clearly seen in the art of Turner. Always devoted to the infinite aspects of nature, he stressed them to such an extreme in his last watercolors and drawings that forms seem dissolved in a sea of colored light and atmosphere. His art was, however, merely symptomatic of the universal interests which prevailed for about fifty years—the maximum momentum of the movement lasting from about 1840 to 1890. During that time France was the leading artistic nation of the Western world, so the impressionist movement has been associated largely with that school and its international followers. Impressionism, like realism, has always been latent in art; signs of it appear in some Roman paintings, in the late work of Titian, and unmistakably in Velasquez' art. But it was only in the nineteenth century that a large body of artists was finally conditioned psychologically and equipped technically to exploit fully the possibilities of the impressionist conception.

The conceptual basis of the impressionist mode can be easily defined: it rests on the belief that the transitory and infinite aspects of reality are of primary importance. When this philosophy is translated into visual terms it manifests itself in a paramount interest in the representation of two kindred types of subjects: those containing rapidly moving objects and those in which the infinite attributes of nature play a dominant role.

The Combat (Fig. 153) by Delacroix is an object lesson in the treatment of the first of these interests—the representation of rapidly moving bodies. Delacroix made this drawing after a trip to North Africa in 1832 with the French ambassador to Morocco. He apparently witnessed or heard about the life-and-death struggles of horsemen and wild beasts while there, and they so fired his imagination that he recreated a number of them on canvas and paper. Whether using a pencil or a brush, Delacroix employed the same technical device of broken outlines and sketchily rendered forms to record the eye's impression of violently struggling combatants. The manner of treatment gives the picture a vitality and variety which are commensurate with the theme at hand—a typical merit of this kind of impressionist drawing. Though repose is necessarily absent, orderliness is not, owing to the perfect consistency of Delacroix's handling.

In the hands of Delacroix, a devotee of the dynamic art of Rubens, the impressionist mode became an excellent method for the repre-

FIG. 153. Delacroix. *The Combat.* "An Arab Rider Attacked by a Lion." *ca.* 1834. Fogg Museum of Art, Harvard University.

FIG. 155. Van Gogh. *Cypresses.* *ca.* 1889. Brooklyn Museum.

FIG. 154. Whistler. *The Thames at Battersea.* *ca.* 1880. Museum of Fine Arts, Boston.

sentation of rapid action. At the same time it bore the seeds of the reaction against it, for it verges on the vague and wild—the love of vitality and fleeting movement being carried nearly to an extreme. Since little more could be safely attempted in this direction, it marked the end of a quest.

The Impressionists' concern with an infinite nature is seen in a lithotint from the hand of Whistler, an American who studied briefly with the French Impressionists at Paris and then became, for the rest of his life, the most controversial figure in British art. Taking for his subject a scene along one of his favorite haunts, the *Thames at Battersea* (Fig. 154), he rendered it in the manner of his painted nocturnes. While it would appear off-hand to have little in common with Delacroix's *Combat,* it expresses the same underlying concept of a transitory and infinite world, the emphasis, however, being on the infinite.

It is difficult to imagine how an artist could be more indefinite without becoming completely nebulous. Whistler's emphasis of a vague and soupy atmosphere at the expense of all tangible forms is appropriate to the representation of a nocturnal scene along the notoriously foggy and smoke-laden Thames. But this raises the question not of appropriateness of treatment, but of feasibility of subject. There is a sound reason why 90 per cent of all pictures represent the daytime hours. Though the night may have been "made for love," it is visually one of the most unrewarding of subjects. Claude Lorrain had put the sun in the sky; Whistler removed it. The effect was like dropping a curtain on a play, for light is essential to all visual experience. In his scenes of night Whistler brought to an end one aspect of the pictorial tradition by pursuing the infinite to the vanishing point.

The merits and limitations of Delacroix's and Whistler's impressionist approaches to reality can be summed up in terms of a few extreme satisfactions and equally extreme deficiencies. Delacroix's broken outlines and sketchy modeling create a feeling of great vitality. Whistler's blurred outlines and nebulous modeling create with equal success a feeling of perfect repose. The capacity of the one to stimulate and the other to soothe demonstrates the wide expressive range of the impressionistic mode and each, within his style, was orderly and consistent.

The extremity of these virtues created equally grave deficiencies. The impressionist interpretation of reality neglected the finite side of our world to an extent that could not be accepted indefinitely. Psychologically viewed, the swing of the pendulum to the infinite had been accompanied by a radical swing to the purely visual. When the tactile sensations were starved to that extent, it was time for a change. It came with the modern reaction.

THE MODERN MODES

The modern modes of drawing arose during the last quarter of the nineteenth century and have continued to the present. What historical stage they have now reached no one can say, but their origins are clear. They were created to correct the excesses and deficiencies of the impressionist mode and were probably meant to re-establish a more balanced outlook. As always, the pendulum tended to swing to the opposite extreme—but not quite.

The modern reaction did not retreat wholly into the past or carry art back to the point where it had started in early ancient times. While disclaiming the excesses of Impressionism, it retained its genuine merits. Out of these it created composite modes which combine old and recent styles in original ways and are to that extent new. Despite similarities with the past, nothing exactly like them can be found in the previous history of art.

Having discussed this phenomenon at length under the modes of painting, we can treat it summarily here, for no matter how bewildering the modern modes may be in other respects, they are consistent in having parallel objectives in both drawing and painting.

A brief examination of a drawing of *Cypresses* (Fig. 155) by Van Gogh should illustrate the modern point of view and methods. First of all, it exemplifies the most prominent common denominator of the modern modes—their return to a high degree of finiteness. This drawing of *Cypresses* is as nonatmospheric as Whistler's *Thames at Battersea* is murky. It does not contain any shadows or light source. Technically speaking it is linear, with a slight respect for mass. This suggests a deliberate return to the finite modes of prepictorial times, probably under the influence of Japanese prints. Yet the *Cypresses* also reminds us of Delacroix's *Combat;* each is, like the men who drew them, vital and dynamic. The difference is that Van Gogh was not drawing an impression of a rapidly moving object. He was depicting a scene which was in actuality as static as Whistler's *Thames at Battersea.* Using Delacroix's broken outlines merely as a device, he projected a personal love of vitality upon a quiet natural scene and endowed it with a completely imaginary activity.

So if he seems to have revived the ancient linear mode, he uses it in an unprecedented way, combining its finiteness with a dynamic conception. The similarity of his outlook to Delacroix's is equally deceptive. To Delacroix, the combat was very real. To Van Gogh,

the cypresses were only symbols of something even more important—
the vitality which he felt in the universe and within himself. He
therefore made no attempt to record individual appearances accurately and realistically. He must have felt that the nineteenth-century realists and Impressionists had both forsaken their conceptual
and creative powers in a pursuit of the material world, and that the
Impressionists especially had gone to an extreme in pursuing the
most fleeting and tangible aspects of that world. He sought to
restore the primacy of imagination, thought, and feeling, and also
to direct our attention back to the permanent and universal—not to
any single instance of vitality, but to the energy which pervades the
cosmos.

He did this in a new way, without trading on the finite-minded,
ideological ancients. In the *Cypresses* he employs a linear, finite
method and a static subject to express their opposites—vitality and
movement. This would be contradictory if he were recording our
ordinary sense perception of actual trees, but it is a highly effective
way of expressing a concept of cypresses which symbolize universal
energy. Van Gogh's cypresses writhe and twist as though some supernatural power were running through them.

This kind of thinking was not far-fetched. It merely anticipated
the appreciation of unlimited sources of power which the scientific
discovery of atomic energy has revealed to our time, making global
concepts of energy and limitless chain reactions an everyday idea.

The difference between the outlooks expressed through the drawings of Delacroix, Whistler, and Van Gogh only illustrates a revolution in artistic thinking and its modes of expression which occurred
during the last years of the nineteenth century. It could have been
illustrated equally well by juxtaposing any group of drawings by
Corot, Géricault, Ingres, and Monet with examples by Cézanne,
Gauguin, Matisse, Picasso, and Rouault. Much as all differ individually, they share attitudes which divide the two groups sharply.

Whether one likes the art of the modernists or not, one thing is
clear: they could not live in a world whose outlook changed profoundly between 1875 and 1950 and continue to repeat the pictorial,
realistic, and impressionist concepts and methods. They had to
devise new ways of expressing new interests and beliefs. They could
not do this merely by reverting to older precedents. Like all creative
artists, they needed both to express their own times and to contribute
something new to the growth of art.

CHAPTER 12

Representation in Sculpture

There are five principal systems, or modes, by which sculptors have represented various aspects of reality and expressed their reactions to the world around them in an organized fashion. They are the *glyptic, plastic, realistic, impressionist,* and *linear* modes.

Besides numbering five they resemble painting and drawing in other respects. Each mode has been favored in different times and places. There is, moreover, a similarity between the modes of sculpture, painting, and drawing during any given period because of that period's common denominators of attitude.

These parallelisms are useful, for they make it unnecessary to repeat the general backgrounds from which each springs. Unfortunately, there is some inconvenience in the fact that we cannot use the same terms that we used for painting and drawing, because sculpture differs from the pictorial media in certain important respects. Its strength lies in the realm of actual tangible forms, its weakness in the field of color, atmosphere, and light where the pictorial arts excel; and no sculptor has been able to overcome this limitation except in degree. Compared to painting, sculpture is at a disadvantage in creating an illusion of deep and atmospheric space. Its actual three-dimensionality, however, always gives it a potential advantage over painting in the representation of massive forms. It takes a Giotto, Michelangelo, or Cézanne to create as convincing massiveness in painting as an ordinary sculptor can achieve in a figure in the round. Also, the literal bulk of round sculpture introduces significant compositional differences between the two media. Because of these several differences we have substituted the word *glyptic* for the sculptural counterpart of sculpturesque painting and *plastic mode* for the corresponding pictorial mode of painting. The connotations of *glyptic* and *plastic* allow a more accurate explanation of the special sculptural properties, but require some clarification.

THE GLYPTIC MODE

Although the term *glyptic* has no simple translation, it was long used effectively by Professor Chandler Post of Harvard. Once understood in the sense it is used in modern German criticism, it embraces an important concept of sculpture.

The glyptic mode, to start with one simple idea, can be identified by the preservation in a statue of the qualities of the material used. The sculptor who employs the mode appears to love the intrinsic nature of his material. He strives to preserve, enhance, and exploit it, inducing in us an appreciation of its essential qualities. Although he may cultivate them in bronze, he is more likely to work in limestone, granite, or marble.

We can define the special interests of the glyptic sculptor further by noting the principal properties of stone. Universally it is characterized by three-dimensional mass, weight, density, solidity, shape, and various types of surface texture. It is with the attribute of shape that the glyptic sculptor is mainly concerned, for it is largely by the manipulation of shape or form that he achieves representation and expression.

A glyptic sculptor is little interested in the possibilities for imitation of surface textures offered by his material. Instead, he tries to retain the inner properties of mass, weight, density, solidity, and cohesive strength. To keep textures in this supporting role, he almost never uses them to represent something foreign to the nature of stone or bronze, such as lace, cloth, or human flesh. These are the concern of the realist but not of the glyptic-minded sculptor.

How best to preserve the intrinsic qualities of stone was demonstrated long ago by artists who discovered that a certain group of universally respected shapes lend themselves especially well to sculpture. These are such well-known geometric shapes as the cube, cone, sphere, and cylinder. One merit of these shapes is that, coming as they do from the abstracting human mind, they epitomize orderliness. Clear-cut, finite, smooth, and more often than not symmetrical, they are the essence of calculated regularity, the opposite of accident and natural irregularity. Taken by themselves they are too austere for the average taste, but are invaluable when combined with the properties and appeal of actual physical materials. This the glyptic mode does, making stoniness and the geometric shapes complement each other. They then form one of the best marriages of material and shape in art. Through them the interests of design can be amply satisfied, yet they permit some representation too, for geometric shapes approximate any number of natural forms, especially the parts of the human body so long favored by sculptors as a subject. Thus by employing geometric shapes sculptors can preserve the essential qualities of their material, obtain a high degree of orderliness, and satisfy the requirements of representation simultaneously.

The glyptic mode may therefore be conceived as fulfilling three requirements. Since the interests of these requirements—material, design, and representation—are to some extent opposed, each example of the glyptic mode illustrates a compromise of interests. The possible compromises are, of course, limitless, resulting in flexibility of individual expression. One artist may approach careful representation while another leans more toward abstract geometric forms. Yet the glyptic mode can always be recognized within these poles. A work of sculpture falls within this mode if the sculptor has kept the underlying geometric shapes reasonably apparent and has refrained from treating surface textures realistically, if, in sum, neither shape nor surface is sacrificed to representation. If they are sacrificed the result is not unsculptural sculpture, but simply sculpture in another mode, the realistic.

In employing the abstract shapes of solid geometry, sculptors are able to present in the concentrated forms of art a distillation of one of the universal types of shape. For though spheres, cones, and cylinders may seem to have been conceived intuitively by the human mind, the original ideas were probably suggested to it by shapes which are around us all of the time. Since these have been present from the beginning of time and are a possible source of inspiration to all, they have played an incalculable role in unifying art. For works of sculpture which used them as a common source could never be entirely without a common unity. Thus we see once more the profundity of Cézanne's observation that all of nature can be reduced to a geometric order. Although he uttered this statement in modern times, he was merely articulating an insight which artists have possessed subconsciously for untold generations.

By a fortunate coincidence Fig. 156, a photograph of a cypress tree and some rocks, illustrates the two types of shapes which are found universally on the planet we inhabit. The picture was taken on Monterey Peninsula, California, but it might have been snapped at a thousand places on our globe. These two types of shape we shall call the geometric and the plastic. The round, massive rock exemplifies the geometric and the tree the plastic; and each gives point to the other by its contrasting characteristics. The boulder

FIG. 156. Cypress tree and rocks. Monterey
Peninsula, Calif.

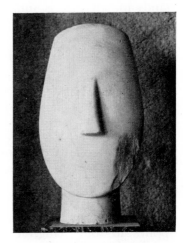

FIG. 157. *Colossal Head of an
Idol.* Cyclades Islands. 3000-2500
B.C. Louvre, Paris.

FIG. 158. Laurana. *A Princess of the
House of Aragon. ca.* 1472. National
Gallery of Art, Washington, D.C.

FIG. 159. Brancusi. *Mademoiselle Pogany. ca.* 1910. Philadelphia Museum
of Art.

291

stands for all that is simply ordered, solid, concentrated, and immovable. It makes a strong appeal to our tactile sense and connotes for both our sensory and conceptual responses the essence of the finite. Any work of sculpture which, while giving a similar shape the greater regularity of art, retains something of this boulder's qualities will likewise appeal to our sense of the finite and stimulate our tactile senses. The glyptic mode seeks to do precisely that.

Plastic shape is at the far pole from the geometric in the natural scheme but is no less universal. It is illustrated by trees the world over, and especially by those which, unlike the boulder, have not been worn smooth by eroding winds and rains, but have been beaten by the weather into tortured and twisted shapes. Since the term *plastic* has been loosely applied to many kinds of painting, let us state clearly that we mean the term in the dictionary sense, namely, as it applies to some tangible mass which is pliable, malleable, and flexible and can therefore be given a new shape by being twisted and turned. A plastic form is one which results from such a shaping process. In Fig. 156 the bent and gnarled cypress tree is a clear-cut illustration. It is as complex and angular as the boulder is simple and round. More than that, it strongly suggests movement by appearing to be responsive to the winds which whistle through its branches. Compared to it the boulder is utterly stable and impervious. The tree suggests movement, too, by thrusting out its limbs like jagged arrows in all directions. And finally, it suggests infinite space by reaching out into space as space flows in between its branches. This process is known as the interpenetration of forms and space. The total effect implies the infinite world as forcibly as the boulder represents the finite.

It is important to point out a basic orderliness beneath this dynamic arrangement, lest we mistakenly assume that while the boulder is orderly looking, the weather-beaten tree is chaotic. On the contrary, the plastic shape of the tree is perfectly orderly, for if consistency is the basis of order, it is consistent in its irregularity.

With this photograph still before us let us consider three possible directions that can be taken by a sculptor who holds one of the shapeless raw materials of his art, such as a lump of clay, in his hands. He might shape the clay into a human head so carefully that it resembles its model in every detail. He might mould it into a shape which simultaneously suggests both a sphere and a head. Or he might knead and press it into an irregular mass of ridges and hollows which represents, nevertheless, a recognizable human image. These three choices exemplify the realistic, glyptic, and plastic modes of representation. They are options which are open to any sculptor and must be elected by him, for the clay itself is neutral and unexpressive. The direction which the sculptor takes will be determined to a considerable extent by the compulsive influences which his society exerts upon him. But within that expression he has freedom to choose how much emphasis he will place upon realistic representation and how much on glyptic or plastic form. The precise formula that he establishes may be called his individual expression. In either case he is asserting the artist's ancient privilege of objectifying his feelings in his own controlled and calculated manner. This interplay between the man and his raw material, his environment and his finished product is the history of art in a nutshell. The following illustrations are but examples of the principle at work, and those that follow immediately illustrate a choice in favor of the glyptic mode.

The glyptic mode is immeasurably old, extending back into early prehistoric times in the famous Paleolithic *Willendorf Venus*. It springs from man's inherent capacity for abstract thought and from the timeless presence of geometric forms in universal nature. The far-reaching historical span covered by the mode is shown by Figs. 157 and 159. The first, a *Colossal Head of an Idol* from the Cycladic Islands, dates from 3000 to 2500 B.C. and carries us back to the Aegean region which Greek art dominated in later ancient times. Though we cannot accurately call this figure Greek, it anticipates in a rudimentary way much of the feeling for the sculptural media which made the Greeks masterful sculptors in their time.

The second example, Fig. 159, is a portrait of *Mademoiselle Pogany* by the modern Rumanian sculptor Constantin Brancusi. Not only is it typical of an international style in modern sculpture, which includes in its illustrious roster the leading sculptors of our time—Maillol, Milles, Městrovič, Manship, Epstein, Archipenko, Despiau, Zorach, Flanagan, Arp, Gill, Lachaise, Laurent, Kolbe, Barlach—but demonstrates the remarkable persistence of the glyptic mode. Modern artists have revived the mode after a lapse of interest during the post-Renaissance period (from about 1550 to 1880) for two reasons; it was a perfect corrective for the excesses of nineteenth-century Impressionism and academic realism which had reached the same extremes in sculpture that they had in painting. It also offered sculptors an opportunity to return to certain timeless sculptural principles. The resemblance of the *Colossal Head of an Idol* and the portrait of *Mademoiselle Pogany* in several important characteristics demonstrates these persisting principles.

Both are excellent examples of the glyptic mode. Their sculptors obviously appreciated the beauty of the marble in which they worked and did everything they could to preserve its special properties in stable, finite, geometric forms. They refused to sacrifice these qualities for the sake of representation. Their feeling for the smooth round forms and clear outlines of the glyptic mode is equally apparent. Both sculptors had a high sense of the geometric's abstract attractions. Brancusi, a modern adherent of form-for-form's sake, makes so few concessions to representation that the *Mademoiselle Pogany* head suggests a geometric form quite as much as it does a human being. Glyptic design has been so stressed that only the barest essentials of a female face are included.

The sculptor of the *Colossal Head of an Idol* stressed design to an even greater extreme. One might assume that this was due to a lack of representational skill. And though this is partly true, the answer is not so simple as that, for progress in art has not been measured by an advance from design to representation; prehistoric artists showed a remarkable capacity for representing images realistically when they so desired. They simply desired more often to express their keen sense of design. Only modern peoples who have lost a sense of form or design see art in strictly representational terms. The *Colossal Head* shows a negligible interest in imitation, yet its design is remarkably sophisticated; though primitive in origin, it is anything but crude. Indeed, Jacob Epstein, a learned and skilful modern sculptor, has proudly carved a marble head of a woman which is virtually its twin. And modern sculptors in general have eagerly studied primitive art in an effort to recapture some of the essentials of sculpture.

Seen historically, the glyptic mode is associated with prehistoric sculpture and with primitive art from ancient to modern times on a global scale. It was the typical mode employed by sculptors through most of ancient civilized history; it returned to favor for another thousand years in the Middle Ages; and was revived again in recent modern times. Oriental sculptors have used it in conjunction with another finite style, the linear mode, for centuries upon end; the part it has played in the history of art is therefore impressive.

Its reputation was further enhanced by its adoption among the leading sculptors of the Early Renaissance in Italy; it was the reigning mode throughout the fifteenth century, owing in great measure to the prestige of the Classical Revival. Sculptural thinking tended to dominate painting during this century, forcing it, as we have seen, into a sculpturesque mode of representation. Because of its ancient roots and its predominance during the Renaissance, the glyptic mode has long been identified with the Mediterranean classical approach. A bust of *A Princess of the House of Aragon* (Fig. 158) by the fifteenth-century sculptor Francesco Laurana is an excellent example of the point of view of the Renaissance Italians, especially in its serenity and composure. These qualities were prized by the idealistic ancient Greeks and their later Italian followers, and the glyptic mode was well suited to express them.

But what strikes us most in this bust is the balance of representation, design, and material. Each has been given its due. There is no doubt about the material; not only is it marble, but marble which is so skilfully finished that it subtly suggests marble and flesh at the same time. Nor is there any doubt about what is represented. Whereas the *Colossal Head* might be a man, woman, or child, Laurana's bust is a young woman with an individual face and personality. The contrast between the universal and individual could hardly be better exemplified. And yet Laurana's sense of design kept him from forgetting the appeal of abstract forms. Consequently, we can enjoy the bust as the likeness of a handsome woman and as a pleasing composition of geometric shapes. Moreover, one is tempted to say that this is the glyptic mode at its best. Standing somewhere in between the extremes of the *Colossal Head* and the *Mademoiselle Pogany,* its balance of representation and design avoids the baldly obvious and relies upon an art that conceals its art.

On the basis of these examples the glyptic mode can be said to possess certain clearly definable merits. Regardless of differences, all three statues denote a respect for the intrinsic beauty of the material itself, a feeling for the esthetic appeal of geometric forms, an appreciation of stable, finite forms, and a due regard for the importance of the tactile sense. The glyptic mode lends itself to an orderliness which is usually more simple than complex; it partakes of the universality of geometric forms without wholly sacrificing individuality except in extreme cases; and is an ideal means of objectifying finite stability.

So selective a point of view must neglect some interests and hence have limitations. If, for example, a sculptor wishes to express a higher pitch of vitality, a greater degree of variety and infinity, and a stronger suggestion of movement, he will do well to turn to another method, such as the plastic mode.

THE PLASTIC MODE

In modern criticism the plastic mode has played a poor second to the glyptic. The glyptic has been called *the* sculptural mode and the *true* way of carving and modeling. Modernists like Brancusi have been outspoken in this respect, while historians have supported the glyptic method with all of the massive prestige of the ancient and Renaissance masters, who worked primarily in this manner. This bias has made them give the plastic mode the name "pictorial" in many instances, the implication being that it is a sculptural reflection of characteristics which are more typical of painting.

There is undeniably some truth in these beliefs. The plastic mode is connected with the historical period from the seventeenth through the nineteenth century when there were certainly more great painters than sculptors, the reverse of the situation in ancient times and at the height of Renaissance sculpturesque painting. Worse still, many sculptors confused their aims with those which can be realized better in painting, such as attempting to represent deep, atmospheric space or filling the backgrounds of reliefs with innumerable accessories.

Nevertheless, there are legitimate aspects of reality which cannot be so well represented in the glyptic mode as in the plastic. Recognizing this truth, many sculptors who happened to be born during the great age of painting employed the plastic mode, not because it resembled painting, but because it can be a sculptural mode in its own right. They have two arguments in their favor. One is that the plastic mode expressed the spirit of their times better than the glyptic—a view lent credence by the fiasco of early nineteenth-century Neo-Classicism. The other is that the plastic mode originated in forms which are as universal as the geometric. To omit them would be to discard a far too significant side of reality.

The argument that, quite apart from painting, the plastic mode can accomplish certain sculptural aims better than any other is demonstrated by Renée Sintenis' figure of the runner Paavo Nurmi (Fig. 162). Nurmi was the great Finnish athlete who created a sensation at the Paris Olympic games in 1924 by shattering a number of long-distance records. His long, easy stride must have aroused Sintenis' admiration and the statue was the result. Granted Sintenis' right to attempt any subject, the only question hinges on the success of his methods. And the answer to that lies in the international popularity of the little figure.

Working in pliable clay rather than the rigid materials of glyptic sculpture, he treated the surface in a continuously sketchy and irregular fashion. Nothing is finished in detail, everything is incomplete. The purpose of the method is twofold: to give us only the kind of quick impression that we ourselves would have of a running figure, and, secondly, to keep our attention on the surface so that we will not be conscious of the weight of the body. The result of this consistent and deliberately indefinite superficiality is a minimizing

Fig. 160. *Menkure and His Queen.* Reigned *ca.* 2794-2771 B.C., IV Dynasty. Museum of Fine Arts, Boston.

Fig. 161. Daumier. *The Burden. ca.* 1860. Walters Art Gallery, Baltimore.

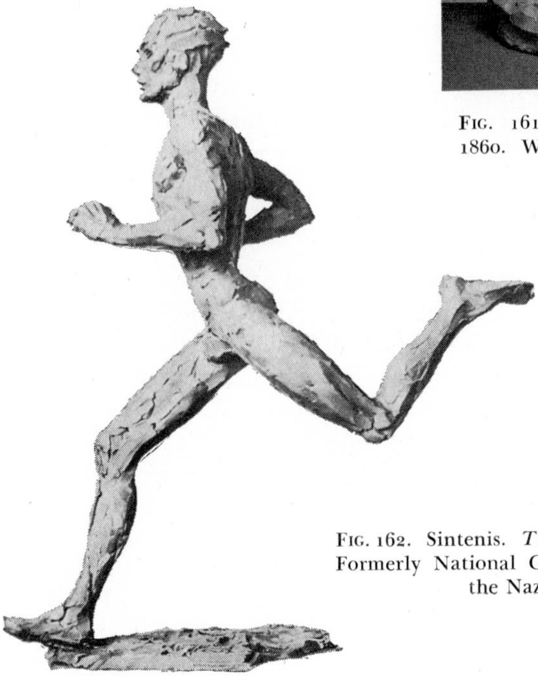

Fig. 162. Sintenis. *The Runner Paavo Nurmi.* 1926. Formerly National Gallery, Berlin. Confiscated by the Nazi régime *ca.* 1938.

of the tactile sense and a strengthening of empathic appreciation. It
is not difficult for us to identify ourselves with this flying figure in a
pleasurable way. What counts in Sintenis' case is the successful use
of the plastic mode, not a blind adherence to glyptic treatment.

The relative merits of the glyptic and plastic modes can be seen by
comparing two pairs of figures, the mother and child by Daumier
entitled *The Burden* (Fig. 161) and the ancient Egyptian *Menkure
and His Queen* (Fig. 160). Each of these pairs expresses a different
idea for which its particular treatment was admirably suited. We
can hardly imagine the treatments of the respective figures being
exchanged without the ideas expressed being radically altered.

The main theme of *The Burden* is the driving movement of a
hardworking, heavily-muscled Parisian washerwoman. She seems to
be straining against a wind as she lugs her heavy bundle. Much of
this impression of powerful movement is conveyed by the bulk
of the figures. But it is an impression that is heightened by the
plastic conception conveyed through the flowing outlines and rough
but consistently irregular surface. Although the heavy stride of the
laundress differs from the weightless, floating grace of Sintenis'
Nurmi, the two figures are both plastic in the way they express a
feeling of movement and vitality, and both appeal strongly to empathic identification. Hence in its own way the tug and pull of the
laundress on her burden is as affective as Nurmi's fleetness of foot.

The stone statues of *Menkure and His Queen* epitomize self-
assured authority. They are dynamic in the sense that they radiate
an inner power. But they do so in a tensely static posture. Long-
range stability and a conservative, simple, and finite outlook are their
outstanding personal traits. For the expression of these ideas the
glyptic mode was ideally suited. The simple, massive, geometric
orderliness of its forms expresses Menkure's personality and dominant station in life with forceful clarity.

Two final examples will allow us to see additional expressive
capacities of these two contrasting modes. While the plastic mode is
well suited to represent various kinds of flowing physical movement
because of its stress on continuity of surface, the same irregular
rhythm can express dynamic inner qualities and spiritual feelings;
this capacity extends its expressive range into an important field.
It has been profoundly realized in a bronze interpretation of
Beethoven (Fig. 164) by the French sculptor Émile Bourdelle.

Like most masters of the plastic mode, Bourdelle was primarily
interested in the vital qualities and meaning of his subject and only
secondarily in its exact physical appearance, giving us only enough
clues to establish identification. A death mask of Beethoven is sup-

Fig. 163. *Head of a Priest.*
XXVI Dynasty, 663-525 B.C.
Museum of Fine Arts, Boston.

Fig. 164. Bourdelle. *Beethoven. ca.*
1910. Metropolitan Museum of Art,
New York.

299

posed to have suggested this head. If so, Bourdelle infused the death mask with vivid life by the force of his own inspiration. That inspiration must have come from his own understanding of Beethoven's powerful, passionate, and tormented creative personality.

Bourdelle's *Beethoven* and the ancient Egyptian *Head of a Priest* in Fig. 163 allow us to contrast the attitudes toward the role of illumination in sculpture expressed by the glyptic and plastic modes. If compared to painting, the glyptic may be said to resemble the point of view of Michelangelo, the plastic that of Rembrandt. The glyptic sculptor who carved the *Head of a Priest* did not ignore the effect of infinite light and shadow in his preoccupation with finite forms, but he placed his principal emphasis upon the tangible world and used light to stress the smooth, round, massive simplicity of his geometric forms. Bourdelle, the plastic sculptor, regarded light and shadow in another way. Being more concerned with the infinite physical world in which light and shadow play major roles, he considered them to be important ends in themselves. His employment of broken surfaces supports this conception in two ways; the rough surface directs our attention away from finite tangibility to the more infinite spiritual qualities, while the alternation of bosses and hollows creates a vibrant pattern of high lights which spells life and vitality. In short, where the light flows around the smooth forms of the glyptic mode, it dances over the surface of the plastic.

The Egyptians possessed a remarkable aptitude for creating fine sculpture in the glyptic mode, a fact which accounts for much of the renown of their school. The *Head of a Priest* is only one of hundreds of equally good examples of the glyptic sculpture which they created. Several conditions lie behind this fact. The Egyptians seem to have known clearly what they wished to do. Deciding on one mode, they used it with perfect consistency. They were not distracted by scores of other modes as our modern museum-conscious artists are, and so they did not flit from one hybrid mode to another. But though ignorance was a blessing in their case at first, some credit must be given them for a determined artistic outlook. In the course of their long history they were subjected to outside influences from Greece and Mesopotamia. Yet for centuries they adhered to the same point of view. This loyalty gave them one great advantage— infinite practice in a single mode. The results can be seen in the sculptural finesse of the relatively late *Head of a Priest*. Centuries of accumulated skill went into it. If the effect is somewhat cold and austere, it is nonetheless impressive, speaking as it does for one of the most persistent, consistent, and ancient stylistic reigns in history.

The plastic mode is comparatively new. Although hints of it can be found in very early sculpture, its full possibilities were not consistently realized until recently. The Gothic sculptors had tended in that direction, but never took the final logical step, while the brilliant seventeenth-century master Bernini, who handled the mode expertly in his small terra cotta sketches, abandoned it for a more realistic finish when he carved his larger works. It was not until the nineteenth century that any large number of sculptors used the plastic mode with full and consistent understanding. Perhaps the mode required the particular kind of environment which appeared in the nineteenth century. Or possibly the mode needed the special knowledge that led to Impressionism. As we have seen, painters were not fully ready for Impressionism until the middle of the nineteenth century, and the same rule might well apply to sculptors. At any rate, the most consistent examples of the plastic mode date from the past hundred years. Moreover, they parallel the points of view of the Impressionists and some of the modernists closely. The conception of form that Van Gogh applied to such pictures as his *Mountainous Landscape* (Fig. 65) and *Cypresses* (Fig. 155) clearly exemplifies the plastic attitude. And it is a moot question whether the *Burden* and the *Nurmi* should be classified as plastic or impressionist. When rapid movement is represented, it is difficult to draw any sharp line between them.

THE REALISTIC MODE

A sculptor who holds a lump of clay in his hands may shape that clay into a head within either the glyptic or plastic modes, relating them as he does to the qualities of certain universal forms. If he molds a head of a priest in the glyptic mode, that head will partake of the universal nature of a spherical boulder; if he depicts Beethoven in the plastic mode, the result will remind us of equally universal trees. His work will not be all likeness or all design but a fusion of the two.

He may also mold the clay so carefully that every individual detail of his living subject is represented as accurately as sculpture permits. His point of view will then be realistic, his main criterion exactitude of likeness. He will not distort appearances for the sake of expression, as did Bourdelle, nor idealize features and proportions to achieve greater physical beauty, as the ancient Greek sculptors were prone to do. More likely, he will accept ugliness where he finds it, including the profusion and diversity of nature, impartially or fondly. As a realist, he will genuinely love nature and regard truth-to-life as a privilege and obligation. His loyalties therefore differ from those of either the glyptic or plastic sculptor. He admires and respects nature as it is; the others maintain that art is only intended to serve man. Whereas practitioners of the other modes select and emphasize mainly to satisfy man's esthetic and spiritual needs, the realist gives us a transcription of nature with a minimum of selection. He gains thereby the least universality but the greatest individuality possible to any of the modes. A few concrete examples will illustrate these points and outline the history of the mode.

The history of sculpture shows that the realistic intention is always present but is likely to flower rather late in any cultural cycle. Both phenomena can be illustrated by the history of ancient art. For its use is not so much a matter of perfected skill as of attitudes and preferences in expression. As early as the IV Dynasty (about 2800 B.C.) the Egyptians showed an interest in realistic representation. They also possessed the acuteness of observation which is a primary requisite of the realistic mode; and they had the technical skill to carve realistically whenever they wished. On several occasions in their long history they did so wish, as during the reign of Ikhnaton. But on the whole they felt that the glyptic mode expressed their outlook more aptly.

If the realistic mode did not find universal favor with the Egyptian peoples, it did find favor with others and has been able to compete side by side with the other modes more than once in history. The reason for this is due, again, to a universal principle: each of the modes persists because it makes a special and unduplicable contribution, and the realistic mode has been no exception.

The history of the mode during the past five centuries bears this out. Roughly speaking, it parallels the rise of the realistic mode in European painting. It arose among the late Gothic sculptors in the North during the fifteenth century and spread to the South. A striking example of it is the figure of a worshipper from Mazzoni's *Nativity* (Fig. 165) in the cathedral of Modena. Not even Van Eyck could have been more incisive in the treatment of every minute detail. It is as true to life as a sculptured figure can be. Two of the signs of its utter commitment to realism are the imitative use of color, as distinct from a symbolical, conventional, or decorative usage, and the inclusion of every wrinkle and blemish in the man's leathery face and hands. Nor have any liberties been taken with normal proportions. The model had small eyes, a large nose and heavy jowls, and these Mazzoni recorded without being moved to idealize or distort them for any expressive purpose. The merits of his honesty are plain. Such a faithful imitation gives us an intense

Fig. 165. Mazzoni. Detail. *The Nativity*. 1477-1480. Cathedral Crypt, Modena.

Fig. 166. Bernini. *Cardinal Scipione Borghese*. 1632. Borghese Gallery. Rome.

Fig. 167. Bernini. *Apollo and Daphne*. 1622-1624. Borghese Gallery, Rome.

feeling of individuality. It gives us, too, a feeling typical of all good realistic sculpture, that the sculptor worked directly from a living, flesh-and-blood model and not from a figment of the imagination. It gives us, finally, the feeling that man is fit to appear in art as he is without apologies or changes.

Commitment to the facts is crucial to the realistic mode, and success or failure depends upon a wise use of this commitment. Since the realist does the least selecting after he has chosen his subject, he must do the most before. A worthwhile subject will survive in spite of physical ugliness or a meticulously realistic treatment, but the realistic mode can rarely make a dull subject interesting. It is the least orderly of the modes, and whatever vitality it communicates must come from the subject rather than the treatment. Mazzoni's worshipper cannot compete in order or vitality with the *Head of a Priest* or Bourdelle's *Beethoven,* but it can challenge them in human interest. Hence the realist must choose his subject well.

Owing to certain differences between painting and sculpture, the realistic mode was not delayed in its development. It did not have to wait as painting did for the perfection of perspective or aerial projection; nor did it have to wait on the refinement of oil painting. Such problems as the representation of atmosphere, illumination, or deep space were no hindrance in its case, and its own compositional problems—a few figures in shallow space—were comparatively simple. Therefore, such sculptors as Mazzoni were able in the short span of the fifteenth century to bring the realistic mode to a high level of development. Technically speaking, they left little that could be desired.

However, the mode enjoyed its widest usage in the seventeenth century alongside its companions in representation, the realistic modes of painting and drawing. The new high level was not due so much to technical superiority as it was to the superior vitality and imaginative brilliance of the Baroque masters. They endowed the mode with a verve and excitement which overrides all of our objections and by sheer success makes them seem petty and captious. They proved once and for all that no mode is intrinsically inferior to the others.

The most irresistible of the Baroque giants is Bernini, whose portrait bust of Cardinal Scipione Borghese (Fig. 166) is a justly famous example of realism in sculpture. In it and similar portraits he lifted the realistic mode to a new level of excellence. Highly skilled in technique, he was able to capture the appearance of textures with perfect fidelity. Yet he did this with apparent ease, conveying a feeling of facility and dash. He avoided especially the air of plodding attention to details that often makes realistic sculpture seem surface-bound, finicky, and dull like the accurate but lifeless figures in a wax-works museum. Bernini illustrated how the realistic mode could be endowed with life because he appreciated the inner qualities himself. He projected something of his own vigor into the image of the Cardinal, giving the head a tilt and erectness that radiate energy. He also responded to the individuality of Borghese and his other sitters and made them true to life in the spiritual as well as the physical sense. By using skill, imagination, and insight Bernini demonstrated how many of the pedestrian and prosaic qualities of the realistic mode can be overcome and truth combined with vitality, inspiration, and excitement. He showed especially the suitability of the realistic mode for vivid, lifelike portraiture.

Bernini reveals his preference for the realistic attitude most clearly in the way he accepts and respects the diversity of natural appearances. If the texture of the face differs from that of the robe, he records that fact. If the shape of the face differs in its roundness from that of the more angular folds of the robe, he retains that difference too. He is also true to life in representing the hair, the puffy cheeks, and the proportions of the features as they are rather than as they might be. He introduces another telltale sign of the realist by representing the pupils and irises of the eyes, even to drilling holes which suggest the high lights in the human eye. He has, in short, carved from the same point of view that Nanteuil engraved his portrait of Louis XIV (Fig. 149) and Velasquez painted the famous one of Pope Innocent X during the same seventeenth century. Indeed, Bernini's *Cardinal Borghese* brings sculpture as close to realistic painting as it can come without the use of color.

Like every other method, the realistic mode has limitations beyond which the most gifted masters go at their peril. One field in which it is at a disadvantage is the representation of rapid movement. Here the plastic mode is unquestionably its superior. Bernini sensed this truth only partially. When doing clay sketches he used the plastic mode fluently, even to endowing quite static poses with a high vitality and lively sense of movement which anticipated the *Beethoven* of Bourdelle. But when he turned to large and serious moving figures in marble he forgot the merits of the plastic treatment. Either he was addicted to realism or he was troubled by the unfinished appearance of plastic surfaces, forgetting that that is their chief means of representing rapidly moving figures.

His *Apollo and Daphne* (Fig. 167) is a noted case of misapplied realism. The postures of the bodies tell us that Daphne is fleeing to elude the amorous grasp of Apollo. But the extremely careful representation of every surface detail connotes something contradictory to our experience with the static. Bernini was not the first master who did not know when the turning point between a vigorous sketch and a highly finished treatment of moving figures had been reached. And he was by no means the last. Not until the nineteenth century did artists in general fully appreciate the advantages of a rough but rhythmic plastic surface in the depiction of movement in either painting or sculpture. Moreover, though this was an early work by Bernini (carved in fact when he was only about twenty-five years of age), he was never able to forego entirely his love of realism for the sake of his dynamic tendencies toward activity. He continued to the end to apply a treatment which is excellent for portraiture but poor for the representation of motion. Hence, though Bernini's *Apollo and Daphne* is more beautiful in many respects than Daumier's rough-looking little *Burden,* it is inferior to it in suitability and consistency of treatment. Both Bernini's brilliance and shortcomings were typical of a stage of sculpture in which there still remained some confusion between the proper uses of realism and plasticity.

The later history of realistic sculpture can be briefly summarized. By the nineteenth century the artists of Europe were so practiced in the realistic mode that minor painters and sculptors such as Vincenzo Gemito possessed a technical competence which left nothing more to be desired or done. Gemito, a Neapolitan who liked to roam the streets and waterfront of his picturesque, song-loving city, found his subjects among its many carefree urchins. Judging by his work at large he was, like scores of other nineteenth-century European artists, a man of genial temperament and little profundity, but undeniably skilful in realistic representation. A typical example of the subjects that he found in everyday life is his *Neapolitan Water-Carrier* (Fig. 168). It is a subject which conveys the eternal charm of happy-go-lucky boyhood. Only a churlish person would resist smiling sympathetically with this quite unembarrassed grinning boy. He is as natural as nature itself. The command over anatomy, posture, and realistic representation is impeccable. Beyond that, it offers little more than an ingratiating but commonplace feeling for everyday life.

If portraiture and everyday scenes were the whole of life, the realistic mode would have had the field to itself. But it cannot keep pace with other modes on the higher levels of human thought and

FIG. 168. Gemito. *Neapolitan Water-Carrier. ca.* 1840. Gallery of Modern Art, Rome.

FIG. 169. Rodin. *The Age of Bronze.* 1876. Metropolitan Museum of Art, New York.

FIG. 170. Rosso. *A Woman Seen Towards Evening.* 1893. Gallery of Modern Art, Rome.

feeling and in the deepest valleys of tragic sentiment. When a realist insists upon rising or descending to these levels, he reveals the shortcomings of realism all too clearly. He does this especially when he treats symbolic, religious, or idealistic subjects in which the spirit, imaginative content, or idea is more important than physical appearances. In such cases an emphasis upon the physical may even be contradictory or antithetical. The very greatest artists have stumbled on this rock. Bernini did so when he carved his *Apollo and Daphne.* So, too, did Rodin when he cast his *Age of Bronze* (Fig. 169), though apart from intent both are superb statues in many ways.

Rodin was living in Brussels when he created the *Age of Bronze,* and used a young Belgian soldier of excellent physique as his model. He submitted a plaster cast of the figure to the Paris exhibition of 1876 and was gratified by its acceptance. Then the rumor was spread that Rodin had made the statue by casting it directly from life. Even an age conditioned to expect miracles of realistic representation found its perfection hard to believe. In order to exonerate himself Rodin had to send casts and photographs of the living model for comparison with the statue. He was eventually cleared of the scandalous charge, and the figure was placed in the Salon of 1880.

This episode illustrates the lengths to which realism can be carried, but it is incidental to the more important question of the appropriateness of such a treatment for symbolic purposes. In spite of the figure's grace, beauty, and depth of feeling, our attention is continually directed from the main idea to the perfect rendering of the flesh which ripples over the bones and muscles of the chest. Hence, instead of being in harmony with the idea, the treatment competes distractingly with it. It is a tribute to Rodin's genius that he nearly makes us forget the cleavage between representation and content in this figure. His inability to do so entirely proves the limitations of the most perfect realistic sculpture in the field of highly imaginative ideas. Yet any mode which shows such powers of survival in spite of the censure of countless critics cannot be scorned. Its continuing power lies in one timeless fact: although the realist does not exploit the artistic means at his disposal to endow his work with a rhythmic order or vitality, he does capitalize on another opportunity—the almost universal appeal of any subject which possesses "human interest." This may seem like a slight contribution to creative art—a new discovery of common gold—but it cannot be dismissed. As long as artists of the stature of Bernini give us vivid representations of human character, realism will have its followers.

THE IMPRESSIONIST MODE

The impressionist mode in sculpture evolved from the general movement toward Impressionism which highlighted European art during the second half of the nineteenth century, with its center in France. The representation of moving forms and infinite scenes either with or without movement were its aims. In suggesting motion it employed an irregular plastic surface which is visually comparable to the broken color of the pictorial Impressionists. It is therefore possible to classify Sintenis' *Nurmi* and Daumier's *Burden* as impressionist statues which use plastic means or as plastic statues which resemble the impressionist mode.

In representing a fleeting impression of an infinite and ever-changing world the Impressionists varied their means. When dealing with the indefiniteness produced by distance or shadows, rather than rapid movement, they did not so much stress consistent irregularity as a regular blurring of outlines and contours. Medardo Rosso's study of *A Woman Seen Towards Evening* (Fig. 170) illustrates this type. The correspondence of his dates and those of the French Impressionists will not be missed, while his Italian nationality shows the international character of the movement. The subject he has chosen is equally significant; Whistler was painting nocturnes and Debussy composing them at about the same time. The night as a theme was in the air of Europe during the eighties and nineties.

The disadvantages of representing the twilight or evening hours have already been discussed in connection with painting. If in spite of them a sculptor wishes to make the dusk his subject, he must render his forms more or less as Rosso has. The logic of his subject dictates that he will keep all forms indistinct, disregard all minute details, and slur over outlines and features. In *A Woman Seen Towards Evening* only the suggestion of a hat casts the face into shadow, rendering it mysterious and elusive. Mouth, nose, and eyes are barely indicated. Nothing but a momentary impression of a figure nearly lost in the dim light of a fading day is conveyed. Yet that impression is conveyed successfully.

The material which Rosso used is significant. It is wax, a medium of which he was especially fond. It lends itself to the representation of such fugitive themes as the woman depicted here; but one can hardly imagine a more fragile or ephemeral sculptural substance.

We can admire the daring of Impressionists like Rosso but not necessarily their judgment. The use of wax is but a symptom of the way they courted the fleeting aspects of reality. In a short time they pushed these possibilities to the limit and prompted the same kind of reaction in sculpture that occurred in painting; Brancusi's *Mademoiselle Pogany* is an example of the return to a more finite, glyptic mode which followed in the twentieth century.

Rosso's *A Woman Seen Towards Evening* is at the far pole from the point of view of either Brancusi or Mazzoni and illustrates the end-of-the-line extreme which Impressionism reached by the end of the nineteenth century. It possesses the indisputable unity of the impressionist modes, and it is mysterious and serene; but its forms are as nebulous as sculpture could afford to be. Those who followed had little choice; since sculpture could not be carried any further in this direction, they had to return to the past or take a new tack. As events turned out, they did a combination of both.

THE LINEAR MODE

The linear mode of sculpture relies primarily upon lines as a means of representation and shows only an incidental interest in the other formal entities. Since it does not exploit the three-dimensional character of the sculptural media or take advantage of their normal massiveness, it appeals little to either the superficial or penetrating aspects of the tactile sense. It is therefore the most concentrated and selective, and usually the simplest, of the modes of representation. For clarity of outline and visual impact, it is unexcelled.

Thus the merits of the linear mode are synonymous with those of line in general. Lines, as we remember, do not exist in nature, where there are only edges of shadows and boundaries between areas of color. Lines, therefore, are the most abstract and strictly artistic of all representational devices. Even more to the point are their special artistic properties and the psychological effects they have on us. Since they are an imaginative invention—a purely artistic convenience—they have no weight or material substance and are thus the epitome of lightness. On the other hand, our eyes can follow and perceive them clearly. When these two characteristics are combined, the result is a kind of paradoxical weightless finiteness.

An artist can put these qualities to excellent use in two ways. He can express the intangible, spiritual quality of inner reality. And he can also represent the flowing, graceful character of certain kinds of movement in the external world. These are the special fields in which the linear artist can be a master.

There is a third province in which line has few superiors—the expression of wit, mental vivacity, and lightheartedness. This does not mean that line cannot express serious ideas, only that its physical

FIG. 171. *Flying Apsaras.* Sui Dynasty, A.D. 581-618. Nelson Gallery and Atkins Museum, Kansas City, Mo.

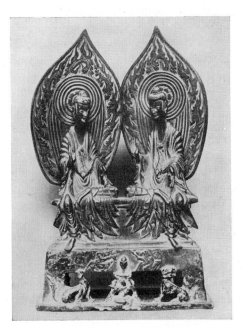

FIG. 172. *Sakyamuni and Prabhuta-ratna.* A.D. 518. Wei Dynasty. Musée Guimet, Paris.

FIG. 173. Calder. *The Hostess.* 1928. Museum of Modern Art, New York.

311

lightness tends to connote lighter themes. We often hear melodies whose "light touch" expresses a kind of sophisticated carefreeness. It is equally easy to find comparable examples of linear art. James Thurber's "*Touché!*" is an instance of the aptness of crisp and deftly executed lines for the expression of wit. Hardly less delightful is Alexander Calder's figure *Hostess* (Fig. 173). Constructed of wire, it is as linear as it is unsculptural in the usual sense. It could have been rendered in pen-and-ink like Thurber's "*Touché!*" without any loss of meaning. Yet its incisive humor is undeniable and its characterization perfect. A dozen more descriptive attributes could not have made it more effective.

Hence there is good reason to agree with an old observation that though line is one of the most ancient of artistic devices it has also been one of the most refined and civilized. Its range extends from the fumblings of children to masterpieces which are among the finest examples of precision and control in art. The reason for this is plain. An artist who relies on his linear skill alone cannot hide poor draftsmanship behind bold modeling or fancy textures. His lines have no competition; the whole stage is theirs. In none of the more complex modes is the quality of a single element so apparent as in the linear mode.

That the potentialities of the linear mode have often been realized can be seen in specific sculptural examples. Fig. 172 is a noted example of Chinese sculpture in the linear mode. It depicts *Sakyamuni and Prabhutaratna,* two holy figures of the Buddhist religion, posed as if engaged in conversation. There is about them an air of geniality, courtesy, and graciousness; they give the impression of men of quick wit and lively minds. But this impression is not due so much to any extraordinary expression of intelligence on their faces as it is to the linear mode's capacity for creating a light and vital spiritual atmosphere. The treatment of this pair is sculpturally crisp and deft. The use of angles and points in the design gives it a sharpness of idea as well as of physical form. But most important of all is the way the unknown sculptor deliberately eliminated any feeling of massiveness by multiplying the representational lines. Our eyes see virtually nothing else.

The effect of this linear emphasis can be appreciated better if one contrasts Fig. 172 with the massive Egyptian statues of Menkure and his Queen (Fig. 160), who are static, glyptic symbols of physical vigor and durability. Besides them the bodies of Sakyamuni and Prabhutaratna appear thin and fragile; their vitality lies in the life of the mind and spirit. A comparison of the Chinese figures with Daumier's *Burden* will show how the linear mode also differs to an equal degree from the form and spirit of the plastic mode. There is hardly any point in comparing it with the realistic mode.

If the bronze figures of Sakyamuni and Prabhutaratna demonstrate the power of the linear mode to endow two perfectly static figures with an air of spiritual vitality, Fig. 171 demonstrates quite eloquently its ability to create the impression of light, airy movement and flowing grace. It represents a Flying Apsaras, a Buddhist religious figure comparable to the angels of Christianity. Like them, the Flying Apsaras is an imaginary figure which is properly conceived as being supernaturally light and capable of flying through the air. The sculptor has conveyed this impression by exploiting the lightness of lines and avoiding any suggestion of mass or corporeality. The relief is of the shallowest possible kind—little more than a flat, slightly raised drawing in stone. A second characteristic of no less importance is the skilful use of directional lines to specify and enhance the feeling of movement. This is one of the principal resources of the linear mode. Rarely has it been used more effectively than here.

A close inspection of the genial face of the *Flying Apsaras* will reveal a characteristic which the figure has in common with the *Sakyamuni and Prabhutaratna* and Calder's *Hostess*—a carefree spirit. Since these three subjects are different, one can only assume that it is the linear mode itself which gives them this easy grace. And an examination of other examples will bear this out.

The fact that the *Flying Apsaras* is sculpture in low relief as distinct from sculpture in the round suggests an important characteristic of the linear mode and something of its history. The mode probably originated in prehistoric times when men drew images on pieces of bone or stones or on the walls of caves with sharply pointed instruments. In other words, the mode started as a kind of drawing in stone. To some extent it never outgrew this procedure. Whereas the plastic and glyptic modes had to be developed in three-dimensional forms, the linear mode could attain a high level of expression within a shallow field, as the *Flying Apsaras* proves. Since shallowness was no disadvantage, sculptors made little effort to overcome it. Indeed, as we look back over the history of the linear mode, we may doubt whether any linear sculptors have ever improved upon the designs incised in clay tiles during the Han Dynasty (206 B.C.–221 A.D.) in China. No other mode of representation reached the peak of its development at so early a date as the linear mode did because of its essentially simple and two-dimensional character

Historically the linear mode has been associated chiefly with the art of the Orient and especially with the religious art of China and

Japan, in which its aptness for the expression of religious ideas was a valuable asset. It profited, too, from the perennial preference of the Orientals for linear methods of representation and from the centuries of practice that they devoted to linear techniques. By concentrating upon linear modes in painting, drawing, and sculpture, they developed the use of lines to the highest level of refinement in the history of art. While the restless West changed from mode to mode, the Eastern artists imperturbably continued their more conservative traditions, handing down skills from master to pupil through generation after generation. Consequently the largest body of fine examples of linear sculpture is to be found in the religious art of the Far East, the *Flying Apsaras* and *Sakyamuni and Prabhutaratna* being typical.

This is not to say that the Asiatic masters never employed the other modes. Japanese sculptors like Unkie created some world-famous examples of realistic portraiture and other Japanese masters showed an impeccable feeling for plastic form, while the Indian sculptors formulated the Eastern version of the glyptic mode. But despite these exceptions one feels the dominance of linear thinking throughout the art of the Orient and not least in the sculpture of India. Massive though the Indian figures sometimes are, they are always framed in sinuous lines whose quality of movement lightens the masses and endows them with a rhythmic sense of life. For all their differences, a love of line united the artists of Asia.

Owing to the prestige of Egypt, Greece, and Rome, Western sculpture developed along more glyptic and realistic lines, adding the plastic and impressionist modes in the course of time. In these more congenial modes it has excelled the Orient. But the honors in the linear mode have fallen to the East.

The two periods in which the West has shown a real predilection for the linear mode and a capacity for understanding and using it well are the Middle Ages and recent modern times. It was, significantly, in the Middle Ages that the West was most open to Oriental influence, for that period saw the breakdown of Roman materialism and the ascendancy of the spiritual doctrines of an Oriental-born Christianity. The flat and shallow Byzantine sculpture of this time was, like linear Byzantine mosaic pictures, at least half-Oriental in derivation. And the Gothic sculpture of the late Middle Ages, while not linear in the sense here intended, had a high respect for the expressive qualities of line. A Gothic sculptor would probably have appreciated the spiritual vitality and physical lightness of the *Sakyamuni and Prabhutaratna* as much as any artist in Western history.

Modern sculptors who have been internally minded and historically conscious to a high degree began to appreciate Oriental art forms, especially Japanese prints, about 1850. The effects can be seen in Calder's *Hostess*. A Japanese artist would feel more at ease with it than with Michelangelo's *Moses* or Bernini's *Apollo and Daphne*. Thus the linear mode of sculpture has had its definable merits and has played an equally definable historical role in the evolution of the world's art.

CHAPTER *13*

The Abstract Arts

Although architecture and the other abstract arts are nonrepresentational, they are capable of arousing sensations and sentiments in the organized ways of art. This is particularly true of architecture, where structure and material can be used to suggest order, excitement, or repose, and a preference for the finite or the infinite. To these ends, the absence of representation is really an advantage. Freed from the demands of representation, the architect can give a more intense sensation of design by concentrating on the formal aspects of his art. He must, of course, remain aware of the practical function of architecture, but that calls for fewer compromises than does representation in painting.

On the other hand, the abstract artists must pay for their privilege of concentrating on a purer order by accepting some misunderstanding or indifference. It is plain that most human minds grasp the concrete and individual ideas in representational painting more readily than abstract or universal concepts. They also perceive the practical values in architecture more quickly than the formal and expressive. When an art form like modern abstract painting or sculpture is neither practical nor representational, the layman usually has a hard time finding any use for it at all. A special effort has then to be made to point out the logic of the approach. Yet one fact favors that effort: human beings will generally appreciate anything for which they are shown a good reason.

ARCHITECTURE

Architecture, the most important of the abstract visual arts, will receive the lion's share of our attention. When compared to the other visual arts, it most resembles sculpture, since both are literally three-dimensional, but it differs from sculpture in being hollow. This hollowness complicates the problem of the designer several-fold but does not change essentially his basic conceptions of forms. We shall be struck by the similarity of the names and types of organization.

The modes of architecture are relatively easy to study. Since no representation is involved they are only two in number—*geometric* and *plastic*. There are innumerable variations and combinations of these modes, but they have remained the basic starting points of architectural design throughout the history of art.

THE GEOMETRIC MODE. From the beginning of architecture men have been building structures which have as their basis clearly discernible geometric forms. The discovery of the usefulness of these shapes did not wait for history or advanced civilizations; they appeared in early and very primitive times. Their antiquity and universality denote their origin in fundamental modes of thinking. They characterize the Eskimo's igloo, the straw huts of the African Negro, the houses of the Pueblo Indians, the Druid monuments at Stonehenge; they are found in peasant architecture the world over. Given a set of blocks, a child will continue the mode as naturally as he breathes; and a boy will build a snow fort in a geometric shape almost without thinking. Unfortunately, apprehending architecture critically is not so intuitive as building. Hence we usually must have the geometric common denominators of architecture pointed out to us before we appreciate them fully.

The two characteristics of geometric forms which recommended them to builders in prehistoric times must have been assets too great to miss even when one was building like the African savage primarily for shelter. First of all, the geometric forms lend themselves readily to the requirements of shelter. A half-sphere can be an Eskimo's igloo and a cone the roof of a straw hut. But above and beyond that every geometric form possesses an orderliness which appeals to man's esthetic instinct regardless of whether he is conscious of it or not. Thus the geometric forms accomplish two ends at once. In sculpture they combine with representation, in architecture with practical function.

The basic geometric forms, although they appear in many variations, are the same in both of the three-dimensional arts: they are the cube, cone, cylinder, pyramid, sphere. Figs. 174b, c, and d, illustrate these shapes diagrammatically and show us two important things about them. First, their proportions can be varied endlessly;

second, the possible combinations of these different units of solid geometry are almost limitless. Together these two attributes of geometric forms have given architects great flexibility in meeting practical requirements within an orderly and expressive framework.

Though the geometric forms can be used singly, they are found in varying combinations in the majority of the world's best known buildings. The Taj Mahal, for example, is composed essentially of a cube, five hemispheres, and four cylinders. But in a structure beauty depends upon the particular proportions and combinations employed, for the geometric is not in itself a guarantee of beauty. It is only a starting point for creation or appreciation, but a most important one. How important it is can be deduced from one indisputable fact. Most of the great buildings of the world have a clear geometric compositional basis, while buildings which are unsatisfactory or confusing lack this clarity. For one reason or another their decorative elements become ends-in-themselves and yet cannot stand alone. The decorative embellishments are to geometric forms of architecture what a sauce is to meat; to mistake one for the other is to invite artistic failure.

The geometric forms have lent themselves to architecture in another important way. They are by their very nature the essence of the finite—clear-cut, stable, and permanent. No architect needs to hold these qualities sacred, for he has the same privilege as the painter, draftsman, or sculptor of expressing the infinite within the limits of his medium. But if he wishes to emphasize the finite, he has a powerful weapon at his disposal in the geometric forms and he will not lose sight of that opportunity.

Since masterpieces of architecture have a way of stating their case with unmistakable force, these several points can be illustrated by a few examples. The collective expression of architecture is in that respect an advantage. Far better than in the more individualistic field of painting, the architectural ideas of vast societies and centuries of time can be summed up by a few outstanding buildings.

The Great Pyramid of Khufu (Fig. 174a) will serve as a starting point. It is one of the oldest and largest structures in the world, and one of the most famous. While its extreme antiquity and its religious significance have their appeal, its real greatness lies in qualities which transcend history. It is a perfect example of a single geometric form on a grand scale, and benefits from all the qualities possessed by such a figure. It could not be simpler; this in itself appeals to the complex human mind. It is the epitome of the finite in a shifting and transitory world. If Khufu's architect sought a symbol of permanence, he could not have done better. The broad

FIG. 174a. Great Pyramid of Khufu. Reigned *ca.* 2900-2850 B.C., IV Dynasty. Gizeh.

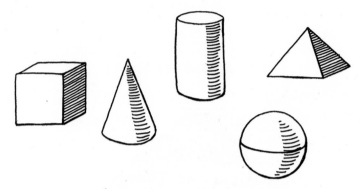

FIG. 174b. Schematic illustrations of basic geometric shapes used in architectural design.

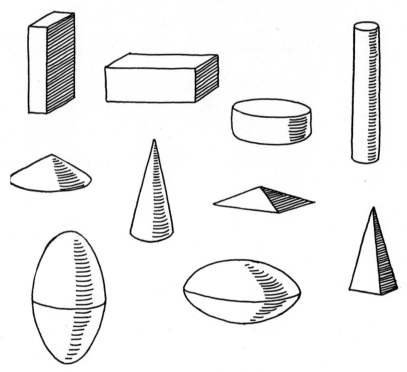

FIG. 174c. Schematic illustrations of basic geometric shapes used in architectural design
with variations in proportions.

FIG. 174d. Schematic illustrations of compositions employing basic geometric shapes in architectural design.

base and low center of gravity of a pyramid make it the most stable of all geometric forms. At the same time, it is the essence of effective orderliness, symmetrical in outline from any point of view and crowned by the ultimate architectural climactic feature—a point.

The inhuman austerity, aloofness, and consistency of the Great Pyramid make it an awe-inspiring tomb but hardly a heart-warming building. Its self-sufficiency in the lonely desert is as asocial as its form is expressive of an iron-willed but lonely authority—the authority of such an exceptional man as Khufu.

Although the Great Pyramid is not alone in employing a single geometric form, it is probably unsurpassed for its undeviating adherence to simplicity; almost nowhere else in the world has so much faith been placed in the power of unadorned consistency. In construction, also, it represents a limited type of building. Where most of the world's buildings are predominately hollow, the Great Pyramid is almost solid. This solidity contributes immeasurably to the feeling of massive finiteness that the structure conveys. But since hollowness means usable space in architecture, solidity on this scale is the kind of luxury that only a pharaoh could afford. The solidity of the Great Pyramid is therefore psychologically impressive but exceptional from the practical standpoint.

The more normal conception of architecture is exemplified by the Strozzi Palace (Fig. 175), whose courtyard and numerous rooms were designed with an eye to the needs of daily living. Like the Great Pyramid, it is a single geometric form and therefore similar to it in some respects. It has the austerity of any massive geometric form, and its cubical design appears strong and durable. This impression was not unintended, for during the socially hectic, often violent, Renaissance, a family palace was both a home and a fortress.

On the other hand, the geometric austerity of the basic cube has been relieved in the Strozzi Palace. This was done for both practical and esthetic reasons. As in most hollow buildings, there was a need for some light and communication. These were achieved by inserting windows and a door. But since both are relatively small, the walls continue to dominate. Esthetically, Giuliano da Sangallo and Il Cronaca could not, any more than their Italian Renaissance contemporaries in general, bring themselves to accept the unrelieved heaviness of an absolutely finite form. So they relieved that heaviness by adding lines to their door and window openings within a limited formula. The lines, though numerous, are mainly horizontal, a stress which is reinforced by the subdivision along storey lines and by the heavy cornice. The total effect is one of some variety within an emphatic geometric orderliness.

FIG. 175. Giuliano da Sangallo and Il Cronaca. Strozzi Palace.
1489-1507. Florence.

FIG. 176. Pantheon. Mainly A.D. 120-124. Rome.

There can be no doubt of one thing: Renaissance architecture resembles the ancient classical style whether found in Rome or Egypt in its essentially static clarity of form, for one of the results of the Revival of Antiquity was a return to the finite. Yet the Renaissance created its own variation of the finite by inventing a style which is more linear and hence somewhat lighter than the average Egyptian or Roman building. The refinement of the Renaissance style is usually traceable to a skilful and sensitive use of lines in lightening geometric forms.

The finest buildings in the geometric mode are usually combinations of different geometric shapes. These are so played against each other as to enhance our enjoyment while satisfying practical needs. In fact, the term *architectural composition* has come to be synonymous with the esthetically effective combination of two or more geometric masses. The Washington Monument, for instance, is basically a tall, slightly tapered rectangular shaft capped by a pyramid. It could scarcely be simpler or more effective. A still better known example of this kind of composition is the Pantheon at Rome (Fig. 176). Seen from the front it is simply a rectangle surmounted by a triangle and a dome (or half-sphere), the dome itself resting on a large cylinder. The width and height of the building are approximately equal, but the general impression it gives is one of massive, earth-bound finiteness; it is a symbol not only of the grandeur of Imperial Rome, but of the durability of its buildings and ideas. The particular combination of geometric shapes which is sometimes referred to as the Pantheon motif has been one of the most popular in history, being repeated in various proportions even in modern times. A well-known version in our own country is Jefferson's original library for the campus of the University of Virginia.

One of the reasons for the success of the Pantheon motif is its skilful application of three compositional principles—balance, contrast, and continuity—in the combination of geometric forms. When these principles are so used as to build up to an architectural climax in a dome, cupola, or spire, the result can be extremely satisfying. Since these principles permit innumerable variations in composition, the architects of the Renaissance were able to stay within the Roman ideals and yet create a style of their own. The Church of Santa Maria della Consolazione at Todi (Fig. 177) presents a varied but satisfying combination of contrasting geometric forms. As in the Pantheon, the progression of the forms leads the eye logically and forcibly to the top. In its general effect, however, the Renaissance church is as different from the Roman temple as the Strozzi Palace is from the Pyramid of Khufu. The ancient monuments are devoted

FIG. 177. Bramante (?) and Caprarola. S. Maria della Consolazione.
1508. Todi.

FIG. 178. Skidmore,
Owings, and Merrill.
University Hospital,
New York University–
Bellevue Medical Cen-
ter. 1949. New York.

to expressions of massive strength and durability, while the typical Renaissance structure expresses a somewhat lighter touch. Compared to the Pantheon, Santa Maria della Consolazione seems taller and more linear. While both exhibit finiteness and have geometric forms as a prominent common bond, one is ponderous, the other more graceful. Yet this difference illustrates the possibilities that were open to architects who wished to work within the geometric mode.

The feeling for geometric forms reached a low ebb historically in the nineteenth century, a period marked by poorly digested revivalism and decorative confusion, but it has been given new life in our time by the modernists. They have rung the changes on geometric composition in such buildings as Skidmore, Owings, and Merrill's University Hospital (Fig. 178) for the New York University–Bellevue Medical Center, employing geometric forms in ways that are strikingly new. Because they departed radically from deeply entrenched nineteenth-century ideals, they have been accused of ruining architecture. Articulate exponents of the new architecture such as Frank Lloyd Wright reply that they have only used age-old principles in up-to-date ways. The truth of this may be suggested by saying that the Greek designers of the Parthenon would feel at home with the University Hospital and probably find it an exciting building. They would recognize in it a point of view that is essentially classical, finite, and geometric.

The Greek architects would also perceive that the University Hospital is a new version of the ancient geometric mode in several outstanding respects. One is a consistency of reliance upon geometric forms hardly matched since the Pyramids. Related to this austerity is a scorn for decorative embellishment, partly owing to a reaction against the excessive and indiscriminate ornateness of nineteenth-century revivalist architecture. In addition, there is a new flexibility and boldness of design that was made possible by new materials and techniques, permitting, for instance, the arrangement of windows and doors in the University Hospital along horizontal lines to an unprecedented extent. Perhaps more important still, the dynamic conception of composition has given a new vitality to the formerly static geometric mode. The Medical Center's wings radiate from a central core as though bursting with centrifugal energy. Thus our modern architects resemble our modern painters and sculptors in certain essentials. All have had a keen appreciation of the importance of the basic forms of design, some to the point of devoting themselves to form-for-form's sake. All have been students of the past and have acquired a high regard for ageless principles. But all have striven to create art forms which, though partaking of the timeless, express the dynamic character of our own age.

THE PLASTIC MODE. Two conceptual ideals may be conceived as extreme points between which every example of the building art falls. The first of these, the geometric mode, we have now described. We have also shown how the extreme finiteness of the Great Pyramid was alleviated within the geometric mode in the Strozzi Palace. It now remains for us to describe the plastic mode which is as opposite in character and meaning as the boulder and the tree in Fig. 156.

These modes diverge especially in their valuations of finiteness and infinity. Granting that any building is of necessity substantial, the geometric mode courts the impression of substantiality while the plastic mode seeks to overcome that appearance to the utmost degree possible in the building media. Psychological reaction, as distinct from physical fact, must thus be taken into account. Ideally, then, that building is most plastic which most thoroughly surmounts the normal finiteness of building materials. Granted this premise, what are the practical steps which an architect can take to shift from the expression of the finite to that of the infinite?

1. He can multiply the lines of his composition, attracting attention to these weightless elements and away from the main geometric masses. The Strozzi Palace illustrates the mitigating effect thus created.

2. He can emphasize vertical lines and pointed arches instead of horizontal, ground-reflecting lines like the cornice of the Strozzi Palace.

3. He can introduce irregularly curved lines which increase the plasticity of any form and suggest movement instead of inertia.

4. He can deliberately weaken the sense of mass by creating lines which run counter to the principal contours of the geometric shapes. And he can intensify this effect by using broken outlines for contours—that is, by bursting the bonds of the geometric shapes, reaching into space with spires and pinnacles, and encouraging an interplay of space and solids. To the extent that space is incorporated into the concept of the design, its infinite connotations will aid the plastic architect's intentions.

5. He can enlarge the openings given to windows and doors and emphasize this openness in his design by surrounding them with splayed enframements and canopies. By these means the solid portions of the building will be proportionately reduced.

6. He can reduce the impression of solidity still further by his

treatment of the remaining walls. He can break up the surface into a series of bosses and hollows with a convex-concave rhythm similar to the consistent irregularity of plastic sculpture. In addition, he can perforate his material forms until they resemble "lace in stone." The most important result of this treatment is to create a play of light and shadow reminiscent of the color vibrations of Impressionist painting and intended to have the same effect. Its real merit is to increase the sense of vitality and to utilize the intangibility and changeability of light and shadow. Such a treatment endows a building with a kind of "life of its own."

7. He can conceive his whole building as a unit composed of flowing, undulating masses not unlike those found in highly plastic sculpture. Such a treatment is contrary to all of our concepts of proper building procedures, and a consistently curvilinear design conflicts with age-old notions of building based on vertical-horizontal systems. But an architect who has the skill and daring to overcome these limitations can give a building a splendid unity and a high degree of rhythmic vitality.

An architect may use all of these means of attaining a feeling of plasticity or any combination. If he uses the first six, he will exploit most of the possibilities of infinite and plastic expression in architecture and create something akin to the great Gothic cathedrals. If he employs all seven, he will create a building in the tradition of the Baroque churches of the seventeenth and eighteenth centuries.

A few examples will show how these methods have been put into practice. The Cathedral of Reims (Fig. 179) is a superb illustration of plastic architecture as it evolved under the hands of the Gothic masters, the first builders in history to understand and exploit most of the possibilities of the plastic mode. Their achievement, however, was preceded by a period in which architecture changed from the ancient classical approach to the full-fledged Gothic ideal. A representative building from this period of transition is the Church of the Holy Trinity at Caen in Normandy (Fig. 180) which is neither Roman nor Gothic but a distinctive mixture of both. In their main outlines, parts, and arrangements the Church of the Holy Trinity and the Cathedral of Reims are similar, for both were built around the needs of Christian worship. Yet each makes a quite different impression upon us because of important differences in treatment.

The church at Caen is called Romanesque, a stylistic name suggested by the round arches and sturdy strength it seems to have inherited from Roman architecture. These were in accord with a love of power and a desire for permanence which the Norman builders of William the Conqueror's day appreciated in Roman architec-

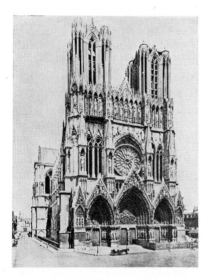

FIG. 179. Cathedral of Notre Dame. Designed by Jean le Loup and Bernard of Soissons. Mainly 13th century; west front, 1380-1420. Reims.

FIG. 180. Ste. Trinité. "Abbaye aux Dames" of Queen Matilda. 1062-1140. Caen.

FIG. 181. Da Sangallo and Il Cronaca. Doorway. Strozzi Palace. 1489-1507. Florence.

FIG. 182. West portals. 1507. Cathedral. Rouen.

329

ture and wished to continue. But there are also signs in Holy Trinity of a different temperament and outlook. The Normans, originally seafaring warriors from Norway, were too restless, super-stitious, and untamed a people to accept the static, rational, disciplined architecture of Rome completely. In building Holy Trinity they erected two towers which burst the self-sufficient out-lines of the old Roman geometric forms, following a practice that had evolved as the Middle Ages gradually broke with Roman prece-dents. Reaching aloft, the medieval towers at Caen give an un-Roman and unclassical vertical emphasis to the compositional lines. Also, some of the bulk of the towers is reduced by spindle-like mem-bers in the openings, anticipating some of the lightness of Gothic architecture. In these ways the Romanesque builders prepared for the coming of the plastic mode. But Holy Trinity, because of its strongly finite character, remained within the province of the geo-metric, and the Romanesque style in general attained a clear-cut, self-sufficient character of its own, illustrating one way in which the geometric and plastic modes can be combined. A blending of Roman geometric logic and engineering genius with northern emo-tional drives, the Romanesque style is vigorously masculine.

Between the last quarter of the twelfth century and the end of the thirteenth there occurred one of the most rapid shifts in outlook ever to transform European life. The reasons behind it have been described with brilliant insight by Henry Adams in his classic *Mont Saint Michel and Chartres* and are too complex to be examined here. But the results of this change can be seen in the Cathedral of Reims and the other masterpieces of Gothic architecture. Exploiting with great boldness structural and esthetic principles which were only suggested by Romanesque architecture, the Gothic designers brought the northern predilections for mysticism, infinity, and plastic form fully into their own. They created a style so different from either the Romanesque or ancient classical that the Renaissance Italians branded it Gothic, or "wild." It was in truth a superb realization of plastic possibilities—a style understood with great thoroughness and pursued with great consistency. Behind it was a new psychology. The bishops and townspeople who built the Cathedral of Reims had come to prize lightness and openness as much as the militant, prac-tical Normans had valued shows of formidable and forbidding strength, thus expressing their appreciation of a new sense of refine-ment, freedom, and enlightenment that spread over Europe during the last stages of the Middle Ages. These qualities appeared in the simultaneous rise of Gothic architecture and the cult of the Virgin, instilling a feminine grace in the Gothic that contrasted physically and ideologically with the masculine severity of the Romanesque. For the expression of these changes in point of view the plastic mode was admirably suited.

In swinging the pendulum so completely away from the blocky, finite massiveness of the Norman Romanesque Church of the Holy Trinity to the soaring delicacy of the Gothic, the builders of the Cathedral of Reims exploited at least six of the ways by which a plastic treatment can reduce a finite, geometric mass to a light and flowing form. They did this thoroughly, turning the classical conception of architecture inside out, and leaving only the undulating, fluid type of plastic form to be exploited by the Baroque designers. There have been few more dramatic or successful architectural revolutions in history.

The contrasting characteristics of the plastic Gothic and the more geometric Roman, Renaissance, and Romanesque styles demonstrate the importance of treatment for expressive effects. A principal difference is the contrasting part played in each by light and shadow. In Romanesque and classical architecture light and shadow are used to model forms and intensify their solid properties. In Gothic the solidity is minimized by a plastic treatment of forms involving irregular and broken surfaces and a vibrant play of light and shadow, resulting in an emphasis upon the variable and infinite.

Two examples will illustrate this difference in attitude. The doorway of the Strozzi Palace in Florence (Fig. 181) expresses the finite, geometric point of view in every particular. Each detail is clear, static, and solid in keeping with the over-all design. The conception of an architecture of heavy walls and small openings is adhered to consistently. Like all finite, geometric art which underscores the qualities of three-dimensional masses, this building appeals strongly to the tactile sense.

It is not by accident that this cubical palace reminds us of the sculpturesque painting of Michelangelo. He must have seen it many times while it was being built in Florence during his youth and have admired its massive strength, for he later helped Antonio da Sangallo the Younger design the Farnese Palace at Rome along similar lines. This is an instance of the way in which the prevailing point of view of a time runs through all the arts.

Quite different from the geometric Strozzi Palace are the portals of the Cathedral of Rouen (Fig. 182). While the sharp edge of the Strozzi Palace's doorway denotes a hole in a thick wall, the splayed portals of the Cathedral of Rouen lead our eyes through the walls gradually and minimize their heaviness. In the upper portions of the Cathedral everything possible was done to reduce the effect of solidity and tangibility. Windows were enlarged at the expense of walls, and the remaining stone perforated at every opportunity. Hence the treatment of this Cathedral's fabric has been aptly likened to "lace in stone."

This antigeometric and essentially plastic treatment caused the appeal to the tactile sense to be weakened, but the visual effect heightened. Deliberately sacrificing finiteness, the Gothic designers expressed their worship of the infinite by stressing the intangibles— light, shadow, and, in their stained glass windows, color. They not only reduced the principal qualities of stone by perforating it, but created, by the same method, a color vibration of great intensity and a strong sense of vitality.

The transcendent qualities of the geometric and plastic points of view can be seen in the attitudes of two famous artists towards architecture. Michelangelo's glyptic and classical biases made him detest the Gothic union of plasticity and complexity. In an oft-quoted diatribe against the style of the northern artists and builders, he flayed their "weakness" for details while missing their genius for achieving both infinite variety and plastic unity on a tremendous scale. The Impressionist Monet saw Gothic architecture with different eyes. He loved the vibrant play of light and shadow which resembled the broken colors in his own paintings and worried little about the attendant loss of massiveness. He not only elected to paint the façade of Rouen Cathedral a number of times, but eliminated altogether any feeling of mass, realizing in paint the intangibility which the late Gothic architect could only aim at in stone.

Although the masterpieces of architecture generally express either the geometric or plastic conceptions with authority, room must be left for mixtures of the two modes, for some extremely satisfying buildings can thereby be appreciated. One of these, the Church of the Holy Trinity at Caen, we have already seen. Although emphatically finite and geometric, its severe orderliness is relieved by a few gestures toward the infinite. Another example of mixed modes, the Mirador de Darraxa in the Alhambra at Granada (Fig. 183), presents this formula in reverse. The designers clearly favored a large measure of plasticity and complexity, but wished to avoid extremes and retain some degree of finite clarity. Their method was to preserve and emphasize those outlines which bounded geometric shapes by a skilful use of decorative lines. The walls were enlivened without being eliminated and the geometric and plastic played against one another successfully, each heightening the effect of the other. The Moorish architects built the Alhambra in this style because, coming from northern Africa, they could not escape entirely the influence

FIG. 183. Detail. Mirador de Darraxa. "Hall of Two Sisters." Begun 1230. The Alhambra. Granada.

FIG. 184. Neumann. Wallfahrtkirche. *ca.* 1740. Vierzehnheiligen.

of the Mediterranean classical tradition. Unconsciously they paid their respects to it through linear definition, geometric compositions, and a balance of verticals and horizontals.

While the possibility of combining the merits of both modes greatly extends the range of architecturally satisfying formulae, it does not preclude poor practice. In every case of good plastic design one principle is apparent; the architect conceived his basic masses and surface treatment together. Every detail of the Cathedral of Reims is related to an underlying form, as, for instance in the interplay between the cubical core and spindle-like surface of the towers. In fine plastic architecture there is no decoration as such. If we must use the term we should think of it as applying to an *integral* part of the plastic form.

The last builders to exploit the potentialities of the plastic mode with great skill and understanding were the Baroque architects of the seventeenth and eighteenth centuries. Some of the most consistent examples of this style were created by the northern architects and by the Germans in particular. Their achievement came somewhat later than that of the precocious and brilliant Italians, but it should not be surprising; for they were surrounded by Gothic examples.

A fine example of the Baroque version of the plastic mode is Balthasar Neumann's Wallfahrtkirche, at Vierzehnheiligen in southern Germany (Fig. 184). Complex but unified, it typifies a kind of integrated plasticity that was long in coming. It had to await a skill which could shape a whole building as though it were clay. It had to await, too, a perfect skill in harmonizing a variety of materials and media—marble, glass, and metals, and architecture, sculpture and painting. The true Baroque church is no piecemeal assemblage. It aims at a total unity of effect and stands or falls on its achievement. When successful, it is spectacular.

In Neumann's Wallfahrtkirche a curvilinear line which meanders rhythmically throughout the design unifies the building. The façade of the church is curved like a cupid's bow. The ground plan is a pattern of areas shaped like clover leaves in which curved outlines predominate. And the interior walls and vaults have been curved wherever possible. The effect favors the infinite and especially the plastic. Solid walls seem to have been bent with an ease which belies their substantiality. More than that, they seem to have been set in a weaving undulating pattern. The static is thus reduced and the vital emphasized. In addition to unifying the design, the curved lines give it a special character, diverting attention from the stationary properties of walls and supports and inducing a roving apprehension.

This is a restless architecture but it is by no means wild. The Baroque architects displayed extraordinary control in relating solids and space so that they interpenetrate constantly. Not only is this shown by their use of large windows, but by the treatment of the interior, where nave, side aisles, and bays seem perpetually to overlap. But the crowning touch is the use of a painting similar to Pozzo's *Glorification of the Company of Jesus* (Fig. 110) to open up the building to the sky. Not even the heaven-aspiring Gothic builders were able with such facility to eliminate the whole vault of a building.

By treating solid materials as though they were putty, the Baroque architects exploited whatever plastic possibilities the Gothic designers had left untouched. They created in this way an inspired architecture which is dynamic, varied, and infinite. Its restlessness is hardly to our own taste and it is worlds apart from the geometricity of the New York University–Bellevue Medical Center, but its brilliance is undeniable.

The historical distribution of the geometric and plastic modes is easily traced. They have alternated leadership down through the centuries, with the plastic evolving gradually from the geometric until carried to excess. Historically the geometric mode reigned from primitive times until near the end of ancient classical civilization. During the later history of the Greco-Roman world, Mediterranean architecture tended toward plastic conceptions of form, but this tendency was cut short by the fall of Rome before it could be exploited. Then the medieval world returned to the geometric mode for another thousand years. It was not until the thirteenth century that the Gothic style broke the age-old hold of the geometric mode and held sway for a period of about two hundred years. With the Italian Renaissance, classical ideals returned to the fore, only to give way in a rhythmic alternation of leadership to the Baroque. In our time, the International Style of modern architecture, while varying from country to country, has brought a return to geometric concepts.

Thus, if the history of architecture is rapidly reviewed, the plastic mode appears to have been adopted, understood, and fully exploited only during two historic periods—the Gothic and Baroque—and for a total of five hundred years at most. During all the remaining centuries the geometric mode has predominated. In numerical terms this means that a majority of the world's famous buildings exemplify that mode.

The geometric mode has predominated because of certain physical and connotative merits. Its structural systems have been simpler than those of the plastic mode, hence they appeared earlier in time and were adopted by more people. Once established, they were hard to dislodge. Reinforcing these practical assets were equally important psychological merits. The geometric mode stands for strength and security; its examples look sturdy and dependable—not only in the protection they give from natural elements, but from human threats. Neither the Great Pyramid nor the Strozzi Palace was made to appear impregnable merely to ward off weather; the Pyramid was designed to thwart robbery, the Strozzi Palace to withstand armed assault. Countless other buildings in the geometric mode express through their substantiality human fears and the universal craving for security. Since these fears have plagued human beings through most of our history, the geometric mode has been favored over the plastic.

The times have been few when men felt an overwhelming urge to express spiritual aspiration or exultation. The Gothic thirteenth century was such a time, the Baroque period was another. Both were marked by extraordinary spiritual vitality. To express that vitality each turned in its own way to the plastic mode.

Let us not be misled, however, in assuming that the feeling of exuberant freedom which abounds in the Cathedral of Reims and the Wallfahrtkirche permeated the Gothic and Baroque societies, for the civic and domestic architecture of the late Middle Ages is as heavy and fortress-like as the Strozzi Palace and Baroque society was torn by wars. Only the religious edifices enjoyed the privilege of expressing men's hopes and aspirations. That is part of their purpose, but it reduces still further the examples of plastic architecture. Indeed, if the history of architecture is viewed from long range, the Gothic cathedrals and other truly great examples of plastic architecture are as exceptional as they are inspiring.

The ultimate merits of the geometric and plastic modes do not depend, however, on quantity or popularity, but on their capacities for fulfilling man's architectural aims and needs. In that respect each mode has been indispensable, and each has proved its worth in many masterpieces.

ABSTRACT PAINTING, SCULPTURE, AND THE MINOR ARTS

Men have often wished over the centuries to free themselves from the demands of representation in painting and sculpture and from the practical requirements of architecture so that they could express their delight in pure form. Until the present century, however, they have found an outlet for this esthetic urge only in subordinate and

less respected art forms, such as the decorative carving or embellishment of architecture, glazed tiles or geometric mosaic patterns, and
the making of furniture, textiles, ceramics, or carpets. These minor
or decorative arts have often brought visual delight, but almost never
without fulfilling some useful purpose. While craving freedom of
expression, men have been inhibited by a strong reluctance to create
any minor work of art which was not useful in some way—the connotation being that such an object was *useless*. So deep-seated has
this prejudice been that not until the twentieth century did artists
bring themselves to create nonrepresentational paintings and statues
and claim for them the status of major works of art. They have by
no means completely won their battle in the eyes of the public, but
this does not absolve us from making an attempt to understand their
aims.

We can approach these aims from several points of view, starting
with the following pertinent fact; although men are forced by circumstances of life to heed the demands of usefulness in almost
everything they do, strong drives in their spiritual natures predispose
them toward certain activities as ends in themselves. The three
strongest drives that affect artistic activity are the urge to play and
to enjoy leisure for its own sake, the urge to know for the sake of
knowing, and the urge to create pure order. The desire to know
gave rise to philosophy and higher learning in the arts and sciences;
the desire to create pure order led to the composition of music and
the pursuit of higher mathematics. Through mathematics the love
of numerical relationships and geometric forms which have no necessary connection with anything in nature could be satisfied. All of
these denoted the pleasure the human mind can derive from abstract
thinking. In addition, the products of this kind of thinking met
with enthusiastic responses from many who appreciated them even
if they could not create them. They have added much to the pleasure of civilized living, a notable instance being the current widespread enjoyment of fine music.

Having found the courage to do what composers and musicians
have done for centuries, modern artists discovered that they could
realize their new aims in single works of art. More important critically, abstract art partook of either the geometric or the plastic mode.
Both modes, for instance, can be used to create abstract forms which
are as pure expressions of order as any algebraic equation and have
no recognizable connection with nature. A well-known example of
this kind of pure abstraction we have already seen in Mondrian's
highly geometric *Composition in Red, White, and Black* (Fig. 55).
Mondrian's prominent lines produce an intense visual sensation

because they are unencumbered with any burden of sentiment. Like all abstract arts, they gain in clarity what they sacrifice in meaning.

An illustration of the plastic mode is provided by the work of William Muir. Giving his figures such general titles as *Growth* (Fig. 186), he deals with essential universal phenomena. His preference is for plastic forms which he handles with such facility that they suggest countless shapes. Some which have been suggested are creeping vines, weather-beaten trees, flames, columns of smoke, and jungle-like roots—so evocative of all these ideas is his imaginative and imagination-stimulating *Growth*. Thus the abstract arts do not have to divorce themselves from nature. They can be used to interpret its universal forms and phenomena in a clear and intensified manner.

Muir's *Growth* was itself originally inspired by a study of skunk cabbages (Fig. 185). But, following a common practice of abstract artists, he eliminated the particular characteristics of his source until he arrived at a concentrated symbol of many living and growing forms. Thus his figure *Growth*, freed from identification with any one specific form, and suggesting all the plastic growth-patterns in nature, allows the spectator to see in it whatever natural form he will.

The evocative power of a figure like Muir's *Growth* derives from a common psychological phenomenon. The human mind can perceive the underlying geometric or plastic forms in representational statues; it can also find natural forms in so-called abstract works of art. Owing to the dual qualities of universality and individuality of all natural forms, either process is possible and valid. The representational artist leans toward the specific, while the abstractionist favors the general. Neither, however, entirely ignores the other. Thus, in the last analysis, the difference between representation and abstraction is only a matter of degree, of how far the artist carries the process of selection, distillation, and concentration which is common to all fine art.

Muir's *Skunk Cabbage No. 1* and *Growth* demonstrate a typical evolution from the representational to the abstract, the one being the beginning of the process, the other the result. According to Muir, artists carry selection and elimination as far as possible in order to give us an interpretation of nature which will have a universal rather than a limited meaning and will possess an infinite power of suggestion. Another more strictly artistic interest is to heighten our esthetic pleasure in the textures and colors that a piece of wood or stone possesses and in the shapes that it can be made to assume. They believe that as representational meaning is reduced or generalized, our minds are freer to appreciate these qualities more intensely. The formula—elimination and clarification produce in-

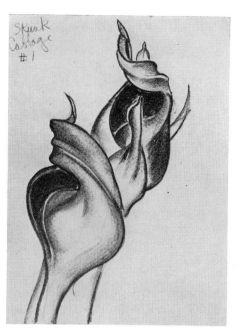

FIG. 185. Muir. *Skunk Cabbage No. 1*. 1950.
Collection of the artist.

FIG. 186. Muir. *Growth*. 1950.
Bowdoin College Museum of Fine
Arts, Brunswick, Me.

FIG. 187. Chinese glazed pottery. T'ang Dynasty, A.D. 618-906. Nelson Gallery and
Atkins Museum, Kansas City, Mo.

tensification—is an old one which they have merely carried to its logical end.

In a different category from modern nonrepresentational paintings are the abstract minor arts which are useful and yet afford great esthetic pleasure. No better example is likely to come to mind than the ceramic ware of the Chinese, such as the glazed pottery vessels in Fig. 187. Artists who produce objects like these do not aim to suggest universal natural forms in the conscious fashion of our modern abstractionists. They feel an obligation toward the practical function of their products as well as concern for their beauty and succeed in varying degrees with this dual problem. We must not assume that all functional forms are beautiful; nor are all beautiful forms functionally efficient. The master of the minor arts is one who strikes a balance between these interests, heeding functional needs which the modern abstractionist ignores.

It is to the credit of the old Chinese craftsmen that they were able to create things whose beauty includes usefulness and whose usefulness does not exclude beauty. Their genius lay in their feeling for the formal entities of outline, mass, color, and texture, with a special genius for orderly, strong, and graceful shapes. Under their hands these characteristics took on a clarity and intensity which have made connoisseurs around the world nearly forget that they were handling vases or pots or bowls in their sheer delight with their formal beauty.

The merits and limitations of the abstract visual arts can be summed up by saying that their most obvious limitation is their inability to convey any specific idea as clearly as can a representational work of art; but against this can be set almost unlimited capacities for expressing universal attributes of reality in forms which can convey order and variety, vitality and repose, and finitude and infinitude with unmistakable clarity and intensity.

In order to avoid attempting too much at one time, we have thus far studied the geometric and plastic modes in connection with the separate media of art and their subdivisions. It might be wise now to note how, like trees and boulders, these modes are universal and run through the world of art without regard for medial lines. We have only to look beneath the surfaces of a number of works of art to see that they are members of a universal family whose forms are essentially plastic. Observe, for instance, the common quality of apparent movement and vitality in Muir's *Growth*, Kokoschka's *Courmayeur* (Fig. 9), Barye's *Black Panther* (Fig. 31), Daumier's *Drinking Song* (Fig. 63), Van Gogh's *Mountainous Landscape* (Fig. 65), El Greco's *Agony in the Garden* (Fig. 90), Hirschvogel's *Landscape with a Curved Wooden Bridge* (Fig. 118), Turner's *Martello*

Towers Near Bexhill (Fig. 146), Dürer's *Flight Into Egypt* (Fig. 148), Delacroix's *Combat* (Fig. 153), Van Gogh's *Cypresses* (Fig. 155), Daumier's *Burden* (Fig. 161), Bourdelle's *Beethoven* (Fig. 164), and Neumann's Wallfahrtkirche (Fig. 184). All of these show the far-flung continuity of the plastic conception of form.

The geometric conception of form has been no less continuous or widespread. A few examples which demonstrate how readily this fundamental way of conceiving form cuts across boundaries of time, place, and media are the *Seated Statue of Khum-Ba-F* (Fig. 2), Cézanne's *Vase of Tulips* (Fig. 15), the *Zeus from Artemisium* (Fig. 50), the *Governor of Lagash* (Fig. 67), Giotto's *Meeting of Joachim and Anna* (Fig. 75), Cézanne's *House in Provence* (Fig. 80), Zorach's *The Spirit of the Dance* (Fig. 84), Wright's Johnson Wax Company Building (Fig. 86), Mantegna's *St. James Led to Execution* (Fig. 106), Lippi's *Portrait of a Man* (Fig. 125), Cézanne's *Louis Guillaume* (Fig. 127), Giotto's *Death of St. Francis* (Fig. 133), Laurana's *Princess of the House of Aragon* (Fig. 158), Brancusi's *Mademoiselle Pogany* (Fig. 159), and *Menkure and His Queen* (Fig. 160). These point with equal eloquence to the long history of the geometric tradition in artistic thinking.

But the mere determination of the mode of organization employed in a work of art is not the end of criticism; it is only the beginning of an analysis of characteristics whose distinctive quality is always individual. Coupled with haste, the guessing of modes can result in some fallacious pigeonholing, such as identifying a pictorial picture as realistic and then "reading into" the picture memorized realistic characteristics. To the point is an old agricultural adage, "Study the animal before you name it; don't name it before you study it."

Nor is the use of a common mode in itself a guarantee of fine quality. The preference for the sculpturesque mode by the Italian painters of the Renaissance gave every new generation a basic inheritance and saved many hours of training. It also gave the Renaissance a coherent style. Nevertheless, the Renaissance produced its share of monstrosities as well as masterpieces. And the same may be said of every period and mode. All *permitted* great expression; they did not *produce* it. Greatness had to be achieved individually in every case, as a comparison of the work of Da Vinci, Raphael, and Michelangelo with that of any of their pupils will amply show. This is an inescapable law of selectivity which applies equally to analysis, criticism, and appreciation. Pigeonholing and categorizing are necessary for systematic study. But they are never more than points of departure toward understanding expressive characteristics and qualities.

CHAPTER *14*

The Visual Media

It is not essential to become a proficient technician in any human activity in order to judge or appreciate it. A general acquaintance with the techniques employed is, however, important in evaluating the proficiency with which the work has been produced. This is notably true of the visual arts, where the expressive effects are so dependent upon the physical characteristics of the medium. Failure to appreciate the limitations as well as the potentialities of a medium will result in a false evaluation of the particular work. This is especially pertinent in the consideration of the first of the pictorial works to be discussed—mosaic.

THE PICTORIAL MEDIA

MOSAIC. A mosaic picture like the *Empress Theodora and Attendants* (Fig. 188) which is a pendant to the *Justinian and Courtiers* (Fig. 121) at Ravenna is composed of small cubes of colored glass and stone. When set into the wet plaster of a wall these become as unchangeable and durable as the wall itself.

Although the Romans knew mosaic and used it extensively to cover floors, the medium is now associated mainly with Byzantine art. The golden age of the medium was the sixth century, when the masterpiece of Byzantine architecture, St. Sophia, was built at Constantinople by Justinian. The medium continued to be used during the spread and long twilight of Byzantine art (as in the mosaics of San Marco at Venice), but never surpassed its early achievements. It gained its greatest eminence at an earlier date than any of the other major pictorial media and then faded from popularity. It is seldom used today, because its purposes, merits, and limitations are foreign to our interests.

Fig. 188. Detail. *Empress Theodora and Attendants.* A.D. 526. S. Vitale, Ravenna.

Fig. 189. Detail. *Festival of Roses.* 1435-1440. Metropolitan Museum of Art, New York.

Fig. 190. Gothic stained glass window. 13th century French. Isabella Stewart Gardner Museum, Boston.

Fig. 191. Fra Angelico. *Madonna of Humility.* 1430-1440. National Gallery of Art Washington, D.C.

Chief among the medium's limitations from our point of view is its tediousness. The pictorial design must be worked out completely in a cartoon or other preparatory design before the painstaking execution is begun. And when completed, the medium has prominent representational and projectional shortcomings.

The nature of the medium limits it largely to the mode of line and local color. Modeling can only be achieved with difficulty, and effects of illumination, atmosphere, and shadow are almost out of the question; consequently, a representation of deep space by perspective or aerial means is beyond its scope, as is the suggestion of natural movement. The medium is stiff, static, flat, shallow, and finite—one of the poorest for realistic representation that an artist could use.

Against these drawbacks can be set mosaic's beauty of design and material. Its flat patterns are an advantage in mural decoration; its durability is unquestioned; and its colors can be magnificent. The thousands of tiny cubes reflect light in a variable, sparkling fashion, like a crown set with jewels, endowing mosaic with a colorful life and vitality which offsets its representational rigidity. Although poor as a means of representation, the medium has great beauty.

Therefore, while the modern artist with his craving for more spontaneous vehicles of expression gives mosaic a wide berth, the medium was excellent for the religious, ideological, and decorative purposes of the sixth century Byzantine artists, and should be appraised accordingly.

TAPESTRY.   A tapestry picture like Fig. 189 is one woven into the fabric of a cloth, usually on a large scale. Like a mosaic picture, it normally depicts a religious or courtly scene and was intended to serve a mural purpose. The big woollen panels were hung on the otherwise bare and cold stone walls of European churches and castles, partly to convey ideas pictorially, but to no small extent to provide some measure of psychological warmth. To this purpose the colors, textures, and connotations of heavy woollen cloth were admirably suited.

Whereas mosaic became a popular medium in the Mediterranean region during the Byzantine ascendancy of the early Middle Ages, tapestry became prominent only in the Gothic art of the late medieval period. The finest tapestries were woven in the northern countries of Europe during the building period of the cathedrals and were often intended to decorate them. That the peoples of the North should appreciate the warm textured qualities of tapestries is not hard to understand.

To weave a picture in cloth on a large scale is difficult. Threads must be dyed many colors; a full-scale colored cartoon must be created in advance and then carefully woven over a period of months and sometimes years. When completed, the fabric was subject to fading, rotting, and damage by moths. Both its stability and durability left much to be desired. Moreover, it offered only a limited means of representation, making possible a semisculpturesque effect at best. Despite the *tours de force* performed by the seventeenth-century French tapestry-makers at the Gobelin works in Paris, tapestry could never compete with the oil painting of its day as a means of pictorial or realistic representation.

In the face of pronounced physical and representational limitations, the question must arise—why does an artist patiently put hundreds of hours of time into such a medium? In the case of tapestry the answer lies, as it does in mosaic, in compensatory qualities of design and decoration. The softly pleasant colors and textural warmth of the large tapestry panels saved many a medieval church and castle hall from utter coldness. To this may be added the general observation that the medieval peoples had a genius for building, and realizing this they used the pictorial media without hesitation for subordinate decorative purposes. We who have less feeling for mural decoration, but a greater awe for the importance and independence of pictures, must remember this relationship if we wish to understand tapestries in the perspective of their original function.

STAINED GLASS. Stained glass was the third major medium that rose to prominence during the Middle Ages. Like tapestry it achieved perfection in the Gothic period of northern Europe. The finest examples in this medium were designed by the thirteenth-century artists of the Île de France for the great cathedrals; the masterpieces are the incomparable windows in the Cathedral of Notre Dame at Chartres. Few of these windows have come to America, but a brilliant example can be seen in the Gardner Museum in Boston (Fig. 190).

The construction of a stained glass window is probably the most difficult pictorial process ever devised. A complete design is made in advance and then translated into pieces of colored glass, which, because of their fragility and the intricacy of the design, must be small. Hundreds of these fragments, each cut individually with the utmost care, went into the making of a single large window. The pieces were held in place by ribbon-like frames of I-shaped lead, and the design as a whole strengthened by crossbars of iron or steel. When placed in a window opening and exposed to wind and weather, it was a fragile medium indeed. Because of this delicacy, the windows of Chartres have in our century been removed at every threat of war.

When, to this fragility and extreme difficulty of execution, one adds the obvious limitations in representation, it is easy to see why modern artists have seldom touched the stained glass medium except to decorate revivalist architectural monuments like the modern Gothic Cathedral of St. John the Divine in New York City. The medium lends itself naturally to representation in the mode of line and local color and geometric projection, but to little more. When, with the onset of the Renaissance, artists wished to extend even a finite point of view beyond those limits, the stained glass medium went rapidly out of favor.

The many limitations of this medium are, however, more than balanced by its superlative qualities of design and decoration. No other medium gives us such an intense sensation of color as stained glass through which light pours directly instead of being reflected from and partly absorbed by an opaque surface. The living quality of the light, which changes with the time and character of the day, contributes much to the living, changeable quality one feels in the Gothic cathedrals. By suffusing the interiors with a mellow light it counteracts the cold effect of stone walls. Contrary to popular supposition, the Gothic cathedrals are not brilliantly lighted by their large windows, but they do benefit from one of the most beautiful kinds of lighting ever invented. Acting together, the vivid colors of the stained glass windows and the variable light that passes through them endow the Gothic masonry with a vitality which is necessary to its expressive purposes. One cannot imagine the cathedrals without these windows.

Like mosaic and tapestry, stained glass is associated historically with the Middle Ages and primarily with the mural decoration of religious edifices, in which all three media played a subordinate but valuable role. Their subject matter, too, is mainly religious with a highly collective bias. Representationally they denote a time when a realistic view of reality was quite secondary to the expression of symbolical ideas. Within these limitations mosaic, tapestry, and stained glass functioned well, but being little suited to express the outlook of the Renaissance, they fell into disuse after the Middle Ages.

TEMPERA. While tempera painting was known throughout the Middle Ages, it came to the forefront of the artistic media during the Renaissance in Italy, when masters of the fame and ability of

Fra Angelico made it and fresco the two predominant media of the day. It was used in the painting of numerous pictures which, though of a religious nature like Angelico's *Madonna of Humility* (Fig. 191) and intended to adorn altars and chapels, were not a fixed part of the mural decoration. Independent of the wall, they were the precursors of the free-hanging easel painting of modern times.

A tempera painting was executed by applying colors mixed with egg yolk to the surface of a fine-grained wooden panel (such as poplar) which was covered with a thin coat of *gesso* (similar to present-day plaster of Paris). This surface gave the painter a smooth, white, luminous background on which to work. He had, however, to build up his picture with hundreds of minute strokes of a pointed brush because of one crucial characteristic of egg-yolk—it dries very rapidly, usually setting in a matter of minutes.

Such a technique virtually demanded a finite style in which outlines would be clear and sharp, but it also allowed a powerful modeling of forms. It was therefore well suited to the sculpturesque mode of the time, as is evident in Fra Angelico's panel.

Since colors in tempera had to be applied quickly in short strokes, an artist had to know in advance what he wished to do and then remain loyal to his original plan. It was not a medium which allowed a brilliant idea to be captured in the heat of inspiration. Spontaneity was not its forte; it could never have given rise to Impressionism. Everything about tempera denotes an age which was still imbued with the medieval ideals of careful craftsmanship.

The vigorous but strong-minded artists of the Early Renaissance accepted the unavoidable tediousness of tempera because of certain outstanding properties. The egg medium is moistureproof, durable, and colorfast; pictures painted in it have remained well-preserved to the present day. Furthermore, it can be made translucent enough to permit some of the white ground to shine through the colors, giving them a high degree of luminosity. If an artist wished, he could employ intense colors, confident that they would retain their pristine brilliance for centuries to come. Fra Angelico's *Madonna of Humility,* with its still bright and gay colors, is an excellent example of tempera's dependability.

Colorfastness has been stressed in this discussion of media because it is more than a pedantic concern of any conscientious artist. He wishes not only to objectify his feelings but to fix them in a permanent relationship. Fading or darkening alters his expressed idea, and uneven fading may destroy it altogether, changing a balanced composition into a discordant one. Hence the centuries-old dread of fugitive colors and the pursuit of permanence by artists has not been a mere fetish.

The tempera medium is associated with some of the most satisfactory pictures ever painted—the masterpieces of the fifteenth-century Renaissance Italians. Speaking for a relatively happy and optimistic time in history, they are cheerful and gay in color and yet executed with impeccable craftsmanship. They express, too, a balanced, transitional point of view, combining the decorative beauty of the Middle Ages with a sufficient measure of realism to create convincing human figures. Compared to Fra Angelico's warmly gracious *Madonna of Humility,* the mosaic image of the Empress Theodora is a stiff and austere symbol. Better still, Angelico and his better contemporaries were able to convey this new humanistic and social grace with little loss of decorative appeal; in decorative quality alone the embossed gold-leaf background of his picture is superb. Thus the development of tempera was a sign of the times and contributed significantly to them.

FRESCO. During the Italian Renaissance another medium, called *fresco,* vied with tempera in popularity. An excellent medium for mural decoration because unlike tempera it could be used conveniently on great areas, it gave the Italian artists a means of painting pictures on large plaster walls of churches and chapels which cried out for embellishment. It gave an extra string to their bow, for most of the masters who used tempera were also trained in fresco painting.

Although fresco was an ancient medium, having been employed widely by the Egyptians for decorating tombs with pictures like *Nakht Watching Plowing* (Fig. 120) and then adopted by the Romans for mural decorations of many sorts (as in the houses of Pompeii), the medium gained its greatest prestige during the Italian Renaissance, when more great examples of it were created by more famous masters than at any other period. Giotto's *Presentation of the Virgin* (Fig. 51), Mantegna's *St. James Led to Execution* (Fig. 106), Raphael's *School of Athens* (Fig. 104), and Michelangelo's *Creation of Adam* (Fig. 126) are all fresco paintings, and the majority, it will be noted, are either religious in subject or located in religious edifices.

The period of fresco's ascendancy can be dated rather exactly. It fell between the time that Giotto painted the interior of the Arena Chapel at Padua (*ca.* 1305) and Michelangelo's decoration of the ceiling of the Sistine Chapel in the Vatican (1508-12); their paintings represent the pioneering and culminating masterpieces of the medium. They are similar in one noteworthy respect; both consist of a group of pictures which are related or illustrate a narrative serially. Called a cycle of frescos, this method of presentation became typical of Renaissance mural decoration. Mantegna, Masaccio, Signorelli, Gozzoli, Perugino, and Raphael, like most of the other leading masters, painted a cycle of frescos at one time or another.

The fifteenth-century Italian artist created a picture in fresco by painting in water color on the moist surface of freshly applied plaster, thus affixing a picture and finishing the wall in one operation. Behind this task lay, however, a good deal of preparation. To take an example, Michelangelo, before painting the ceiling of the Sistine Chapel, had first to construct an elaborate wooden scaffold and design a complete cartoon or design on paper. The cartoon was necessary because plaster sets in the course of a few hours, during which an artist could complete only one or two square yards of his picture. Moreover, working close to it, he needed something to insure that the small area he was painting would be properly related to the composition as a whole.

An ingenious method was invented to save the artist time and take advantage of the full-scale preparatory drawing. The outlines of the drawing were transferred to the section of new plaster by dusting charcoal powder through holes which were perforated along the drawing's outlines by means of a revolving disk not unlike the rowel of a western spur. With these lines to guide him, the painter could be sure the positions, proportions, and perspective relationships of his figures were correct; he could then concentrate his attention on modeling his forms and completing his color design.

But before a cartoon could be used as an over-all guide, it had to be worked out at a cost of much labor. The amount of effort that went into this process is eloquently revealed by the many drawings of figures that Michelangelo did before painting the Sistine ceiling. One such drawing, that of Adam for the *Creation of Adam,* can be seen in Fig. 58. Michelangelo not only made scores of similar drawings before he was ready to paint, but drew such details as heads, hands, and toes until he was satisfied. Before an artist could paint a fresco picture he had to know what he was going to do. Clearly, it was not a medium for the impetuous; the care that went into these Italian mural decorations made them the masterpieces they are.

This procedure contributed to one very noticeable characteristic of the Italian Renaissance. It was, of necessity, an age of outstanding draftsmen, for whether an artist painted in fresco or tempera, he had to do a large amount of drawing in advance. The center of this art was Florence.

Two changes occur as a fresco painting dries. The colors applied on the wet surface sink into the wall to a depth of about one-eighth of an inch, becoming a permanent part of the plaster and making the picture nearly as durable as the wall itself. On the other hand, the colors fade somewhat in drying. This can be regarded as an advantage, for the softer colors are more harmonious, a characteristic especially to be valued in large wall decorations. Sir Charles Holmes has wisely observed that there is a relationship between area and our tolerance of color intensities; the hues which seem bright and gay in a miniature Persian illumination like the *Polo Game* in Fig. 112 would appear garish in a fresco as large as Perugino's *Christ Delivering the Keys of Heaven to Saint Peter* (Fig. 102a). The Italian masters benefited by the fact that it is hard to be garish in fresco. They had, too, another reason for liking the soft hues of fresco: living in a sunlit land they felt less need for the brilliant colors employed in stained glass windows by the peoples of the North.

Some exceptions, of course, were inspired by the desire for greater realism which appeared with the Renaissance. Giotto, for instance, not only abandoned the medieval gold background, but introduced blue skies which he wished to make as intense as those in nature. To do this he had to add washes of strong color to the dry picture. This process, called *fresco a secco,* became common in the Renaissance for purposes of addition or correction, but it was seldom a good practice. We can see the results in Giotto's *Presentation of the Virgin* (Fig. 51); the parts painted in true fresco are in excellent condition, the sky which was applied *a secco* has flaked off badly.

The fresco medium has long been identified with the sculpturesque mode of painting favored by the majority of Italian Renaissance artists from Giotto through Michelangelo. It was ideal for their representational purposes. When the finite interests of the fifteenth-century artists faded before the new emphasis upon infinite light and shadows, blended colors and atmosphere, fresco painting went out of favor. For though it was not impossible to paint frescos in the pictorial mode, as Andrea del Sarto proved, pictorial interests could be achieved much more easily in other media. And as a general rule the busy artists of the Renaissance and post-Renaissance periods always preferred a medium which could achieve their aims both effectively and easily.

In the twentieth century the fresco medium has staged a kind of comeback. It has been revived and widely used for mural paintings by the artists of the Mexican school headed by Diego Rivera and Orozco. No less significant has been a revival of tempera painting by contemporary artists such as Peter Hurd. Rivera revived fresco in order to paint in a sculpturesque manner. And Hurd's Renaissance-like portraits are a part of the widespread return to a finite conception of reality which runs through modern art. Whenever there is a revival of older art forms there is likely to be a corresponding resurrection of the appropriate older media. Artists do not possess an unlimited number of media, and by perceiving the special merits of the older media they have often been able to use them for present purposes.

THE FLEMISH MIXED METHOD OF OIL PAINTING. Before the Gothic period faded the artists of northern Europe felt the urge to set painting on the way to realism. They were not able to begin this trend with the older tempera medium, but by the early years of the fifteenth century they had discovered a medium—oil—which allowed them to start. Eventually it was to revolutionize the art of painting.

Jan Van Eyck and his brother Hubert are usually given credit for having recognized, if not discovered, the artistic possibilities of the oil medium early in the fifteenth century. They began, too, to paint in a new and distinctive manner. Thus the part played by oil cannot be disconnected from the remarkable advance in realistic painting which Jan Van Eyck made when he painted his *Marriage of Giovanni Arnolfini* (Fig. 193).

It is our good fortune to possess a picture which Jan Van Eyck did not complete, the *St. Barbara* (Fig. 192) at Antwerp. It exemplifies graphically what laboratory scientists can now tell us about the method of painting used by Van Eyck and the other fifteenth-century Flemish masters.

It is called a mixed method because the artists built up their pictures in two stages and with two different media. Judging by the *St. Barbara,* they painted a tempera picture on a panel after the fashion of their Italian contemporaries, but with this important difference—this initial picture was monochromatic, with only the outlines and modeling rendered. The merit of this procedure was to separate the problem of form from that of color. This was especially advantageous for Van Eyck and the other Flemings because they liked to paint complex and microscopic details; note for example the intricacy of St. Barbara's tower.

As a second procedural step the Flemish painters added color by applying thin films of oil pigment until they attained the effect desired, which, in Van Eyck's case, was a realistic one. The section of his *Marriage of Giovanni Arnolfini* shown in Fig. 193 illustrates

FIG. 192. Jan Van Eyck. *St. Bar-bara*. 1437. Royal Museum, Ant-werp.

FIG. 193. Jan Van Eyck. Detail. *Marriage of Giovanni Arnolfini and Giovanna Cenami*. 1434. National Gallery, London.

FIG. 194. Tintoretto. *Diana*. 1570-1580. Fogg Museum of Art, Harvard University.

FIG. 195. Titian. Detail. *Rape of Europa*. 1559. Isabella Stewart Gardner Museum, Boston.

what the *St. Barbara* panel would have looked like if it had been finished.

Using the more or less complete underpainting (as in the *St. Barbara*) as a guide, an artist like Van Eyck would apply translucent glazes or thin films of colored oil pigment to his panel until the color design itself was finished. Glazes were used insofar as possible because their physical beauty is usually superior to that of opaque pigment, as a glass of wine contrasts with a glass of milk. They offered, too, new possibilities in realistic and pictorial representation, the translucent films of color lending themselves especially well to the representation of such infinite intangibles as luminous shadows and distant atmospheric effects. The general rule was to use glazes for these effects and more opaque pigment for substantial masses like Arnolfini's face and hand, but this rule was not inviolate. Since glazes, as any painter knows, are extremely difficult to control, much of the painting had to be rendered in opaque pigments. The only certainty is that the final effect was achieved through a succession of carefully thought-out stages. The well-known conservator, Alfred Jakstas, has stated that this gradual procedure and the convenience of a complete underpainting should be stressed more than the use of glazes in the Flemish method; they were the crucial aspects of the technique.

In addition to being well adapted to the realistic aims of the early Flemings, the medium possessed other merits. The practice of painting slowly and carefully in thin films insured long life, making the fifteenth-century Flemish paintings among the best preserved works of their times. Brilliant, enamel-like colors also make them as decorative as they are realistic, so that they are among the most popular pictures ever painted. Though small in scale, their hues still sing a merry song. They must have been a delight to the light-and-color-hungry peoples of the North who added them to the medium of stained glass. Moreover, though less scintillating than that most brilliant of all media, they permitted the greater accuracy of representation that the dawning Renaissance demanded.

There is only one apparent drawback to the Flemish mixed method of painting in oil over a tempera base. The tempera underpainting required great patience. So long as it was used by a people who loved minute details, who were not in a hurry, and who were thoroughly imbued with the ideals of craftsmanship instilled by the old guilds, this was an advantage instead of a hindrance. The attitude implied links the method with earlier media, from mosaic through fresco, which necessitated careful planning and patient execution. It was clearly a technique which would be unsuited to a more restless, individualistic and spontaneous time, as we shall see in tracing the subsequent history of oil painting.

THE VENETIAN MIXED METHOD OF OIL PAINTING. Near the end of the fifteenth century the oil medium was brought by Antonella da Messina or some other itinerant Italian master from Flanders to Venice. Giovanni Bellini became interested in the possibilities of the medium, and his pupils Giorgione and Titian adopted it avidly. They were on the verge of creating a revolutionary change in Italian painting from the fifteenth-century sculpturesque mode to the pictorial mode that brought the Venetian school to the forefront in painting and inaugurated the post-Renaissance style.

One of the changes that they sought to express was a new interest in the infinite aspects of reality which neither tempera nor fresco could render easily; another was the growing restlessness of European life. Symbolized by the Reformation, it demanded a new and more fluid medium of expression.

Oil painting seemed the answer to these requirements. But before it could fulfill them completely, the method of using it had to be altered to suit the purposes and conditions of sixteenth century Venetian life. Whereas the Flemings of the North desired small but jewel-like panels for their dark and relatively small houses, and wanted an art that reflected their own patient natures, the Venetians craved large pictures in the Italian mural tradition for their palaces. At the peak of their prosperity, they wanted pictures which would do honor to Venice's sumptuous grandeur. The small-scale, delicately detailed paintings and tedious methods of the Flemings were hardly suited to their more impetuous temperament. So, adopting only the oil itself, they devised a new method for their own purposes.

First, they abandoned painting on panels in favor of canvas. This change permitted them to work on a large scale and at the same time revolutionize mural decoration. Instead of having to spend four years lying on his back atop a scaffold in a damp chapel with paint and plaster dripping on his face, as Michelangelo did, an artist like Tintoretto could paint in the comfort of his studio and affix the canvas in its permanent position afterward.

The advantage gained in speed alone was enormous; it allowed Tintoretto to become one of the most prolific decorators in history, measuring his output by the acre. The gain in ceiling decoration was even greater. As a result, this method of painting on large pieces of stretched canvas in the studio became the standard procedure for mural and ceiling decoration until the revival of fresco in very recent years. It was used by Picasso in 1937 when he painted the huge *Guernica* (Fig. 1) for the Spanish Pavilion at the Paris World's Fair.

In painting on canvas the texture of the cloth and its slight springiness under the touch of a brush produce a different sensation from painting on a hard panel. It is a pleasant sensation. More to the point, however, is the fact that it encourages a broader and more fluid type of brush stroke. It is as natural a surface for the pictorial and impressionist modes as the *gesso* panel was for the sculpturesque mode.

Even more important than canvas was the nature of oil paint itself. It can be applied as thin as water or as thick as butter, making possible the most infinite or the most finite effects. But this comprehensiveness hinges upon one especially important characteristic—the oil medium, in contrast with tempera and fresco, dries slowly. It thereby allows a painter to blend colors one into another, to suppress or stress outlines as he chooses, and to capture any effect of atmosphere and illumination. The art of Rembrandt and most of the other post-Renaissance masters grew out of this technical capacity of oil paint.

In transforming the Flemish oil method, the vigorous, large-thinking Venetians not only substituted canvas for gessoed panels but abandoned the difficult tempera underpainting for one composed of oil, thus employing the one paint from start to finish. Furthermore, though they recognized the merits of a monochromatic underdrawing which separates the problem of form and color and provides a compositional guide, they greatly simplified the underlying design. For they had much less interest than the Flemings in small pictures, minute details, or painstaking realism, but a greater interest in sweeping effects and grand designs. Their art was conceived in bolder terms and for mural decoration.

How this method was put into practice can be seen in Fig. 194, for we are again fortunate in having an unfinished picture by a master of the school. This *Diana* is especially illuminating because it shows how easily the brilliant Tintoretto thought in terms of oil painting from the moment he began his picture. Unlike Van Eyck, who made careful drawings on paper before setting brush to panel, Tintoretto dispensed with such preparations and drew directly on the canvas with a broad and loaded brush. His first objective was merely to establish the main outlines of the composition in brownish monochromatic colors and with a minimum of details. The underpainting is little more than a sketch in oil.

Having blocked in the main forms and areas of his design without worrying much about color, he then began to work toward the ultimate hues of his picture in an evolutionary process. In this way the transition from the problem of outlines, modeling, and spatial composition to the color design and more complete representation was made by a succession of logical and easily controlled stages. Thus the method should not be conceived as consisting of two complete and separate stages, but rather as a process of continuous development. Its special merit was to give the artist an opportunity to work out his ideas step by step instead of committing himself to a completed picture at the outset. X-ray negatives show how even as highly experienced a painter as Tintoretto took advantage of this flexibility by making changes as the painting grew under his hand.

In general the Venetians worked from a uniformly brownish tone to a pattern of light and dark areas, from thin glazes or films to thicker *impastos,* and from monochromatic to chromatic designs. As a rule, those portions of the picture devoted to shadows and atmosphere were thinly. painted, while substantial forms (like Diana's shoulders and head) were built up in layers. This technical procedure for representing the infinite and the finite was admirably suited to give each its due.

One effect of this method was far-reaching. The practice of painting in glazes and impastos over a brown-toned canvas gave the Venetian pictures much of their chromatic richness and atmospheric quality. It also meant that post-Renaissance painting would be not only more pictorial than the sculpturesque work of the early tempera and fresco painters, but darker as well.

THE POST-RENAISSANCE DIRECT METHOD OF OIL PAINTING. Once adopted, the medium of oil has retained its popularity from the fifteenth century to the present with no end of its reign in sight. During that span of time the methods of using oil paint changed nearly as much as the history of Europe. The main direction of this change was from an elaborate, painstaking procedure, exemplified by the art of Van Eyck, to a simpler, more rapid, spontaneous, and direct approach.

Part of this change was a reflection of historical pressures. As the tempo of European life accelerated from the patient, time-ignoring ways of the Middle Ages to the haste of modern times, there was a corresponding demand for quicker means of expression. The early response to this demand is shown by the difference between the practices of Van Eyck and Tintoretto, and the progressive character of the change by the even greater contrast between the procedure of Van Eyck and Monet. The lightning-like execution of Monet made Tintoretto himself seem slow of hand.

The most critical period of European oil painting, when changes occurred in rapid succession, was the transitional sixteenth century.

Venice played a leading role in these changes, and its master of masters, Titian, was a leader in them technically as he had been representationally. Learning oil painting from his master Giovanni Bellini, he first applied it in a smooth, cautious manner (as in his *Madonna of the Cherries,* Fig. 129). Afterward, he painted in the method employed by Tintoretto and his fellow Venetians, building up his composition through a succession of stages. Neither he nor his great followers, Rembrandt and El Greco, ever entirely abandoned this admirable procedure. Owing to the fact that Titian developed his natural talents over an active life of ninety-nine years, he acquired a skill granted to few men. In technical terms this meant that in his later years he could abandon underpaintings altogether and paint directly on virgin canvas as fast as he could apply the pigment. When he retained the mixed method it was from preference, not from dependence or lack of ability. A detailed study of one of his mature works, the *Rape of Europa* (Fig. 195), painted when he was eighty-two, shows that he could paint complete forms directly on the canvas. In this particular picture much of Europa's wind-blown drapery was begun and completed in a single, spontaneous operation. Titian had, among many other gifts, an unerring instinct for technical appropriateness and knew exactly when rapid and direct execution would convey an appropriate vitality of movement.

Once started, Titian's judicious practice became widespread in the ensuing centuries as the tempo of life increased and artists gained more and more practice. Within a century of Titian's death painters like Velasquez were able to dispense with underpainting entirely. More than that, they also seem to have been able to bypass any kind of preparatory drawing either on paper or canvas, setting to work on a bare white or neutral canvas and completing most or all of a picture within the course of a day. Remarkable stories have been handed down about the speed of execution developed by the post-Renaissance masters, stories which the volume of their completed work supports. Hals was celebrated for his rapidity, and Van Dyck hardly less so, while Rubens' studio turned out pictures almost as fast as a modern mass production factory.

Contrary to popular beliefs based on an awe of old-fashioned craftsmanship, there is no special virtue in taking forever to finish a picture. The busy post-Renaissance masters used all their common sense to speed up the painting process wherever this could be done safely. They had, therefore, an urge toward direct painting which enormous practice allowed them to achieve.

One consequence of a more direct approach is neither a fault nor a virtue, but a mere historical result. Whereas the Italian Renaissance artists bequeathed us a gallery of superb preparatory drawings and their period will always be known as a period of great draftsmen, many of the post-Renaissance masters left few drawings, unless, like Rembrandt and Van Dyck, they also enjoyed etching or some other drawing medium. Hals and Velasquez are instances of renowned masters who created few preparatory sketches, though the decline in drawing begins even earlier with Titian.

It is not hard to imagine why direct painting would appeal especially to portrait painters and other artists to whom spontaneity and the avoidance of a "frozen look" was important. Thus we find Goya carrying on in the footsteps of Velasquez at the court of Spain in the closing years of the eighteenth century. As with Velasquez, one of his duties was to paint portraits of the important court personages, who, thinking they were busy, would not sit indefinitely. Under the spur of these conditions, he painted their portraits without previous preparation. Whether true or not, the story that he painted his famous *Clothed Maja* in a few hours attests to his reputation for speed-of-hand.

One of Goya's most celebrated court portraits depicts the whole family of King Charles IV, a group which not even Goya could paint at one sitting. He had the royal family pose for him one at a time and composed the picture synthetically from his studies. These, executed in oil, show how little time was required in posing, for they represent only the heads and the mere suggestion of backgrounds. One of the most appealing of the series portrays the old-young face of the *Infante Don Carlos Maria Isidro* (Fig. 197). It is especially to the point for this discussion because, like Van Eyck's *St. Barbara* and Tintoretto's *Diana*, it is unfinished. Such pictures allow us to look, so to speak, over the shoulder of an artist while he is painting. Being unfinished, the clearly discernible brush strokes in them tell us better than any words not only what his methods were, but whether he painted slowly or rapidly, cautiously or boldly.

Titian, Velasquez, Goya, and Hals are some of the men who contributed most to this heritage of experience in direct painting, with Hals being especially outstanding. Called the "laureate of laughter," he demonstrated brilliantly how a momentary, spontaneous expression could be painted with a quickness rivaling the modern candid camera. It is difficult to catch such an expression by photography; it is awe-inspiring to be able to capture it in paint, but Hals achieved the near-impossible in his *Malle Babbe* (Fig. 196) with every appearance of ease.

Behind this deceptive ease lay genius and vast experience, but

FIG. 196. Hals. *Malle Babbe*. "The Witch of Haarlem." *ca.* 1628. Kaiser Friedrich Museum, Berlin.

FIG. 197. Goya. *Infante Don Carlos Maria Isidro.* 1800. Prado. Madrid.

neither would have prevailed without a method for painting directly. If Hals had lived in Flanders during the time of Van Eyck, he could not have painted his *Malle Babbe* as he did, with all the will in the world. The difference between its high vitality and *Giovanni Arnolfini's* respose is partly a matter of temperament and partly of representational modes, but it is also due to no small extent to the expansion of technical means.

Hals's *Malle Babbe* illustrates some of the important changes which attended the rise of oil painting. The Italian Renaissance artists expressed themselves primarily through their shaping of forms; the post-Renaissance masters placed a greater stress on color, illumination, and textures. While tempera or fresco painting minimizes the character of brushwork, the thick, butter-like properties of opaque oil pigment permit an artist like Hals to exploit it, making his handling of the medium as autographic as a signature. So great was the expressive advantage of this practice that it has been adopted widely from the time of Titian to the present day.

The rise of opaque painting was attended by loss of translucency. Whereas the thin films of pigment used by the early Flemings and High Renaissance Venetians resembled a glass of wine, the thick, opaque pigments used from the beginning of Impressionism on have the cloudy character of milk. Being opaque, they prevent both colors and background from shining through the various layers. They have not the depth of tone of thinner paints; their entire character is on the surface. Thus what was gained in autographic painting was sacrificed in color translucency.

Oil paintings dating as far back as the Venetians have always been subject to certain faults. The canvas backing on which the pictures are painted is likely to rot. Hence it is a rare old master painting which has not been relined at least once. The canvas also expands and contracts under various weather conditions at a rate different from that of the layers of paint, causing the pigments to crack and sometimes peel. The pigment itself often becomes faded or discolored, destroying the original color design. Thus the chemistry of painting cannot be ignored. Whistler's pictures have faded badly; Sargent's have cracked, owing to hasty painting upon half-dried surfaces; and the bitumin underpaintings of some seventeenth-century artists have penetrated to the surface, turning shadows opaque black. Coats of varnish applied to pictures as preservatives have darkened them with a false "golden glow." Correcting these faults has cost large sums of money, more having been spent on the conservation of oil paintings than on all other types of painting combined.

Yet oil painting has flourished for five hundred years because it has had far more virtues than faults. It is the most versatile medium ever invented, permitting artists to paint in any linear, sculpturesque, pictorial, realistic, or impressionist mode or variation thereof that they desire. Its versatility has been demonstrated by such diverse and contrasting artists as Tintoretto and Grant Wood or Rembrandt and Charles Sheeler, all of whom used the oil medium. It has never had any serious limitations in the full range of expression of order or variety, finitude or infinitude, and vitality or repose. And it can be so used as to appeal with equal strength to either the tactile or visual senses. Little more could be asked of any medium.

PASTEL. Unlike oil, the medium of colored chalk called *pastel* has had a limited history and usage. It gained some degree of popularity in the eighteenth century, notably in France. It suited the elegant spirit of that time and country and satisfied the ambition of a few portraitists like Perronneau and La Tour to capture a kind of feminine vivacity. It was continued in the nineteenth century for kindred reasons by the Impressionists Manet, Renoir, and Degas.

Degas gave the medium an unprecedented status by his own stature and sense of fitness. He saw its suitability for representing the lithe movements, feminine grace, and fluffy costumes of ballet dancers, and used it for a large number of his famous pictures, such as the *Dancer with a Bouquet* (Fig. 107). He also employed pastel for suggesting the quick movements and colorful, shimmering costumes of mounted jockeys at the race track.

Thus a common denominator of subject and intention runs through the pastel pictures of the eighteenth and nineteenth centuries. There is about all of them an air of lightness, vivacity, color, and charm. Little wonder that Mary Cassatt used pastel frequently for her gentle studies of mothers and children, or that the rugged, masculine artists of the "Ash-Can" school found it unsuited to their purposes.

The dry, powdery effect pastel creates has neither the translucence of oil glazes nor the substance of opaque oil impastos. Having no depth, it keeps our attention on surface textures and other superficials, favoring lightness and working against any sense of mass. In addition it is a fragile medium. Unless the chalk is "fixed" by spraying a film of shellac or varnish over it, it smears or falls off under any kind of handling; and up to recent times there was no well-known "fixative" which would not discolor the picture to some extent.

The merits of pastel lie in its cheapness, its lightness of weight for any traveling artist, and the speedy, sketchy type of execution it allows. These characteristics recommended it to the eighteenth-century portraitists and the nineteenth-century Impressionists who, within these limitations, created some beautiful pictures.

WATERCOLOR. Painting with watercolor on paper has a history quite different from pastel. It has been practiced widely for many centuries in Europe and universally in the Far East. Its popularity has steadily increased until thousands of amateurs now attempt it and professional artists regard it as a major medium. It became as important in the art of Turner and Winslow Homer as etching was in Rembrandt's.

Though watercolor painting was known for many centuries, it has been truly exploited for only about a hundred years. Prior to Turner's activity in the first half of the nineteenth century, water-color was used mainly as a means of tinting rather pale colors on very precisely executed drawings. Inheriting this practice, Turner applied it to his own early drawings, but his tendency toward a greater emphasis upon light, color, atmosphere, and movement, coupled with long practice with watercolor, eventually made him reverse the older concept by making the drawing secondary to the water-color.

In short, Turner discovered once and for all that watercolor is used best when kept wet and washy and handled with breadth and zest. He discovered these essential qualities at the same time that he was pushing his love of the infinite close to modern Impressionism. So joining medium and expressive aims, he became simultaneously one of the pioneers of Impressionism and the father of modern water-color.

The art of Homer, whose life overlapped Turner's, illustrates the close connection between the rise of watercolor and landscape painting in the nineteenth century. For watercolor is a natural medium for painting anywhere in the out-of-doors and a wonderful traveler's medium. The two facts are joined in the careers of both Turner and Homer, the Englishman having journeyed all over Europe and the American up and down the Atlantic seaboard. While traveling, they painted mainly in watercolor. Each could carry enough paper and color in a satchel to produce a hundred pictures, something that would obviously be an impossible undertaking with unwieldy canvases and oil.

Watercolor is thus a cheap, handy, and highly transportable medium, but it is by no means an easy one to control. In few other media is the qualitative difference between the work of beginners and masters so great. As a rule high skill with watercolor denotes excellent training and years of self-discipline; the watercolor masterpieces of both Turner and Homer came, for instance, relatively late in their careers.

This difficulty is connected with the highly desirable spontaneous and washy look. In order to preserve that look in a modern water-color which contains a minimum of pencil outlines, an artist must paint quickly, for one of the crucial properties of watercolor is rapidity of drying. The watercolorist must know what he is doing. If he does, he can achieve an admirable freshness of handling. If he does not, he must correct; and when that is necessary the colors become muddy and the signs of fumbling apparent.

Watercolor is not, like pastel, a fragile medium, for it adheres to paper much better than colored chalk; and paper, contrary to popu-lar belief, is a durable material. There are watercolors painted by Albrecht Dürer in the sixteenth century which are still in excellent condition.

The principal virtues of watercolors are exemplified by the art of Homer. An avid traveler and lover of the out-of-doors, he used watercolor to produce hundreds of landscape paintings like the *Coming Storm* in Fig. 119. In these he siezed upon the virgin quali-ties of nature and the dynamic aspects of reality. He loved changing lights and shadows and the heavy atmosphere of deep space, and used watercolor as an extremely rapid means of capturing them. Effect-ing a union of concept and medium, he pushed watercolor beyond the degree of boldness attained by Turner.

The artists of the twentieth century have gone even beyond Homer. Among them John Marin has been outstanding because of his perfect understanding of the essential properties of watercolor. His pictures are even wetter looking than Homer's. Like Turner and Homer a lover of nature, he has stressed its infinite and dynamic aspects. Being primarily a watercolorist and landscape painter, he has run counter to the return to the finite which marks twentieth-century painting in oil.

A long list could be made of the merits of watercolor from the evidence of Turner's, Homer's, and Marin's pictures alone without beginning to do justice to younger artists like Dehn, Burchfield, Whorf, and Wyeth. The expressive range of watercolor is great; its colors, for instance, can be intense or dull, gay or somber. Yet the medium has its limitations, as Homer himself discovered. While admirably suited to represent coming storms and other aspects of the transitory world, its very thinness and lightness make it in-capable of representing the heavy, substantial side of nature. Homer realized this shortly after settling on the coast of Maine when he attempted to paint massive rocks and ocean waves. After a few trials with watercolor, he turned to oil pigment whenever he wished to convey the power of the sea and the immobility of the cliffs, thus staking out clearly the realm in which each medium is at its best.

THE MEDIA OF DRAWING

Unlike paintings, the majority of which are meant to be unique and complete, most drawings are intended either to be mere sketches or to be reproduced; and their media were designed accordingly. Michelangelo's preparatory study for the Adam in the Sistine ceiling (Fig. 58) and the unique but fragmentary drawings that Leonardo da Vinci included in his private notebooks are simply sketches. The Florentine artists of the time drew a great many similar pictures by way of practice. And Thomas Eakins probably drew his *Masked Nude Woman* (Fig. 150) for much the same reason. The comparatively simple, quick, and inexpensive media of drawing with pencils, crayons, and pen-and-ink on paper has long provided a means of practice, private expression, or preparation. A good deal of the appeal of such drawing lies, therefore, in its informality.

It was not until the eighteenth century that artists consciously created single drawings as finished works of art which were intended for direct sale. This practice arose because the demand for paintings by popular artists like Fragonard and Boucher exceeded the supply. When hard-pressed, they found that they could sell even quickly executed sketches of pretty girls at excellent prices, and naturally cultivated this market. Drawing for sale has been standard practice ever since, and, in some cases, quite lucrative. Today, the merest sketch by Picasso is a highly negotiable product. The fact that a drawing was produced for a patron did not, however, change the artist's unique and essential technical treatment.

An earlier type of drawing arose in the fifteenth century with the advent of printing; it was the practice of drawing for reproduction and widespread distribution. Thus appeared the printed or graphic arts. Numerous to start with, they become still more so because of refinements and combinations. We shall limit ourselves to the consideration of woodblock engraving, copper engraving, etching, mezzotint, aquatint, and lithography. This sequence is about the order in which they became historically prominent, and allows us to consider the significance of any evolutionary similarity they may have with the history of painting. Since in the graphic arts we never deal, as we do in old master drawings, with the original work of the artist but with a reproduction of it, the technical processes by which this indirect expression is achieved are much to the point.

WOODBLOCK ENGRAVING. Woodcuts or woodblock prints, as they are commonly called, mark the first response of visual artists to the invention of printing. The first examples appeared in the homeland of printing, Germany, hard on the heels of its invention, initially as illustrations to printed texts, an illustrative beginning which the graphic arts never wholly outgrew. Development of the new art was rapid, partly due to an inherited skill in wood-carving and partly to an affinity for the graphic arts that has lasted to the present time. Within a century the German school had progressed from crude beginnings to the golden age of the art in the first half of the six-teenth century. Woodblock engraving became one of its major contributions to the Renaissance. The leader of the German school, Albrecht Dürer, was also the leading master of woodblock engraving in Western art.

Before the invention of printing each drawing was unique and hence useless for book illustration. The advantage that came with multiplication is illustrated by Dürer's fame. For while a very few people knew his paintings and drawings, thousands of people throughout Europe knew his art in his own lifetime through prints like his *Siege of a Fortress* (Fig. 198). What could be done to repro-duce such a drawing had, of course, to be geared to the capabilities of printing in his day. Indeed, the development of the graphic arts reflected the development of printing in each century following.

Dürer achieved the reproduction of his *Siege of a Fortress* by drawing his picture on a block of hard, fine-grained wood with a pen or pointed brush, much as he would on paper. The untouched portions of the block were then cut away with a gouge, leaving the drawn lines as ridges. Because of these ridges this process became known as relief printing as distinct from the other general types of intaglio and planographic printing. When ink was applied, it ad-hered only to the ridges, which printed the picture on paper.

The cutting of a woodblock was as difficult to practice as it is easy to describe. Despite long practice in wood carving, the cutting of a block with a gouge was an awkward, painstaking procedure at best. While pushing the gouge forward, the engraver had to exercise great manual control. Care had to be taken to move with the grain of the wood without cutting through any of the ridges. Such patience would have been rewarding if the ridges could have been made to print fine lines, but they were necessarily coarse, as we can see from Dürer's *Siege of a Fortress*. In sum, woodblock engraving permitted bold, clear, vigorous drawing, but little refinement.

Accepting these limitations, Dürer exploited the medium fully, extracting a maximum of expression from the woodblock print. As

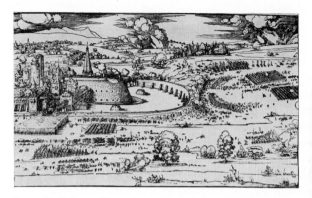

FIG. 198. Dürer. *Siege of a Fortress.* 1527. Bowdoin College Museum of Fine Arts, Brunswick, Me.

FIG. 199. Dürer. *St. Jerome in His Study.* 1514. National Gallery of Art, Washington, D.C.

FIG. 200. Rembrandt. *The Three Trees.* 1643. National Gallery of Art, Washington, D.C.

366

a result, his *Siege of a Fortress* is outstanding for its finiteness. It is, of course, deficient in any sign of infinity which we associate with atmosphere and changing lights and shadows. Any depth that it may have is conveyed through purely linear means. The clouds are hard and razor sharp, the whole picture dry, rigid, and static. So, strong and virile though it may be, it represents only the beginning of progress in the graphic arts.

COPPER ENGRAVING. The second forward step in the graphic arts was through the medium of copper engraving. Significantly, it was Dürer who took the longest initial stride. An artist of many interests, he was sensitive to the change from the finite to the infinite which occurred in painting in the sixteenth century. Following the leadership of the Venetian painters, he wished to represent light, shadow, and atmosphere in graphic form with a much greater degree of refinement than was possible through wood engraving. He therefore adopted copper engraving and became its first great master.

A comparison of Dürer's *St. Jerome in His Study* (Fig. 199) with his *Siege of a Fortress* will show the different effects which can normally be achieved through the two media. Whereas the woodcut of the fortress may be described either as being evenly lighted or containing no discernible source of illumination, the engraving of St. Jerome is outstanding for the way in which the light enters the windows, reflects from the sills, and plays throughout the room. Illumination plays as important a role in this picture as outlines and contours do in the wood engraving. The difference may remind us of the similar contrast between the sculpturesque painting of the fifteenth century and the pictorial mode which came into prominence during Dürer's lifetime. It may remind us, too, of the concurrent rise of realistic painting, in which a softer and more natural rendering of illumination and atmosphere played an increasingly prominent part. Hence Dürer was merely keeping step with general trends in art which led in time from Jan Van Eyck's *Marriage of Giovanni Arnolfini* to the expressive luminosity of Rembrandt and the realistic luminosity of Vermeer in the seventeenth century.

The luminous effect of the *St. Jerome* was made possible by the fact that an artist can engrave much finer lines in a polished and grainless plate of copper than he can by gouging away wood until a picture in ridges remains. He pushes a V-shaped burin along the copper surface, cutting a furrow after the fashion of a plow. Each furrow will retain ink and print as a line. Its width or darkness will depend upon the pressure put on the burin by the engraver. Thus precise control over direction and pressure are crucial to his art and make it a difficult one. Added to this difficulty is the fact that it is never easy for the human hand to control a forward or pushing movement. The advances in representation made by copper engraving were notable but hard won.

Despite the patience it demands, copper engraving has remained popular to the present day, because it provides a satisfactory way of reproducing the effect of a realistic drawing. The French court portraitists of the seventeenth century discovered this capacity and exploited it so fully that their style became universal in the making of paper money from that day to our own without being improved upon. An excellent example is Nanteuil's portrait of *Louis XIV* (Fig. 149). Engraving of a portrait did not, of course, improve its realism, but it made it duplicable. Hence the noted monarch could distribute copies throughout Europe, much as we order and send out prints of a photographic portrait. A century later Hogarth used the same capacity for reproduction to advantage when, unable to sell his satirical paintings to the aristocracy, he engraved and sold copies of them to the populace. For a long time his fame rested on such engravings as the *Enraged Musician* (Fig. 72).

The very real technical merits of copper engraving are offset to some extent by limitations. The character of the engraving process favors accuracy of representation but minimizes any spontaneity of expression. A prominent feature of Nanteuil's *Louis XIV* is the mechanical appearance of the numerous parallel lines, a stiffness even more noticeable in works of lesser quality. A realist will accept this rigidity of means for the sake of accuracy but an artist who values vitality of expression over appearances will not. Finding himself put in a kind of strait jacket by copper engraving, he will seek more flexible media, like copper etching.

COPPER ETCHING. The process of etching with acid upon metal was used in medieval times for incising designs on suits of armor, but it was not developed widely for reproducing drawings until the sixteenth century. It found its greatest exponent in Rembrandt in the seventeenth century, and has not been substantially improved upon since.

One of the motives behind its adoption was the desire of artists to capture infinite aspects of reality with greater ease and effectiveness than could be done by engraving in copper. An early clue to this ambition can be found in Hirschvogel's *Landscape with a Curved Wooden Bridge* (Fig. 118) which, though etched less than twenty years after Dürer's *Siege of a Fortress* was engraved, is its superior in the rendering of a distant atmospheric effect. Hirschvogel's landscape was only a step on the way to Rembrandt's etching of *The Three Trees* (Fig. 200). In that noted print the possibilities of representing a dynamic, weather-ridden, spacious, atmospheric, and luminous nature were realized through etching as never before. A comparison of it with the *Siege of a Fortress* will reveal how emphatically the early engraving epitomizes the finite world and the later etching the infinite.

Besides enabling the artist to create atmosphere with ease, etching allowed him greater freedom of expression. The very appearance of an etching suggests spontaneity. Compared to an engraving, it is sketchy instead of mechanical-looking. It may be described as a means of reproducing a very freely rendered drawing in pen-and-ink, though realistic exactitude can be attained if the artist so desires. The possibility of freedom of execution gives it a greater lightness and vitality than can be normally found in any engraving.

These expressive potentialities hinge upon a crucial difference between the way an engraving and an etching are made. The engraving, as described earlier, is created by pushing a burin through the copper, a process in which manual control is difficult. An etching, by contrast, is made by sketching on a waxed copper plate with an etching needle. The process is not unlike sketching with a pen and not much more difficult. The point is as light as a feather as it races over the surface and only negligible pressure is needed to trace a line through the wax. Thus, while the hand of the engraver must be tautly controlled, the hand of an etcher can be relaxed and playful. By crisscrossing his strokes he can achieve an infinite gradation of values down to deepest shadows, which intensifies the luminosity of his lights, as Rembrandt did in his *Christ Healing the Sick* (Fig. 151) and *The Three Trees*.

This ease and refinement of execution derives from another crucial difference between the engraving and etching processes. In etching the principal work of incising the lines is done chemically instead of manually. For when the waxed plate is immersed in an acid bath the exposed copper lines can be etched to any depth desired by allowing greater or less time. Refinement of gradations can be carried to great lengths by stopping out certain lines while others are bitten deeper by the acid. In this way the process can be carried forward in a series of controllable stages. But the chief merit of this procedure is that it places a premium on artistic judgment rather than manual effort and so emphasizes the mental side of creativity.

Etching ranks in versatility with the oil medium which arose alongside it in the field of painting and was used with equal mastery and for kindred artistic ends by Rembrandt. But etching has two shortcomings which encouraged the continuation or invention of other graphic media. Because acid bites laterally as well as downward, it etches tunnel-like troughs whose edges are fragile. Only about a hundred impressions can be printed before wearing of the plate produces a fainter image. First-class prints of Rembrandt's etchings constitute, therefore, limited editions. By contrast, the V-shaped lines of an engraved copper plate can safely produce a thousand prints.

Furthermore, even in the hands of a Rembrandt, etching remained a linear means of representation which could not capture tonal effects perfectly. Thus, insofar as artists were bent in that direction, they sought further means.

MEZZOTINT. Mezzotint is a cousin to etching in that it employs a copper plate with the aim of creating realistic or pictorial effects. It differs from etching in emphasizing gradations of light and shadow in even greater degree, but usually at the sacrifice of etching's linear crispness.

A mezzotint is made by scoring a polished copper plate with a metal rocker covered with tiny teeth. The plate, when pitted in this manner, would print a uniformly dark tone, so gradations from this background are created by scraping away the pitted surface to various depths, high lights being created by deep scraping while medium values are established by lesser pressure. The artist works from dark to light, instead of from light to dark, as in etching and engraving. Mezzotint therefore favors dark and shadowy effects, and is at its best when producing them.

Mezzotint, with its softer and more atmospheric appearance, can give shadows a velvety richness. This soft richness of tone made it popular in the eighteenth century, when it rose to prominence, and highly satisfactory as a realistic means of copying famous or popular paintings. It has also often served the purpose of modern photography.

The rise of mezzotint was in line with the steady trend of both painting and drawing toward a greater realism and pictorialism. Those who raised mezzotint to a high qualitative level used it as a method of capturing in reproduceable form the characteristics of pen-and-wash drawings. Probably its greatest exponent was Turner, who employed it for his *Liber Studiorum*, examples of which are *Little Devil's Bridge* (Fig. 11) and *Norham Castle* (Fig. 25). Missing the linear crispness of etching, but wanting the tonal richness of mezzotint, Turner usually started with an etched drawing which he finished in mezzotint. His drawing of *Martello Towers* (Fig. 146) illustrates the first stage of this process, the *Little Devil's Bridge* and *Norham Castle* the finished products.

By and large, mezzotint has never attained the popularity of etching. When a pure mezzotint is compared to an etching (Turner's mixed method excepted), it lacks etching's clarity of line; and while it has a velvety lusciousness and softness of tone, it suffers from a more mechanical appearance. The excessive softness is not necessarily a merit in the long run, for it suggests a cloying absence of virility, while the mechanical look, which comes from the technical process, cannot be avoided.

The mechanical look is caused by the fact that the signs of the rocker cannot be eliminated. But the principal difference between etching and mezzotint can be traced to their respective tools and processes. Not only is the etching needle light and pointed, but it can create either sharp lines or cross-hatched shadows with ease because the hard work of etching is done by acid. The mezzotint rocker can create only broad effects, and is a comparatively clumsy tool to handle. Lacking the aid of acid, it must be controlled entirely by manual manipulation. What is true of the rocker is also true of the scraper.

The principal merit of mezzotint lies in its minute control over gradations of value, making it a medium which is primarily useful for realistic and highly pictorial effects. The cottony forms and deep shadows which characterize it have seemed unduly soft and formless to many critics, but elicited lavish praise from its devotees during the period of its popularity in the eighteenth century.

AQUATINT. Aquatint is a means of reproducing the effect of a pen-and-wash drawing. As in etching, a needle is used to achieve the crispness and clarity of outlines common to etchings and to avoid the extreme softness of mezzotint. The wash effect is reproduced by dusting resin powder or some other acid-resisting substance over the copper plate. The acid, which can eat only in the spaces between the tiny particles, bites the plate in proportion to the density of the powder. Where it has been sprinkled lightly, the acid will cut a surface which will print as a dark shadow; where the powder is heavy, the acid will be resisted and the printed result will be light and luminous. By manipulating the density of the dust, any degree of darkness or sequence of gradations can be achieved. The method therefore provided a simple way of capturing many sorts of luminous and atmospheric effects. On the other hand, the areas of tone could be kept relatively flat and poster-like. The use of an etching needle in combination with powder and acid enabled artists to gain chemically most of the virtues of mezzotint and etching easily and quickly without having to accept the mechanical and representational limitations of mezzotint.

The process had much to recommend it. Its chemically bitten areas of tone are not only less mechanical looking than comparable mezzotint tones, but possess a speckled quality which delights the aquatint artist. Less velvety than mezzotint, it is sharper and more virile in character.

Aquatint's merits were demonstrated by its greatest practitioner, Goya, who employed it for his three tremendous satirical series, the *Caprices, Proverbs,* and *Disasters of War,* (Fig. 4), the latter one of the most scathing denunciations of human viciousness ever uttered through visual means. Unlike mezzotint, aquatint is capable of providing the punch and biting expression needed by a hard-hitting work of art.

Aquatint arrived late on the historical scene. It was invented in the second half of the eighteenth century and quickly adopted. By the beginning of the nineteenth century it was a popular medium on the Continent and in England. Pertinent to its high development at that time was a general emphasis upon pictorial values in both painting and drawing which it was well-suited to express.

As the nineteenth century progressed aquatint declined for the same reason that engraving and mezzotint lost their popularity. Unlike the painting media, color was not their strong point, hence they could be replaced by photography for the reproduction of realistic and pictorial effects. The strength of etching was shown in this mortal competition. It persisted and survived owing to characteristics which could not be easily and cheaply duplicated by photographic means. Etching excepted, the decline of the graphic arts was closely related to the rise of the camera.

One newcomer defied this trend. It was lithography, which arose and flourished side-by-side with the photographic arts.

LITHOGRAPHY. Lithography, which literally means drawing on a stone, is one of the few graphic media which can be credited to a definite inventor. The process of printing from a stone plate was discovered in 1796 by Aloys Senefelder, a native of Prague, who perfected the process two years later. It was a late-comer to the graphic repertory, but its merits were so outstanding that it was widely adopted almost immediately and knew its golden age within fifty years of its invention. Between 1796 and 1830, Goya created some of his finest drawings of the bullring in the medium and shortly thereafter Daumier mastered the art in innumerable examples. His

Women Gossiping (Fig. 152) illustrates to perfection what can be done in reproducing a drawing by lithography.

So effective was the medium that it has survived even the inroads of photography, which virtually eliminated engraving and mezzotint. Though past its golden age, it has rivaled etching in popularity in our century. The American artist George Bellows used lithography as a major means of expression. The lithographic reproduction of his *Stag at Sharkey's* (Fig. 77) is nearly as famous as the oil painting and has certainly been seen by more people.

Lithography differs from the other media in several respects. It is, for one thing, called a planographic medium because it employs a flat surface in printing, as distinct from one whose image is carved in relief, as in wood engraving, or incised in intaglio fashion, as in copper engraving or etching. The great advantage that a lithographer enjoys over, say, an etcher is that the drawing which develops under his hand is nearly identical with the image which will emerge from the press. Hence he knows while he draws what his results will be and can develop or correct them freely without having to make and correct a succession of proofs. The appeal of this spontaneity, immediacy, and flexibility to artists can easily be imagined. These properties are especially important in lithography, enabling it to reproduce the freedom of execution common to a drawing in pencil or crayon. Lithography can preserve the sketchiest effects perfectly and is an excellent medium for the representation of light and shadow, atmosphere, and subtle shades of modeling. In it one can duplicate any kind of representation which can be achieved with a pencil.

Basically, the discovery of lithography hinged on the fact that grease is attracted by grease and repelled by water. Senefelder found that when he drew with a grease pencil on the flat surface of a certain kind of Bavarian stone and then moistened the surface, the greasy drawing would repel the water while the untouched stone would absorb it. Conversely, when he rolled an oily ink over the plate, it would be repelled by the moist areas (which would then print as white), but absorbed by the drawing. Furthermore, the ink would be absorbed and later printed in exact proportion to the darkness or lightness of the drawn lines. Consequently, a facsimile of the drawing could be reproduced with all of its gradations perfectly matched. The process could be repeated indefinitely, so long as the plate was moistened and then inked in that order. It was later discovered that this technique could be refined by bathing the drawn stone with nitric acid and gum arabic. This bath had a twofold effect. It fixed the drawn image, integrating it permanently with the stone; at the same time it reduced the untouched stone by the slightest fraction of an inch. The image was thereby left in an imperceptible relief. If one wishes to be technically literal, lithography as modified today is not a planographic but a relief process.

The printing press and the black ink employed permit darker lines than one can normally draw with a pencil without digging into the paper. Thus the reproductive process actually improves on the original drawing; it increases the value range and produces velvety black lines and shadow areas which delight the followers of the art. That intensified value scale is well illustrated by Daumier's *Women Gossiping*.

Lithographic drawing can be used perfectly well for the sculpturesque mode or to model figures strongly, as Daumier and Bellows both demonstrated. But the medium was invented at a time when the pictorial mode held the center of the stage, with the realistic mode near at hand and the impressionist mode waiting in the wings to make its entrance. And though this timing was a historical coincidence, the widespread and rapid adoption of lithography by artists of that particular time governed the development of lithography to a considerable extent. Fortunately, the medium was excellently suited to their purposes. Child Hassam proved this point when he produced a large number of effective impressionist pictures by lithography.

Daumier also indicated another merit of lithography which was in harmony with the temper of his times when he reproduced a vast number of drawings through the medium for popular distribution. In assessing the qualities of lithography, one cannot overlook the part played by increasing populations and their demands. Lithography was particularly suited to the reproduction of drawings in the burgeoning daily newspapers of the nineteenth century because its virtually indestructible stone plate could print hundreds of impressions without any serious loss of quality. Daumier and a host of his contemporaries took advantage of this durability, using such Parisian journals as *Le Charivari* and *La Caricature* as outlets for their humorous and satirical commentaries on politics and daily life. In the twentieth century a way was found to use a zinc plate instead of a stone. Since the zinc plate could be curved around a rotary press, impressions numbering into the thousands could be printed for the daily press. In this way the centuries-old ambition to disseminate drawings widely was realized beyond anything Dürer ever dreamt of. Duplicability, durability, quantity, and spontaneous representation were thus joined on a popular level by the special properties of the lithographic process. If anything, the medium and its masters suffered from its fertility. It was a long time before people convinced themselves that an artist like Daumier could be both a popular humorist and a great master.

The advantages of the lithographic process are numerous. Execution is very direct, and this directness minimizes the limitations encountered when several stages and tools are involved. Inspiration is not lost on the way, for the artist does not have to limit himself to what can be done with one implement but not with another, as Dürer had to do when he drew a woodcut design which had to be carved with a graver. In these qualities of spontaneity, directness, and simplicity the lithographic process has few rivals.

Over the years the media of drawing paralleled those of painting. When there was a radical change in the mode of representation and a desire for greater spontaneity, directness, and speed, there was a corresponding change in the media employed. As in painting, new representational aims inspired a search for new procedures. Whether one gives primacy to the discovery or the desire is not important; together they made an evolutionary progress in the graphic media possible.

THE SCULPTURAL MEDIA

The distinguished modern sculptor William Zorach has pointed out that all of the materials and most of the techniques of sculpture have been known from early ancient times. Unlike painting, architecture, and the graphic arts, sculpture did not have to wait until relatively modern times for revolutionary new materials and techniques. This accounts for the early eminence of sculpture and for the absence of epoch-making improvements that appeared from time to time in painting and architecture.

With its rapid technical start, sculpture was the first of the visual arts to achieve lasting greatness on a broad front. The sculptural media need not be considered for any contributions to an evolutionary process. Rather we may judge them for the great possibilities and the few limitations they have offered to the artist.

All of the sculptural media have lent themselves from prehistoric times to the two principal forms, sculpture in the round and in relief. And all four of the classic methods of creating sculptural figures by subtraction, addition, manipulation, and substitution have been known for at least two thousand years.

Michelangelo described the first of these processes when he said that in order to carve a figure one has only to conceive it within a block of stone and then cut away the excess material. Genius is prone to this kind of off-hand oversimplification, but it explains the essentials. Michelangelo's own "unfinished" *Captive* (Fig. 66) illustrates such a figure in the making.

Renée Sintenis' *Runner* (Fig. 162) exemplifies the additive method. In it the figure is developed from a metal skeleton or armature to its final form by the addition of masses or layers of clay. The process assumes the use of a soft, malleable material. Sintenis also manipulated the surface of the clay to create his final effect. An even better example of manipulation is furnished by Daumier's *Burden* (Fig. 161). A statue of this type is formed by twisting, stretching, and kneading a mass of clay from its raw formless state to an artistically expressive shape. The potter with his wheel has exemplified this procedure for centuries.

The last method, substitution, is based on the desirability of converting the form of an easily worked material like clay or wax into a more durable substance, such as bronze, and usually involves the use of molds. The classic method for making this substitution is known as the *cire-perdue* (or lost wax) process. This technique allows a sculptor to shape a figure in soft wax over a fireproof core and then, after covering it with an outer heat-resistant mold, replace the wax with hard metal. He does this by pouring molten bronze into the top of the mold. The heat melts the wax, which is between the two molds, causing it to drain through a hole in the bottom of the outer mold until it is completely replaced by bronze. After the bronze has cooled and solidified, the casing is removed and the cast statue stands revealed.

It is easy for us to explain the antiquity of the first three methods. A cave man can be imagined carving a stone with a rude ax or shaping a figure out of mud by hand. But we are surprised to learn that the *cire-perdue* method is as old as it is ingenious, and testifies to the technical proficiency of our distant ancestors. The Chinese had developed this skill to a high point by the time they cast the *Bronze Spiral Finial* in Fig. 236. It predates the birth of Christ by at least eight centuries, while certain ritual vessels go back as far as 2000 years B.C.

Another method of making an easily molded material more durable is equally ancient. Men discovered at an early time that clay could be shaped and then baked, a fact that made possible the universal art of pottery-making and the highly popular medium of terra cotta. They discovered, too, that baked clay figures could be reproduced indefinitely by the use of molds, thus anticipating by many centuries the duplication of drawings by the graphic media. The renowned Tanagra terra cotta figurines were cast in Greece at least three hundred years before the Christian Era, and Chinese sculptors were able to make terra cotta tomb figurines in hundred lots by the time of the Han dynasty (206 B.C.–220 A.D.). Later, the Chinese became world-famous for their ability to glaze terra cotta pottery and porcelain with such rich, translucent colors as we find on the tenth century *Lohan* shown in Fig. 3 and on the glazed pottery vessels in Fig. 187.

A broad view of sculpture will reveal two other striking technical characteristics. First of all, sculptors have exhibited an unusual perseverance and hardiness from the earliest periods. Given an opportunity to use soft and easily worked materials, they have deliberately chosen the hardest kinds of stones procurable, sometimes, as in Assyria, sending long distances for them.

They have never been daunted by difficulties in pursuing their representational aims. This is especially true of realism. By the time of the Old Kingdom (*ca.* 2980–2475 B.C.) Egyptian sculptors had achieved a realism in such statues as *Menkure and His Queen* (Fig. 160), despite the use of extremely hard stone, that was far in advance of anything achieved by contemporary Egyptian painters. In some respects their realistic skill has never been excelled.

Much has been written in praise of the ability of the Baroque artists to unite many different sculptural materials in large, complex projects. They have been lauded, too, for their ability to handle marble and other substances as freely as putty, capturing every kind of imitative effect from lace and satin to flesh and clouds. Bernini was especially proficient in this kind of sculptural versatility.

We should be wrong, however, in concluding that his skill indicates any such progress in sculpture from ancient to modern times as we find in painting. For by late antiquity the sculptors of Greece could have matched Bernini's competence. Any limitation they imposed on their realism was self-imposed. No such statement can be made about ancient painting or architecture.

One can extend this assertion to the other modes of sculpture. By the time of Christ the sculptors of antiquity had mastered every important material and technique, giving the world a tremendous gallery of masterpieces. They had perfected the realistic mode and left little to be desired in the glyptic mode. If they failed to carry the plastic mode to the logical conclusion that was ultimately reached, it was not from lack of suitable materials or technical skill but because their view of life did not favor it.

One limitation has influenced sculptors generally because, unlike the painter or draftsman, their materials are often heavy and hard to transport. As a result, proximity of materials has figured prominently in the history of sculpture, as in that of architecture, enabling us to identify whole schools by their use of local media.

But within the materials at hand, artists may and have selected those which satisfied their personal preferences. Egyptian sculpture is a notable example of this selectivity. As everyone knows, the Egyptians employed some of the hardest stones in the world for sculpture, often on a large scale. The statues of *Menkure and His Queen* (Fig. 160) show sculptors using a very tough green slate early in their history and the *Head of a Priest* (Fig. 163) reveals them still carving in a dense material, basalt, some two thousand years later. The Egyptians also carved in diorite, basalt, granite, and obsidian because these materials were plentiful in Egypt and furthered their religious craving for permanence. But another motive of no little significance probably influenced ther choice, too. Since they did not lack softer materials like clay and limestone, they must have used intractable stones because they derived a sense of accomplishment from mastering them. Glorying in a difficult task and triumphing over a self-sought obstacle, like climbing a mountain peak, is not an uncommon token of strength in human life, and it undoubtedly has played its part in the history of sculpture. Egyptian sculpture exudes the kind of virility that comes from meeting such a challenge.

Another highly specialized instance of a cultivated difficulty is found in the use of ivory. This material is not native to either of the lands where it became a typical badge of art. The Byzantine sculptors of Asia Minor and the Balkans had to import ivory from afar, and this was truer still of the Japanese sculptors; yet both used it extensively. The Byzantine designers seem actually to have prized the intractability of ivory, feeling probably that it reinforced the dignity of compositions like the *Harbaville Triptych* (Fig. 354). The Japanese carvers also prized the intractability of ivory, but with a different aim in mind; treating it with a realism that amounts almost to a *tour de force* allowed them to display, even to flaunt, their remarkable technical virtuosity.

The Chinese demonstrated the mastery of a material obstacle in still another way. Although they possessed all kinds of easily wrought media in their vast land, they showed from ancient times a special preference for jade, endowing it mentally with values approximating the diamond's. Jade can be an extremely handsome substance, but it is one of the most difficult to carve. Yet this difficulty never deterred the Chinese sculptors, who became extraordinarily facile in the handling of this material.

The willingness to overcome an obstacle is illustrated in another way by ancient Assyrian art. The sculptors of that period had only thin, fibrous local palm trees from which to carve. Nothing daunted, they hauled colossal blocks of stone from the northern mountains to their homeland on the plains between the Tigris and Euphrates, as we see them doing in Fig. 111. But not even their vigorous efforts could entirely overcome the local scarcity of stone and their primitive methods of transportation. On the whole they had to be content to decorate the palaces of their kings with low-relief carvings on slabs of stone, like the *Winged Deity* in Fig. 336 and the *Wounded Lioness* in Fig. 286, which they could transport in quantity. Assyrian sculpture provides us a classic example of the effect of distant sources of supply.

The history of sculpture demonstrates how availability of materials governs artistic output. Sculptors may learn to perform miracles in handling difficult materials, even to treating ivory and basalt in highly realistic manners, but they cannot change the intrinsic qualities of the materials at their disposal; they can only exploit them as fully as possible. Therefore, it has made a difference to sculptors what kind of media they found around them. And since we cannot fail to notice the intrinsic or unchangeable properties of these materials or help associating each artistic group with its media and methods of coping with them, a brief discussion of the various materials is in order.

Stone has contributed the main material of sculpture universally and from prehistoric times. It is found in most places throughout the world, Mesopotamia being a striking exception; and men attained competence in carving it as early as the Paleolithic Age. But stone varies in type, and that is its differentiating quality.

We have already mentioned the connection between Egyptian sculpture and the several extraordinarily hard stones which are native to the Nile Valley. These, in common with hard stones all over the world have certain characteristics which affected Egyptian sculpture and are likely to affect sculpture wherever they are used. Hardness encourages the composing of statues in single, compact masses and discourages the representation of complex, active figures. *Menkure and His Queen* illustrates this type of composition well, as does the Sumerian *Governor of Lagash* (Fig. 67). Coupled with compact treatment, the forms are endowed with an aura of indestructibility and permanence, a massive, immovable strength or resistance to change. Physically, the color and grain of these stones leave something to be desired, but both the Egyptians and Mesopotamians found ways of polishing the surfaces to make them acceptable and often handsome, the dark glossy surface of the *Governor of Lagash* being an especially good example.

In ancient and medieval times, periods of intense activity in sculpture generally, men found and worked other kinds of stone and bone which were either easier to carve or somewhat pleasanter to view than granite, diorite, and basalt. Among the hard materials were ivory and jade, which were adopted because of distinctive properties in which faults and merits are about equally balanced. Ivory is hard, tough of grain, and has a tendency to split. It is limited in size by the diameter and curvature of an elephant's tusk. Statues or reliefs carved in it must be comparatively small, even when pieced together, and they tend to yellow with age. Both the Byzantine and Japanese sculptors accepted these limitations and turned them to good account. The Byzantines, energetic merchants and travelers, used ivory for small statuettes and altarpieces, like the *Harbaville Triptych,* which they sold from one end of the Mediterranean to the other when northwestern Europe was in a state of barbarism, thus spreading the Byzantine style widely throughout the early Middle Ages. They made small scale and its attendant transportability an advantage, and so popularized ivory that it was frequently used by the French Gothic sculptors as late as the fifteenth century for statuettes of the Madonna and Child. The Japanese sculptors put the small scale of ivory to good use by identifying it with exquisiteness of craftsmanship. Their tiny *netsuke* figures are among the most popular of all artistic minutiae.

Carving in jade suggests a similar patience and refinement in the Chinese temperament with which it has always been associated, for though jade is found in other parts of the world, the Chinese alone have used it extensively. Like ivory, it is a hard material to work, which encourages working on a small scale and in a linear style. The Chinese, masters of line for many centuries, found these characteristics to their liking. They also sought and prized three other qualities in jade which are at variance with our common notion of that material. The finest jade, in their opinion, is a milky white, not an olive green; the Chinese call the latter jadeite and assign it the same value as glass has in relation to the diamond. When carved in thin pieces, this milk-white jade is both translucent and iridescent, and possesses a physical beauty which more than offsets its hardness of handling. A superb example of these revered characteristics is the *Jade Disk of the Type Pi* (Fig. 220) at Kansas City.

If ivory and jade suggest special cultures and purposes, marble is almost synonymous in our minds with all sculpture in stone, probably because it was a favorite material of the Greeks whose genius made a deep impression on Western thought. In addition, marble was widely used by the Romans in antiquity and by European masters from the Renaissance to the present day in a tradition that includes such giants as Donatello, Michelangelo, Bernini, and Rodin.

Marble recommended itself to all of these artists because of its special properties. It was, for one thing, plentiful in Greece and Italy. Being relatively easy to carve, it permitted the representation of as much realism of appearance or action as a sculptor wished. Since the Greeks were keenly interested in the human figure in motion and the Romans in realistic portraiture, marble was ideal for their purposes and the European tradition they established. It had only one serious drawback. Being soft, it was likely to break along any slender, projecting member, such as an arm, ankle, or neck, and in the course of time hundreds of Greek and Roman statues were broken at these points. Against this weakness the sculptors could set several outweighing virtues in addition to ease of handling. Chief among them is physical beauty. Whether finished plainly or polished to a high gloss, the texture and color of marble are pleasant to the eye. Its color may even improve with age, often turning, as in the Parthenon sculptures, to a warm and mellow honey color.

What may be regarded as the weaknesses and strengths of marble are reversed in bronze. The Greeks used it extensively to complement their activities in stone. With the exception of the brilliantly corroded ancient Chinese ritual vessels, bronze cannot compete with marble in color and is regarded by many as dark and unpleasant looking. But compensating for this drabness are representational merits of the first order. Bronze permits almost any mode of representation, ranging from the realism of Rodin's *Age of Bronze* (Fig. 169) through the vigorous plasticity of Bourdelle's *Beethoven* (Fig. 164) to the formality of Maillol's *Torso* (Fig. 5). It kept no sculptor from taking any representational direction he wished.

Grasping at this versatility the Greeks used bronze to express their love of action without the risks of breakage inherent in marble. They were able to cast confidently many figures like the *Zeus from Artemisium* (Fig. 50) whose extended arms would long ago have been broken off had they been carved in marble. The Greeks eventually did remarkable things with marble, such as the violent poses of the *Laocoön Group* (Fig. 406), but the use of bronze allowed them to express their ideas more fully and freely at an earlier date than they could have with marble alone.

The advantage of starting with a malleable material like moist clay or wax and ending with terra cotta or a hard metal like bronze is eloquently illustrated by Daumier's *Burden* (Fig. 161) and Rodin's *Aged Courtesan* (Fig. 6). Either of these figures might have been carved in stone, but only at the cost of great labor. One is tempted to believe that the plastic mode could not have been developed to the point it reached under the hands of Daumier and others if they had not been able to work initially in soft clay. The contrast between the restricted plasticity of Bernini's *Apollo and Daphne* (Fig. 167) and the flowing forms of his clay and bronze statues tends to confirm this belief.

The transposition of soft clay figures into terra cotta or bronze is desirable; in the case of wax it is virtually obligatory. Since the means of making this transposition were discovered in early ancient times, the Chinese used wax extensively in the creation of their bronze ritual vessels. Since then wax has never been without its adherents, Michelangelo being one. Nevertheless, the use of wax has always been comparatively limited. Owing to its extreme brittleness and fragility when dry and its tendency to powder and crack, wax figures which have not been cast into bronze are rare. We know that Barye modeled many small figures of animals in wax but only as studies, not as finished products. One such group of a *Young Man Mastering a Horse* at Bowdoin College is noted because of its rarity; most of Barye's other wax studies having long ago been broken into pieces and lost.

Medardo Rosso's *Woman Seen Toward Evening* (Fig. 170) is another artistic rarity because Rosso apparently intended it and a number of similar statues to be regarded as finished. One must observe that only an Impressionist of extreme persuasions would use wax as a final material. To represent a fugitive theme in a fragile medium is consistent but perilous; few sculptors have been willing to carry consistency so far.

These anomalies excepted, the sculptural media used by the Greeks and Romans have been revived and perpetuated by all Western societies which continued the Hellenic traditions. Hence both the forms and favorite materials of the Greeks were passed down to us together from Renaissance times, while the more remote Egyptian culture and media have affected us less. The result is that for every statue in granite, European sculptors of the Renaissance and post-Renaissance periods produced a hundred in marble, terra cotta, or bronze.

North of the Alps, however, this preference for marble was slow in being realized. At the time when the French sculptors were raising the Romanesque and Gothic styles to their heights, they possessed inexhaustible supplies of limestone for building and carving, whereas they would have had to import marble from Italy. The post-Renaissance and modern masters did import their materials without a second thought after transportation methods had improved, but in the Middle Ages the problem was a serious one. The medieval artists used the limestone which they had at hand; as a result, it is the material that we associate most commonly with Romanesque and Gothic art.

These artists did not suffer from using limestone. The material contributed much to the realization of their aspirations. Being plentiful, it permitted the building of huge and generously decorated monasteries and cathedrals. If its soft grey or creamy color is less handsome than marble's milk-white or honey-colored tones, limestone's textures and sober hues at least suited the temperament of the more romantic northerners. And there are still those today who prefer the restrained and subdued colors of the weather-beaten cathedrals to the effects of marble. The two materials seem appropriate to the two contrasting cultures which favored them and complement each other well in our heritage.

The workability of limestone allowed the Gothic artists of France to build on a scale and carve with a freedom which they must have accepted with gratitude. The material became part and parcel of their expression, making possible the soaring towers of Reims (Fig. 179), the lacelike decoration of Rouen (Fig. 182), and the vital fluidity of such statues as the *Madonna and Child* on the Cathedral of Notre Dame in Paris (Fig. 419). At the same time it did not keep them from being realistic and probably fostered that tendency in late Gothic sculpture exemplified by the *Tomb of Phillipe Pot* (Fig. 398) in the Louvre.

Wood has played a prominent part among the materials used in the history of sculpture. Its use dates back to ancient times. One of the most famous of statues, the *Sheik-el-Beled,* was carved in Egypt during the Old Kingdom, some two thousand or more years before Christ. Geographically, too, wood has been widely employed, having been popular in Egypt, Japan, and northern Europe. It has been favored by primitive societies all over the world, from tribes in Africa and Australia to the Indians of the American Northwest.

Several properties have made wood a popular material. It is found all over the world, except in desert or arctic lands, and in some cases is superior to local stone. This was noticeably the case in Japan, where the tradition of wood carving took precedence over stone sculpture. Certainly, the plenitude of wood in northern Europe and the relative scarcity of it in Italy and Greece were not without their effects upon the scultpural production of those regions; the Egyptians, who imported wood for sculpture, were the exceptions. The Swiss, Germans, French, English, Poles, and Norwegians made some of their chief contributions to art through wood. Wood carving has remained a vigorous tradition in Middle Europe to the present, but the artistic peak was probably reached in France in Gothic times, when such statues as the boxwood *Madonna and Child* in Fig. 420 and the polychromed wood *Virgin* in Fig. 421 were carved and the incredibly intricate wooden choir stalls of the cathedrals completed.

In modern times there has been a revival of wood sculpture, with artists like William Muir adopting it as their principal material. His *Growth* (Fig. 186) is an example of what can be done to exploit the special properties of wood. Carved from California redwood burl, its form has been made to appear alive, while its surface has been polished so as to enhance both the flowing plastic curves and the warm colors of the wood.

Wood sometimes cracks, rots, burns, or falls prey to worms and termites, but it possesses merits which have endeared it to thousands of carvers. Its color, grain, and texture can be so treated as to appeal to man's sensuous nature. It comes in a great variety of types, permitting a choice of an easily worked material or a very durable one. Hence, it allows a wide range of expression and virtually any mode of representation that one desires, though there is some indication that the nature of wood favors linear and plastic rendering and tempts sculptors in the direction of complexity. Probably the main drawback of wood is the grain which distinguishes it from clay and stone. Grain increases the difficulties of any carver, who cuts against it at his peril. But the beauties of wood have compensated, attracting devotees who prize it above all other sculptural materials. Its appeal can perhaps be summed up by saying that, whereas stone always connotes a certain coldness, wood inspires a feeling of warmth.

One statement that can be made about sculpture in general is that its media make all its practitioners highly conscious of physical properties. Hard, heavy, and dense stones like granite almost invariably influence a sculptor toward the static, geometric, glyptic mode which was given classic form by the Egyptians. Stones like marble and limestone steer the artist in a more realistic or plastic direction, and malleable materials like clay and wax further this tendency even more. Similarly, the lightness and living qualities of wood tempt an artist to work along plastic lines. In each case the special physical attributes of the material affect the formal thinking of the sculptor.

One sweeping generalization is worth risking in order to correlate architecture, sculpture, and painting. Stone sculpture has predominated when architecture and sculpture have been the reigning arts, as in antiquity, and when the outlook was mainly finite. By contrast, bronze sculpture has been noticeably popular when painting has tended to dominate visual expression, as it did during the post-

Renaissance period and nineteenth century, and when the attitudes of the times have favored the infinite.

THE ARCHITECTURAL MEDIA

The history of the architectural media consists of the triumph over two physical obstacles to man's building aims and the putting of his triumph to expressive account. These two obstacles have been called the "tyranny of the wall" and the "tyranny of the post." The problems which persist through the centuries in the building arts all revolve around these obstacles and the means men have evolved to overcome them.

In this continuing battle the history of architecture has been almost the reverse of the history of sculpture. Whereas sculptors faced comparatively simple technical problems which they mastered at an early date, architects constantly met more difficult problems than they could solve quickly. Sometimes the lag between intention and solution continued for more than a millenium. When new structural materials and methods finally overcame a vexing impasse in a striking way, the revolutionary improvement was properly attributed to technical advances. The media have therefore played a more dramatic role in the history of architecture than they have in sculpture or even painting.

Architects can never forget one requirement that painters and sculptors can ignore: their designs must fulfill practical functions. And central in these functions is the need for shelter which provides usable space—the more of it the better. Gaining a maximum of space with a minimum of protective means has therefore been one of the universal quests of architecture. In order to provide this sheltered space architects have had to build and support walls and roofs from earliest antiquity. Hence the Great Pryamids, in which solids predominate over interior space by a thousand to one, are as exceptional as they are impressive. They illustrate the exact opposite of what is customarily meant by a building.

The basic practical problems of architecture are thus easy to perceive. They consist of the natural elements, weather and gravity, and of the construction of walls and roofs that men have had to build to attain shelter. We say *had* to build because the walls and roofs they were able to construct robbed them of the light and air they desired almost as much as space. The villain in this drama was not weather so often as we might think, but gravity. So, in one sense, the history of architecture is a gradual conquest of gravity.

The main structural systems which men have used to overthrow the tyranny of the wall and the post are: the post and lintel; the arch, vault, and dome; the dome on pendentives; the ribbed vault and buttress; the truss; and the cantilever.

The principal materials which have been used are stone, brick, wood, glass, metals, and concrete. Uniting these materials and techniques in some kind of geographical-temporal context is the history of architectural engineering.

THE POST AND LINTEL SYSTEM. Old as the Pyramids are, they do not mark the beginning of building, for building in the normally accepted sense implies the creation of usable hollow space. One of the most ancient of methods for creating that space is called the post and lintel system.

The post and lintel system is a method of supporting a roof or floor by a series of posts and cross-pieces. No one knows how ancient this simple system is or how it originated. There are good reasons for believing that it lay within the spontaneous ingenuity of men at an early stage in their development. It could have occurred to any prehistoric man with a glimmer of intelligence who saw a tree which had fallen across a gully, for by substituting posts for the sides of the gully he could have constructed a rudimentary system of support. Such a method of support was known and mastered on a grand scale by the time the gigantic circular monument was built at Stonehenge, England, in the Late Neolithic or Early Bronze Age. It seems to have sprung up spontaneously all over the world among primitive peoples. Indeed, we can see the origin of this kind of building any time a child starts to play with blocks. The child will first stack them in a solid pile, as the ancient pyramid builders did. But soon he will set a series of blocks upright and place other blocks across them. In some such fashion was the post and lintel system born again and again in the mechanical mind.

Although Stonehenge is a splendid monument and a fine example of the post and lintel system, it is not, any more than the Pyramids, a building, for its open top gives no shelter. For an ancient example of a true building we must go to Egypt, where, at the time the Pyramids were being constructed, the Temple of the Sphinx (Fig. 201) was erected nearby. It is a classic example of the post and lintel system, illustrating both the strength and weaknesses of the system and of Egyptian architecture.

The Egyptians have been given credit for cradling civilization because, though they did not settle down earlier than the peoples of Mesopotamia, they built structures of far greater durability. The dried-brick buildings erected between the Tigris and Euphrates are nothing but archaeological memories, but the massive temples and pyramids of the Nile Valley still stand—symbols of indestructibility.

Part of their survival is due to the materials used. The Egyptians employed stone in constructing the Temple of the Sphinx and most of their other important monuments, for it was plentiful and it expressed the craving for permanence which ran through their religious beliefs. It was a symbol of material security in a harsh climate and insecure world.

Part of the durability of Egyptian monuments like the Pyramids and the Temple of the Sphinx is due also to the static systems of construction used—the piling of blocks into a huge mass in the one and the use of static uprights and cross-pieces in the other. The thrust in such a system is wholly downward; its dead weight could not be less dynamic or absorbed in a simpler fashion. Hard materials and structural simplicity together gave the Egyptians the permanence they desired. However, they paid a penalty for this permanence by lifting hardly a finger to combat the tyranny of the wall or the tyranny of the post. Rather, they set in motion a tradition of masonry architecture which perpetuated these tyrannies for nearly three thousand years, until Gothic times.

The masonry construction exemplified by the Temple of the Sphinx thwarts all attempts to introduce an abundance of light, air, and space into a building. The cause lies in the intrinsic characteristics of stone. A stone post like any of those in the Temple of the Sphinx can support enormous loads of crushing weight providing it is thick enough. But even a thick cross-piece of stone is so weak at its center that it is likely to crack under its own weight and is almost certain to crack if it is required to carry any heavy load; it is adequate for a roof, but a poor means of supporting a floor. This means, in turn, that the posts must be close together, as they are in the Temple of the Sphinx and in such vast buildings as the Temple of Karnak. The latter is a forest of mammoth columns in which masonry predominates over usable space by a ratio of at least two to one. To the extent that columns intrude into the floor area of a building the tyranny of the post is in command. Egyptian architecture bowed to this tyranny in extreme degree.

Another fault of masonry construction in stone can be demonstrated with a set of children's blocks. Any wall built by stacking these dry (mortarless) blocks in courses must be thick if it is to mount very high. If unsupported it will topple sideways. At best it cannot be built up more than the equivalent of two or three building storeys, making high multi-storeyed structures impossible. Unfortunately, the thicker a wall is, the smaller must be the windows in it;

FIG. 201. Temple of the Sphinx. (Valley Temple of the Pyramid of Khafre.) Khafre reigned *ca.* 2850-2794 B.C. Gizeh.

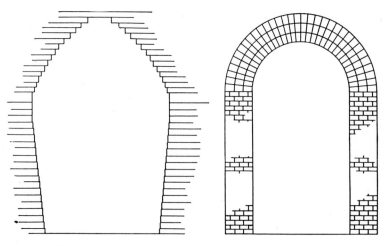

FIG. 202. Types of early Mesopotamian vault. 2000-700 B.C.

any large windows would weaken it dangerously. If, in addition, one forces the walls to support the outer ends of the lintels (as in the Temple of the Sphinx) and to play a part in holding up floors and roofs, they must be thicker still. In the Egyptian buildings these faults of numerous heavy parts and massive walls combined to rob the interiors of the three principal desiderata of the building arts—space, light, and air. They were crowded, dark, and stuffy.

Let us assume that the Egyptians, living as they did in a hot, dry country, actually desired a moist, dark coolness in their interiors; and, furthermore, that both the aura of massive permanence and the darkness fostered the sense of mystery that the priests required. Nevertheless, the system of masonry construction that the Egyptians accepted offered little chance for progress to the rest of the world. Quite to the contrary, it endowed masonry construction with a prestige that retarded architectual thinking for centuries, even among northern peoples whose need for light and space was more urgent than their need for permanence. Once enthroned, the tyranny of the wall was not easily or quickly dislodged.

The post and lintel system is not confined to masonry. Over the world it has probably been employed ten times as often in wood construction. Literally millions of houses in America have been built recently with a system of framing which is based on the simple post and lintel support. The Egyptian buildings which contain stone lintels are therefore exceptional; they grew out of and expressed the particular needs of the ancient inhabitants of the Nile Valley.

Long before the birth of Christ the Greeks combined stone walls and columns with wooden lintels in order to overcome the limitations of Egyptian architecture. Less bent on massiveness and more desirous of space and light, they achieved a greater openness through wooden lintels and wood and tile roofs. These, being much lighter than stone, had a double merit; they could span larger areas without intervening posts, and they permitted lighter outside walls. The Parthenon was covered in this way, which partially accounts for its lighter appearance in comparison with the Temple of the Sphinx or the Temple of Karnak.

This compromise, however, was not all pure gain. The Greeks traded durability for space because wood splits, rots, and burns. Sheer decay prevents any wooden structural member from ever lasting as long as masonry. If much of ancient Mediterranean architecture has survived to represent these cultures, it is because the Egyptians and Greeks built predominantly in stone.

Whenever the Greeks substituted wood for stone they invited eventual destruction. In spite of a rather dry climate the ancient wooden structures have entirely vanished. Presuming that these were of minor value, no great historical loss was entailed. When the Greeks sought permanence for an important structure, they substituted stone for wood. They are said to have done this literally when they replaced the rotting wooden columns of the Heraeum at Olympia with masonry members until the whole building was, so to speak, artificially petrified.

When, conversely, the Greeks used wood in spanning the interior of the Parthenon, time exacted a penalty. The roof of the temple has disappeared, as has that of nearly every other Grecian temple of its time. The roof of the Parthenon was destroyed by an explosion; many wooden roofs rotted and caved in; others were consumed by fire. In any case, each was as vulnerable as the wooden city of Chicago at the time of the great fire.

THE ARCH AND VAULT. Egyptian architecture was governed by the building materials at hand. Possessing unlimited quantities of stone but only a poor supply of fibrous palm wood, the Egyptians built accordingly. Necessity was no less the mother of invention in the history of early Mesopotamian architecture. In ancient times the silt-covered land between the Tigris and Euphrates was, thanks to elaborate irrigation ditches, a garden spot; yet it offered little to builders in the way of either wood or stone. Clay was its most abundant material. So, faced with the need to provide shelter from the sun, the builders based their system of construction on the ubiquitous sun-dried brick and evolved the arch, vault, and dome for covering space. They thus paved the way for many later developments. At the time, however, their own achievement was a modest one, owing to the characteristics of their crude bricks.

These bricks were not without their merits: they could be made easily, cheaply, quickly, and in quantity by slave labor and, being small, readily moved from place to place. They permitted the building of vast fortress-cities by the Early Babylonians and Assyrians and one of the seven wonders of the ancient world, the Hanging Gardens of Babylon, by the later Babylonians. When finished on the outside with colored glazes, they were acceptable and even brilliant in appearance. They had, on the other hand, one grave weakness—in the long run they were fragile. The cities of which they were built are now nothing but mounds of dirt. Great Nineveh literally crumbled into dust.

Even new buildings of sun-dried bricks had marked disadvantages, owing to the system of building which the brick forced upon its users. Since the brick was useless as a lintel and stone was scarce, the Mesopotamians had to find another way to cover space with small bricks in a dry, mortarless system. To meet this need they invented the arch and its extension, the vault. It is an ingenious system, depending on the fact that when wedge-shaped bricks are arranged over a half-circle, as in Fig. 202, they will lock themselves together against the downward pull of gravity. The wedge-shaped pieces are called *voussoirs* and the wedge at the top the keystone, the latter being fitted into place last. Until that moment the arch or vault is not self-supporting and must be held up by a wooden framework called a centering; it is an indispensable part of the structural system.

A crucial difference between the post and lintel and the vault comes from the dynamic activity of the vault. For while the pressure of the lintel is downward, the thrust of the vault is both downward and outward. It tends to spread apart like a man on stilts. This is especially true in vaults of sun-dried brick which lack a mortar adhesive.

In order to counteract the outward thrust of plain barrel vaults, the Mesopotamians had to construct massive walls. The dead weight and inertia of these walls stabilized the system. At the same time they created an extreme predominance of solid over void, reducing interior space to a minimum and drastically cutting out light and air. These fortress-cities must have resembled mountains through which a few tunnels had been burrowed. All spacious living was necessarily in courtyards or on roof-tops, but without benefit of shelter. Thus, if the post did not intrude in Mesopotamian architecture, its sun-dried brick vaults imposed an unparalleled tyranny of the wall.

There are, of course, several ways to look at anything. The Mesopotamians probably welcomed the cool darkness of their vaulted homes as a relief from the blazing Near-Eastern sun; and they undoubtedly felt secure behind thick walls. Herodotus, who was greatly impressed by the outer ramparts of Babylon, says that they were 800 feet high and 110 feet thick. Even allowing for Herodotian exaggeration, they must have been among the most massive fortress walls of ancient times and nearly as awe-inspiring as the Pyramids. Yet they did not last and, like the masonry post and lintel of the Egyptians, contributed little to the quest for usable space.

MOLDED CONCRETE. Augustus asserted that he found Rome made of brick and left it in marble—more accurately, marble veneer. He might have taken even greater pride in another contribution of his people, the mastery of molded concrete. For through their perfection of this great plastic material the Romans contributed infinitely

more to the progress of architectural engineering than anything they
achieved through superficial decoration. In this one way they bested
the Greeks artistically, for though the Greeks created a masterpiece
of refinement in the Parthenon, they added nothing radically new to
structural progress. Under the leadership of Rome the building arts
took tremendous forward strides toward greater variety and greatly
increased space.

The Romans were under heavy pressure to improve the modes
of building. Having created the first truly modern empire, they could
not maintain it with the limited building types that had persisted
through most of antquity—the house, the tomb, and the temple.
Their political organization and swelling population demanded new
edifices. The city of Rome had increased to over a million inhabitants, by far the largest metropolis the world had ever seen. The
hordes of people in it needed huge temples like the Pantheon (Figs.
176, 203, and 204), meeting places (or basilicas) for public purposes,
and several kinds of governmental buildings. They had also developed a taste for bathing and recreational centers on a vast scale
like the Baths of Caracalla, and for huge amphitheatres like the
Circus Maximus and the Colosseum (Fig. 207). They needed, moreover, a complex system of highways, sewers, and aqueducts. They
were obliged, too, to extend the material benefits of their civilization throughout their Empire by building temples, amphitheatres,
roads, and aqueducts on only a slightly reduced scale. Indeed, the
Pont du Gard (Fig. 206) which they built near Nîmes is one of the
truly impressive monuments of architectural history. It illustrates
how the Romans added a new dimension to architecture not only by
creating unprecedented quantities of interior space, but by linking
hundreds of miles of country with a network of roads and aqueducts.
They conquered space both indoors and outdoors with a boldness
no previous peoples had shown. Architects prior to this time had
been unable to overcome the tyranny of the wall and the post, and
had made a virtue of solidity. The Roman architects probably were
the first to conceive space as the primary objective of building and
to mold and shape voids as though they were material forms. Thus
a new conception of the purpose of architecture was born.

Without this conception Rome could not have existed and grown
as it did. If the aqueducts alone had been removed Rome would
have perished. Equally important was the realization of this conception in practical terms. The demand for many large and unprecedented types of buildings had to be met with a bold and
competent technical knowledge. Here the Roman genius was at its
best, for, while conquering the world, the soldiers had developed a

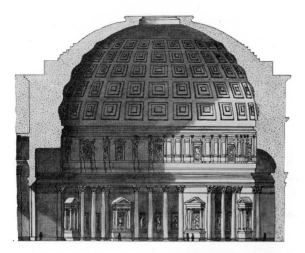

FIG. 203. Cross-section. Pantheon. Mainly A.D. 120-124. Rome.

FIG. 204. Piranesi. Interior of the Pantheon. *ca.* 1760. Bowdoin College Museum of Fine Arts, Brunswick, Me.

FIG. 205. Berg. Centennial Hall. 1913. Breslau.

FIG. 206. Pont du Gard.
ca. 19 B.C. Near Nîmes.

FIG. 207. The Colosseum. A.D.
72-82. Rome.

FIG. 208. Anthemius of
Tralles and Isidorus of Miletus. Santa Sophia. A.D. 532-
562. Istanbul.

military engineering which could be applied in numerous ways to civil construction.

The development of the Roman Empire depended in no small degree upon finding a way to meet their building needs quickly, cheaply, and extensively. The Romans found the answer to their problem in molded concrete. It was a revolutionary discovery, for even though the ingredients of its material and the crucial cement had been available for centuries, it was the Roman imagination which grasped its possibilities.

The disadvantages of concrete—such as its unpleasant color and texture—are far outweighed by its many merits. Cement is plentiful in many parts of the world, is comparatively inexpensive, and can be easily hauled in small bags to a building site. Although a good deal of technical knowledge is required for the designing of the forms, this could be done by a few Roman engineers, while crews of slaves could do most of the work. The actual pouring of concrete demands much muscle but little thought. It thus lent itself admirably to the distribution of ability and manpower that Rome possessed.

The virtues of concrete are that its ingredients—sand, water, and cement—can be carried separately to a building site and then poured into any shape desired. It will even harden under water, making it ideal for the piers of bridges and the foundations of wharfs. Once hardened, it forms a monolithic mass which is proof against water, fire, and rot, and is exceedingly durable—witness the longevity of the Pont du Gard, Pantheon, Colosseum, and other Roman buildings. Though battered on the surface, their concrete cores stand almost intact.

Consider specifically what the mastery of concrete allowed the Romans to accomplish. It permitted them to leap over rivers and chasms with gigantic spans like those of the Pont du Gard, carrying water, food, goods, people, and information—the life-giving elements of the Empire—speedily across hundreds of miles. It enabled them to erect the prototype of all modern stadia, the Colosseum, whose 80,000 seating capacity was not equaled until recent times and whose traffic arteries were superior to those serving most of our present-day arenas. Above all it allowed them in the Pantheon (Fig. 204) to shape a dome over an unbroken interior measuring 142 feet in diameter and the same dimension in height. No ancient structure in Greece, Egypt, or Mesopotamia had ever provided so much usable space.

The casing of the Pantheon is a monolithic mass of concrete ingeniously poured between molding walls of brick, so that the two bonded together have the appearance of brick but the strength of concrete. Such a monolith reduces the columns and pilasters which the Romans borrowed from the Greeks to merely decorative members. They support nothing, and could be removed with no destructive effect. We are prone to resent this debasement of the Greek columnar system. But two things must be borne in mind in fairness to the Romans. They could never have solved their building problems through the post and lintel system. On the other hand, concrete, the one material that answered their needs, is ugly to look at. While excellent for the cores of large buildings, it makes a poor exterior. The Romans were not the last to recognize concrete's lack of beauty and seek to improve it by adding decorative pilasters and brick or stone veneers.

Although the Romans conquered the tyrannical support brilliantly, they did not overcome the tyranny of the wall. The ponderous shell of the Pantheon (Fig. 203) is at some points 28 feet thick. Let us assume that the Romans liked such massiveness when it did not reduce interior space; indeed, that they valued the psychological support that it gave to their imperial ideals and appreciated its contribution to the grandeur of Rome. But welcome or not, so long as the tyranny of the wall remained, there was room for further architectural progress. That progress came with the development of the dome on pendentives in the Near East.

Meanwhile, there was an interlude in building in Italy which was to influence the future of architecture in Western Europe. The Early Christian builders, after the official recognition of their religion in the early fourth century, took over a progressively larger part of the leadership of a declining Rome. Emerging from their hiding places in the catacombs, they began to build churches with great rapidity, and during the ensuing two hundred years erected in and around Rome most of the famous Early Christian centers of worship—Santa Maria Maggiore, San Lorenzo, Sant' Agnese, San Clemente, San Pietro, and San Paolo Fuori-le-Mura. There was, in short, a "religious building boom."

This rapid growth was marked by good and bad ideas. Both are illustrated by San Paolo Fuori-le-Mura, the largest and grandest of the Early Christian churches still in existence, the original San Pietro having been demolished in the early sixteenth century to make room for the present edifice. On the credit side is the cruciform shape and general arrangement of the church. Called *basilica* after the Roman meeting places on which it was based, its nave, side aisles, and altar end provided such an appropriate setting for Christian congregational worship that the type has persisted to the present day.

On the debit side is the structural system used. It contributed nothing to the advancement of architectural engineering; rather, it was a retrogression, for the Early Christian builders reverted to the post and lintel system, abandoning the fireproof methods of covering space that the Romans had invented. They spanned their interiors with wooden trusses, much as the Greeks had covered the Parthenon nearly a thousand years before. To be sure the builders of San Paolo and San Pietro bridged great widths, reaching in San Pietro nearly a hundred feet of unbroken space. But the wooden trusses they used were, as always, vulnerable to fire and decay, which, in more cases than one, justified their worst fears. Thus, while the Early Christian basilica bequeathed to the Middle Ages an admirable arrangement for worship, it posed, at the same time, a structural problem which plagued people for almost five hundred years—how to cover the basilica with a fireproof ceiling and roof.

Behind this structural defect lies a general truth. No great system of engineering is evolved overnight. The Roman builders and military engineers had developed a tradition and acquired their technical skill over a period of centuries, and the Early Christians could not borrow more than its superficial aspects overnight by zeal alone. Being largely recruited from the have-not classes, the Early Christians possessed the least of Rome's organizational and practical abilities and were mentally opposed to all of the kindred materialistic sciences that were the Roman forte. They were able to borrow where borrowing was easiest—in the general functional arrangements of the older buildings. But where borrowing is hardest—in the engineering devoted to the covering of space and the mastery of materials—they failed. Stealing ravenously from the pagan temples for the glory of God, they gathered up odd assortments of columns (as in San Clemente) whenever they could not find a complete colonnade. Hence the handsomest parts of their buildings were almost always of Roman origin; the walls they actually built were by comparison poorly constructed. It took a long time for Western Europe to overcome that part of their example. The fourth great contribution to the advancement of the architectural media did not occur in the Western half of Christendom, but in the Eastern division where the dome on pendentives was evolved.

THE DOME ON PENDENTIVES. When Constantine moved the capital of Rome to Constantinople in 330 and laid the foundation of the Byzantine Empire on the site of the old Greek colony of Byzantium, he seems to have carried with him most of the technical brains left in the service of Rome. At Byzantium these were united with a tradition of Greek logic and manual skill and a Near-Eastern genius for domical and vaulted construction. Constantine also brought with him a Christian worship which was best housed in a square or rectangular building with an altar at one end which served as a focus for the mass. The Early Christian cruciform basilica had served this need well but at the sacrifice of structural finesse which little suited the Near-Eastern mind.

In this new situation the problem was how to construct a fireproof dome over a square space so as to satisfy Christian requirements and utilize the best features of Near-Eastern building at the same time. The solution lay in one of the handsomest and most ingenious systems for covering space ever invented—the dome on pendentives. Evolved rather than invented suddenly, it was not brought to perfection until the time of Justinian, two centuries after Constantine. Perfected, it enabled Justinian to build one of the world's truly superb buildings, Santa Sophia at Constantinople. The architects were, significantly, two Greeks.

It is now certain that the peoples of Asia Minor had been able to build small domes at least as far back as Assyrian times. But a vast dome over a square plan had been beyond their reach because of the limitations of building without mortar. No brick or stone dome which is merely held together by gravity could span a large room; and the walls which supported it would necessarily have been thick.

The Byzantine builders did not wish simply to create a variation of the Pantheon dome, for their practical and spiritual aims were different. The need for a rectangular plan was only one of them. Another of no less importance was to achieve an impression of logic, lightness, and spaciousness at the same time. In other words, the spiritual character of Christianity in the ancient Hellenic world called for an expression quite unlike that for which the massive walls of the Pantheon sufficed. How well the Byzantines succeeded in achieving their special goal of expressing a spiritually inspired logic, as distinct from the soaring mysticism of the Gothic architects, is shown by the interior of Santa Sophia (Fig. 208).

Yet the Byzantines owed the Romans a great debt. For one essential difference between the ancient Near-Eastern dome and the dome on pendentives was due to the presence of a material which binds stones into a solid wall. The Romans had given mortar, a variant of concrete, to the world; and without it the building of Santa Sophia would have been impossible.

The other essential in Santa Sophia was the system of the dome on pendentives. Basically, as one can see in Fig. 208, it consists of four inverted triangles whose upside-down apexes rest on piers at the four corners of a square plan but whose upper portions curve inward until they join in a circle, thereby providing a base for a dome. The triangles, or pendentives, effect the transition from a square to a circle in a smooth and efficient fashion. One of the principal virtues of this arrangement is that the outward thrust of the dome is absorbed and transferred gradually downward to a set of four pier buttresses (at the corners) and two inward-facing semi-domes. The latter serve to elongate the ground plan to meet the liturgical needs.

The most important consequence of this distribution of weight and thrust was to lighten the structure. This was in keeping with a major Byzantine aim which the builders of Santa Sophia accomplished so successfully that they reduced the walls to a thinness that seems almost fragile beside the Pantheon's massiveness. This lightness strikes one forcibly because of a special physical characteristic. Unlike the monolithic walls of the Pantheon, the shell of Santa Sophia is perforated and lightened by windows and other openings. Nowhere is this more apparent or effective than in the dome itself, which took on the character of an inverted saucer around whose rim the designers had cut a ring of windows. As a result, the dome seems to float in the air over a halo of light.

By these several means the architects of Santa Sophia excelled even the Romans. The Pantheon, the Romans' largest domical building, is vast; but Santa Sophia is vaster still. Its actual dimensions are awe-inspiring even to moderns who take architectural wonders for granted; the dome rises 180 feet above the floor and is 107 feet in diameter. It carried architecture beyond anything that had been done before and still maintains its place as one of the world's great buildings. Owing to its calculated design the psychological effect of spaciousness it creates exceeds that of the Pantheon more than can be accounted for by the difference in actual measurements.

The secret of Santa Sophia's eminence lies in a double triumph. Like the Pantheon, it overcame the tyranny of the post and provided a vast, unimpeded, and beautifully articulated volume. But it went beyond the Pantheon in overcoming the tyranny of the wall. Its thin shell appears light in weight and its numerous windows permit an abundance of illumination to flood the interior, creating the effect of a soaring expansiveness. This quality was the Byzantine's reward for perfecting the dome on pendentives. That system allowed them to master the two most ancient problems of architecture in spectacular fashion.

THE RIBBED VAULT AND BUTTRESSES. The next epochal advance in architectural engineering, the ribbed vault and buttress system which was finally perfected as an essential part of Gothic architecture, was as spectacular as the dome on pendentives. But it came long afterward because the Dark Ages which followed the decline of Rome were not uniformly dark. While the Byzantine Empire in the Eastern Mediterranean was at a peak of civilization in the sixth century A.D., Western Christendom was in a barbaric state. Nowhere was this more apparent than in the technical side of architecture where the Romans had excelled; the decline there was precipitous.

The cross-section of the Cathedral of St. Pierre at Beauvais (Fig. 210) and the interior of the Cathedral of Amiens (Fig. 209) show what heights the Gothic builders would reach structurally and expressively before the end of the thirteenth century. But a prolonged development had to come first, starting with the efforts of the Early Christian builders, for it was from their conception of a church, rather than from the Byzantine, that the Gothic cathedrals evolved.

The Early Christian builders fixed the shape of the church—a Roman basilica in cruciform. Compared to the dome-on-pendentives church, with its central climactic element, the cruciform basilica, with its high nave, side aisles, and transept, is long and narrow. Because it focuses attention on the drama at the altar, it is the logical arrangement for Christian worship. Once fixed, it persisted for centuries. Thus no matter how far beyond the Early Christian churches the Cathedral of Amiens may seem to have progressed in its stirring beauty it is still a variation on the Early Christian plan and section.

The Early Christian deficiency was not a functional but a structural one. The wooden timbers which were used to span the naves of San Pietro and San Paolo at Rome were long enough to cover large spaces, but they were impermanent. To protect against fire and rot has always been a primary aim of conscientious builders, and it soon became the aim of the architects of Western Europe who were made to appreciate the merits of fireproof covering by the Vikings. These pagan invaders from the North delighted in putting the torch to Christian churches, and burned thousands of them during their devastating raids of the eighth and ninth centuries. These disastrous forays taught the Christian builders one important lesson: while the wooden roofs would go up in flames, masonry walls remained to be used again.

When the medieval builders sought to replace combustible roofs with masonry, they started on a long and difficult road. Two sources of help were open to them. They could have adopted the Byzantine dome on pendentives and did so in several sections of Italy and France; but they preferred the elongated basilica nave, over which the dome on pendentives is contradictory. A more logical fireproof

FIG. 209. Nave. The Cathedral.
1220-1288. Designed by Robert
de Luzarches. Amiens.

FIG. 210. Cross-section. Cathedral
of St. Pierre. 1225-1347.
Beauvais.

covering was the Roman barrel vault. It was this they adopted and used well into the Romanesque period of the eleventh and twelfth centuries with one important change: whereas the Romans had performed their wonders of space-coverage with monolithic cement, the Christians preferred to work in stone and mortar masonry which exerts a stronger outward thrust. In order to contain this sideward pressure, they had to use heavy walls and pier buttresses. This put them back at the mercy of the wall and the heavy interior support with all the ponderous, dark, and low-ceiling rooms those tyrannies imposed.

Just when the peoples of France and Italy began to resent this chronic heaviness no one can say, for spiritual and physical rebellions of that sort are not formally documented. But the story of architecture in Western Christendom from the eleventh to the fourteenth century revolves around the means that were devised to master these problems in a Christian way. The triumphant solution in Gothic times is therefore the conclusion, not the beginning, of the story.

Signs of slow but steady progress appeared in the eleventh century in northern Italy and western France, especially in Lombardy and Normandy. Sant' Ambrogio in Milan, though still dark and heavy-looking, offered architecture an embryonic ribbed vault and buttress system, and the builders of the Church of the Holy Trinity at Caen (Fig. 180) carried this system even further. With the Burgundians the concept of the flying buttress developed, paving the way for this most striking feature of the Gothic in the nearby Île de France.

Whether at Milan, Caen, Cluny, Amiens, or Beauvais, the problem of the late medieval religious architects was essentially the same. Confronted with heavy vaults and ponderous supporting walls which robbed interiors of light, the architects had to find some way of lightening both in order to get illumination. Their solution was to subdivide the barrel vaults with transverse arches and diagonal ribs which criss-crossed in each bay. This skeleton assumed the major role of supporting the vault and concentrating its lateral thrust at a few points. These points were then strengthened by pier buttresses and later by flying buttresses. The principle involved is common in nature. The leaf of a plant is divided into two components: membranes of tissue, and strong but very light, thin ribs which stiffen the membranes like stays in a corset.

The Gothic designers applied this principle to the barrel vault with a gain in two directions. The lightened vaulting could be lifted higher in the air, giving a sense of both space and height. To accentuate height and minimize the intrusion of supports, the vertical lines of the design were stressed. At Amiens, for instance, the columns are constructed as compound piers, with no loss in support but a considerable gain in lightness of effect.

When carried to a high point of development in the Cathedral of Beauvais (Fig. 210) the ribbed vault and buttress system became a cage of slender masonry supports held in a delicate balance. With this skeleton assuming all of the work, the need for walls was virtually eliminated, and the areas gained by raising the vaults could be filled with windows. Light and lightness, height and spaciousness were the results made possible by this system. So if the Gothic architects did not eliminate the post, they used it to their advantage, and they mastered the wall in breath-taking fashion, earning the respect of engineers and the awe of laymen of all subsequent times.

One of the most noticeable characteristics of Gothic architecture is a kind of consistent irregularity. North and south towers frequently differ, while variations from true right angles are present in the vaults of Amiens and other cathedrals. Corners are often slightly askew. This could be excused as a carry-over from the poor techniques of the Dark Ages or justified as a picturesque characteristic of Gothic romanticism. This apparent haphazardness is even said to promote the living, growing quality in Gothic architecture. Indeed it does! But careful study by Goodyear and others has brought out the consistency of these irregularities. They were not haphazard, but artistically calculated. Their purpose was to introduce the variety which buildings need if they are to avoid a rigidly mechanical appearance. These departures remind us of the refinements the Greeks incorporated into the Parthenon for the same reason. They are signs of technical finesse, not ineptitude. We can easily believe this of the intellectual Greeks, but overlook it in the case of the Gothic artists. If anything, they were even more skilful than the Greeks, for they employed their calculated variations in many more important buildings and on a much larger scale.

Something of the achievement of the Gothic engineers can be conveyed by statistics. The north spire of Chartres Cathedral (Fig. 385) is a towering 377 feet; the edifice is 440 feet long, 150 feet wide across the choir, and 121 feet high in the nave. Reims (Fig. 179) and Amiens are even larger. Amiens is 469 feet long, while its nave vaults are 140 feet above the floor. The dimensions of Reims are about the same. To build the wooden scaffolding and centering alone for masonry on this scale must have been an exacting feat of engineering.

One cannot emphasize too often that the Gothic architects employed these technical abilities for expression and design. Practicality alone does not explain why they built as they did. By Gothic times the problem of creating a permanent, fireproof masonry vault had been solved. To raise the vaults higher in the air did not make them stronger, nor did greater height permit the housing of larger congregations. It did allow more light to enter the interiors, which was undoubtedly a practical gain. But once the problems of construction were solved, the main concerns of the medieval church-builders shifted from the practical to the expressive. Their driving ambition became a desire for an inspiring religious setting, tinged with not a little desire to build higher and higher in the air for the sheer excitement of conquering vast spaces and dizzy heights.

This ambition is dramatically illustrated by the history of Beauvais Cathedral. Its builders sought to float their vaults higher in the air than any others in France and on slimmer piers, creating a sensation not unlike watching an acrobat balance on a 20-foot pole. In the choir they reached the man-dwarfing height of 154 feet, making it the Everest of Gothic vaults. Unfortunately, they overreached themselves. The first attempt, of 1247, ended disastrously; the vaults collapsed. They were rebuilt in 1274, only to fall again ten years later. Undaunted, the architects doubled the number of bays in 1320 by building intermediate piers between those of the earlier scheme. The vault on this doubled support has remained stabilized at 154 feet; but the people of Beauvais had spent themselves on the choir and transept and were unable to complete the forward part of the cathedral. Today we tend to feel that the less lofty but more stable-looking vaults of Amiens and Reims, rather than the precarious-looking piers of Beauvais, represent the happy medium in Gothic.

Even Gothic genius had its limits. These limits were partially determined by economics and partly by the exhaustion of human energies and will; but they were dictated, too, by the nature of stone and mortar and what can be done with them. No one doubts that the Gothic peoples exploited them with zeal, boldness, and skill. Building to the glory of God and the fame of their cities, they gave abundantly and scorned half-measures. Their outpouring of time, money, and energy is the more extraordinary when we remember that cities like Chartres are not large today and must have been smaller then. For a city of a few thousand people to build a church of the size of Chartres Cathedral would be amazing in any age. Measured in terms of medieval resources, it set a lofty standard.

The competition among the French cathedral-builders to erect the highest structures in their land was repeated in the race to build the tallest skyscrapers in Manhattan in the 1920s. In each case the love of height for its own sake and the technical ability to achieve it drove builders far beyond the mere call of practicality.

If one compares the Gothic masterpieces with Santa Sophia, the latter is larger, and superior in other ways. But whereas the Byzantine builders were able to erect only one Santa Sophia, the Gothic masons completed a score of vast churches across the face of northern Europe, showing an ability to repeat this high-level performance again and again. Their productivity can be interpreted as a sign of inspired vitality. It can also be attributed to the combination of ingenuity and soundness arrived at in the ribbed vault and buttress system. Though a few men may invent and perfect a system, the system must not remain dependent upon them if it is to be useful for a long time and over a wide area. The ribbed vault and buttress system evolved in Romanesque times and perfected by the Gothic designers was used by builders for six hundred years.

THE MODERN PLASTICS. Throughout most of the history of architecture builders were dominated by the limitations of wood and masonry. Masonry, though heavy, was nearly indestructible and imposed its character everywhere, perpetuating the two tyrannies of wall and support. It was the common enemy of all seekers of light and lightness in Byzantine, Gothic, and Baroque times. It even governed the Romans, making them think in terms of heavy vaults despite the fact that they possessed concrete.

A climactic point was reached in this development in 1755 when Soufflot designed the Panthéon in Paris. Outwardly a sturdy-looking stone and mortar building, the internal character of the dome reached the peak of post-Renaissance control of masonry construction. The thrust was so distributed that the shell of the dome attained an extremity of thinness without any metal reinforcing. The limit of progress in masonry had been reached. If any further improvement was to be made, new materials and structural systems would have to be found.

These new materials began to appear with the Industrial Revolution and gained wider usage with each succeeding century. We call them the modern plastics because the majority of them, though using natural materials, reshape and transform them for building purposes. They include three main groups: glass, concrete, and metals, though synthetic stones and wood substitutes such as Masonite are being added yearly.

Not literally new, glass, concrete, and metals have been known and used from ancient times. Yet their properties have been so improved that they have acquired a new importance. Glass was an essential element in Gothic design, as it was later in the Hall of Mirrors at Versailles. Until recent times, however, glass had to be poured in thin, small, bubbly sheets; hence the necessity of the subdivided French window. Today, perfectly clear, smooth, plate glass can be poured in huge sheets, allowing broad expanses for unimpaired vision, an abundance of light, and greatly increased strength.

Concrete was used on an Empire-wide scale by the Romans. But the discovery of Portland cement by Aspdin early in the nineteenth century (1824) placed in modern hands a material ten times as strong as Roman concrete. This meant that a modern concrete wall a foot thick would be as durable as a Roman wall ten feet thick. Subsequently modern engineers, using powerful labor-saving machines, found ways of mixing vast quantities of concrete much more rapidly than the Romans could. Equipped with these machines, men were able to surpass the huge bulk of the Great Pyramid (Fig. 174a) for the first time in history, in Boulder (Hoover) Dam, in less than a tenth of the time needed by the Egyptians.

The modern architectural revolution was made possible by widespread scientific and technical innovations. If architects today possess unprecedented structural materials and techniques, it is because they have benefited from the efforts of men in many laboratories and on distant engineering projects. The pooling of these discoveries has made modern architectural progress a victory of teamwork. The invention of powerful engines is but one example. Yet it is an important one, for without these machines the improved materials and techniques would have been useless. Machines have not replaced the human brain, but skyscrapers cannot be built without them.

The third major plastic, metal, has also been known from early times. The Italians used it, though awkwardly, for tie rods in buildings. Only during the past two centuries, however, have the architectural potentialities of metals been even partially utilized. As substitutes for wooden framing, they contributed enormous new strength. Unfortunately, they exhibit the same vulnerability to fire as wood. Gutted by flames which softened the metal framework, some of the first metal skeleton buildings collapsed like wet spaghetti.

This weakness against heat inspired modern engineers to imbed metal in concrete. They thereby produced reinforced concrete, a material whose elements were old but whose combined strength was new. Equally revolutionary was the use of metal framing for windows and steel girders. These changed the whole conception of window and other openings. Wide horizontal windows, balconies, and doors can now be freely used. The streamlined horizontality of the

New York University–Bellevue Medical Center and Wright's Kaufmann House (Fig. 213) at Bear Run, Pennsylvania, is typical exploitation of this new possibility.

The pioneer experiments which took place behind the scenes of
respectable architecture, and in areas far removed from the fine
arts, were adopted only slowly by conventional builders. They originated in answer to the need for many new types of structures created
by the impact of the Industrial Revolution. The swelling population of Europe was adequately equipped with fine churches, schools,
and public buildings; but it needed railroad bridges and stations,
factory buildings, public markets, and other structures which conventional architectural concepts could not supply. In the course of
the nineteenth century there appeared another phenomenon of the
times—the international expositions, destined to play an important
role in modern architecture. Although they presented unprecedented problems, their temporary character allowed architects to
solve them with greater originality than was permitted in more permanent buildings. The expositions offered excellent opportunities
for experiments with new materials and techniques.

New needs, materials, and structural systems were thus joined to
overcome the impasse created by Soufflot's final refinement of masonry and to permit progress in architecture. The progress set in
motion inaugurated one of the most epochal advances in architectural history. Its end is by no means in sight, but its beginning is
clear. It started in England and France, the two European countries
which launched the Industrial Revolution. The beginning came
earlier than is commonly realized in the behind-the-scenes field of
utilitarian architecture. Even during the eighteenth century architectural engineers on both sides of the Channel were vying with each
other in the solution of old problems and the satisfaction of the
new needs created by the industrial, economic, scientific, political,
and social revolutions that were beginning to transform Europe and
are living issues still.

For instance, Smeaton showed how the age-old desire for durability could be fulfilled more cheaply, quickly, and satisfactorily than
ever before when he built the Eddystone Lighthouse off Plymouth in
1759. Using a streamlined design which deflected the force of the
waves, he succeeded in making a lighthouse stand where previous
masonry lighthouses had crumpled before the Atlantic storms. Here,
far from fashionable architectural circles, a new era in functional
design was born.

Meanwhile, other engineers attacked the old problem of spanning
out-of-door space in order to meet the new need for stronger and

longer railroad and highway bridges. Wood was inadequate and masonry cumbersome and costly, so they turned to metal. Darby's iron bridge of 1779 at Coalbrookdale represents only a modest beginning, but it touched off a period of rapid progress. Before a quarter century had passed, Telford offered (in 1801) to replace the burnt-out wooden London Bridge with a single metal arch. Sixty-three years later Brunnel spanned the gorge at Clifton with a spectacular suspension bridge. Following in his footsteps, Roebling started a new era of bridge construction in America with his similar Brooklyn Bridge of 1883. The suspension bridge was not new, but the use of steel cables permitted dimensions never seen before.

In the twentieth century engineers have made gigantic bridges commonplace. Their progress can be measured by noting that Roman bridges and aqueducts, like the Pont du Gard (Fig. 206), which remained unsurpassed for seventeen hundred years, have now been dwarfed by such distance-devouring structures as the Golden Gate Bridge across San Francisco Bay.

The expansion of interior space has been no less marked. The war against the tyrannies of the wall and the support was declared early in the modern architectural revolution and advances made almost at once. By using a steel framework, Brunet built a Grain Market as large as the Roman Pantheon at Paris in a single year (1811). Its domical form sheltered a huge interior within paper-thin walls without the aid of any posts.

Brunet's achievement was only the beginning. In 1851 Paxton, an English greenhouse designer, made a spectacular contribution to space-coverage. The occasion was the Exposition of World's Industry at London sponsored by Prince Albert, for which a gigantic shedlike structure was desired. Where all of the conventional architects failed, Paxton solved the problem by erecting an oversized greenhouse 1851 feet long—one foot for each year of the Christian Era.

Constructed exclusively of metal and glass, his Crystal Palace eliminated the wall as it had been conceived for centuries. Simultaneously, he reduced the post nearly to zero, for the metal columns which supported the central vault were as slender as reeds. Walls and supports together occupied only 1/200 of the building's volume; the rest was usable space. A landmark in architectural history, the Crystal Palace dramatically reversed the relationship of solid and void which prevailed in architecture as long as masonry was the reigning material. The walls now did nothing but protect against the weather.

The people who flocked to the Exposition of 1851 were fascinated by the sensations of lightness, luminosity, and openness that

Paxton's design produced. It was they who called it the Crystal Palace. It did more than any other single building to reveal and dramatize the possibilities of glass and metal. Long a favorite with the public, it was re-erected at Sydenham in 1854 and called the "First Modern Building," but its subsequent collapse during a fire showed the need for greater attention to fireproofing.

Following Paxton's time many other improvements in the covering of space were developed. Outstanding among them was Cottancin's Gallery of Machinery at the Paris Exposition of 1889. It was as light and airy as the Crystal Palace, and larger. Its special contribution was to publicize the merits of cantilever construction whose principle is illustrated by a child's seesaw—a lintel balanced on a single support. If no other building has made quite such an epochal impression on people as the Crystal Palace, progress has at least been steady. Today the tyranny of the wall and the post are things of the past, and spacious, well-lighted interiors are taken for granted.

Max Berg's Centennial Hall of 1913 at Breslau (Fig. 205) is a striking example of these qualities. A modern-style arena, it resembles a great predecessor, the Roman Pantheon (Fig. 204), but surpasses it in several respects. The old Roman engineers would have danced with joy if they could have matched it in either construction or design.

The Centennial Hall demonstrates what modern designers can do with reinforced concrete. Its combination of lightness and strength allowed Berg to cover the entire arena with a domical spider web whose many interstices admit a flood of light. The relation of walls and openings used in the Pantheon has been reversed. Hence Berg's dome floats in the air with an ease which reminds us of the dome of Santa Sophia. This ability to perform prodigious feats of engineering with apparent ease is a principal factor of modern architectural engineering.

Superb materials and brilliant engineering would, however, have gone to waste if Berg had not known how to combine them with an expressive design. His use of a shallow dome with lines bursting from the center makes the ultimate effect of the Centennial Hall emotional, not technical. It radiates the vitality of modern times.

Through the use of the modern plastics architects have realized another human ambition—to build high into the air. Part of this craving is practical, part of it purely psychological, but it dates back to early times. One of the seven wonders of the ancient world was the lighthouse tower at Alexandria, and the great height of the Pyramids was no small factor in their fame. Another monument which thrilled men was the "Leaning Tower" of Pisa. It was by no means the only tower built at the time. The people of San Gimignano built seventy-two of them to satisfy a similar desire. Men built towers all over the world, from the beginning of history until the Gothic architects extracted the last ounce of effectiveness from verticality of design.

Until modern times, they were limited by the properties of masonry. Then an engineer named Gustave Eiffel showed the world what men could do to build upward by using modern materials when he designed the Eiffel Tower (Fig. 211) at Paris for the Exposition of 1889. Constructed of metal, it greatly exceeded any tower the world had ever seen, and its 984 foot height was not surpassed until the Empire State Building was erected in 1930.

Thrilling as the Eiffel Tower is, it did not satisfy the normal requirements of a building. A show-piece, it provided neither shelter nor usable interior space. When architects sought in modern times to satisfy these requirements in multi-storeyed buildings for factory or office use, their progress was slower. Here they again encountered their ancient enemy—the masonry wall. The stone or brick wall was adequate for low buildings; it was useless for multi-storeyed structures before the advent of the modern plastics. The story of the skyscrapers hinges upon this battle for freedom from the wall.

The first progress was made in the England of the early Industrial Revolution, where the need for multi-storeyed buildings was forced upon the designers of factories. James Watt, the versatile inventor of the steam engine, was among the first to perceive a solution to the problem. The gist of the problem was to free the wall as much as possible from the necessity of supporting the floors. That done, a brick wall could be erected to a height of three or four storeys without making it unduly thick at the base; such a thin wall also allowed a reasonable amount of window space.

As a step in that direction Watt devised a post and lintel system using iron instead of wood. For it he invented a T-shaped lintel which was the precursor of our steel I-beam. This substitution of metal for wooden lintels marked a turning point in modern framing because of metal's superior carrying capacity. Watt's ingenious T-shaped beams, while light and strong, would not bend in any direction, and were able to support most of the floor load. The walls were required to hold up only themselves and the few beam-ends which extended to them. The cotton mill at Manchester in which Watt employed this system in 1801 represented a long stride forward in multi-storeyed building.

FIG. 211. Eiffel. Tower. 1889. Paris.

FIG. 212. Hood, Corbett, Reinhart, Hofmeister, and others. Rockefeller Center. 1932. New York.

FIG. 213. Wright. Edgar J. Kaufmann residence. "Fallingwater." 1936. Bear Run, Pa.

Another forward step was taken in 1850 by Fairbairn when he designed a mill at Saltaire for Sir Titus Salt. Employing a cantilever system of long metal girders balanced seesaw fashion on slender steel posts, he built a factory five storeys high. Here the walls merely anchored the girders and played no part at all in supporting the floors, while the columns which assumed the principal loads look like pin-points on the plan. The wide-open interior provided plenty of space for men and machines.

Fairbairn covered Sir Titus Salt's mill with a type of trussed roof which is now universal. His system itself was not new; it had been used in wood in the Parthenon and the Early Christian basilicas, its principal merit being that, unlike a vault, it absorbs thrusts internally and needs no buttressing. The substitution of metal for wooden trusses made the system much stronger with little increase in weight.

Despite the truss's merits, a limit in multi-storeyed building was reached in Fairbairn's and similar mills. A brick wall could not be built higher than five storeys without thickening its base. To do that would have defeated the builders' purpose by creating narrow, tunnel-like windows. Thus, beyond a certain point, the ancient tyranny of the wall still prevailed.

That tyranny was finally overthrown about 1882 by a still little-known middlewestern architect named Buffington. His insight was revolutionary in recognizing the true strength of the steel skeleton. He decided that it was capable of supporting not only the floors of a tall building but the outside walls as well. He saw no reason why the outside walls, now reduced to the role of a weather sheathing, needed to be built in thick, monolithic form from ground to roof. Instead, the wall for each floor could now rest on a metal ledge attached to the steel skeleton. In that way a wall which extended only from one floor to the next could be thin and its window openings large.

Buffington's ingenious principle was not readily accepted by the always conservative conventional architects. In 1889 the Chicago firm of Burnham and Root designed a multi-storeyed structure, the Monadnock Building, which was the antithesis of Buffington's idea. Its monolithic brick walls, extending fifteen storeys high, were so thick at the bottom that windows were reduced to tubelike portholes; the interior was dark and gloomy. The defects were so apparent that it was the last attempt to erect a tall building on this outmoded principle. Within a few years, first at Chicago and then on Manhattan Island, the tyranny of the wall was overcome once and for all in the skyscrapers. Buffington, calling his project a "cloudscraper," had envisioned a twenty-eight-storey building. A bold thought for the time, he never developed it beyond the paper stage. But he had perceived the great structural strength of steel.

Once the strength of steel was fully appreciated, the sky became the limit. Men no longer had to limit themselves to small towers or open-framework giants like the Eiffel Tower. Using Buffington's principle, they could stack usable office space storey upon storey to dizzy heights. The Woolworth Building of 1913 was but a sample of what was to come. Within a dozen years the Chanin Building had soared to fifty storeys, only to be dwarfed soon afterward by the Empire State Building of 1930.

In the race to excel which characterized the skyscraper building of the fabulous twenties, practical considerations such as the high value of street-level real estate on Manhattan Island were only part of the motivation. Held down for centuries by masonry walls, architects seemed bent upon building upward for the sake of uninhibited accomplishment. They erected skyscrapers on the midwestern plains where land was cheap. In fact, they designed buildings taller than even commercial demands warranted; neither the Empire State Building nor the Chrysler Building has often been fully occupied.

Having proved their point, men eventually lost their desire to reach the moon by means of buildings. The Empire State Building remains the tallest building in the world, without a rival in sight. An end to the craving for height was finally reached when men no longer felt earth-bound by the tyranny of the wall.

The time also came in the search for space when men were able to build larger enclosures than they could use. This occurred during the Second World War when a mammoth factory was erected at Willow Run. Since the end of hostilities, only part of its vast interior has been fully occupied; the remainder has lain idle. This is a self-defeating anachronism, for architecture will always be held within certain limits by practical considerations. It is too expensive to be extended indefinitely to satisfy man's desire for space and height.

Architects discovered without being told that there is more involved in the esthetic of the skyscraper than height or space alone. Within two years after the Empire State Building's completion, Raymond Hood and his associates turned the design of office buildings in another direction. Commissioned to design Rockefeller Center in New York (Fig. 212), they made no attempt to match the altitude of the Empire State Building, but emphasized instead the proportional relationships of each building and its arrangement in the group, creating the most satisfying of all the skyscrapers. The tallest tower does not necessarily arouse the strongest sensation of soaring verticality or give the most esthetic pleasure. Yet we must remember that neither Rockefeller Center nor the Empire State Building could have been erected if Buffington had not invented the sectional wall or Otis the elevator. Technical mastery had to precede the refinement of design.

Spectacular as the development of the skyscraper was, the modern plastics have probably been most dramatically used in cantilever construction. The system itself was not new. Archimedes understood it, and architects applied it for centuries in constructing balconies and overhanging roofs, but they were limited to the modest projections that could be accomplished with wood or stone. Only when steel girders and reinforced concrete became widely available could the cantilever be fully exploited. Here was an ancient principle at work: creative human imagination perceiving the possibilities at hand and applying them to newly arisen needs.

Outstanding among those who have appreciated this need for creative exploitation is Frank Lloyd Wright. His insight into structural principles and the nature of materials has made him an inventor of many brilliant techniques. His mastery of the modern plastics has been conclusively demonstrated in his use of the cantilever—as in the Kaufmann House at Bear Run, Pennsylvania (Fig. 213). This striking house owes its thrilling quality to Wright's full exploitation of the cantilevered porches and overhangs which can be built with reinforced concrete. The house, which rests on the rock ledge of a waterfall, appears to be suspended in the air, so skilfully has Wright played down the vertical supports. It is a technical triumph over gravity and space arousing an almost heady sense of power in the observer. The tyranny of the wall is ended—here is a new dimension in architecture, expressing the dynamic spirit of our times.

The achievements made possible by the strength of the modern plastics have put the architects of our century in an enviable position. They have overcome problems that restricted builders for thousands of years. They have given us more space, light, air, and height than we can use. Yet the history of architecture is not at an end. New problems and new materials will always challenge the ingenuity of man. And these challenges will be met, as they have in the past, with vigor and imagination.

In closing this cursory study of the media, let us heed the same warning that applied to the modes of representation. The media are an indispensable means to the controlled objectification of feeling, but they are not a substitute for, or a guarantee of, quality of feeling. We must therefore be on our guard against confusing technique with inspiration. The Parthenon, thanks to the imagination, thought, and feeling that went into it, is still, despite its simple structural system, a more inspiring building than our towering sky-scrapers or gigantic factories. Technique is not to be scorned, but if it were the final answer to art, the Empire State Building should be more beautiful than the Cathedral of Chartres. Few would say that it is.

CHAPTER *15*

Spatial Design

Whether design is called order, control, rhythm, the antithesis of chaos, or a projection of intelligence, its function is to create an arrangement of visual elements in any art work which will satisfy the human need for both order and variety in a world which is profuse and confusing on the one hand, and monotonous and boring on the other.

Granted the need for such an ordering of forms and colors in works of art, how is it accomplished? The key is consistent limitation of some sort. One way, as we have seen, is through the organization of representation; another is through organization of ideas; the third is through the kind of organization of physical elements we call composition. It is design in this limited sense which we shall consider here.

An artist who is bent upon supplanting confusion with a sense of design, coherence, and control employs certain recognized principles of order. Although he uses these subconsciously after years of practice, we must analyze them consciously to read the language of the visual arts.

Fortunately, they are only three in number: harmony, sequence, and balance. They are not the special property of the visual arts, but are universally apparent in the organization of literature, music, the dance, drama, or wherever else order is essential.

No particular time or place has ever had a monopoly on them. They can be aptly illustrated by works of art created by the most primitive artist and the most highly civilized. The African Negro's sense of musical rhythms, the Navajo Indian's feeling for patterns, and the most cultivated European's handling of light and shadow, all attest the universality of these principles. We have therefore drawn illustrations from the world's art without any special concern for chronology or locale.

In the visual arts the principles of order are related to the attributes of forms and their colors as these are arranged in space. For the sake of convenience we shall deal first with spatial design and then with color design.

The so-called terms of space to which the principles of order are applied are attitude, direction, interval, measure, shape, and surface. The first three—attitude, direction, and interval—pertain to the positions of forms in space, the last three—measure, shape, and surface—apply to the attributes of forms themselves or, in the case of surface, to a characteristic of a work of art as a whole.

For purposes of analysis it is convenient to arrange the principles of order and the terms of space in two columns and consider the possible relationships one at a time.

The Principles of Order ⟶ *The Terms of Space*

Harmony	Attitude ⎫
Sequence	Direction ⎬ Position
	Interval ⎭
Balance	Measure
	Shape
	Surface

Generally speaking, an artist will apply the principles of order to the terms of space in such a way as to establish a predominance of order without entirely eliminating variety. He may use any or all of the principles of order in a single work of art. Usually the artist will concentrate upon one principle and upon certain spatial terms, such as diagonal attitudes, curvilinear shapes, or smooth textures. As a result, his personal style will illustrate one or two possibilities of design.

A discussion of all the principles of order and terms of space and color together would only produce confusion. If we remember that a work of art ultimately affects us totally, we can subdivide the problem of design into its elements and study separately the methods by which an artist achieves control over them.

HARMONY

Basically, the principles of order describe the means by which consistent limitations can be achieved. In Denman Ross's opinion harmony is the most important. By *harmony* we mean a general similarity producing an accord among several parts. The crew of an

eight-oar rowing shell are in harmony if they are "pulling together."
The term "general" implies slight variation for the sake of variety.

HARMONY OF ATTITUDE. By *attitude* we mean the *position* of any
form in relation to the ground or horizon. The possibilities are
threefold: horizontal, vertical, and diagonal, the latter being one of
degree between the other two.

A harmony of attitude denotes the general similarity of attitude
arrived at by a consistent limitation to one of these possibilities.
An excellent example is Jacopo della Quercia's *Sin of Adam and Eve*
(Fig. 214). We are struck at once by the similarity of pose between
two figures based on a harmony of vertical attitudes reinforced by a
bow-shaped curve in each figure. These graceful figures assume an
almost dancelike harmony of posture which is further accentuated
by the similar curvature of the tree. Because of the simplicity of the
relief, the harmony of attitude stands out especially in the identical
positions of the legs and feet. Yet Quercia took care to introduce
some variety in the placement of the arms and in the contrasting
directions in which the heads are turned.

Professor Pope has stressed that variety is not to be confused with
complexity. The orderliness of a design must be visually appreciable if we are to enjoy it. Usually it can be indicated with a few
lines. Many of the world's masterpieces are great because their designs are basically simple. This is true of Quercia's *Sin of Adam
and Eve*.

The *Waterfall and Pine Tree* (Fig. 215) illustrates a variation on
this theme. The orderliness conveyed by the picture is due to a
harmony of diagonal lines, from the lower left to the upper right.
However, the harmony is not so apparent as that in Quercia's relief,
for unlike the relief, which contains two standing nude human
beings, the four harmonized elements—earth, rocks, tree, and waterfall—contrast strongly in appearance and connotations. The Chinese
were especially fond of reconciling these universal elements in designs which are microcosms of the terrestrial elements.

Winslow Homer performed a similar feat in his *Northeaster* (Fig.
18), which contains a huge wave, a rock, and a cloud of spray. Together these symbolize the eternal conflict between the land and the
ocean, but in the design they are harmonized by the similarity of
their diagonal attitudes.

Two other paintings in which harmony of attitude is the striking
feature are Giorgione's *Sleeping Venus* (Fig. 79) and Michelangelo's
Creation of Adam (Fig. 126). In the one the principal lines are
nearly horizontal; in the other they are consistently diagonal.

FIG. 214. Della Quercia. *Sin of Adam and Eve.* 1425-1438. Portal, S. Petronio, Bologna.

FIG. 215. *Waterfall and Pine Tree.* Sung Dynasty, A.D. 960-1279. Museum of Fine Arts, Boston.

419

Although our main impressions of these relatively bold designs are of an over-all harmony of attitude, some room must be allowed for subordinate harmonies of attitude. Though minor, these can provide much pleasure. In Homer's *Fog Warning* (Fig. 61) there is a harmony of attitude between the angle of the dory and the streamer of fog and another between the position of the oars and the ocean's horizon.

Excellent examples of attitudinal harmonies can be found in architecture. Gothic architecture is noted for its stress upon vertical lines in such cathedrals as those at Reims (Fig. 179) and Amiens (Fig. 209), while the Roman architects tended to stress horizontal design as in the Pont du Gard (Fig. 206) and the Colosseum (Fig. 207). The architectural styles of whole civilizations can often be identified by the preference for a particular harmony of attitude.

Modern architects have stressed both vertical and horizontal harmonies, but they have done so consistently. The skyscraper designers naturally emphasized vertical lines, as Raymond Hood has done in Rockefeller Center (Fig. 212). Architects of smaller structures have shown a marked preference for harmonies of horizontal lines. Frank Lloyd Wright is a master of this kind of design. Note how skilfully he emphasized the horizontal by his treatment of the brickwork in the Johnson Wax Company Building (Fig. 86a) and by his suppression of the vertical supports in the Kaufmann House (Fig. 213).

As a general rule harmonies of attitude are most apparent in architecture, because there are no representational distractions in that abstract art. They are nearly as apparent in painting and sculpture containing similar figures, like Quercia's *Sin of Adam and Eve*, Michelangelo's *Creation of Adam, Menkure and His Queen* (Fig. 160), and *Sakyamuni and Prabhutaratna* (Fig. 172). They are least obvious in pictures and statues composed of a variety of elements, such as the Chinese *Waterfall and Pine Tree* and Homer's *Northeaster*. Our delayed reaction to this type of harmony and the subordinate harmonies in a painting like Homer's *Fog Warning* can give us much enjoyment. The artist must make certain, however, that they are visually appreciable.

HARMONY OF DIRECTION. By direction we ordinarily mean the position in which a figure faces, or the lines of movement from one part of a composition to another. The commonest possibilities are left or right, up or down, and backward or forward. Harmony occurs when any one of these possibilities is emphasized to the exclusion of the others. It can be understood best by imagining a scene in which a contrary situation prevails, as it does during recess time in a school yard when the children run in every direction at once, or by looking at Hogarth's deliberately jumbled *Enraged Musician* (Fig. 72) which depicts the swarming vitality of eighteenth-century London.

A treatment of attitude which is the opposite of either of these situations must be marked by an orderly or concordant movement of most of the figures in the design—to wit, in the same direction. Two men walking together along a road or even facing in the same direction would illustrate such an accord. Bernini's *Apollo and Daphne* (Fig. 167) and Daumier's *Burden* (Fig. 161) have this characteristic in common, as do *Justinian and Courtiers* (Fig. 121) and *Menkure and His Queen* (Fig. 160); in both the mosaic and Egyptian statues all figures are facing forward or toward the spectator.

A common instance of directional agreement is a band of marching soldiers, of which there are innumerable examples in art. We have already seen such bands in Meissonier's *1814* (Fig. 28) and Orozco's *Zapatistas* (Fig. 29). Different as the two pictures are, they are similar in that respect, fortunately for the Meissonier, for the harmony of direction exemplified by Napoleon's disconsolate army gives the picture at least a minimum of order.

The universal symbol of direction—the arrow—is not to be limited, however, to these apparent instances. It is implied in the principal guiding lines of numerous landscapes, both reposeful and dynamic. A fine example of the dynamic is Turner's *Seascape with a Squall Coming Up* (Fig. 48) in which all the evidence of sails, waves, flags, and clouds indicates a strong movement of the wind from left to right. Sesson's *Boat Returning in a Storm* (Fig. 401), though different in other ways, is unified by a similar harmony of direction.

Harmony of direction must not be taken for granted. Like the cadets marching in perfect unison on the parade ground at West Point, it is a product of organization. There are many works of art in which variety of direction prevails, for example Velasquez's *Maids of Honor* (Fig. 94), Hiroshige's *Traveller Buying an Otsu-E* (Fig. 115), Gauguin's *Mahana No Atua* (Fig. 141), and Rembrandt's *Christ Healing the Sick* (Fig. 151). In these pictures there is not even a contrasting or balancing of one group against another. But when variety of direction is so pronounced, one may be sure of two things: the artist had a reason for stressing disorder in this particular spatial term, yet he counterbalanced it through orderliness of other kinds.

The general principle underlying all design is based on the multiplicity of possibilities. When variety is emphasized in one term, orderliness can be achieved in other ways. In this way artists satisfy both requirements at once. The possibilities of the formula are almost limitless. There is, nevertheless, a general agreement with Pope that in this formula order should be the dominant factor and variety but the accent or relief.

A comparison of either Orozco's *Zapatistas* with Meissonier's *1814* or Barye's *Black Panther* (Fig. 31) with Bonheur's *Lion and Lioness Resting* (Fig. 30) would seem to support this opinion. The first of each pair is now deemed superior because the sense of orderliness is strong, while in the second cases one's main impression is of profusion and diversity.

HARMONY OF INTERVAL. Space in nature is often what Pepper has called "pure emptiness": in art it can become almost tangible as if shaped and molded. It is a real and important factor in design. Nowhere is this more evident than in harmonies of interval.

Interval is the series of spaces between three or more forms ranging from wide to narrow. In harmony of interval the critical factor is not the distance but the uniformity which results from a consistent limitation of these choices.

Harmony of interval is illustrated by the regularly spaced supports or decorative members in buildings. In a frame house, for instance, the upright studs and most of the beams are centered sixteen inches apart. Similarly, the spaces between the piers and pilasters of the Colosseum (Fig. 207) are equal on all levels and around the entire structure, giving it a pronounced quality of orderliness. But the most memorable harmonies of interval are found in colonnades and porticos, such as the Doric colonnade of the Parthenon (Fig. 423) and the equally celebrated portico of the Pantheon (Fig. 176).

The abstract arts have, as usual, an advantage over the representational here because their harmonies are so visually appreciable. Persian carpets, like other fabrics, are full of highly enjoyable harmonies of interval.

In painting and sculpture uniform intervals, though less obvious, often play an important esthetic role. Harmony of interval contributes importantly to the orderliness of the *Festival of Roses* tapestry (Fig. 189) in which the figures, while not facing in the same direction, are equally spaced. Another instance is the detail of the Byzantine mosaic, *Empress Theodora and Attendants* (Fig. 188); the intervals between the three heads are almost identical. By contrast, there is a slight but significant difference between the intervals of the Madonna and her two attendants in Titian's *Madonna of the Cherries* (Fig. 129). This subtle variation illustrates a general difference between the compositional preferences of painters and sculptors who came before and after the end of the Middle Ages.

The medieval designers subscribed more often than not to a high degree of regularity in intervals and other spatial terms. Their work creates an impression of strict orderliness, verging on rigid monotony and denoting a collective social attitude, characteristic of the authoritarian Byzantine society.

Post-medieval artists like Titian seem, on the other hand, to have sought a progressively greater degree of flexibility and a freer type of design. They were no less interested in an appreciable order, but were conscious of the desirability of greater subtlety. We get the impression that the medieval artists, like the church fathers, took their audiences for granted, while the later masters felt obliged to hold attention. Consequently, there arose a perceptible difference between early medieval art and post-Renaissance paintings and statues; a difference which expresses two contrasting ideals of design.

HARMONY OF MEASURE. *Measure* is the impression of size conveyed by the terms *large* and *small*, though more limited terms like *tall* or *short, light* or *heavy, thin* or *thick,* are acceptable when they describe some special characteristic. Harmony of measure depends, like the other harmonies, more upon consistency than quantity.

The idea of measure or size looms large in design because of the importance of its numerous connotations. The words *colossal, mammoth,* or *puny* are apt to mean more to us than any terms of interval because they are related to physical factors which affect us daily. This, of course, is more a matter of expression than design, but it influences our reading of designs insofar as we project certain practical norms upon them. The following examples will show how often we project preconceived standards of measure upon any scene or object.

There is, for instance, the scene which contains adults of different sexes, such as Rubens' *Rape of the Daughters of Leucippus* (Fig. 216), Jacopo della Quercia's *Sin of Adam and Eve,* and *Menkure and His Queen.* Ordinarily, we think of males in these scenes as being larger than the females, a condition which is true to life but not artistically harmonious. The artist who would give both life and art their due must effect a compromise by making the men only slightly larger than the women. This was done by Rubens, Quercia, and the unknown portraitist of *Menkure and His Queen.* Rubens carried the adjustment even farther by reducing the scale of the horses; they are much smaller than they would be in actuality, but the resulting harmony of measure is so pleasing that we scarcely

FIG. 216. Rubens. *Rape of the Daughters of Leucippus. ca.* 1618. Alte Pinakothek, Munich.

FIG. 217. *Diadumenos.* 1st century B.C. Based on Polyclitus' statue of about 450 B.C. Metropolitan Museum of Art, New York.

FIG. 218. Bronze ritual vessel, Type Ting. Late Chou Dynasty, 600-250 B.C. Nelson Gallery and Atkins Museum, Kansas City, Mo.

notice a discrepancy. Rubens was not the only master to reduce the sizes of men and animal figures according to a female norm; he had an excellent precedent in the frieze of the Parthenon (Fig. 267), whose horses would be mere ponies in real life.

Harmony of measure is therefore not a matter of literal similarity of size but of appropriateness to a general norm. This is illustrated by any scene which contains both children and adults. When Michelangelo, who loved large human figures, made both Adam and God the Father huge in his *Creation of Adam* (Fig. 126), he was careful to make the cherubs who fly through the air with the Lord equally gigantic. Daumier did the same when he modeled his terra cotta group, the *Burden* (Fig. 161). Having decided upon a broad-shouldered, powerful-looking figure for his laundress, he made the child at her side commensurately husky. One can easily imagine it growing up to be the same kind of woman. Both Michelangelo's and Daumier's figures are of an artistically arrived-at type.

An imaginative artist can populate his world with any size people he chooses, so long as he is consistent. Typical instances are the *Menkure and His Queen* and the *Sakyamuni and Prabhutaratna* (Fig. 172). It does not matter that the pharaoh and his queen are large while the saints are small and thin; each is consistent within its context. The base and background of Menkure are properly massive, those of Sakyamuni linear and delicate. The creation of a setting in a scale appropriate to the figures in it is a common and admirable aspect of fine art, especially in portait painting.

Distinctive harmony of measure is a prominent stylistic feature of much of the great masters' work. The paintings of Titian, Rubens, and Renoir and the statues of Maillol show a persistent preference for ample human types. El Greco preferred leaner, almost neurotically emaciated types, while Van Dyck took twenty or thirty pounds from the figures of his master Rubens in order to express a personal preference for more elegant and aristocratic-looking people. Thin or heavy, a consistently used measure is an outstanding characteristic of many personal styles. It has the further merit of being both orderly and expressive.

The same observations can be extended to architecture. Significant preferences for massive members run through Egyptian, Roman, and Romanesque architecture; typical examples are the Church of the Holy Trinity at Caen (Fig. 180), the Temple of the Sphinx at Gizeh (Fig. 201), the Pont du Gard (Fig. 206), the Pantheon (Fig. 176), and the Colosseum (Fig. 207), the latter being a perfect example of the Roman ideal.

Measure also plays an important part in the three orders which the

Greeks bequeathed to architectural design—the Doric, Ionic, and Corinthian. These orders permitted a choice of the sturdy, the elegant, and the ornate; but the difference may be refined by noting that, whereas the Doric column is about five diameters in height, the Ionic and Corinthian are seven or eight diameters. The parts of each order are commensurately large and simple or small and complex.

Gothic architecture is notable for a consistent preference for an open and airy lightness. the Cathederal of Reims (Fig. 179) and other Gothic masterpieces like Rouen Cathedral (Fig. 182), or Beauvais (Fig. 210) were not likened to "lace in stone" without reason. A comparable lightness and harmony of measure is noticeable in much Islamic architecture, as in the Hall of Two Sisters in the Alhambra at Granada (Fig. 183). There is a general resemblance between the Gothic and Islamic that goes beyond their common use of the pointed arch and sets them apart from the Egyptian, Roman, and Romanesque. That is not to say that either is superior to the other, only that each group had similar ideals of measure.

There is no competitive right or wrong in design; the important criterion is internal consistency. No nation or period has had a monopoly on the instinct for harmonies of measure, although a certain conception of measure will permeate the art of a whole society at a given time and become an essential attribute of its style of expression. The minute parts and complexity of the stained glass window make it suitable to adorn almost any of the French Gothic cathedrals. The *Menkure and His Queen* would be equally at home in the simple, massive Temple of the Sphinx, but we cannot imagine the window in the Temple or the *Menkure* in a cathedral.

Each of the modes of projection, no matter how realistic or unrealistic it may appear for representational purposes, is saved artistically by exemplifying a principle of order. In the case of the geometric and diagonal modes long used in the East but strange to our eyes, harmony of measure is a prominent feature. Typical examples are the small Persian painting of *A Polo Game* (Fig. 112) and Masanobu's *Playing Cards* (Fig. 113). In neither is there any diminution of scale from foreground to distance; the emphasis is upon orderly design rather than realism.

No discussion of harmony of measure is complete without some mention of proportion, a term that bothers most laymen, who use the expressions "good proportion" or "out of proportion" without explaining what they mean. It may be helpful to observe that proportion is always based on a norm which is individual for each work of art. Harmony results when this norm is followed consistently. The bronze ritual vessel in Fig. 218 and the Greek *Diadem-Binder* in Fig. 217 have little in common except that each creates the impression that its parts, while not identical in size, are in proportion as they are used. The norm of a heavy vessel set by the main body of the vessel is echoed by the handles and legs, each of which is sturdy for its type. As a result, there is a harmony of measure among the various parts.

The strong but moderate-sized body of the *Diadem-Binder* sets a norm for that figure which is reflected by the arms and legs. The Greeks, who handed down to us a good deal of shrewd, conscious thought about proportions, generally favored the ideal of the happy medium between extremes exemplified by this work. It was part of an attitude toward life which embraced their conceptions of both athletics and athletes. Avoiding, at least in the earlier days, the overdeveloped, specialized professional athletic type, like our 250-pound football player, they favored the well-rounded youth whose legs and arms were strong and agile enough to perform the varied activities of the decathlon. Something of the same ideal of diversified moderation runs through their architecture, even the relatively sturdy Doric. In both sculpture and architecture this policy of restraint without excess produced proportional norms which have pleased many generations.

Size alone is not the determinant of harmony. We mentioned the professional athletes of our day only as examples. Compared to the norm or average of men they verge upon the freakish because of the extremities of size engendered by their specialized sports. Moreover, there can sometimes be found among them ultra-freakish figures whose freakishness gives them an advantage even among specialists. Babe Ruth, whose power was concentrated in his arms and shoulders, was likened, because of his comparatively slender ankles, to a barrel on match sticks. Bob Fitzsimmons had the arms of a blacksmith and the legs of a ballet dancer, an arrangement which allowed him to achieve championships in three different divisions of boxing. Great athletes both, they were, artistically speaking, the opposite of the ideal expressed in the *Diadem-Binder*.

When relationships of measure are handled with the finesse characteristic of the Greeks, we instinctively call the resulting proportions beautiful. Harmonies of measure are important contributions to our esthetic experience and give us a means of describing one of its aspects more precisely. The same observation is true of the other aspects of design, for there are few words about which human beings are more vague than *beauty*.

HARMONY OF SHAPE. No less eye-catching than measure in a design is the factor of *shape*. Psychologists say that it has a high "attentional value." When exploited it adds greatly to the feeling of order in a work of art.

The types of shape which an artist employs are of two main groups: the straight-lined and the curvilinear. The rectilinear composition strikes us as the more abstract and artificial; there are few straight lines in nature but many in things that men build. Straight lines and right angles are outstanding characteristics of the world of architecture, and give its products an appearance of both abstract artificiality and orderliness. The highly geometric square-cut character of Dudok's school at Hilversum (Fig. 223) is an example.

Harmonies of curved lines and forms are more likely to reflect the flexible, flowing, and plastic quality of nature. Owing to the profound influence of nature, examples of such harmonies are plentiful. The art in them lies in a consistent selection of curves drawn from the profusion and diversity of natural forms, giving us a distillation of one of nature's aspects. A fine example of this kind of microcosm is the Cretan *Octopus Vase,* Fig. 219. The vase itself is round and bulbous; the octopus, whose tentacles enclose it, equally curvilinear. Between the two shapes there is an accord which demonstrates decorative embellishment excellently.

The *Octopus Vase* and the Chinese glazed pottery dish in Fig. 221 are alike in that both exhibit this common denominator of harmonious design. In both, the figure which decorates a round form is itself predominantly curvilinear.

A vivid example of the harmony of curved lines is the jade disk (Fig. 220) at Kansas City. Its circular shape harmonizes perfectly with the swinging curves of the decorative dragons—the favorite fantastic animal form of the Chinese who were at their best in endowing it with living, flowing lines.

Like measure, shape is a hallmark of the major architectural styles. The round arch is invariably associated with Roman architecture. It is outstanding in the Colosseum and the Pont du Gard; hardly less so in the Romanesque. Santa Sophia (Fig. 208), and Byzantine architecture in general, owes much of its reputation to the harmony of curved forms inherent in the dome on pendentives structural system, while Islamic architecture derives a good deal of its flavor from the widespread use of the peculiar but distinctive horseshoe arch seen in the Hall of Two Sisters at Granada (Fig. 183). The onion-bulb dome of late Russian Byzantine architecture is almost a signature of that style. And the proclivity of the Baroque designers for curvi-

FIG. 219. *Octopus Vase. ca.* 1500 B.C. Metropolitan Museum of Art, New York.

FIG. 220. Jade Disk, Type Pi. Late Chou Dynasty, 600-250 B.C. Nelson Gallery and Atkins Museum, Kansas City, Mo.

FIG. 221. Glazed pottery dish. Sung Dynasty, A.D. 960-1279. Museum of Fine Arts, Boston.

linear forms, illustrated by Neumann's Wallfahrtkirche at Vierzehn-heiligen (Fig. 184), is well known.

The most famous example of an identifying shape-character is the architecture of the Gothic cathedrals. The north European design-ers created symphonic masterpieces in the great naves of such cathe-drals as Amiens (Fig. 209), adding melodies of genuine charm even in minor details, like the portal arches of the Cathedral at Peter-borough, England (Fig. 222), where repetitions of the pointed arch are handled with an eye for both harmony and variety.

Harmony of shape is a prominent characteristic of modern archi-tecture, whose designers have shown a marked predilection for the square geometric form. The rectilinear quality of Dudok's school at Hilversum (Fig. 223) is by no means unique, as a glance at the straight lines and right angles of the New York University–Bellevue Medical Center (Fig. 178), Wright's Kaufmann House at Bear Run, Pennsylvania (Fig. 213), and Rockefeller Center (Fig. 212) will re-veal. Modern designers have also occasionally proved their aptitude for handling predominantly curvilinear compositions consistently and even brilliantly, as Max Berg did in the Centennial Hall at Breslau (Fig. 205).

A study of modern architecture confirms the timelessness of the principles of design and the antiquity of man's ability to use them well. For though the rectilinear geometricity of modern structures exhibits a commendable respect for variety in composition, while the ancient Temple of the Sphinx (Fig. 201) is monotonously simple, they are basically similar in their harmonies of shape, and both are akin to Mondrian's vividly rectilinear *Composition in White, Black, and Red* (Fig. 55).

The harmonies of shape found in architecture, abstract painting, and the nonrepresentational arts in general are often rather apparent. Without detracting from the intense sense of order they can convey, one can safely say that the less obvious but more subtle harmonies of shape found in painting and sculpture are sometimes more enjoy-able. While one usually discovers the art that is concealed in this kind of art after noting the representational message, this delayed discovery carries with it a special sort of pleasure.

The reader can perceive much by viewing the following with an eye for underlying but unifying harmonies of shape-character: Mail-lol's *Female Torso* (Fig. 5), Kokoschka's *Courmayeur* (Fig. 9), Barye's *Black Panther* (Fig. 31), Marc's *Two Deer* (Fig. 32), Van Gogh's *Mountainous Landscape* (Fig. 65), Cézanne's *House in Provence* (Fig. 80), Wright's interior of the Johnson Wax Company Building (Fig. 86b), El Greco's *Agony in the Garden* (Fig. 90), Michelangelo's *Crea-*

FIG. 222. Portal Arches, 1237. Cathedral, Peterborough, England.

FIG. 223. Dudok. School. 1922. Hilversum.

431

tion of Adam (Fig. 126), Gauguin's *Mahana No Atua* (Fig. 141), *The Dwarf of Murad II* (Fig. 145), Turner's *Martello Towers* (Fig. 146), Delacroix's *Combat* (Fig. 153), Van Gogh's *Cypresses* (Fig. 155), Brancusi's *Mademoiselle Pogany* (Fig. 159), Daumier's *Burden* (Fig. 161), the *Flying Apsaras* (Fig. 171), Hals's *Malle Babbe* (Fig. 196), Muir's *Growth* (Fig. 186), Calder's *Hostess* (Fig. 173), Quercia's *Sin of Adam and Eve* (Fig. 214), Rubens' *Rape of the Daughters of Leucippus* (Fig. 216), and the bronze ritual vessel in Fig. 218. These are but a sampling of the many possible types.

Curvilinear harmonies predominate in these examples, which were selected without proof of that point in mind. But one's search for harmonies of shape should not be limited to works of art in which either the curvilinear or rectilinear runs throughout the design in a grand rhythm, admirable though such harmonies may be, for there are many enjoyable examples to be found in minor passages of pictures, as, for instance, in Hirschvogel's *Landscape with a Curved Wooden Bridge* (Fig. 118). Harmonies of shape are least frequent in examples of the realist mode, but abundant in those modes which took liberties with nature freely and, as Konody would say, imposed on her a rhythm of the artist's own creation. The paintings of Van Gogh illustrate vividly an art in which design takes precedence over nature. One of the most important harmonies of shape by which an artist may unify a picture comes from the character of his brush strokes. Like a handwritten signature, they express both his personal temperament and his sense of order. Van Gogh can again be cited as an example of the artist with a signature-like stroke, but Frans Hals and others were no less effective.

PICTORIAL METAPHORS. Literary artists have a device called a metaphor by which they reinforce one idea by playing upon its similarity to another. They then gain emphasis without bald repetition. Pictorial artists use a comparable means of underlining an idea through a part of a design. Their method involves several of the harmonies we have been discussing, especially harmony of attitude, but its chief characteristic is a deliberate coincidence of shape. Hence mention of it at this point is as fitting as at any other.

A pictorial metaphor, to be effective, or, as Pope would assert, visually appreciable, must be reasonably near the form to which it calls attention by a kind of echoing of general shape-character. Metaphors of this type, though found in art the world over, came into special favor with the rise of the Renaissance. The unusual literary consciousness of that period made it concerned with the importance of conveying ideas forcefully and artfully. The Renaissance masters were dedicated illustrators; they were also among the most conscious and articulate designers we have ever had, relying upon hard work and clear thought as much as they did upon strokes of genius or flashes of inspiration. Brilliance was their reward; they created models of sophisticated design whose subtle pictorial metaphors established a pattern for post-Renaissance art. Most of the illustrations we shall mention come from the period since 1400.

Giotto, the father of Renaissance painting, early displayed an adeptness at handling the pictorial metaphor. The Arena Chapel at Padua, where he painted his most noted cycle of frescoes, contains many examples. A cogent one is the *Flight Into Egypt* (Fig. 224) in which he created a double metaphor by having the mountain repeat the pyramidal shape of the Madonna and Child and by having a tree, symbolic of the Christ Child, grow out of the side of the mountain. Its position on the right side of the mountain directly above the Child is more than a coincidence. One is supported in this view by the frequency with which Giotto united both the form and meaning of the human and background elements in his paintings.

A concern for the picture as a whole became a sign of good composition in the following centuries to such an extent that quite ordinary men were able to employ architectural or rural settings competently in the backgrounds of pictures. Routine but effective examples of this type of harmonization of accessories are common in portraiture; furniture, columns, and drapery are used to echo and frame the figures and faces of sitters, with Van Dyck among the masters of the tradition.

The pictorial metaphor lent itself to more sophisticated and interesting use in illustrative painting. Millet's masterpiece, the *Gleaners* (Fig. 225), shows how Giotto's example was continued; the two haystacks and the haywain in the middle distance serve the dual purpose of drawing the eye toward the horizon along the diagonal line set by the three figures and of repeating the massive group character of the gleaners.

Another nineteenth-century example of the pictorial metaphor can be found in Turner's *Seascape with a Squall Coming Up* (Fig. 48). Following the lead of Claude Lorrain and Ruysdael, illustrated by their *Landscape with Cattle* (Fig. 117) and *Wheatfields* (Fig. 116), Turner assembled the elements of his marines and landscapes with the care of an architect constructing a building. In the Malden *Seascape* he arranged his clouds with particular effectiveness, placing one which is shaped like the dark sail on the right immediately above it and another above the flag, repeating its form.

The Venetian masters of the sixteenth century excelled in the use

Fig. 224. Giotto. *Flight into Egypt. ca.* 1305. Arena Chapel, Padua.

Fig. 225. Millet. *The Gleaners.* 1856. Louvre, Paris.

434

of the pictorial metaphor, with Titian their most adept genius. A superb composer conscious of literary values, he gave infinite thought to the problem of illustrating stories in ways that would be intellectually, artistically, and emotionally effective. He used the pictorial metaphor deliberately and shrewdly. To study his pictures is to see this means at its best.

The results of his efforts can be observed in his *Entombment* (Fig. 62), where a scarf droops beside the limp arm of the dead Christ and crinkles on the ground in the same shape as His fingers—an impeccable touch. In his complex but beautifully calculated *Meeting of Bacchus and Ariadne* (Fig. 89) there are a number of excellent metaphors. One is the tree branch above the flowing cape of Bacchus which frames its outline, while the cape itself repeats the attitude and shape of Bacchus' arm and hand. Another is the group comprised of the boyish satyr, his dog, and the boar's head he drags behind him; together they form a triangle which repeats the pyramidal form of Bacchus immediately above. Ideologically, the satyr's group provides a comic relief for the serious adult drama of his betters. Also, the attitude of the satyr is in counterpoint to the forward leap of Bacchus, one instance among many of a richly integrated composition.

El Greco became an accomplished composer by following in Titian's footsteps after studying the master's work briefly at Venice. His *Agony in the Garden* (Fig. 90), while a far cry from Titian's *Bacchus and Ariadne* spiritually, is its equal in adroitness of design. This can be noted especially in the appropriateness of the backgrounds El Greco provided for the dominant figures of Christ and the Angel of the Lord. Behind Christ is a conical-shaped rock which echoes His figure, while a cloud repeats the outline of the Angel's body and wings. Completing the idea are the implications of the earth-bound, harassed Savior and the supernatural Angel, and the rocks of the earth and the clouds of Heaven.

Giorgione, Titian's short-lived Venetian contemporary, was a master of the metaphor in a more reposeful manner. Indeed, it is possible that Titian learned the rudiments of his method from this quiet genius and their common master Giovanni Bellini. A typical example of Giorgione's compositional skill is contained in his *Sleeping Venus* (Fig. 79); the long curve formed by the goddess' hip and leg is reiterated and emphasized by an identical curvature in the hill above it.

HARMONY OF SURFACE. The world about us consists of a confusing diversity of surfaces, ranging from the extremely rough to the perfectly smooth. An artist who wishes to paint realistically will respect or at least strongly suggest this profuse variety. The artist who values artistic unity above accuracy of imitation generally transposes the different textures of reality into a more uniform surface. If he is reasonably realistic in other aspects of representation, harmony of surface will have the merit of adding that minimum degree of unity which even the most realistic painting requires. Consistency of surface is one of the most useful types of order that an otherwise imitative artist can impose on his vision of nature, as was skilfully illustrated by Velasquez and Vermeer.

The artist who has no particular interest in imitating nature imposes a harmony of surface upon his work without any hesitation. His twofold guiding principle will be to create a unity of surface within each design and to devise a surface texture which will appeal to sense perception. He may find these in nature or invent them himself. In either case he will achieve harmony of surface by limiting himself consistently to one type of texture throughout his picture or statue.

An artist who is technically sensitive to his media will come to love the materials in which he works as much as any textures he finds in nature. Harmony of surface is one of the principal ways of expressing the kind of pleasure he derives from handling oil pigment, watercolor, wood, marble, or bronze regardless of what they may represent. This is perfectly plain in the work of William Muir (Fig. 186).

In painting his *Sunday on the Island of La Grande Jatte* (Fig. 226), Seurat united the variety of textures which one would find in such an outdoor scene by using a perfectly uniform brush stroke. Seen close on, its effect is one of thousands of tiny colored dots. As a result, the method was called *pointillist* technique. Its fine, granular surface unifies the picture from edge to edge, a fact of considerable importance in such a large and complex scene.

Akin to this procedure is Rouault's treatment of *The Old King* (Fig. 227). He too invented his own surface instead of relying upon a natural source. Endowed with a keen appreciation of the sensuous quality of his artistic material's textures and colors, he applied the oil pigment thickly, almost like butter spread with a knife. Students, in describing its visual effect, have often compared it to colored stucco. Rouault's consistent use of one type of texture gives his pictures harmony of surface, peculiarly appropriate to the tense themes he represents, as is Seurat's dotlike technique for his more serene subjects.

FIG. 226. Seurat. *Sunday on the Island of La Grande Jatte.* 1884-1886. Art Institute of Chicago.

FIG. 227. Rouault. *The Old King.* 1916-1936. Carnegie Institute, Department of Fine Arts, Pittsburgh.

FIG. 228. Veronese. Detail. *The Family of Darius Before Alexander.* ca. 1566. National Gallery, London.

FIG. 229. Arp. *Configurations.* "Three Forms Movable on One Large Form." Collection of the artist, Paris.

437

The detail from Veronese's *Family of Darius Before Alexander* (Fig. 228) illustrates another way of obtaining a harmony of surface. Where Seurat and Rouault superimposed striking techniques upon smooth canvas, Veronese painted on a coarse canvas whose heavy weave plays a discernible part in the over-all texture of the picture, the uniform coarseness of the fabric imparting a basic unity to the composition. Titian and Tintoretto, like others of the Venetian school, had a similar appreciation of the tapestry-like properties of heavy canvas, as we can see in Tintoretto's *Diana* (Fig. 194) and Titian's *Rape of Europa* (Fig. 195). They likewise delighted in the rich, pasty character of oil pigment, and in sumptuous materials like velvets and brocades, human skin and hair. It is plain to see that when Veronese was painting materials of this sort in his *Family of Darius Before Alexander* his heart was in his work.

Tactile sensitivity to the sensuous appeal of the material world is a hallmark of the Venetian school from Giorgione through Tintoretto, but many single artists who followed after them were their equals in creating harmonies of surface. One thinks immediately of Gauguin, who painted pictures like the *Mahana No Atua* (Fig. 141) on canvas that is nearly as heavy as burlap. He loved the fabric on which he painted even before he touched a brush to it and took care to preserve its character.

Chardin, although Gauguin's equal in textural sensitivity, had more interest in the buttery impasto of his pigment (Fig. 287). The same may be said of Van Gogh, who loved to paint with a loaded brush. Renoir, on the other hand, kept his pigment thin and gained his harmony of surface by weaving a kind of uniform texture upon the canvas with feathery strokes.

Hans Arp's *Configurations* (Fig. 229) exemplifies the point of view of the artist who so delights in the artistic media that he presents them in pure form, without any representational reference to other forms. Where Bernini carved and polished the marble to represent flesh, cloth, and hair in his portrait of *Cardinal Borghese* (Fig. 166), and Mazzoni carried imitation still further in his *Nativity* (Fig. 165), Arp has treated the marble as a thing of beauty in itself. Whatever he did was intended only to display its properties to the fullest advantage. To that end he projected a harmony of curvilinear forms and smooth surfaces upon his material which allows us to see its textures and shapes intensified, without any distractions.

Because a feeling for materials is almost universal among capable visual artists, the examples of harmonious treatments of surfaces are numerous. But lest we become lost in sensuous appreciation, we should remember that consistency is the crux of harmonious design:

the type of limitation is optional. The rough has no advantage *per se* over the smooth; an abundance of examples of unified surfaces—rough, medium, and smooth—can be found among the world's fine works of art.

The following are a few, selected at random from architecture, sculpture, and painting. While unlike, all are characterized by a visually appreciable harmony of surface. The *Seated Statue of Khum-Ba-F* (Fig. 2) shows what can be done to preserve the intrinsic quality of coarse-grained granite, a procedure in which the Egyptians were adept. The Sumerian *Governor of Lagash* (Fig. 67) illustrates the same end attained by exploiting the capacity of a hard fine-grained stone to take a high polish.

It is worth noting that several of the artistic media which do not lend themselves to realistic representation possess compensating characteristics; mosaic, tapestry, and stained glass all possess distinctive qualities which give unity to any picture. A study of *The Empress Theodora and Her Attendants* (Fig. 188), the *Festival of Roses* tapestry (Fig. 189), and the Gothic stained glass window in Fig. 190 will confirm this fact.

Almost all of the artistic media possess characteristics which can be exploited. Painters and sculptors have only to guard against placing realistic representation above unity of surface; the architect must refrain from mixing together too many different materials. Wright's Johnson Wax Company Building (Fig. 86a) shows how unity of surface can be gained by emphasizing one material while introducing other materials for accentuation and variety.

To an equal extent artists have gained harmony of surface by a consistent handling of their medium, regardless of its physical properties. Van Gogh, Hals, Kokoschka, Renoir, and Daumier are all artists whose brush strokes played prominent parts in the unification of their work, partly because they placed a high premium on the autographic character of oil paint. Bourdelle in his *Beethoven* (Fig. 164) and Daumier in *The Burden* (Fig. 161) vigorously exploited the malleable character of clay. Conversely, Michelangelo and his fellow fresco and tempera painters, who worked on smooth plaster, conceived their forms in harmoniously smooth terms. Each group was in accord with the characteristic of its media and appreciated the value of a harmonious picture surface.

A HARMONY OF ALL TERMS. There is a simple relationship between unity and variety in the esthetic order of a work of art. Remembering that a choice between an extreme of either orderliness or variety is open to any artist, we can observe the one extreme in any work of art where harmony has been imposed on every term. A perfect instance is the Temple of the Sphinx (Fig. 201), in which there is a harmony of attitude, interval, measure, shape, and surface. Such complete uniformity, especially common in architecture, comes dangerously close to monotony. Judging by the silent testimony of most visual artists, such an extreme should be avoided, especially in representational works where perfect orderliness would have the effect of freezing all life. Since variety is an essential characteristic of life, the majority of artists have, when stressing several harmonies, such as attitude and interval, deliberately varied others, like measure and shape. It is variety of this sort which gives life to the orderliness of Rubens' *Rape of the Daughters of Leucippus* (Fig. 216).

SEQUENCE

Sequence, the second principle of order, adds another string to the artist's bow. It permits him to extend a harmonious relationship indefinitely or to create a form of order in which change, rather than similarity, is the essential feature, thus gaining greater variety without any loss of order. A *series* is the everyday word which best suggests the basic idea of a sequence.

The extension of an idea through a series can be achieved in three different ways: sequence of continuity, sequence of gradation, and sequence of alternation.

SEQUENCE OF CONTINUITY. Sequence of continuity, the simplest possible type, resembles harmony and may differ from it only in the idea of an extended series of forms. The distinction can be understood by comparing the soldiers on the *Warrior Vase* in Fig. 230 with Della Quercia's *Sin of Adam and Eve* (Fig. 214). The soldiers, instead of being only two in number, are arranged in a long line. They are as harmonious as Quercia's relief, but they are orderly to the point of monotony because of an extended application of harmony to all six spatial terms. Six soldiers in line, like six identical columns, create a stronger impression of harmony than two. Hence sequence of continuity is a simple but effective way of reinforcing the idea of harmony.

In the *Warrior Vase* this reinforcement of harmony to the exclusion of all variety is appropriate for a scene of regimental life. A not uncommon phenomenon, this type of sequence of continuity can be described as military order. Stiff and unvarying, it applies to the representational arts the same kind of uniformity which is normal in architecture.

FIG. 230. Detail. *Warrior Vase*. Late Helladic III period, 1400-1100 B.C.
National Museum, Athens.

FIG. 231. Meunier. *Return of the Miners*. Designed for his "Monument to Labor."
1895-1905. Meunier Museum, Brussels.

There is room among sequences of continuity for a quite opposite type of order in which complex variety is permitted. This may be called, when applied to a group of marching men, a loose order. It is illustrated by Meunier's *Return of the Miners* (Fig. 231). In this relief a group of hard-working but unenthusiastic laborers shuffles toward the mine entrance to begin their wearisome shift. As long as they do their jobs, Meunier seems to be saying, they do not have to march like soldiers; their loose order is realistic.

Like military order, the loose order is common in everyday life. It can be found repeatedly in the serpentine line of boys playing crack-the-whip in a school yard. The boys may differ in size, shape, and dress, but as long as they hold hands in a chain they preserve more order than if they were running wildly around the school yard. Yet when the bell ends the recess, they will march to class in as automaton-like fashion as the soldiers on the *Warrior Vase*.

We have in a single principle of order the possibility of representing truthfully two extremes of human behavior, the dynamically regimented and the dynamically free. Sequence of continuity is, because of this flexibility, a valuable artistic means. Its range from perfect unity to great variety can be illustrated by the contrast between the Pont du Gard (Fig. 206) and Tintoretto's *Miracle of St. Mark* (Fig. 256): sequence of continuity is a common denominator of both. It is very apparent in Tintoretto's painting, for the serpentine arrangement of the milling throng is the one thing that gives order to the melodramatic scene. Compared to it, Meunier's returning miners appear almost regimented.

Sequence of continuity allows an artist to carry the unity of a colonnade, or variety, as in Tintoretto's painting, to the *n*th degree. Most sequences of continuity fall in between these two extremes; Orozco's revolutionary soldiers, *Zapatistas* (Fig. 29), is one good example; another is Meissonier's somber *1814* (Fig. 28), which depicts an army of men who have lost their *esprit* but preserved their military ranks.

Although sequence of continuity is an excellent means of creating a sense of movement (as in any of the examples by Meunier, Tintoretto, or Orozco) it can also be used to give to a static design like a colonnade or aqueduct a subtly dynamic quality. In the paintings or reliefs the movement is represented; in architectural designs it is the eye which moves sequentially during perception. This undoubtedly plays a part in the feeling of movement conveyed by the Pont du Gard and other spectacular bridges and aqueducts. This motion is crucial in our response to any work of art in which a sequence of continuity is skilfully articulated.

SEQUENCE OF GRADATION. The principal characteristic of sequence of gradation is a change in form which is progressive, uniform, and slow, not sudden or abrupt. It is a gradual thing. The merit of gradation is that it allows an artist to introduce variety into his design without going to extremes of contrast. He thus achieves order and variety at the same time. Moreover, gradual changes in a design induce an easy sense of change in perception, which produces a feeling of pleasure. This gradation is what gives grace and coordination to athletic action and the dance. Sequences of gradation have figured prominently in a large proportion of those works of art which we call especially beautiful, such as the sculpture of Praxiteles, and his *Hermes and Dionysus* (Fig. 409) in particular. Although no single characteristic accounts for this statue's reputation for beauty, the graded curve of its S-shaped posture contributes importantly to that fame.

A sequence of gradation can be applied to any or all of the terms of space. Gradation of attitude is exemplified by the spokes of a wheel or the ribs of a fan; radiating from a center, they appear to our eyes to change gradually from the horizontal to the vertical and back. The same principle is found in arches; a good example appears over the windows and doorway of the Strozzi Palace (Fig. 181). The Scopasian *Battle of Greeks and Amazons* (Fig. 333) is a variation of the same idea in a somewhat freer representational form. There is a gradation of the battling figures from the almost vertical Amazon in the center to the supine figure on the right.

Gradation of direction, though common in architecture, is rather rare in painting. Rembrandt built a masterpiece around it when he painted his *Anatomy Lesson*. Here a gradation of direction appears in the arrangement of the heads, whether one reads from left to right or up and down. In the bottom row, for instance, the left-hand head is in profile, the next turned slightly, the third in three-quarter position, and the fourth almost full-face—a four-step change from side to front view. Van Dyck's *Triple Portrait of Charles I* is another example. Wishing to show all aspects of the king's head to enable the sculptor Bernini to do a bust in Italy, sight unseen, Van Dyck represented the right profile, the full face, and the left profile in a single composition. Although a practical *tour de force,* the picture is strikingly novel.

A gradation of interval is one of our main impressions of a fluted column, like the Doric columns of the Parthenon (Fig. 425) and the Ionic columns of the Erechtheum (Fig. 426), and accounts for some of the beauty they possess. The flutes are uniform in width, but as we see them on the round columns they appear to grow gradually narrower—a phenomenon which the designers anticipated and exploited. Gradation of interval also plays an important part in realistic painting, for that mode respects the fact that the intervals between forms narrow gradually as they recede into the distance. Perugino underscored this idea in his *Christ Delivering the Keys of Heaven to Saint Peter* (Fig. 102a) by introducing a striped pattern into the pavement of his piazza setting.

Perspective projection appears both realistic and orderly. In that system there is a gradual narrowing of interval as architectural forms converge toward the vanishing point; even more noticeable is the gradation of measure. A gradual diminution of scale is the common factor in the otherwise dissimilar pictures by Bruegel and Rubens—the *Wedding Dance* (Fig. 232) and *Autumn, the Château de Steen* (Fig. 223). This is true of all paintings based on the perspective mode of projection. Each of the two artists held a multitude of details in perfect relationship. Rubens' precise control over minute gradations of size appears miraculous to anyone who has tried to create such an effect. It is also the basis of the composition's unusual spaciousness.

Gradation of measure is one of the best and most universal attributes of beauty in architecture and in the decorative or minor arts. Examples in which this principle of order has been turned to good account number into the thousands. Any architectural design in which there is a gradual decrease from a broad base to a narrow or pointed top utilizes this principle. The Great Pyramid of Egypt (Fig. 174a) and most domical and vaulted structures are so designed, for the arch, whether round or pointed, employs a gradation of measure. The splayed portal arches of the Cathedral of Peterborough (Fig. 222), which are typical of Gothic entrance-ways, employ this principle in the pointed arches, and in the arrangement of arches within arches in funnel-like fashion. A similar gradation of forms is found in Santa Sophia (Fig. 208) and adds much to the beauty of its interior; there the eye is led upward from small half-domes to the great dome above.

The tapered form is another instance of gradation of measure, whether its sides are straight or curved. A famous example of the former is the Washington Monument in our national capital, while the Eiffel Tower at Paris (Fig. 211) spectacularly exemplifies the latter. A simpler though no less effective example is the bronze ritual vase in Fig. 237. The resemblance of its design to that of the Eiffel Tower underscores the universal applicability of the principle.

The portal arches of the Cathedral of Peterborough are not alone in demonstrating gradation of measure. Any set of concentric arches

FIG. 232. Pieter Bruegel the Elder. *The Wedding Dance.* 1566.
Detroit Institute of Arts.

FIG. 233. Rubens. Detail. *Autumn, The Château
de Steen.* 1636. National Gallery, London.

FIG. 234. Malwiyah Minaret. Abbasid period,
845-852. Samarra, Iraq.

445

or circles would possess a similar appeal—a fact that Berg exploited when he designed the Centennial Hall at Breslau (Fig. 205). So also did the designers of the coffered pattern for the dome of the Pantheon at Rome (Fig. 203) centuries before.

Although pyramidal and domical structures are deservedly popular in the architectural field, there are other ways of grading measure from a broad base to a narrow top. The Malwiyah Minaret (Fig. 234) at Samarra, Iraq, gains its effect through a spiraling gradation of measure. This telescope-like design, akin to the stepped pyramid common in both Egyptian and Mayan cultures, was made more graceful than either by the use of a continuous curve. Like the Eiffel Tower, it has the dual appeal of harmony of shape and gradation of measure.

The Eiffel Tower, the Washington Monument, the Pantheon, Santa Sophia, Santa Maria della Consolazione, the Pyramids, the Malyiwah Minaret, and many other architectural monuments have a common characteristic: the eye is led from a broad base to a narrow or pointed top. In the crowning masterpieces, like Santa Sophia, the eye is guided unerringly along a path that is varied enough to interest and delight; the artist never lets us wander or become lost. There is a sense of climax, a focus of attention, and the logical place for it is at the top of a dome, pyramid, spire, or gable. This accounts for the popularity of these forms in architecture. But something else accounts for their effectiveness; each exemplifies in some way that basic principle of design—gradation of measure.

Closely allied to the type of extended spiral in the Malwiyah Minaret is the simple scroll. Based on a gradation of measure through progressively expanding arcs, its universality is shown by the resemblance between its most noted form, the Ionic capital (Fig. 235), and the Chinese bronze finial in Fig. 236. Called, in the case of the Ionic capital, a volute scroll, this popular design is found in the uncoiling fronds of young ferns and in the snail shell.

Artists, pottery makers, and architects discovered early in history that a graded curve could be made more graceful still by being extended in reverse to form an elongated S. Praxiteles became famous as a creator of beautiful statues by taking advantage of this fact. At about the same time in ancient Greece the designers of buildings in the Ionic style introduced the *sima reversa* into architecture, where it has remained ever since. A means of effecting a smooth transition from a vertical to a horizontal plane, especially at the juncture of wall and cornice, it is, as its name implies, an S-curve. In order to prove that their achievement was not accidental, the same designers

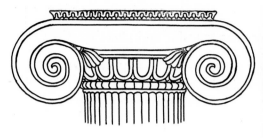

FIG. 235. Ionic capital. 4th century B.C.

FIG. 236. Bronze spiral finial. 9th–8th centuries B.C. Chou Dynasty. Nelson Gallery and Atkins Museum, Kansas City, Mo.

FIG. 237. Bronze ritual vessel, Type Ku. Early or Middle Chou Dynasties, 1100-600 B.C. Isabella Stewart Gardner Museum, Boston.

FIG. 238. Oxblood porcelain vase. K'ang Hsi period, 1662-1722. Museum of Fine Arts, Boston.

447

contrived for similar purposes the graceful and effective triple curvature of the Ionic base (Fig. 426).

Probably the most assiduous and successful of all employers of the
graded S-curve were the ceramic designers of China. Making the
name of China synonymous with beautiful porcelain everywhere,
they achieved their reputations partly through the quality of their
colors, glazes, and textures, but even more through the grace of their
shapes. They made the use of exquisitely graded curves a hallmark
of their art for century after century, as is amply shown by the
examples from the T'ang dynasty in Fig. 187 and the later oxblood
porcelain vase in Fig. 238.

The omnipresent principle of gradation of measure is shown in
rudimentary form by every stairway, ramp, or inclined plane of any
kind. However, the context in which any of these is used is the artistic determinant. Only when related to a monument like the
Great Pyramid of Khufu does the inclined plane contribute to and
partake of the nature of great art.

A gradation of shape is less often met in the visual arts, for there
are few convenient ways by which a designer can shift from a straight
to a curvilinear form. If some latitude is employed in interpreting
the character of shape, the Romans may be said to have created an
example of gradation of shape in the Colosseum (Fig. 207). Their
method was to separate the crucial forms in space, so that the gradation could be made in stages. Specifically, they decorated the ground
level with simple Roman Doric pilasters, the second tier with slightly
more elaborate Ionic, and the third and top stories with the most
ornate style of all, the Corinthian. They thus progressed gradually
from the simple to the complex in logical steps. It was so effective a
solution that it inspired imitation in later centuries, notably in
Alberti's Ruccellai Palace in Florence.

Gradation of surface is as noteworthy as it is rare. For practical
reasons architects have preferred to employ either harmony or contrast in the treatment of building surfaces, probably because gradations of surface entail costly extra effort. But the few examples that
do exist are striking. One thinks immediately of Michelozzo's
Medici-Riccardi Palace at Florence, because the handling of the
surface in it is an outstanding feature. The walls of the three storeys
are, starting at the ground level, rough, semirough, and smooth, the
latter providing an effective contrast with the heavy, ornate cornice.

A less renowned, but perhaps artistically superior gradation of
surface may be found in the exterior walls of the Strozzi Palace
(Fig. 175). So subtle that it almost eludes the eye, the gradation is
not, as in the Medici-Riccardi, effected in obvious stages; it progresses

continuously from a rough surface at street level to a nearly smooth surface beneath the cornice. To gain this effect both the sizes of the stones and the grooves between them were decreased gradually; the operation required unusual skill and patience, but the reward was an architectural design which illustrates gradation of surface in a distinguished way. Indeed, it is an excellent representative of the merits of gradation as a general principle.

SEQUENCE OF ALTERNATION. An alternation in design is a repeated change as distinct from uniformity or gradual change. A principle which applies to life at large, we find it in the alternation of day and night, in the action of a bird's wings, and in the ebb and flow of the tides.

When organizing his spatial design, an artist can apply the principle of alternation to any or all of the terms of space. He can alternate left and right attitudes or directions, rectilinear and curvilinear shapes, and rough and smooth surfaces. More often than not, however, one striking use of alternation within a harmonious or balanced design is sufficient.

An example is Perrault's design for the east façade of the Louvre (Fig. 239). Working within the classical idiom, he created a composition which exemplifies symmetrical balance and illustrates various types of harmony, such as the harmony of attitude, interval, measure, and shape found in the ground-storey windows and to a considerable extent in the second-storey columns. But with the Baroque period's penchant for variety he wished to break up this regularity. The device he used was the ancient principle of alternation; especially an alternation of interval in the colonnade. By repeating a change from the wide to the narrow in a sequence, he broke up the tendency toward monotony intrinsic in any highly regular colonnade and earned a lasting reputation as a designer.

The east façade of the Louvre illustrates one of the principal merits of an alternation of terms. This alternation enables a designer to increase the element of contrast or change in any composition while retaining all of the benefits of an orderly principle. The higher degree of conflict thus introduced creates a more staccato effect, but that effect may be desirable or necessary to offset an overdose of harmony.

Not only in visual design is alternation apparent. The alternation of sound and silence established by the tom-tom-like beating of drums is an essential element in primitive music and its modern descendant, jazz. Not only do the drums set a basic pattern, they din it into our ears by repetition. The effect of such music is

FIG. 239. Perrault. East façade of the Louvre. 1665. Paris.

FIG. 240. The Great Temple. Mayan renaissance, *ca.* A.D. 980-1200. Tikal, Yucatan.

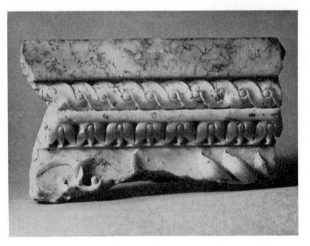

FIG. 241. Fragment of an architectural cornice moulding. Probably Republican Roman, 1st century B.C. Bowdoin College Museum of Fine Arts, Brunswick, Me.

hypnotic and stimulating. In the case of savages who are whipping themselves into a fury before engaging in battle, the alternation of a drum beat arouses a frenzy of emotion, and the influence of jazz upon civilized crowds is hardly less intense. Its appeal is to something deeply rooted in human nature, and we do not have to search far to find it. It has its source in the human pulse which is the bulwark of all life.

Any design marked by an alternation of elements, whether musical, verbal, or visual, speaks directly to the human psyche because it reflects a phenomenon which is both essential and universal. When the alternating pulse of life beats strongly in musical compositions, as it does in the work of Bach and Beethoven, other qualities seem secondary; all the skill in the world will not compensate for a feeble pulse.

Konody, in his definition of art, makes rhythm synonymous with order and regards it as indispensable. Order is indeed essential to all art—but rhythm is not, although it is a powerful and vital agent. The stately music of Bach and the mighty measures of Homer's verse owe much of their appeal to the use of rhythm.

A rhythmic alternation of terms endows a work of visual art with an extra measure of vitality through rapidly repeated changes which it introduces into a sequential pattern. An alternation is as crucial to the expression of vigor as a gradation is to the sense of beauty. Our present study, however, is the role of alternation in the creation of orderly designs. Its function in that respect contrasts with gradation; for where a slow change is typical of a gradation, an alternation is characterized by an abrupt or sudden shifting of terms. Where the one permits us to adjust to variations slowly, the other forces us to adjust rapidly and repeatedly. It agitates our minds, but in an orderly way. The principle difference lies in a much greater degree of variety.

A very striking work of architecture, the Great Temple at Tikal (Fig. 240), was created by taking advantage of the variety to be gained through the use of alternation. A pyramid of the stepped type, it resembles the Great Pyramid of Khufu (Fig. 174a) at Gizeh in the gradation of measure from a broad base to a narrow top. But whereas this change occurs slowly and steadily in the Egyptian monument, it takes place abruptly in the Mayan temple in an alternation of vertical walls and horizontal steps. Although both structures are orderly, they generate quite opposite effects in our minds. The mass by the Nile is smooth, austere, like the desert; the temple at Tikal is as harsh and broken as the jungles of Yucatan.

Alternation can add greatly to the interest of a work of art, contributing more to vigor of design than it detracts from smoothly flowing beauty. It has been used repeatedly to enliven the character of architectural forms which were in danger of appearing monotonous. The in-and-out rhythm of the fluting of a column is an instance of alternation used to break up the monotony of a too-smooth surface. An even better example is the cornice molding used by the Greeks and Romans to adorn the upper edges of their buildings. In the typical example shown in Fig. 241 alternation and continuity are strongly marked, with variety of design included for good measure. The rhythmic movement is established in the upper band by the over-and-under and up-and-down progression of the pattern. Coupled with a harmony of shape, it is a handsome motif; it is even more effective because of its contrast with the lower band, in which a vertical series of leaves is alternated in simple left-and-right pattern. Alternation is thus not only a principle of order in its own right, but enhances the beauty of other forms of order with which it is associated.

Alternation strikes us most forcibly in the abstract arts. In human life people do not normally arrange themselves in rhythmic postures, and the artist who would represent life truly is thereby handicapped. The abstract artist, being free from representational obligations, can stress rhythmic accents as freely and strongly as he wishes throughout the entire range of the decorative arts. They provide, in company with architecture, a veritable encyclopedia of alternations in design. Borders on furniture, textiles, and ceramics, which are by their nature sequential, are sequences of alternation.

Although alternations are less obvious to the eye in the representational arts than in the abstract, where pulsating rhythms can virtually dominate, good examples can be found in painting and sculpture. They are especially vivid in any scene depicting human beings marching or walking—like the *Warrior Vase* from Mycenae (Fig. 230) and Meunier's *Return of the Miners* (Fig. 231)—for the act of walking or marching in step is no less an example of alternation than the human pulse or the meter of a poem. What we describe as graceful walking or skating involves essentially an undulating or rhythmic progression in time and space—a fact that is borne out by the number of human activities, like dancing, skating, or marching, that are accompanied by some kind of musical beat or counting. Less apparent but no less effective are the subtle rhythms which artists impose upon their designs quite apart from any representation of movement. The life that an artist can bestow upon the most static scene by the use of rhythm has often been used as an index of his personal vitality.

True, this strong feeling for rhythm does not pervade all great art. It is noticeably absent in the calm art of Van Eyck. But it is a striking feature in the art of Michelangelo, Tintoretto, El Greco, and Rubens; it permeates the work of Van Gogh and weaves through the canvases of Gauguin and Matisse. A marked attribute of modern art, it either inspired or was inspired by a new appreciation of the pulsating rhythms of primitive music, sculpture, and dancing. It has a way, moreover, of uniting spiritually and stylistically works of art from diverse historical backgrounds, and thus serves as a universal leavener. One need go no farther than the superbly rhythmic pre-historic *Bison* (Fig. 33) and the *Two Deer* (Fig. 32) by Marc to see how an undulating line can create a family of pictures transcending time. Taken as a whole, they speak for men in whom the sense of life beat strongly.

We should appreciate each sign of pulsating life and enjoy rhythmic vitality wherever we find it without demanding that it be present at every turn. There are other principles of order whose claim to attention has been well earned. Harmony is one of these; gradation, a bountiful contributor to beauty, is another. A third, which we must consider now, is balance. In the field of design no one of these is supreme in the creation of order or beauty. In their complementary relationship each is necessary and indispensable.

BALANCE

Unlike harmony or sequence, in which there is a general similarity or an orderly change, balance is characterized by a uniformity of opposition. Orderly because of the one property, it is varied because of the other. An essential feature of its dual nature is contrast, conflict, or opposition of some kind which is resolved by the act of balancing or equalization. While designs employing balance can be static in nature, they can also contain a high degree of inner tension. And since tension generates vitality, balance is capable of achieving that desirable quality along with a considerable amount of variety. Thus, while balance is by its nature less suited than sequence to give order to movement, it is not its inferior in vitality and variety and is in both respects superior to harmony. It rounds out, complements, and completes the artist's compositional resources, permitting him to accomplish certain ends of design that cannot be attained in any other way.

Balance in art reflects ancient and widespread conditions of life. Reality abounds in opposite and conflicting attributes which require some kind of stabilization, or which present a balance already achieved by natural forces. While man cannot always resolve his conflicts, he has always admired the symmetry exhibited by natural forces. The Greeks extended this principle to social relationships and to personal and intellectual aims as a major ideal or way of life, Aristotle's doctrine of the mean being perhaps the best known exposition of their particular attitude. The same principle applied to art merely reflects this ancient concern of the human mind.

Balance can be illustrated by a game of tug-of-war in which a temporary stalemate, or uniformity of opposition, has been reached. In such a game the participants are not pulling harmoniously or moving progressively in the same direction, but are pitting the strength of one group against that of the other. The more perfectly matched or balanced the two sides are, the more effort must be exerted to break the deadlock. The combination of uniformity and opposition, or balance, forces the contestants to expend more energy than they would if running unhindered in the same direction. Conflict probably generates more vitality than any other condition in nature, life, or art.

The artist who stresses balance in a work of art is dealing with a visual tug-of-war. The pictorial, sculptural, or architectural balance depends upon qualities of visual attraction which, though not so concrete as weights on a scale, affect us nonetheless strongly. We seem to have a physiopsychic mechanism (or kinesthetic sense) that measures optical balance as the inner ear measures physical equilibrium.

There are two principal approaches to the problem of balance. One pertains to the balancing of conflicts which already exist, like the mediation of a labor dispute, while the other is devoted to the creation of opposing elements in balance. It is the latter approach that the creative artist exemplifies. His application of the principle is dynamic and unique, for in the process of creating a picture he will bring his design into balance and then throw it out of balance many times. Ultimate balance being his objective, he must know when the picture is finished and the balance perfect, a decision which requires acute judgment.

Within the field of spatial design there are four possible methods of attaining balance. Two arise from the fact that a visual artist can stabilize his formal entities to either side of a real or imaginary axis or around a central point. In the pictorial arts the axis will bisect the frame, while the central point of balance will be at its geometric center, making the frame in either case an important factor in the design. In the free-standing architectural and sculptural arts the axis or center will be related to the building's or statue's silhouettes which are their frames.

Two additional methods of balancing a design stem from the

possibilities inherent in symmetrical and asymmetrical groups. In the parlance of design these are called obvious and occult balances. The four possibilities which emerge can be demonstrated diagrammatically in the following fashion:

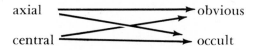

The crossing arrows are intended to indicate that an axial balance can be either of the obvious or occult type and the same option is available to central balance, making a total of four varieties in all.

AXIAL OBVIOUS BALANCE. An axial balance is one which is arranged to either side of the real or imaginary vertical axis of an enframement or form, the axis having the effect of dividing the design area into two equal parts. Within these halves a balance of elements or uniformity of opposition is created. The term *obvious* is used to describe this condition of equilibrium when the two areas are symmetrical or nearly so. The word *obvious* is used to include both because it permits a greater latitude than symmetry implies. Within that latitude, however, there must be a highly appreciable matching of elements to left and right of the axis.

Two everyday examples will clarify this point. Almost every child has created in school an obvious axial balance by folding a piece of paper and then cutting out a simple pattern along the two free edges. When the paper is unfolded the pattern on one side will be a mirror-image of the other. The design may suggest a Christmas tree or a symmetrical leaf, but its balance of elements will be obvious. Similarly, we have all seen an obvious balancing of elements when six children of about equal size and weight have distributed themselves on either side of a seesaw.

The same principle of obvious axial balance is manifest in countless works of art. A clear-cut illustration is the portal of St. Trophîme (Fig. 242) at Arles. A typical example of French Romanesque architecture, it exhibits the regularity and symmetry which southern French builders inherited from classical Rome. Beyond that it exemplifies the preference for symmetry which runs, like a strong tide, through the entire history of architecture. Applied to the façades of buildings which were symmetrical within, it made the portal side unusually prominent—so much so that our modern architects referred to this unmitigated respect for regularity and emphasis upon the front as the "tyranny of the façade" and took steps to invoke a new principle of design that would alleviate it. Prior to modern

FIG. 242. Portal. St.
Trophime. *ca.* 1180-
1190. Arles.

FIG. 243. Bronze ritual vessel, Type Yu.
Early or middle Chou Dynasty, *ca.*
1100-600 B.C. Museum of Fine Arts,
Boston.

FIG. 244. Cimabue. *Madonna Enthroned. ca.* 1285. Louvre, Paris.

456

times, however, the architectural façade was a perfect demonstration of axial obvious balance. The revolt against it is of comparatively recent date.

The portal of St. Trophîme illustrates in architecture the principle employed by the school boy who draws the pattern on a piece of folded paper. At a modest distance every spatial term incorporated in the building is found on both sides of the central axis; attitudes, intervals, shapes, and sizes are identical. There are three columns and two saints on the left and comparable units on the right; one side of the arch and the sloping roof is a reverse image of the other.

With the exception of the arch and the roof, there is a minimum of opposition in this design. Quite to the contrary, the vertical columns and front-facing saints present more uniformity than conflict. The result is a highly stable design as well as an emphatically frontal one. Granted that such stability has been deemed a desirable attribute of architecture throughout most of its history, one can also appreciate the modern architects' rebellion against static and symmetrical designs and the worship of a building's front.

Historically viewed, the portal of St. Trophîme expresses the acceptance of symmetry and regularity by the collectively conditioned medieval people. It is a trait which one finds extending from Byzantine art of the sixth century—note, for instance, the rigid and uniform frontality of Justinian and Courtiers (Fig. 121)—through the façade of the Cathedral of Rouen (Fig. 182), which dates from the sixteenth century. Not even the vigorous and daring Gothic builders escaped its hold. But what is acceptable and even desirable in architecture has the effect of putting the representational arts in a strait jacket.

When an obvious axial balance is imposed upon a painted subject it freezes the life from the scene. Human beings do not normally align themselves in balanced groups as though anticipating the visit of a photographer. When they are thus presented the effect is static and artificial.

Cimabue's *Madonna Enthroned* (Fig. 244) is an illustration of the medieval worship of symmetry applied to painting. Characteristic of its time, it presents the Madonna and Child squarely on the central axis, flanked by matching angels to either side. A group photograph of an athletic team could hardly be more stiffly posed. While this stiffness was suited to formal religious pictures proclaiming the dignity of the Madonna, and undoubtedly did not appear over-rigid to medieval eyes, the artists of the Renaissance rebelled against this essentially Byzantine type of design. One of the first signs of the Renaissance was a marked departure from obvious balances by Cimabue's own pupil Giotto and all of the latter's followers. Giotto's asymmetrical *Presentation of the Virgin* (Fig. 51) is a typical example of an output in which obvious axial balances are rare. In this way, and for these reasons, the hold of obvious symmetry on the representational arts was broken some six centuries before it was cast off by architecture and the other abstract arts.

The designer who is not obliged to represent the flexibility and informality of human life—as Giotto did deliberately—may court orderliness as zealously as he pleases. This would apply to any one of thousands of designers of the so-called decorative arts, a field in which the axial obvious balance has enjoyed a continuity quite equal to the favor it has found in architecture. A striking example is the bronze ritual vessel in Fig. 243, shaped by an unknown ancient Chinese designer. Its age is not important; it is no more symmetrical than hundreds of other vessels, carpets, or chairs that date from later centuries. More to the point is the way it illustrates a difference between architecture and the decorative arts. The architect's assumed duty to express stability accounts for the static symmetry of the portal of St. Trophîme. The decorative artist, on the other hand, may feel a primary obligation to the expression of symbols of life rather than security. Freed of the burden of being as practical as the architect, he can create livelier compositions. At least, that is his option, and the designer of the ritual vessel availed himself of it.

In his design there is no less uniformity than in the portal of St. Trophîme, but there is a good deal more opposition. The horns of the highly stylized water buffalo radiate from the axis in diametrically opposite directions, and there is a strong effect of conflict in the bristling, arrow-like projections. The composition is a tug-of-war of contrasting elements which gives it a remarkable variety and vitality.

The high content of opposition in the bronze ritual vessel produces an air of tension and life which is as expressive of the ancient Chinese animistic religion symbolized in it as the stability of St. Trophîme or Cimabue's *Madonna Enthroned* is of medieval Christian collectivism. In another respect, however, all three designs are typical of axial obvious balances the world over. In each the central axis is stressed, making it apparent rather than implied. Cimabue did this by placing his most important figure on the central axis in a way characteristic of medieval painting; it is identical with the Austrian *Virgin Enthroned* in Fig. 49. The architect of St. Trophîme brought out the axis by a column, the apexes of arch and roof, and the figure of Christ. Similarly, the designer of the bronze ritual vessel made a series of important shapes coincide with the axial dividing line.

The advocate of an axial obvious balance makes his equilibrium as emphatic as possible. As a consequence, this method has both merits and drawbacks. Its orderliness is unquestioned, and designers have always used it for the sake of that quality. The results of this method are clear and stable. On the other hand, these very merits have their limitations, clarity leaving too little to the imagination and stability verging on the lifeless and monotonous. The medieval people were not so disturbed by uniformity as later peoples, but in the long run the axial obvious balance appeared to have grave deficiencies for representational painting, a limited capacity for holding our interest being prominent among them. It is too clear, and not sufficiently elusive or infinite. The subsequent history of design in painting therefore took a different and opposite direction by exploring and exploiting the possibilities of the occult type of balance.

AXIAL OCCULT BALANCE. Axial occult balance resembles obvious balance in that it is predicated upon a central axis which bisects a frame or outline. But it differs from the obvious balance in several important ways. In the three examples which are offered to illustrate this method—Ribera's *Martyrdom of St. Bartholomew* (Fig. 245), Holbein's *Christina of Denmark* (Fig. 246), and Degas' *Dancers Practising at the Bar* (Fig. 247)—the central figure is not placed on the central axis. Each artist seems to have deliberately avoided stressing the dividing line. That is the common method of avoiding the obvious, the intention being to increase the interest-holding qualities of the composition. As a method this requires a deliberate use of indirection, elusiveness, and infinity. The degree to which these qualities are utilized is of primary importance.

The term *occult* grows out of this intention. The opposite of obvious, it denotes an elusive quality which we perceive subconsciously, rather than directly and clearly. Although difficult to measure with a ruler or to describe in terms of matching figures, it is a very real quality. Common agreement can be reached on the question of when a design has reached the point of balance or gone beyond it. If the designer is an artist of acute sensibilities, his sense of balance can be trusted exactly, and the nicety of judgment that he reveals through his pictures can be a source of intense esthetic enjoyment for us.

This phenomenon of definite but unexplainable appreciation is more widespread than we generally realize. We have many capacities whose proof lies in action rather than explanation, our sense of equilibrium being outstanding among them. We know when a skater does not go to the other extreme and sprawl on the ice. We

FIG. 246. Hans Holbein the Younger.
*Christina of Denmark, Duchess
of Milan.* 1538. National Gallery,
London.

FIG. 247. Degas. *Ballet Dancers Practising at the Bar.* 1875. Metropolitan
Museum of Art, New York.

can calculate this balance, appreciating both its exactness and difficulty. For we are painfully aware of the instant when a skater starts
to lose his equilibrium, and our discomfort increases as the imbalance
develops into a catastrophe. Self-identification, empathy, a sense
of equilibrium—call them what you will—are all-important to our
sense of pleasure in order and our dislike of gracelessness. They provide the universal appreciative equipment to which the designer of
an axial occult balance appeals.

The merits of axial occult balance correct the deficiencies of the
obvious type of balance. Courting just the slightest measure of disequilibrium for the sake of more infinite appeal, this method teases
our imagination by remaining outside our ultimate grasp. Its infinitesimal lack of clarity holds our interest. This explains why the
term *occult* is substituted for *asymmetrical*. Though related, their
psychological implications are different, asymmetrical implying a
physically off-center design. Whereas an asymmetrical design may
not be balanced, an axial occult balance must seem to be.

An outstanding merit of axial occult balance is its dynamic effect
upon the spectator. In the subtlest possible way it suggests the hidden disequilibrium which is inherent in all movement, for there is
no such thing as perfect balance in human activities, even in the
most accomplished skater. The possibility of a fall is always present
and lends drama and interest to the procedure. Equilibrium and
disequilibrium are thus present in an exquisite tension, the interest
being heightened by the narrow line between them. Our experience
with this fact of existence carries over into our apprehension of the
axial occult balance and causes us to connect it with dynamic forms
of order. When a static scene is represented, as in Holbein's
Christina of Denmark, it appears less rigid than an obvious balance
like Cimabue's *Madonna Enthroned.* When action is represented,
as in Ribera's *Martyrdom of St. Bartholomew,* the dynamic quality
of the design is increased proportionately. Thus, in several ways,
the axial occult benefits by and cultivates our associations with equilibrium. Being primarily concerned with action, both endow the
occult design with an added measure of vitality.

A commonplace example will illustrate another important difference between the two types of balance. We referred previously to a
seesaw upon which three children of about equal size are grouped
on one side and three similar children on the other, like the angels
on either side of the Madonna in Cimabue's altarpiece (Fig. 244).
Similarly, one could place three bricks on one pan of a scale and
three identical bricks on the other. However, there is another way
of gaining balance. Two large boys could be placed on one end of a

seesaw and five smaller children on the other, offsetting size with numbers. Balance, the ultimate aim, would thus be attained by a uniformity of opposition among unlike elements. This dissimilarity of elements on either side of the axis is as crucial to an axial occult design as is the attainment of balance. It is by this process that the artist gains the variety which the obvious balance lacks. As a result, variety and vital instability are more frequent in occult balance than is normal in obvious balance.

The visual artist gains these qualities by playing one spatial term against another—size against irregularity, roughness against smoothness, verticality against horizontality, and one direction against another. A word will be added later about the extent to which the visual attractiveness and attentional values of these contrasting attributes has been understood and systematized. Here our attention should be focused upon the importance of employing and then reconciling dissimilar forms on the two sides of the composition.

The three paintings by Holbein, Ribera, and Degas in Figs. 245–247 not only illustrate these points exceptionally well, but they speak for a historical trend. They stand apart from the medieval group of *Justinian and his Courtiers,* Cimabue's *Madonna Enthroned,* and the Austrian manuscript illumination of the *Virgin Enthroned* by virtue of their occult treatment of balance. Holbein, Ribera, and Degas continued in their respective centuries a trend away from the obvious that had started as early as Giotto. Compared to any painting by Cimabue, Degas' composition is highly occult, representing the nineteenth-century and modern point of view. So continuous was this quest for greater variety and vitality within the field of compositional order that obvious balances became as rare in modern painting as they were typical in the Middle Ages.

These paintings by Holbein, Ribera, and Degas are worthy of study for their own sakes. Fine examples of design, each illustrates interesting aspects of axial occult balance in a unique manner. The story behind Holbein's portrait of *Christina of Denmark, Duchess of Milan,* is not without human interest or bearing upon the design. Her reputation for beauty attracted the attention of Henry VIII during one of his numerous wife-hunting periods. Rather than ask for her hand, sight unseen, he sent Holbein to make a likeness of the lady. Although she never became Queen of England, her portrait hangs in the National Gallery at London today. She was a widow wearing mourning, a condition which Holbein respected by portraying her in a quiet, symmetrical pose. But the artist had to do something to give interest to such a somber and static scene and found the means to do that with occult axial balance. Moving the duchess slightly to the left of the central axis, he balanced the picture and served an ideological end as well by placing a small but eye-catching notice of her identity on the wall to the right. The size and placement of the legend are exquisitely adjusted to the needs of the design. It is in almost every other respect too a model of simple but adroit understatement.

Ribera's *Martyrdom of St. Bartholomew* is a more complex and dramatic picture. If he had followed the medieval tradition, he would have arranged his crosslike instrument of torture symmetrically, as in the *Crucifixion* at Daphni (Fig. 87). Instead, obeying the Baroque instinct for a more dynamic composition, he placed the post and cross-bar to the left of the central axis, thus preordaining an occult balance. His next problem was to equalize the visual weight of the two areas, a solution which he achieved by extending the body of St. Bartholomew toward the right and by pitting various attitudes and directions against each other. Final equilibrium was established by introducing the two columns and five spears in the upper right-hand corner.

Degas' *Dancers Practising at the Bar*, coming later in time, bears the least resemblance to medieval symmetrical compositions. It appeals strongly to the occult sense of balance. Degas went out of his way to avoid the angles of view and positions normally associated with an obvious symmetry, and viewed the scene as though he were above it and to the left, making the interior horizon assume a sharp angle. It creates a seesaw instability appropriate to the activity represented. Furthermore, though the heel of the central figure is near the picture's center, no form actually coincides with the axis; Degas' treatment was too subtle for that.

At first glance the upper right quadrant of the composition seems favored and almost to outweigh the rest. But Degas, with his customary ingenuity, balanced the picture in two ways. One was by painting the floor in a vigorous, eye-catching manner, so that the lower half of the design receives its due; the other was to insert his own signature and the powdered resin shaker at just the place in the picture where it would give the weight needed for balance, Few people have excelled Degas in the resolution of such visual problems or in giving interest to supposedly uninteresting floors and walls. He seemed to take pleasure in posing compositional difficulties and then overcoming them. He leaves us, too, with no doubt about one matter: his precisely controlled occult balance is far more interesting than the easier axial obvious type.

Degas' design resembles that of the later Japanese prints. Like

Degas, the makers of these prints courted compositional difficulties for the sake of the greater interest that came with their solution, both for the artist and the spectator. The designs which they created in the period from the seventeenth through the middle nineteenth century are predominantly asymmetrical but exquisitely balanced. Hokusai's *Great Wave* (Fig. 377) and *Fujiyama in Clear Weather* (Fig. 265) are only two examples among many.

The West has produced many masterpieces of occult axial balance. Raphael's *Mass of Bolsena* (Fig. 59), a triumph over an unusually difficult problem, has already been discussed. Since the ability to manage occult balances increased with time and experience, it is appropriate to mention three modern examples. Cézanne's *Vase of Tulips* (Fig. 15), Bellows' *Stag at Sharkey's* (Fig. 77), and Eakins' *Between Rounds* (Fig. 78) are superb examples of intrinsic interest in problems of design and their solution.

Occult axial balance can be applied to sculpture as readily as to painting, and with a comparable increase in interest. The ancient Greeks made this discovery about midway through their history and pursued it vigorously. The turning point came during the time now called the Transitional Period, which fell between 480 and 450 B.C., just prior to the Golden Age of Pericles. The statues by Greek sculptors before the Transitional Period mainly adhered to the law of frontality. This convention, which the Greeks inherited from the Egyptians, prevailed in the eastern Mediterranean world throughout early ancient history. It is exemplified by the rigidly vertical, frontal, and symmetrical *Menkure and His Queen* (Fig. 160), the Sumerian *Governor of Lagash* (Fig. 67), and the early Greek *Apollo of Tenea* (Fig. 405).

The active, inquisitive, and democratic Greeks broke with the old authoritarian conventions by the time of Myron. One incentive was their love of the well-developed athlete in action, a subject for which axial obvious balance was little suited. Myron, in representing a discus thrower in his best-known statue (Fig. 371), chose a highly asymmetrical pose, the young athlete having leaned far off-center as he prepared to throw. Myron also demonstrated the sureness of his judgment by selecting that dynamic instant between the upward and downward swing of the arm—a moment of poise which implies action without strain.

The balance of directional forms and attitudes in Myron's *Discus Thrower* is characteristic of a change which was occurring throughout Greek sculpture. It can be observed in the development of the groups that were created to decorate the spaces under the gables of temples. There, too, the trend was from the obvious to the occult type of balance. The progress made during the Transitional Period prepared the way for the Golden Age and the brilliant use of the occult balance in the east and west pediments of the Parthenon.

When the evolution of Greek sculpture is compared to European compositional trends from the Giotto to Degas, and with the evolution of Japanese painting and print-making, it leads us to conclude that the normal development in design is from the obvious to the occult. This change also seems to be connected with social changes toward greater variety, complexity, activity, and individuality. Accompanying this desire is an increased capacity on the part of spectator and artist in dealing with more intricate types of both subject and treatment. This increased ability denotes a greater attention span and artistic maturity which can safely be evaluated as genuine artistic progress.

Another implication of the history of Greek design is that a marked shift from the obvious to the occult is more than a historical tendency—it indicates a significant break with established traditions. It connotes what we mean by "going modern." If we accept the fact that the world has "gone modern" many times, we can see that it did so about the time of Giotto, during the seventeenth century in Japan, and, long ago, in Greek times. Civilization progresses, as Toynbee has pointed out, in advances and pauses and periods of acceleration which are reflected in the history of design.

CENTRAL OBVIOUS BALANCE. Central balance derives its meaning from the relation of the formal entities of a design to the center of a framed area or a form. There is, of course, a natural tendency to arrange a central design around the center of a circular enframement, but such circularity is not necessary. The enframement can be square, hexagonal, or rectangular. What is crucial is the arrangement around the central point.

The study of central obvious balance need not delay us long. It is a design type which lends itself but little to representational painting or sculpture, for human life rarely arranges itself in a central obvious balance and appears artificial if so composed. On the other hand, central obvious balance is easy to identify in the arts where it is common. By and large these are the abstract architectural and decorative arts. Plates which are symmetrically decorated in every direction are abundant. So, too, are such centrally balanced symmetries as star designs, and any kind of spoked wheel.

Equally prevalent are architectural examples of the central obvious balance. The insides of domes or regularly shaped towers seem to our eyes to be distributed evenly around a central point or vertical axis. This is clearly true of the crossing vault and lantern (Fig. 248a) of the Cathedral of Ely when we view it from below. Though such a design is only a part of the structure as a whole, it possesses an independent and noticeable integrity.

Our perception of the central point or vertical axis in a building is likely to be an additional way of seeing a horizontal axial design. Yet it gives pleasure in itself, for there are many ways of viewing a work of architecture from within or without, and a central balance may well be found among them. For example, the interior of Santa Sophia (Fig. 208) disposes us to read it as an axial obvious balance with strongly marked areas to left and right. The same observation applies to the interior of the Pantheon (Fig. 204) and Max Berg's Centennial Hall at Breslau (Fig. 205). But in each of these buildings we can also look upward from the center of the floor to the center of the dome and find there a perfectly symmetrical central balance.

Something of the same experience enters into our appreciation of the Colosseum at Rome (Fig. 207). As we approach the building from a distance, its strong horizontal lines force us to observe it from left to right. But upon closer inspection the curved character of the walls impresses our consciousness and conditions us for what we find within the amphitheatre. There the focus of attention is the oval-shaped floor upon which the ancient combats were staged, and the tiers of seats ringing the oval concentrically one above the other repeat and stress the oval shape. We become progressively more aware of the centrality of this arrangement the higher we mount in the stadium. From every position in the enclosure our eyes are attracted inward toward the oval and its center. Though we look down upon a floor instead of upward toward a dome, the effect is fundamentally similar. This secondary viewpoint, coming as a kind of esthetic dividend, is a bonus well worth looking for.

Central obvious balance lends itself naturally to perfectly static symmetry, as in Fig. 248b. But a more stimulating way of treating such patterns is illustrated by the several designs found in Figs. 248c-g. These involve movement revolving around the center; radiation from the center (centrifugal action); convergence toward the center (centripetal action); curvilinear convergence (whirlpool fashion); and curvilinear radiation (like a Catherine wheel). The various frames are meant to show that a circular enframement is usual but not obligatory. These designs are not definitive; scores of other patterns can be constructed from them by combination, but these are basic.

The common element in these designs is movement of some sort in relation to a point and, in many cases, a circle. This is not sur-

FIG. 248a. *Crossing Vault and Lantern*. Alan of Wasingham. 1323-1362.
Cathedral, Ely.

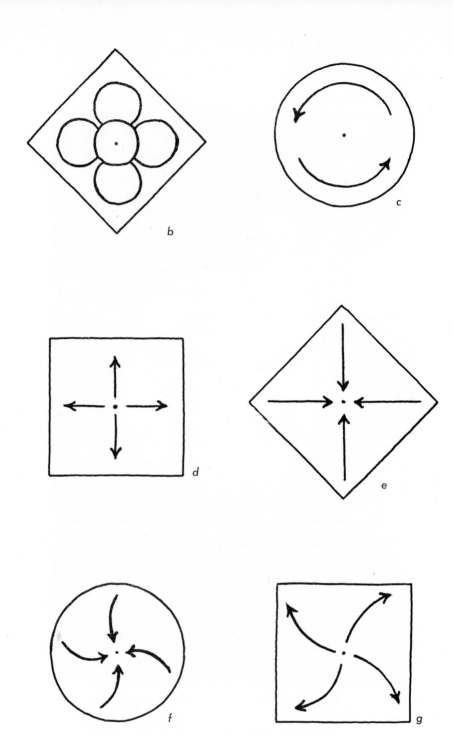

FIG. 248b–g. Diagrammatic illustrations of central balance.

prising, for few forms in the world imply movement as readily as a wheel; its shape automatically sets us thinking in circular terms. The centripetal, centrifugal, and circular movements that are associated with revolving action are among the most dynamic in human experience. Little wonder that designers the world over, from the unknown ancient inventor of the Indian swastika to the modern creator of a Turkish coffee-table top, have responded to the circle and exploited this principle of central obvious balance.

CENTRAL OCCULT BALANCE. Central occult balance stands in the same relation to central obvious balance that occult designs of the axial type bear to obvious axial balance. Its comparable limitations and merits consequently need not be repeated in detail here. We shall focus our attention on the historical role played by central occult balance.

This kind of design has been an important factor in the evolution of painting and sculpture, but its most significant impact has been on the development of a modern style in architecture. Architecture, a practical and conservative art, was retarded by its addiction to axial obvious balance for a longer period than either sculpture or painting. This devotion to symmetry perpetuated a worship of the façade which prevented the exploitation of architecture's three-dimensional character. Too much emphasis was placed upon the front of buildings, to the neglect of the remaining sides. Although this simplified the designer's problem, it kept him from realizing the full possibilities of his art. A three-dimensional form intended to be viewed only from the front offers but a single composition; one which invites inspection on every side gains immeasurably in esthetic interest by its infinity of appreciable relationships.

The Greek sculptors discovered this quality of the three-dimensional media as early as about 450 B.C. Myron's *Discus Thrower* (Fig. 371) invites inspection and gives pleasure from every point of view. Anyone who has not walked around the figure and looked at it from the sides and rear has missed its full effect. Once established, this method of composition was available to all sculptors; and it has been consciously continued by the modern classicist, William Zorach, in his *Spirit of the Dance* (Fig. 84). But the same Greeks were wedded to a frontal emphasis in architecture, with an ironical result. Whenever Greek architecture was emulated in later times, the temple "front" was its principal feature. The exception to this long domination of the shallow façade was Gothic architecture, in which north and south portals were often prominent. On the other hand, the apse end of a building was of minor importance compared to the front. Hence the truly four-sided or façade-less building remained a matter for future exploitation.

The nearest that the older builders came to an all-around building was in the small circular temples at Rome and Tivoli. When they built their largest temple, the Pantheon, they reverted to a strongly emphasized façade. No matter how centrally balanced it may be internally (Fig. 204), the exterior is dominated by a Greek-Roman temple front (Fig. 176).

This tradition of symmetry and frontality persisted through the nineteenth century, until modern architects discarded it in order to exploit architectural possibilities more fully, and gain greater interest. Their attack was two-pronged. First they abandoned obvious symmetrical balances, like those of St. Trophîme (Fig. 242) and the Strozzi Palace (Fig. 175), in favor of the occult type. The result can be observed in the Kaufmann House (Fig. 213), by that pioneer of the movement, Frank Lloyd Wright. From any point of view its balance is occult rather than obvious.

Then the architects of the modern movement placed an unprecedented stress on a central vertical axis instead of on the old-fashioned longitudinal axis. The latter had been associated with the façade and aligned a building to left and right of a line extending from the front to the rear, as in the ubiquitous Christian basilica-type church. The new alignment retained a left and right reading of design, but radiated from an axis which rose from the center of the ground plan to the center of the top. This arrangement of forms around a central vertical axis was not in itself new. The Great Pyramid of Khufu (Fig. 174a) was arranged with four equal sides ascending to a point, as were Santa Maria della Consolazione at Todi (Fig. 177), the Washington Monument, and the Eiffel Tower (Fig. 211). The Colosseum at Rome (Fig. 207) also presented at least four uniformly important sides for appreciation, manifesting the three-dimensional character of architecture.

Modern architecture differs radically from the old by the union of the central vertical axis and a use of occult balance. The uniting of these two concepts produced more than the sum of two ideas: it gave modern buildings an immeasurable amount of extra interest. Wright's Kaufmann House can be used for demonstration. It has literally no one façade, but a series of equally interesting aspects. The pivotal axis which makes this circumferential observation possible remains stationary. Located in the vicinity of the chimney it holds our eyes as we walk around, just as the forms radiate from it in the ground plan. Something radically different from house designs which had persisted for centuries was gained here through the com-

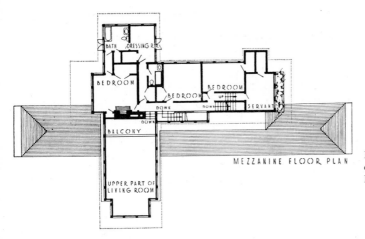

FIG. 249. Wright. Plan of the mezzanine floor, Frank J. Baker house. 1909. Wilmette, Ill.

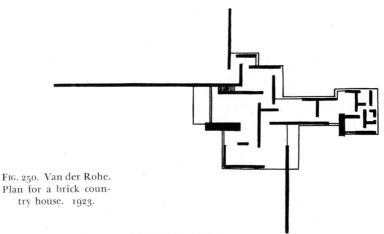

FIG. 250. Van der Rohe. Plan for a brick country house. 1923.

FIG. 251. Skidmore, Owings, and Merrill. Model of the New York University–Bellevue Medical Center, 1949. New York.

bined effect of occult and central balance. It is also infinitely more engrossing, stimulating, and fully developed than earlier designs.

This new design concept has run through modern architecture like a unifying theme, joining in a common style men, like Wright and Gropius, who think of themselves as opposites in international modernism. The attitude toward design that both share with Mondrian will not be lost on the close observer. The rectilinear harmony and occult axial balance of the painter's *Composition in White, Black, and Red,* while historically allied with Gropius' Bauhaus school, is constructed on many of the design principles of Wright's Kaufmann House.

The best proof of this universality of style can be found in a series of architectural examples. Wright began to experiment with non-façade, many-sided house designs early in the present century. By 1909 he was committed, as in his Baker House (Fig. 249), to a plan which radiated in occult fashion from a central vertical axis—a forerunner of the Kaufmann House. Whether under Wright's influence or not, Mies Van der Rohe advocated an essentially identical arrangement in his plan for a brick country house (Fig. 250) of 1923. The similarity between his viewpoint and that expressed in Mondrian's abstract paintings is apparent. In 1926 Walter Gropius incorporated this kind of occult central balance in an actual building, his famous Bauhaus school at Dessau. Later, Skidmore, Owings, and Merrill employed this formula in their design for the New York University–Bellevue Medical Center (Fig. 251) of 1949. This is the Bauhaus design transplanted from a German school to an American hospital. But it is also a design come home, for it owes much of its character to Wright's early efforts.

It has been said that the central occult balance in architecture really came into its own when the airplane added a new dimension to our perception of buildings and cities. Although a dome like that of the Pantheon or Santa Sophia encourages an upward-looking appreciation, the Bauhaus or Medical Center type of design can probably best be seen from above. Skidmore, Owings, and Merrill seem to have had the airborne viewer consciously in mind when they laid out the plan of their hospital. When even the bird's-eye view of architecture is taken into account, it would seem that architectural potentialities are being fully exploited—possibly for the first time.

In the decorative arts obvious symmetries are plentiful and occult balances rare. But an exceptional example, like the six-foil bronze dragon mirror (Fig. 252) in the Freer Gallery, makes up for scarcity with brilliance. The designer of this mirror hit upon the happy idea of decorating the circular surface with a dragon which chases its

FIG. 252. Six-foil bronze dragon mirror. T'ang Dynasty, A.D. 618-906. Smithsonian Institution, Freer Gallery of Art, Washington, D.C.

FIG. 253. Raphael. *Madonna of the Chair*. *ca.* 1510-1512. Pitti Gallery, Florence.

FIG. 254. Tintoretto. *Marriage of Bacchus and Ariadne*. 1578. Ducal Palace, Venice.

tail around the center. In this way the vitality associated with the dragon by the Chinese is given full play rather than being cramped or stultified. It would be hard to find a better example of the exploitation of the dynamic potentialities inherent in central balance. Basically, this mirror resembles Fig. 248c.

The Chinese have tended to favor certain stylistic characteristics over many centuries. Their love of dynamic curvilinear design conveys a keen sense of life and vitality; they show an enduring appreciation of the disequilibrium necessary for an expression of lifelike variety. The Chinese attitude toward order is subtle, flexible, and yielding, compared to Western classical standards. Another excellent example of central occult balance, also Chinese, is the glazed pottery dish in Fig. 221. Its designer has shown a typical Chinese talent for adapting a representational image to a ceramic shape, enhancing and satisfying the requirements of both. This floral motif in a circular dish is a harmony of curved shapes, suggesting a logical connection between a harmony of curves and a central balance, whether occult or obvious.

Raphael's *Madonna of the Chair* (Fig. 253), the most familiar example of central occult balance in Western painting, illustrates this principle perfectly. Raphael employed a harmony of curved shapes throughout most of his design and, in addition, adapted these shapes to the circular pattern. The Madonna's head is bent inward to fit within the frame. So, too, is the figure of the youthful St. John. Raphael was too sophisticated to place any important point exactly in the center, but located the elbows of the Christ Child and Madonna above and below it. By making all the forms and lines revolve around the center as well as fit into the frame, he created a strong sense of circular organization which gives order, life, and interest to the picture. The design accounts in no small measure for the renown and popularity of this picture.

Despite the success of the *Madonna of the Chair,* neither Raphael nor any other artist has used the tondo frame, as the Italians call it, frequently; it remains an unusual form. The reason for this avoidance of the circular enclosure is fairly plain. Having no sides, top, or bottom, it suggests a rolling wheel. This inherent mobility gives it a dynamic quality, but produces an uncomfortable feeling of instability. Raphael himself felt it necessary to introduce some stabilizing element into the circular design of his Madonna, and did this by giving a prominent place to the straight, vertical post of the chair. Furthermore, the round format does not accommodate itself to normal human postures. Instead, representation has to be accommodated to the character of the frame, as in the *Madonna of the Chair.*

Scenes which lend themselves to circular representation are few. But artists occasionally compress their figures into a tondo frame for the sake of its dynamic form. When they succeed as well as Raphael in mastering this difficult composition, they accomplish something rare and noteworthy.

The special merits and difficulties of central occult balance are illustrated by the works of Tintoretto. Although a prolific and tremendously talented painter, he undertook this kind of design only a few times. His most successful attempt, the *Marriage of Bacchus and Ariadne* (Fig. 254), is regarded as one of the finest of his paintings. A successful central occult balance is usually accorded exceptional attention and credit.

One of the artist's problems is *when* to use central occult balance. Tintoretto showed excellent judgment in this respect. By using a central balance of the type in Fig. 248f, he achieved the combination of grace and movement which attends a whirlpool-like design of converging lines. At the same time he told his story well, focusing attention upon the critical joining of hands by placing them in the center of the composition.

Tintoretto simplified his problem by working within a rectangular rather than a round frame. This is the common procedure; Raphael's was the extraordinary one. While it sacrifices something of the possibilities open to consistently circular design, it greatly extends its representational uses, for many more scenes can be adapted to a rectangle or square than can be fitted into a circle. Making the figures in a central balance appear credibly posed instead of forced and artificial is difficult, and it is doubtful whether Raphael himself could have created more than one *Madonna of the Chair*. On the score of naturalness Tintoretto was brilliantly successful; the figures of his *Marriage of Bacchus and Ariadne* move within the revolving design with effortless grace, making his art appear perfectly natural.

The rectangular frame used by Tintoretto bears upon a difficulty a student meets when he attempts to distinguish between central and axial occult balance. A sharp distinction is not necessary. The left and right scanning movement of our glance, the situation of our feet upon the plane of the earth, and the flatness of the horizon all condition us to read compositions in a left-right axial fashion. We cannot escape this habit even when analyzing such designs as the Chinese dragon mirror, Raphael's *Madonna of the Chair*, or Tintoretto's *Marriage of Bacchus and Ariadne*. Everything in our nature favors axial perception. Central occult balance must therefore be construed as a type of design which is superimposed upon axial balance. Complicating a picture in this way increases the interest of the design, adding an extra string to the compositional bow. This same duality can be observed in architectural design such as that of the Pantheon, the Great Pyramid, and the Colosseum which can be appreciated in both axial and central fashion.

A noted use of this double principle in painting appears in Rubens' *Rape of the Daughters of Leucippus* (Fig. 216). The level horizon makes the design seem at first to be in axial balance of a highly occult sort. But the horizon is only a stabilizing element in a design which revolves around the center in a dynamic fashion, and with perfect appropriateness to the theme. Rubens' design is basically a diamond or swastika pattern within a squared rectangle. Moreover, the diamond is balanced on one of its points—a precarious equilibrium. Rubens, a shrewd composer, courted this tense equilibrium for the sake of heightened activity, and intensified it by multiplying the diagonal attitudes until they became a complex of balanced criss-cross forms.

Rubens' use of diagonal lines as substitutes for the curvilinear forms of Raphael possesses an outstanding merit. A dynamic effect is created when these lines pass through or near the center and use it as a fulcrum. Many paintings contain this kind of composition; Michelangelo's *Creation of Adam* (Fig. 126) is a celebrated instance, and Degas' *Dancers Practising at the Bar* (Fig. 247) is another. There is a marked circular movement in Botticelli's *Annunciation* (Fig. 263) and in Hokusai's *Great Wave* (Fig. 377) which has undoubtedly contributed to their fame.

Central occult balance is a concept with many possibilities and applications. In Giotto's *Death of St. Francis* (Fig. 133) it plays no part at all; in Raphael's *Madonna of the Chair* it is the dominant compositional pattern; in Rubens' *Rape of the Daughters of Leucippus* it is superimposed on an axial balance and contributes only partially to the design's total effectiveness. But whether playing a primary or secondary role it can add much to the vitality and interest of a composition. It is one of the most difficult types of design to handle well and yet one of the most valuable ever conceived. Though rarely found in fully developed form, its contribution has been widespread and conspicuous.

THE COORDINATION OF TWO– AND THREE–DIMENSIONAL DESIGNS

We tend, in analysis, to divorce the organization of two-dimensional surface and three-dimensional space. Painters must think of both, at least subconsciously; we miss some of their problems of design if we fail to combine the two.

A wide range of coordinative ability is expressed in works of art. Some pictures, like Mondrian's *Composition in White, Black, and Red* (Fig. 55), are exclusively two-dimensional. Others, like Cimabue's *Madonna Enthroned* (Fig. 244), imply only a shallow space; in them the coordination between picture plane and recession is of limited interest. But there are many other pictures whose surface and space are so varied and subtly coordinated as to add greatly to our enjoyment.

A classic example of sophisticated spatial coordination is Raphael's *Sistine Madonna* (Fig. 255). It is his most famous Madonna. It treats a subject which had been done to death by his predecessors; but he lifted it above the crowd and gave it new interest by his design. Throughout the Early Renaissance painters had treated recessional planes in sequence parallel to the picture plane. This applies equally to Giotto's *Death of Saint Francis* (Fig. 133) of 1325 and Perugino's *Christ Delivering the Keys of Heaven to St. Peter* (Fig. 102a) of about 1481, Mantegna's diagonal recessions being unusual for his time. Raphael wished to avoid this too-regular, if orderly, method of recession. He did so in the *Sistine Madonna* by the simple but effective variation of having the Virgin enter the scene as though she had walked upon it from the wings on stage left. The curtains even suggest a theatrical set. Mary's walking motion and billowing garment replace the old static poses with graceful action, adding an interest that was novel for the time. Her path has followed an arc, the pivotal point of which is established by St. Barbara's spiral posture as she ushers the Madonna upon the scene. St. Sixtus looks up at the Virgin in a gesture which balances St. Barbara's attitude. The feet of the three figures form an arc which echoes the path of the Virgin. Thus Raphael, by deceptively simple inventions, gave new interest to an old theme.

Raphael was only one of many sixteenth-century masters who, dissatisfied with the old symmetries and planear recessions, felt that a new and more dynamic type of recession was in order. By the seventeenth century his point of view had become typical of the Baroque. One artist who contributed to the change was Tintoretto. Younger than Raphael, he was not a pioneer of the new mode, but he had few superiors in the coordination of dynamic, asymmetrical two-dimensional and three-dimensional designs. The variety and power of his compositions virtually carried the day for the new manner.

Two of his most famous pictures, the *Miracle of St. Mark* (Fig. 256) and *Adam and Eve* (Fig. 257), both in the Academy of Venice, owe much of their appeal to his skill in coordination. The former illustrates an episode in the life of St. Mark, the patron saint of Venice; he saved the life of a Christian convert by shattering the

FIG. 255. Raphael. *Sistine Madonna. ca.* 1515. Royal Painting Gallery, Dresden.

FIG. 256. Tintoretto. *Miracle of St. Mark.* 1548. Academy, Venice.

FIG. 257. Tintoretto. *Adam and Eve.* 1550-1551. Academy, Venice.

478

hammer of his would-be executioner. A lover of the dramatic, Tintoretto depicts the Saint descending abruptly upon the crowd, some of whom have not yet seen him. It is in the grouping of the crowd that Tintoretto shows his capacity for coordinating the two- and three-dimensional designs. He has arranged the string of figures along the lines of a **W** and then repeated the same pattern in depth, a difficult but effective thing to do.

Tintoretto was able to match this performance repeatedly, varying his designs according to the subject. In the *Adam and Eve* he created a harmony of attitude between the two figures along a strong diagonal which extends from the upper left to the lower right corner. He carries our eyes into the distance along an equally marked diagonal path which progresses from the lower left to the upper right quadrants of the composition. Thus the two- and three- dimensional designs form a cross coordinated by their common diagonal character.

By coordinating surface and depth in an asymmetrical fashion Tintoretto and his fellow artists of the late Renaissance opened up a fertile field of design. Several centuries passed before artists had largely exploited the interest values of coordinated diagonal or meandering design. Our purpose here has not been to explore this vast field, but simply to indicate how much interest a skilful coordination of two- and three-dimensional designs can add to a picture's esthetic richness when designing in depth is exploited. A comparison of the Tintoretto *Adam and Eve* with Martini's handsome but shallow *Annunciation* (Fig. 101) should make this clear. An appreciation of this advantage attended the development of perspective projection. The possibilities were perceived during the late Renaissance and fully developed in the seventeenth century Baroque style.

The use of the double diagonal from left to right and back into space is typically but excellently illustrated by De Hooch's *Mother by a Cradle* (Fig. 98) of about 1660. An equally good example of the consistent use of meandering diagonals on the surface and in depth can be found in El Greco's *Agony in the Garden* (Fig. 90) of the same century, while Degas' *Dancer with a Bouquet* (Fig. 107) shows how artists, once shown the way, were able to compose in depth in the nineteenth century on a par with artists of any other time.

These examples refute the common belief that there is no improvement or progress in art, but only change. Insofar as each work of art is a unity in and by itself, this is true. But in the capacity to improve the coordination of two- and three-dimensional designs, it plainly is not so.

CHAPTER 16

Color Design

Color is the visual artist's second major esthetic resource. Properly organized, it can be esthetically as effective as spatial design, although in a different way. Static in character, color appeals strictly to visual sensations, though often with great intensity. Any sense of movement suggested by a design must be credited mainly to sequential spatial arrangements, with color allowed only a supporting role. Its effect upon the tactile and motor half of our appreciation is negligible.

Color appeals to us in another way which may be powerful and important or relatively secondary. Historically, there have been those who regarded it as a mere adjunct to line and form, agreeing with Ingres that line is the probity of art. Another Neo-classicist, David, considered color merely decorative, something applied superficially to the all-important forms of a composition. In their more moralistic and doctrinaire moments both artists condemned color for its sensuous softness or effeminate prettiness. By no stretch of the imagination can color be said to have the virile strength of mass or the crispness of line. Classical art has always tended toward that attitude, stressing drawing, modeling, and spatial composition over color and illumination.

Today such a qualitative separation seems like asking a great distance runner which of his two legs is more important to him. By the widespread use of color in photography, especially in the Technicolor motion picture, we have become aware of the impact of color over monochrome representation.

The most fervent classicists were, in practice, aware of color's contribution to beauty, and numbered among their ranks some of the finest colorists, such as Michelangelo and Raphael. The romantic and impressionist artists of history have been unabashed worshippers of color and illumination. Monet was interested predominantly in those elements. Most modern critics agree that, while color sensibilities vary, no artist, classicist or romantic, can be called a great painter unless he was competent in the field of color as well as that of spatial design.

Our joint reaction to color may be a sensuous one, but unless we appreciate color's compositional value, we miss its full appeal. Those who have felt the impact of Van Gogh's colors will not be unaware of their contribution to expression. In its ability to express vitality or establish the mood of a scene, as in John Sloan's *Wake of the Ferry* (Fig. 76), color is supreme. Our present task, however, is to consider the methods by which an artist can control and organize the colors of his design to express his sense of order. We shall emphasize painting because color has been most fully exploited in that medium.

Color design resembles spatial design in two important respects: a painter organizes his colors within a formula which includes both order and variety, and he applies the same principles of order to colors as he does to spatial design. But the terms of color are different. Every color is characterized by its hue, value, and intensity. Therefore, though color design may result in many different combinations of order and variety, it always involves the application of the principles of order to the three universal terms of color, as in the simple diagram here:

The Principles of Order   ⟶   *The Terms of Color*

Harmony	Hue
Sequence: gradation	Value
alternation	Intensity
Balance	

Here, as in spatial design, all of the principles of order may be in operation, but generally one or another of them will assert itself, making one picture an outstanding example of harmony, another of gradation or alternation, and a third of balance. Most critics agree that a color design may excel in one form of order without having to excel in all.

We must also remember a peculiarity of all design, and of color in particular: theory is one thing, practice is another. Compromises and adjustments must be made to adapt the ideal to the several objectives of painting because of specific representational requirements. The landscape painter, for example, is caught between the need to select a color scheme from nature's profuse and diverse colors and the need to keep his picture reasonably recognizable. He must, in find-

FIG. 258a. Turner. *Fighting Téméraire.* 1838. National Gallery, London.

FIG. 259a. Da Vinci. "Mona Lisa." *La Gioconda.* 1503-1506. Louvre, Paris.

FIG. 260. Rose window and canopy. Central portal. *ca.* 1507. Cathedral, Rouen.

FIG. 261. Matisse. *Girl in a Striped Dress.* *ca.* 1940. Collection of Mr. and Mrs. Alfred K. Stern, New York.

ing typical colors, discover a mean between truth and art. Only the completely nonrepresentational or abstract painter can utilize ideal color design without limitation or compromise.

HARMONY OF COLOR

Harmony, as stated in Chapter 16, denotes a general similarity of certain visual terms (such as harmony of attitude or measure) without implying exact agreement. Appreciation of it should therefore allow some variety. Applied to the terms of color the possibilities of harmony are similarity of hue, value, or intensity. The best way to understand these possibilities theoretically is to refer to charts based on the color circle and two triangles illustrated in Figs. 91a and 92a.

Harmony, like all other forms of order, depends upon a consistent limitation. Its particular method involves the emphasis of similarities and the suppression of differences within the range of possibilities, which means in color terms the range of choices in hues, values, and intensities.

Considered in order, the range of hues is indicated by the color circle or scale of hues in Fig. 258b. One way of narrowing differences in this field is to divide the circle into two groups of colors, with the family of "warm" hues on the left and the so-called "cool" hues on the right. A glance at the actual colors in Fig. 91a will show that the "warm" hues resemble each other in partaking of yellow and red in various degrees, with red-orange the "hottest" hue in the group and red-violet the least warm because it contains some blue. The "cool" hues are banded together by the common denominator of blue, with that color being the "coldest" of the group. A second glance will show that red-orange and blue are nearly opposite in the color circle; they are therefore extremely dissimilar or disharmonious.

Harmony of color will be given to a design by cultivating these similarities and avoiding the more obvious differences. Theoretically, harmony would ensue so long as an artist remains within the respective families. But yellow and red-violet, though both warm colors, are comparatively far removed from one another in the circle of hues and thus difficult to reconcile if harmony rather than contrast is the objective. Therefore, most artists will simplify their problem and insure harmony by narrowing their range of hues. Knowing that neighboring or analogous hues are the most harmonious or similar, they limit themselves to three or four of these and build their designs around them. This use of only a pie-shaped segment of all the possibilities in the full scale of hues is indicated by Fig. 258c.

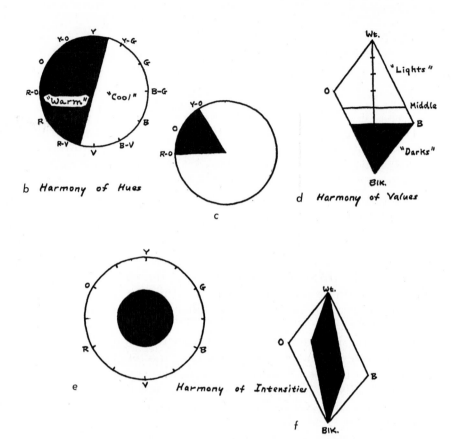

b *Harmony of Hues*

c

d *Harmony of Values*

e

Harmony of Intensities

f

FIG. 258b–f. Diagrammatic illustrations of color design.

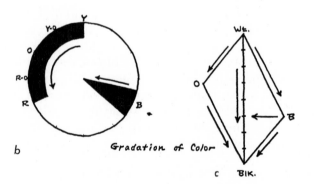

b

Gradation of Color

c

FIG. 259b–c. Diagrammatic illustrations of gradations of hues and values.

484

Any other sector of hues from either the "warm" or "cool" side of the color circle would be as effective; the crucial factor is a limitation to closely associated "warm" or "cool" hues. On the other hand, the use of three or four of these endows the design with variety. Nature has given us a perfect example of harmony in the chameleon, which can blend into its surroundings to the point of invisibility; other examples are to be found in the protective coloration of innumerable animals, birds, and insects.

A few examples will illustrate how limitation for the sake of harmony works out in the practice of painting. An obvious instance is the art of Rembrandt, which is known for its predominance of golden tones. The *Portrait of Nicholas Bruyningh* (Fig. 135), for example, is characterized by a general similarity of tones, the harmony deriving from an emphasis of the warm family and of the yellow and brown neighbors in particular. The *Bruyningh* portrait illustrates in practice what Fig. 258c points to in theory. Burchfield's *November Evening* (Fig. 27), a quite different picture in other respects, illustrates equally well what may be called a harmony of analogous "warm" hues.

The two principal possibilities of a harmony of hues lie in a general emphasis of "warm" or "cool" hues. Three noted pictures which exemplify the latter are Whistler's *Nocturne, Blue and Silver* (Fig. 139), El Greco's celebrated *View of Toledo* (Fig. 367), which is as cold in tonality as the *Bruyningh* is warm, and Van Gogh's *Mountainous Landscape* (Fig. 65), a picture in which blues and greens predominate. Whistler, an advocate of art for art's sake, revealed his conscious interest in color harmonies by giving his pictures such titles as *Nocturne, Blue and Silver* and *Symphony in White*. Similarly, Van Gogh filled many letters with references to his striving for particular color harmonies. He undoubtedly thought in terms of limited palettes that deliberately aimed at a harmony of hues.

Many other artists have theorized about the nature of color design. Homer studied a book on color by a physicist, Chevreul, until it was dog-eared. Seurat attempted to reduce his own ideas on color to a formula which would turn every Frenchman into an enthusiastic "Sunday painter." This knowledge helped them, as it does the critic, up to a point. But it is not in the long run a substitute for an instinctive color sense. No amount of reading Chevreul will turn an ordinary artist into a master of color. Conscious color organization is an interesting proof of artistic thinking, but secondary to the results obtained by painters like El Greco, Homer, and Seurat.

Whether consciously arrived at or not, the color harmonies which artists tend to favor over a period of time become important hallmarks of their personal styles. Rembrandt's predilection for warm hues has been mentioned as an outstanding case. Another example is Daumier, who used warm hues frequently and to great effect in his masterpiece *The Uprising* (Fig. 316). Hogarth's warm-toned *Shrimp Girl* (Fig. 301) and Eakins' brown and gold *Between Rounds* (Fig. 78) are as typically characteristic as Corot's cool silvery green landscapes.

The term "general similarity" has been used to avoid any implication that an artist like Rembrandt would limit himself to the segment of hues contained in Fig. 258c. A great colorist will rarely be that obvious. He will usually introduce contrasting hues—greens, blues, or violets—into his yellow-orange harmony with the deliberate intention of giving it variety. So long as these contrasting hues are kept unobtrusive (i.e., low in intensity), they will not disrupt the harmony but enhance it. Often these variations are nearly invisible except on close inspection, though they contribute importantly to our subconscious esthetic appreciation.

A sharp accent is permissible within a harmony so long as it is kept only an accent. Both Corot and Winslow Homer were fond of introducing a small but brilliant touch of vermillion into a harmony of silvery green hues. As a result, they achieved a predominance of order with enough variety to avoid monotony. In so doing they were thinking essentially as artists have thought for centuries. The need for some degree of variety within a general order pertains to harmonies of all sorts, but the principle which underlies most outstanding color designs can be appropriately mentioned here. Painters who clearly aim at a harmony of one term, such as hue, have insured variety in their pictures by employing a spread of one of the other terms. For example, Rembrandt's *Portrait of Nicholas Bruyningh*, while containing a twofold harmony of "warm" hues and low intensities, is characterized by a wide range of values from high lights to low darks.

It does not matter which terms of color an artist harmonizes, so long as he employs variety in one of the remaining terms. Value is elected to provide variety in the majority of paintings because of its connection with light and shadow and modeling, in both of which some range of attributes is necessary. A favorite color scheme used by Winslow Homer, to mention one example, contains a harmony of low intensity colors (often with "cool" colors in the majority) in company with a wide range of values, the ancient formula of variety within order being thus respected. His *Schooners in the Moonlight, Saco Bay* (Fig. 20) is one instance, his *Fog Warning* (Fig. 61) another.

HARMONY OF VALUES

The scope of possibilities contained in the value scale ranges from white to black. Theoretically, therefore, a harmony of values would be characterized by a limitation to one segment of the value scale, such as white, high-light, light, and low-light; or high-dark, dark, and low-dark. Middle occupies a neutral position, ready to join either group. For simplicity these two subdivisions of the scale can be referred to as a harmony of light values (or "lights") and a harmony of dark values (or "darks"), as indicated in Fig. 258d. Any or all of the colors in the scale of hues could be so arranged, as well as the orange and blue suggested in Fig. 258d. Indeed, a harmony of "lights" could contain every hue in the rainbow as long as the predominating values were kept above the level of middle. This process is well demonstrated by the work of Monet.

The theory of harmonies of values would thus seem to be simple. We have, however, suggested why artists prefer to use a wide rather than a narrow, or harmonious, range of values in actual practice. They need differences in value to describe forms in space. In the sculpturesque mode this is attained by modeling; in the mode of line and local color by differences in values among adjoining areas, as in the mosaic of *Justinian and Courtiers* (Fig. 121). Neither type of representation would be possible in a completely dark or light picture. The same optical requirement arouses an instinctive distaste for wholly dark or light pictures, causing us to describe them as either gloomy or "washed out." Their chief effect upon us is one of excessive vagueness, of the infinite carried too far.

A few pictures actually illustrate these two extremes. One thinks especially of Whistler's nocturnes, the *Lagoon, Venice* in Fig. 139 and the *Thames at Battersea* (Fig. 154), and of Turner's late watercolors which are often symphonic arrangements of pale yellow and blue washes. In both types forms are almost indistinguishable, in the one because of enshrouding shadow, in the other because of blinding light. They are bound to be exceptional in the normal course of representational painting.

If, on the other hand, a harmony of values is conceived in terms of predominantly but not exclusively dark or light pictures, its application can be greatly extended. Titian's *Christ Crowned with Thorns* (Fig. 130), Caravaggio's *Death of the Virgin* (Fig. 134), and Rembrandt's *Nicholas Bruyningh* (Fig. 135) are all harmonies of dark values. Other pictures, such as Raphael's *School of Athens* (Fig. 104), are predominantly light. After allowance has been made for modeling, 90 per cent of the picture remains in the upper range of values. Thus, if modeling and high lights are excepted, many pictures are harmonies of either light or dark values.

In an effort to enrich their colors, Titian and Tintoretto tended to use quite dark values in the paintings of their final periods. Caravaggio and his followers carried this tendency so far as to earn the name "tenebrists" (painters of shadows). And Rembrandt, like many post-Renaissance painters, pushed the trend still further. El Greco's darkly somber *View of Toledo* (Fig. 367) and Goya's grisly nighttime scene, the *Execution of the Madrileños* (Fig. 136), show this common style of treatment. As a consequence of this wide-spread emphasis upon darker and richer colors, we generally think of the seventeenth and eighteenth centuries as a period of dark pictures.

Owing partly to the white plaster bases of the Renaissance tempera and fresco media, and partly to general outlook, the paintings of the fifteenth century are light in character. So, too, is the extensive body of painting which grew out of Impressionism in the latter half of the nineteenth century. Unlike the "tenebrists," the Impressionists aimed at filling their pictures with light. Indeed "luminism" might better describe their stylistic aims than Impressionism. Monet and his associates favored colors high in both intensity and value, causing critics to speak of their palettes as being in a "high key." The part played by high-key and low-key palettes has been an important if not a major role in the history of art.

HARMONY OF INTENSITIES

Harmony of intensities is one of the most frequently used and effective forms of order in the repertory of color design. It exploits to the full the capacity of colors to create a brilliant and stimulating effect, as in a parade with its gaudy flags and banners. Rare is the person who has never responded to the gaiety of a carnival.

Weak, or low intensity, colors serve an almost opposite purpose. They avoid two dangers inherent in harmonies of high intensities: obviousness and garishness. The combination of these two qualities makes for a high attentional value, and is suited to a poster or circus banner. This "punch" or impact may also be the ruin of interest, however, causing us to tire of potency as quickly as we are attracted by it, as we do popular but short-lived jazz records. Hence strong colors are often described as loud. Whether the loudness is due to sound or color, it is a fault to be avoided. High intensity colors must therefore be carefully handled if their merits are to be exploited and their dangers avoided.

Low intensity colors are not without faults. They may suffer from weakness, or feeble vitality—a kind of tonal anemia. Too muted or suppressed, they may hold interest if they catch it, but their attentional value is low. On the other hand, they have the advantage of inherent subtlety. Being far removed from any possibility of loudness or garishness, they are in little danger of tiring us. The excellent record of low intensity harmony indicates that these pitfalls can be avoided and good qualities exploited. Many of the world's most cherished works of art are based on harmony of low intensities. The theory underlying these and other harmonies of intensity is illustrated diagrammatically by Figs. 258e and 258f.

The principle involves only a choice between high and low intensities. In Fig. 258e high intensities are illustrated by the outside of the color circle, where all hues are at maximum brilliance; low intensities are contained in the inner ring of the circle, adjacent to the middle value neutral center. An artist achieves harmony of intensities by drawing his hues primarily from either of these circles. At the same time he can avail himself of a wide range of hues and values, for the differences between yellow, violet, and the intermediate hues are nearly as great as the value scale itself. Commonly, however, an artist with a tasteful sense of color will recognize that taking full advantage of the value range offered by the outer circle would lead to confusion. He will limit at least one of the terms, contenting himself with a variety of hues and some harmony of values, or with a spread of values and a limitation of hues—in short, with a dual harmony and a single variation. Because of the strong colors and wide range of values and hues in the outer circle, limitation is more advisable there than in the inner circle.

Fig. 258f illustrates the other common approach to the harmonizing of intensities. High intensities fall along the outer edges of the triangles and low intensities in the inner area, next to the neutral value scale. Maximum intensities are found at the apexes marked by O and B, respectively, or low-light and high-dark, the normal saturation points of orange and blue. Intensities decrease or increase according to their proximity to these summits, but generally speaking the outer scales are relatively high in intensity, while those nearest the neutral value scale are naturally weaker.

Fig. 258f contains only two complementary hues (any pair or single hue can be substituted), in contrast to the wide range of hues in Fig. 258e. This limitation guarantees some harmony of hues if analogous hues are used, and balance if complementary hues are selected, as in the diagram. At the same time the vertical range, which embraces the full value scale, insures a wide variety of values. If, therefore, a painter desires to retain the subtlety of a harmony of low intensity hues, he can avoid a feeble effect by emphasizing a spread of values. He would limit himself to the colors within the black area of Fig. 258f, or even to the "warm" or "cool" half of that area. This rather involved theory of organization has been described in some detail because it is the principle underlying a large portion of the world's most satisfying pictures. Probably more fine pictures exemplify the method implied by the simple diagram in Fig. 258f than any other.

A survey of the art of painting will show that a large number of pictures that we call fine, subtle, beautiful, or refined are painted in a harmony of low intensities. Instinctively, sensitive artists have known that a little strong color goes a long way, and that human reactions favor a temperate use of color strength. This does not mean that soft colors necessarily make weak pictures, for two compensating sources of strength are always available—the vitality inherent in light and the special vigor that comes from contrasts of value. Through these, artists have had at their disposal the possibility of combining refinement and strength.

The harmonies of low intensities illustrated in this book alone are numerous. Among them is one of the most famous paintings in Western art, Leonardo da Vinci's "Mona Lisa" (Fig. 259a). Its color design is based upon a harmony of low intensities and a limitation to two contrasting hues, a warm yellow-orange and a cool bluish-green. Strength of color is insured by the wide range of values, yet the subdued effect created by the low intensities is outstanding and has a marked bearing on the picture's reputation for subtlety and refinement. The quietly posed figure speaks to us in a very gentle voice. Rembrandt's *Nicholas Bruyningh* (Fig. 135), another masterpiece of psychological interpretation, is a further example of effective use of low-intensity colors. In it a dual effect is created by the alert and active pose and a strong value contrast. This is combined with a harmony of low intensity and warm colors—a contrast of terms which gives the picture unusual vitality.

A harmony of low intensities is used in conjunction with a warm palette in Burchfield's *November Evening* (Fig. 27) to give that painting its rich but somber air, whereas a marked value contrast in Homer's cool, low intensity *Schooners in Moonlight* (Fig. 20) endows it with the harmonious but exciting beauty of moonlight sparkling on water. Another use of low intensities can be found in Ruysdael's *Wheatfields* (Fig. 116), a vastly spacious but somber picture because of its muted and predominantly dark colors. Winslow Homer used low intensity colors and contrasting values repeatedly to capture the same brooding quality of the north woods in his Adirondacks and

Canadian watercolor landscapes. Raphael, by contrast, combined low intensities with high values to create a relatively cheerful intellectual atmosphere for the philosophers in his *School of Athens* (Fig. 104), demonstrating the versatility of this method.

The prevalence of low intensity harmonies in the history of color design points to a fundamental psychological basis for conservatism in color. Artists held to this conservatism a long time, preferring to gain the effect of vivid coloration by other means. Titian, though noted as a master of rich colors, such as "Titian red," rarely painted any hue stronger than half intensity; he made his colors appear brilliant by a skilful manipulation of value and intensity contrasts. This method gains vividness and richness without the risk of garishness. It is a method well known to colorists. Many brilliantly colored paintings owe their effectiveness to the vitality inherent in luminosity. Van Gogh, a painter who has been erroneously accused of painting directly from his tubes, was too skilful a colorist to pull out all the stops in so obvious a manner. Although using more intense colors than Titian, he too placed more reliance upon luminosity and color contrasts than upon intensity alone. Harmonious color design, as both artists knew, is less a matter of strength than of relationships. Those rare examples of successful high intensity harmony occupy a special place in artistic favor. This is notably true of the brilliant and beloved medieval stained glass windows.

Viewed comprehensively, there are several outstanding groups of painters. The medieval artists, who used color with more regard for symbolic and psychological effect than representational truths, were often uninhibited colorists. The designers of Byzantine mosaics, such as *Justinian and Courtiers* (Fig. 121), manuscript illuminations like the Austrian *Madonna Enthroned* in Fig. 49, miniatures, altarpieces, and stained glass windows like those in Figs. 190 and 260 delighted in using brilliant color. Medieval tradition persisted into the Renaissance, and many painters of the fifteenth century also employed color harmonies that are more brilliant than truthful, Fra Angelico (the *Madonna of Humility,* Fig. 191) among them. The rise of realism had a subduing effect upon color intensities, so that only uninhibited geniuses like Rubens used high intensity colors boldly in the post-Renaissance period. Romanticists like Delacroix and Impressionists like Monet had to wage an artistic war to restore brilliant colors to the painter's palette. The Impressionists as a group became notorious and were ultimately cherished for their devotion to high-key color schemes. Thanks to them a new freedom of color design was attained and the old dark browns and olive greens were made to seem drab and dull. There were, of course, exceptions among their predecessors, notably Rubens and Turner; but a great debt is owed to the Impressionist and such of their sympathizers as Lautrec and Renoir for revitalizing the field of color harmony. Owing to their staunch efforts the post-Impressionists and Modernists have been able to create high intensity harmonies without any apologies.

This form of organization has been prominent in the work of the foremost modern masters. Specific examples of pictures which are brilliant in color are Cézanne's *House in Provence* (Fig. 80), Van Gogh's *Sunset over a Plowed Field* (Fig. 140), Gauguin's *Mahana No Atua* (Fig. 141), Seurat's *Sunday on the Island of La Grande Jatte* (Fig. 226), Rouault's *Old King* (Fig. 227), and Matisse's *Girl in a Striped Dress* (Fig. 261). These paintings almost summarize the chief methods of employing high intensity colors. One type is illustrated by Cézanne's *House in Provence* and Van Gogh's *Sunset over a Plowed Field;* in them a harmony of high intensity colors is used in conjunction with a harmony of high values, producing a high-keyed, luminous effect. Another popular type is illustrated by Matisse's *Girl in a Striped Dress;* in it there is a wide spread of values among the high intensity colors. Moreover, dark and light values are sharply contrasted, creating a shock effect in which balance is more to the point than harmony. A large number of modern paintings in which vitality seems to be a major aim must be interpreted in this way. But the important point in both cases is that value and intensity relationships are so interrelated that they must always be considered together.

The general stepping-up of color intensities in modern painting has been paralleled by a comparable trend in architecture. Seldom has color been used so freely, vividly, and enthusiastically as an adjunct of form. An increasing emphasis upon lightness of values has aided and intensified the effect of increased illumination from larger windows. Openness and lightness have been twin keynotes in the psychology of modern architecture, compared to which Victorian thinking was cautious and staid. The French rococo builders, with their love of pastel shades, approached the modern outlook, but not even they equalled modern design in the introduction of strong colors into the conservative field of architecture. Kitchens and bathrooms, formerly hospital-white and coldly utilitarian, are now frequently warm and glowing, while monotonous institutional grays and creams are fighting a losing battle in offices and schools. Few past architectural periods have been more color conscious. Vividness as well as lightness of color has become a hallmark of modern architecture, bringing to Western building a colorfulness hitherto confined to the medieval styles of the Byzantine and Gothic designers, and the Persians, Indians, and Japanese in Asia.

The Oriental group suggests a further aspect of the history of color design. Color can be organized with three different purposes in mind: representational, symbolic, and esthetic. Though interrelated, these aims are subject to different degrees of emphasis. Color has most often been subordinate to representational purposes in the West, especially during the post-Renaissance reign of realism. This suppressed color intensities through increased introduction of shadows and atmospheric effects. The Asiatic and medieval artists, to whom representation was usually secondary to symbolic, esthetic, and expressive purposes, handled color much more arbitrarily and freely. The result was a widespread display of man's natural love of bright and intense colors—natural, that is, if we judge by the uninhibited preferences of youthful or primitive painters. The collective societies of the Middle Ages and the East, with their greater emphasis upon symbolism, also used high intensities unreservedly whenever these suited their purposes. Persian miniature paintings are famous for their brilliant colors, while many of the later Japanese prints, like Hokusai's *Fujiyama in Clear Weather* (Fig. 265), are excellent examples of high intensity harmonies.

When the modernists departed to some extent from the post–Renaissance European tradition, part of their break took the form of a new direction in color. They turned for inspiration and revitalization to the art of peoples who were not inhibited by realistic doctrines —to the art of children, primitives, the Middle Ages, and the Orient. The similarity between the high intensity color harmonies of Van Gogh and Japanese prints, between Gauguin and primitive art, Rouault and medieval stained glass windows, and Matisse and Persian miniature paintings will come as no surprise.

Looking at Persian miniatures and similar brilliantly colored pictures, Sir Charles Holmes arrived at a principle of some importance a few years ago. There is, he observed, a connection between size and our toleration of color intensities. The Persian miniatures, for example, are as small as they are vividly colored, and the larger medieval stained glass windows present strong colors to us only in minute fragments. The same rule was followed by Fra Angelico when he painted altarpieces, like the *Madonna of Humility* (Fig. 191). Everywhere sensitive colorists have recognized that the danger of garishness increases geometrically with the enlargement of areas. They have kept high intensity harmonies small, or subdivided them into tiny areas. When called upon to paint frescoes on a large scale they have employed harmonies of much lower intensity. Fra Angelico did so when he painted his *Annunciation* (Fig. 46) in San Marco; Michelangelo followed suit in the decorations for the Sistine ceiling (Fig. 126); and Picasso reduced the intensities of his huge *Guernica* (Fig. 1) virtually to zero. Rubens proved his genius by painting large, violently active, and intensely colored pictures which are vibrant and alive without being loud. But few can match his energy or organizing ability. By and large, the high intensity harmonies found in the world of art are in pictures of small or medium size.

The technical terms of color harmony can be translated into a simple and practical appreciative system. All color harmonies depend upon an accord within a context, a process that can be described as a "pulling together." If any passage in a picture "jumps out" of its context and attracts special attention to itself, harmony will be disrupted and some other kind of order (such as balance) must be sought.

SEQUENCE: GRADATION OF COLOR

A sequence of gradation in color, as in spatial design, is characterized by a steady, progressive change. The major possibilities are uniform change in hue, value, or intensity. This may be through a sequence of neighboring hues, from light to dark values, or from high intensity to low intensity color strength respectively.

The theory of gradation of hue is illustrated diagrammatically by Fig. 259b. The circular arrow indicates a progression from yellow to red through the intermediate hues of yellow-orange, orange, and red-orange by graduated stages. Comparable changes are frequently met in the sunsets and rainbows of nature and in the physicist's spectrum.

Gradations of value are basic in the value scale, which extends from white to black in graded steps, and in any color chart which is related to it, as in Fig. 259c. As the eye follows any of the arrows it must assume that regular changes are implied.

Gradations of intensity are suggested by both Figs. 259b and 259c. In Fig. 259b gradation is illustrated by the arrow which points from the blue hue on the outer, full intensity rim of the color circle inward toward the low intensity inner ring and neutral center. In Fig. 259c it is indicated by the arrow from the full intensity blue at the apex, marked *B*, to the neutral value scale. As the eye moves from one part of these diagrams to another, changes occur in a regular fashion.

These possibilities are extended by the fact that double changes occur in most progressions and triple in many. For example, the sequence of hues from yellow to red involves not only a change of hues but of values (from high-light to high-dark); only the intensity remains constant or high. There is also a double change along most of the arrows in Fig. 259c. The arrow pointing from *O* down to *Black* traces a dual gradation in values and intensities; the color becomes both darker and duller. The horizontal arrow from *B* to the value scale diagrams a singular change—a gradation of intensities in which the blue hue and high-dark value remain constant. Gradations of all three terms are common in painting.

These are the theories which underlie gradations of colors in actual works of art. Because of representational requirements, they are subject to compromises and adjustments as in the field of color design at large. Their most notable contribution has been in the realm of beauty. Owing to the slow, steady change inherent in gradations of all sorts, they have a pleasant effect upon the human psyche, and have a high esthetic value. A picture which owes much of its fame for beauty and representational subtlety to gradations is Da Vinci's "Mona Lisa" (Fig. 259a). The modeling of the hands is noteworthy, and the enigmatical smile which plays around the eyes and mouth is unexcelled. Both were achieved by a superb control over minute gradations of colors. Individually imperceptible, so gradual is their change, they create an effect of infinite softness in the picture as a whole.

Few artists have possessed the manual steadiness and visual sensitivity that created the "Mona Lisa," but those who have approached Da Vinci's control have created superlative works of art. Vermeer, usually cited as a master realist, also had a highly developed sense of beauty. Thanks to a command of gradations, his *Cook* (Fig. 93) can be enjoyed for both its realistic accuracy and its esthetic order. Vermeer showed his true skill in the darker passages of his pictures, where distinctions of form and gradations are hard to control; his mastery there is enough to delight any painter.

The examples of Vermeer and Velasquez demonstrate how realism that rises to a high esthetic level generally does so through skilled use of gradations. Realism which is not pleasing in spite of its truthfulness is usually marked by crude gradations. This is noticeably true of the work of Bonheur and Meissonier, the nineteenth-century literalists, and the paintings of Vermeer's imitators. Their pictures will not stand comparison with his; the qualitative differences can be accounted for in no small measure by technical inferiority in the management of this difficult form of order—gradations of color.

Gradations are difficult to handle and are highly prized because they denote an important artistic quality—personal sensitivity. Theirs is not the shock effect exemplified by the more blatant, commonplace types of poster or advertising. Rather, it depends upon the rarer virtues of poise, restraint, or natural repose expressed through artistic control. Thus Caravaggio, for all his impact, was a heavy-handed artist compared to Da Vinci, as he was also a coarser man. The difference is concretely observable in his *Death of the Virgin* (Fig. 134). Although his picture is not without merits, his sense of beauty, when judged by his harsh gradations, is not in a class with Leonardo's.

There is a close connection between the modes of representation and design. Design is their saving grace, because works of art cannot stand on representational interest alone. Additional esthetic values which derive from pleasure-giving orderliness are essential to their survival. Each of the modes of representation that we have studied exemplified one or more forms of spatial and color design at the same time that it was depicting reality. Gradation of color, for example, is crucial in all modes of representation which employ the modeling of forms in sculpturesque fashion or in a crosslight. It serves both representation and design in the sculpturesque, the realistic, and in the post–Renaissance pictorial modes of painting. Typical examples are Lippi's fifteenth-century *Portrait of a Man* (Fig. 125), Vermeer's seventeenth-century *Cook* (Fig. 93), and Rembrandt's *Nicholas Bruyningh* (Fig. 135). All three illustrate the theory of modeling from light to dark contained in Fig. 259c. Gradation contributes in them a feeling of massiveness, truthfulness, and psychological vitality respectively. Rembrandt's art, like Leonardo's, depended heavily on a mastery of nuances of modeling and illumination, meaning, in practical terms, a supersensitive control over gradations.

Gradation has also provided an orderly basis for the modes in which a representation of distance was important. This was achieved in all pictures based on perspective and aerial projection by a combination of converging lines, diminution of scale, and a progressive reduction of intensities toward a middle value bluish-gray. Gradation of color thus played a central role in spatial representation.

The wedge-shaped area in Fig. 259b illustrates the theory underlying all representation of distance through color design, the arrow indicating the direction the color changes take as forms recede into the distance. Among works of art a good illustration of this principle is Monet's *Marée Montante à Pourville* (Fig. 137). Here a progression of colors from high intensities in the foreground to low intensities in the background simultaneously creates a sense of space, atmosphere, and orderliness. It offers precisely the esthetic values which make a realistic or impressionistic painter like Vermeer or Monet an artist instead of an optical machine. Design makes the difference between art and a mere record of visual appearance.

Gradation of colors characterized most of European painting in one way or another from the onset of the Renaissance (Giotto's powerful tactile sense was expressed through it) through the impressionist period of the nineteenth century, spanning both the tactile and visual reactions to reality recorded in that impressive body of pictures. In Matisse's relatively flat paintings, like the *Girl in a Striped Dress*, and in other modern art which reverted to the mode of line and local color, gradation plays a lesser descriptive part, yet Cézanne, Gauguin, Seurat, Picasso and other moderns clung staunchly to it; hence it has continued to be a living factor in design.

Two types of gradation appeared in this historical period whose chronology is of some significance. Between the time of Giotto and the middle fifteenth century it was common to model figures in what Pope called the early Renaissance gradation. It is illustrated by Fra Angelico's *Madonna of Humility* and is characterized by a modeling from pale high lights to full intensity areas in what would normally be the shadows. The effect resembles that obtained by modeling with white and pure color without any use of black. The two upper arrows in Fig. 259c diagram the theory of this system. Its visual merit is in the preservation of the color scheme in the upper values and high intensity range, making it brilliant and light. It accounts for much of the cheery, luminous, and colorful aspect of Fra Angelico's panel paintings.

Fra Angelico and some of his contemporaries also modeled forms by employing gradations of hues, progressing from yellow in the high lights down to red-orange or blue-green in the so-called shadows, as implied by Fig. 259b. The rainbow character of this system preserved the gay colors which they loved and yet suggested the sculpturesque modeling that was then coming into favor. This lyrical, essentially medieval type of painting was arbitrary—a far cry from the realistic painting of the following centuries. In most respects it was backward-looking or transitional and more medieval than modern. But only a pedestrian realist lacking in color sense will fail to see its merits and derive some joy from it.

The late Renaissance and post-Renaissance system of modeling by gradations of colors contrasts diametrically with the late medieval and early Renaissance type. When realism began to supplant arbitrary symbolical, expressive, and esthetic emphases, natural shadow as well as illumination entered the pictorial arts. Modeling was thenceforth achieved by grading from high intensity high lights to low intensity shadows along the paths marked by the lower arrows

in Fig. 259c. The result was a general darkening of pictures throughout the time extending from Titian's somber *Christ Crowned with
Thorns* (Fig. 130) to Whistler's *Nocturne* in Fig. 139. While there
was undoubtedly a gain in realism, the darkness of such pictures eventually induced a reaction. Today both painters and critics view the
arbitrary, shadowless systems of the prerealistic painters with renewed
appreciation, recognizing that medieval arbitrariness had the merit of
creating some of the most joyous color gradations we have ever had.
Historically the post-Renaissance period of European painting was
characterized by a special type of realistically oriented gradation of
color, and the remainder of art history by another. In view of the
prominence of the old master tradition in our eyes, it is well for us to
see that it actually represents a minority expression in any global
perspective of art.

Since gradations of color are naturally apparent in painting, we
are apt to overlook their importance in sculpture and architecture.
The nonartist usually considers color only in its limited aspect of hue.
Blacks, whites, and grays (the neutrals) cannot be dismissed from the
world of color. In the fields of sculpture and architecture, it is with
these neutral values that we are primarily concerned. The value
gradations of these neutral colors deriving from the play of light and
shadow is crucial in the effects of three-dimensional mass conveyed by
the glyptic masters. Though the sculptor and architect cannot control effects of light and shadow precisely, each can anticipate them.
In fact, they cannot function without them.

No great perception is needed to see how gradations of value are
anticipated and exploited in the geometrically based sculptural and
architectural masses of the glyptic and geometric modes. Within
them gradations of value are exploited especially by the creation of
spherical, conical, and cylindrical shapes. In any cross or side lighting these will automatically create a gradation of values. Hence this
principle of order is one which the sculptor and architect must always
have in mind.

A few examples from each medium will illustrate these points.
Laurana's *Princess of the House of Aragon* (Fig. 158), Brancusi's
Mademoiselle Pogany (Fig. 159), *Menkure and His Queen* (Fig. 160),
the late Egyptian *Head of a Priest* (Fig. 163), and Hans Arp's *Configurations* (Fig. 229) are all examples of smooth, round sculptural
forms which we read as gradations of values. Their wide separation
in time indicates the ageless universality of this principle, and Arp's
Configurations shows its application to abstract sculpture.

Bernini's *Apollo and Daphne* (Fig. 167) is considered a beautiful
work of art, despite certain representational faults; much of that

beauty stems from a rippling, undulating treatment of surfaces which creates a soft, mellow, and varied gradation of lights and shadows. Bernini's Italian sense of beauty thus transformed his most realistic intentions.

Greek sculpture is similarly marked by an attention to both truth and beauty, making the two, in their case, almost synonymous. Technically speaking, they were able to carve sculptural surfaces so that they presented a gradation of values that is pleasing to the eye. And sculptors everywhere who have succeeded in pleasing the eye have done so repeatedly by applying the principle of gradation. The Greeks' sense of beauty stood them in good stead in their architecture. There, too, a gradation of values was a central means. The column which they used conspicuously is a round form which turns light and shadow into a gradation of values. Admiring this effect, the Greeks repeated and emphasized it through the creation of colonnades.

Since the creation of gradations of values by round forms is a universal phenomenon, this principle of order abounds in architecture. Other instances where it was invited into the design are the Colosseum (Fig. 207), the Malwiyah Minaret (Fig. 234), a notable example, and the Pantheon at Rome (Fig. 176). The Pantheon, which combines columns with a cylindrical rotunda and hemispherical dome, is virtually a definitive illustration of this kind of gradation.

Gradations of value abound in the abstract arts wherever round forms are found. The makers of Chinese ceramics like those found in Figs. 187, 221, and 238 rang the changes on this method in older times, and abstract sculptors like Arp and Muir (Fig. 186) have done the same in modern times. The common element in their efforts was a love of round forms, which leads one to believe that in the three-dimensional arts generally a spatial harmony of curvilinear shapes goes hand in hand with a gradation of colors. United, they aid and enhance each other.

Gradations of color are found in all architecture and in most sculpture. They play their smallest role in linear sculpture and in its pictorial counterpart, the mode of line and local color painting. However, Pope has pointed out that the tones in the finer types of line and local color painting are seldom perfectly flat. They customarily contain gradations of color within the separate areas. These gradations are carefully limited, but they are none the less esthetically effective. This is true of scores of Chinese masterpieces on silk which were painted, like Western watercolors, in a wet and fluid medium. The washes in these are among the most subtle, restrained, and sophisticated examples of gradation in all art.

The acme of exploitation of color gradations in Western art was

reached in the post-Renaissance period of painting. During that
time painters came to control gradations with extraordinary competence, while the outstanding men handled them superbly. What
was exceptional in Giotto's time became a stylistic characteristic of
post-Renaissance painting in general. Three factors lay behind this
improvement. One was the adoption in the sixteenth century of two
media, oil and watercolor, which are perfectly suited to and encourage the blending and grading of colors. Then the accumulation
of practice in these media reached widespread and high levels in the
nineteenth century. Finally, the combination of these two facts
with the trends toward more realistic, pictorial, and impressionist
painting in this historical period was reflected in gradations of colors.
They are inseparable from the interests in the representation of
three-dimensional form, atmosphere, illumination, and distance,
which characterize all of these aims.

Numerous artists combined these several facets of the time in pictures of great beauty. Renoir used gradations of color with infinite
invention and skill, as can easily be seen in his *Dance at the Moulin
de la Galette* (Fig. 41) and *Nude in a Brook* (Fig. 43). Another
definitive example is Turner's *Fighting Téméraire* (Fig. 258a). In
this picture Turner synthesized the trends of three previous centuries
and anticipated many of those in the impressionist period that ensued. His attitude made him the archetype of the painters of infinity. What is pertinent here is the part played by a gradation of
colors throughout the canvas in realizing the major esthetic and
representational aims of the post-Renaissance period. Turner has
exploited gradation to the full, creating gradations of hues, values,
and intensities which, although less subtle than Leonardo's, still
define the possibilities. Much of the fame of this picture depends,
therefore, on the handling of this particular kind of organization.

SEQUENCE: ALTERNATION OF COLOR

Alternation, like gradation, is a sequential form of order, but
artistically quite dissimilar. Involving an abrupt rather than a progressive change, it is used for different and often nearly opposite
purposes.

The theory of alternation is simple. Applied to color design, it
employs a repeated shift of hues, values, or intensities, or of all three
terms. Since the effect sought is one of continuous contrast, these
terms are usually selected from opposite poles of their respective
scales. Typical examples would be an alternation of complementary
hues, such as red and green, or blue and orange, black and white val-

ues, and brilliant and dull intensities. The degree of contrast desired can be controlled by exploiting these contrasts or by choosing more closely related parts of each scale. One can be either potent or subtle, though the purpose of using alternation is normally to achieve a strong effect. Theoretically, the fullest possible contrasts of hue, value, and intensity would attain that end.

Alternations of color normally possess a high attentional value and are used with that quality in mind. On the other hand, they verge on the obvious and are always in danger of being low in interest-holding value. The designer must steer a course between these merits and limitations. A fabric which we call loud is generally an overdone example of the plaid or similar design. The best example of alternation is what we ordinarily call stripes, and the most blatant examples of these are the convict's clothes or the ubiquitous awning. Though high in attentional value, they are hardly subtle.

The difference in esthetic effects created by gradations and alternations is well illustrated by the contrast between Leonardo da Vinci's "Mona Lisa" (Fig. 259a), an unsurpassed example of gradation, and Henri Matisse's *Girl in a Striped Dress* (Fig. 261), a striking example of alternation. The *Mona Lisa* is a profound-looking woman painted with great refinement; Matisse's *Girl in a Striped Dress* is empty-faced but visually gay and stimulating. This is no disparagement of Matisse; he was a shrewd composer who knew precisely what he was doing. His humanistic interests were moderate, but his control over design was exact. Although he possessed an extensive knowledge of the world's art—he copied the old masters in the Louvre for ten years and visited exhibitions widely—he deliberately chose to return to the mode of line and local color painting and to such pre-Renaissance sources as the art of early antiquity, the Middle Ages, and Asia. In the Oriental field Japanese prints and Persian miniatures replete with stripes and high intensity colors were his favorites, and he admired the freshness of primitive and childlike art. The common qualities of these types are simplicity and straightforwardness coupled with high vitality. Generally finite and precise in visual character, they capture our attention but sometimes fail to hold our interest. Matisse showed his great talent by succeeding in both these respects.

Alternation of color is a principle which appears not only in painting, but in all the visual arts. Like gradation, it is a welcome byproduct of certain treatments of three-dimensional form. Its virtues are, moreover, not confined to shock effects, but can be exploited with a high degree of sophistication. This possibility made alternation a favored technique during the Renaissance and post-Renaissance periods. Hence there was no time from which this form of order was really excluded. The important distinction is therefore between obvious type of alternation already described (i.e., stripes and similar patterns) and other, more subtle types.

The three-dimensional arts of sculpture and architecture, which seem colorless compared to painting, depend upon patterns of light and shadow to convey their meanings; without light they are meaningless. When their forms are so arranged that there is a repeated raising and lowering of surfaces, the visual result is an alternation of values. Thus, in alternation, as in gradation, there is a cause-and-effect relationship between spatial and color designs. Examples in which an undulating or boss-and-hollow surface treatment produces an alternation of values are Bourdelle's *Beethoven* (Fig. 164) and Daumier's *Burden* (Fig. 161). Because of their alternation of surfaces and illumination, these sculptural figures are as different from the *Menkure and His Queen* and the Egyptian *Head of a Priest* as Matisse's *Girl in a Striped Dress* is from the "Mona Lisa." They underscore the difference between the smooth glyptic treatment of form and the broken surfaces of the plastic mode. If gradation is intrinsic to the design of the one, alternation is no less important to the other.

In architecture any surface which is marked by a succession of recesses will be interpreted visually as an alternation of values. Examples which will occur to anyone are colonnades, bands of windows, or similar openings, and regularly variegated surfaces. The portico of the Pantheon (Fig. 176) illustrates the first; the New York University–Bellevue Hospital Medical Center (Fig. 178) and Colosseum (Fig. 207) the second; and the Strozzi Palace (Fig. 181) and the cornice molding in Fig. 241 the third. In all of these an alternation of light and dark is a prominent feature.

The handling of color alternations subtly instead of obviously can be achieved in several ways. They are important enough to warrant careful consideration. One way to avoid obviousness is to add some complexity to an oversimplified arrangement like stripes. This can be done by breaking up the stripelike pattern into smaller units to produce a shimmering effect. The visual effect is a kind of dancing of hues, values, or intensities, technically known as color vibration. The checkerboard is a common example; the salt-and-pepper tweed or polka dot tie are others. Wherever found, color vibration lives up to the implications of its name by imparting a sensation of sparkling life. It delights the eye with its vitality and pleases it esthetically by its variety.

Its variety often means the difference between an artistic and a merely utilitarian treatment. For example, when paint of a uniform color is applied to a wall, it colors the wall and protects it physically, but its appearance is comparatively flat and monotonous. An artist can break up this monotony. One method is to introduce gradation of color. Turner's *Fighting Téméraire* is a masterly representative of this method.

The other method is to introduce a consistent vibration of colors. This is done in rudimentary fashion even by house painters and decorators when they employ stipple or speckle techniques. Artists can carry these techniques to their ultimate development. They have consistently used either color blending or color vibration for at least five centuries to overcome a boardlike effect. Practitioners of oil and watercolor, media which lend themselves to either treatment, have regularly exploited their ability to add interest to flat surfaces. Vermeer excelled at making the bare wall of a room beautiful with subtle gradations, while Degas could make a board floor vibrate with color.

The medieval artists who worked in mosaic and stained glass made much of the vibrant effect resulting from their use of vitreous fragments and painters of tempera altarpieces in the late Middle Ages and Early Renaissance broke up flat gold backgrounds with incised designs after the fashion of Fra Angelico's *Madonna of Humility* (Fig. 191). The need for gradation or alternation of surface was widely appreciated. As Pope points out, few paintings in the line and local color mode are literally flat, and the best of them present variations of either the graded or alternating sort.

The Islamic and Gothic architects of the late Middle Ages were adept at giving stone a lacelike, shimmering appearance, as can be seen in the Hall of the Two Sisters at the Alhambra (Fig. 183). Judging by Neumann's Wallfahrtkirche (Fig. 184), the late Baroque designers were also expert at achieving a vibrant and vital effect in buildings. The Baroque architects used alternations of value enthusiastically to further their interest in theatrical qualities and in a so-called pictorial type of architecture; all three styles combined color vibrations and plastic forms to stress the infinite.

Color vibration also establishes a basic similarity between Gothic architecture and impressionist sculpture and painting. Bourdelle's *Beethoven* (Fig. 164) is notable for this quality. So, too, is Monet's *Marée Montante à Pourville* (Fig. 137). The impressionist oil painters carried color vibration to its climax. By their deliberate use of broken colors, the paintings of Renoir, Sisley, Monet, and Pissarro dance and shimmer before our eyes. It is not strange, then, that Monet painted the façade of Rouen Cathedral many times. Its perforated surface presented a vibrant alternation of lights and darks which was made to order for his own broken-color technique.

This technique was a valuable part of Impressionism's general style, so much so that Seurat, Cézanne, and Van Gogh adopted it for their own uses at the same time that they rebelled against some impressionist excesses. Seurat's pointillist manner, a polka dot type of color vibration, was carried to the level of high art in his *Sunday on the Island of La Grande Jatte* (Fig. 226). Cézanne's more vigorous treatment can be seen in his *Forest of Fontainebleau* (Fig. 39) and *House in Provence* (Fig. 80); color vibration was an important element of his art. But it remained for Van Gogh to carry this method to its highest development in such pictures as his *Mountainous Landscape* (Fig. 65), *Sunset over a Plowed Field* (Fig. 140), and *Cypresses* (Fig. 155). Between them the Impressionists and post-Impressionists explored color vibrations thoroughly and rapidly, bringing them to a peak which left little more to be done along that line.

Another way of relieving the obviousness of stripes and adding interest to any visual field was the combination of alternations of color with gradations. Whereas color vibration endowed striped effects with sophistication, the combination of alternation and gradation added subtlety. Artists could stress either vigorous or subtle sophistication, and even found ways of combining color vibrations with alternating gradations to give a further effect of extraordinary interest.

The possibility of joining alternation and gradation was discovered early in history. The fluted Greek column owes its striking and lasting beauty to this ingenious partnership. The cylindrical character of the drums creates a gradation of light and shadow in any normal crosslight, while the fluting establishes an alternation of light and shadow. If the Greeks had merely incised vertical lines in smooth round columns, some alternation would have resulted, but their esthetic sensibility led them to carve concave grooves (as in Fig. 425) with sharp outer edges. The sharp-edged shadows thus produced formed an inner sequence of gradations within the general gradation, the net effect being one of the most satisfying in the history of art. When other refinements of this caliber were added to the Greek architectural orders, their historical popularity was assured.

A combination of alternation and gradation in sculpture is illustrated by Bourdelle's *Beethoven*, which has been mentioned often because it is rich in compositional and technical merits. Since a series of ocean waves is essentially like the fluting of a Greek column, the same principle of an alternating gradation is present in Monet's *Marée Montante à Pourville*, another work of art which is full of variations of design. It illustrates the general point that though we may seek and find only harmony on one inspection of a picture. great works of art have a way of exemplifying many principles of design. After we have returned to them repeatedly, their interest-holding qualities seem almost inexhaustible.

The Baroque canopy discussed in connection with aerial projection is another instance of an alternating gradation. In Ruysdael's *Wheatfields* (Fig. 116) a gradation of intensities from foreground into the distance is accompanied by an alternation of light and dark bands. These carry the observer's eye to the horizon, and preserve the picture plane. So successful was this superimposition of one form of order on another that it was adopted by most subsequent painters of the out-of-doors. Both Turner and Homer used it in the marines in Figs. 48 and 119. There are very few landscapes in which only a straightforward gradation of intensities is used. The alternating gradation was more successful than either alternation or gradation alone and rightly became one of the most popular methods in the designer's repertory.

One important characteristic of alternation remains to be stressed. Whether applied to the terms of space or the terms of color, its rhythmic quality comes as close as any art form can to capturing the pulse of life. This alone is enough to insure its preservation.

BALANCE OF COLOR

Balance is used in color design when, instead of a general harmony, there is a dissimilarity of color attraction, with some areas standing out more prominently than others. This dissimilarity allows the artist to avail himself of the high attentional value of contrasts within an orderly form and gain, at the same time, flexibility of representation, for actuality is more often characterized by contrasts than by harmony.

Balance is achieved by equalizing the visual attraction of colors on either side of an axis, or around the center of an enframement or defining outline. This is done by increasing or decreasing the contrasts of hue, value, and intensity of the various areas which make up the compositional pattern. Generally speaking, the greatest weight can be given a color area by playing it against one or more opposite color characteristics. Hence a full intensity red-orange of middle value would stand out most vividly if placed against a dark low intensity blue-green background.

Color design therefore illustrates pointedly the fact that all design is a matter of relationships. Juxtapositions of neighbors are crucial in color balance, as is a factor borrowed from the realm of spatial design—measure. A large area of pure red-orange will take precedence over a small area of the same pigment. Adjustment proceeds along these lines, with the artist who seeks to balance a set of contrasting colors tending to stress oppositions of hue, value, and intensity in contradistinction to harmony in which differences are narrowed.

Since color designs function in conjunction with spatial designs, they are arranged in axial and central balances which may be either obvious or occult. There is little need to elaborate here on the central balance as a special type, for it is gained by the same methods as the axial, while the obvious axial balance can be illustrated summarily by Cimabue's *Madonna Enthroned* (Fig. 244). The color design is as symmetrical as its spatial arrangement, which accounts for its rigid orderliness. The colors of the angels' garments on the left are matched by identical colors at each level on the right. Stressing the concept of symmetrical balance is the large blue area of the Madonna's robe which is located firmly on the central axis.

Manet's *Fifer Boy* (Fig. 262), a quite different picture in numerous respects, is a good illustration of an occult axial balance. Although the figure is centrally placed, its easy stance suggests an asymmetrical balance of considerable subtlety. Manet's methods of creating a striking color design are worthy of study because of their general application to the whole problem of balance.

Unlike the *Madonna Enthroned,* which has a uniform brilliance of colors, Manet's youthful fifer stands out because he contrasts strongly with the background. Whereas the background is a low intensity brownish hue of almost uniform value, the boy's costume is a pattern of bright colors and sharp value contrasts.

Catching our eye at once, the boldly outlined figure holds our attention because Manet skilfully balanced the colors from top to bottom within the outline. He painted the trousers a brilliant red-orange, but offset their intensity by the sharp value contrast between the blue jacket and white sash. He also allotted equal emphasis to both the top and bottom of the figure by value contrasts in the shoes, and hue and value contrasts in the red, yellow, and blue cap. Thus the *Fifer Boy* contains many of the devices universally used to gain color balance. The practice of making a figure stand out by giving it a high color attraction against a neutral background is widely employed in painting, especially in portraiture.

Another popular method of balancing colors is suggested by Manet's use of the primary hues—red, yellow, and blue. They have been the favorite color triad of artists for centuries. Two excellent

FIG. 262. Manet. *Fifer Boy*. 1866. Louvre, Paris.

examples are Fra Angelico's *Madonna of Humility* (Fig. 191) and Rouault's *Old King* (Fig. 227), in which red, blue, and yellow predominate. The perennial popularity of this triangle probably arises from its wide range of color characteristics: the red satisfies the desire for a warm hue, the blue for a cool hue, and the yellow for one that is light and brilliant. Furthermore, there is normally a distinct spread or contrast of values between the comparative darkness of red and blue and the lightness of yellow. There are other triads, such as orange, green, and violet, but none has been as favored as the triangle of the primaries. Its closest rival has been a soft yellow ochre, cobalt blue, and a reddish orange burnt sienna. This palette, when mixed to include various shades of green, permits an admirable range of effects, and was widely used by European landscape painters from the time of Claude Lorrain to Turner.

Pope has described the practice of consistently limiting a design to a few colors as painting from a fixed palette, and he has shown how often the masters employed this kind of limitation to gain a balanced, orderly variety. Closely allied to painting with one or another triad is the practice of balancing complementaries. Complementaries, being opposites in the color circle, recommend themselves as naturally to the designer of balanced compositions as analogous or neighboring colors do to the designer of color harmonies. Instead of working in narrow triangular sections of the circle, the master of balance works across it.

The best known complementaries are hardly less popular than the red-blue-yellow triad. They include red and green, yellow and violet (or blue), red-orange and blue-green, and orange and blue. Most of these have, like the red-blue-yellow triad, the merit of containing contrasts of both high and low values and warm and cool colors. They cover a wide range of territory for two hues.

Vermeer was fond of balanced complementaries and handled them adroitly. He especially liked yellow and blue in combination, making it almost a trademark of his style. But in his *Cook* (Fig. 93) he included two pairs of complementaries, yellow and blue and red and green. These, used in close conjunction with the figure of the woman, make her stand out against the neutral wall of the room.

Any juxtaposition of areas whose color terms contrast will attract the eye according to the degree of contrast. Using this principle, an artist can adjust a design until it is balanced by increasing or decreasing the various measures of colored areas and their relationships of hue, value, and intensity. In a painting he makes these adjustments within the picture's frame and in relation to its axis or center. Thus

Manet thought not only of neighboring color relationships when painting his *Fifer Boy*, but of their position in the design as a whole —whether above or below, or to right or left of important determining compositional lines or points.

He was merely following a universal practice. All other artists have had to do the same when they sought to create a balance. There are four common approaches to the problem of color balance. In one that is found widely, the artist, instead of emphasizing the central axis by placing a principal figure on it, as Cimabue, Manet, and Vermeer did in their respective *Madonna Enthroned*, *Fifer Boy*, and *Cook*, avoids the central axis, placing his principal figures in the right and left halves of the composition and balancing them in an occult fashion; a favorite method is to pit a color and intensity attraction against an equally strong contrast of values. Van der Weyden's *St. Luke Painting the Virgin* (Fig. 97), in which St. Luke's red robe provides the color and intensity attraction and the Madonna and Child the balancing value contrast, illustrates this method. It is only one among many similar treatments. Homer's *Northeaster* (Fig. 18), Turner's *Fighting Téméraire* (Fig. 258), Rubens' *Queen Tomyris with the Head of Cyrus* in the Museum of Fine Arts, Boston, Chardin's *Still Life* with a bowl of plums in the Phillips Memorial Gallery, and Eakins' *Will Shuster and Blackman Going Shooting* in the Clark Collection, New York, are fine pictures which, though very different in subject, are basically of this common compositional type. Its popularity springs from the fact that the emphasis upon the sides rather than the center of the picture is especially suitable to an asymmetrical balance. The departure from a centralized focal point is only a matter of degree, but it is a significant change, for it permits two major centers of interest instead of one. The resulting advantage or gain in interest is shown by Turner's *Fighting Téméraire* in which the ship and the sunset are complementary and equally important.

A second major method of attaining color balance is to cast one side of a picture into shadow while illuminating the other side. Giorgione, in composing his *Sleeping Venus*, employed this kind of association of dark and light with left and right, and it continued to be a favorite device of the Venetian masters through the sixteenth century. Their practice was to divide the picture into two approximately equal halves. Later schools, while retaining the general principle, tended to oppose larger shadow areas against small but brilliantly illuminated areas, relying on the high attentional value of the latter to establish the balance. This distribution also expressed their greater interest in the representation of concentrated luminosity. De Hooch's *Mother by a Cradle* (Fig. 98) is an outstanding example of this sort of design.

A third method of balancing the color design of a picture consists of a uniformity of opposition among four quadrants. The aim is to avoid too strong a stress on either the central axis, as in Fra Angelico's *Madonna of Humility,* or the left and right halves of the picture area. Instead, an equal apportionment of eye-catching color is distributed through all four quarters. Though there is some sacrifice of emphasis in favor of diffusion, the picture as a whole gains in interest. In Matisse's *Odalisque with Raised Arms* (Fig. 123), where this method is used, the decorative design on the wall in the upper right section of the picture attracts the eye strongly instead of being entirely subordinate to the human figure. Matisse used the same distribution of attention in his *Girl in a Striped Dress* (Fig. 261). Making every section of the canvas visually important seems to have been one of his guiding principles of design.

An equal assignment of color attraction to all sections of a picture is essential in any balance of the central type. This can be done in either an obvious, symmetrical fashion or in an occult manner, but examples of the obvious central balance are rare in painting although plentiful in the decorative arts, Persian carpets being typical of the obvious symmetry. Matisse's *Odalisque with Raised Arms* is too thoroughly stabilized by vertical and horizontal lines to be read as a central balance, but this is not true of Rubens' *Rape of the Daughters of Leucippus* (Fig. 216), Raphael's *Madonna of the Chair* (Fig. 253), or Tintoretto's *Marriage of Bacchus and Ariadne* (Fig. 254), all of which revolve around a central focal point. Furthermore, the strategic spotting of colors and illumination is quite as important to the sense of balance they convey as their spatial designs.

A fourth widely used type of balance depends on the fact that a balance of judiciously placed areas of color attraction can be conceived in three-dimensional space as well as on a two dimensional surface. These color areas play an important role in projectional design, causing us to think not only in terms of left and right and above and below, but of backward and forward relationships.

The areas of strong color interest can, of course, be organized in planes that are parallel to the picture surface, though this is an obvious and only moderately interesting arrangement. A more interesting method consists of organization along diagonal, zigzag, or meandering recessional lines. This type of asymmetrical design came into prominence in Baroque times and has continued in use to the present day. Turner's *Fighting Téméraire* is a fine example; in it

the eye is drawn backward from the dark buoy in the right foreground to the luminous ship in the left middle distance and thence
to the brilliant setting sun in the right distance.

Few artists handled this kind of occult design better than Degas,
whose pictures exemplify its many possibilities. His *Dancer with a
Bouquet* (Fig. 107) is typical. Though of a very different subject
from the *Fighting Téméraire*, its color design is basically similar.
The eye is again led from a dark object in the right foreground back
into the distance along a zigzag path. These examples illustrate the
principal types of balanced color design—a process requiring great
inventiveness and judgment, but one which, skilfully performed,
gives profound esthetic pleasure.

CHAPTER 17

Coordination of
Representation and Design

An artist often simplifies his problems by subdivision, making individual studies of the figures in a complex composition or preliminary sketches of the design, as Michelangelo and Picasso did when painting the Sistine ceiling (Figs. 58 and 126) and the *Guernica* (Fig. 1); or he may divide form and color into separate problems, as Van Eyck did (Fig. 192). But eventually he must synthesize all of these formal and dramatic entities into a unified whole.

We, as spectators, do the reverse. Starting with the finished product, we perceive the work of art as a whole by an almost instantaneous and usually subconscious process of mental synthesis. But we can gain added insight by occasionally analyzing consciously the many steps an artist takes as he constructs and coordinates the elements in a work of art.

Artists who limited themselves to shallow axial balances and symbolical pictures, like Cimabue's *Madonna Enthroned* (Fig. 244), found their problem of coordination relatively simple. But when, under the influence of Giotto, they began to cultivate more lifelike representation within asymmetrical balances developed in deeper space, their difficulties were multiplied. Like the director of a play, a painter of any asymmetrically balanced representational picture is dealing not with a uniformly attractive image, but with areas which he must treat as the stars, supporting players, and supernumeraries of his pictorial drama. To tell his story well, he must weld these different parts into a visual image which is esthetically, emotionally, and representationally unified.

To balance spatial, color, and representational elements with different powers of attraction, the artist must play many compositional factors against each other. Psychologists call these attentional values, reflecting certain universal psychological traits. The masterful composer understands and exploits these traits while the weaker designer is less sensitive to them.

Balance is regularly and strongly affected by the following attentional values whenever representation and design are combined. Tests show that the eye normally favors the area to the upper left of center in a picture and then tends to read clockwise. An artist will do well to make his main representational subject coincide with this natural spatial center of interest and then distribute his forms in a slightly circular fashion. Painters have not always followed either of these rules rigidly, but many fine pictures exemplify them. The Japanese print most popular in the West, Hokusai's *Great Wave* (Fig. 377), illustrates centralized circular composition perfectly.

Akin to the trait is the tendency of the eye to ascend to the peak of any pyramidal, conical, or vertically graded form. Architects and painters have exploited this habit for centuries. Raphael is noted for placing the head of a Madonna or a similar center of interest at the peak of a pyramidal design.

When coordinating spatial design and representation an artist can usually assume that the eye is more strongly attracted to an animate form than to an inanimate; to the natural more than the symbolical or abstract; to the large rather than the small; to a vertical or leaning figure more than to a seated, prone, or reclining figure; to a moving figure versus a stationary one; to the rough over the smooth; to an irregular over a regular shape; and to the frontal, not to the silhouetted. Moreover, the eye will tend to follow the direction in which any figure is facing, pointing, or moving. It is also attracted by deep space, as in the distant portions of a landscape, though a large foreground figure will naturally occupy a favored position.

Both deep space and large foreground figures, however, are secondary to the use an artist makes of the principal guiding lines in his composition. Employed with skill they can lead the eye irresistibly to the leading subjects—a fact that Raphael exploited superbly when he placed Plato and Aristotle over the vanishing point of his perspective scheme in the *School of Athens* (Fig. 104). Though surrounded by a multitude of other men, they are the dominating figures.

In the competition among colors, the eye will favor intense colors, large areas, and high values. It is especially attracted to strong light, a fact which may account for much of the "pull" of distance or of any figure or group which is spotlighted. Centralization and illumination, for instance, focus attention on the figure of Christ in Rembrandt's *Christ Healing the Sick* (Fig. 151).

Above all these considerations, the strongest attraction will be exerted by contrasts, whether spatial or tonal. One dynamic figure can be made to outweigh a crowd. The late medieval and Renaissance religious illustrators proved this when they made Christ stand out from a multitude by isolation, a commanding gesture, and a general focus of attention upon Him. Giotto's *Raising of Lazarus* is an illustration. His *Death of Saint Francis* (Fig. 133) demonstrated how one strategically placed supine figure can be made to dominate a group of standing men by virtue of its singularity.

No group of artists has applied these principles of attention with greater astuteness than the directors of stage productions. A summary of their practices in creating living pictures is an object lesson for all types of visual coordination. The stage director is no abstractionist; his task is to put over a set of ideas and emotions in the handsomest and most effective manner possible. He will assign the center and front of the stage, spotlighting, and eye-catching costumes to his stars in any complex scene and require the supporting actors to remain quiet and still. The importance of this arrangement may be overlooked until some veteran scene-stealer attempts to "upstage" the star, maneuver him out of the spotlight or center, or detract attention by slight bits of business.

The similarity between effective pictorial composition and stage direction is quite close. Giotto must have seemed to his contemporaries much like a skilful director of plays. He was adroit at using backgrounds to set off his human action, as when he placed the mountain behind the Madonna and Child in his *Flight into Egypt* (Fig. 224) or framed the group in the *Meeting of Joachim and Anna* (Fig. 75) by an arch. The Golden Gate of Jerusalem was thereby made to serve both design and representation. In his *Presentation of the Virgin* (Fig. 51) he arranged his actors shrewdly: the youthful Virgin is emphasized, despite her small size, by her location in the center of the picture and at the top of a stairway—always a prominent position. In addition, she is framed, as between parentheses, by her mother and the priest, while all of the spectators except one look in her direction. It is no accident that she is the center of attention.

Giotto was hailed almost at once as a master artist, not only because he observed human behavior with a new insight and social sympathy and painted storytelling pictures, but because he told his stories in an effective way. The difference between his art and that of his less capable followers is not wholly due to compositional superiority, yet design is a noticeable factor. One can confirm the difference painfully by comparing his *Presentation of the Virgin* with the picture of the same subject by his follower, Taddeo Gaddi.

An essential quality of really great works of art is the seeming ease and grace with which the creator coordinates his design. But Gaddi's picture reminds us forcefully that this process is not automatic or to be taken for granted. Although using the same people and story, he allows the architecture to dominate the scene. The lines which should lead our eye to the central drama and unite the setting confuse us by pointing in every direction, and elements which should make minor contributions become major distractions.

The eye-catching powers of objects must be judiciously used by any composer, lest they draw attention from the principal theme, for scene-stealing does not occur on the stage alone. It is the common mark of a poor composer, and the sign of a lapse in the skill of a master. All artists have "bad days" which account for variations in the quality of their work. Veronese, as we shall see, did not integrate and control the elements of his *Supper at Emmaus* (Fig. 326). Stumbling over the ever-present distraction, he allowed minor elements to distract or even dominate.

This almost theatrical skill in handling value relationships and compositional elements is common to most artists of great ability, and is especially apparent in those works which rank highest in appeal. Perhaps that is why we often refer to them as "dramatic". In the *Supper at Emmaus* (Fig. 325), for example, Rembrandt has concentrated attention on Christ by a perfectly calculated placement of His figure and by a shrewd handling of directions; since all of the figures look toward Christ, we do too. More important still, there is nothing to detract our attention. Rembrandt made his reputation by the completely logical composing of his earlier *Anatomy Lesson*. The principal characters, Dr. Tulp and the cadaver on which he is demonstrating anatomy, are so placed that our eye is drawn to them. Tulp stands almost alone near the center of the picture and in strong illumination. He is quiet and poised while his listeners register alert attention. Like Christ before His disciples, the isolated figure commands attention. The arrangement of the heads in a parallelogram pattern leads the eye to the figure of Tulp. Thanks to a skilful gradation of directions, this painting is a model of integrated variety and focal emphasis.

No fine compositions are identical, yet all reflect keen intelligence —judgment applied to a hundred and one decisions relative to the coordination of spatial design, color design, and representation. Botticelli's *Annunciation* (Fig. 263) is a masterpiece of balanced contrasts. Broadly speaking, it is an axial occult balance with circular overtones. Within this pattern the standing figure of the Virgin is contrasted with the kneeling Angel Gabriel; these two active, com-

Fig. 263. Botticelli. *Annunciation. ca.* 1489-1490.
Uffizi Gallery, Florence.

Fig. 264. Titian. *Venus of Urbino. ca.* 1538. Uffizi Gallery, Florence.

plex human figures contrast with the simple, static setting. The curvilinear diagonal postures of the figures are played against the rigidly rectilinear architecture. The right foreground, in which the Virgin is dominant, is contrasted with the left background, and the left made to hold its own by virtue of the combined "pull" of distance and light. The asymmetrical placement of the door is the key to the design; had it been located in the center, the composition would have been commonplace. Foreground and distance have also been handled shrewdly. For although Botticelli emphasized the perspective projection that engrossed his day by introducing a patterned pavement, he made it an illustrative asset, not a distracting end in itself.

The master composer Titian showed a similar shrewdness in painting his *Venus of Urbino* (Fig. 264), the prototype of a noted line of famous reclining beauties continued by Velasquez, Goya, and Manet. She marks a break with Giorgione's idealized *Sleeping Venus* (Fig. 79) in favor of a living, wide-awake woman whose title of goddess is a mere tag. Prominently situated in the foreground, she tends to dominate the composition. Moreover, our tendency to look at faces is reinforced here by the drapery. Its plain dark areas not only divide the design, but sharply set off the head and torso. Hence Titian had to exert himself to give equal weight to the right side of the canvas. He did this by putting a sleeping dog on the foot of the couch, and then adding two women to the background whose apparent search for clothing arouses our curiosity. They were given extra attentional value in two ways: the kneeling woman by value contrast and the standing one by the color attraction of her intensely red dress. In this way left foreground and right background are neatly balanced, as are the diagonal line of the Venus and the vertical edge of the drapery. The total effect is not a balance of spatial, color, and representational elements in separate layers but a coordination of all three.

On the other side of the world Hokusai spoke for the perennial Oriental grasp of the essentials of design in scores of pictures, but in none more simply or clearly than his *Fujiyama in Clear Weather* (Fig. 265). Like Titian, he was obliged to balance a picture in which he had deliberately allowed one side to assume predominance. Avoiding the obvious by locating the famous volcano asymmetrically, he accepted the fact that our attention would be drawn to it. He strengthened this ideological attraction by coloring the mountain a brilliant red-orange and adding an eye-catching value contrast to the snow-ribbed peak. The base of the mountain he colored an intense green which contrasts with the red-orange cone, giving it additional

FIG. 265. Hokusai. *Fujiyama in Clear Weather*. From "Thirty-Six Views of Fuji," *ca.* 1825. Museum of Fine Arts, Boston.

FIG. 266. Degas. *The Rehearsal*. *ca.* 1874-1875. Frick Collection, New York.

518

weight. In the face of this formidable array he had to build up the upper part of the picture, and the left section in particular. He did this by color intensity (the brilliant blue of the sky), value contrast (created by the white clouds), and shape interest (of the irregular cirrus clouds). In the over-all pattern the horizontal clouds counteract the sweeping diagonal lines of the mountain. To insure balance, he set the signature and title against the sky, placing it with that precision for which the leading Japanese print-makers are justly famous. Here again spatial terms, color, and idea are balanced and coordinated in such a way as to enhance and support each other.

When Japanese prints were brought in numbers to Europe in the nineteenth century, Western artists like Degas learned much from them but added to them significant ideas from the Western tradition, notably a keener appreciation of three-dimensional space. In Degas' *Rehearsal* (Fig. 266) there is a hint of the Oriental diagonal mode of projection typified by Masanobu's interior scene *Playing Cards* (Fig. 113), but the sense of depth is much greater. The eye is first attracted to the musician because of the value contrast between the light background and his dark coat, and then to the dancers because of their numbers and activity. Consequently, the foreground and right side of the picture might have monopolized attention had not Degas exploited two counterbalancing factors: our tendencies to follow directional lines, such as the arrow-like pointed feet of the dancers and the lines of the floor, and to look toward the distance when it is strongly illuminated. Degas, like Botticelli, Titian, and Hokusai, has also played vertical against diagonal lines. More important, he has thoroughly integrated his spatial design, color design, and representational ideas. Although they may be analyzed separately, they cannot be fully understood apart from each other. This is the mark of a superior design, of which Degas created many. His *Rehearsal* is an outstanding illustration of that organizing ability possessed by the masters of art.

CHAPTER 18

Part-to-Part Design

Any work of art is conceived and must be appreciated in its entirety. But since it is composed of a carefully organized series of parts, our apprehension of it must be of a dual nature—perception of the work as a whole, plus a deeper study of its components and their relationships. Theodore Meyer Greene asserts that in a great work of art these relationships are virtually inexhaustible. They provide an infinite series of "pictures within pictures" which can be appreciated only by a penetrating part-to-part analysis.

The layer-like, sequential character of observation which passes from general impressions to an awareness of refinements can be demonstrated by common experience with a large picture like Rembrandt's *Night Watch*. When a visitor to the Rijksmuseum in Amsterdam first sees the huge painting at the far end of a long gallery, he does have an impression of the composition as a whole; indeed, he cannot have any other. As he moves forward he begins to observe things that he missed at first. Upon coming close to the picture, he notices refinements of relationships that eluded him entirely at a distance. He may spend an hour, a week, or even a lifetime in close study without exhausting the picture's part-to-part organization. Meanwhile, close to the picture, he cannot see it as a whole. He therefore probably backs away from it for a third and different inspection. Ultimately, he synthesizes his distant and close observations mentally into the impression of the picture as a whole which he carries away with him and remembers. Only in this ultimate sense does the statement that we see a picture as a whole accord with common experience.

Anyone who has painted a picture or watched an artist at work will recognize how studio practice anticipates the spectator's multiple perception. Because he must paint within arm's length, an artist constantly retreats from his canvas to check the relationships he has developed at close range; for he must not only relate these to their neighboring elements, but to the composition as a whole. The need of both spectator and artist to observe a work of art close-up and at a distance is due to the physical limitations of human eyesight; we do not see things in detail from far away, nor can we observe them comprehensively when very near. Complete perception is a fusion of both types of seeing.

This fusion is especially necessary when a work of art combines a strong compositional center with a center of human interest, as is likely to be the case in the majority of works of art. In Rembrandt's *Christ Healing the Sick* (Fig. 151) the figure of Christ is made to stand out by virtue of His ideological significance, central position, and brilliant illumination. Our eyes go immediately to him, but we gain only a general impression of the crowd. People who have seen this etching a hundred times cannot recall the three figures near the left margin with any degree of accuracy. They may well have other new things pointed out to them indefinitely in the peripheral regions of the picture. A picture is not only comprised of many parts, but of parts which possess different degrees of attractiveness. In this case our limitation is one of attentional capacity. When joined to our physical limitations it makes part-to-part analysis obligatory.

Part-to-part observation is therefore recommended as an antidote to excessive concentration. It forces one to take one's time, to allow a set of complex relationships to register in the mind. They cannot be absorbed as a whole or in a hurry. Without sufficient time one never goes beyond impressions and misses much of the esthetic nourishment offered by any work of art. Critically speaking, the results of the usual hurried museum visit are seldom more than a series of snap judgments.

An excellent illustration is provided by the frieze of the Parthenon (Fig. 267). Despite its length and richness, the composition conveys a sense of grace and ease. This can easily deceive us into assuming that we can absorb its meaning at a glance when, in fact, we have hardly begun. The Panathenaic Procession created under the guidance of Phidias did not gain its reputation merely by being simple and easy to understand. The sequence of movement, ideas, and forms that unfolds in it has been likened to a symphony. It is comprised of a wealth of interrelated harmonies, sequences, and balances, with motifs woven through the *fabric* of sound, then varied endlessly while various other types of audible design are played against each other contrapuntally.

FIG. 267. Studio of Phidias. *Youths and Horses*. From the "Panathenaic Procession" of the Parthenon frieze; north side. 447-432 B.C. British Museum, London.

FIG. 268. Michelangelo. *Soldiers Bathing in the Arno*. "Bathing Soldiers Surprised." Engraved after the grisaille copy of the lost cartoon (1504-1506) for the Hall of the Great Council, Florence.

The detail of *Youths and Horses* in Fig. 267, while deceptively simple at first glance, illustrates the symphonic quality of the frieze. In it continuity is established by the lines of the horses' bellies, but monotony is avoided by this line's subtle variations, and by the intermittent vertical legs of both men and beasts. Far from being a straight line, it ripples along in a sequence of undulating curves. In a similar way the straight legs of the principal horse and youth harmonize with each other but contrast with the diagonal and angular legs behind them. The four human figures are also carefully related to one another; three of them look forward, while the fourth looks backward. Viewed together, their heads form a long arc which repeats the flat curve of the horse's neck and mane. The ultimate refinement is found in the nude youth whose arms seem to point to two directions at once, a posture in perfect accord with the basically sequential character of the processional frieze. These refinements are not seen as a whole or absorbed in a moment. But to miss them is to overlook most of the composition's beauty.

An even stronger argument for careful analysis is contained in the drawing which Michelangelo did for a proposed fresco decoration in the Grand Council Hall at Florence (Fig. 268). Long since destroyed, the cartoon is known only through a grisaille copy and old engravings, but is deservedly one of his most celebrated designs. It represents a group of nude Florentine soldiers who were surprised while bathing and are hurriedly preparing to meet an attack. The subject offered the sort of swarming masculine nudity that Michelangelo loved to depict.

No one would call this a simple picture. It seems at first complex to the point of confusion. No one can read it quickly, yet a careful study will reveal both its unity and variety. The common denominator is a balance of contrasting attitudes and directions. It weaves through the composition, linking each figure with the others in a network of counterpoint. Thus seen, the picture ceases to be confusing and becomes a superbly coherent composition, one of the high points of Renaissance design.

Michelangelo did not integrate this intricate group in a flash of inspiration. There is evidence that he worked long and hard on the design, developing each individual figure in drawings which are counted among his masterpieces. The *Study of the Back of a Nude Male* in Fig. 147 is typical of the care he devoted to the project. Michelangelo did not originally envision or create this picture as a whole. Like every other artist, he built the composition up part-by-part through trial and error. He poured into it time, energy, and thought. And if we are to gain from it even a fraction of what he put into it, we must observe it in a commensurately cumulative and thorough manner.

A part-to-part analysis of works of art reflects the way they are created and extracts the fullest benefit from them. Yet we can reduce the problem to relatively simple terms. The part-to-part organization of works of art in all the media falls into four main groups: the ensemble of parts; the fusion of parts; the closed contour; and the open contour. The ensemble of parts and the fusion of parts pertain to the internal relationships of any work of art. The closed contour and open contour pertain to the external relationships, meaning the relationship of a pictorial design to its frame, and a statue or building to the surrounding space. There is a relationship between the two groups which further simplifies the problem. The ensemble of parts is in accord with the closed contour type of design, while the fusion of parts is in harmony with the idea of the open contour.

THE ENSEMBLE OF PARTS

The adherents of the ensemble and the fused design both aim at unity but proceed in opposite ways. Typical of the ensemble of parts is any painting in the sculpturesque mode of the Renaissance, for example Michelangelo's *Creation of Adam* (Fig. 126). While no one would question this painting's unity, the parts are, nevertheless, clearly discernible; each retains a measure of prominence and independence.

Michelangelo preserved this clarity of parts by conceiving the scene as though it were illuminated by a strong, even, frontal light. In this lighting, forms and outlines stand out clearly. Shadows are few and atmosphere entirely absent, for Michelangelo suppressed or eliminated both of the elements which tend to soften outlines and merge forms and deliberately preserved the independent boundaries of each figure. The result is a composition in which the part contributes to the whole but is not sacrificed to it; the figure of Adam is magnificent by itself and yet participates in a harmony of attitudes. Michelangelo's design thus expresses a love of the finite and tangible aspects of reality and an antipathy toward the infinite and mysterious. Although powerfully emotional, it is clear and concrete—an art of sharp outlines and solid forms.

Clarity of form is not confined to the sculpturesque mode of painting, nor is organization by means of an ensemble of parts. Both apply to the ancient mode of line and local color and many of the modern modes, linking them into a timeless and world-wide point of view. Despite differences, the *Nakht Watching Plowing* (Fig. 120),

FIG. 269. Maillol. *Mediterranean. ca.* 1901. Museum of Modern Art, New York.

FIG. 270. Bernini. *St. Longinus.* 1629-1638. St. Peter's, Rome.

Justinian and Courtiers (Fig. 121), Masanobu's *Playing Cards* (Fig. 113), Matisse's *Odalisque with Raised Arms* (Fig. 123), and Michelangelo's *Creation of Adam* all partake of a single tradition. To it we might add Thurber's *"Touché!"* (Fig. 143), the Greek *Youth and Maiden* in Fig. 144, and the *Dwarf of Murad II* (Fig. 145); whether paintings or drawings, a clarity of outlines and parts is an outstanding characteristic in each.

The method of organization which aims at an ensemble of parts transcends the different modes of representation which separate and distinguish works of art. It is common to all media and applies with equal force to architecture. Brunelleschi's Pazzi Chapel (Fig. 273) is as good an example of an ensemble of parts as Michelangelo's *Creation of Adam*. Though one appreciates the unity of its design, the parts stand out vividly in the memory. Brunelleschi intended this to be so and did everything in his power to promote it. If he had desired a greater unity, he would have suppressed the differences in color; instead, he stressed value contrasts which make every medallion, cornice, and pilaster stand out in bold relief. A contrasting but balanced ensemble of parts, not a blended harmony, was his calculated goal.

The same desire was expressed in the Parthenon at Athens in the fifth century before Christ and in the New York University—Bellevue Medical Center (Fig. 178) of our own time. In sum, the ensemble of parts knows no boundaries of medium, time, or place. Once appreciated, that fact leads us to even broader implications. Whether we are talking about Brunelleschi or Masanobu, Phidias or Cézanne, Michelangelo or Matisse, we are dealing with men who shared a love of clarity of parts. This bias linked them with the Greek classical point of view, an attitude which recurs whenever an artist or group admires the finite in reality and art above all else. The ensemble of parts has always been one of their principal means of expressing that concept.

Music abounds with examples of the classical point of view. Whether we call Mozart and Brunelleschi classicists or associate them by other labels, their art identifies their fundamental similarity, for the motifs of Mozart's compositions are as clear and distinct as Brunelleschi's capitals. The same rule extends to literature. It was not by chance that Gibbon wrote nostalgically of the decline and fall of the Roman Empire; his mind gravitated toward classical clarity. Observe his sentence, "I sighed as a lover, but obeyed as a son." It speaks volumes, yet, like the Roman Pantheon it is balanced, clear, and complete.

The ensemble of parts expresses a universal type of human thought which joins men, not only because they lived in classical antiquity, Renaissance Italy, or neo-Classic France, but because they placed a premium upon clarity in every part of a design.

THE FUSION OF PARTS

The fusion of parts expresses a point of view which is as universal as the ensemble of parts, but opposite in character and aim. An artist who uses such a method places a higher value upon the unity of a composition than upon any of its parts. Accordingly, he seeks to blend and merge them to a higher degree than the classical composer, stressing continuity over contrast and balance. His treatment of color is an example. Whereas in a typical painting in the mode of line and local color or the sculpturesque mode each color area is clearly outlined and the color design as a whole is an ensemble of parts, there are no sharp dividing lines between colors in a fusion of parts; they are blended and graded one into another.

The paintings of Rembrandt, the most noted exemplar of this method of organization, are quite unlike the pictures of Masanobu, Michelangelo, or Matisse. If we take his portrait of *Nicholas Bruyningh* (Fig. 135) as an example, the reason seems to lie in his emphasis of light and shadow. Whenever shadow is allowed to play a prominent part it has the effect of softening and obscuring outlines and forms. In the Bruyningh portrait much of the form is nearly lost in shadow. The larger result of any such suppression of details and dividing lines is to induce the spectator to read the composition more comprehensively. The optical principle is that as detail decreases, the capacity to grasp the picture as a whole increases.

At the time when Rembrandt adopted the pictorial mode of Titian's later years, the baroque artists in general were moving toward a greater fusion of parts in all kinds of design. Rembrandt continued this trend as long as he lived, developing it to a high point in his *Christ at Emmaus* of 1661. A comparison of this composition with his *Christ at Emmaus* of 1648 (Fig. 325) will show how much he progressed in the direction of the infinite. This late masterpiece by Rembrandt illustrates a common characteristic of fusion of parts—it appeals to the imagination, the emotions, and our sense of the mysterious and infinite. In Rembrandt's design this is achieved by a reliance upon implication. Throughout the shadowy picture the spectator's mind must fill in what he barely senses. The mood emotions are appealed to strongly.

The landscape painters of the nineteenth century followed Rembrandt's lead by stressing the atmosphere which blends and softens outlines in deep space. The Impressionists carried this method to its final development, tying their pictures together at the expense of almost every detail or part. Monet did this in his *Marée Montante à Pourville* (Fig. 137); Renoir was plainly not interested in the part itself when he painted his *Umbrellas* (Fig. 138); and Whistler cared only for the over-all effect when he created his *Nocturne, Blue and Silver* (Fig. 139). The representational emphasis which this sort of painting permitted has already been discussed; here we are concerned with the kind of feeling favored by the fusion of parts. John Sloan's *Wake of the Ferry* (Fig. 76) is representationally akin to these impressionist paintings, and, like them, appeals primarily to the mood emotions.

When a fusion of parts emphasizes light and shadow, atmospheric backgrounds and blended colors, the infinite over the finite in the physical world, and stresses imaginative implication, understatement, moods, and nuances of feeling in the psychological realm, the result is called *romantic*. This romanticism can be identified with specific historical periods and modes of representation, such as nineteenth-century Romanticism. But it also expresses a recurring point of view which runs through history as a basic attitude—sometimes dormant but always there. It links artists, whose superficial differences and separation in time divides them in our minds, into an important family in the history of art. Conceived as one member of the great triad of classic, realistic, and romantic biases, it helps us to see the history of art comprehensively.

The romantic approach has often pervaded literary and musical thinking. Poe consciously sought to make his readers forget words and sentences and remember only a total impression in the *Pit and the Pendulum* or the *Fall of the House of Usher*. Beethoven created in his string quartets and the *Great Fugue* especially a continuous flow of swelling and ebbing sounds. The word *fugue* itself suggests a subtle but fugitive artistic character. Debussy composed his nocturnes and *La Mer* at about the same time that Whistler and Monet painted their nocturnes and marines. Without trying to force this connection between music and painting, it is plain that the underlying structural principle—a fusion of parts—was the same in all. The common denominator of this principle is a minimum of independence and a maximum of interdependence of the parts in a composition, whether it be pictorial, musical, or literary. The individual forms in a Monet hardly make sense; they must be read in relationship to neighboring areas, and even these must be read in the context of the picture as a whole. In literature the fusion of parts is marked by a repeated use of conjunctives, introductory and other

FIG. 271. Michelangelo.
Tomb of Lorenzo de' Medici.
ca. 1523-1533. Medici Chapel.
S. Lorenzo. Florence.

FIG. 272. Bernini. *Chair*
of St. Peter. 1657-1666.
St. Peter's. Rome.

linking words. Each sentence refers to the one before it and the one that follows in a chain of ideas.

A sentence by Gibbon can stand by itself. And while a figure by Michelangelo gains something from its position in a design, the *Adam* (Fig. 58) is an imposing figure alone. The sense of completeness created by Michelangelo's preparatory drawings for larger compositions bears this out. A simple practical test will demonstrate the relative independence of parts in an ensemble of parts, as opposed to the relative dependence upon contexts of the elements in a fusion of parts. With a pair of scissors one can easily cut from a photograph a figure by Michelangelo, a building by Giotto, a capital by Brunelleschi, or a part of any design that is classical in the broadest sense. But he would be at a loss where to cut among the shadowy outlines in Rembrandt's *Nicholas Bruyningh* or Whistler's *Nocturne*. Even if he were moderately successful, the figures would look incomplete. The significance of the context as distinct from the part can be illustrated by the quotability of ideas from Shakespeare and the Bible. They make sense either in or out of their contexts. So pregnant with meaning are they that they seem to carry their own contexts within them. Conversely, while many people read Poe, almost no one quotes him.

The fusion of parts is an organizing principle in all the visual arts. In Bourdelle's *Beethoven* (Fig. 164), for instance, the parts are as indefinite and dependent upon the whole as the parts of Rembrandt's *Nicholas Bruyningh,* and both contrast with the Egyptian *Head of a Priest* in Fig. 163 and Lippi's painted *Portrait of a Man* (Fig. 125), in which ears, eyes, and mouths are sharply delineated. Wölfflin, observing that this principle runs through sculpture and painting alike, described the difference between the classical ensemble of parts and the romantic fusion of parts as the difference between absolute and relative clarity. However, the principle of fusion is carried so far in Medardo Rosso's highly impressionist *Woman Seen Toward Evening* (Fig. 170) that clarity is almost eliminated, placing it at the far pole from either Laurana's Renaissance-classical *Princess of the House of Aragon* (Fig. 158) or Brancusi's modern-classical *Mademoiselle Pogany* (Fig. 159).

Also far removed from any ultra-clear classical buildings are the masterpieces of Gothic and Baroque architecture. In the interior of Amiens Cathedral (Fig. 209) the eye will not find pilasters standing out darkly against a light wall or contrasting with abruptly horizontal cornices. Instead, it will be led from floor to vault and from doorway to apse by continuous lines that embrace the entire fabric like a gigantic net. One will remember the interior as a whole without being able to recall any particular medallion or capital. This does not mean that no horizontal lines interrupt the upward sweep of vertical piers and curved vaults, but only that the relatively small capitals and cornices provide variety and accents without creating a break in the major emphasis.

The baroque artists of the North created a style of their own, but retained a number of features of the Gothic principle of a fusion of parts. Though the Cathedral of Amiens and Neumann's Wallfahrt-kirche at Vierzehnheiligen (Fig. 184) look quite different at first glance, they are kin in many respects. As one contrasts either or both of them with the Pazzi Chapel or the Pantheon their common points become more apparent. Chief among these is a mutual adherence to the fusion of parts as a principle of part-to-part organization. In their case, as in others, it is a principle which unites superficially dissimilar buildings in a world-wide, timeless, and basically similar family. It is at the heart of one of the great traditions of art.

The masterpieces of architecture illustrate one or another of these modes of organization by adhering to an even more important principle of design—consistent limitation. For an architect who has limited himself to an ensemble of parts or a fusion of parts on the interior of his building will apply the same system to the exterior. Hence the Pazzi Chapel and the Pantheon are ensembles of parts inside and out, while the Cathedral of Amiens and the Wallfahrt-kirche are externally and internally just as definitely of the opposite type.

CLOSED AND OPEN CONTOURS

A work of visual art possesses a set of internal relationships which may be fused or arranged ensemble. But it is also related to the external world. In a picture this relationship is adjusted to the frame; in a statue or building, whose silhouette is its frame, the relationship is to surrounding space. Since space is intangible and a frame is often unobtrusive, we tend to overlook this important relationship. We can appreciate its importance by noting that the whole of city-planning is based upon the relationships of buildings to each other and the surrounding space.

A painter can use a frame to great advantage, making it far more than a means of hanging a picture on a wall or separating it from the wall. Ingres realized this opportunity and exploited it when he painted his portrait of *Madame Rivière* (Fig. 274a). At first glance a photographically realistic image of a beautiful woman, it is, on closer inspection, a masterpiece of design. The internal relationships

FIG. 273. Brunelleschi. Pazzi Chapel. 1429. S. Croce. Florence.

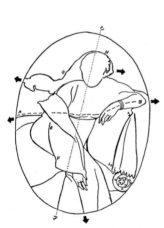

FIG. 274b. Compositional diagram of Ingres's *Madame
Rivière*.

FIG. 274a. Ingres. *Madame Rivière*. 1805. Louvre,
Paris.

of the linear pattern comprise a most beautiful complex of graded S-curves, harmonies and balances of attitude, and linking sequential lines. The harmony of curvilinear shapes is a fascinating network of continuous forms, leading the eye along flowing lines and creating an intense sensation of grace, clarity, and poise. No aristocratic beauty could have asked for a more advantageous presentation.

The internal relationships constitute only half of the picture's appeal. The other half derives from the brilliant way in which Ingres utilized his oval frame. Avoiding the obvious, he balanced his design asymmetrically, bisecting the oval in two directions by diagonal lines (*A–B* and *C–D* in Fig. 274b). Their tilt gives the subject her dynamic, alert appearance. Even more impressive is the way Ingres played his main directional lines against the frame, echoing its curvature (*E–F* and *G–H*), balancing it (*I–J*), and cutting it at right angles. The arrows in the compositional diagram (Fig. 274b) are intended to show how systematically Ingres employed this device. The radiating lines seem almost to burst the bounds of the frame, giving the design a high degree of vitality. It is a picture whose design cannot be fully understood apart from its frame.

Not all artists have handled this external relationship as expertly as Ingres. Yet it is a factor in every other work of visual art. The basic relationships are implied by the terms *closed contours* and *open contours*. In the closed contour there is a deliberate exclusion of the surrounding world. Raphael's *School of Athens* (Fig. 104) is an excellent example. He clearly intended his picture to be as self-sufficient as possible—an intellectually created, man-made realm which owes nothing to nature and little to the outside world. He therefore painted a heavy enframement and organized his picture so that nothing within it challenges that boundary. It is a finite, limited scene.

The open contour expresses an opposite conception of the role of the frame. It is but a necessary practical limit to a segment of a larger reality. In that respect Velasquez's *Maids of Honor* (Fig. 94) is the converse of Raphael's *School of Athens*. The Spanish master did everything possible to imply a world outside his picture. He therefore let his frame cut through the large canvas on his easel to the left and the window and boy on the right. Our eyes, supplying the remainder of these forms imaginatively, penetrate beyond the frame. Velasquez invites us to extend our vision into the outside world as surely as Raphael excluded it by blocking our way. Whereas he hems us and his painted figures in, Velasquez suggests a participation in a larger, infinite reality.

Many other pairs of paintings could illustrate these fundamentally opposite conceptions. Fra Angelico's *Madonna of Humility* (Fig.

191), like Raphael's *School of Athens*, is a strongly centralized, inward-looking picture, sufficient unto itself. On the other hand, Rembrandt's *Nicholas Bruyningh* (Fig. 135) directs the spectator's imagination outward in the direction of Bruyningh's gaze. To that extent it is not self-sufficient, nor was it intended to be. Rembrandt appreciated the infinite too much to cut his figures off from it; he directs our attention to it at every opportunity.

Rubens, judging by his *Rape of the Daughters of Leucippus* (Fig. 216), shared Rembrandt's appreciation for the larger world. Although more of a classicist than the Dutch master, he participated in the expansive attitude of the seventeenth century. His composition seems to burst with energy, his forms to radiate from the center.

The picture conceived with open contours seems to override the confining frame, as though resenting narrow physical limitations. This can be appreciated by contrasting the Rubens with Raphael's *Madonna of the Chair* (Fig. 253). Both are central designs, but opposite in their centrality, for Raphael's circularly arranged figures make no attempt to burst outward; they reflect the frame and appear perfectly happy within it. Spiritually, the two pictures represent a sort of claustrophobia on the one hand and contented confinement on the other.

In the nineteenth century Degas and the Impressionists followed Rubens and Velasquez rather than Raphael. Degas' tendency in that direction was reinforced by his love of Japanese prints. In them human figures and architectural forms are frequently cut down the middle by the frame. Degas carried this technique inherited from Velasquez and the Japanese to a high point in his *Rehearsal* (Fig. 266). The frame crops the elderly violinist at the waist and severs the foot of one of the ballet girls while allowing another dancer's foot to protrude into the scene. Hence our imaginations are deliberately directed to areas and forms outside of those actually shown. This casual but skilfully framed segment of reality has the natural and lifelike quality of a close-cropped candid camera shot.

The necessity for some kind of frame in painting makes the closed or open contour largely a mental concept. The artist who prefers the closed type will accept the frame, respect it, and unite it with his composition. The painter who prefers the open type will regard the frame as an unfortunate necessity and use organization and implication in every way that he can to overcome its limiting presence. The artist who conceives the world in finite terms will be happiest within the closed contour, while the lover of the infinite will gravitate toward the open contour method.

The concepts of open and closed contour apply to sculpture and architecture with even greater force; in them contours are literally open and need not be implied. If anything, sculptors and architects must exert themselves to create a sense of enclosure among their normally open forms, but their intention is usually clear. For instance, Michelangelo said that a well-conceived statue could be rolled down hill without having any limbs broken. He favored compact figures over more exuberant, outward-thrusting types, and put this attitude into practice in such statues as his *Captive* (Fig. 66) and *Bound Slave* (Fig. 358). Like the painter who respects the frame, he revered the block of stone and preserved something of its compact character in the finished work.

The continuity of this point of view is illustrated by Maillol's modern masterpiece, the *Mediterranean* (Fig. 269). Like Michelangelo, Maillol created a frame with his own figure by linking the head and the upraised knee through the arm. He thus formed an unbroken line or closed contour around the figure. The bowed head and introspective orientation of the figure reinforce this effect. Self-contained, it is lost in its own world.

A simple but practical way of distinguishing the closed contour from the open contour in sculpture is to imagine the closed type of statue in a single looping outline, while any outline around the open type would wind in and out; one would be simple, the other complex. The complex outline would clearly be demanded by Bernini's *St. Longinus* (Fig. 270). His conception of sculptural form was as outgoing, expansive, and uninhibited as Michelangelo's was constrained. His work tends to remind us more of his exuberant contemporary Rubens than either the great Florentines before him or Maillol afterward. A dynamic spirit, Bernini preferred centrifugal action and cross-shaped designs to the centripetal or circular. Whereas Maillol's *Mediterranean* is introspective, with head bowed down, Bernini's *Longinus* is extroverted and upward-looking. It illustrates, in contrast to the Maillol, another significant difference between the closed and open contour in sculpture—opposite treatments of surface. The surfaces of the *Mediterranean* are smooth and round, and in accord with the simple outline. The surface of the *St. Longinus* is full of bosses and indentations. It is as consistently broken up and complex as the figure's outline. The part-to-part organization is consistent in each case with the dominant conception.

The closed or open contour can be employed in both the outline and parts of a statue. They can also be applied to the composition of any sculptural group, extending the consistency of the individual figures to the design as a whole. True to their views, Michelangelo and Bernini demonstrated this principle when they created the *Tomb*

of Lorenzo de Medici (Fig. 271) and the *Chair of St. Peter* (Fig. 272).
In Michelangelo's tomb at Florence each figure is contained within a
closed contour, spiritually isolated and introspective. This is so true
of the portrait of Lorenzo that the nickname-loving Italians have long
called him "Il Penseroso." The general effect created by the *Tomb*
is one of a carefully balanced ensemble of independent parts. The
human figures form a symmetrical pyramid, but each stands out
against the architectural setting. In it there are bases for the reclining figures and a frame for Lorenzo. This idea of an ensemble of
enclosed and underlined parts extends throughout the composition.
The tomb itself is sharply defined by a dark enframement which sets
it apart from the rest of the room. The principle of the closed contour was applied individually and collectively throughout Michelangelo's design.

Bernini's *Chair of St. Peter* is the converse of Michelangelo's
Tomb. It illustrates that there is a strong affinity between a fusion of
parts and open contours, just as there is between an ensemble of parts
and closed contours. The *Chair* is a fine illustration of one affinity,
the *Tomb* of the other. The governing principle in both is consistent limitation carried throughout the composition. The individual figures in Bernini's *Chair of St. Peter* are, like his *St. Longinus*,
characterized by open contours. The extroverted figures look outward and spread their arms, forming complex, open, moving shapes
which direct our attention from part to part in a continuous linking
movement. The draperies, too, are characterized by numerous swirl-
ing folds, giving a sense of activity. Openness, continuity, and vitality are the keynotes of this design just as inclosure, separation, and
stability are of Michelangelo's *Tomb.* Bernini's figures are so linked
that no one of them stands out strongly, as do Michelangelo's; their
merit lies, instead, in their interrelationships. There is also a noticeable difference between the ways by which Michelangelo and Bernini
related their groups to the larger architectural settings. The *Tomb
of Lorenzo* is self-contained and sharply bounded; the *Chair of St.
Peter* reaches out in every direction to join its surroundings. The
crowning touch in the *Chair* is the treatment of the Dove of the Holy
Spirit; it is framed in an eye which admits the light of the whole outdoors through an actual window. Though small, it is a perfect symbol of the open-contour concept of design.

A helpful way of distinguishing between the closed and open contour is to perceive that the former excludes the surrounding space
and the latter embraces it. The open contour reaches out toward
space like the fingers of a hand, seeking to create a union of forms and
space through an interpenetration of the two. The devotee of the

closed contour cares nothing for space itself. Favoring the tangible solid, he is indifferent toward the intangible space that surounds it. In broader terms he cares little for the infinite or in effecting any union between his forms and it; more often he tries to shut it out. The adherent of the open contour extends his appreciation imaginatively to include space. To him the interstice is as real and important as the solid form around it. The one derives its meaning from the other and cannot be understood without it. He therefore invites space into his buildings in numerous ways and seeks by implication to make his structure a part of infinity.

The signs of these two opposite attitudes are manifold in the history of sculpture, but are especially prominent in architecture—an art of hollow forms. Let us turn for examples to three noted structures, the Great Pyramid of Khufu (Fig. 174a), the Pantheon (Fig. 176), and the Strozzi Palace (Fig. 175), and consider the connection between finitude and the closed contour which contains each of them. The finite closed contour is itself the result of a use of geometric forms for the basic masses and composition of each structure. Working together, the closed contour and the regular, balanced geometric forms give these buildings that appearance of independent self-sufficiency which is a common characteristic of finite, closed contour design. The most striking exception to this general rule is modern architecture. Although its proponents have returned to geometric masses, they have grouped them in dynamic, out-thrusting patterns and stressed a new openness in the treatment of walls. Their tradition-breaking combination of closed-contoured geometric masses and open-contoured designs accounts in no small measure for the revolutionary quality of such outstanding examples as the New York University–Bellevue Medical Center (Fig. 178 and 251) and Wright's Fallingwater (Fig. 213).

A consistent way of employing open contours architecturally was discovered long ago by the Gothic architects. Lovers of the plastic form and the fusion of parts, they allied these to open contours to suggest the infinite profoundly. The Cathedral of Reims (Fig. 179) and the façade of Rouen Cathedral (Fig. 182) illustrate their attitude. The outlines of Reims are broken at every point by towers, spires, pinnacles, and canopies as the building reaches up into the sky. The flying buttresses leap over space like so many bridges, and every part of the building pushes out into space or draws it into baylike forms. The eye meets an intermingling of forms and space in every direction. In this respect the wide-open, lacelike Cathedral of Reims could not be more different from the massive Pyramid of Khufu.

A similar contrast exists between the entrance to the Strozzi Palace

(Fig. 181) and the façade of Rouen Cathedral. Despite the presence of an entrance in the Florentine palace, its thick walls and closed contours seem to exclude the outside world both socially and spatially, like a fortress or a tomb. The light and airy cathedral, with its many windows and large doors, implies an inviting interior and seems to welcome us into it. Yet when we enter a typical Gothic cathedral, like the large one at Amiens (Fig. 209), our attention seems to be directed toward the exterior, for much of the genius of the Gothic builders lay in their ability to make one imply the other and the building as a whole to imply infinity. They achieved this effect by suppressing the dividing line between exterior and interior, bringing the sunlight of the outside in through large windows and pointing their vaulted arches like arrows toward heaven. Inside and out their buildings are as open as they could be. We feel in them a sense of spaciousness which is the opposite of claustrophobia.

One can appreciate the spaciousness of the Gothic interior by comparing the nave of Amiens with the rotunda of the Pantheon (Fig. 204). In spite of the generous dimensions of the Roman temple and its famous "eye," one feels hemmed in by ponderous walls and a downward-pressing dome. The earth-bound Roman building does not soar; nor was it meant to. The spiritual purpose was to inspire a feeling of permanence, dependability, and protection. This it does superbly. The Gothic cathedral is, by contrast, the epitome of a dynamic freedom and confidence.

It is interesting to note in passing how Max Berg's Centennial Hall at Breslau (Fig. 205), while resembling the Pantheon, is new because of its adaptation of Gothic openness.

The instinct for an interpenetration of forms and space was inherited from the Gothic builders by the Baroque masters. Given a new, more horizontal direction, it was employed brilliantly to imply the union of the tangible and the infinite in reality. We need go no further than Vierzehnheiligen (Fig. 184) to observe how a Baroque structure attempts to burst its physical limits by pushing out into space at every opportunity. The open contour is the heart of its architectural design, as it was crucial to Bernini's Baroque sculptural groups. The fusion of parts and open contours at Vierzehnheiligen permeate the structure. The curvilinear lines of the plan of the Wallfarhtkirche are so integrated that they appear to envelop, push inward, and radiate all at once. The exterior joins this concerted movement by undulating in and out like a cupid's bow or serpentine. Its cross-shaped plan resembles the out-reaching arms of Bernini's *St. Longinus*; the open contour is basic in both.

The use of closed and open contours in sculpture produces effects comparable to those found in architecture. The use of closed contour in architecture makes a building appear comparatively heavy and earth-bound, even when it is tall and thin. To test that principle, compare the monolithic Washington Monument with the Eiffel Tower; the difference in effect is not due to height alone. Closed contours also make a building appear to rest upon the ground but be distinct from it (as in the Parthenon), whereas the Gothic cathedral seems a part of its surroundings, growing out of the ground and reaching toward the sky. The three elements are not separated as they are by the Parthenon's prominent base and heavy horizontal roof; instead, the decorative statues on the cathedrals form vertical links between whatever is below and above them.

The classical conception of the relation of forms to ground and surrounding space runs through both architecture and sculpture. *Menkure and His Queen* are enveloped in a closed contour which excludes space and plants them independently but heavily on the ground. Everything about them suggests self-contained solidity. The same observation applies to the Egyptian *Head of a Priest* in Fig. 163. The unison of the closed contour and the ensemble of parts is characteristic of the classical style in all media and times. Consequently the Egyptian *Priest* and Laurana's *Princess of the House of Aragon* (Fig. 158) are stylistic cousins and both are foreign to Bourdelle's *Beethoven* (Fig. 164), in which there is a fusion of parts and open contours.

An open contour endows a sculptural figure with an aura of movement and vitality—a common characteristic of Bourdelle's *Beethoven* as well as of Bernini's *St. Longinus* and *Chair of St. Peter.* When actual motion is implied, as in Bernini's *Apollo and Daphne* (Fig. 167) and Sintenis' *Runner* (Fig. 162), the figures appear to glide over the ground instead of resting heavily upon it. They seem literally to have entered the scene from one side and to be on the point of running out of it on the other, thus implying a larger world of space on the order of the frame-cropped violinist and dancers in Degas' *Rehearsal* (Fig. 166). In each case the use of open contours creates a feeling of physical lightness that is contrary to the closed contour's effect of weight and stability.

These samples fall into groups which lead to certain general conclusions. There is a natural affinity between the closed contour and ensemble of parts and the open contour and fusion of parts regardless of medium. Their constant appearance together indicates that they are integral components of two different systems of design which express two opposite expressive purposes. How these express, in turn, comprehensive philosophies of reality has already been suggested.

The distribution of these systems of part-to-part organization in time follows the historical ebb and flow of two unlike conceptions of parts. The closed contour prevailed in classical antiquity in all media and has enjoyed renewed prestige whenever the classical view of life has been revived, notably in the period of the Renaissance and, to some extent, in modern times. Meanwhile, the fusion of parts and open contours has enjoyed favor in a rhythmic alternation, reaching peaks of achievement in the Gothic period, in Baroque art, and to some degree in the nineteenth century. As evidence of mastery in the seventeenth century one need only mention the Baroque genius for relating buildings to one another and to their environments. By extending their appreciation of space to a building's surroundings the Baroque masters laid the foundations of modern city planning and landscape architecture and immeasurably enhanced the effectiveness of their own buildings. In this regard they were at least different from the Gothic masters, for where the medieval designers fused their structures with existing surroundings, the Baroque architects achieved control by creating their own environment. Their two masterpieces of controlled settings, St. Peter's (Figs. 85a and 85b), with its colonnaded piazza, and the Palace of Versailles, with its tremendous gardens, influenced scores of later designs.

Yet the Baroque feeling for space was demonstrated most vividly in the field of painting. Because of their love of openness, modern landscape painting was born in the seventeenth century. In the outdoor scenes of Claude Lorrain (Fig. 117) and Ruysdael (Fig. 116) the distant horizon and vault of sky are, for the first time, not mere backdrops for more important human affairs, as they are in Perugino's *Christ Delivering the Keys of Heaven to St. Peter* (Fig. 102a) and Titian's *Rape of Europa* (Fig. 132 and 195), but are continuously fused recessions and unlimited invitations into infinity. The Baroque painters thus applied the principle of open contours to the three-dimensional space of their pictures as well as to the two-dimensional frames. To prove that the Baroque mastery of space was not an accident, artists like Pozzo fused their ceiling designs (Fig. 110) and opened up contours to such an extent that they made the vaults of churches seem to disappear, achieving a triumph of spatial organization.

CHAPTER 19

The Expression of Ideas
The Subjects of Art

Expression is the result of *what* is presented and *how* it is organized or designed. In the representational arts the first of these ends is achieved by employing likeness in some degree. In the abstract arts, in which there is no subject matter in the usual sense, ideas and emotions are conveyed through a combination of form and symbolism.

The task before us is to explore and illustrate these premises in two stages. We shall ultimately consider the coordination of form and content in a series of specific examples, arriving thereby at a principle which is generally valid without being a "fixed idea" or a single standard of beauty or expression. But prior to that we must at least introduce ourselves to the range of ideas that has been expressed through the visual arts.

THE MAJOR TYPES OF SUBJECT MATTER

The visual arts have been called the picture-book of civilization. They have embraced the life of man in such a powerfully illustrative manner as to rank among the foremost historical means of discerning man's past. They tell us of his interests, hopes, aspirations, and fears. And in man's art we find the key to his capacity for understanding his world.

Artistic subject matter comes from man's observations of inner and outer reality and his urge to control and understand them. The subdivisions of these interests are the various orientations of perception as discussed in Chapter 3—naturalistic, humanistic, social, religious, and introspective. We shall translate these general terms into the specialized vocabulary of the visual arts without any loss, for the

Fig. 275. Totonac ceremonial axe head. *ca.* 1000-1200. Albright Art
Gallery, Buffalo.

Fig. 276. Ch'en Jung. Detail. *Nine Dragon Scroll.* Mid-13th century, Sung Dynasty.
Museum of Fine Arts, Boston.

542

principal categories of subject matter found in painting, drawing, and sculpture embrace also every aspect of life. These are: religious art, symbolic art, allegory, visionary art, satire, caricature, literary illustration, historical illustration, genre, portraiture, human anatomy, animal life, outdoor scenes, and still life.

RELIGIOUS ART. The religious attitude is the most universal in human life. It has been defined as the worship of higher powers from a sense of need, a need based on man's inability to control or understand reality in any final sense. From this inability stem his most profound awe and worst fears. Judging by the number of paintings and statues which express this, man's control and understanding of reality has been slight throughout most of history. Religious art declined as man's knowledge of natural reality and his control over it was increased by modern science. That decline, however, was only a matter of a few hundred years. If works of art of all ages are taken into account, religious art clearly comprises two-thirds or more of all the art in the world. Fear, awe, superstition, and exaltation move men deeply, and intense feeling is the strongest motivation of art.

The West has interpreted religion in a narrow sense, hardly thinking beyond Christian symbols or the representation of Biblical episodes. But human needs arising from a sense of inadequacy before the infinite and unknown have also been embraced by Mohammedanism, Buddhism, Hinduism, and innumerable primitive religious, each with its own artistic expression. Hence we can first illustrate religious art by a Totonac ceremonial axe-head (Fig. 275) and a detail of Ch'en Jung's *Nine Dragon Scroll* (Fig. 276).

The Totonac axe-head speaks for the fear of a jungle-dwelling people of harm from natural enemies. The enemies they propitiate are a serpent and a feline, probably a jaguar. Fears of this sort are commonly expressed in primitive art. The *Nine Dragon Scroll* expresses a happier adjustment to nature, for the Chinese dragon is not the fearsome beast of Western lore but a symbol of natural forces which may be benign as well as destructive. These dragons sport through the clouds and upper air with wonderful abandon, bringing not only thunder, lightning, and wind, but also crop-nourishing rains. This scroll speaks for many human views, for nature-oriented religions have been frequent in human history.

The worship of higher powers from a sense of need was naturally attended over many centuries of time by expectations of practical help. Men propitiated images or idols in the hope of avoiding evil or gaining some benefit from either human or natural sources. Prehistoric and primitive art contains countless examples of this type.

The Chinese bronze ritual vessel pictured in Fig. 243 combines both ideas in an interesting way; it is decorated with thunder-scroll motifs which signify rain for crops and also with highly stylized designs of the cicada, or locusts which destroyed the crops. The dragon heads and water buffalo patterns are tokens of a so-called animistic religion. Generally speaking, the artists of primitive agricultural societies everywhere have always expressed an alert consciousness of the whims and favors of a capricious and all-powerful nature. Unable to control or understand it, they could only propitiate it. Similarly, the artists of nomadic, hunting societies have reflected their people's respect for the element of luck in unpredictable wars and hunts. Art of this sort dates back to prehistoric times. The prehistoric *Bison* in Fig. 33, while denoting a careful observation of natural appearances, was also painted with an eye upon good fortune in the hunt.

A survey of religious art must include many Christian examples, but it should also include examples from other lands and past societies. Typical examples shown in this book which represent the world's religious art are Tintoretto's *Miracle of St. Mark*, Giotto's *Presentation of the Virgin*, Rubens' *Elevation of the Cross*, Fra Angelico's *Madonna of Humility*, Ribera's *Martyrdom of St. Bartholomew*, El Greco's *Agony in the Garden*, Rembrandt's *Supper at Emmaus*, Titian's *Entombment of Christ*, Gauguin's *Mahana No Atua*, Raphael's *Three Graces*, Rubens' *Rape of the Daughters of Leucippus*, the Greek *Zeus from Artemisium*, the Byzantine *Crucifixion* at Daphni, the Chinese *Sakyamuni and Prabhutaratna*, and the Indian *Kali* and *Dancing Siva*. Many of these come from the field of Greek mythology, a source of religious art which played a tremendous part even in Western Christendom.

These and other works of religious art tell us much about man's spiritual life. They express his conceptions of the origin of the natural world and cosmos, the origin of human life, the character of death, and of life beyond death. They express his speculations on the meaning of premature death despite goodness, and of longevity despite evil. They recognize the effects of natural phenomena, from beneficent sunshine and rain to natural calamities. They explore, too, the social relationships of man to man.

These works of art illustrate several important approaches to the expression of religious ideas. One of great popularity is the symbolic approach exemplified by the *Crucifixion* at Daphni. Another that is found all over the world, with the outstanding exception of iconoclastic Mohammedism, is of a historical nature, and illustrates a specific episode, like Titian's *Christ Crowned with Thorns*. Since the human mind craves demonstrations of religious ideas, this identi-

fication of religion with individuals and incidents has been even
more universal than symbolical art; Hinduism, Buddhism, Christianity, and Greek paganism abound in it. It is a special mark of protestant art, as in Rembrandt's Biblical illustrations.

The world's religious art can also be divided into two vast groups
according to origin of inspiration. In one group, containing Buddhism and Christianity, are those religions which grew out of the
ideas and examples of towering historical personalities. In the other
group are innumerable religions developed amorphously from the
ideas and superstitions of myriad anonymous people. The classic
example is ancient Greek mythology, but the group includes the
whole of Hinduism and countless mythological and legendary early
religions, including much of the Judaism of the Old Testament.
This type has gained the allegiance of the overwhelming majority of
human beings. However, many believe that the religions founded
by such prophets as Christ, Mohammed, and the Gautama Buddha
have transcended the superstitious religions qualitatively by encouraging a higher ideal for the human potential. If this view is
tenable, the contention that Christianity and Buddhism have inspired
the finest religious art can also be justified.

The most important offer of the prophet-founded religions was an
ideal of brotherly love instead of fear. The artistic realization of this
ideal depended, however, on favorable historical conditions. The
Christian art of the medieval West, for instance, expressed an authoritarian, collective, and highly symbolic attitude. Only with the
comparative individual freedom of the Renaissance were artists like
Giotto and Rembrandt able to cultivate the democratic, social, and
positive tenets of Christianity.

Common, too, are examples of supplication for divine intervention in time of need, and acknowledgment of miraculous help. Illustrations of Christ's miracles, like Rembrandt's *Christ Healing the
Sick* (Fig. 151), are many. Another famous example is Tintoretto's
Miracle of St. Mark (Fig. 256) which commemorates the spectacular
rescue from martyrdom of an early Christian convert. But Christianity had no monopoly on the respect for divine intervention. In the
Freer Gallery at Washington there is an excellent example from India depicting Krishna Holding the Hill Govardhana to Protect the
People of Brindaban and Their Cattle from the Rain Poured down
by Indra. Two other objects of worship for intervention of some sort
should be mentioned. One inspired the Cult of the Virgin in the
West, which reached its peak in the late Middle Ages. The other,
which shows the universality of basic human needs, inspired the Cult
of Kuan Yin in the Buddhist lands of Asia, China, and Japan. Both

of these cults were sustained by the prayers of women for help in their special needs—for marital happiness, fertility, and comfort during childbirth.

A sketch of religious art makes one thing plain: no other type of art can compare with the insight it can give into man's spiritual life —his bed-rock hopes and fears, virtues and limitations. Beside it other art often seems superficial. Nor can one avoid the conclusion that the majority of human beings who have lived on this planet have been haunted by fear. The evidence of art on this score is plain. The examples which express joy, exaltation, or uninhibited love can be quickly named. Bellini's *St. Francis in Ecstasy*, the *Assumption of the Virgin* by Correggio and Titian, and the *Glorification of the Company of Jesus* (Fig. 110) by Pozzo are as exhilarating as they are rare. Most human beings have truly found life a vale of tears.

SYMBOLIC ART. Every entity has both universal and individual attributes; anything can be construed as a symbol. In artistic parlance, however, a symbol has a special meaning. We have already noted something of this meaning in distinguishing between the symbolical and illustrative intentions of such pictures as the *Crucifixion* at Daphni and Titian's *Entombment of Christ*. Religious art is full of symbols and symbolic meanings, but it has no monopoly on the use of symbolic expression.

This type of expression can be defined indirectly by determining the motives behind its use. When and where has it been employed? Why? With those questions answered we should be able to recognize good and bad practices in symbolic expression. Judging by prehistoric, primitive, and child art, an artist's first instinct is to represent what he sees. But as knowledge accumulates in a society its store of ideas becomes more comprehensive, complex, and abstract. Mathematicians, religious leaders, and artists must resort frequently to symbols for the communication of ideas.

An artist commonly resorts to symbolic expression when he wishes to convey the idea of something supernatural and hence invisible— such as figures of gods, angels, and devils. Since, in the visual arts, these must be seen to be appreciated, he makes them tangible by creating symbols for them. A large group of symbols for the moods, forces, and phenomena of nature—Chinese thunder scrolls, Sotatsu's wind gods, Michelangelo's *Dawn, Twilight, Day,* and *Night* on the Medici Tombs (Fig. 271)—represent a similar expedient. Often the idea to be conveyed is too vast, complex, or remote for the ordinary limits of a painting, drawing, or sculptural group. So the artist reduces it to a single figure or simple group. The Greeks showed special aptitude for this kind of summary simplification. Humanistically inclined, they personified intangible ideas, creating wood nymphs, river gods, and deities for every occasion. They conceived them so well that they have continued to populate Western literature and art for three thousand years. Later societies followed suit when they wished to create national signs or to summarize large ideas.

The figure of Uncle Sam illustrates why a painter must employ a symbol for anything so complex as a country. An author or songwriter can include enough descriptive detail to elaborate many of the aspects of a nation (as in the words "I love thy rocks and rills, thy woods and templed hills"), but the visual artist must confine himself to what the eye can see. The alternative is to employ a series of pictures in medieval or comic strip fashion—not now regarded as satisfactory—or express the idea symbolically. Even relatively concentrated visible entities often elude direct representation. Hence the adoption of figures of Alma Mater for colleges and universities, for example.

When an artist desires to stress notable individual attributes or crucial events in the lives of important personages, he frequently finds symbolism valuable. Medieval art abounds in examples of this ideological sign language—the money bags of St. Nicholas, the arrows of St. Sebastian, the stones of St. Stephen, and countless other signs of martyrdom or holiness: palms, crowns, halos, etc. The same system was also used to identify Justice (scales), Father Time (a scythe), and Cupid (a bow and arrow).

When an artist wishes to emphasize certain human traits indirectly he often employs symbolic references to animal characteristics—the fox's intelligence, the lion's strength, the eagle's swiftness, the donkey's stubbornness, the coyote's cowardice, or the wolf's voraciousness. Aesop and La Fontaine exploited these associations with classic success in literature. Their meanings were not lost when adopted for the visual arts. The statue of the Sphinx is a world-famous example, while the colossal Assyrian guardian figures that combine the strengths of men, eagles, and lions or bulls are noted examples of composite symbolism employing animal attributes.

Symbolism has many uses; it is a great convenience. Like shorthand, it saves time, relieving the artist of the necessity of describing the story of St. Sebastian's martyrdom in detail. The figure of a man, a column, or even a single arrow is sufficient to convey the story. More important still are the general merits of symbolism. It allows an artist to emphasize the universal rather than the individual aspects of an idea. Since a nation like the United States or a religious con-

ception like the Holy Spirit cannot otherwise be depicted, symbolism
is the only visual means of communicating certain ideas.

Two faults of symbolism should be recognized along with its
merits. It puts a premium on knowledge and demands a capacity
for abstraction. Lack of knowledge may cause works of art to become meaningless in the course of time to all except scholars. Prominent instances today are those demanding a knowledge of the Bible,
church history, or classical mythology. Owing to the rapid decline
of this kind of knowledge in our society, most of the subject matter
of medieval religious art and ancient and Renaissance classical art is
now lost on the majority of people.

Abstraction is sometimes extremely difficult to understand, even
for well-educated persons. Recognizing this, artists like Goya have
symbolized the evils of war by representing specific scenes. These are
without doubt easier to grasp than such highly symbolic treatments
of war as Picasso's *Guernica*. Furthermore, though Picasso's *Guernica* is charged with passion, most symbolic art seems emotionally
colder than illustrative art.

There is a case for employing a fair degree of realism in the type
of expression illustrated by Goya's *Disasters of War* or *Execution of
Madrileños*. Conversely, symbolism calls for a considerable degree of
generalization if not of outright idealization. Thus an artist who
wishes to stress the universal implications of any idea, as Picasso did
when he painted the *Guernica*, is justified in not being explicit in
details. This connection between symbolism and generalization for
the sake of universal meaning is basic. Missing that point is almost
sure to produce bad results, the most glaring being the paintings of
the nineteenth-century French academicians. Endowed with more
snobbishness than understanding, they produced tons of highly realistic marble figures of justice, hope, virtue, and the like. This was a
mistake which the Greeks seldom made. Masters of both idealization
and explicit realism, they never mixed these incompatibles in their
finest periods of art.

ALLEGORY. An allegory is a story told wholly or partially through
symbols, or symbolic expression with an illustrative purpose. The
distinction can be made clear by a few examples. The Statue of Liberty tells no story; it stands for a general idea of freedom. In Delacroix's painting *Liberty Leading the People* (Fig. 315) in the Louvre,
the figure of Marianne also represents freedom, but freedom in the
context of a specific event, the Revolution of July, 1830, in France.

On the other hand, allegorical and symbolic expression are similar
in several respects. An artist who resorts to either of them generally

wishes to stress the broader, more universal aspects of an idea, and avoid the explicitness of the realistic mode of representation. He must also avoid unduly abstruse ideas and treat themes which are a part of common knowledge if he wishes to be understood—a point that Rivera and other proponents of communist doctrines have often missed. Finally, he must strive to overcome the coldness that always threatens symbolic expression because of its inherently abstract character. Its very loftiness may make it seem remote. To overcome this austerity he must provide vitality, warmth, passion, or sincerity, along with knowledge and logical intelligence—a large order for any artist.

Allegory goes beyond symbolism in another respect which adds to the artist's difficulties. It not only relates a story but generally points a moral in the telling. The moral must be significant rather than trivial, and of almost universal and timeless meaning. If genuine breadth is not attained, the failure is usually described as banal. Allegorical expression is not a form to be undertaken lightly. While its successes are impressive, its failures have been numerous.

Among the successes one must certainly list the *Contest of Carnival and Lent* painted by Pieter Bruegel the Elder. A man of encyclopedic knowledge and interests, and abounding vitality, humor, and warmth, Bruegel was able to see and reveal the extremes of abstinence and gluttony. He could treat a subject in the broadest terms and yet make it seem like life itself.

Bruegel was a giant, a unique and exceptional artist. But one cannot help feeling in the presence of his work that the time in which an artists lives has a bearing upon his success with allegorical expression. The Middle Ages and Renaissance were schooled in allegorical and symbolic representation. To artists and spectators alike religious, classical, and philosophical ideas were part of the atmosphere. Bruegel, while contributing his own genius, also inherited this aptitude.

The nineteenth and twentieth centuries lost touch with this tradition, making effective examples of allegory all the more remarkable. In addition to Delacroix's *Liberty Leading the People*, Daniel Chester French's *Death and the Sculptor* (Fig. 277) and Albert Ryder's *Death on a Pale Horse* (Fig. 278) are good examples, and Picasso's *Guernica* one worthy of Goya or Bruegel himself. Goya, incidentally, created the last great series of allegories, among the greatest of all times, in the old tradition—the aquatints called *Proverbios* and *Caprichos* (Fig. 281).

In his *Death and the Sculptor*, Daniel Chester French tells of a gifted young sculptor, Martin Milmore, whose life and talents were cut

FIG. 277. Daniel Chester French. *Death and the Sculptor.* (Martin Milmore Memorial.) 1892. Metropolitan Museum of Art, New York.

FIG. 278. Ryder. *Death on a Pale Horse. ca.* 1910. Cleveland Museum of Art.

short by death. It is a theme which could only be conveyed allegorically, but might have been presented vaguely, melodramatically, or sentimentally. French presented the story so clearly that we can grasp its general meaning immediately. Moreover, he rose above several obstacles which trapped his fellow academicians. In this case the realistic treatment of both the youth and Death unites the relief stylistically and makes the event seem real and immediate. French had something that his contemporaries lacked—a sincere feeling for an allegorical episode. His genuine sentiment gives warmth to the scene, while his dignity, restraint, and gentle poetry contribute to its unity. Since philosophical speculation about death has been rare in a generally optimistic America, French's competent handling of this subject is as unusual as it is exceptional—a personal accomplishment, as it were, in spite of the times.

Another personal success is Albert Ryder's *Death on a Pale Horse* (Fig. 278). More poetic than French and much less realistic, Ryder was far from a typical American. He was a dreamer, recluse, eccentric, and mystic rather than a down-to-earth, gregarious man of action. Living in his own dreams in the middle of Manhattan Island, he seldom ventured out in public. This picture grew out of one of his rare contacts with other people. Briefly, it was occasioned by the suicide of a waiter who sometimes served Ryder at his brother's hotel. The waiter, an inveterate gambler, had put all of his savings on a sure tip and tried to persuade Ryder to do the same. The horse, of course, lost the race, and the waiter shot himself. The tragedy moved and shocked Ryder into trying to convey the evils of gambling. The result was the *Death on a Pale Horse*.

It is sometimes helpful to put one's self in the place of an artist who has decided to treat a theme of this sort. Would realistic illustration express one's thoughts and feelings? If so, will any one scene in the episode express its broadest implications? The answer to both questions is plainly negative. Sensing that, Ryder wisely adopted allegorical means. This is no particular race track, yet it is all race tracks where Death might ride. The light is an eerie, luminous yellow; the shadows a dark and somber brown; the forms generalized and shadowy—the general treatment mysterious, indefinite. This pictorial but nonrealistic representation creates a stark and sober mood and leads one to conclude that the establishment of a proper mood is probably as important in allegorical expression as narration on a high philosophical plane. Indeed, it is a crucial and saving element. It is feeling that lifts Ryder's *Death on a Pale Horse* above naïveté and French's *Death and the Sculptor* above mere realism. It is lack of feeling that betrays the pretentious academic allegory.

VISIONARY ART. Visionary art is a special type of the introspective orientation discussed broadly in Chapter 3. It expresses man's exploration of the world of inner reality, lying in the semiconscious and subconscious recesses of the mind. We normally refer to the products of these mental caverns as dreams, hallucinations, or visions. We often think of them as signs of insanity, morbidity, obsessions, and neuroses. Our tendency is to avoid them out of a kind of fear. Art shows an awareness of fantastic mental quirks haunting and fascinating human beings. The most normal people are fascinated by the monstrous, grotesque, and irrational at the same time that they are repelled by them.

Historically, men have given artistic and literary expression to introspective preoccupations to convey their horrified fear of the unknown within themselves and in the supernatural world; to express personal insight into the workings of the mind; and to make objective scientific studies of these phenomena. These approaches apply to different periods of history.

The first prevails in a time when general education is rare and economic misery and religious superstition rife. The Middle Ages, and the Dark Ages especially, bred this attitude. The second approach would be common in an age of comparatively free inquiry, when a few men of genius would explore the subconscious world under the impact of personal or historical times of troubles, like the period of the Counter-Reformation wars and the Inquisition. Post-Renaissance Europe was a breeding ground for such ideas, with El Greco and Goya leading the inquiries into the infinite. The third approach, the scientific, denotes a period when science is in the ascendant, but when the world is troubled by spiritual and practical upheavals. Our own time has exemplified this kind of introspection, giving rise to Surrealism, Dadaism, and other products of the soul-searching mind. Dali, the best known artist of this school, combines scientific calm and knowledge with admitted obsessions with the horrible and irrational. He differs in that respect from his ignorant, superstitious medieval precursors and even from later men who, like El Greco and Goya, had the insight of genius but lacked scientific support. The artists who have gravitated toward the intellectual and spiritual hinterlands are numerous. This mental interest is still widespread in our time.

The outstanding historical exception to this preoccupation is Greek art. The Greeks lived up to their philosophical ideals through most of their history. They cultivated the finite in both inner and outer reality, disliking and avoiding the unknown. When their confidence was undermined by fear-breeding wars and other troubles,

they too succumbed to mystery cults like that of Mithras. But meanwhile, their Egyptian and Near Eastern neighbors kept visionary art
alive by producing innumerable statues of monstrous gods out of the
visionary imagination. Hence visionary art has known an unbroken
history from the earliest to the latest times. It is capable of shedding
a strong light on the character of man.

The most real product of the visionary mind is a feeling rather
than an image, a sense of revulsion, guilt, fear, or outright horror.
Translating such feelings into visual terms is difficult; the only
premise an artist can assume is that certain fears are common among
men. Visionary art, like allegorical expression, is replete with symbols. Its distinctive character lies in its special subject matter and in
the prominence it gives to moods arising from morbid fears. French's
Death and the Sculptor would not fall within the visionary field in
spite of the presence of an imaginary figure, nor would Ryder's
Death on a Pale Horse, despite its dreamlike quality. Both artists
were inspired by objective events. Visionary art, by contrast, orig-
inates in subjective reality. Its purpose is to reveal the general workings of the subconscious mind.

Hence the emphasis in visionary art should be upon conditions of
universal or wide significance, and realism of style should be avoided.
The artist's problem is to be convincing, not merely realistic. In
this pursuit one liberty is permitted him: his pictures are freed from
the normal relationships and contexts of wakeful life. External logic
is illogical when visions and dreams are expressed; instead, an artist
must invent a new but credible body of logical relationships. This is
a task of formidable proportions which is accomplished only by the
most penetrating kind of thinking. It is never, as we might suppose,
merely painting crazily. Paradoxically, an insane person rarely paints
intelligible visionary pictures, those who do display a curious mixture of the imaginative and the lucid.

Visionary art is exemplified well by the paintings of Hieronymus
Bosch, a Flemish artist of the late fifteenth century. Whereas most
artists have regarded visionary art as a side line, he made it a full-time
occupation. Several forces seem to have bent him in this direction
and qualified him to excel in it. He lived at the end of the hob-
goblin-haunted Middle Ages in a northern land which had inherited
both the romantic disposition toward the infinite and the vivid im-
agery of the Gothic peoples. In Italy, where Raphael was to glorify
rationality in the *School of Athens* (Fig. 104) within a decade, he
would have have been deemed a lunatic.

Actually Bosch had, despite his love of eccentricity, an extraordinarily keen mind. Added to this mental clarity were an irrepressible

sense of humor, a searching into human psychology, and an unsurpassed ability to invent vivid symbols. His was almost the perfect mental equipment for an artist who wished to plumb the mind as well as to delight his audience. His complex pictures are both entertaining and revealing to anyone who will study them. Bosch was a precursor of an even greater genius, Pieter Breugel the Elder, and resembled him in his encyclopedic knowledge of human nature. Like Bruegel, his insights were not merely droll or lurid; his exposure of human lusts, while smacking of the moralism of his day, is as modern as Freud.

Although much time, patience, and knowledge are required to fathom the symbolism of Bosch's pictures, his meanings are clear. The *Temptation of St. Anthony* (Fig. 279) is an excellent illustration. It deals with the mental struggles of a man who wanted to be holy and good and tried to put all carnal desires, worldly ambitions, and fleshly appetites behind him, only to find that memories of lifelong habits plagued and tortured him. His voluptuous dreams were called sinful and his saintly aims laudable in his day, but they still speak with an objective ring of the Jekyll-and-Hyde struggle in human nature. Bosch's genius lay in expressing these ideas through symbols which are as lucid as they are amusing.

Bosch's psychological researches were continued in the eighteenth century by another penetrating student of human personality. Visionary art was only one of many fields in which Goya excelled. He is a link between a persisting medieval tradition of the supernatural and modern scientific surrealism. He inherited the medieval belief in witchcraft and many of its symbols but anticipated the verifiable truths of psychiatry. No more important pioneer of modern art can be cited. His concern with man's inner life was far ahead of his time. Goya differs from Bosch in being more modern in both time and attitude. He exemplifies the deadly serious attitude of the Freudians as distinct from the capriciousness of Bosch, Thurber, or Paul Klee. Part of this was personal and part historical; Goya, a passionate, troubled man, lived in a decadent and tragic period in Spanish history. Even before Napoleon's army ravaged his country, life had been no joking matter.

Goya's temperament and circumstances made him take a dim view of human nature. His *Proverbios* record it as evil, stupid, and habit-ridden; his *Caprichos* as wayward and unreliable; his *Disasters of War* as brutal and savage. Goya, a man of profound intelligence, sympathies, and democracy, was strongly affected by these failings and he lashed out at them furiously. His hard-hitting art is too bitter to be funny, and too true to be ignored. Although one-sided

FIG. 279. Bosch. *Temptation of St. Anthony.*
ca. 1500. Royal Museum, Brussels.

FIG. 280. Goya. *Nun Frightened by
a Ghost. ca.* 1819. Metropolitan
Museum of Art, New York.

FIG. 281. Goya. *The Sleep of Reason
Gives Birth to Monsters. ca.* 1799.
From "Los Caprichos." Museum of
Fine Arts, Boston.

in its grimness, it deals clearly with universal, timeless, and important attributes of our mental life. Some insights Goya inherited; others were his own, but he treated all lucidly and vividly; and while his imaginative inventiveness did not excel Bosch's, he spoke in larger and bolder stylistic terms. Impact, not detail, is the essence of his art.

Goya's point of view is illustrated by his drawing of a *Nun Frightened by a Ghost* (Fig. 280) and *The Sleep of Reason Gives Birth to Monsters* (Fig. 281), an aquatint etching from *Los Caprichos* series. The former may be interpreted in several ways, but the most plausible explanation is that Goya, like Bosch, has externalized the thoughts of a person who has taken a vow of chastity and renounced all worldly pleasures, but cannot entirely control her thoughts. The memory of past loves is symbolized by a man who strums beguilingly on a guitar. Clad as a monk, he may be a churchman who reminds her of the past, a suggestion which makes him appear horrible. Worse still, he catches her off guard, frightening her by his ability to steal into her thoughts. Goya's artistry lies in the creation of a pantomime which objectifies this woman's spiritual struggle in terms that have a universal ring. Her gesture and facial expression are eloquent signs of the conflict between good and evil in every human conscience.

The Sleep of Reason Gives Birth to Monsters, Goya's own caption for this *Los Caprichos* aquatint etching, considers another facet of the mind—the suspension of rationality during sleep. This psychological phenomenon is symbolized by a man who is surrounded by monstrous creatures of his own imagination when sleep lulls his reason; an evil-looking cat and a swarm of bats, they seem to have emerged from symbolic mental caves. The sleeping man looks like someone tortured by a nightmare. A kind of temporary insanity is implied. Weird as is Goya's presentation of the case, the morbid tendency of the mind called manic depression is now recognized as a widespread characteristic.

Bosch, Goya, and similar introspective artists have put their fingers on major attributes of the human psyche—the problem of lust, the warring of good and evil in the best of consciences, and the conflict between instincts and inhibitions, conscious rationality and sleep-engendered irrationality in all human life. Antedating modern psychiatric science, the insight of artists penetrated deeply the hidden recesses of the mind.

SATIRE. Satire is identified most conspicuously by its revelation of human sins and transgressions. It expresses a humanistic orientation in that its primary subjects are exclusively human or man-made.

More than that, its humanism is social, for it deals chiefly with the behavior of people toward one another. Consequently, the term *social satire* is used almost as a single word.

Satire is an art form with a definite slant. Its spiritual character is generally described by such adjectives as ironic, bitter, caustic, pessimistic, tragic, and, if somewhat humorous, sardonic. In extreme forms it is referred to as a scathing denunciation of human vices and evils. It expresses a negative report on human conduct, and a rather dim view of life. Yet satire aims at constructive criticism and improvement. By exposing evils the satirist hopes to bludgeon people into mending their ways. Satire is not the way of love or kindly persuasion, but a forceful approach; hard-hitting bitterness, sarcasm, exasperation, and ludicrous humor are among its most effective weapons. While it runs the risk of shortening its effective life by creating a reaction of irritation, withdrawal, or repulsion, it is at its best an art of great virility and vitality. It can rarely be ignored, and may exemplify the peak of human rationality.

Neither maximum rationality nor the gadfly's exposure of faults is, as Socrates discovered, what human beings usually want. The complex, acid art of satire has often played second fiddle to art that was simply beautiful or realistic. While beauty pleases, truth hurts. Caught in their own irony, men of intelligence and insight like Hogarth and Daumier have often had to watch second-raters and conformists carry off the laurels, true appreciation coming to them only after death. The good satirist accepts these hazards.

The formal and dramatic entities of satire are not unlike the means and methods of symbolic, allegorical, and visionary art. While a narrative approach is stressed, the illustrative devices are often imaginative and may include a good deal of symbolism and allegory. There is, however, one marked difference between satire and these other forms. Unlike visionary art, satire deals with problems of the external world. Hence Goya's *Nun Frightened by a Ghost* is visionary but not satirical; Daumier's *Women Gossiping* satirizes maliciousness, but is hardly visionary. French's *Death and the Sculptor,* a still further type, is an allegory containing a symbolical figure, but is neither satirical nor visionary in intention.

An outstanding feature of satire which may or may not appear in visionary art is exaggeration. Since the satirist not only points a moral but underscores it, he must stress the enormity of the vice he is dissecting; and this calls for a penetrating understanding of his subject. Also he must exercise a subtle command over physical distortion—the visual satirist's principal means—if effectiveness rather than mere grotesqueness is to be achieved.

Few other artists wrestle harder than the satirist with the problem of how much distortion, emphasis, and artistic license should be employed. Meeting this problem successfully requires intellectual equipment of a special, and apparently rare, sort. It must combine analytical and critical faculties of a high order with artistry which is tasteful as well as intense. It is not the mental equipment of an objective, sensuous realist like Velasquez, a fact which accounts for the numerical preponderance of noted realists over successful satirists. Satirists must possess profound minds as well as sharp eyes and disciplined hands.

At or near the summit of great satire is the work of Pieter Bruegel the Elder. His *Blind Leading the Blind* (Fig. 282) exemplifies the satirical approach superbly. He was one of the giants of art, a master who could match strokes with any realist but was infinitely more—a profound and encyclopedic student of human life. An unexcelled social philosopher, he dealt not only with the bad elements in humanity but the better side as well, as in *The Wedding Dance* (Fig. 232). Neither Swift nor Bunyan had a broader understanding of human virtues and weaknesses. With Hogarth, Daumier, Cervantes, and Fielding, and unlike the utterly serious Goya, Bruegel had a sense of humor. He laughed at and with his fellow men while grieving over their seemingly incurable failings.

The *Blind Leading the Blind* is outstanding among Bruegel's many masterpieces because it contains so much of his complex mixture of love, sympathy, exasperation, and rambunctious humor, and because it highlights clearly and vividly a message of far-reaching significance. The theme, borrowed from the Biblical parable, reiterates one of the persistent tragedies of life: as long as mentally blind people follow equally blind leaders, they will end up disastrously. In the picture they are stumbling downhill into a morass.

Bruegel's *Blind Leading the Blind* pertains to political mistakes of universal significance. He had cause to know them well, for he lived in Flanders when it still lay under the yoke of a Spanish tyranny which his countrymen fought and accepted with mixed courage and confusion. But Bruegel was too shrewd to limit himself to a political cartoon; he created, instead, a picture whose message applies to human ignorance wherever it may be found.

Bruegel's satire is not so cynical as it may seem. Actually it denotes a disappointed idealism, a paradoxical mixture of laughter and tears. It stems from high standards for the human potential which are disappointed by actual performance. The satirist implies only that the performance is poorer than necessary. He registers disgust. His commonest complaints are against the dearth of good will and

FIG. 282. Pieter Bruegel the Elder. *Blind Leading the Blind*. 1568. National Museum, Naples.

FIG. 283. Toulouse-Lautrec. *Yvette Guilbert Taking a Curtain Call. ca.* 1894. Rhode Island School of Design, Providence.

intelligence, or even common sense, in human affairs. He cries out against malevolence, muddling, sloth, and downright stupidity.

The creation of enduring satire requires a combination of unusual personal attitudes, high artistic skill, and keen judgment. The unusual personal attitudes must be the kind that make a man *care* what his fellow men do and be bitterly disappointed when they fail through viciousness, laziness, or stupidity. High artistic skill is required because the message in satirical art is deliberately intensified by exaggeration, causing spectators to overlook the merits of design and representation. Unless these are of a high order, the picture will not outlast a potent but temporary message. Better still, excellence of design and representation should be combined with ideas of universal and timeless significance. Selecting such themes requires keen judgment and a broad understanding of human life. Keen judgment is also required of the satirist if he is to know how much exaggeration to employ. If he overplays his hand the result will be merely ludicrous or comical.

The outstanding satirists in the history of art have been relatively few—Bosch, Pieter Bruegel the Elder, Hogarth, Goya, Daumier, and a few lesser men. In our own century Georges Rouault and George Grosz have been prominent, while a number of younger artists, like Aaron Bohrod, Peter Blume, and William Gropper have also left their marks. The Far East contributed one satirist of world stature, the Japanese Toba Sojo, but on the whole Oriental artists have not been given to satirical painting.

These men all illustrate several special characteristics of satire. Historically, they fall within relatively modern times, indicating that some freedom of enquiry is necessary if satirical criticism is to be pursued and tolerated. Collective societies of an absolutist make-up will neither encourage nor condone satirical criticism. Satire is significantly absent from the art of ancient Egypt, most of Asia, and most of medieval Europe. On the other hand it was permitted and prospered in democratic Athens and in republican Rome. The political, social, or religious censor can kill public satire over night. It never raised its head during the Spanish Inquisition, and even Goya employed it at his peril later on; nor did it have an easy time under such nineteenth-century rulers as Louis Philippe, who tested Daumier's sincerity with a term in jail. The acceptance of satire in any society is a sign of health, for, despite the evils the satirist condemns, there is at least liberty of expression and tolerance for criticism. Lacking freedom or gagged by tyranny, the satirist must display both caution and courage to survive, as Bruegel, Goya, and Daumier discovered.

The similarity between the mental qualities of the literary and the pictorial satirist need hardly be stressed. Both thrive or disappear under like historical conditions. The heydays of satire in the two media show a striking parallelism. Hogarth and Daumier, for instance, lived in periods of active literary satire; the Englishman was a contemporary of Jonathan Swift and the Frenchman of Honoré de Balzac. Both arts suffered from similar weaknesses. The emphasis which satire places upon exaggeration tends to obscure esthetic merits, especially among the satirist's contemporaries, who are apt to say, "He is a sharp fellow, but hardly an artist." Hogarth and Daumier are masters who knew what it was to amuse the populace but be overlooked by the critics. The writer or painter who makes people laugh or jolts their complacency is almost certain to be taken lightly or resented. Mark Twain complained that everyone credited him with a funny bone but no brains, and Bruegel was similarly underrated because of his drollness. Their contemporaries would have hooted the suggestion that any of these men was a greater artist than the self-serious, awe-inspiring Sir Joshua Reynolds or the facile Meissonier.

The heyday of political satire coincided with the period of political ferment which started with the Renaissance and gradually fostered modern democracy. Such a trend encouraged a vast production of satirical political cartoons. The eighteenth, nineteenth, and twentieth centuries produced bumper crops, with Thomas Nast, the exposer of the notorious Tweed Ring, and the Britisher David Low being among the best known of many cartoonists. But the contrast between the voluminous output and the small residue of enduring satirical art only stresses the temporary character of most political issues and the necessity of satirizing broader human failings. The majority of satirical masterpieces are nonpolitical; they treat, instead, shortcomings that seem part of human nature without regard to time or place.

CARICATURE. On first sight caricature and satire may seem indistinguishable. Both employ exaggeration and distortion as primary means, and satire in the hands of a Hogarth or Daumier can be funny. Even Bruegel's *Blind Leading the Blind* (Fig. 282) appears ludicrously comical until one perceives its underlying meaning. But there are fundamental differences in intention behind the uses of satire and caricature. Despite its surface humor, satire is serious, moralistic, and corrective; caricature is critically congenial, tolerant, and sympathetic. The difference can be illustrated by such serious journalistic political cartoons as those of Kirby, Herbert Block, and

Fitzpatrick, and the humorous illustrations of Darrow, Steig, and Price which appear in *The New Yorker*. The latter are not without some instructional value but they highlight the foibles rather than the vices of human nature.

Caricature as a fine art is exemplified by the work of Henri de Toulouse-Lautrec. His drawing of *Yvette Guilbert Taking a Curtain Call* (Fig. 283) is deservedly known for its incisive qualities of wit and execution. This is caricature, not satire. Lautrec habitually distorted forms, but he exaggerated Yvette Guilbert's appearance from amusement, not to ridicule her. How much he distorted is shown by Degas' pastel portrait of a *Singer Wearing Black Gloves* in the Fogg Museum. The similarity ends with the title; for Degas' treatment is straightforward, his proportions normal. His picture represents a theatrical performance, but tells us little about the personality of the singer. Lautrec ignores the setting, but tells us much about Yvette Guilbert's personality, as well he might, for she was one of the outstanding theatrical celebrities of Paris in the Gay Nineties. Hardly a beauty, she was awkwardly proportioned but graceful of movement. Other contradictions made her a fascinating performer. A talented eccentric dancer, she was a born comedienne who could sing, mimic, and pantomime superbly. She exaggerated her thin, angular frame by wearing long black gloves and used her hands with masterly expressiveness. She also had bright red hair. Her versatility has been likened by older theater-goers to the talents of Beatrice Lillie.

Lautrec has brought out Guilbert's characteristic whimsy, her love for her audience, and her own enjoyment in amusing them by employing a caricaturist's two best resources—a controlled exaggeration of unusual features and an eye-catching economy of means. Lautrec designed similar posters of many of his friends in the Parisian entertainment world, but none finer than the series he did for Yvette Guilbert. A close friend and a frequent diner at her table, he intended no satire or ridiculing of her peculiarities. This, like much of his work, is a kindly and sympathetic caricature done in gratitude for friendship.

Caricature might be misjudged as a minor partner of satire or as a mere element in much satire. It could also be underestimated as a kind of tongue-in-cheek and not very important portraiture or everyday art. It does not take itself very seriously, and hence is related to satire as scenes of everyday life are to historical illustration. Yet caricature serves a purpose that cannot be fully served in any other way. It responds to subjects with unusual and prominent physical features and personal traits, who virtually invite caricature, like

Yvette Guilbert and Theodore or Franklin Roosevelt. To say that these people of strong personality lend themselves to caricature does not mean that they deserve to be satirized. Caricature merely confirms their exceptional qualities by the use of a kind of visual underscoring. Hence the basis of caricature rests on an element of truth; its distinctive qualities lie in its particular presentation of that truth.

Not all human subjects invite caricature. George Washington did not; Abraham Lincoln did. He invited both satire and caricature at every turn during his lifetime. The second Roosevelt was a readymade subject; the caricatures of him by J. N. Darling and others show one of caricature's principal merits—its ability to capture a vivid and vital personality more convincingly than would a serious, formal portrait. On the other hand, Stuart's celebrated portraits of George Washington, James Madison, Thomas Jefferson, and John Marshall are probably more successful than any caricatures could have been. One cannot imagine these dignified, intellectual men understanding Lautrec or being appropriately understood by him.

The artist must have the ability to see appropriate subjects and the requisite treatment, preferably an impeccable eye for essentials, and a style which is, like Lautrec's, clear and concise. Linear drawing and painting in the mode of line and local color undoubtedly fulfil these visual requirements and are found most often in the world's finest caricatures. The other qualifications lie in the artist's mind and personality, with a sense of humor and a natural gusto prominent among them.

These demands on both subject and artistry have limited the amount of caricature which has risen from the level of journalism to fine art. In the West, Hogarth, Rowlandson, Daumier, Constantin Guys, Lautrec, Paul Klee, and James Thurber come to mind. In the East there are the ink drawings of Toba Sojo, the theatrical poster prints of Sharaku, and some comical drawings and prints by Hokusai. The number of great caricatures that one can garner from even a global survey is not extensive. By and large the masters of art have dealt seriously with serious problems. They may have suspected what Mark Twain consciously observed, that those who treat serious subjects with any levity are not taken seriously on any artistic count, and eschewed caricature for that reason.

Yet even the greatest men have their lighter moments, when they engage in a little fun-making. Many of the best loved caricatures in the fine arts were created in moments of diversion by the ranking satirists. Hogarth could dissect social vices to the core, but he was clearly in a joking mood when he drew his *Enraged Musician* (Fig. 72), a theme in which satire would have been out of place. Nor was

Daumier always bitter. He detested viciousness and exposed it unsparingly in his *Women Gossiping* (Fig. 152), but he knew and loved many good and simple people whom he depicted with a keen sense of fitness, sometimes in a friendly, straightforward way, and sometimes with a kindly touch of humor.

LITERARY ILLUSTRATION. Since all paintings inspired by the Bible and other religious writings are, in a sense, literary illustrations, this type of subject matter constitutes the largest and greatest gallery of art in the world. In general, however, a special category is reserved for religious illustration because much of its source has obscure, often legendary, origins, comes from the pens of many authors, and is often believed to be divinely revealed truth. Of illustrations of literature in the more modern, fictional sense, such as the imaginative prose or poetry of single authors like Shakespeare, Cervantes, and Tolstoy, there have been many. If we add to the acknowledged masterpieces, like Tolstoy's *War and Peace* and Poe's *Raven,* all of the illustrations in popular magazines which have come and gone monthly or weekly over many years, the total is astronomical. But only a very small amount of this tremendous production has lasted. Most of it is as ephemeral as the political cartoons or humorous illustrations in our daily papers—a great outpouring of energy devoted to a kind of writing in sand.

It is difficult to determine why so much of the world's great literature has not inspired comparable visual illustrations. Dostoievsky's *Crime and Punishment,* for instance, is a profound, deeply moving novel which contains many illustrable episodes, yet it has never evoked illustrations of any great merit. Stranger still is the fact that Shakespeare's dramatic and highly visual poetry has elicited so few first-rate illustrations. Several factors militate against the union of fine writing and worthy illustrations. One is the neglect of many literary masterpieces by talented illustrators. Secondly, a novel or poem must be enduring itself before it can inspire lasting visual interpretation. There is not, to my knowledge, a single instance of outstanding visual art which emerged from a second-rate literary source. While all the possibilities of literary illustrations may not be grasped, they must always be present before they can be exploited.

There must be compatibility of temperament between a great writer and a great artist who illustrates his work. The examples of literary illustrations which have survived bear this out. Outstanding among them are Blake's illustrations of Dante's *Divine Comedy,* Daumier's *Don Quixote* series, and Delacroix's paintings illustrating Scott's *Ivanhoe,* notably the *Abduction of Rebecca.* Anyone familiar with the personalities of Blake and Dante, Daumier and Cervantes, and Delacroix and Scott will recognize their similarity. The writings of Dante were made to order for Blake, while Daumier, the ideal illustrator of Cervantes, would have been ill-suited to depict the Florentine's epic dreams. Delacroix, who loved lion hunts (Fig. 346) and the dashing, adventurous life, was perfectly equipped to speak for the swashbuckling novels of Scott. Out of such spiritual congeniality is born the great literary illustration. Dostoievsky, it would seem, lacked a spiritual counterpart among the great visual artists, as did Shakespeare, Homer, and Milton.

In this union of art and authorship time is not crucial. Delacroix was a contemporary of Scott in the international Romanticism of the early nineteenth century, but such a parallelism is rare. Daumier and Blake both lived centuries after the authors who inspired them. The work of an author frequently must wait a long time for an artist who can interpret it truly. It is of paramount importance that that kindred spirit be a master of his own medium rather than a mere visual translator of literary episodes. Daumier was an artist before he was an illustrator and would have been immortal without illustrating a single book, as would Delacroix. Neither of these men trained to be illustrators, but rather brought fully developed talents to that field. It is doubtful, however, whether any of Daumier's *Don Quixote* illustrations or Delacroix's *Ivanhoe* pictures would have gotten by the art editor of an ordinary modern magazine, for they were not painted to play a subordinate role. Neither artist paid the kind of attention to accuracy of detail which is so important to the journalist. Nor did either illustrate a clearly definable episode which coincides with a line in the text. Instead, they created works of art which are only incidentally illustrations and can stand with or without textual caption. More important to Delacroix and Daumier than accuracy of time, place, episode, costumes, and accessories was the interpretation of the general spirit of *Ivanhoe* and *Don Quixote,* and in this they had no superiors. David and Meissonier might have recreated every button in a scene exactly, but one can safely wager that Cervantes would have been more pleased with Daumier's general interpretation.

Daumier and Delacroix show us what lasting literary illustration requires: it is not accuracy of representation, but creative imagination, spiritual compatibility, and vitality. The artist is under the same obligation as the writer to make his work credible and alive. These are qualities which he cannot borrow but must bring to the task himself. The masterpieces of literary illustration point to a further rule. None of them was ever commissioned, like the modern magazine story illustration. Delacroix lived at the same time as Scott but had no contact with the author or his publishers. His illustrations of *Ivanhoe* were inspired by his spontaneous interest in that novel. Spontaneous interest of this sort has been the motivating force of all outstanding literary illustrations. Such interest must be present if the painting is to have the feeling that is essential to art. It is a quality that cannot be ordered.

Many of the foremost masters have done little or no illustration of fiction. Many literary works do not lend themselves to illustration within the limits of painting and drawing. Try, as a test, to select a scene from *Hamlet* which would be meaningful without the spoken words. The soliloquies, while superb theatre, are not illustrable, and the scenes of action, like the climactic duel, do not present the psychological heart of the play. This problem of condensing the gist of a novel or play whose meaning unfolds temporally into single pictures confronts the illustrator repeatedly. Those literary works which have a permeating spirit which can be summarized in paint have the best chance of being illustrated well; the others cannot be, regardless of their literary merits. Each medium has limitations which prevent at many points a marriage of the two arts.

Religious literature has motivated much great art. One reason stands out because of its capacity to inspire men by dealing with bedrock problems of human experience, compared to which even the psychological struggles of a Hamlet seem of secondary importance. On both counts the Old and New Testaments are superbly illustrable books. In them most of the old masters found enough material to fill a lifetime without turning to lesser literary sources. Religious literature presents the artist with the sum of human experience in a treasury gathered by many men over centuries of time. Not even Shakespeare's genius could match its wisdom as a source of artistic inspiration.

The plenitude of noted religious illustrations and the contrasting dearth of other kinds can be traced to another reason. The illustration of fictional literature requires a considerable education. Literature is not something that one grasps over night. Indeed, literary and visual understanding are so often poles apart that few writers have yet produced an acceptable treatment of the visual artist's aims, Kipling's *Light That Failed* being typically wide of the mark. Conversely, artists have rarely been searching readers of novels. Delacroix, an educated man who read widely and consorted with talented literary men, was exceptional in this respect. Most of the great visual artists have been verbally illiterate or ordinary men. Their training lay along other lines. In antiquity and the Middle Ages they were neither more nor less than talented craftsmen for whom book learning was unnecessary. Not until the Renaissance was the artist regarded as a special individual, a genius, or a recipient of divine inspiration. Even then the Botticellis and Michelangelos who sat in Lorenzo de Medici's choice literary circle were exceptional and privileged characters, and Leonardo da Vinci is not to be taken as representative on any score.

The majority of Renaissance artists learned their trade as members of the goldsmith's guild and enjoyed the same advantages, duties, and respect as members of that craft. As late as the eighteenth century artists and authors alike were respected but not coddled. If they ate in a lord's house it was in the kitchen; no one thought of them as gentlemen or educated men, except possibly in the case of Sir Joshua Reynolds. Only recently have a few artists taken college degrees or explored the complex world of written words with any thoroughness. This alone would account for the scarcity of outstanding literary illustration.

How, then, can we explain the many superb religious illustrations? Because there are many ways of becoming educated without reading. Religious wisdom, by contrast with other types, permeates the air of a society and can be absorbed by word of mouth through generation after generation. Rembrandt, a failure at academic education, proved this possibility conclusively. Moreover, wisdom so absorbed is the cream of human experience and is likely to produce art of lasting significance. Equally important for the visual arts is the fact that the primary significance of religious literature is spiritual and its episodic character only incidental. Better still, its episodes sum up the pith of accumulated truth with unmatched clarity, intensity, and concentration. No other literary source can compete with them as a supplier of illustrative material.

Only when the theme of a literary work inspires intense feeling is the artist able to objectify it in pictorial form. It is this feeling, not the episodic content of writing, that engenders a work of art.

HISTORICAL ILLUSTRATION. To the average person, history consists of momentous events and turning points in the march of human affairs rather than the continuity of daily life. So defined, this spectacular facet of the social humanistic orientation has been the subject of a large amount of artistic illustration.

There are two common features of such illustrations: the event illustrated must have actually occurred even if reported only legendarily, and it must have been momentous in its effect upon the course of events. Events of this caliber have inspired artists to depict them in large numbers. Although the illustrations of this book were not chosen with that idea in mind, many of them are historical illustrations. Some of the great or well-known pictures which qualify as historical illustrations are Orozco's *Zapatistas* (Fig. 29); Velasquez's *Surrender of Breda;* Goya's *Uprising in the Plaza del Sol: May 2, 1808,* and *Execution of the Madrileños: May 3, 1808* (Fig. 136); Géricault's *Raft of the Medusa* (Fig. 378); Meissonier's *1814* (Fig. 28); Veronese's *Family of Darius Before Alexander* (Fig. 320); Leutze's *Washington Crossing the Delaware;* Vanderlyn's *Columbus Landing in America;* Trumbull's *Signing of the Declaration of Independence, Battle of Princeton,* and *Surrender of Cornwallis at Yorktown;* David's *Death of Socrates, Battle of the Sabines, Oath of the Tennis Court, Death of Marat, Napoleon Crossing the Alps,* and *Coronation of Napoleon;* Gros's *Napoleon on the Bridge at Arcole, Napoleon at the Battle of the Pyramids,* and *Napoleon at the Battle of Eylau;* and Delacroix's *Massacre at Scio, Death of Sardanapalus,* and *Liberty Leading the People: July 28th, 1830.* And we must not forget sculpture when such works are available as Saint-Gaudens' *Shaw Memorial* (the departure of the first Negro soldiers for the Civil War front) and Rude's *Departure of the Volunteers,* an event of the French Revolution.

All of these examples have one quality in common: they hint of adventure, action, and mighty deeds; they are dynamic and vital in theme; they express the heroic side of man's history, and make the blood run a little faster. As such they have an initial advantage in their claim upon our attention and interest. They have to be very bad pictures before we will condemn them.

History has had a good representation in art, often by masterpieces of the first rank. If pictures of average or ordinary quality are brought into the fold, few events of any consequence have failed to be represented; an encyclopedia of history could be illustrated nearly as thoroughly with pictures as with words. The problem of artistic quality, or excellence in historical illustration, is, of course, another matter.

A high percentage of the examples we have mentioned come from the nineteenth and twentieth centuries, with a preponderance dating from the neoclassic and romantic movements of the early nineteenth century. These two movements doted on history, whereas the following impressionist movement treated it indifferently. Napoleon, a contemporary of the neoclassic and early romantic painters David and Baron Gros, received as full a propagandization through art as any celebrity in history, even granting that his magnetic personality inspired such fulsome treatment. The appearance of a large group of historical paintings at this time is in itself expressive of trends in both history and art. The past hundred and fifty years have been as dynamic as any in the history of civilization and have thus lent themselves to a kind of self-illustration.

Previous centuries were less self-conscious about their own historical development, not because they lacked stirring events and profound upheavals but, probably, because of the slower dissemination of news. The masters of the Renaissance and post-Renaissance periods paid little or no attention to historical illustration. The major exception was the encyclopedic genius Rubens, whose pictures of the *Death of Decius Mus* (part of a series), *Battle of Constantine and Maxentius, Battle of Greeks and Amazons, Bishop Ambrose Repelling Theodosius,* and *Queen Tomyris with the Head of Cyrus* are among his masterpieces, which is to say among the finest paintings of Western art. The series of designs which epitomizes his art—as the Sistine ceiling does Michelangelo's—the Henry IV–Marie de Medici series in the Louvre, is a historical interpretation.

Historical illustrations originate in four main ways. Foremost among them is the illustration of a historic event which the artist actually witnessed. The classic example is Goya's pictures of the Napoleonic invasion of Spain, with the *Execution of the Madrileños* (Fig. 136), a masterpiece among masterpieces. Goya watched these events with his own eyes. One of his captions for the *Disasters of War* series says, "I saw this!" If this is not to be applied literally to the details of the picture, one important thing is that Goya not only saw numerous scenes of this sort but reacted to them emotionally and visually. Personal experience of this type usually aids a historical painter in achieving accuracy and credibility.

David was present during the Oath of the Tennis Court, Gros was at the Battle of Eylau, Trumbull was Washington's aide at the time of Cornwallis' surrender at Yorktown, Delacroix saw the July Revolution of 1830, and Orozco watched the Zapatistas marching on Mexico City—facts which lent credibility to their reports and inspired firsthand emotional reactions. That experience of this kind can make a picture more alive and believable is apparent when one compares the compositions which David drew from his own revolutionary and Napoleonic times with those he took from ancient history. His *Battle of the Sabines* is not half so convincing as his quiet *Death of Marat,* despite its frantic display of action.

A second origin of historical illustrations is contemporary but indirect information. Velasquez's *Surrender of Breda* is a noted case. The artist was not present at the surrender of the heroic Dutch city to the Spaniards, but received a detailed description of the event from the commander-in-chief, the Marquesa de Spinola, when the painter and warrior were shipmates en route to Italy. Although the trust-worthiness of such an account must have been colored somewhat in recollection and transfer, it is second only to direct experience in reliability. Since artists, like witnesses to murders, are seldom in the thick of crucial actions, second-hand reports must be accepted and valued, especially when the painter shared the current environment of the event. Indeed, indirect experiences outnumbr direct, on-the-spot observations. Delacroix was not at the massacre of Scio, nor was David on hand when Charlotte Corday stabbed Marat. What is important is that these historic events fired the painters' imaginations and that, moreover, they had the benefit of living at the time.

A third source of historical illustration finds the artist removed by a generation or two from the events he depicts. A typical case is Meissonier's *1814* (Fig. 28). He was born a year after this episode in Napoleon's career and grew up in the different atmosphere of the middle of the century. He gained his impressions of the Napoleonic era from men who had lived through it and from reading on his own. His view would therefore have been affected in two ways: his information had been altered by time and he lacked the vitalizing experience of contemporaneousness. He saw Napoleon's career through his grandfather's eyes, through the eyes of his own later generation, and through history books.

In a fourth kind of historical illustration the artist is still further removed from the events and times he represents, sometimes thousands of years away from them. Famous examples of this group are Veronese's *Family of Darius Before Alexander* (Fig. 320) and Delacroix's *Death of Sardanapalus.* Rubens' *Queen Tomyris and the Head of Cyrus* is based on an episode related by Herodotus. Herodotus himself is full of folklore, tradition, and public knowledge, and if one goes that far, subjects patently based on legendary history should be admitted, like Burne-Jones's *King Cophetua and the Beggar Maid,* Edwin Abbey's *Knights of King Arthur's Round Table,* and Watt's *Sir Galahad.*

If a scale of informational reliability can thus be set up, what bearing does it have on the artistic or even historical value of an historical illustration? Is the painting of an eyewitness automatically superior to one by an artist who lives nine centuries after the scene he paints? Can any further scale of proximity versus remoteness be adduced on any proportionate basis? The answer is clearly negative. To prove that point let us consider some specific cases, starting, for comparative purposes, with two men, Goya and Rubens, who rank among the foremost of historical illustrators.

Goya painted and etched scenes he actually saw; Rubens drew

mainly upon the distant past. But in neither case was proximity crucial, for while direct experience stimulated Goya's emotions, lack of it did not prevent Rubens from creating vividly real historical compositions. Two methods may be employed to overcome a gap of time. One is to turn to research in the hope of recreating the appearance of the scene down to the last button. This is the archeological method. David and Meissonier put great stress on it, as did Gérôme, the painter of *L'Éminence Grise* (Fig. 34). In their pictures the costumes, settings, and accessories are perfectly trustworthy. Though no one would condemn this accuracy, it does not by itself bring a historical scene to life for us. Rubens was indifferent toward such research, or at least was not pedantic about it. His *Queen Tomyris with the Head of Cyrus* contains costumes and backgrounds of the Baroque period, not of Cyrus' day. Likewise, Veronese's *Family of Darius Before Alexander* takes us back to sixteenth-century Venice instead of ancient Persia. Yet Rubens' and Veronese's people and pictures live for us, while Meissonier's and Gérôme's are half-alive at best.

Something more than research, painstaking realism, and accurate information is required to create a living work of art. And if the picture does not live, the history will not either. A classic instance is provided by the contrast between David's *Coronation of Napoleon and Josephine* and Rubens' *Coronation of Marie de Medici*. David took infinite pains to portray the setting and each of the many figures exactly to the last marble grain and whisker. But despite his hard work, the huge and pretentious canvas is devoid of feeling. Rubens' design, though containing recognizable likenesses, is also full of symbolical figures and makes no pretense of transporting us back to the actual time and place. Yet it overflows with feeling, and in so doing lives for us.

Is there, then, any specific way by which an artist can paint a satisfactory or great historical illustration? It would seem that there is none that is special to historical illustration as such. The capacity for historical illustration is identical with the ability to commit human activities of any sort to art. In addition to a command over the organization of representation and esthetically pleasing spatial and color design, it is a capacity for sympathetic and emphatic identification, a feeling for the drama in large events, and a perception of the timeless lessons in historical episodes.

A great historical picture invariably has two meanings: it is an individual surrender of a particular place; at the same time it implies surrender and failure everywhere. Meissonier's *1814* suffers because it is too individual, exact, and self-limiting. A good historical illustration it may be, but it is not a great work of art. David's *Coronation* is also an accurate illustration, but it lacks the transcendent excitement of Rubens' *Coronation* which speaks not only for the drama of one coronation but of all coronations. If there is a difference between the historical illustration which is that and little more and the historical picture which is also a work of art, it stems from a given artist's superior grasp of the larger messages that are implicit in the single scene—in short, from its universal significance. Goya has given us the ideal example in his *Execution of the Madrileños*. A picture based on a specific historical incident by a man who knew whereof he spoke, it is a precise illustration. Yet to anyone with half an eye, it is a violent protest against man's inhumanity to man wherever it may be found.

GENRE. In the visual arts the term *genre* is used to describe scenes from everyday life as distinct from the illustration of momentous historical events. It is a facet of the humanistic orientation which is devoted to the usual social activities of human beings.

A popular and outstanding example of this type of subject matter is Murillo's *Boys Eating Grapes and Melons* (Fig. 284). It virtually epitomizes the character of genre painting. Like historical painting, it represents something that actually happened, and something that Murillo saw with his own eyes. It thus originated in external reality rather than in the artist's visionary mind. Consequently, it is concerned more with observation than invention. Note, for instance, Murillo's observation of the beggar boys' clothing, of the way one lad rolls his eyes as he sucks on the pilfered grapes, and of the stuffed mouth of his melon-eating companion—all points which carry the look of actuality. This close scrutiny of the details of human customs, behavior, types, and environment is typical of good genre painting.

Observation of this sort places genre painting at the far pole from visionary art. It removes it, too, from the realm of satire and caricature, as well as from historical illustration. Like most genre studies, Murillo's subject is presented in a straightforward, simple, and unpretentious manner. The scene stands or falls on its ability to be ingratiating without being either imposing or weird. No one would liken it to Goya's *Execution of the Madrileños*, Bruegel's *Blind Leading the Blind*, or Bosch's *Temptation of St. Anthony*, or judge it in the same way.

The genre scene has its own kind of truth and profundity. We would get a very limited and exaggerated impression of past life if we gained it solely from history books and historical illustrations. These furnish the high lights of human endeavor, but most of life

FIG. 284. Murillo. *Boys Eating Grapes and Melons.* 1670-1682. Alte Pinakothek, Munich.

FIG. 285. Houdon. *John Paul Jones. ca.* 1785. Pennsylvania Academy of Fine Arts, Philadelphia.

573

transpires on a more routine, humdrum level. It is this side of life that genre art records, filling in the broad areas that make up the bulk of our activities. Its emphasis is upon the continuity of life, upon ordinary events, like *Boys Eating Grapes and Melons,* or Vermeer's *Cook* (Fig. 93). Nothing could be simpler or, in a way, more appealing. To miss that appeal is to experience nothing in life except the spectacular, or hear nothing in music except the *fortissimo* passages.

Genre painting also has its favorite mode of representation. Murillo's picture, compared to his softly saccharine religious compositions, is painted in a pictorial mode which tends toward a moderately realistic style. This treatment is appropriate, for realism has a definite place in the field of genre painting and sculpture. There its merits can be exploited while its limitations are minimized. The realistic mode makes no great demands on our imagination. It enables the artist to state, simply and clearly, "I saw this." Both Murillo and his contemporary, Velasquez, were most effective when painting from direct experience, but inadequate when attempting to compose imaginatively; Velasquez was heavy and lifeless, Murillo fuzzy and sentimental. Velasquez's closely observed early *bodegones* (peasant scenes) and his late *Maids of Honor* (Fig. 94) are clear and convincing; his *Coronation of the Virgin* is unsatisfactory. The same evaluation applies to Murillo's many Immaculate Conceptions in contrast to his groups of genre scenes of which the *Boys Eating Grapes and Melons* is the finest. Any artist who is at his best when he paints what he can see without too much cerebration does well to devote himself to a realistic treatment of genre subjects, leaving loftier themes and abstract methods to more imaginative men like Raphael.

Genre, like all other types of subject matter, has its historical contexts. Reference to a few examples will help to clarify this point. In addition to the *Boys Eating Grapes and Melons* and the *Maids of Honor* already cited, De Hooch's *Mother by a Cradle* (Fig. 98) and Gemito's *Neapolitan Water-Carrier* (Fig. 168), Degas' *Laundresses* (Fig. 49), and the Hellenistic *Old Woman Going to Market* (Fig. 404), *Boy and Goose* after Boethos (Fig. 414), and *Peasant Going to Market* (Fig. 415) may be properly interpreted as straightforward genre scenes.

Most of these masterpieces of genre come from the late Greek and post-Renaissance periods and the nineteenth century. In all of those periods there was a drift away from the idealistic toward realism. The rise of genre can be related inversely to the decline of religious art of the symbolic type. Already marked in the century of Vermeer, Velasquez, De Hooch, and the Dutch little masters, this trend reached its peak in the nineteenth century. Giotto stood at the beginning of this slow change in Western society; his approach was a compound of the genre and the religious. Rembrandt, who also desired to give his pictures the look of life, continued this attitude in his scenes from the daily life of Christ, such as his etching of *Christ Healing the Sick* (Fig. 151). But by the nineteenth century the shift from faith to a materialistic outlook was complete. Only a few lofty souls like Delacroix clung to religious themes; the majority of artists were committed to genre.

This shift in viewpoint was, of course, a change; but it was not a decline. If art was less lofty, it was often more warm-hearted. Compare Daumier's genre *Drinking Song* (Fig. 63) with the Daphni *Crucifixion* (Fig. 87). The far-reaching interest in scenes of daily life led artists to explore and bring into the fold of subject matter many fields that had lain untouched. Notable among these were the treatments of sports and theatrical life exemplified by Goya's bullfight lithographs, Géricault's and Degas' racecourse studies, Degas' innumerable ballet dancers, Bellows' prize fighters, Eakins' rowers, and numerous representations of circus life backstage and out front. All of these give us an honest and invaluable insight into the thoughts and interests of the people of the nineteenth century. Art would be poorer without them.

Historically, the full flowering of the genre attitude cultivated by the artists and encouraged by the public is always a relatively late stage of development in any cultural continuity. This fact helps us to place the art of Hellenistic Greece and the post-Renaissance and nineteenth-century periods in their proper places. It also helps us to relate Japanese prints like Masanobu's *Playing Cards* (Fig. 113) and Hiroshige's *Traveller Buying an Otsu-E Picture* (Fig. 115) to the long history of Japanese art. Called Ukiyoe prints, these pictures were consciously devoted to scenes of "the passing world." They arose and thrived under tendencies which were very like those of Europe. In both hemispheres genre art expressed a decline of the feudal system in favor of a middle-class freedom which one may call, according to one's beliefs, vulgar or healthy and true-to-life. It produced a host of ordinary pictures, but it also gave us the art of Frans Hals, Vermeer, and Daumier.

PORTRAITURE. Portraiture can be partially defined by describing what a portrait is not, for there are innumerable pictures of people which are not portraits. No representation of Christ is a portrait because His appearance is still a matter of conjecture. One of the striking phenomena of history is that His personality and character were so dominant as to make men oblivious of His physical appearance, and none of His contemporaries left us any description of how He looked.

A portrait is an actual, rather than an imaginary, representation of a person who was seen by the artist or carefully described to him. It is an accurate record of his appearance in which reliability of such details as the color of hair, shape of the nose, and other features is a primary requirement. Some degree of realism is essential, at least in the treatment of the head. Historically, therefore, the full flowering of portraiture has generally coincided with a fair degree of realism in representation and a considerable amount of individualism in the upper ranks of society. Roman art illustrates these two conditions definitively; the art of Europe from the Renaissance to our own day is not far behind.

The Roman school, which was addicted to portraiture, produced no better example than Houdon's *John Paul Jones* (Fig. 285). In its presence one has the feeling that he is looking at a completely trustworthy record of the great sailor's physical appearance. True, much of his forceful character is also implied, but the outstanding characteristic is accuracy of representation.

The humanistic orientation toward man's appearance, which portraiture expresses, tells us much about history. Of primary significance is its immense antiquity. It had reached a high state of development by the time of *Menkure and His Queen* (Fig. 160), some 2700 years before Christ. A second quality of portraiture is its universality. It is found in the art of societies all over the world. A third, and perhaps even more impressive, fact is its persistence from early times to the present day. This tells us much about human nature. For the ego which inspires the commissioning of portraits seems to have been no less extensive and ancient than the curiosity which responds to them. People have always wanted to show others what they looked like and to perpetuate their appearance through art.

The expression of these urges has, of course, fluctuated through history. Hundreds of Egyptian portraits tell us of the strength of this motive which was justified by religious tenets in early ancient times. The Romans discarded the religious excuse and indulged in portraiture to their hearts' content. In both of these celebrated schools portraiture was confined to the ruling classes. Not until the invention of photography made cheap likenesses available could any but the wealthy afford portraits. Hence one can ascertain who possessed the powers conferred by office, church, money, or fame in any given era by noting who was portrayed in painting or sculpture.

So lasting have been the traits of curiosity and vanity that portraiture has thrived in all societies where there was a modicum of opportunity for anyone. It even crops up in the middle of the ego-suppressing other-worldly medieval epoch, entering, as it were, through the back door, in representations of donors of religious pictures. Artists have also had a way of sneaking their own portraits into their works. One of the gems of portraiture thus introduced is a small figure of Peter Vischer the Elder which adorns a shrine at Nuremberg. This practice was common in the self-conscious Renaissance and was indulged in frankly by Raphael, who placed himself among the mathematicians in his *School of Athens*. Similarly, Velasquez painted himself prominently in the *Maids of Honor*, while Rembrandt, to the north, was carrying self-portraiture to a high level. Artists have contrived to keep portraiture alive almost continuously.

Portraiture prospered under encouragement during the ancient and modern epochs and declined under medieval discouragement. The other major gap is found in Asian art. Its significance there is minor compared to the importance of religious art, but such examples as one finds are often masterpieces. Mughal art contributed not a few, as did Japanese. Unkie's portraits must be counted among the most incisive ever carved.

In view of the portraitist's devotion to an explicitness and accuracy which are often artistic stumbling blocks, the high quality of much portraiture is impressive. Any reckoning of the world's art must include many portraits among its masterpieces. Jan Van Eyck's *Marriage of Giovanni Arnolfini* (Fig. 95), Laurana's *Princess of the House of Aragon* (Fig. 158), Verrocchio's *Equestrian Portrait of Bartolommeo Colleoni* (Fig. 380), Bernini's *Cardinal Scipione Borghese* (Fig. 166), the *Menkure and His Queen*, the *Governor of Lagash*, and the portrait of an unknown Roman in Fig. 307, all warrant consideration for any selection of outstanding works of art. Much of the art of Velasquez, Hals, Rembrandt, and Ingres would be included, for portraiture played in their work a prominent, if not a dominant, role.

Portraiture is a complex subject, but the major categories are easily defined. A large percentage of portraiture consists of single figures like Houdon's *John Paul Jones*. These may include only the head or extend to bust, waist, three-quarter, or full length. Another prominent category is known as the group portrait. Frans Hals favored this type, but probably no one has excelled Rembrandt in it; his *Anatomy Lesson, Night Watch,* and *Syndics of the Cloth-Makers' Guild* are all in this class. A third designation is the self-portrait, and a fourth the equestrian portrait. Finally, there is the portrait which is introduced subordinately into a picture, such as the donors and self-portraits mentioned above.

These types have no qualitative significance; great, mediocre, and poor examples exist in each of them. The standards of excellence by which they are judged derive rather from the possibilities and limitations that lie within the avowed intentions of portraiture. A high degree of explicitness and accuracy in representation is regarded as a primary requirement in portraiture. On that ground Brancusi's *Mademoiselle Pagany* (Fig. 159) leaves some question despite its formal beauty, but Houdon's *John Paul Jones* does not. A study of this and other portraits by Houdon will show why he ranks high among portrait artists. He recognized the physical-spiritual duality of human beings and endowed his most faithful representations with an inner life and character. He was able to do this because he himself possessed a sharp eye and a sensitive mind and spirit. Accurate representation alone does not make a portrait, but only a map of the subject's features. To be completely successful, a portrait must show not only what the subject looks like, but something of what he is. It must suggest his character as well as his appearance. Houdon's emphatic sensibilities responded to the vitality of his sitters, while his sympathies enabled him to portray young and old, male and female, and all classes and types with equal understanding. He had a feeling for both the individual and typical characteristics of his sitters. His *John Paul Jones* is a fighting man; his *Thomas Jefferson* a thinker and statesman; his *Washington* a high-minded leader; his *Daughter of Brogniart* the quintessence of youthful femininity. He was an artist with an extraordinarily comprehensive understanding; Rembrandt's portraits excel his only in their sense of beauty. Houdon therefore exemplifies almost ideally the art of portraiture.

THE HUMAN FIGURE. The face, which is the main subject of portraiture, has played a major role in the humanistic orientation of artistict subject matter, but the human body has run it a close second in interest. Attention to these complementary aspects of our total make-up has been so closely associated that their histories are nearly identical. What we said about the historical fluctuations in portraiture applies so aptly to the study of the figure that the latter's history in art can be summarized quite briefly, allowing us to turn to general considerations.

The human body was a principal subject throughout the whole history of ancient art in the Mediterranean area and was an outstanding aspect of pagan art and Greek art in particular. The Greeks explored the subject so thoroughly that many think they left little unsaid. Since the complex human body is a rich field for observation, this was hardly true. With the Renaissance revival of antiquity, figure studies again became popular, and were considered from many new points of view. This enthusiasm has continued to the present day.

Owing to the religious taboos of the Middle Ages against the exposure of human flesh, this pagan and supposedly indecent subject was more or less forbidden, and there was a hiatus of about a thousand years duration in this progression. Meanwhile, Asiatic artists, who had no scruples about nudity, continued to represent the human physique assiduously. This was particularly true in India. All in all the works of art in which the human figure plays a prominent part are innumerable.

The human body has received much attention in the arts, and this is natural; nothing in the physical world is closer to us, or affects us more profoundly. In addition, there are many artistic reasons for the popularity of the body as a subject. Its complexity gives it a high degree of interest and it can be a thing of great beauty, as witness the stress placed upon beauty contests from the time of Greek mythology to the present. It provides a fascinating field of study for the scientifically minded artist, like Pollaiuolo, Michelangelo, Leonardo da Vinci, and Thomas Eakins. Its proportions can be related to a mathematically conceived or semi-abstract ideal of beauty, as in the famous canons of Polyclitus (the *Diadem-Binder,* (Fig. 217) and such modern advocates of "form for form's sake" as Maillol *(Female Torso,* Fig. 5). Finally, it can express innumerable social conditions, like those implied by Rodin's *Aged Courtesan* (Fig. 6), and countless shades of human feeling, like the healthy strength expressed by Rubens' *Rape of the Daughters of Leucippus* (Fig. 216) or the humble attentiveness of the Egyptian scribe *Khum-Ba-F* (Fig. 2). All told, this versatile instrument of expression is to the visual arts what the piano keyboard is to music. It is hard to think of any vehicle that is its superior or has enjoyed a more illustrious history.

Approached from many points of view and with many expressive purposes in mind, the human figure has been employed artistically with great variety. The classical Greeks used it to personify ideas, attest their love of healthy outdoor activities, and express their sense of beauty (the *Zeus from Artemisium,* Fig. 50). Objective realists like Eakins have catalogued its appearance (*Masked Nude Woman,* Fig. 150) and romanticists have exploited its ability to convey the emotions. Social realists like Meunier and Gemito (the *Return of the Miners,* Fig. 231, and *Neapolitan Water-Carrier,* Fig. 168) have used it to reveal the effects of social environment and occupation on its development. The artists of India have made it a thing of sensuous grace or abounding vitality (*Siva as Nataraja, Lord of the Dance,* Fig. 372); Goya and Matisse have exploited its sensual allure (*Nude Maja,* Fig. 359, and *Odalisque with Raised Arms,* Fig. 123); and Giorgione identified it with perfect repose (*Sleeping Venus,* Fig. 79). Michelangelo, perhaps the greatest master of the human nude, did all of these things and more, making it a major element in his art and expanding its possibilities as much as Beethoven later expanded those of the symphony.

In achieving their ends artists have represented the body as it is in actuality, idealized it, smoothed it up, glossed over its defects, improved its proportions, twisted it, elongated it, distorted it, and manipulated it in a hundred ways. There is little that they have not attempted. And although every new generation finds possibilities in it that have not been exhausted, artists have already made it the means of a powerful and infinitely varied statement. To remove its contribution from art would leave an unimaginable gap.

ANIMALS. Animals, by which we mean all of the subhuman animate species, always have been a popular field of artistic expression of the naturalistic orientation of perception. Representation of animals like the *Bison* at Altamira (Fig. 33) and the *Mammoth* at Combarelles (Fig. 142) must be counted among man's earliest artistic records. This interest has enjoyed an enviable continuity to the present, even persisting through the Middle Ages. There was in its case no such moral taboo as that which disrupted the representation of human anatomy. Consequently, much fine animal art can be found in the output of almost every period and country in history. It was a major concern throughout antiquity and has been universally popular in the art of Asia, while the representations of animals in European art from Renaissance days to the present are innumerable. For example, Egyptian art almost automatically suggests the *Geese of Medum,* Cretan art the *Octopus Vase,* Greek art the horses of the Parthenon, Assyrian art the wild animal hunts of Ashurbanipal, Roman art the wolf of Romulus and Remus, Indian art the beasts indigenous to that whole peninsula, Rubens and Delacroix violent scenes of crocodile and lion hunting in Africa, Géricault the *Derby at Epsom,* Chinese art the superb glazed pottery figurines of camels and Bactrian ponies, and Japanese art numerous studies of birds, fish, and animals of all sorts. The tigers and monkeys of Tohaku and others are among that nation's favorites.

Animals have been introduced into art in three main ways: as a secondary or incidental subject in a landscape or primarily human theme, such as in Rubens' *Autumn, the Château de Steen* (Fig. 83) and Hals's *Malle Babbe, the Witch of Haarlem* (Fig. 196); as a subject on an almost equal footing with the landscape setting or human beings, as in Courbet's *Stag Thicket, Lao-Tze on a Water Buffalo* (Fig. 379), and Delacroix's *Lion Hunt* (Fig. 346); and as the primary subject, as in the Egyptian *Cat* in Fig. 313.

It would be impossible to count the animals that have played an incidental role in works of art. A better evidence of absorption with this side of nature is the work of first-rate artists who specialized in the representation of animals. In the Japanese school there have been many, while in China Han Kan, a painter of horses, has always been listed among that country's masters. In the West, Frans Snyders, Barye, and Marc are associated almost exclusively with this field. Barye, the painter and sculptor of the *Black Panther* (Fig. 31), *Jaguar Killing a Young Wild Ass* (Fig. 314), and *Prancing Horse* (Fig. 343), is regarded by many critics as one of the foremost sculptors of the nineteenth century. Devotion to animal subjects has not kept artists from creating on the highest level.

Quite as impressive as the wealth of material representing animal life is its high quality in general. There is an abundance of fine work, and some of the masterpieces rank high among the world's great works of art. This is certainly true of the *Wounded Lioness* in Fig. 286. This celebrated figure expresses the passion for hunting that enthralled the virile warriors and hunters of the ancient Assyrian ruling class. It was a passion which eventually ruined them, for the cruelty with which they treated both men and beasts in their conquered empire led to a violent revolt that wiped the Assyrians from the pages of succeeding history. In this study of a wounded lioness, the masterpiece of a series, sympathy is absent but there is a profound and exceptional respect for a worthy foe. The sculptor elected to depict the lioness in her death throes; wounded mortally in the spine, she drags her paralyzed hind quarters valiantly toward her tormentors. One can almost hear her snarl of defiance. The conviction of this scene is absolute; it was based on a complete scrutiny of every detail important to the principal idea and an unerring concentration upon the essentials.

Animal life has been the source of so much fine art because it has inspired careful observation, elicited much sympathy, like

FIG. 286. *Wounded Lioness.* Reign of Ashur-bani-pal, 668-626 B.C. British Museum, London.

FIG. 287. Chardin. *Still Life. ca.* 1754. Frick Collection, New York.

FIG. 288. *Lotus Flowers and Leaves.* Ming Dynasty, 1368-1644. Museum of Fine Arts, Boston.

Franz Marc's (Fig. 32), and generated a great deal of feeling, like the fearful awe expressed in the serpent and jaguar heads on the ceremonial axe-head in Fig. 275. We have perforce always lived quite close to animals. For century after century we have hunted them for sport or food, worshipped them, fled from them, captured them, domesticated them, studied them scientifically in the field and in captivity, kept them as household guardians and pets, harnessed them, ridden them, driven them. And though most of them are minute compared to other natural forms they have the inestimable advantage of being alive, an attribute which gives the smallest of them more interest than any mountain. That this interest has been universal throughout man's history is amply demonstrated by his fondness for animals as the subject of his art.

OUTDOOR SCENES. The greatest and most readily apparent part of reality with which man has had to reckon is his external physical environment. It would be remarkable if it had not entered extensively into his artistic comments on life. What we called in an earlier chapter the naturalistic and architectural orientations of perception were only inevitable responses to man's surroundings that have impinged upon his consciousness from the beginning of human history, affecting him profoundly.

Indeed, the remarkable fact is the extent to which he has excluded his surroundings from works of art. This in itself is significant. There is a considerable difference between being unable to escape one's environment, accepting it neutrally or without fear, being keenly interested in it, and loving it. All of these reactions are manifest in the history of the painting of outdoor scenes and each is an eloquent spokesman for the attitudes of various times, places, and individuals. They demonstrate that the representation of nature in art has not by any means been continuous, that for much of human history men have not liked nature, and that only in relatively recent centuries have they loved it.

The people of the ancient world admitted their physical environment into art only incidentally. They believed that nature was capricious and hostile and that man was infinitely more important and interesting. Their philosophy set the pattern for the Mediterranean world and was counteracted only by a brief but strong love of nature in Roman times. In the Middle Ages the earthly setting was crowded from the picture by a different but equally influential concept, the absorption of that time with things religious. A really extensive attention to physical surroundings had to await the decline of the medieval outlook and the rise of the Renaissance.

From that time on man's environment began to compete with the humanistic and religious orientations and to receive progressively increasing attention. One can trace this progress through the Renaissance to the point where there is a balance in the sixteenth century between man and his setting (as in Giorgione's *Sleeping Venus*). When that point was reached the way was opened for artists to paint pure landscapes, which Ruysdael and Claude Lorrain did in the seventeenth century. The acme of this trend was reached in the nineteenth century, when men who were primarily landscape painters—Turner, Constable, Corot, Rousseau, Monet—constituted a high percentage of the first-rank artists. By that time the ancient Greek and medieval attitudes had disappeared to such an extent that a lyrical enthusiasm for nature could be freely and fully expressed.

Hand in hand with this enthusiasm for nature came an increased knowledge of it, the one promoted and benefited by the other. Turner, Constable, Monet, Winslow Homer, and many of their contemporaries possessed an impressive factual knowledge of nature. Part of this knowledgeable enthusiasm was due to the advances of science which called attention to scores of hitherto unnoticed phenomena, explained them rationally and eliminated many of the old aversions. The nineteenth-century atmosphere in which artists lived was a nature-conscious environment. At the same time it was marked by a decline in religious faith. It is hard to avoid relating the history of landscape and environmental painting to the histories of science and religion. The rise of landscape painting as science developed and religion declined may be partially explained by an ancient observation of Aesop that "we fear most what we understand least." Science dispelled most of the old superstitious fears and offered a new control and understanding. With that release from fear of nature came the freedom to study and enjoy it.

Landscape painting rose to its full development at a late date in the Orient (in the Sung period of Chinese history and in the Ashikaga and Tokugawa periods in Japan—the periods of Tung Yüan, Fig. 374, Sesson, Fig. 401, and Hokusai, Fig. 377) only after the religiosity of the Asiatic Middle Ages had weakened. It is significant that India, which retained its religious preoccupations, has never developed pure landscape painting. It is also significant that Eastern art was unaffected by European science, a fact which created a noticeable difference in the art of the two hemispheres. The crucial factor in man's representation of his environment is not so much the objective appearance of what he records as what it signifies of his attitudes. For example, man's size in relation to the out-of-doors has not changed, but this relationship has varied greatly in his mind's eye over the years.

To understand this complex subject, some categorizing is necessary. We must, for instance, subdivide man's painting of the out-of-doors so as to include closely allied themes in addition to pure landscape painting. Though this is probably the most important category, marine painting of the sort that Winslow Homer created is a type that must be recognized, as is the depiction of urban scenes like those by Utrillo.

Further characterizing of this broad field can best be pursued through the examination of some typical contrasting examples. For instance, three different conceptions of man's size and importance in nature are illustrated by Bruegel's *Blind Leading the Blind* (Fig. 282), Perugino's *Christ Delivering the Keys of Heaven to St. Peter* (Fig. 102a), and Tung Yuan's *Clear Weather in the Valley* (Fig. 374); in the first the human figures are large and dominating; in the second, in balance with their setting; in the third, minute.

Three aspects of the finite approach to nature are shown by Thomas Cole's *Oxbow of the Connecticut near Northampton*, Cézanne's *House in Provence* (Fig. 80), and Carl Hofer's *Italian Landscape*. The first resembles a portrait of a person in its individual exactitude; the second is a more general analysis of a particular scene; the third a presentation of the universal characteristics of mountainous landscapes in general. The infinite view of the out-of-doors is exemplified by Homer's *The Artist's Studio in an Afternoon Fog* and Turner's *Tempest of Snow*. These are as indistinct as Cézanne's and Cole's pictures are sharp and definite.

Associated with the finite and infinite conceptions of reality are the various limitations of view. Constable's *Trunk of an Elm Tree* (Fig. 376), like Courbet's *Stag Thicket,* is finite in the sense that it is both close-up and exact. Wu Chen's *Bamboo in the Wind* (Fig. 375) shows the variety of ways in which these different concepts can be mixed; though close, it is generalized. Other limited views of the out-of-doors are the vista and corner types illustrated by Hobbema's *Avenue of Trees at Middleharnis* and Wyant's *A Clearing in the Woods*. Similar limitations were applied by Utrillo to such urban vistas as his *Church of Sacré Coeur de Montmartre* (Fig. 22) and Vermeer to his *Little Street in Delft*. The description *intimate* is often given to pictures like Vermeer's *Little Street* and the Wyant, as distinct from the grand and heroic rocky mountain scenes by Bierstadt. Contrasting with these fractional views are the sweeping, comprehensive panoramas that one finds in Rubens' *Autumn, the Château de Steen* (Fig. 83), Constable's *Weymouth Bay* (Fig. 373), and Tung

Yuan's *Clear Weather in the Valley* (Fig. 374). The latter, because it is more generalized and infinite, has an almost cosmic character.

The relation of man-made architecture to nature has been explored by more than one artist of a philosophical turn of mind. Turner's *Norham Castle* (Fig. 25) implies the decay of human things in a continuously replenished nature; Burchfield's *November Evening* (Fig. 27), with its pathetic and drab setting, expresses a similar fatalism. Kokoschka's *Courmayeur* (Fig. 9), by contrast, depicts a snug village which persists happily and harmoniously in its mountain valley.

The dynamic side of nature has been treated extensively within the realistic and infinite concepts of reality. Straightforward but dramatic observations of weather and other phenomena are contained in Hiroshige's *Shower on Ohashi Bridge* (Fig. 68), Homer's *Coming Storm* (Fig. 119), and Rembrandt's *Three Trees* (Fig. 200). Equally spectacular for their beauty are the sparkling moonlight in Homer's *Schooners in the Moonlight, Saco Bay* (Fig. 20) and the glowing sunset in Turner's *Fighting Téméraire* (Fig. 285a). The reposeful side of nature, while less striking, has not been neglected. Whistler praised it often in his peaceful nocturnes and Corot in his placid harbors, rivers, and ponds.

A broad field of study has been man's relation to this changeable nature. Homer's *Fog Warning* (Fig. 61) shows man threatened by a sudden change, as does Sesson's *Boat Returning in a Storm* (Fig. 401); while Géricault's *Raft of the Medusa* (Fig. 378) shows him completely victimized by the sea. The ocean has often been represented as a principal villain in man's efforts to survive and to earn a living, though dry-land threats to life and limb have been recognized too, as in John Steuart Curry's *Tornado over Kansas*.

The vicissitudes of life have naturally loomed large in men's minds, but the beneficent side of nature has also been given some attention; a notable example is George Inness' *Peace and Plenty*. Others have sung songs of praise in even more lyric terms, stressing the abundance and fertility of nature. Rubens and Renoir are noteworthy for the sense of natural energy and growth their landscapes convey, and Van Gogh is internationally celebrated for the bursting vitality that permeates his sunflowers, olive groves, sunsets, and cypress trees. On a quieter plane Giorgione, too, conceived nature in rich and luxuriant terms. As is to be expected, these men have their opposites. Giotto and Michelangelo included only the barest kinds of landscape settings in pictures like the *Flight into Egypt* (Fig. 224) and the *Creation of Adam* (Fig. 126). They illustrate the attitude of those in whom humanistic, social, and religious interests predominate, and who neither know nor care much about nature. In this respect Michelangelo was like a later-day Greek.

Outdoor scenes can express a preference for the civilized or for the wild. Claude Lorrain's are models of the civilized, for though scenes like his *Landscape with Cattle* (Fig. 117) depict the countryside, they are always as neat as a park. Those of his Italian contemporary Salvatore Rosa cultivate wildness, often depicting robbers and brigands in their mountain haunts. Three centuries later Winslow Homer showed a similar fondness for the untamed backwoods in his *Coming Storm,* and populated his Adirondacks and Canadian watercolors with fishermen, guides, and hunters.

Certain broad types can be discerned among paintings of urban settings. They range from the representation of narrow side streets to broad avenues, spacious parks, and panoramas, as found in Bellows' *Cliff Dwellers,* Pissarro's *Boulevard Montmartre,* and Turner's mezzotint of a *View of London from Greenwich.* Our normal experience of cities is such that the views of streets outnumber those of skylines, though the character of Venice lent itself to numerous representations of the broad lagoon along the Riva by Guardi and Canaletto.

A further distinction can be found between the recorded types of urban civilization. It is easy to see the fondness of many artists for lower-class settings. Bellows, Sloan, Hopper, and Burchfield are among those one recalls, the first two being described as members of the "Ash-Can" school because of this predilection. Perhaps these artists felt that tenements and slums have more color, life, character, picturesqueness, or mood than more genteel surroundings.

Marine pictures, too, vary. The true seascape is illustrated by Frederick Waugh's *Roaring Forties* (Fig. 17), a scene of mid-ocean. More common is a type which has been referred to as the surf-and-rocks school. Winslow Homer set a precedent with such pictures as his *Northeaster* (Fig. 18) which has been repeated by the thousands along the New England coast. The underlying theme here is the ceaseless conflict between the ocean and the land, the dynamic and static, the Yang and the Yin. There are numerous other marines which typify the oceans and seacoasts of the world in their calmer moments, like Bonington's beautifully serene *Coast of Picardy.* And there are many pictures representing the diverse facets of man's relationship with the sea, both at work and at play. The former are, perhaps, more dramatic and memorable; but unpretentious little pictures like those Boudin painted of bathers and vacationers at the French seashore resorts have great charm.

Out-of-doors paintings of all varieties extend from the literal to the imaginary. Most of those that have earned fame were inspired by some actual scene but they do not necessarily transcribe its appearance as literally as Church's *Niagara Falls,* which seems to include every wave, ripple, and wisp of spray. Instead, the rule seems to have been to clarify, intensify, and interpret the natural scene. Painters have not often gone to the other extreme—pure invention. Albert Ryder's *Death on a Pale Horse* (Fig. 278) is so subjective that it can hardly be described as having a true landscape quality. On the other hand, El Greco's *View of Toledo* (Fig. 367) strikes an almost perfect balance between normal license and extreme subjectivity; it is rooted in reality but heightened by a powerful imagination. This is precisely what makes it one of the great pictures of the world.

The artistic exploration of man's out-of-doors environment has been remarkably thorough. It is clear that man's settings have been able to inspire artistic excellence of the highest character, making the rich field of outdoor painting one of the foremost categories of subject matter, and one of the most enjoyable to look at.

STILL LIFE. With our final category of subject matter, still life, we seem to descend from a major to a minor realm. Most still-life pictures are, like the one by Chardin in Fig. 287, small and unpretentious. Compared to a landscape they show reality fragmentarily and close up, as though through the wrong end of a telescope. They also seem philosophically trivial and emotionally thin. Yet a great number have been painted, often by the foremost masters, and their history is quite ancient. So they cannot be dismissed out-of-hand.

An interest in painting fragments of reality goes back to early times. In the ancient Egyptian fresco *Nakht Watching Plowing* (Fig. 120) there is a group of vessels containing fruits, cereals, and various liquids which possesses the kind of independence that identifies the still-life subject. The number of baskets of fruit and vases of flowers which have appeared in large pictures and yet been worthy of close study is great indeed and extends through the history of painting. Garlands of fruit abound in Roman sculpture and are among the most carefully executed figures in that field More than one later master was at his best when painting a still-life group in the corner of a picture—notably Caravaggio, Courbet, and Renoir. Still life has had the capacity to arouse the interest and stimulate the talents of major, as well as minor, artists. The universality of its appeal is shown by its presence in the art of all countries and both hemispheres —like the *Lotus Flowers* from the Ming Dynasty of China in Fig. 288.

Still-life groups have appeared in pictures in an incidental role throughout the history of art, but still life as an end in itself did not come into its own until the seventeenth century, when its popularity rose markedly among such groups as the Dutch little masters. Since that time its popularity has been unabated. It reached its zenith in the nineteenth century, when masters of the caliber of Renoir, Cézanne, and Van Gogh made still-life painting a major part of their art.

One of the reasons for the long life and popularity of still-life painting pertains to the matter of quality. Still life, in the hands of a master, has the merit of being able to say much with little. Thanks to both our imaginations and those of the artists, fine still-life pictures can imply realms of reality out of all proportion to their size or the seeming triviality of the subject. Sensitive critics see the picture of the *Lotus Flowers* as a microcosm, as a bit of nature which somehow stands for the whole world of growing plants and foliage. They see in Chardin's *Still Life* implications of all the intimate and all-important domestic life that centers in the kitchen. The small format of the still-life picture can be an ideal place in which to exploit the capacity of individual objects to suggest universal ideas.

There is nothing in the nature of still-life painting that limits the expression of a sense of order or variety or a sense of vitality or repose. Compositions like Cézanne's *Vase of Tulips* (Fig. 15), Van Gogh's magnificent *Sunflowers,* and Chardin's *Still Life* are excellent examples; so are the decorative quality of Braque's still-life pictures and the sheer gaiety of Matisse's colorful lemons and brocaded backgrounds. These qualities are expressed with a maximum of technical and compositional artistry and a minimum of ideological dependence. They make a strong case for still-life painting.

The main varieties of still-life painting are easily discovered. Chardin's *Still Life* in Fig. 287 typifies a common category. It contains items anyone could gather up around an ordinary kitchen and arrange on a table. These are the essence of the domestic, everyday, and familiar. They could be subdivided into various man-made articles—glasses, bottles, baskets, and pots and pans— and natural products like fruits and vegetables, but are usually painted together. These have been the stock-in-trade accessories of a large group of painters, of whom Cézanne is perhaps the most noted modern master.

A second category depicts such natural items as fish, fowl, and other game. Called *nature morte,* this department was also mastered by Chardin, whose pictures of dead rabbits are superb. It was a

field to which the Flemish and Dutch little masters of the seventeenth
century were devoted. Usually these trophies of the hunt or market place were painted resting on a table.

A third group is known as the flower-piece. As a rule it represents
flowers arranged in a vase or bowl against a simple background and
exploits the advantages of color and variety which are associated with
flowers everywhere. It has enjoyed universal favor. Rubens, a lover
of all things that bloom and grow, thought enough of this subject
to keep a specialist in flower-painting, Jan Bruegel, in his employ.
Contemporaneously, Jan Van Huysum, a Dutch little master, devoted
most of his career to the painting of luxuriant flower-pieces. In later
centuries, particularly the nineteenth, flower-painting gained high
popularity, encouraging Courbet, Monet, Renoir, Cézanne, Van
Gogh, Gauguin, and Matisse to paint outstanding examples.

There is a basic similarity in these examples of European still life.
The elements in all of these types—whether pots, flowers, or dead
rabbits—are arranged in isolation from their normal contexts, though
they are consistently related to each other. This removal from usual
experience, this careful separation and ordering, creates a certain
artificiality. While not bad, and indeed an esthetic merit, these characteristics explain why still-life paintings sometimes appear contrived.
Oriental still-life artists avoided this extreme of abstraction by going
to nature instead of lifting natural forms out of their normal contexts and arranging them on a table or in a vase. There is little still-
life painting of Chardin's sort in Asiatic art, but there is a great deal
like the *Lotus Flowers* in Fig. 288. Whereas Chardin's *Still Life* is
good in spite of its separation from normal experience—for we almost
never see kitchen items arranged in this manner, the *Lotus Flowers*
is good because it is both artful and natural. While carefully selected
and composed, its art is subtly concealed. It seems identical with our
commonest experiences with nature as we see it close to, and yet
strongly suggests the natural world at large. Here is the microcosm
at its best.

The still-life pictures of the Occident and the Orient thus express
two opposite conceptions. The Western still-life tradition has clung
in the main to the closed contour conception of design; the Eastern
to the open contour. This difference was emphasized in the nineteenth century when the infiltration of Japanese prints into modern
French art created a temporary meeting of minds. At this time Van
Gogh painted what was for the West a new kind of still-life picture
when he depicted a flowering pear tree or a luxuriant bed of irises
growing in their natural sites. It was a short-lived precedent, for soon
afterward Matisse, Picasso, and Braque reverted to the customary

European type. Within a generation Western still-life painters had gone farther away from, rather than closer to, nature by using still life as the jumping-off point into complete abstraction.

Still-life paintings clearly express many points of view. There are pictures by the Dutch little masters which place a premium on realistically depicted content and give little heed to esthetically satisfying design. They are often crowded to the point of confusion with dozens of dead fish or a marketful of food, but seem to have satisfied their owners if they appeared "good enough to eat." These artists held the mirror up to nature but created little of lasting value. The exceptions, like Pieter de Ring and Pieter Claesz, are few in number.

There is another important body of still-life pictures featured by an acute sense of design, and perhaps by a momentary preoccupation with form rather than content. Among them are some of the best-loved pictures from the brushes of Chardin, Courbet, Manet, Cézanne, and Matisse. All of these masters painted serious human themes, but occasionally turned to still-life painting for the sheer fun of concentrating on problems of design and execution. These problems delight any sensitive artist and bring out some of his finest abilities.

The observer who can forget the burdens of intellect for a moment and join the master still-life painters in a little artistic play will find superb examples of textural studies and composition in Chardin's excursions into still life, beautifully rich and free-flowing brushwork in Manet's, masterpieces of form and formal organization in Cézanne's, and colors that sing like a rainbow in Matisse's. Thus, while still-life painting has never been the *pièce de résistance* of art, it has given us some wonderful desserts. Even more, it has given us, in the still-life pictures of Cézanne, examples of composition which have few superiors in any field of art.

One thing remains to be said about the field of artistic subject matter. Much was made of the limitations of the visual arts in an earlier chapter, but when we study the far-reaching inclusiveness of content in the visual arts and the number of subjects that artists have treated in so many different ways, art seems to be limitless indeed.

CHAPTER 20

The Conditions of Man

A great many paintings and statues perform their most valuable function by offering us insight into aspects of human life which are of timeless significance and as universal as hunger and hate. They contribute importantly to man's quest to understand and control reality, and further the humanistic orientation in art. No subject interests human beings so much as other human beings, and no other phase of reality is closer to our understanding. Yet man's nature is endlessly complex. We never understand it absolutely or finally, and this ultimate elusiveness fascinates us.

Human beings have understood each other with widely differing degrees of profundity. The wise men of history have possessed exceptional insight, but their numbers are few. Fewer still are those who have possessed the ability to express their insight in art forms which lastingly benefit the rest of us. By common agreement this group has always included the great seers and prophets, the famous philosophers and orators, and the noted authors and poets. Articulateness in words has been the mainstay of their insight. To this group we may add the masters of painting and sculpture. Though they expressed their observations in a silent medium, their insights are none the less profound. The great artists have been more than virtuosos, more than mechanics, more than technicians; they have been men with penetrating minds whose works can teach us much about the nature and conditions of man and what is important to him.

The works of visual art which treat what is of timeless and universal importance in man's physical, mental, and spiritual life can be divided into two contrasting groups. In the group which we shall consider first are the statues, drawings, and paintings which depict conditions conducive to man's well-being. In the other group are representations of those conditions which undermine or destroy his welfare. Artists, like other thinkers, have concerned themselves with the age-old problem of what is good or evil for man. Far from pretending to a detached, scientific, impersonal objectivity, the greatest of them have loved life passionately and identified themselves sympathetically or empathically with their fellow men even when saddened by their plights or their failings.

We shall consider the positive side of life under the following headings: sexual desire, romantic love, marital love, maternal love, benevolence, confidence, modesty, mental vitality, alcoholic animation, *joie de vivre*, physical strength, physical grace, and nervous vitality. Of these, none has received more consideration than the first five, which make up the realm of human love.

THE SEX URGE

Without debating the morals of the sex function, let us merely accept the fact that nature planted this drive in human beings to insure the perpetuation of the species, and made the biological urge too strong to be ignored. The uncontrolled sex urge is little different in men and animals, as Robert Louis Stevenson showed in portraying his "Mr. Hyde"; it is desire on a purely sensory level. Neither subtlety of expression nor difficulty are its distinguishing features; even imbeciles feel its lash. Its dominant characteristics are compulsiveness, brevity, indiscrimination, and ubiquity. After hunger it is the most urgent and universal drive in man's nature and the sensation which allies him most closely with the animate world. The propagation of the species is of primary biological importance to men, as it is to every member of the animal kingdom.

Yet sexuality has not inspired a proportionate number of fine works of art. A vast number of the many devoted to the subject, such as the numerous erotic Japanese prints, Greek vase paintings, and the wall decorations at Pompeii, never rose above the level of pornography. Nevertheless, a considerable body of masterpieces remains which cannot be dismissed. For whatever their titles may be, the following treat this theme: Maillol's *Desire* (Fig. 289), Rembrandt's *Susannah and the Elders* and *Joseph and Potiphar's Wife*, Tintoretto's *Adam and Eve* (Fig. 257), Bernini's *Apollo and Daphne* (Fig. 167), Rubens' *Rape of the Daughters of Leucippus* (Fig. 216), Titian's *Rape of Europa* (Fig. 195), Correggio's *Jupiter and Io,* Hogarth's *Harlots' Progress*, and Fragonard's *Swing* (Fig. 290)—all of them noted works of art.

Two threads of historical significance run through these examples. One is rooted in the Greek tradition. Herodotus wrote that the Greeks were notorious among antique peoples for their sexuality and an emphasis on hedonistic paganism reappeared with the Greek tradition in the Renaissance to challenge St. Paul's conception of Christianity. The second thread traces back to the Old Testament studies of human nature, which by no means ignored the role of lust. It came to light whenever the Bible was illustrated narratively, as in the art of Rembrandt. With two such precedents to draw upon, the great artists were able to lift their depictions of lust above the level of pornography and make them express the efflorescence of health and vitality.

In the age-old observation of artists there is a common formula for the lust-motivated relationship of the sexes: men are represented as the active, aggressive agents, women as the passive, with the female exhibiting various degrees of resistance—genuine, half-hearted, or token. On the Greek vases the satyrs always pursue the nymphs, never the other way around. The notable exception to this rule is Rembrandt's *Joseph and Potiphar's Wife*.

A frank and convincing treatment of this theme is Maillol's *Desire* (Fig. 289). Giving his relief a forthright, truthful title, he avoided the usual circumlocutions that mask sexuality in Renaissance pictures and statues. Thus freed of pretense he was able to present his subject in this Greek-style metope in an honest and forceful fashion. The raw ardor of the naked male is undisguised, the aversion of the female to his animal directness seems sincere, and the purely physical nature of the relationship exposed and even underscored. Maillol was no prude; yet in the end his figures give a dominant impression of youth and vigor.

At the far pole from Maillol's Homeric conception is Fragonard's *Swing* (Fig. 290), a gem of a picture which typifies the attitude of the eighteenth century. Far too polite to call a spade a spade, the century of Casanova and the Versailles aristocrats was engrossed with lustful thoughts but cloaked them with a veneer of respectability. No century ever played harder or more exquisitely at disguising its intentions. Lust among the well-bred had always to be given an air of good manners. Fragonard's *Swing* is, consequently, as chicly clothed and sophisticated as Maillol's *Desire* is lusty. In it there is a narrowing of differences between the sexes, with the lady giving encouragement boldly to an eager but effeminate gentleman in an atmosphere of naughty intrigue. An elderly husband in the right background dutifully swings the young wife, while she kicks her slipper toward a

FIG. 289. Maillol. *Desire. ca.* 1904. Museum of Modern Art. New York.

FIG. 290. Fragonard. *The Swing.* 1765. Wallace Collection, London.

FIG. 291. Rodin. *The Kiss.* 1886. Luxembourg, Paris.

half-concealed young lover. In such fashion did the French aristocrats dally with love while the Revolution was brewing.

Fragonard, Boucher, Watteau, and their eighteenth-century French
school as a whole made lust naughty and enticing. The profundity
and general application of their conception can be questioned, but
the beauty of their pictures and the breadth of their interests cannot.
Their work cannot be ignored in any consideration of this theme.
In the long run, however, men of the stamp of Rubens and Maillol
best justified lust as one of the positive forces of life.

ROMANTIC LOVE

While romantic love contains a substratum of lust, sensuous desire
is only one element in its bond. It must possess sentimental and
psychological ingredients which lift it above the animal level and are
an important measure of human and civilized development. The
capacity for love is a mark of highly civilized man; it is almost non-
existent, according to Havelock Ellis, among many primitive tribes-
men, who often have not even a word for it.

Among the civilized, tributes to the importance of love are myriad,
and in many instances inspired. The love story is central in nearly
every major novel, opera, or play in the literature of every nation.
It abounds, too, in works of visual art. The artists of Japan, Persia,
and India gave it lyrical and tender treatment, while the painters of
eighteenth-century France made it their major subject matter, as the
titles of pictures by Watteau, Boucher, and Fragonard indicate: the
*Lesson of Love, Reunion of Love, Venus Disarming Cupid, Venus
Consoling Love,* the *Lover Crowned, Invocation to Love,* and the
Love Letter are only a few examples among many which dwell upon
this theme. The eighteenth-century aristocracy of France was engrossed in the subject, and gave every aspect of it a sophistication and
refinement rarely excelled in art. Their pictures comprise its book
of etiquette, with Watteau's *Embarkation for Cythera* (Fig. 319)
probably the masterpiece.

But for a definitive treatment of this subject, Rodin's *Kiss* remains
the ideal example, the work of visual art which rings the truest, has
the widest meaning, and presents this complex emotion at its best.
It is to romantic love what Maillol's *Desire* is to the physical, and a
study of their similarities and differences will sum up the topic.

Both Rodin's *Kiss* and Maillol's *Desire* present the relationship
between a man and a woman in a state of frank undress. They are
not French of the eighteenth century, but Man and Woman of every
place and every time. Beyond that their differences are marked.

The physical action in the Maillol is violent and one-sided; in the Rodin it is mutual, quiet, and tender. This mutuality is an important distinction, for it is what spiritualizes an otherwise animal act and allows a fulfilment of human personality.

In the *Kiss* Rodin has made the female soft, small, and curvilinear, the male large, strong, angular, and slightly awkward: in this way he shows us how, under the influence of love, the woman takes on some of the man's strength and draws his head to hers in an ardent embrace, while the rough man becomes tender and unwontedly considerate; his huge hand rests gently on her hip, his other arm is restrained. The impetuosity of Maillol's *Desire* is absent, and in its place is a complementary fulfilment and blending of two human personalities, making for a union of the finest attributes of femininity and masculinity. Where sex predominates in Maillol's relief, it is only part of the richer and more enduring relationship in Rodin's *Kiss,* as it is in all finer representations of romantic love in art, like Frans Hals's *Yonker Ramp and His Sweetheart* and Harunobu's *Lovers Walking in the Snow.*

MARITAL LOVE

Like most other people, artists have observed, participated in, and speculated on the nature of the marital relationship for many centuries. The following, which range far back in time, all deal in one way or another with this subject: *Menkure and His Queen* (Fig. 160), Giotto's *Meeting of Joachim and Anna* (Fig. 75), Hals's *Artist and His Wife,* Grant Wood's *American Gothic* (Fig. 96), Jan Van Eyck's *Marriage of Giovanni Arnolfini* (Fig. 95), Rembrandt's *Self-Portrait with Saskia* and *Shipbuilder and His Wife,* and Rubens' *Self-Portrait with Isabella Brant* (his first wife). Many of these are self-portraits, reminding us that the artists have known something of what they have said from personal experience. The examples date from at least 2700 B.C. and represent five different centuries; so they should give us a cross-section of opinion.

The aspects of the many-sided marital relationship presented in these works naturally vary, but together they provide a picture of the field as a whole. *Menkure and His Queen* meet the world together. They share the same pride in their high position. And though Menkure is master, his Queen is not unimportant. With an arm around his waist, she seems to stand ready to help and advise him. The Iowa farmers in *American Gothic* and Giovanni Arnolfini and his wife face the world together, too, but in different ways. Grant Wood's country people are stolid but staunch, typical "salt of the earth" characters. Arnolfini and his wife, on the other hand, are gentle and refined; he holds her hand with protective tenderness. Giotto's *Meeting of Joachim and Anna* shows us still another manifestation of marital love. Their gentle but eloquent kiss is the culmination of years of waiting for a child.

The three self-portraits by Hals, Rembrandt, and Rubens illustrate individual variations in marriage. Frans Hals and his wife beam at the world with healthy, apple-cheeked faces, the epitome of comfortable Dutch middle-class domesticity. Rembrandt's *Self-Portrait with Saskia* depicts him when he was at the peak of his popular success, and a joyously happy young husband. The picture, which seems to represent a tête à tête party, is filled with gaiety. It contrasts, in that respect, with Gainsborough's *Morning Walk*, which depicts a pair of honeymooning young aristocrats; typically British, they appear devoted but self-consciously on their best behavior. Rubens' own nuptial self-portrait with the beautiful young Isabella Brant is also quietly dignified, but easy, natural, and unpretentious, like that superb master himself. Finally, Rembrandt's *Shipbuilder and His Wife* examines the state of a marriage that has endured into old age. In it the wife enters a room to deliver a message. Her husband is working over a drafting board. Half-preoccupied, he turns toward her, while she keeps a hand on the door for a prompt withdrawal. The essence of their union is a consideration born of long understanding and adjustment. Like *Menkure and His Queen*, they have a job to do in life, and they do it together, suppressing self-interest for the common good.

Each of these examples tells us in its own way something of the admirable side of marital love and the elements which make for its success. Are there, however, any special traits which distinguish marital love from romantic love and lust? Let us turn for an example to one other fine interpretation of marital love, David's *Lavoisier and His Wife* (Fig. 292). The perfection and warmth of this marriage, which David had the perception to appreciate, redeemed him from the frigid academic pieces he ordinarily painted.

Lavoisier was a well-known French scientist of the eighteenth century, a fact which David conveys by showing him at his work. Even more important is the way in which his wife quietly encourages and supports him in his researches, a relationship which the painter has shown clearly. The devotion of the couple is obvious without being sentimental. Moreover, the picture convincingly asserts that two people can, through marital love, attain the highest development of the human potential that is possible to the equation. For Lavoisier and his wife have achieved in marriage the fulfilment of

Fig. 292. Jacques Louis David. *Lavoisier and His Wife*. 1787. Rockefeller Institute for Medical Research, New York.

Fig. 293. Hans Holbein the Younger. *The Artist's Family*. 1528. Museum, Basle.

Fig. 294. Kollwitz. *Family Group*. *ca.* 1928. Bowdoin College Museum of Fine Arts, Brunswick, Me.

their whole personalities. The picture takes on an extra meaning when we learn that Lavoisier and his wife were wantonly guillotined five years later (in 1799) by the Revolutionary Assembly, though his scientific work for the King had been done for the benefit of all French agriculture.

Sexuality is subordinated in David's masterpiece, as in the others described above, to higher attributes of human personality—companionship, maturity, tolerance, steadfastness, tenderness, consideration, mutual respect, and admiration. These are the attributes of happiness as distinct from pleasure, and connote quiet but long-range attainments instead of fiery but short-lived feelings. Marital love, according to these works of art, is a cumulative and slowly won condition based on innumerable experiences, and is superior to physical love by virtue of its difficulty of achievement, and its more lasting rewards.

If romantic love is the normal prelude to marriage, there is yet a difference between them. For neither David's *Lavoisier and His Wife* nor any of the other illustrations of marital love we have cited contain the kind of sexual demonstration that is present in Rodin's *Kiss*. They stress affection rather than passion, implying that it is the real cement of any enduring relation. Hence, while sex is not eliminated, its fires are banked for the long-run purposes of marriage.

MATERNAL LOVE

Countless works of art extol mother love. A tremendous outpouring of them began with the Cult of the Virgin in late Gothic times and continued to the end of the post-Renaissance period, with Raphael making an immortal reputation on his paintings of the Madonna and Child. But religion alone cannot account for this popularity. Rather, it is recognition of one of the most important kinds of love in human life.

This love, completely nonsexual in character, is distinguished by devotion, sympathy, tolerance, and tenderness. By bringing out the unselfish qualities of womanhood it has inspired the admiration of artists around the world. Among the noted works of art devoted to this subject are Giotto's *Presentation of the Virgin* (Fig. 51), Daumier's *Laundress* (Fig. 311), De Hooch's *Mother by a Cradle* (Fig. 98), Raphael's *Madonna of the Chair* (Fig. 253), Utamaro's Japanese prints of mothers and children, Mary Cassatt's numerous paintings of the theme, and Käthe Kollwitz's *Family Group* (Fig. 294). These pictures present nearly every facet of maternal love. Mary Cassatt's canvases are full of affection; Giotto's *Presentation of the Virgin* brings out a mother's pride; Daumier's *Laundress* shows the solicitude of a mother for her child as she assists it up a stairway, De Hooch's *Mother by a Cradle* points out the care mothers devote to the very young, and Utamaro's prints underline the long and patient education that must go into the rearing of children during the helpless or awkward years of their lives.

In her *Family Group* Käthe Kollwitz, a woman of great heart and profound understanding, has given us a kind of summation of mother love. Having lived through the bitterest years of the post-war depression in Germany, she saw it tested well and missed nothing of its character. In the lithograph, the *Family Group*, the mother's face is not shown, yet one senses her pride of motherhood and the tenderness in her large hands. It could not be simpler or more true to life. This scene gave Käthe Kollwitz one of her few light-hearted moments, for the poverty and starvation that surrounded her in Germany and struck especially at the children made her sympathetic art predominantly tragic and poignant.

On a quieter but no less moving plane is Hans Holbein's *Artist's Family* (Fig. 293). A masterly study of mother love, it is characterized by a quality of patient care that any woman will appreciate. More than that, it possesses a poignant sadness. Although comparable in composition to the contemporary pyramidal designs of Raphael, it is worlds removed from the Italian master's pictures in its realism. A pathetic personal experience moved Holbein to paint it. The story is briefly this: the first years of Holbein's marriage to Elizabeth Schmid were happy. A charming and pretty girl, she appears serenely beautiful as the Madonna in his early pictures. But the Reformation ruined the arts in Basle, forcing Holbein to go to England to earn a living. Eventually he became the celebrated portraitist of Henry VIII and his wives and court. There was apparently no place at court for Holbein's family, but he visited them at Basle in 1528, when he bought them a house and painted this picture. It it not far-fetched to read in the family's expression the premonition that Holbein would soon desert them for his career abroad. The children are prematurely serious and the once-pretty mother is careworn, but they are united by a strong bond of loyalty. Holbein must have been torn between his family and his career, for this is the most deeply felt of all his pictures. It is a moving example of maternal love, and under the circumstances is doubly effective because of its restraint. There is therefore little for us to add about this subject that Käthe Kollwitz and Holbein have not already expressed.

BENEVOLENCE

When Christ told all men to "love one another," He set them their most difficult task. The social love that He meant is not prompted by normal instincts, blood relationship, sexual desire, or hope of gain. It requires a high degree of altruism, generosity, and magnanimity, and is probably the most mature attitude that human beings can attain. The supreme examples of it, like the immortal story of Ruth and Naomi, Abraham Lincoln's "With malice toward none and charity for all," the utter self-sacrifice of Father Damien, and the lifelong compassion of Albert Schweitzer are Himalayan peaks in the history of human behavior.

Because of the rarity of this virtue in its highest degree, it has not been widely illustrated in art, but the available examples are often among the finest works. Think of the many representations of the lives of the saints, such as El Greco's several versions of the *St. Martin Dividing His Cloak with a Beggar* and Giotto's frescoes of the life of the gentle and devoted St. Francis of Assisi. Two specific pictures which represent human sympathy and good will with inspired artistry are Ghirlandaios *Old Man and a Boy* (Fig. 344) and Hals's *Rommelpot Player* (Fig. 345).

Another fine example is Andrea della Robbia's *Visitation* (Fig. 295). Here the emotional rapport and bond of sympathy between the young Virgin Mary and the elderly St. Elizabeth are complete. The incident represented is the visitation of the Virgin who was soon to bear the Christ Child to the friend who was carrying the future St. John the Baptist. If their positions were reversed, it would be an equally good illustration of the love of Ruth and Naomi. As an illustration of benevolence it is definitive as well as beautiful.

CONFIDENCE

Fear plagues the human mind. The ideal antidote to this condition is a self-confidence which does not need constant bolstering. Where it exists short of arrogance it is a valuable and healthy attitude. It is a primary characteristic of the dynamic type of leader, who radiates it in a contagious fashion, and no less important among those leaders who reassure others by calm and poise. An extreme lack of confidence in a person makes everyone else ill at ease. The degree to which confidence exists in the face of obstacles and on the basis of achievements is therefore a factor of prime importance in determining the condition of man.

FIG. 295. Andrea della Robbia. *Visitation*.
ca. 1485. S. Giovanni Fuorcivitas, Pistoia.

FIG. 296. Detail. *Khafre*. Reigned
ca. 2850-2794 B.C., IV Dynasty. Egyptian
Museum, Cairo.

FIG. 297. Van der Weyden. *Portrait of a
Lady*. *ca.* 1455. National Gallery of Art,
Washington, D.C.

Confidence has traditionally been associated more closely with men than with women, and is indeed one of the chief qualities by which the male character is judged. So the principal examples in art usually represent outstanding men, such as Napoleon or Christ or John Paul Jones (Fig. 285). The great sailor gave us a ringing instance of confidence when he proclaimed in battle, "Sir, I have not yet begun to fight." It is words of this kind which inspire less intrepid men to outdo themselves, and are the mark of the dynamic leader.

As Henri Bergson asserts in his *Creative Evolution*, human history is not fixed; its course has been altered for good or ill by creative men. Confidence has been central in the shaping of things because our empathic reactions are as acutely sensitive to its influence as they are to lack of confidence, fear, and panic. We therefore do not need to have the signs of confidence defined for us; we know them when we see them. We can see them plainly on the face of Houdon's portrait of John Paul Jones. His vigorous, upright bearing, clear eyes, firm mouth, and strong chin are the outward signs of an inner assurance —an assurance which generates a similar quality in us. Confidence, here as always, is measured by a specific kind of feeling, and that feeling lifts this portrait above a mere physical record and makes it a masterly objectification of emotion.

Confidence cannot be bluff. We are quick to detect sham and demand achievements. In a historic leader, the appearance of confidence and a record of success go hand in hand. A superb example of this combination is the portrait of *Khafre* (Fig. 296) in the Egyptian Museum in Cairo. This massive seated figure is a man of great physical strength and immeasurable confidence. He is the essence of imperturbable calm, and rightly proud of his position and achievements. Yet his attitude is not offensive or arrogant, for his self-assurance rests on one of the supreme accomplishments in history. Khafre was the pharaoh who built the second Pyramid at Gizeh (Fig. 381). Taller even than the Great Pyramid of Khufu, it is one of the mightiest structures ever erected by man. It was not until our own century that architects, with modern materials, techniques, and machines, were able to construct buildings which exceed the sheer bulk of Khafre's Pyramid. To obtain its completion Khafre had to command the services of thousands of men over a period of many years. To say that he kept his hold by threats and coercion is probably to oversimplify his power. He must also have been a man of inexorable will and purpose who derived the confidence expressed in his portrait from actual exploits. His was an assurance based on a stupendous success. It epitomizes the representation of confidence in the visual arts.

MODESTY

In their characterizations of human beings, people have universally distinguished between the primary character traits of men and women. The Chinese used the terms *yang* and *yin* which are more or less equivalent to our *active* and *passive*. A German biologist has referred to the role of one as *force* and the other *harmony*. As a whole they have assigned to the male the attributes of strength, confidence, and restless activity, and to the female, opposite or complementary qualities. Shakespeare expressed a common opinion in describing Cordelia, the youngest daughter of King Lear: "Her voice was ever soft, gentle, and low—an excellent thing in woman." The characteristics which we accept as proper and admirable in men and women are different and cannot be exchanged without creating a distasteful air of effeminacy on the one hand and misplaced masculinity on the other.

The importance of this propriety can be seen by contrasting Houdon's *John Paul Jones* and the portrait of *Khafre* with Fra Angelico's *Madonna of Humility* (Fig. 191), Laurana's *Princess of the House of Aragon* (Fig. 158), Rembrandt's *Portrait of a Woman* (Fig. 365), and Rogier van der Weyden's young lady (Fig. 297). The widely admired portraits of the men radiate confidence and strength and those of the women modesty and gentleness. The qualities of restraint and modesty are exemplified especially well by Weyden's *Lady*. She is serenely posed, with hands clasped calmly together. Her chin, compared to Khafre's, is cast slightly downward and so too is the direction of her gaze. She is the opposite of aggressive. Moreover, her general appearance is echoed by the mien of Laurana's *Princess of the House of Aragon*, Rembrandt's *Woman*, and Fra Angelico's *Madonna of Humility*. Their similarity in this regard is striking. Inasmuch as these artists are widely recognized for their understanding of femininity, the prominence they have given to modesty in their characterizations expresses a common attitude.

MENTAL VITALITY

One of mankind's greatest pleasures has come from exchanges of ideas in conversation. Closely allied to this joy in talk is mental vitality, for the exchange of ideas is usually attended by signs of accelerated thought; nothing would be more incongruous than a lively flow of ideas and a "dead pan" expression. When amused or pleased the mobility of our smiles and the sparkle in our eyes mirrors the momentary vivacity of our minds. When depressed or serious our faces grow dull or sober. Mental vivacity and a warm, expressive personality are therefore regarded by almost everyone as social assets. Two things make the social condition of man possible and pleasurable. One is the expressiveness of the human face; the other is our empathic response to signs of mental vitality and the fun and relaxation we derive from them. So sensitive is this mutuality that a bright smile or a frown are both almost inescapably contagious and emotionally effective.

In the silent, visual arts, the viewer's empathic identification is crucial for any representation of mental vitality. For no painter or sculptor can convey through a face alone either the intelligence of the person represented or the specific ideas that are running through his mind. He can only suggest that we are in the presence of a mind that is vigorously alive. Hence the only part of mental vitality that is actually communicable through painting or sculpture is the feeling that attends it. Yet that is no mean asset, for we can smile with a person regardless of whether he speaks.

Appreciative psychological-minded artists have endeavored to give the faces they painted the signs of an inner life. A main characteristic of Giotto's art is the intensity of expression that typifies his people, like the smile of motherly pride on the face of St. Anne in his *Presentation of the Virgin* (Fig. 51). He was a pioneer in this field, but while his command over the representation of living faces was intense, it was not complete. With experience artists gained remarkable control over this phase of their art. Among the examples that would stand out in this field are Van Dyck's superbly alert *Cardinal Bentivoglio* and Houdon's marble portrait of Voltaire in the foyer of the Comédie Française in Paris. The intellectual vigor of these two men is striking compared to almost any portrait by Holbein. The German master's people are robust but sober, whereas *Bentivoglio* and *Voltaire* are lean and almost frail but very much alive. Voltaire's eyes seem to dance to the tune of his irrepressible, witty mind.

No small portion of Rembrandt's appeal rests on the signs of intelligence in the faces of his subjects, ranging from the intensely thoughtful to the light-hearted. We find this quality of intense mental activity in his own superb *Self-Portrait* in the Imperial Gallery at Vienna; one can almost read his thoughts. It is an outstanding characteristic of his portrait of *Nicholas Bruyningh* (Fig. 135)— a perfect picture of a man enjoying a casual but delightful conversation. In portrait after portrait by Rembrandt, like the *Woman* in Fig. 365, one finds a twinkle in the eyes and a subtle smile that are

FIG. 298. Maurice Quentin de la Tour. *D'Alembert*. *ca.* 1750. Louvre, Paris.

FIG. 299. Hals. *The Jolly Toper*. *ca.* 1627. Rijksmuseum, Amsterdam.

FIG. 300. Carpeaux. *The Dance*. *ca.* 1868. Louvre, Paris.

FIG. 301. Hogarth. *The Shrimp Girl*. *ca.* 1750. National Gallery, London.

sources of measureless pleasure. It is a dour man indeed who cannot enjoy them.

Maurice Quentin de la Tour, a French artist of the eighteenth century, specialized in the representation of mental vitality in a series of pastel portraits. Though his work cannot compare in scope with that of Rembrandt, Rubens, and others, it is superb within its limitations. His faces gleam with life. Among other things he perfected a sketchy handling of pastel which exploited that medium fully, and captured the spirit of his subjects effectively. What we know of La Tour indicates that he was a man with a lively Gallic wit and was attracted to kindred spirits. A spritely look runs through his whole portrait series and may have been projected upon the visage of *D'Alembert* (Fig. 298). Yet there is a limit to the sort of projection that made Rembrandt see a philosopher in every beggar. D'Alembert was, in fact, a brilliant intellectual. In most cases in art, both artist and subject contributed to the final result. In this instance the result was what is called "a speaking likeness" and a brilliant example of mental vitality.

ALCOHOLIC ANIMATION

Alcoholic animation is a kind of mental and physical vitality. And although its beneficence may be questioned, the subject cannot be ignored by the student of art or its sources in life. For men have drunk alcohol, smoked tobacco, and praised both for centuries. One of the most copied of all poems is a drinking song written by Anachreon in the sixth century before Christ.

Men drink and seek solace in tobacco because the best of them are neither free nor self-sufficient but are shackled by a host of personal inadequacies and social restrictions and compulsions. To find release from these cares, they turn to the mild euphoria induced by alcohol.

Artists have accepted the lapses of their fellows from strict morality tolerantly and have recorded them in an extensive gallery of pictures. More than that, they have often entered unreservedly into the spirit of the occasions represented. Consequently, the paintings which depict alcoholic animation are among the most infectiously ingratiating in art and, in numerous cases, of considerable artistic quality. There is a wonderful bounce in Daumier's *Drinking Song* (Fig. 63), gusto in Rubens' *Triumph of Silenus* (Fig. 318), and great dexterity of brushwork in Hals's *Malle Babbe* (Fig. 196). No other subject caused these masters to work more vigorously or brilliantly.

Drink, it is said, brings out the true nature of man, making some

aggressive and others amiable, gay, or hilarious.   Artists have run the
gamut in their interpretation of the individual effects of alcohol.   Rubens' *Triumph of Silenus* and Daumier's *Drinking Song* are hilarious.
Clodion's statue of a *Nymph and Satyr Drinking Wine* is, in keeping
with the mores of eighteenth-century France, gay but well-mannered.
On a quieter level still are Hals's genre masterpieces *Malle Babbe* and
the incomparable *Jolly Toper* (Fig. 299).   Both are delightful representations of social amiability.

The *Jolly Toper* is one of the great pictures of Western art.   Its
technique is brilliant and the characterization of its content perfect.
We have all attended parties or known the type that Hals has represented here so well; he is the good-natured fellow who, made even
more congenial by a little drink, wanders around at a party fraterniz-
ing with everyone, a benign gleam in his eye and a ready smile on his
face.   All men are his friends.   He will tell a story to any who will
listen.   In Hals's *Jolly Toper*, a *bon vivant* of this sort has been caught
in his rounds with the lightning perception of genius.   The picture
is a spontaneous, lifelike image.   For our purposes it justifies temperate alcoholic animation.

JOIE DE VIVRE

There are people whose vitality is attributable to abounding health
and sheer joy in living. They possess an exceptional capacity for a
radiant optimism, what the French call *joie de vivre*.   The spirit of
youth shines from their faces and permeates the activity of their
bodies.   They appear young, free, and without a care in the world.
They may be neither intellectual nor profound, but theirs is an enviable personality.

The quest for a fountain of youth and all it symbolizes of happiness is centuries old, as is the craving for a carefree existence.   In the
ordinary circumstances of life the complete freedom from care is at-
tainable only in our dreams, or with the help of alcohol or other
drugs. Hence those who are supremely happy day after day without
the aid of either seem especially blessed.   Yet there is evidence that
we would not know what to do with the fountain of youth were we
to find it, and strong suggestions, like the stories of Adam and Eve
and Pandora and her box, that we would use it poorly.   We cannot
believe unquestioningly that freedom from care is entirely what we
want.   A sense of maturity, accomplishment, and social worth are in
the end more fulfilling than pleasure.   We deliberately choose not to
be children, lotus-eaters, or playboys all of our lives.   We court cares
and responsibilities and accept their consequences.   So while we love

to see children having a good time and join them on occasion, we cannot accept *joie de vivre* as the principal aim of life. Seen in that perspective, the great examples of *joie de vivre* give us a glimpse into paradise without setting a pattern for the whole of life or art.

Outstanding among works of art which exemplify this quality are the statues of the nineteenth-century French sculptor Jean Baptiste Carpeaux and some of the pictures of William Hogarth. A sense of gaiety runs through the whole of Carpeaux's work and nearly bursts the bounds of his noted group, the *Dance,* on the façade of the Opera House in Paris (Fig. 300). While these figures are appropriately graceful, it is their bounding vitality and youthful joy that dominate our impression. Similarly, Hogarth's universally popular *Shrimp Girl* (Fig. 301) wears a frank and infectious grin of natural joy. The artistry and discipline with which Carpeaux and Hogarth have captured this quality are not to be discounted. But we feel that skill was, in their cases, only the servant of a natural gift for optimism and buoyance. Carpeaux's gaiety was celebrated in his day. A principal facet of his personality, it made him the darling of the pleasure-loving court of Louis Napoleon's Second Empire. And Hogarth, though a philosopher of life who could be serious and even scathing, personally possessed a wonderful sense of fun and an irrepressible courage. If optimism in the face of discouragements is a test of strength, he was one of history's strong men. Thus the *Dance* and the *Shrimp Girl* express qualities that sprang from the personalities of their creators quite as much as from the subjects themselves, though Hogarth must have been inspired from without when he saw this simple but glowing girl in the market place. Whistler proclaimed Hogarth the greatest of English painters upon seeing it.

The term *joie de vivre* describes the essential quality in Carpeaux's *Dance* and Hogarth's *Shrimp Girl,* allowing us to distinguish between them and Hals's *Jolly Toper.* The shrimp girl's personal appeal, for instance, does not derive from alcoholic amiability, as does the jolly toper's, nor from such qualities of sparkling wit and mental agility as fill the picture of D'Alembert. It comes from a simpler and more naturally ebullient source—pure joy of living.

These masterpieces of good cheer are among the world's best-loved works of art. Others which pay tribute to man's persisting good spirits throughout a history of adversity are Hogarth's own delightful *Laughing Audience,* Pieter Bruegel's jolly *Wedding Dance* (Fig. 232), and a host of pictures by Renoir, all of which are blessed with an abundance of animal spirits and a love of life. They form one of the cheeriest galleries in art.

PHYSICAL STRENGTH

Human beings set great store by signs of physical strength that attest an abundance of vitality. But some attention can be given to the different ways in which man's physical strength has manifested itself.

The handiest reference for determining the typical categories of physical strength is the realm of track and field events. Better than any other, that composite sport has recognized that men possess different kinds of physical strength and has provided outlets for each. Its separate activities run the gamut of physical requirements and aptitudes, from the fleetness-of-foot of the sprinter to the stamina of the long-distance runner, the sheer power of the shot-putter, the springiness of the high-jumper, and the vigorous snap of the javelin-thrower, with other events like the hurdles and pole-vaulting testing strength and skill in various combinations.

Artists have shared in the perennial empathic pleasure of watching strong men in action and have distinguished between the diverse displays of strength, power, stamina, and agility. More important still is their capacity for observing and recording these qualities exactly in works of art. It has been their way of paying homage to the inner life of the body as well as to its physical beauty. The Greeks, as Elie Faure asserts, were no less engrossed in the "life of the muscles" than in canons of ideal proportions, and bequeathed this twin enthusiasm to a Western world which adopted it without much coaxing.

In the Greek mind the supreme example of strength was the imaginary figure of Heracles, an idea that was given powerful expression in the metope of *Heracles and the Cretan Bull* at Olympia (Fig. 407). The Greeks also combined an unsurpassed observation of the body in action with high artistic skill to give us other memorable studies of human physical strength, like the tense tug-of-war in the Parthenon metope in Fig. 356 and the frantic power of the *Laocoön Group* (Fig. 406).

From the classic period to the present (with the usual exception of the Middle Ages) artists have used this theme of man's bodily strength to produce a wealth of powerful and appealing works. Michelangelo's *Captive* (Fig. 66) nearly bursts with the power of a Herculean weight-lifter, a kind of strength for which his art is famous. Quieter but nonetheless powerful is the taut strength in the figure of *Menkure* (Fig. 160). Pollaiuolo's *Hercules Strangling Antaeus* (Fig. 64) illustrates tremendously the crushing strength of a wrestler. Daumier's *Burden* (Fig. 161) is so imbued with power that we can feel the force of the husky laundress as she bucks a galelike wind. Sintenis' *Paavo Nurmi* (Fig. 162) depicts the winged stamina of the noted distance runner, allying a wiry strength to agility. Rubens' *Rape of the Daughters of Leucippus* (Fig. 216) represents a ponderous kind of power.

These are celebrated instances of physical strength—power in motion. There is another type of strength which should be remembered, lest we identify strength only with activity. That is strength held under tight control. Far from being static, this poised balance of momentum and inertia conveys the most highly charged dynamic sense of all. Its tautness is filled with life. Michelangelo understood this principle of restraint and used it superbly throughout his art, as in the *Captive*. Other examples of contained energy with great effective powers are the Sumerian *Governor of Lagash* (Fig. 67), and the Egyptian pharaoh *Khafre* (Fig. 296). Though apparently in repose, these men radiate strength through the clasp of a pair of hands, the firm set of a jaw, or the line of tightly compressed lips. These displays of latent strength and power in reserve are subtle and immensely effective.

PHYSICAL GRACE

To the fine artist or acute observer physical strength is not always enough, despite its ability to excite. An additional quality which has been universally prized is physical grace. It gives a sense of order to power which might otherwise be awkward, ponderous, or wild. Though often associated with physical strength as an esthetic bonus, it can be the primary quality of a figure, adding flowing, coordinated movements to a handsomely proportioned but only moderately muscular physique. This possibility offers the feminine form an important channel of appeal. Most of the examples of physical strength that we have cited are masculine, but the field of physical grace naturally includes many instances of the feminine form. Where men have dominated the more muscular activities, women have at least been their equals in grace. In the dance Pavlova's name is as famous as Nijinsky's.

The different emphatic effects of strength and grace can be illustrated by the power of an elephant and the grace of a deer. Men have always appreciated both qualities. Physical grace can be divided into three types in art. One type unites grace with power; a second is exemplified by strong, well-coordinated male athletes; the third is found in the softer grace displayed by such activities as skating and dancing.

The versatile Greeks were masters of all three forms. The *Zeus from Artemisium* (Fig. 50), the *Diadem-Binder* after Polyclitus (Fig. 217), the Phidian *Ilissos* from the Parthenon (Fig. 408), and Myron's *Discus-Thrower* (Fig. 371) all combine masculine coordination with ample strength. Praxiteles has been celebrated through the ages for the grace of both his male and female figures. Other masters, too, have contributed outstanding examples of grace to the endowment of art. In our own time Paul Manship has continued the tradition of gracefulness found in Greek sculpture and in the art of the Asiatic Indians who worshipped the dance, as exemplified by the *Siva as Nataraja, Lord of the Dance* (Fig. 372). Manship captured exquisitely one of the pervading qualities of Indian art in his *Dancer and Gazelles* (Fig. 302). Here harmony of curvilinear lines and flowing gradations are combined to express graceful dancelike movements and poise in a beautifully balanced composition.

This quality of grace has been so closely associated with order and beauty, and so much the aim of artists, that we have many outstanding examples. Grace is one of the qualities that makes Michelangelo's art great. It goes hand-in-hand with heroic strength in masterpiece after masterpiece from his chisel and brush, but nowhere more impressively than in his renowned *Creation of Adam* (Fig. 126). Those who followed in Michelangelo's footsteps with understanding have likewise cultivated grace. Raphael stressed this quality in his *Three Graces* (Fig. 394), Tintoretto repeated it in his *Marriage of Bacchus and Ariadne* (Fig. 254), and Rodin made it a principal attribute of his *Age of Bronze* (Fig. 169). Others who courted it are the sculptors Bernini and Maillol; Bernini's *Apollo and Daphne* (Fig. 167) and Maillol's *Nude Torso* (Fig. 5) are excellent examples. In addition, Degas created a whole series of works which are devoted to the study of grace—his famous oils, pastels, drawings, and statues of the ballet dancers of the Paris Opera House, like the *Dancers Practising at the Bar* (Fig. 247) and the *Rehearsal* (Fig. 266). In these he examined the dancers from almost every point of view. The artists of the Orient also extolled grace extensively. In the art of India, China, and Japan it is a quality of the first importance.

Physical grace may be either grace of proportions or grace of movement. Usually an artist who appreciates the one also prizes the other and even combines the two, as Raphael did in his *Three Graces* (Fig. 393) and Michelangelo in his *Back of a Nude Male* (Fig. 147), gaining a twofold beauty. In addition, he can unite these qualities with physical strength to exploit an even richer type of appeal. Praxiteles did not do this when he created his beautiful but languid *Hermes and Dionysus* (Fig. 409), preferring serenity and repose; but

FIG. 302. Manship. *Dancer and Gazelles*. 1916. Art Institute of Chicago.

FIG. 303. Daumier. *Two Clowns.* ca. 1855-1865. Metropolitan Museum of Art, New York.

FIG. 304. Rembrandt. *An Old Woman in an Arm Chair*. 1635. Metropolitan Museum of Art, New York.

Rodin did when he cast his tensely supple and superbly proportioned *Age of Bronze*.

Grace is, of course, not indispensable in all works of art and may, in fact, be antithetical in some cases. It would be out of place in Goya's *Disasters of War* (Fig. 4). It would be unnecessary and perhaps incongruous in Meunier's *Return of the Miners* (Fig. 231) and in Bellows' *Stag at Sharkey's* (Fig. 77). Nor would anyone find grace in Eakins' *Masked Nude Woman* (Fig. 159) in anything like the degree that it is stressed in Zorach's *Spirit of the Dance* (Fig. 84). These works have their profundity of meaning apart from physical grace. And there are other deeply moving masterpieces of art in which grace is negligible or absent; their force of meaning lies in other qualities, sometimes even a deliberate harshness. Physical grace is therefore a dividend of beauty which we should prize, but not demand.

NERVOUS VITALITY

Nervous vitality, like grace, is distinguishable from physical strength, and differentiates human beings in an important manner. It is nature's way of balancing the scales. She makes the sandpiper fragile but quick, the elephant strong but slow. In human circles the same difference exists between the bantam-weight and the heavy-weight boxer. Football players may be as unlike as the tortoise and the hare because of the difference in their endowments of nervous energy. The same division extends through all the animate world, where variety is created by different combinations and degrees of strength and vitality. It is a complex but fundamental determinant of the pattern of life.

Nervous vitality probably makes its greatest contribution to human intelligence, personality, and activity. It is to mental vitality what grace is to physical strength, and is usually found in combination with it. A man with an alert mind may lack grace and be unable to lift a heavy weight, but he is almost certain to be a person of considerable nervous energy. His mind reflects its driving and sustaining force.

Nervous vitality is the principal attribute of vivid personalities. It makes them exciting, alive, and magnetic. The outstanding case is the personality of Christ. He performed no unusual feats of physical strength, but He impressed all who saw him with his mental energy, dynamic activity, and nervous vitality. He made these qualities paramount in human development and set an electrifying example that makes Hercules seem dull.

Michelangelo and Leonardo da Vinci excepted, the famous artists, too, have seldom been noted for unusual muscular strength. They have been strong men in some cases, but have been esteemed more often for the abundance of nervous energy shown by their creative activities. Nervous vitality is expressed through a kind of vibrancy or suggestion of rapid, pulsating movements. Held in restraint, it gives the impression of an inner tension. As a form of energy it resembles the effect of an electric conductor. Though still, it shocks or tingles our nerves. Physiologists tell us that thought and motor impulses are measurable electrical phenomena, and it is perfectly logical to call a person of great nervous vitality a "live wire."

Two examples of nervous energy in art will help to define it further. One is Daumier's *Two Clowns* (Fig. 303), a drawing in which nervous vigor is outstanding. The clowns who are trying to drum up interest in their circus or side show do not impress us primarily with their strength, as does Michelangelo's *Captive,* or with the kind of physical grace conspicuous in Manship's *Dancer and Gazelles;* but they quiver with energy. The standing, shouting clown is truly a "live wire." Daumier's extreme sketchiness of technique here plays an important part in objectifying this nervous energy. Though not the only method, it is universally found among works of art devoted to the expression of this aspect of life. Nervous energy is also manifested in a kind of tension arising from restraint or inner conflict, an implied pressure which is especially effective because of its quietude. An example is Rembrandt's *Old Woman in an Arm Chair* (Fig. 304). This is an apt illustration because Rembrandt himself was apparently impressed by the vigor of this robust elderly Dutch woman. He carefully noted that she was seventy when he painted her portrait. Not only did he take care to inscribe this fact, but he stressed energy in every aspect of her pose—in her firm grasp on the chair, her alert expression, and her erect posture. Here are signs of nervous energy expressed with mature and poised restraint. They are doubly effective because they are present where we least expect to find them.

If vigorous old age is an excellent demonstration of nervous energy, so too is vitality in a man who is physically frail and frequently ill. Houdon's statue of Voltaire in the Comédie Française in Paris illustrates such a case. The famous philosopher and dramatist asserted that he spent more of his life convalescing in bed than out of it. His body was so frail that Houdon hid most of it under a nondescript classical toga. Yet the parts that show—the hands and the head—are extraordinarily alive with energy, mental vitality, and wit. Voltaire probably could not have lifted a ten-pound weight;

his vitality existed apart from muscles and was sufficient to make him one of the most brilliant and prolific writers in history. In sum, of all the forms of physical energy, nervous vitality is the most productive of creative and spiritual things. It is the mainspring of the world of ideas.

THE REPRESENTATION OF PHYSICAL, MENTAL, AND SPIRITUAL ILLNESS

Life is made up of whites, blacks, and grays—a fact that critics have sometimes forgotten. They have attempted to limit art only to what is beautiful, calling all else ugly or unartistic. Most artists, however, have recognized the evil conditions of man and have drawn from the tragic side of life some of the most moving of all works of art. Hence for every stirring picture of love, confidence, and strength there is an equally powerful representation of their opposites—hate, fear, and physical debility. These complement the good and help to present life as a whole. To neglect them is to cut ourselves off from some of art's most profound masterpieces.

The tragic elements most often represented in art are fear, hate, pride, stupidity, debauchery, hunger, and physical debility. By tragic elements we mean the causes of man's frustrations and failures, and in studying the visual arts our first task is to recognize the look, or outward signs, of these defeating symptoms.

Fear. There is no need to define fear; every human being has experienced it. In mild forms it is a stimulus to action and, overcome, a measure of bravery. Its real significance in a work of art begins when it is represented as a chronic state or a specific condition of such magnitude as to cause near-paralysis. The fear of imminent death is the most obvious and extreme example.

Fear is so universal an affliction that there are many illustrations among the great masterpieces. In Ribera's *Martyrdom of St. Bartholomew* (Fig. 245) stark fear is written on the face of the saint who knows that he is about to be flayed alive. His eyes are feverish and glazed, his mouth parched, his brow beaded with perspiration. A variation on this theme of violent death is the Niobe Group in Florence (Fig. 310). It illustrates a Greek myth in which Niobe boasted that her many children were superior to Leto's two children, Apollo and Artemis. As a punishment Niobe's sons were slain by Apollo and the daughters by Artemis. Like St. Bartholomew, Niobe's eyes are filled with horror as she helplessly watches her tormentors, the executioners. Her daughter displays fear by turning her back and hiding her face in her mother's garment; fright has overcome her entirely.

Fear of pain and death is the subject of the *Laocoön Group*. So tortured with anguish is the face of Laocoön (Fig. 416) as he is crushed to death by the serpent that it is difficult to look at the group with any esthetic pleasure. Yet unpleasant as it is, the work is too powerful an expression of fear to be ignored. Goya's *Execution of the Madrileños* (Fig. 136) verges on the same extreme, yet compellingly appeals to our sympathy and anger, probably because it represents an event of fairly recent times, rather than a remote and ancient myth. Raw and harsh as it is, the brutal slaying of the Madrileños carries the conviction of reality. The poses and expressions of the men who look into the muzzles of the firing squad comprise a masterly study. True to life, they offer a universal demonstration of the effects of stark fear.

In the *Laocoön Group* and in Goya's *Execution* and *Disasters of War* series the response to fear is pushed to the extreme. Most representations of fear have been tempered with some restraint and probably gain in effectiveness thereby. A less intense and overwhelming treatment gives us a better chance to notice and enjoy other qualities. Van Gogh, for instance, worshipped nature with uninhibited ardor, but exercised restraint when he dealt with human tragedy. His *On the Brink of Eternity* depicts a man who has recognized both his own insanity and the end it will lead to. He bows his head hopelessly; but his fear of death (a self-revelation on Van Gogh's part) is contained within tolerable bounds; it is a fear turned inward, but all the more moving for its restraint.

Considering their situation, the Adam and Eve in Masaccio's *Expulsion* (Fig. 306) have restrained their grief and fear of the future. Instead of flinging their arms about and tearing their hair melodramatically, they hide their faces and cover their bodies. Their anguish is plain enough without being overdone. The secret of this effectiveness is twofold: a respect for the classical tradition of dignity and self-control and a skilful use of closed contours for dramatic purposes. The two techniques were often combined during the Classical Revival.

Masaccio's *Expulsion* was a landmark in Italian Renaissance painting. He was the first painter of great talent to follow in Giotto's footsteps, understanding human emotions from firsthand observation and representing them convincingly in his work. A comparison of Giotto's paintings with any in the preceding Byzantine tradition will illustrate how he gave life and feeling to human figures. And Masaccio went even further in this respect. A perceptive and ac-

FIG. 305. Detail. *Death of a Gaul and His Wife.*
"Arria and Paetus" group. 241-197 B.C., Hellenistic
period. National Museum (Terme), Rome.

FIG. 306. Masaccio. *Expulsion*
ca. 1427. Brancacci Chapel.
S. M. del Carmine, Florence.

FIG. 307. Portrait head of an
unknown Roman. 1st century
A.D. Metropolitan Museum of
Art, New York.

curate representation of human emotions was thus one of the major contributions of the early Renaissance masters and a principal accomplishment of their followers down to the present.

The ancients, too, were no mean students of human behavior. An artist who worked at Pergamum in the third century B.C. created an example of fear which could have set a precedent for Masaccio and all other later artists. It represents an instance that actually occurred and was observed with profound understanding. Presented with both sympathy and restraint, it is pathetic but not melodramatic. The statue depicts the *Death of a Gaul and His Wife* (Fig. 305). These brave people wandered into Greek territory in search of a homeland and were repulsed in a series of desperate battles. This stalwart warrior killed his wife and then committed suicide rather than accept capture and slavery. We see him as he looks hopelessly over his shoulder at the pursuing Greeks and holds a sword to his own breast as he gauges the number of seconds that he has left to live. The mixture of fear, regret, and courage in his face makes this figure live before our eyes. It is a movingly restrained and poignant representation of fear.

HATE. Hate, like fear, manifests itself in many guises—in anger, cruelty, scorn, meanness, and outright sadism. But unlike fear, it is not an instinct. Socrates said that men are not born bad; and a song in the musical comedy *South Pacific* asserted truly that we have to be taught to hate. Hate brings out the worst in human nature and makes the comeliest face ugly. A poisonous sickness, it is a sign of a mind gone sour and, in extreme or chronic cases, actually deranged. It is one of the spiritual illnesses which Christ combatted most energetically with its opposite, love.

Hate is a sign of fear, weakness, and inferiority. It shows itself commonly in a desire to strike back at any human cause or threat to one's physical safety or mental security with physical violence or character assassination. Socially it promotes the blind irrationality of mob violence and lynchings. Infecting a group, it makes them strike out at the superior person or symbolic enemy like wolves tearing at a victim. Under its influence the human potential is at its lowest, most bestial level. Yet hate is not a special mark of primitivism, but a glaring weakness of the most sophisticated international civilizations. Probably the weakest link in our cultural armor, it is hardest to excuse when it is founded upon the calculating, cold-blooded intelligence of a Genghis Khan or a Hitler.

Artists have recognized the signs of hatred and exposed their principal forms in some thoroughly perceptive works of art. With few exceptions the best examples have been rich in feeling, for hate, being an extreme reaction to fear, is an intense emotion. Goya's *Disasters of War* series was meant to reveal the terrible effects of fear on human beings when raised to the pitch of hatred by war. His *With Reason, or Without* (Fig. 4), illustrates how men can be driven out of their minds by hatred (note the insane fury of the peasant who wields the axe), and how they strike in that state with blind savagery at any soldier who symbolizes the enemy. All capacity to discriminate between one human being and another has been destroyed by the dementia of hatred.

Another penetrating student of mass hatred was George Bellows. His First World War lithographs of German atrocities lack the measure of objectivity that Goya preserved, and are inferior to the *Disasters of War* because of prejudice and special pleading. But Bellows' denunciation of lynching in such lithographs as *The Law Is Too Slow* is as hard-hitting and close to the mark as anything Goya etched. Both exposed hatred in its most virulent social forms.

The subject of Christ crowned with thorns is a pre-eminent instance of hatred because of the contrast in it between demoniacal cruelty and goodness. It opposes in concentrated form all that is good and evil in man. Titian, thinking that the theme was horrible enough without any emphasis, played down sadism and brutality in his *Christ Crowned with Thorns* (Fig. 130) and stressed a mood of sadness and resignation. It was thus left to Hieronymus Bosch to present the subject in all its horror; his tormentors are so crazed with hate that they verge on caricature. Titian was therefore wise in handling hate with some restraint while indicating its causes clearly. Indeed, this wisdom is well applied to any emotions as intense as fear and hatred if melodrama and caricature are to be avoided. Our tolerance for them has a definite turning point and saturation limit.

In his youth Rembrandt was guilty of emotional exaggeration, but as a mature artist he created one of the finest of all representations of hate. His *Christ Healing the Sick* (Fig. 151) contains on the left a group of spectators who cynically hope that the Savior will fail. Their sneers of smoldering hatred will reward a close examination, for they attest Rembrandt's wide knowledge of human feelings. Each face is individually characterized, while the group hatred is treated with a subtlety that makes this etching deservedly famous.

In our time George Rouault has dwelt upon the subject of hate in such pictures as his own *Christ Crowned with Thorns*, the *Three Judges,* and the *Old King.* A combination of hatred and stupidity has so distorted the faces of the *Three Judges* that they resemble a pig, a wolf, and a vulture rather than three human beings. The ugliness of intense malevolence is also the theme of his *Old King* (Fig. 227), which is alleged to represent the Biblical Herod. The scowling, Assyrian features are contorted into a symbol of vindictive evil.

Hatred does not have to assume a spectacular form. One of the worst of its forms is the everyday variety vented through malicious gossip, with ill will distorting truth for the sake of character assassination. Daumier has given us a memorable illustration of this process in his *Women Gossiping* (Fig. 152). Viciousness is written on their faces as they tear down some other person's reputation. It is a revelation of hatred which should give all of us pause.

PRIDE. Pride in the form of arrogance, conceit, or self-righteousness is a type of blindness. The Old Testament prophets and Christ hit at it vigorously because it not only distorts truth in one's own favor, but usually at the expense of other people. It is therefore a double evil. When Socrates, following the spirit of the old Greek proverb, said, "Know thyself," he was not speaking against self-confidence but against the unwarranted self-importance of the Sophists. The difference between confidence and pride, which seems slight at first, actually leads in opposite directions.

The effects of pride on an imperial scale are inscribed in the history of ancient Rome and written on the faces of hundreds of its leaders who were portrayed in stone. They apparently reveled in this kind of self-love and cared not whether their egotism, bullying, and braggadocio made their subject peoples love or hate them. In the name of patriotism they distorted confidence and the opportunities of leadership into ruthless exploitation. Their pride was salved, but they were not happy in proportion to their riches. They were, according to such written confessions as those of Seneca and Marcus Aurelius, a miserable people during their decline, when pride was all they had left. An air of sickness and guilt hung over their empire even in its better days and infected the expressions of the Roman rulers, politicians, businessmen, lawyers, soldiers, and even the women. The faces in the skilfully executed portrait heads of the time are those of intelligent but cynical men and women. This frame of mind poisoned the Roman leaders and the lives of all who were under their domination. Through all these figures there runs one expressive thread—stubborn, self-deluding pride.

One of these portraits by which the Romans presented their face to the world, the *Unknown Roman* in Fig. 307, seems nearly perfect; its expression cannot be mistaken. It is the image of a man who was intelligent, vigorous, and physically strong but whose mind had been warped by arrogance. His furrowed brow, glaring eyes, and scowling mouth show why the Romans of the first century A.D., the zenith of their Empire, were able to rule the world. They also reveal why no one loved them.

Compare this hard, cold, bitter face—the face of a man who is spiritually ill despite his domineering strength—with some of our other illustrations. The unknown Roman, while keen-looking, is quite different from the mentally vital D'Alembert; his pride offends and antagonizes, whereas the French philosopher's friendly smile ingratiates and attracts. The Roman elicits, too, a different reaction from the figures of Khafre or John Paul Jones; his exaggerated self-importance repels as much as their logical confidence inspires admiration. Finally, the impression the Roman makes differs from that created by the harassed dying Gaul in Fig. 305; one figure arouses sympathy, the other repugnance. The last effect is crucial in the scale of human attitudes where pride or self-praise stands comparison with modesty or justifiable confidence.

In the human visage, pride runs to type. It has been especially prevalent among the world's autocratic rulers and military leaders. The look is too prominent and recurrent to be missed. Its characteristics are stamped on the face of this unknown Roman; they appear again on the hard face of the Italian Renaissance general Bartolommeo Colleoni (Fig. 380). And they frown upon us once more from the faces of Hitler's Prussian marshals. We know that Napoleon favored a similar, detached mien, and Genghis Khan and Attila must have looked down on the world with the same cold stare. The final proof of this professional continuity is found in the practice of the old Japanese actors. Whenever they impersonated a member of the military caste, they assumed a proud and cruel expression. Shunsho's *Ichikawa Danjuro V as Kudo Suketsune* (Fig. 341) is an example.

However, Daumier and Rembrandt remind us that while military leadership may foster pride and develop its worst aspects by putting arrogant men in a position to do vast harm, pride is universal even among lesser men, because it is closely allied to fear and hate. Daumier's *Women Gossiping* (Fig. 152) is not confined to the representation of one emotion; it is a compound of suspicious fear, hatred, and self-righteousness. Filled with the hatred born of fear, the women are gossiping to bolster their own petty egos. Like the unknown Roman who remained a bully all his life, these women betray the marks of permanent immaturity. Rembrandt's *Christ Healing the Sick* (Fig. 151) also points up the kinship of pride, fear, and hatred. The scribes and Pharisees watch Christ's ministrations like hawks in the hope that he will fail. Their pride, supported by their entrenched position, has made them smug. The elements of fear, hate, and pride can be arranged in different formulae, but the aggregate effect on human personality is always ugly.

STUPIDITY. Since there is no perfect mind, every intelligence has its blind spots. We all miss the logical connection between cause and effect at times and in various degrees. One philosopher contented himself with pointing out the difference between stupidity and ignorance, saying to a new class that they were present because they were ignorant but *not* stupid. Stupidity itself is of several kinds: stupidity due to temporary ignorance; to occasional blankness; to subnormal mental development; and to chronic blindness. This differentiation makes room for all of us on a relative basis.

Despite man's history of missed opportunities, human beings at large are ingenious and intelligent. The chronic vacuity of the moron is a rare phenomenon in our world of generally intelligent people. Democratic government is based on this distribution; so is our jury system.

The scarcity of representations of stupidity in the visual arts therefore reflects the fact that stupidity is not met in gross form nearly as often as fear, hatred, or pride. It also elicits a neutral response because it is a condition which arouses neither strong sympathy nor condemnation (resignation is perhaps the commonest reaction). It is a dull and unpromising condition to represent; we cannot love stupidity, yet it is a difficult thing to hate. At most it leaves us with a feeling of annoyance, indifference, or disappointment.

Apart from the blankly expressionless faces of much Byzantine art, there are few representations of stupidity among fine works of art. Only four small groups present themselves with any prominence. Van Gogh is one of the few major artists who has represented moronic stupidity with all its blank, dull opacity. It is the theme of a few drawings that he made of the potato growers of his native Holland at the outset of his career. One of these in particular epitomizes the signs of stupidity. It is a profile drawing of a young woman of the potato fields. Her face is the complete converse of *D'Alembert* or Hogarth's *Shrimp Girl*. Her features are ugly and ill-formed, her expression listless; the weak chin droops, the mouth hangs open, and the eyes stare vacantly downward. Only in the medical illustrations of imbeciles does one ordinarily find anyone so brutish. The light of intelligence was withheld from this young woman in extreme degree.

Van Gogh did not continue to explore this depressing field. Near the end of his life, however, he had ample cause to consider one form of stupidity—the suspension of faculties imposed by insanity. Discerning the symptoms in himself, he paid close attention to them in other victims and created one of his most moving pictures, *On the Brink of Eternity*. Its theme differs from moronic stupidity, for it implies an intelligence that is beset by illness and which, during lucid moments, is aware of its own decline. Whereas the *Potato Grower* moves us only little because we cannot identify ourselves with her, the man portrayed in *On the Brink of Eternity* frightens us; his tragic condition is one that could capriciously attack anyone.

This stupidity arising from insanity has been studied by two other artists, Géricault and Velasquez, with the latter raising it to an immortal level in his portraits of the dwarfs and buffoons of the Spanish court of Philip IV. The image of the little moron *El Bibi de Vallecas,* with his vacant face and stunted, ill-coordinated body, was recorded with Velasquez's usual objectivity and, probably for that reason, makes a strong appeal to sympathy. The superb brushwork and color prove that there is nothing in the painting of stupidity to prevent the creation of a masterpiece.

Géricault's pictures of the insane have gained less notice than Velasquez's because they are less skilfully painted and less objective. Géricault could not resist the temptation to exaggerate the already-distorted personalities of his *Mad Woman* and *Mad Assassin*. Stupidity and insanity are grievous enough in their natural states, and are best handled, as Velasquez did, with objectivity or restraint. Géricault showed a callous streak by treating these victims as wild-eyed freaks.

Hogarth is another famous master who represented dementia. It was, as with Van Gogh, an exceptional subject with him, but he included it in the eighth scene of his *Rake's Progress* series, in which Tom Rakewell ends up in the notorious lunatic asylum, Bedlam. Hogarth's conception of Bedlam verges on caricature, but escapes the callous air of Géricault's treatment. The extremely objective studies of moronic stupidity by Velasquez and the intensely personal studies of insanity by Van Gogh are pre-eminent in this field.

Artists have had their chief opportunity to deal with stupidity where it is commonplace rather than exceptional or freakish. Examples of temporary stupidity, or stupidity that is economically or socially understandable are common. Usually the result of boredom or fatigue, or caused by alcohol or narcotics, it is an easily grasped phenomenon. Emotionally we examine such instances of stupidity with liking or disliking. An illustration of the first is Meunier's *Return of the Miners* (Fig. 231). Meunier, a keen observer of the effects of hard and monotonous labor on men, shows how unending toil in the mines bows the bodies and blunts the minds and spirits of the workers. They trudge back to work with an utter lack of enthusiasm. These men are not naturally stupid, but have been rendered so by the nature of their labor and the subsistence level of the lives they lead.

The other kind of externally induced stupidity is illustrated by Degas' *Absinthe* (Fig. 308), a picture noted for its fine, Japanese-type composition. In it Hélène Andrée, the female friend of the Montmartre poet Marcellin Desboutin, is in a temporary stupor, the combined drug and alcoholic effects of absinthe drinking. Both her mind and body are dulled as she slumps in her seat and stares vacantly at nothing, as though under hypnosis. Her posture and mien remind us, as do the slouching, brutish figures in Meunier's *Return of the Miners,* of the expressive connection between body and mind; wherever stupidity is represented in the face there is an attendant lethargy in the body. Conversely, where the mind and spirit are alive, as in Houdon's *John Paul Jones,* the body is also erect, alert, and vigorous, even though it be as frail as Voltaire's.

The commonest kind of stupidity is social boredom. Schopenhauer, terming it ennui, said it is as prevalent as air; he called it the greatest curse of mankind, and the worst cause of restlessness. It is depressing to experience or behold; hence artists have tended to avoid it as a subject. Degas, however, has given us a vivid example in his *Absinthe.* Mlle. Andrée has been caught in that vicious circle wherein one drinks futilely to escape boredom. She looks as though her companion and her surroundings, accepted out of habit, had ceased to interest her. This Maupassantian realism is far from the sordid naughtiness of Lautrec's conception of Montmartre (Fig. 40) or Renoir's rosy view of Gay Paree (Fig. 41). Yet its uncompromising truth makes it a great picture. Like most examples of stupidity represented in art, this is a penetrating study. But it is one of a small group. The nature of this mental condition makes it a negation of man's intellectual potential. And artists have in general preferred to depict more lofty and stimulating facets of man's complex mind.

DEBAUCHERY. A Chinese writer once said that all pleasure is sensuous. From a medical standpoint that is true. Only a puritan maintains that sensuous pleasure is intrinsically harmful to mental and spiritual health, but only a libertine claims that sensuous pleasure can be pursued indefinitely. Debauchery begins when sensuality begins to exact a penalty in health, causing the pleasure-seeker to defeat his own ends. He then becomes a victim of appetite and lack of control. An instance of this good turning into bad through excess

FIG. 308. Degas. *Absinthe*.
Hélène Andrée and
Marcel Desboutin. 1876.
Louvre, Paris.

FIG. 309. Kollwitz. *Bread!*
1924. Bowdoin College
Museum of Fine Arts,
Brunswick, Me.

is the difference between mild animation from alcohol and drunken stupor or acute alcoholism.

We refer to debauchery as "burning the candle at both ends" or dismiss it by saying that "boys will be boys." This is a tolerant way of admitting that the human race is not as rational or self-controlled as it could be and that its waywardness is not to be appraised too severely. Man is tough enough to survive a vast amount of over-indulgence in pleasure. Debauchery has always been the subject of a great deal of slapstick humor and joking.

Perfectionists speak of debauchery as a perpetuation of original sin or a malevolent, self-destructive streak that human beings have never been able to exorcise. Less extreme or more balanced minds accept a tendency toward debauchery as an inherent element in human nature, but join in drawing a line between overt debauchery, or uncontrolled excess, and the normal desire to enjoy a reasonable amount of pleasure in life.

The effect of these views can be seen in the representation of debauchery in art. Artists have reflected each of the attitudes, with some pointing the finger of moral scorn at excessive dissipation, others showing in a more or less objective way the physical effects of chronic depravity, and still others treating the subject in a jocular manner. In the latter case the intention is not to uphold debauchery as a good thing: rather, it is to say that there are various kinds and degrees of dissipation, some of which, if temporary, are relatively harmless. Hogarth, for instance, was a hard-working, intelligent, admirable artist, and a devoted husband, but he was not averse to an occasional "night out with the boys." He represents such an experience in his *Mid-night Modern Conversation,* a caricature of heavy drinking that is too funny to be taken seriously. Another group of artists has considered the social, psychological, and economic consequences of degeneracy.

Broadly viewed, artists have not made debauchery a major field of artistic exploitation, but have, rather, kept it a side issue in life. The number of first-rate artists who have given close attention to the "problem" of debauchery is not great; the tacit implication is that there are worse evils among fallible men—such as greed, hate, cruelty, and hardness of heart. The fine examples that do exist, however, are worth consideration. They deal, as a rule, with one or another of the three main forms of debauchery—gluttony, sensual excess, and drunkenness.

Moral scorn for debauchery has been assumed by only a few artists, notably Michelangelo and Rouault. The great Florentine was spartan, ascetic, and deadly serious in his religious and personal views. His *Drunkenness of Noah* in the Sistine ceiling is an outright condemnation. Even more censorious is his statue of Bacchus. Whereas the pagan Greeks had conceived Dionysus, as they called him, as the god of conviviality and healthy animal spirits, Michelangelo castigated him as a leader in drunkenness, as one who has lost control of his faculties and reels about with glazed eyes and a silly smile on his face. Rouault, a devout Catholic, views debauchery with even greater horror. His *Two Prostitutes* employs every device of artistic exaggeration to make carnal sin appear as revolting as possible.

Rodin arrived at the same result in shaping the bronze figure of his *Aged Courtesan* (Fig. 6). A worse human wreck could hardly be imagined. But Rodin seems to have been content to present the evidence and let us deduce the lessons of abuse ourselves. The spirit of his work is sad, resigned, temperate—perhaps even compassionate; Rouault's is exaggerated, gross, scornful, and punitive. Between the two, Rodin's conception is less forceful but possibly more poignant. Neither, however, leaves any doubt about the physical decay that comes with debauchery.

The jocular "boys will be boys" attitude is illustrated by Brouwer and even better by Hogarth. Brouwer, a seventeenth-century Fleming who ruined a brilliant talent prematurely by debauchery of his own, is one of the few important artists in history who made a career of both practicing and representing dissipation. A genuine playboy and "good time Charlie," he was naturally suited to the task. During his short, whirlwind life he frequented the taverns and participated in the card games, carouses, and brawls that he depicts, a kind of moth who sacrificed himself in the flame of dissipation. Rubens, who thought highly of Brouwer's talent, lamented his sad end. One thing can be said for him: his art and life were one. His pictures ring true because he knew whereof he spoke.

Brouwer's paintings are unusual in another respect. He lived at a time when hard liquors and tobacco, an importation from the New World, were enjoying a kind of new-toy craze. The more boorish addicts did not cease to imbibe and inhale until they were physically ill. Brouwer's pictures of peasant smoking sprees are therefore as rare in art as they are forthright. So long as his scenes were true to life he spared no details. The consequences of excess are revealed unhesitatingly in such compositions as *Peasants Smoking, Quarrelling Gamesters, Quarrelling Peasants, The Tap Room,* and *The Barroom.* Brouwer proved the power of artistry to surmount almost any kind of subject matter. A superb technician, he made his *Smoker* in the Louvre a masterpiece in spite of its lowbrow theme.

Hogarth was not so obsessed with carousing as Brouwer, but gave it some attention in his art. It is the primary theme of his *Gin Lane* (the vicious pendant to his beneficent *Beer Street*), and runs through his noted series pictures: the *Harlot's Progress,* the *Rake's Progress,* and *Marriage à la Mode.* In all of these the protagonists are helped along the primrose path by a variety of vices which they pursue with great relish and gusto. Hogarth's irrepressible good humor and tendency toward caricature keeps these tableaux from seeming censorious, though, ironically, they were used by preachers of his day to illustrate sermons on morality. Hogart himself probably felt that an artist can convey a serious lesson better through laughter than sermonizing. It is also necessary to view his *Mid-night Modern Conversation* and other revelries in the context of his time. The eighteenth century in England was not so genteel an age as we assume, but a rowdy time when Britain was at the height of her expansive vigor. Gambling was universal, and gin, rather than tea, was the national beverage. Historically, *Gin Lane,* a catalogue of all the ills arising from overindulgence with hard liquor, was not so much of a caricature as it seems.

A number of intelligent, level-headed artists have, without making a career of it, felt disposed to comment on the economic, psychological, and social consequences of debauchery, that is, the effect it has upon us and our relations with others. Artists have every right to observe this aspect of life, and their success has been impressive when they have appeared to be documenting facts instead of moralizing. A particularly imposing sculptural example dates from the Hellenistic period. An illustration of Greek genius for genre, it depicts a drunken old woman. More pathetic than comic, it points out the social consequences of poverty, toil, and monotony.

George Bellows, a journalist by background, observed and reported the social effects of vicious or uncontrolled debauchery in a number of powerful lithographs. His *Bacchanale,* which represents a scene of the German occupation of Belgium during the First World War, shows the brutal results of drunkenness combined with ruthless military rule. Universal in its meaning, like Goya's *Disasters of War,* it is an uncompromisingly realistic illustration of the military side of debauchery.

The peacetime tragedy of alcoholism is presented graphically by Bellows in a lithograph entitled *The Drunkard.* In it a father who has been made wild by habitual drinking is struggling with his distraught wife and children. Their bedroom is a shambles, their family life ruined. In pictures such as these Bellows expresses the mature view that, while none of us has the right to a "holier than thou" opinion and temporary debauchery may be jolly, its consequences are seldom funny in the long run.

HUNGER. The pangs of hunger have afflicted most people but artists have treated the theme reluctantly. The inhabitants of Asia, though suffering most from gnawing hunger and famine, have elected to survive hunger by stoically ignoring it; even their artists have treated this condition as though it did not exist. Western artists have avoided the subject of hunger for understandable reasons. It is a harrowing sight to behold. When it is so overwhelming that little can be done about it, it badly frustrates our sympathies. Christ recognized that some problems are nearly insurmountable when he said sadly, "The poor are always with us." Hunger does not, like hatred or arrogance, lend itself to critical analysis, moralizing, or correction through art. It demands action along such practical lines that either depicting it impersonally or preaching against its causes in pictures seems like callousness or misplaced zeal.

The intensity of hunger also militates against its inclusion in works of art. It is probably the strongest and most harassing drive that nature instills in us to ensure self-preservation. When it exists it momentarily overwhelms almost every civilized thought or benevolent instinct. Similarly, when presented with appropriate intensity in a work of art it tends to dominate all esthetic and technical considerations—an extremism that most sensible artists wish to avoid. Degas' *Absinthe* (Fig. 308) can be used as an illustration. We can appreciate the beauty of Degas' occultly balanced, open-contour design because his subject, stupidity, does not overwhelm us. Knowing that the condition represented is temporary and not particularly serious, we can look at it with some detachment, perhaps even smile at it. We cannot observe a scene of hunger with anything like that kind of objectivity. The more powerfully it is represented, the more it destroys esthetic appreciation and negates any possibility of recognizing artistry in representation and design. As a consequence artists have limited their studies of hunger to special contexts. These, apart from the famines caused by natural catastrophies, usually have a strongly social connotation, presenting hunger as an evil inflicted by man upon man. The worst causes, of course, are wars and economic depressions. In short, hunger, despite its world-wide scope, does not lend itself to general or symbolical treatment; the moment it becomes vague it loses its essential acuteness. It must be represented in specific contexts, with universal applications being assumed. The outstanding examples of hunger in art are all of the specific instances; the failures are invariably of the generalized, symbolic sort.

Two examples of the symbolic type are a painting of *Saturn Devouring His Own Children* which Goya painted in one of his more distraught moments on the wall of his own dining-room, and Carpeaux's sculptural group of *Ugolino Eating His Children.* Goya's painting is so nightmarish in character that it is revolting; the instance of cannibalistic episode that Carpeaux represented is quite alien to his temperament. The chief liability in these works is a kind of abstract remoteness, a gap between them and anything in our own experience. The same deficiency applies to ancient myths or representations of them.

The Wars of the Reformation (known in Germany as the Thirty Years' War) left in their train hunger and beggardom which account for some of Rembrandt's etchings of beggars and for Jacques Callot's celebrated *Miseries of War.* It remained, however, for Goya to lash out with the fullest fury at the hunger inflicted upon war-ridden nations. In his *Disasters of War* series he includes a picture of several fat war profiteers leering at a group of enfeebled, starving adults and children. His scathing title is: *Are They of Another Race?* The same inhumanity and greed were later pilloried by George Grosz, an artist who lived through the post-war years of disillusion, black-market profiteering, and famine in Germany, and saw after the First World War the same conditions that blighted Goya's Napoleonic Spain.

More recently, depression-born hunger was delineated sharply by Reginald Marsh in such studies as his *Holy Name Mission,* and with almost unparalleled force by Käthe Kollwitz in a series of lithographs like *Bread!* (Fig. 309). It represents a scene which Kollwitz witnessed many times during the terrible period of the twenties in Germany and to which she responded with sympathy but without moralizing. We identify ourselves with this mother as Käthe Kollwitz, a motherly woman, did out of sheer compassion. The helplessness of the children and the impotent anguish of the mother hit one of our weakest points. This ghastliness is a point of some importance. Käthe Kollwitz was, as we saw in the *Family Group* (Fig. 294), a person of profound social sympathies. She also possessed great organizing intelligence and artistic ability. Her compositions are outstanding, her handling of lithography worthy of Goya or Daumier. Yet to point out the powerful modeling of the mother's form and the simple but astute balance of the design in the picture called *Bread!* seems trivial. The human message overwhelms all artistic considerations, making analysis seem callous.

Géricault's most famous painting, the *Raft of the Medusa* (Fig. 378), illustrates this point. Here is hunger attended by insanity, violent fighting, cannibalism, and long suffering. The cause was a mixture of natural catastrophe and malevolent stupidity on the part of the ship's officers after a wreck at sea. Can we react to this situation with sympathy or only with disgust? Whatever our attitude, the picture makes a strong but unpleasant impression on most observers. They are prone to turn away from it before they perceive its fine composition. The *Raft of the Medusa* is another instance of the calculated risk an artist takes when he represents the horror of hunger.

PHYSICAL DEBILITY. Among the factors affecting man's well-being, physical debility occupies a prominent place, for as our bodies fare, so also do our minds and spirits. By physical debility we mean all the ills that human flesh is heir to, but especially the burdens of senility, weariness, illness, impairments like blindness, and, in the end, death itself. Much of Christ's ministry was aimed at the alleviation of these ills. That is one reason why Rembrandt's etching of *Christ Healing the Sick* (Fig. 151) is such a meaningful picture. Death is certain for all, and every sign of physical debility is an anticipatory reminder of it. A prominent physician has indicated the scope of this condition by saying that most human beings hurt somewhere every minute of their lives. Pain or discomfort of some kind eternally plagues our existence. Nothing is of more immediate concern, or leaves us feeling more helpless. It is the great objective fact which must be accepted. The treatment of physical debility in art, for these reasons, contains appeals for sympathy. For this treatment, realism of idea is called for, with or without realism of representation, though both forms of realism are often found together. Caricature has played a small rôle in the representation of physical debility. It is a subject that strikes home too closely to be a laughing matter. Neither can it be viewed with cool detachment. Its characteristics usually induce seriousness, sadness, and resignation.

Physical debility is so universal that it has been presented widely through the arts by many masters. One of the treasures of the Metropolitan Museum, *An Old Woman Going to Market* (Fig. 404), is devoted to the representation of senility. It dates from the Hellenistic period of Greek history, as does another famous treatment of old age, the *Peasant Going to Market* (Fig. 415) in the Glyptothek at Munich. The signs of physical breakdown and decline are here presented with great realism; bent bodies, halting steps, muscular feebleness are objectively true to life; their sculptors are clearly saying that senility is a sad and depressing condition. Blindness is another frequently represented affliction. The Hellenistic period dwelt upon its characteristics—staring eyes, vacant expressions, uncertain steps—in a number of noted figures, like the *Blind Fisherman* in the Vatican and a series of heads of the *Blind Homer*. Blindness elicits as much sympathy as any affliction of man short of death itself. No exaggeration is necessary. Straightforward realism is the order in these pieces.

Like the Hellenistic sculptors with their blind Homers, Rembrandt used the well-known Biblical story of the blindness of Tobit as an excuse to express his own deep sympathy for blindness. His etching *Tobit Blind* is deservedly famous for its observation. It contains, in addition to the helplessly wandering figure of the solitary Tobit, one of those touches by which Rembrandt made his pictures live. Tobit's dog, seeing that its master has missed his way toward the door, is pushing his foot to guide him. Rembrandt was a close observer of old age and its afflictions. Even as a young man his interests were not only mature but serious. Picasso, too, was drawn to various conditions of debility as a young man by the seriousness of his own disposition and the poverty of his youth. In his *Woman Ironing* (Fig. 45) he represents physical debility due to an exhausting task rather than to old age. His theme is chronic fatigue. Less normal in young people than in old, it is nonetheless depressing.

Ultimately, death overrides physical debility. It has about it a conclusiveness and explicitness that can be represented well by the visual arts. It is the theme of some of the most famous works of art in the world, such as Giotto's *Death of St. Francis* (Fig. 133), Caravaggio's *Death of the Virgin* (Fig. 134), and the celebrated *Dying Gaul* (Fig. 413). Here are represented the death of a famous person, the death of a well-loved person, and violent death met heroically. Despair at death was the theme of Goya's *Execution of the Madrileños*. With all the concern of artists for death under heroic or unusual circumstances, none has dealt with the slow decline and fading into death that is the natural termination of old age. Perhaps they feel that the subject lacks drama; perhaps its sad and inevitable nature is so unanswerable that it leaves nothing more to be said.

THE HIERARCHY OF VALUES

There is no fixed scale of values among the subjects of art which automatically guarantees superiority. This fallacy stems from a tendency among human beings to generalize from a false premise. Two common misconceptions are that beautiful subject matter is superior to ugly, and a noble theme better than an ordinary or vulgar one. If the first were true, there should be no place in our regard for Goya's *Disasters of War*, Rodin's *Aged Courtesan*, or Kollwitz's *Bread!*, which are brutal, depressing, and harrowing. Instead, we should prefer any representation of the Three Graces by a suitably trained academician. If the second assumption were true, there would be no question about the excellence of David's *Oath of the Horatii* and the coarse triviality of Adrian Brouwer's *Smoker*. The plain fact, however, is that artists have been able to endow many disagreeable subjects, like the *Dying Gaul,* with greatness. The so-called noble and beautiful pictures which the École des Beaux Arts ground out by the dozens in the nineteenth century now seem insipid. Objective consideration of subject matter in actual works of art soon turns these theories upside-down; experience shows that the final opinion of the expressive quality of a work of art is determined less by the subject than by the intelligence, feeling, and skill of the artist.

The French Academy attempted for three centuries to invert this sense of values and did untold harm in the process. The Academy set up a hierarchy of subject matter as rigid as a feudal caste system. History, mythology, and religion were placed at the top of the scale because they were noble. Landscape was important only as a setting for human activities—a bias taken over blindly from the classical tradition. At the bottom of the scale were genre and still life. This scheme implied that a historical picture was inherently superior to a genre or still-life painting. Artistic considerations like design, sincerity, and appropriateness of treatment were rated as secondary to the subject. This attitude prevailed from the seventeenth through the nineteenth century.

The hierarchy of values was instituted during the reign of Louis XIV, a monarch who conceived both government and the production of art in dictatorial terms. His need for vast amounts of art works arose initially from his desire to decorate the huge Palace of Versailles with a grandiose array of paintings and sculpture. Since only a few talented artists were available, it was necessary to create a factory system in which method could be substituted for talent. He placed in charge of the project Charles Le Brun, an energetic, autocratic designer who had great organizing ability but meager talent. Le Brun got results. He saw to it that the walls of the Palace were covered with acres of painted and sculptured figures, all of them lofty and noble, usually depicting Louis XIV in the guise of *Alexander Entering Babylon* or as *Caesar Crossing the Rhine*. They are large, confused in design, and quite devoid of feeling; the *Alexander Entering Babylon* is a monstrosity.

This debacle was the inevitable result of the method imposed by Le Brun. He forced his army of artists to treat themes that were completely foreign to anything in their personal experience and for which most of them were only superficially educated. Poorly schooled artisans at best, they knew nothing of the classical history they purported to interpret. Worse still, Le Brun substituted stereotyped convention for the emotions of real life. He provided his corps of workmen with handbooks of emotional expressions reduced to standardized faces. Any clever brushman could represent anger, fear, or joy merely by copying the book. He also provided examples of the nude figure in a wide variety of poses. These could be fitted into the proper places in a design without any need to study anatomy or relate it to the emotional contexts of life. This kind of art could be taught so easily that hundreds of young men mastered it sufficiently to fulfil Louis XIV's voracious ambitions. How bad the results are on close inspection has to be seen to be believed. The historical effect of this method was to create the machine-piece in art, a type of historical illustration full of clever handwork, but lacking both unity and feeling. Behind it all was the hierarchy of values, as snobbish and rationalized as the Sun King's own autocratic court.

If the academy of Le Brun had been a historical flash-in-the-pan, it could be dismissed along with most of the arguments for an official, governmentally regulated national art. But it gained a strangle hold on French creative activity and thinking that for three hundred years stifled the artistic genius of that nation. We meet it again in the eighteenth century when Chardin, a master second only to Watteau in natural ability, was reluctantly admitted to the Academy as a mere genre and still-life painter. We find it reappearing in the nineteenth century in the studio of David, who ruled his students' minds with even more dogmatism than had Le Brun, and in the overbearing arrogance and snobbery of Ingres, who fought tooth-and-nail for years against the admission of the brilliant but unorthodox Delacroix to the Academy. And we see it in the hostility of officialdom toward the paintings of Daumier, Courbet, Monet, Manet, and Cézanne because they were unorthodox, experimental, and individual. When the stigma of vulgarity could be included in the official denunciations, as in the cases of these men, the hostility knew no bounds; the Empress Eugénie personally led the attack against Courbet by striking at one of his nudes with a riding crop. France, instead of being the most civilized and artistic nation in Europe, was artistically great in spite of her Philistine efforts to suppress all progress.

Unfortunately, the academic virus and its hierarchy of values were not confined to one time or country. The "system" crossed the Channel and gave rise, especially in the nineteenth century, to a vast and mediocre output of lofty but dull historical pictures by the Royal Academicians. So seldom are these pictures seen today that we forget what a crucial influence Sir Lawrence Alma-Tadema and his

fellow members wielded in their own time. Sir Lawrence's archaeologically contrived conceptions of ancient Rome, so admired in their
own day, now seem tedious and banal in their studied realism and
lack of sincere feeling.

The spread of the academic system also accounts for the hold that
so-called life drawing gained in art schools everywhere. Twice removed from a living context in Le Brun's day, it was preserved in an
even more remote vacuum in the decades after David and the neo-
classic reign. American schools did not escape this aspect of academicians, which persists as a standard fixture, despite the fact that
it was rarely employed by the old masters of the nude.

One of the ironies of history is that the most vigorously courted
beliefs of public and artists themselves are often reversed. John
Singleton Copley was a superb portrait painter during the days when
he was creating likeness of his native American compatriots with
consummate simplicity and straightforwardness. These pictures ring
true. But, dissatisfied and ambitious, he moved to England and tried
to improve his art by painting more elegant portraits and more
"worthwhile" historical canvases, the latter on a large scale. Under-
rating the gallery of colonists which is now the basis of his fame, he
put his stock in his English output. But he could not beat the British
at the aristocratic style and saw his historical pictures fall short of his
hopes.

An even more conspicuous instance of inverted self-appraisal is
the career of Ingres. The painter of *Madame Rivière* (Fig. 274a)
was one of the most gifted portrait painters in history. He was also
narrow-minded, dogmatic, and snobbish, subscribing adamantly to
the hierarchy of values both in and out of Academy meetings. He
belittled his own strength in portraiture, regarding it as a vulgar and
usually boring way of adding to his income. He truly believed that
his real fame would rest on a series of painfully noble religious, historical, and symbolic designs. History has reversed this self-valuation
in no uncertain terms; his historical pictures are hard to take, his
portraits nearly priceless.

The most blatant of Ingres' would-be masterpieces is his *Apotheosis of Homer* (Fig. 312). It is easy to dismiss its ambitious emptiness
with a shrug, but more profitable to consider why and where Ingres
went astray, for his mistakes are common ones. Ingres, like Velasquez, was a man who could paint anything that would hold still before his eyes; but he had not an iota of imagination, sympathetic
warmth, or feeling for living movement. Moreover, though he could
place a single figure like Madame Rivière in a frame superbly, he
could not imagine a group and especially a group in action. Con-

FIG. 310. Bouguereau. *Madonna of Consolation*. 1877. Luxembourg, Paris.

FIG. 311. Daumier. *The Laundress*. 1861. Louvre, Paris.

FIG. 312. Ingres. *Apotheosis of Homer*. 1827. Louvre, Paris.

638

sequently, his *Apotheosis of Homer* is literal, cold, and static. It is also painted in the realistic manner which the Academy was determined to apply to symbolic subjects throughout the nineteenth century. In that respect Ingres' failure was a common failure. His other failures were personal. He regarded himself as one of the intellectual élite of his time—a self-appointed guardian of Raphael and all that was fine and high-minded in art. Actually, he was a prejudiced, despotic, and poorly educated man. Not only did he lack a classical education, but he had none of the indispensable insight into the themes he reviewed and even less experience with the human beings around him. Thus, lacking a feeling for either history or life, he could hardly breathe the breath of life into his historical concoctions. Regarding most people as vulgarians, Ingres loved to make fun of them from his ivory tower. It is doubtful whether the rosy glow of antiquity really made him care about Homer or what he stood for. An apotheosis of Homer, however, was then an acceptable, almost sure-fire way to maintain the prestige that Ingres required.

Ingres was not the only artist in history who, misinterpreting his own talents, painted pictures for the wrong reasons, and owed his immortality to genius in some other direction. Velasquez, Raphael, Manet, and many others, including the great Michelangelo, occasionally got into paths which they were badly fitted to follow. The nineteenth century produced many such errors; it tried to perpetuate a classical tradition with which it had lost contact, and insisted on imposing a realistic manner on every subject it treated. At the same time, it harassed every artist who, like Courbet, Manet, Monet, and Degas, sought to employ realism in representing a very real world.

The course in art followed by any time is profoundly influenced by the ideas of the majority. If these ideas are founded on experience that is a part of the time, their art will be genuine. If their premises rest on some preconceived hierarchy of values and they paint pictures primarily to make money or fulfil ambitions, unfortunate results are almost bound to follow. There will be an overestimation of the false artists who play up to and echo these fallacies. Even worse, the public will disdain and persecute that creative minority of courageous, original thinkers who will some day be the glory of their time. It was in spite of officialdom that Cézanne persisted, survived, and ultimately adorned the art of his day.

The conflicts engendered by the beliefs that men hold are illustrated vividly and specifically by the contrasting fortunes and work of two nineteenth-century artists, Bouguereau and Daumier. Bouguereau, little noticed today, was in his own time a social and artistic lion. Collectors avidly bought at high prices everything he painted.

The idealistically conceived but realistically painted *Madonna of Consolation* (Fig. 310) is typical of Bouguereau's outlook and style. Lofty in theme and photographic in execution, it was acclaimed in its day, but to us it seems specious and the actions incongruous. There is complete emotional separation of the three figures, as though each were a professional studio model posing independently. There is, of course, nothing wrong with using models, but the artist must make them bear some resemblance to life. This he does by drawing upon memory and imagination. Bouguereau could do neither. His pictures gives the impression that he had neither seen nor felt anything about motherhood or a mother's grief over the loss of a child. Like so many of his contemporaries, he thought that a noble theme would produce a noble picture. It may, but only if grounded in keen observation and sincere feeling.

Daumier's position in life was the converse of Bouguereau's. A cartoonist for the popular press, he was not taken seriously in official artistic circles, and made only a meager living. Despite hard work, he had to be supported in old age and blindness by Corot. Long hours over lithograph stones left him time to produce only a limited number of oil paintings. Today they are counted among the masterpieces of nineteenth-century art, but in Daumier's lifetime they went unnoticed. One of these is the *Laundress* in Fig. 311. Like Bouguereau's *Madonna of Consolation,* it deals with the general subject of maternal love; but there all resemblance ends. It is simple and unpretentious. Daumier did not have to contrive a melodramatic tableau to represent motherhood. He understood its essentials from watching scenes of this sort from a studio window above the Seine. Presenting only the ordinary solicitude of a mother for her child, he lets us assume that she would weep for it in tragic circumstances. His style is equally simple; the Venetian pictorial mode outlines the design and principal masses boldly and clearly. When we compare Bouguereau's and Daumier's conceptions, the one is as pretentious as the other is natural. In the end Bouguereau's hierarchy of values did him no good, and Daumier never needed one. This discussion may seem to leave us without any standards of measurement, but a principle of evaluation will be offered in a later chapter.

The human mind usually views other human beings with more interest than it accords landscape or still life. This generalization needs to be qualified, for human interest has only a moderate appeal for some. Claude Lorrain loved nature quite as much as he did the human drama, and Cézanne took more interest in the formal relationships of three apples and a jug on a table than in the burial of Christ or the wedding of a neighbor. Human life is not always more important than landscape or still life to all men, but that order is generally true. One still life by Chardin or a landscape by Monet is worth ten historical "machines" by Le Brun; yet the painting that sheds wisdom on human life will win the support of the largest number of men over the longest period of time. In short, there are good and natural reasons why so much great art deals with human and natural life and so little with still life. That is the one sense in which a hierarchy of values can be justified. Even so, the only situation in which a safe comparison can be made is when a single artist paints both human and still-life subjects, as did Chardin, Courbet, Manet, Cézanne, and Van Gogh. Yet when we stand before a still-life painting by Van Gogh which bursts with life or one by Cézanne whose formal relationships give us the sharpest kind of esthetic pleasure, comparison seems pointless.

This line of reasoning can only lead to one conclusion—we should avoid any hierarchy of values, and substitute a simple principle of judgment for that of subject. The chief defect of a hierarchy of values is rigidity, what the French themselves called an "idée fixe". A more flexible and comprehensive principle is needed, and we shall seek it in the ensuing chapters.

CHAPTER *21*

Organization of Ideas

To the perceptive beholder everything that an artist does—even what he omits—is expressive. This expression can be an incidental result of representation, or it can be the result of intention and design. Only through design can the expressive possibilities of art and full control over the objectification of feeling be exploited. Now we must consider how the expression of ideas is clarified and intensified by design.

To the layman design means primarily the arrangement of lines, forms, and colors in space so as to appeal to the esthetic sense, and we have used the term with this connotation. But it also implies organizing power on any level, and of ideas as well as sensations. Assuming that flexibility, let us consider something of the thought that goes into the organization of ideas.

The young artist, for example, who lives in New York City possesses, like artists from the beginning of time, a superabundance of artistic raw material. He is surrounded by every conceivable human emotion and condition. He can present but a tiny fraction of this material in a single picture, and only a small portion of it in a lifetime. Even if he were able to achieve the impossible, the effect would be confusion rather than clarification and intensification. He must therefore choose relatively small sections of the kaleidoscope and be content with implying the rest. The choice itself is not so much a matter of selecting a noble theme instead of a trivial one as it is of perceiving the significance of any subject. Daumier demonstrated this phenomenon, showing how the artist not only discovers significance but contributes to it. By perceptive intelligence and creative insight he reveals what we miss in quite ordinary subjects. Intelligence of observation, not quality of subject matter, is one of

642

the great differences between a Daumier and a Bouguereau. No less important is the degree of organizing power that an artist brings to his task. This skill will separate widely any group of artists in New York City who have the same opportunities of subject matter, precisely as it did the many Florentine painters of the fifteenth century. In that respect there has been no essential change in the process of controlling the objectification of feeling. This artistic organizing power consists of an insight, varying in degree of consciousness or subconsciousness, into the application of the principles of order and a sense of fitness of treatment. The young Manhattan artist who has selected his subject, as John Sloan did when he started to paint his *Wake of the Ferry* (Fig. 76), will display organizing power to the extent that he includes in his pictures only what is suited to his chosen theme and deliberately excludes whatever is incongruous. This he must do himself; neither nature nor the city will do it for him. Nor is this merely a matter of being simple rather than complex, for Rubens proved in his *Autumn, the Château de Steen* (Fig. 83) that a picture can be highly intricate and yet perfectly unified; indeed, it may be the richer for its complexity. The crux of the matter is a capacity for consistency. The artist must achieve this consistency and convey both his sense of order and his conception of certain ideas and emotions through one design, which makes his task complex. Fortunately, however, when skilfully controlled, design can be both orderly and expressive simultaneously. This synthesis is not automatic; it must be sought deliberately, usually through long years of training and experience. But it can be mastered, as great works of art demonstrate. For the remainder of this chapter we shall examine some of the ways in which organizing power has achieved this duality, this expressive order.

FINITUDE AND INFINITUDE OF IDEAS

One of the major choices of an artist in organizing his representation of reality is between the finite and infinite. This usually means a choice between the individual and the universal aspects of any subject, an emphasis of one quality or the other, since no entity in reality entirely lacks either. No qualitative distinction is intended; great works of art can be found among both types. The important thing is difference, not superiority.

Having already touched upon this subject, we need only to observe a few illustrations of each type with an eye to the practical methods used by artists to stress the infinite or the finite. As an example, turn to the *Cat* in Fig. 313. This is a universal symbol of the

Fig. 313. *Cat.* Late Dynastic, *ca.* 500-300 B.C. Dumbarton Oaks Research Library and Collection of Harvard University. Dumbarton Oaks, Washington, D.C.

Fig. 314. Barye. *Jaguar Killing a Young Wild Ass. ca.* 1850. Metropolitan Museum of Art, New York.

cat family and has all the feline characteristics; it is sleek, strong, silent, alert—utterly still, but ready to spring. Like cats everywhere, it is composed, self-assured, introspective, cruel, and watchful. If a single cat was the model for this figure, all traces of unique individuality were suppressed. This is all cats in one.

The Egyptians studied the cat family for centuries. They painted them on the walls of their tombs with knowledge, awe, and respect, or molded them in religious figures which symbolized the cruel and austere forces of nature and the supernatural. This *Cat* is such a figure, based on generations of accumulated observations, reduced to the basic elements, with the essence of cathood retained and with all that was superficial eliminated. The sculptor of this *Cat* followed a method common to idealistic artists of classical antiquity. Motivated by a desire to capture essential characteristics and follow established standards, he deliberately avoided any details that would identify this statue with a specific cat. This result did not come from vague observation; it denotes the shrewdest kind of scrutiny and selection. Every artist since who has been similarly motivated has proceeded in much the same way.

Barye, the great nineteenth-century French sculptor of animal life, took a different direction when he created his *Jaguar Killing a Young Wild Ass* (Fig. 314). Barye was no less observant than the ancient Egyptian sculptor of the *Cat*. He spent hours watching the appearance, habits, and movements of animals until his knowledge was encyclopedic. He was also interested in universal traits; note, for instance, the typical cruel twist of the jaguar's tail as it sinks its teeth into the throat of its prey. A cat crunching a sparrow on a fence rail could not be more characteristically feline. But Barye was as much a realist as an idealist. This tendency, coupled with the trends of his time, led him to be much more specific than the Egyptian artist in the rendering of individual details. He did not slur over muscles and surface textures in favor of major geometric forms (like the *Cat*'s torso and forelegs), but delineated tendons and sinews so that they ripple under the sheath of flesh. As a result, we have the feeling of an actual life-and-death struggle. Barye's temperament made him love the kind of power that he expresses in the *Jaguar Killing a Young Wild Ass*. He was not content to generalize the idea, but sought instead to intensify its effect. This meant, in practical terms, multiplying the signs of strength in the separate straining muscles, with a greatly increased sense of force. By contrast with the aloof repose of the Egyptian *Cat*, his jungle combat is ferociously vital, individual, earthy, and complex. His method, in turn, has been followed over many centuries by artists with a like interest in explicitness.

Two of the most famous paintings of the nineteenth century illustrate the same divergence of choice between an emphasis of the finite and individual or the infinite and universal. In this case, too, both artists were dealing with a theme which offered many possibilities for observation and interpretation—war and revolution. In the nineteenth century the people of France fought a series of bloody revolutions before the eyes of Delacroix and Daumier, each of whom recorded his reactions to the fighting.

Delacroix gave his picture a resounding title—*July 28, 1830: Liberty Leading the People* (Fig. 315). He depicts a poorly organized but determined band of insurgents who began the overthrow of Charles X, the hated Bourbon who replaced Napoleon. The fiercest fighting took place in Paris, where the opposing forces clashed along the boulevards and over the barricades across the narrow streets. Delacroix has done everything in his power to represent this particular revolution. He identifies the country as France by the tricolor flag and the French goddess of Liberty, Marianne, the city and street by the distant towers of Notre Dame, and the period by the gun-bearing man in the tailcoat and stovepipe hat. On the other hand, he kept his sympathies and ideas detached. An artist, not a politician, he was at heart an old Bonapartist who, though he had not much to gain, merely hated the Bourbons more than he loved the people. Aristocratic and aloof, he probably regarded them as "rabble in arms." Despite the physical energy in the picture, there is a marked spiritual reserve on Delacroix's part. He seems to be saying essentially that, although revolution may grow out of complex causes and present many facets—misery, idealism, hysteria, pain, and death—it also includes a good deal of irresponsible opportunism. During the chaos of the fighting the rowdy elements of the population have a grand time "shooting up the town." The pistol-waving boy, like an American cowboy on a shooting spree in the old Wild West, is the most convincing figure in the composition. It is more than likely that he expresses Delacroix's own opinion of the fighting of July 28, 1830.

By representing this limited scene directly and exactly, Delacroix has shown only one side of revolutionary warfare, but what he shows is true and forcefully presented. His picture is not without universal implications, but it pertains unmistakably to the revolutions of his own day. Daumier's painting, though drawn from the same violent source, is quite different. He called it simply "L'Émeute," *The Uprising* (Fig. 316). The picture was probably painted between 1848 and 1850, the interim between the fall of Louis Philippe and the

FIG. 315. Delacroix. *Lib-erty Leading the People.* (July 28, 1830.) Louvre, Paris.

FIG. 316. Daumier. *The Uprising. ca.* 1849. Phillips Collection, Washington, D.C.

FIG. 317. Chavannes. *La Guerre. ca.* 1861. Philadelphia Museum of Art.

647

coup d'état of Louis Napoleon. He undoubtedly witnessed some of the bloody fighting of February 22 to 24, 1848, which dethroned Louis Philippe, whereas he was only twenty years old during the Revolution of 1830, hardly mature enough to have conceived *The Uprising*.

The Revolution of 1848 is best known from Victor Hugo's account of it in *Les Misérables*; his description of the fighting before the barricades, the wounding of Marius, and Jean Valjean's heroic rescue of Marius in the journey through the sewers of Paris with the police officer, Javert, at his heels, is one of the greatest episodes of nineteenth-century literature. It is that kind of fighting that Daumier has represented. But his approach to historical illustration was his own. He could have painted a picture not greatly different from Delacroix's; instead, he chose another way of interpretation. His *Uprising* is revolution in the most general terms, yet it brings before our eyes the causes of revolution and the most powerful protest that can be used against them—a misery-born outbreak of moral indignation. Though his people carry no guns, their protest against tyranny, hunger, and oppression has the force of a tidal wave.

Daumier's method rose to the level of the infinite and universal. Almost nothing in his picture is temporary or exact. The one limiting detail which specifies time is a tall hat on a single man. Otherwise, the city could be any city, the mob any mob, the uprising any uprising. However, he was too wise an artist to be both general and vague. While merely suggesting the crowd, he concentrated his meaning in one heroic figure. The man with the upraised arm has been called one of the most haunting figures in all art. In him are embodied all the miserable, hungry, long-suffering peoples of the world. He is a universal representative of men whom we might find anywhere at any time there is an explosion of despair.

Daumier's conception of a revolutionary uprising differs from Delacroix's in another respect. Although he did not identify himself with this event, his sympathies were whole-heartedly with the insurgents. He, himself, was from birth to death one of the poor. A great humanitarian, he was no detached observer, but with every visual resource at his command an opponent of oppression, tyranny, and war. He even proved his sincerity by serving a term in jail for his expressed convictions during the reign of Louis Philippe.

An example which suggests strongly that indefiniteness can be overdone is Puvis de Chavannes' *La Guerre* (Fig. 317), an exposition of war which is meant to reveal its horrors, but misses the mark. Chavannes probably composed this picture about 1861, the year he painted his large *War* and *Peace*, now in the gallery at Amiens. He was fond of generalized themes, like the *Work* and *Rest* which he gave to the same museum.   More than that, he favored a highly idealized allegorical treatment.   It is apparent that he was impressed by the penchant of the École des Beaux Arts for lofty and noble themes and symbolism.   And though he avoided the incongruous realism of the academicians, his feet were, ideologically, miles above the ground.

It is not easy to explain at once why Chavannes' *La Guerre* does not ring true.   It is no more generalized or universal in conception than Daumier's *Uprising*.   The most plausible reason is that it does not convey any emotion that Puvis himself gained from observing human conflict.   Rather, it seems carefully contrived—conceived from beginning to end in a studio by a young man who wished to affirm that war is an evil thing, and posed by models who neither knew nor cared what subject was being treated.   As a result his picture fails to show what war does to human beings in real life; Daumier's *Uprising* does.

Chavannes and many other nineteenth-century idealists failed because they tried to convey a moral in universal terms without first being moved by direct experience or imaginative identification.   It is as though they were working from a book or an algebraic formula. An understanding of life is a prerequisite for the revelation of experiences in either limited or infinite terms.   In this respect Delacroix's painting, while less comprehensive than Daumier's, was at least grounded in genuine inspiration and emotion.   It is a work of art in expressing an interpretation of reality through feeling rather than an intellectual concoction.   The same principle can be applied to the clarification, interpretation, and intensification of reality through painting and sculpture in general.

HARMONY OF IDEAS

A harmony of ideas within a work of art is not to be taken for granted; it is only attained by careful selection.   The subject can be tragic, comic, heroic, or, indeed, very ordinary, but there must be consistency, a quality which comes from logical judgment in the many decisions which must be made in the conception and creation of a work of art.   To that extent, art is mental, and a work of art a revealing demonstration of an artist's mental powers.

But art is also a product of feeling.   A harmony of ideas therefore demands a consistent and appropriate mood.   If an artist elects to work on the high plane of epochal thought, he cannot indulge in trivial slapstick unless, as in the case of Shakespeare, he purposefully introduces comic relief.   Failure to select and maintain an appropriate mood has accounted for many failures in every medium of artistic endeavor. A classic example is Ingres' *Apotheosis of Homer* (Fig. 312), which is lofty in theme but stone-cold in feeling. It is devoid of a mood of any kind. Burchfield's somber *November Evening* (Fig. 27), by contrast, is rich in mood, as is Orozco's tautly urgent *Zapatistas* (Fig. 29).

Regardless of what idea is portrayed, two things must be present if there is to be a harmony; everything in the work must be consistent in thought and feeling unless there is a reason for the departure. Michelangelo understood this principle instinctively. Having elected to decorate the Sistine ceiling (Fig. 126) in a heroic and lofty style, he avoided every triviality of idea and composition. His figures are massive, dignified, simple. Yet he was the worst possible model for lesser men who could imitate only the outward appearance of his muscular giants, without being able to endow them with vitality and life. This going through the motions is a common weakness. It occurs, as in Ingres' case, when an artist attempts more than he can master, often out of a snobbish, mistaken worship of some hierarchy of values. Michelangelo, Orozco, and Burchfield knew their own powers and worked within their limitations.

Because of these obstacles and demands, the way of art is strewn with works which have failed to achieve a harmony of ideas within their special realms. But it is also adorned with some masterful examples of sustained consistency. Few artists illustrate these several points better than Rubens. A really versatile genius, he could work within any one of many moods and subjects and keep each feeling proper to the theme at hand. He knew when and how to be noble, comic, or tragic, without confusing these qualities. In view of the quantity of his production, his triumphs of judgment were many and his errors few. Consider the variety of moods and aptness of treatments in his *Rape of the Daughters of Leucippus* (Fig. 216), *Triumph of Silenus* (Fig. 318), *Elevation of the Cross* (Fig. 335), and *La Ronda* (Fig. 351). No two are alike, yet the themes of lustiness, revelry, anguish, and gaiety that they express are fitting in every respect. It is on such scope and aptness that Rubens' fame is deservedly based. Compared to him, Renoir's cheery view of the world, and, indeed, that of almost any other artist, is a limited view; even the mighty Michelangelo was uniformly sober.

Another master who possessed great scope of feeling was Titian. His moods range from overwhelming sadness and dark cruelty in the *Entombment* (Fig. 62) and *Christ Crowned with Thorns* (Fig. 130) to the gusto of the *Meeting of Bacchus and Ariadne* (Fig. 89); each is consistent within itself. Little wonder that Rubens fell in love

FIG. 318. Rubens. *Triumph of Silenus.* 1625-1627. National Gallery, London.

FIG. 319. Watteau. *Embarkation for Cythera.* 1717. Royal Palace, Potsdam.

651

with the Venetian's art when he saw it in Italy. They were kindred spirits.

Two important aspects of an artist's expression are range of feeling and consistency within each mood; the latter is all-important to unity of idea. An artist's problem in this regard is two-sided. He must establish an over-all pattern of feeling for each new work of art, and then bend every detail in that direction, for it is disharmony of details that often causes failure. Rubens' command over these elements is delightfully illustrated by his *Triumph of Silenus* (Fig. 318).

Artists have used harmony of ideas to great advantage in the creation of architectural or landscape settings for their human figures. In well-conceived paintings and some sculptural reliefs the backgrounds are so appropriate for the theme as a whole that we take them for granted. But they do not appear automatically, and they vary in quality from picture to picture. They also have a historical significance, for most early medieval artists ignored the setting in favor of a blank wall or gold-leaf background. It remained for the Renaissance and modern artists to develop this field—an undertaking which they pursued with increasing effectiveness. In the finest works from their hands the setting makes a substantial contribution to both the narrative and spiritual sides of expression.

David's *Oath of the Horatii* (Fig. 88) and the Crucifixion at Daphni (Fig. 87), in which no setting is represented, show the difference between the painstaking attitude of the modern historical illustrator and the indifference of the medieval religious symbolist. David's attitude was that of an archaeologist. He achieved a harmonious setting for his Roman patriots by making a careful study of all available data about ancient history. His main concern was accuracy. Most of the great artists have used a different approach. They were primarily concerned with creating settings which, though not ignoring the physical and narrative requirements of a subject, aimed mainly at capturing and reinforcing the spirit of the theme. Their backgrounds are for the most part imaginary, yet, because of their appropriateness, they seem natural and real. Though they may differ widely among themselves, each is in harmony with the figures it supports.

A setting can contribute greatly to the mood and meaning of a picture in a unique, highly appropriate way. The stormy background of El Greco's *Agony in the Garden* (Fig. 90) is in keeping with that anguished subject, as Tintoretto's melodramatic setting is with his dynamic conception of the *Annunciation* (Fig. 47). Fra Angelico, by contrast, conceived his *Annunciation* (Fig. 46) in quiet terms, setting it in the still of a cloister. Similarly, the utter peacefulness of Giorgione's *Sleeping Venus* (Fig. 79) is augmented by a serene and verdant landscape. Another masterpiece of suitability of setting is Raphael's *School of Athens* (Fig. 104). The dignified surroundings which he provided for Plato, Aristotle, and the other philosophers bear, of course, no resemblance to the actual ancient Athenian Lyceum. They were invented by Raphael, yet they could hardly have been more fitting. On a lesser but quite effective plane are such other examples as Meunier's *Return of the Miners* (Fig. 231) and Bellows' *Stag at Sharkey's* (Fig. 77). The rough treatment of the background in Meunier's relief suggests the grimy atmosphere of an industrial town, the dark blue-gray setting of Bellows' painting the smoke-filled haze of a boxing arena. Each of these examples typifies one of the methods by which a harmony of ideas can be exploited.

SEQUENCE OF IDEAS

A sequential organization of ideas is used less frequently than harmony in the visual arts because of limitations of space. Unlike an author or dramatist, who counts the gradual unfolding of a theme among his principal expressive means, a painter has to work within a restricted area, and he has less control over what the viewer will regard as the beginning, middle, and end of a subject. Some of the most successful examples of sequence in painting and sculpture are found in the horizontal scrolls of the Far East (called *makemonos*) and in the sculptured friezes of the ancient Greeks. The shape of these formats almost forces the observer to view them in the proper order, a circumstance which both the Orientals and the Greeks knew how to exploit.

A well-handled sequence of ideas can be unusually effective. Bruegel's masterpiece, *Blind Leading the Blind* (Fig. 282), is an outstanding example of gradation of ideas. The picture is so arranged that we are compelled to read it from left to right and thus observe the pertinent changes which lead to the disaster of the blind men. Part of this progression is created by a diagonal axis which forcibly suggests a downward journey into a morass. But the most brilliant feature of the picture is a masterly adjustment of details: the blind man on the left is nearly vertical and firm on his feet; his garment, too, is unruffled. From him the eye is led by stages that denote, through leaning positions, unsteadiness, and more rumpled garments, an increasing insecurity leading to catastrophe. The shrewdest touch of all is the arrangement of the staffs which link the blind men and lead the observer's eye toward the swamp.

Although different in spirit and subject, Watteau's *Embarkation for Cythera* (Fig. 319) illustrates the universal principle of sequence in the organization of an idea. The theme is the departure of a group of youthful lovers for the island presided over by Venus. In its refined treatment of romantic love and its exquisite technique it is typical of Watteau's art and probably his masterpiece. The picture contains a sequential arrangement of subject from right to left. The girl in the right foreground sits without a suitor but heedful of a tiny cupid. Behind her, to the left, is a beautiful young woman who listens half-tentatively, half-willingly to a suitor. Farther toward the left are two pairs of lovers who have agreed to journey to Cythera together. One suitor is helping his beloved to rise, the other is walking with his arm around his sweetheart toward the waiting bark. Completing the idea on the far left is a group of lovers who have assembled for the embarkation. Thus a gradation of ideas is carried out in perfect sequence.

Veronese's *Family of Darius Before Alexander* (Fig. 320) is a variation of this method. In it the gradation of ideas proceeds from the outsides toward the center, where the climactic meeting takes place. The picture deals with the appearance of Darius' widow and three daughters before the all-conquering Alexander after Darius had died ignominiously in flight. Only a faithful elderly courtier remains to plead for the helpless captives. Through his composition Veronese has skilfully built up the interest in this meeting. On the outer side are several soldiers, dogs, monkeys, and dwarfs who regard the drama before them with callous indifference. Nearer to Alexander, on the right, the soldiers are more attentive, but he is the dominant figure as he receives the widow with a magnanimous gesture of forgiveness. Especially skilful is the arrangement of Darius' family. Not only is it grouped in pyramidal form, with the compassionate, dignified courtier's figure at the apex, but it, too, contains a perfect sequence of dramatic interest. The youngest and smallest child, on the left, looks casually away from the group. The older sister by her side is attentive but uncomprehending. The eldest sister, however, is well aware of the gravity of their plight, and leans forward anxiously; while the mother is a picture of maternal concern and supplication. In this way the dramatic interest is gradually built to a peak.

No shape of surface is better adapted to the presentation of a sequence of ideas than that of the horizontal makemono scrolls used by the Chinese and Japanese. As these are unrolled from one hand into the other, they narrate an idea in an order akin to a literary sequence. In fact, word descriptions were often added to further that purpose. Among those who exploited these possibilities to the full was the unknown painter of the so-called Heiji monogatari. His command

Fig. 320. Veronese. *The Family of Darius Before Alexander*. *ca.* 1566. National
Gallery, London.

Fig. 321. Studio of Phidias. *Procession of Youths and Maidens*. From the "Panathenaic
Procession" of the Parthenon frieze. 447-432 B.C. Louvre, Paris.

over design accounts in no small measure for the fame of this Japanese scroll.

The Heiji monogatari, illustrated partially in Figs. 322a–322c, deals with the rise and fall of the Taira family's dominance but it too fell in 1185 before the onslaught of a noted warrior, Minamoto no Yoritomo, who became supreme. The period was torn by civil strife hardly matched anywhere else in world history. In the 117 years between 1068 and 1185 Japan had fifteen nominal rulers and many more contestants for the throne.

The scroll shows the flight and capture of one of these harassed rulers and the burning of the old palace of the Sanjo emperors. As the scroll is unrolled from right to left the headlong flight of the hapless emperor appears first. Preceded by his panic-stricken householders, he seeks escape in an ox-drawn wagon. Then comes the fierce attack of the armed samurai who set fire to the palace and murdered any stragglers trapped in the courtyards. Thanks to the bird's-eye view afforded by the diagonal projection employed, there is a sweeping, panoramic impression of action. Also worth noting is the skill shown by the Asiatic painters in the conventionalization of smoke and flames as they crackle through the timbers. With their mission accomplished—the palace aflame and the emperor captured —the warriors slack their pace to a walk. Thus the tempo is carried to a crescendo and then gradually reduced. For skill in the organization of a sequence of ideas this painting has few superiors.

Quite different in subject but related in treatment is the world-famous *Pan-Athenaic Procession* from the Parthenon (Figs. 267 and 321). It is the finest example in existence of the Greek exploitation of the frieze—the architectural band between the colonnade and roof of a temple. The *Pan-Athenaic* frieze, carved for the Parthenon under the direction of Phidias, depicts a celebration that was held every four years in Athens to honor the city's patron goddess. Although simple, the pageant involves a cross-section of nearly the entire Athenian population. The procession, which includes men, women, youths, maidens, children, and horsemen, makes it way up the Acropolis to the Parthenon where a youth presents a *peplos* (a kind of woolen shawl) to a priest of the temple on behalf of the citizens. In the relief the presentation is witnessed by a conclave of gods.

In the sculptural representation, the procession begins at the southwest corner of the temple, where several horsemen are adjusting sandals and bridling their horses. Facing in a variety of directions, their attitudes are casual and informal. Along the long north side this attitude gradually changes into that of a serious, purposeful procession as the marching figures form their ranks and the horse-

FIG. 322a–c. Details. *Burning of the Sanjo Palace*. Mid-13th century. Kamakura period, "The Heiji Monagatari." Museum of Fine Arts, Boston.

657

men urge their mounts to a gallop. As in the Heiji monogatari, the action reaches its peak at mid-point and gradually subsides. On the Parthenon this occurs as the procession nears the presence of the priests, city fathers, and assembled gods and goddesses. The marching maidens and youths slow their pace to a dignified walk and thence to a quiet watchfulness. Tempo is thus a principal feature of the work. Because of its rise and fall it has been likened to a symphony. Its grandeur has made it deservedly loved and admired as one of the great works of Western art.

The artists of the Renaissance devised a third way of organizing visual material sequentially, one that falls between the single easel picture, like Watteau's *Embarkation for Cythera,* and the continuous Asiatic scroll and Greek frieze. This is the series of related panel or fresco pictures, such as Duccio painted on the back of the *Majestas* and Giotto designed for the Arena Chapel. Giotto's *Meeting of Joachim and Anna* (Fig. 75), *Presentation of the Virgin* (Fig. 51), and *Flight into Egypt* (Fig. 224), though separate pictures, are parts of a connected story, and present an idea sequentially in a manner not unlike the modern cartoon strip. These pioneers handed the method down to their Italian followers, who used it repeatedly throughout the fifteenth century. Michelangelo created the crowning example in the Sistine ceiling decorations. In that mighty cycle of frescos he unfolded the epic drama of the creation of the world, the *Creation of Adam* (Fig. 126), and the sins and downfall leading to the flood. This great work is an illustration of a typical sequence of ideas, but executed in so lofty and magnificent a manner that it remains the undoubted masterwork of this style of painting.

BALANCE OF IDEAS

Balance, one of the major principles of order and a primary ideal of life among peoples like the Greeks and Chinese, has been widely used in the organization of ideas in works of art. When used well it adds greatly to the effectiveness of a picture or statue.

The artists of the Italian Renaissance were particularly fond of balancing ideas, partly because of their respect for the classical tradition. We find it present in many of their works, and handled with skill. In Della Robbia's *Visitation* (Fig. 295) the Virgin is standing and looking downward, her face young and unwrinkled; St. Elizabeth is kneeling, looking upward, her face old and wrinkled. A similar contrast is found in Ghirlandaio's *Old Man and a Boy* (Fig. 344). The old man is large and unusually ugly, the boy small and exceptionally handsome. In this picture, as in Della Robbia's *Visitation,* a bond of sympathy overrides the physical differences and creates a spiritual unity. To emphasize this point, Ghirlandaio painted a pictorial metaphor in the open window, making a bare hill on the left stand for old age and a verdant hill on the right for youth.

The masters who were nurtured in the intellectual atmosphere of the Renaissance were adept in the balancing of ideas. Raphael plays one idea against another in his *School of Athens* and *Disputa*, posing the intellectual against the spiritual sides of life, with a third aspect, the artistic, included in the other fresco in the Camera della Segnatura cycle—the *Parnassus*. Michelangelo balanced two mighty themes, also, in the Vatican when he painted the *Creation of Adam* (Fig. 126). Adam lies languidly naked and alone on the earth as he slowly receives the gift of life; God the Father is clothed and well-attended as he vigorously flies through the air to bestow life upon Adam. Titian, another giant of the time, continued this tradition and added to it; his paintings are a textbook of well-organized ideas. In his *Entombment* (Fig. 62) he contrasted death and life with profound understanding. The same sharp contrast is found in French's *Death and the Sculptor* (Fig. 277), where the stately, shrouded female figure of Death stands out strongly beside the lightly clad, active young sculptor.

Those who inherited the intellectual ideals of the Renaissance carried on this tradition of imaginatively balanced organization instead of pursuing the visual appearance of reality. In time this attitude declined under the impact of nineteenth-century materialism, but it was still strong in the days of Bruegel and El Greco, and appears in the nineteenth century in the work of Turner, Goya, and others who studied life philosophically. Bruegel thought deeply about the significance of what he saw, and expressed in the *Blind Leading the Blind* (Fig. 282) a conclusion which runs through most of his art, that nature continues on its serene way with sublime indifference while man muddles ludicrously through his brief tragedy. The beauty and calm of the landscape in this picture are in marked contrast to the disastrous human parade. This is the cynical view of the satirist summed up in the saying, "every prospect pleases and only man is vile."

El Greco, who had little interest in nature but much in the otherworld, also played with large ideas when he painted his *Agony in the Garden* (Fig. 90). In it he balanced an angel, the representative of Heaven, against Christ, then sorely tried by earthly woes. El Greco continuously stressed this contrast between the ethereal and the mundane; it is the principal theme of his masterpiece, the celebrated *Burial of Count Orgaz* in San Tomé at Toledo.

Working within the humanistic tradition of the Renaissance and post-Renaissance periods Da Vinci and Rembrandt created excellent examples of balanced ideas in the *Last Supper* (Fig. 323) and the *Supper at Emmaus* (Fig. 325). In both of these the personality of Christ is brought out strongly by contrasting His calmness with the agitation and consternation of ordinary men.

Rodin, an admirer of the Renaissance masters, and, like them, a profound student of human life, used a balance of elements when he carved his famous *Kiss* (Fig. 291), making the man appear large, angular, awkward, and muscular, and the woman comparatively small, rounded, and supple. Goya, another humanist, dealt with human relations of a more violent sort in his *Execution of the Madrileños* (Fig. 136). Depicting hate rather than love, he contrasted anguish against discipline, individuality against regimentation, tortured chaos against order, passion against coldness, and brilliant light against deep shadow.

With the increased interest in the natural world that developed in the nineteenth century, artists like Turner turned their attention to the relationships of man and nature, natural and man-made things, the old and new, the dynamic and static, and the continuous and ephemeral; they balanced these broad philosophical ideas pictorially. Turner, a supposedly uneducated man, was fond of dwelling upon the meaning of life and especially the effect of natural phenomena on men; the conflict between human beings and the elements runs through many of his pictures. The underlying theme of his *Norham Castle* (Fig. 25) is the contrast between the persistence of natural cycles and the perishability of the man-made castles. His *Dunstanborough Castle* expounds the same idea with a secondary subject in the contrast between a decaying abandoned castle and a humble but inhabited cottage.

Turner brought this temporal-physical drama to a grand climax in the *Fighting Téméraire* (Fig. 258a). In that most famous of his pictures, the discarded man-o'-war symbolizes the passing of the old era of sailing ships and the tug, which pulls her to the graveyard, the ugly, huffing and puffing industrial era that was then transforming England. The sunset symbolizes the end of the once-proud vessel, a ship of the line at Trafalgar. Turner, who loved sailing ships, filled the picture with an air of nostalgia.

Homer, too, was a student of the sea, but less sentimental about human life than Turner. His conception of the conflict between man and the ocean is presented factually and starkly in pictures like the *Fog Warning* (Fig. 61); there are no comments, biases, or regrets.

His *Northeaster* (Fig. 18) is an equally impartial representation of the endless global conflict between the land and sea and the attributes of each.

In keeping with a widespread naturalistic orientation, the artists of the nineteenth century were keenly aware of the savage aspects of natural reality. The subject fascinated Darwin and Stevenson, among others, in the scientific and literary fields and Barye in art. Deadly combats between contrasting types of animals were a preoccupation with Barye. This is illustrated powerfully by his *Jaguar Killing a Young Wild Ass* (Fig. 314), in which the jaguar is large, powerful, and predatory, its victim small, fragile, and helpless. Through a repetition of balanced but contrasting ideas Barye expressed a belief that power rules; the strong and vicious almost always prevail, as in his *Lion Killing a Deer, Jaguar Devouring a Hare,* and *Greyhound Killing a Rabbit.*

This balancing of ideas is an effective way of intensifying and clarifying a subject while interpreting it. There is a vividness that marks any juxtaposition of radically different entities—like black against white, or angular against curved forms. The contrast gives each extra clarity and greater prominence than it would have alone or if subordinated to a harmony of terms. Barye's *Prancing Horse* (Fig. 343), for instance, is a captivating figure, but it does not rivet our attention as compulsively as the ferocious *Jaguar Killing a Young Wild Ass.* The same may be said of the youth in Ghirlandaio's *Old Man and a Boy* (Fig. 344). Handsome though he is, he would not catch our eye nearly as much if he were alone. In conjunction with his ugly elder, his beauty becomes enhanced. This is true wherever a balance is achieved. Properly exploited, it is one of the best methods of organization known to art.

QUALITY OF IDEAS

Is a work of art great because of the acclaim of the critics or because it can be understood and appreciated by the ordinary intelligent person?

We have shown that greatness in a work of art does *not* lie in its adherence to a preconceived hierarchy of values in subject matter. And we have implied that the superiority of one painting or statue over others of a similar character is generally due to those differences in organization that we call design. Let us consider two paintings that have been famous for so long and called superlative by so many critics that the layman accepts this opinion unquestioningly. The

FIG. 323. Raphael Morghen after Da Vinci. *Last Supper*. Original (1495-1498) in the Refectory, S. M. delle Grazie, Milan.

FIG. 324. Rosselli. *Last Supper*. 1482. Sistine Chapel. Vatican, Rome.

two paintings are Leonardo da Vinci's *Last Supper* (Fig. 323) and Rembrandt's *Supper at Emmaus* (Fig. 325). Are there sound reasons why these pictures deserve to be so celebrated?

This illustration of the *Last Supper* is not a photograph of the original painting. Owing to Leonardo's tendency to experiment, the original picture was painted on a poorly prepared ground which began to flake in his own lifetime and is now a wreck. This engraving by Raphael Morghen is the best evidence we have of the picture's appearance in the eighteenth century. Though only a copy, it gives us an inkling of how impressive the original composition must have been. In trying to understand this picture's superiority let us consider first the subject and then the organization of the theme. The subject, the Last Supper, was an imposing and significant one for any member of Christendom. There would be much in its favor in any evaluation of themes. But that alone did not make Da Vinci's picture great. The story was common property; it had been depicted over and over by Giotto and his many followers. In fact, it had become so conventionalized that numerous Renaissance artists could have painted it with ease. Leonardo took his first step toward a superior interpretation when he brought a fresh, unconventional, penetrating mind to the already hackneyed subject.

Despite their long familiarity with the Biblical theme, Leonardo's predecessors had not exhausted its possibilities or even touched on its essential features. Indeed, it was as though Leonardo was the first artist in three hundred years who read the story for himself instead of accepting it second-hand. Seeking a different way of interpreting the subject, he was certainly the first artist to penetrate to the heart of its meaning. Leonardo might have utilized any of seven approaches, the moment:

1. When Jesus announced to the disciples that He would never again eat the feast of the Passover with them on earth.
2. When, starting with Peter, Jesus washed the feet of the disciples (a task usually performed by slaves) to illustrate humility and gently rebuked them for having quarrelled about who would be the greatest among them in Heaven.
3. When Jesus said, "Verily I say unto you, One of you which eateth with me shall betray me." He had twice before told His disciples that He would be betrayed, but now He placed the crime in their own midst.
4. When, in answer to enquiries, Jesus passed a sop of wine to Judas, indicating that he would be the betrayer.
5. When Judas, confused by the revelation, remained irresolutely at the table, Jesus said, "That thou doest, do quickly," and Judas left like one under a hypnotic command to fulfill his evil destiny.

6. When Jesus subsequently announced that others of the disciples would deny or desert Him before His execution (as they did), causing further protests of loyalty.

7. When Jesus finally carried out his purpose in calling the meeting and, Judas gone, instituted the rite of the Sacrament, or Eucharist.

The story of the Last Supper was plainly rich in illustrative material, though some of its episodes lent themselves better than others to visual exposition, and certainly Christ's prediction of the betrayal was the most dramatic and climactic. It is curious that previous artists had passed it over. When Da Vinci selected it as the moment to be represented, he took an important step toward creating the world's most famous painting.

Christ's announcement startled the gathering at the Last Supper. Recovering from their amazement, each of the disciples asked, "Is it I?" protesting his innocence and fidelity. Each did this according to his particular temperament. Only Judas and the gentle John remained aloof. In past times it had been the custom to single Judas out by setting him rather obviously alone on the opposite side of the table—a prearranged position contrary to the unexpectedness of Christ's announcement. This convention appears in Rosselli's *Last Supper* (Fig. 324), but Leonardo was too logical and subtle to use so transparent a device. He quite purposely placed Judas among the other disciples, identifying him by a small bag of coins and an attitude of guilty withdrawal.

Since Da Vinci comprehended the psychological effects of Christ's announcement, he understood the excitement of the scene and its need for careful organization. It was in achieving a suitable composition that he showed his supremacy. First, it was necessary to bring order into the chaos of twelve gesticulating men. This he did by subdividing them into four groups of three, then emphasizing their positions with the four trestles that support the table. A series of hangings on the side walls of the room further emphasizes the division into groups. Yet within each cluster of men there is an internal play of contrasting gestures, directional lines, and colors—a fourfold variety within unity.

A method had also to be devised to give Christ the central position that He deserved. Leonardo did this in four ways. Not only did he place Christ in the geometric center of the picture area, but made Him coincide with the vanishing point of a perspective system of projection; the converging lines lead our glance to His head. This made perspective projection a superb dramatic means rather than a mere tool of realism and a scientific plaything. Moreover, he set Christ against an open door whose light and distance draw the eye to His vicinity, and surmounted the door with an arched pediment which augments this emphasis. Finally, he caused every disciple save John either to look at Christ or point in His direction. He thus made the Savior the center of attention in every possible way.

The specific, point-by-point organizing intelligence that Da Vinci brought to bear on the representation of the *Last Supper* has elicited the world's acclaim. It is demonstrably superior to the effort of any other artist who treated the subject. Behind that acknowledged fact lies a principle of general importance. It is said that in his greatest work an artist sums up the accumulated experience of a lifetime; that he cannot give unless he has absorbed, and that his efforts will reveal these hard-won capacities. This is abundantly true of the long effort that preceded Leonardo's painting of the *Last Supper*. In a sense he had spent his whole career preparing for the task, but he made special studies as well. Much of his life had been devoted to the study of personality and the way the activity of the mind is expressed through the body and face. When preparing to paint the *Last Supper* he spent hours in taverns and wherever else men gathered, watching their expressions and gestures as they reacted to various ideas. A noted raconteur, he may well have told them stories that would elicit expressions of shock or surprise, and added the results to his observations of human behavior. A series of drawings shows the thoroughness of his explorations. When the time came to give a picture of the *Last Supper* the force and conviction of life itself, Leonardo was ready.

These are some of the factors that go into the creation of a masterpiece. We too often take such performances for granted in spite of our awe. But we have only to compare this great picture with another representation of the same theme, such as Cosimo Rosselli painted a few years before Leonardo reached the heights of his career in Milan (Fig. 324). It is typical of the Renaissance conceptions of the Lord's Supper that Da Vinci inherited and improved upon so vastly.

The chief dramatic fault of this picture it its resemblance to any banquet. There is nothing momentous about it. The twelve disciples are arranged along a table, but nothing distinguishes one from another, and Christ, the supposedly central figure, is even less prominent than Judas. There is not only a lack of crucial action and emphasis but much distraction—supernumeraries to the sides, vessels and two playful cats in the foreground, and three eye-catching scenes from the Passion of Christ in the background. The architectural setting contains a multitude of details, but few that direct the eye to the figure of Christ. Rosselli's *Last Supper* is thus the antithesis of Leonardo's and greatly inferior to it.

Da Vinci's *Last Supper* is an example of shrewd perception of the right psychological moment and of an artistic organization that exploits its dramatic possibilities to the full. Rembrandt's *Supper at Emmaus* (Fig. 325) is a masterpiece of the same order, but famous for different reasons. Its strength lies in the expression of the spirit of a less spectacular Biblical episode than Christ's prediction of betrayal at the Last Supper, but infinitely subtle and appealing. The artist's problem was to fathom the exact import of the story and bend all means to its effective representation—a difficult and elusive task. Two very capable painters, Caravaggio and Veronese, had failed in this effort, and Rembrandt himself had produced one fiasco.

Before deciding why Caravaggio and Veronese failed, we must give some thought to the meaning of the *Supper at Emmaus*. The New Testament records that on the afternoon of Christ's Resurrection two of his lesser followers, Cleopas and one who remains unidentified, were walking from Jerusalem toward Emmaus. On the way they were joined by Jesus, whom they did not recognize. Perceiving their despondency and bitterness over the shame of the Crucifixion, He began to explain to them that it had been a necessary part of the Messiah's mission and was foretold by the prophets. Amazed by His knowledge, they begged Him to dine with them at an inn in Emmaus. After the table was spread, He took bread and blessed it as He had done with the Sacrament at the Last Supper. The manner of His prayer was inimitable. Instantly the disciples recognized Him; then He was gone. His presence, however, seemed to remain vividly with them, confirming again what the Master had often told them in anticipation of His departure and the years that they would have to carry on without His physical presence; He had said, "Where two or three are gathered together in my name, there am I in the midst of them." Christ was again stressing at Emmaus the unimportance of His corporeal presence and the all-importance of belief in His spiritual presence. Once He had made this point, He vanished. The servant who had waited on them did not see Him at all. The story is one of the tenderest, subtlest, and most spiritual in meaning in the Bible, a point that Caravaggio and Veronese missed completely. Caravaggio, an artist who strove to make everything he painted as real as possible, placed the utmost stress on materiality in his *Supper at Emmaus* (Fig. 327). A master of still life, he made the food on the table look real enough to eat. But in his realism Caravaggio was unimaginative, spiritually insensitive, and dependent on models. He endowed the Christ with no better or worse characteristics than

FIG. 325. Rembrandt. *The Supper at Emmaus.* 1648. Louvre, Paris.

FIG. 326. Veronese. *The Supper at Emmaus.* *ca.* 1565. Louvre, Paris.

FIG. 327. Caravaggio. *The Supper at Emmaus. ca.* 1605. National Gallery, London.

he found in a commonplace young model. The other carefully posed figures appear overdramatic, and the elaborate, precisely painted food distracting. It seems improbable that Caravaggio had ever read the story of the *Supper at Emmaus* for himself. If he had, his mind was incapable of understanding its deepest meaning. Added to this was a characteristic lack of discrimination and philosophical judgment. Caravaggio was a superb realist with an ordinary mind. He painted many things—old men, card-playing boys, and still life, aptly and well; but his interpretation of the *Supper at Emmaus* was not among them.

Veronese was beyond his depth for another reason when he, too, painted a *Supper at Emmaus* (Fig. 326). A different kind of man from the rowdy, studiously vulgar Caravaggio, Veronese resembled him only in his materialistic outlook which took the typically Venetian direction of a love of luxury. He possessed a courtliness of manner which enabled him to paint the *Family of Darius Before Alexander* (Fig. 320) in an exemplary fashion, but it did not prepare him to understand any intellectual or spiritual idea profoundly. His limitations are, like those of Caravaggio, revealed by his interpretation of the *Supper at Emmaus*. Chief among his faults for this particular subject was his worship of sumptuous display. He sets the scene not in an inn but a palace and clutters the picture with supernumeraries, including portraits of an entire Venetian family and a distracting set of children and dogs in the forefront of the stage. Although his Christ is of a higher type than Caravaggio's, He is nearly lost in the crowd. This *Supper at Emmaus* is therefore no better a Biblical illustration than Caravaggio's; its Venetian sumptuousness is as out of place as the Roman painter's insistent realism.

We can probably accord Rembrandt no higher praise than to say that when he painted his *Supper at Emmaus* (Fig. 325) of 1648 he avoided all of the mistakes of Caravaggio and Veronese and, like Leonardo, showed an unerring grasp of the sacred episode's essential meaning. It was one of many instances in which he proved himself a careful and penetrating student of the Scriptures. As a Biblical illustration it leaves little to be desired. In keeping with the New Testament account, Rembrandt made his setting simple, his actors few. Jesus is properly made to dominate, but the disciples are given their due by skilful arrangement and by the expressiveness of their gestures of recognition. The converse of Caravaggio's and Veronese's posed models, these are men who avoid melodrama and are genuinely surprised. Rembrandt made them convincing by identifying himself imaginatively and sensitively with their situation, and by drawing upon his years of close study of human behavior. In his picture the servant is appropriately oblivious of the Master's presence or identity. Above all, Rembrandt conceived the episode in quietly reverent terms; the scene is suffused with soft light, and the action restrained. In this manner he captured and emphasized the spiritual nature of the story, which his predecessors had missed.

Like Leonardo's *Last Supper*, the *Supper at Emmaus* by Rembrandt was a reflection of the artist's character, mind, and life. He had not achieved profundity overnight. In his youth he painted a version of the *Supper at Emmaus* which is a dreadful example of exaggerated melodrama and misplaced theatricality. It is characteristic of the generally boisterous tenor of his early work. Only after he lost his popularity through the disastrous misunderstanding of his *Night Watch*, and lost his wife as well, did he mellow into the quiet, infinitely thoughtful man the world now reveres. Only then was he ready to understand the real significance of the *Supper at Emmaus*. He had the capacity to learn from experience; that is an ability which lies behind much that we call great in art.

Da Vinci's *Last Supper* and Rembrandt's *Supper at Emmaus* are, as we have seen, similar in some respects to other representations of the same themes. Yet they are different, and more than that, each is outstanding for reasons which are demonstrable in the light of commonly accepted standards and values. Though neither is perfect in any absolute sense, each is great because it is superior to all other attempts at accomplishing the same end. The question of quality need not be evaded; it is not only a matter of comparative values but also one of the norms of evaluation upon which we agree. It can be solved within reason by patient and determined study.

DISRUPTION OF IDEAS

An artist spends most of his life developing a systematic way of organizing his ideas and methods into a style that will express his own personality and yet be in accord with the spirit of his time. In doing so he contributes to the orderly continuity of art. At the same time he departs, if ever so slightly, from his own norms in everything he paints, making each picture from his brush unique. In this way he contributes to the variety and enrichment of art. The history of art fluctuates ceaselessly between these two poles.

Much of this variation of conventions is gradual, almost imperceptible. It is accepted as a normal part of art. Occasionally, however, a group of artists feels compelled to break with the prevailing manner for the sake of artistic progress. This is most likely to occur when some mode has reached a state of near-perfection after a long period of development, as the Italian Renaissance sculpturesque mode finally did in the hands of Da Vinci, Raphael, and Michelangelo. Then, even if no historical changes require new modes of expression, a change is needed, for continued exploitation soon degenerates into repetition. In this sense the history of art has its own internal compulsions and rules.

An example of slow but steady change can be found in the history of perspective projection. Mantegna varied the type by altering the line of vision; Correggio and Pozzo experimented still further by painting objects as they appear from below; Ruysdael, Claude, and others added aerial projection and meandering recessional lines to the system; and Degas gave new life to the time-worn method by depicting scenes from many different positions. These changes were introduced over a period of five hundred years, allowing every generation ample time to become used to them. The public remained in accord with this artistic enterprise because it was not asked to adapt itself to the changes abruptly.

There is another kind of artistic progress which has periodically produced crises. This foment occurs when a highly original artist becomes impatient with conventions which have outlived their usefulness or, by repetition, ceased to present a challenge. He departs from the past with radical suddenness. The slower-moving public falls behind for a generation or two, resents his disruption of its customary ideas, and rejects him in one way or another—through neglect, misinterpretation, or vilification. This is most likely to happen during a period of far-reaching historical changes, in which there is simultaneously considerable freedom for the artist, entrenched officialdom, and a tenaciously conservative middle class. The nineteenth century was such a period of rapid artistic progress and ultra-conservatism; the great disrupters of the old ideas, Monet, Manet, Cézanne, Van Gogh, Seurat, and Gauguin, were not thanked for their innovations, but had life made miserable for them.

They were not the first masters to suffer for their departures from established conventions. Long before them Caravaggio had seen that even the perfection of Raphael wears thin if it is repeated endlessly. He sought to breathe new life into art by introducing an intensified realism. For a long time his pictures were resented. The public did not want its artistic habits changed. Rembrandt also ran afoul of tradition when he painted his now famous *Night Watch*. Because its informality and unusual lighting made it unlike any kind of portraiture the burghers of Amsterdam had ever seen, they disavowed Rembrandt for the rest of his life. They thought he had either lost his wits and forgotten how to paint and draw or was insulting them with an ill-conceived hoax. Two hundred years later history repeated itself when the same epithets were hurled at Manet, Cézanne, and Van Gogh. The violence of the charges was extreme. A radical disruption of ideas and what we now call progress have long gone hand-in-hand and, with equal consistency, been misunderstood.

The adoption of a new approach by a truly creative artist is a deliberate, purposeful procedure whether or not his contemporaries recognize the fact. It is inseparable from the element of control in his objectification of feeling. But it is equally true that an artist may depart unintentionally from norms of almost universal validity and common sense. If these variations from accepted style represent only change and not progress, the work will sooner or later be adjudged bad, no matter what the temporary fame of the artist. This inexorable squaring of accounts and inversions of fame has produced many ironies in the history of taste. The difference between a purposeful and unintentional disruption of ideas is illustrated by the expert clown-on-ice who purposely falls with great skill and control, and the serious figure-skater who slips accidentally. The one is acknowledged to be good skating and the other bad.

There are many ways in which an artist can disrupt a pattern of ideas. He can depart abruptly from his time's favorite modes of representation and design; diverge radically from the prevailing norms of content; or digress from long-term values in favor of a fad in either content or form. Any of these dissents from temporary or long-range custom will cause him to run counter to some artistic trend. So there must ultimately be a reappraisal of his reputation, in the light of which it will go up or down. Considered appraisal of the congruity of innovations in style will often exalt a forgotten artist and expose an overrated one. The verdict of time in these matters is slow but very sure.

A classic instance of purposeful disruption of form is the work of the pioneers of modern painting, Van Gogh, Cézanne, Gauguin, and Seurat. With the exception of Gauguin, none of these artists confronted the public with anything radically new in the realm of subject matter, but layman found their pictures extremely hard to understand and have only begun to feel at ease with them after a lapse of half a century. The main causes of difficulty lay in their modes of representation and design, and especially in their organization of forms in space. Van Gogh is an outstanding case. When his pictures began to appear in the nineties, the public thought him literally mad, unable to draw in proper perspective, and condemned him for using screamingly garish colors. Actually Van Gogh had merely carried certain Impressionist principles of color design a logical step further and with an acute sense of their interrelationship. But the public, which had barely adjusted itself by then to Impressionist colors, was far from being ready for Van Gogh's. The immediate verdict was that he exhibited an inexcusable disregard for every artistic precedent because of lunacy.

Van Gogh's deliberate disruption of the accepted way of arranging forms in space is illustrated by his *Artist's Bedroom at Arles* (Fig. 328). When he began to paint, the accepted way of organizing forms in space was based on the single-vanishing-point system of perspective projection. Mantegna, Pozzo, Correggio, Degas, and others had introduced variations on that mode, but without departing from its cardinal recessional principle. Van Gogh had other ideas. He felt that perspective projection had become time-worm, that something radically new was needed to revive interest in it. His approach was the use of a multiple-vanishing-point system. By using four different vanishing points for as many planes instead of the customary one, he made the floor in the *Artist's Bedroom at Arles* appear to slope steeply upward, while the walls and ceiling slope sharply inward and downward. The effect is an intensification of our feeling of space in what was actually a small room. Furthermore, Van Gogh inverted the normal conceptions of finite-infinite relationships by outlining clouds sharply while making mountains appear to roll and heave, as in his *Mountainous Landscape* (Fig. 65).

Van Gogh's contemporaries attributed these disruptions to stark insanity and the breakdown of normal controls. But today we recognize that there was a purpose in his distortions, and that he created a system which was logical within itself, and employed it consistently. He was also remarkably consistent in his organization of colors, brushwork, and spatial relationships. We can recognize his manner anywhere and find the same principles running through picture after picture. Considering the tempestuous strength of his feelings, he possessed extraordinary artistic control and brought new interest to color and spatial design.

Each of the other pioneers of modern art made a similar contribution in his own way. In his short life Seurat developed a dotlike type of brush stroke which was strikingly new. Although it was suggested by the Impressionist broken-color technique, it avoided the hasty appearance of that method in favor of one which seems scientifically precise and orderly. Seurat put an infinite amount of patience into his organization of forms in space in such a picture as the *Sunday on the Island of La Grande Jatte* (Fig. 226), taking great care to relate every form to its neighbor. He departed from standard perspective

FIG. 328. Van Gogh.
*The Artist's Bedroom
at Arles.* October, 1888.
Art Institute of Chicago.

FIG. 329. Greuze. *The
Punished Son.* 1765.
Louvre, Paris.

FIG. 330. Forain. *The
Prodigal Son.* 1908.
Metropolitan Museum
of Art, New York.

projection, but developed a system which was both orderly and new. Those who study it carefully find it still fascinates.

Cézanne, living longer than either Seurat or Van Gogh, contributed even more than they to the rejuvenation of a perspective system which had come to be taken for granted. Artists could control it easily; the public could read it without effort. Consequently, it had lost its ability to excite either the artist or the viewer. Cézanne overcame that lethargy by emphasizing (with lines, colors, and planear contrasts) every juxtaposition of forms in a picture like the *House in Provence* (Fig. 80), thus revitalizing the part-to-part relationships.

Cézanne's treatment of forms in shallow space was no less novel than his intense feeling for deep space, demonstrated through his superb still-life paintings like the *Vase of Tulips* in Fig. 15. Believing that we had lost the sharpness of our appreciation in this field too, he used many devices to shock us into a fresh awareness of shapes, masses, colors, and their compositional interplay. One of his methods stemmed from the visual fact that we rarely see all the forms in a given scene to best advantage. We may see the graceful outlines of a vase, but miss the round shape of its mouth and the top of the table on which it stands. To overcome this optical limitation, Cézanne began to paint a vase's profile and circular mouth from the best angle of view for each. Then he did the same for the tabletop. This synthetic, composite procedure is clearly visible in the *Vase of Tulips*. It was not unprecedented, for the Egyptians had freely employed a similar system in paintings long before Christ (as in the combination of profile and frontal elements in *Nakht Watching Plowing*, Fig. 120), but it seemed new to Cézanne's contemporaries. It shocked them, fascinated them, but eventually captivated them. In time it opened up numerous long-forgotten possibilities in the field of pictorial design and helped to reinvigorate painting.

Gauguin broke with the immediate past by returning to much older principles of color design. When he painted orange dogs and yellow Christs, his point of view was esthetically medieval in its arbitrariness, but without the medieval symbolism. Breaking with the long-established tradition which had begun with the Renaissance rediscovery of (objective) reality, he painted dogs orange and Christs yellow if, in his opinion, it improved the color scheme. Up to a point his governing ideal was art for art's sake. Today the color patterns that he devised seem strikingly beautiful. But to the public of his own time they were profoundly disturbing. Yet Gauguin was painting logically; he had a reason for what he did and excellent control over its objectification. His logic merely conflicted with the set ideas of his day and required time to be understood. This was also true, in his case, of the exotic subject matter that he found in faraway Tahiti. Even today the undercurrent of primitive superstition that sets the mood for his *Mahana No Atua,* "Day of the God" (Fig. 141) is foreign to the thought-patterns of Christendom.

A more typical disruption of ideas of content was Millet's *Gleaners* (Fig. 225). As we look at the picture today, it seems natural, sincere, and harmless. But Millet's contemporaries raised a storm over it because it upset their traditional conception of France's agricultural workers. The Parisian élite imagined these people to be respectable and hard-working (which they were) and also bright-eyed and well-fed, as depicted by such eighteenth-century dreamers as Greuze and Fragonard. When Millet, a farm boy himself, cast aside the satin-clad, idealized shepherds and milkmaids for true scenes of farm life and farmers, some of them brutish and stupid-looking, he was accused of not only perpetrating ugliness, but insulting the "backbone of France." His masterpiece, the *Gleaners,* now in the Louvre, was reviled as the "Three Fates of Poverty."

Few centuries have had their favorite notions jolted harder than have the nineteenth and twentieth. This was a rich but rocky ground into which modern art had to sow its seeds. Millet was not the only belittled purveyor of the truth. When Géricault exhibited his *Raft of the Medusa* (Fig. 378) in 1819, it aroused a furor because the reigning neo-classicists had imposed a ban on unsparingly realistic treatments of contemporary events, especially any tragedy which implied criticism of the government.

There are, of course, many ways in which an artist can disrupt the prejudices or complacency of others. Courbet found another, not without some glee, when he painted a picture of two *Stone-Breakers* (road menders). The public construed his perfectly straightforward representation to be propaganda for socialism—then a touchy subject—and condemned the picture for this presumed fault. Since no period can avoid social, economic, and political prejudices, there must be a review of allegations at a later and calmer time.

Almost any distortion of form or content is likely to disturb people on first acquaintance. A tolerance for the new comes slowly, a genuine liking slower still. El Greco's distortions of shape and measure caused him to fall into neglect for over two hundred years. Even now he is an acquired taste for a few enthusiasts and a disconcerting figure for the majority. His spiritual descendant Picasso is in somewhat the same position. Many respect his fame who do not pretend to comprehend him. In his case genius goes almost unquestioned. We forget, though, what a long time it took to grow used to emaciated, elongated Grecoesque figures like his *Woman Ironing* (Fig. 45), painted over fifty years ago. At present we cannot easily fathom the reason for his two-eyed profiles and eight-fingered hands unless we ponder the meaning of his *Guernica* (Fig. 1). In that picture Picasso does violence to every normal idea of civilization with the deliberate intention of showing the savagery of war itself. Since war is the epitome of social disruption, to represent it extraordinarily is perfectly logical. We may therefore assume that the intelligent Picasso has equally good reasons for other practices which merely elude our present understanding.

Somewhat easier to understand now, owing to a longer acquaintance, are the disruptions of ideas introduced by Giorgio de Chirico prior to the First World War and developed by Dali and others in the twenties. These not only reflect the disruptions created by the first global war, but express profound insights into the human psyche. Chirico has described how the idea of surrealism came to him through an experience that is not uncommon. Basically it would occur whenever we suddenly meet something out of its normal context; if, for instance, we happen upon a bed and a refrigerator left in the middle of a sidewalk by someone in the process of moving. Any such experience pulls us up short. To imagine a tree growing up through the middle of that bed or flowers blooming in the refrigerator is only to carry the disruption a step or two further. Chirico recognized that our subconscious minds mix up our thoughts in exactly that fashion when liberated by sleep. A weird disruption of contexts may be illogical for the everyday wakeful hours, but it is entirely logical for the world of dreams. Indeed artists had to invent such devices if they were to communicate any of the character of the subconscious realm brought to light by Freud, Adler, Jung, and others through psychoanalytic research.

The artists who undertook to reveal the subconscious world through artistic means shouldered a difficult problem with varying degrees of success. But we must not attribute their efforts to capriciousness or lunacy, much as these explanations may appeal to us. We should appreciate, rather, the remarkable consistency that some of them attained, as Dali did in his *Persistence of Memory* (Fig. 53). In that apparently perplexing picture every normal idea is inverted in a way that few can account for fully, but anyone can admire the consistency with which Dali has carried out his idea. Whether inverted or not, normal or disrupted, the consistent exposition of an idea is the gist of artistic control.

As for the faults which appear in art, competent critics do not call pictures bad without reason. A common error is the unintentional disruption of an idea because of some mistake in judgment—sometimes in the thinking of a whole period in which the weak artist is merely a tool.

An example is the art of Greuze, an eighteenth-century French painter. His failing was a common one, a weakness for incongruous exaggeration. This fault may take two directions, sentimentality or melodrama. Greuze's *Punished Son* (Fig. 329) fails on both counts. The picture supposedly represents the final illness of a father whose errant son has returned home too late—a play on the Prodigal Son idea. Everyone in the household is distraught, including the wayward son. In theory this is a perfectly acceptable theme; the fault lies in Greuze's conception and execution of it. None of the individual expressions and gestures rings true. Each is an exaggerated disruption of the way people actually behave in tragic circumstances. In the whole picture only the dog behaves normally. Greuze also hurt his representation by painting every texture and surface as though it were satin, thus giving the death room the paradoxical air of a boudoir. He did the same when he depicted shepherdesses, farm boys, and milkmaids.

Why did Greuze miss the mark so badly in representing a death scene, when Titian depicted the *Entombment* (Fig. 62) superbly? Where, for instance, did he get the upturned, rolling eyes, rhetorical gestures, and teeth-gnashing that do not appear in life? One reason was lack of either sympathetic imagination or a perceptive experience with such episodes. Coupled to that was the practice of getting emotional signs second-hand out of a book, like Le Brun's manual of standarized expressions, or from theaters like the Comédie Francaise. Without imaginative sympathy or experience neither of these is a trustworthy source of artistic inspiration. Greuze added another mistake. He not only painted for the wrong people, but for the wrong reasons. His motivation, coming as it did from the precepts of intellectual dictators like Jean Jacques Rousseau and Diderot, was synthetic and intellectual. In the so-called Age of Reason, these influential men decreed that it would be a good thing for artists to reveal the admirable traits of the lower classes and extol the simple life. Greuze, a susceptible man, obediently painted such pictures as the *Village Wedding*, which simpers with false sentiments, and the excruciating *Punished Son*. Returning to the simple life while comfortably established in a fashionable Parisian studio is not that easy.

At heart Greuze neither knew nor cared anything about the people he was representing. He depicted them because such scenes were the mode at the influential annual salons of the day, where Diderot's voice was powerful. Reputation-hunting is almost bound to produce values that will not survive. Of course, Greuze's principal audience

knew no more than he about the tragic emotions and behavior of
ordinary people. Chic, elegant, and superficial, they encouraged him
and Diderot in the perpetuation of ideas which were divorced from
reality and hence due to disrupt any later standards based on actual
experience. Thus we see how influential the combination of the
merely clever artist, clever critic, and clever patronage can be in the
formation of taste, and how that taste as a whole can stray from reality
so badly that it must be reversed later on. Greuze was only one of
many men who fell into the same trap. Lacking both strength of
character and true insight, they could only be conformists.

That a whole period can go awry under the impact of far-reaching
social changes and breed a generation of ill-advised artists is an accepted historical phenomenon. The period of the Counter-Reformation engendered a vast production of melodramatic religious art, full
of horrible martyrdoms and sadistic executions of mythological characters, like Ribera's *Death of Prometheus,* and Guido Reni's *Ecce
Homo.* Not even Rubens entirely escaped the influence of this overwrought transitional period. The troubled nineteenth century over-
burdened the sense of restraint of many artists in the field of social
relations. Labor was beginning to assert itself and to be represented
in art—in the agricultural paintings of Millet (Fig. 225) and the industrial sculpture of Meunier (Fig. 231). Meunier's straightforward
representation of labor, unusual for his period, has given his work
lasting value. More typically artists such as Vela expressed sentimental biases in works like *Labor's Sacrifice.* Their one-sided picture
of labor's lot now seems limited and propagandistic. But their mistakes were only characteristic of a too-close view of life and its immediate problems.

Incongruous triviality, another weakness, is distracting and dis-
rupts the mood of an otherwise serious picture. What is permissible
in a scene from ordinary life may be an off-key intrusion in a more
momentous event. We do not expect to find two monkeys playing
in the foreground of Titian's *Entombment.* Yet something akin to
that appears in the center of Rosselli's *Last Supper* (Fig. 324). Even
a major master like Veronese will sometimes be guilty of this im-
propriety; a comparable triviality appears in the foreground of his
Supper at Emmaus (Fig. 326). Indeed, his own contemporaries
frowned on this departure from good taste and accused him of
sacrilege.

Why an artist violates the spirit of a theme is not easy to understand. There is a place for the light touch, but it must be appropriate in context and arrangement. Veronese introduced the same children, dwarfs, and monkeys which had appeared in the *Supper at*

Emmaus into the *Family of Darius Before Alexander* (Fig. 320) to the advantage of that picture. Placed on either side, instead of in the foreground, they provide an effective contrast with the serious, adult drama in the center. Titian added to the value of the *Meeting of Bacchus and Ariadne* (Fig. 89) when he placed a prancing little satyr on the central axis. A touch of comic relief, it is in harmony with the rollicking behavior of the grown-ups.

A third pitfall which awaits the artist is incongruous pomposity. Ingres was notorious for this failing. Extremely proud and self-conscious, he was a pillar of officialdom who lorded it over quieter and more sensible men. Pompous rather than inherently dignified, he craved the support of honors, position, and prestige. Little wonder, then, that his *Apotheosis of Homer* (Fig. 312) is subtly lacking in simple dignity. Like Ingres himself, each of the great men therein assumes a pose of dignified importance. To appreciate this one has only to look at representations of men whose natural dignity needed no pretence: *Khafre, John Paul Jones,* and Meunier's calmly confident *Blacksmith.*

Reynolds projected the same kind of self-importance upon his sitters. Self-conscious and proud, they exhibit a sense of class-consciousness, arrogance, and lack of ease. The women whom he portrayed are especially marked by this lack of natural grace. The deficiency became all the more apparent when Reynolds deliberately strove to capture that quality, as in his large, ambitious *Three Graces* in the National Gallery. A bachelor, he seems not to have really understood women, though he painted many portraits of them. Some empathic and sympathetic deficiency forced him to rely on poses that are supposed to convey nobility, breeding, and grace, but more often suggest only a fashionable and superficial elegance. The pretentious, affected air of his Viscountess Crosbie strikes us today as silly. Although the mode of his day, these affectations are not the sources of great art. Some of an artist's mistakes may stem from the attitudes of his time, but others must be charged to the defects of his own personality. An almost excusable fault is the misplaced pomposity or grandeur of the architectural setting in Veronese's *Supper at Emmaus.* Addicted to luxurious backgrounds of the grand opera variety, he used them indiscriminately. Such richness is out of character with the spirit of the Biblical episode, which Veronese probably never bothered to read directly; the simple background of Rembrandt's *Supper at Emmaus,* suggesting a country inn, is more appropriate. On the other hand, grandeur of setting is exactly suited to the royal meeting of the *Family of Darius Before Alexander;* sumptuousness, like triviality, has no fixed value, but depends on circumstances. Here is one reason why the *Family of Darius Before Alex-ander* is regarded more highly than the *Supper at Emmaus* by the same artist.

Indiscriminate use of realism has been a frequent offender against unity of form and idea. For example, the realism that Caravaggio brought to Italian art during the decline of High Renaissance ideal-ism was appropriate for certain subjects, but out of place in the *Sup-per at Emmaus;* it made the incidental properties on the table unduly noticeable, the participants in the drama commonplace, and the pic-ture deficient in spiritual quality. The Christ in particular is poorly conceived compared to Rembrandt's or Da Vinci's Saviors. Caravag-gio's capacity for painting beards, clothes, and wrinkled flesh exactly and his skill in still life was often a drawback. Ingres' photographic realism was an asset in portraiture, but a liability when he attempted a lofty theme, like the *Apotheosis of Homer*, which called for ideal-ism in both conception and execution. Most of the nineteenth-cen-tury academicians flooded the annual exhibitions of the time with pictures of Justice, Truth, Innocence, Hope, Liberty, which were idealistically conceived but photographically rendered. Bougue-reau's *Madonna of Consolation* (Fig. 310) is but one of many ex-amples of incongruity of form to content.

Reynolds, who portrayed admirals and generals superbly, demon-strated an incongruous idealism when he painted children, which he did frequently but with a curious lack of understanding. He in-variably made them sweet and angelic beyond recognition. His *In-fant Samuel, Angel Heads*, and *Age of Innocence* are bad enough, but the *Strawberry Girl* is absolutely insipid. None of them is on a par with the forthright interpretations of childhood by Rubens, Holbein, Hogarth, or Daumier.

Idealism is usually incongruous in the representation of war. Puvis' *La Guerre* (Fig. 317) fails for this reason. Not only is it rendered with classical idealism, but nothing in it suggests the real-ities of actual war. Compared to Goya's *Disasters of War* (Fig. 4) or *Execution of the Madrileños* (Fig. 136), Daumier's *Uprising* (Fig. 316), or Picasso's *Guernica* (Fig. 1), it is a vapid picture, little better than the ordinary wartime poster.

Looking back over the pitfalls that trap artists, it is easy to see that death, mother love, childhood, and war have been perennial obstacles. Others, too, have lured artists into sentimentality, melodrama, mis-placed realism or idealism, and kindred inconsistencies. But diffi-culty does not mean impossibility. Forain's unpretentious little etching of the *Prodigal Son* (Fig. 330) shows that an artist can succeed where others have failed. His theme presented no less difficulty than

Greuze's *Punished Son;* both deal with the return of an errant son under circumstances of stress. Forain might have fallen into the trap of melodrama, sentimentality, and lack of congruity between form and content. But he was drawing not for the public, the critics, or officialdom, but to express something that he genuinely felt. There is nothing pretty about his etching, yet it is moving and effective. The gestures are restrained and true, and demonstrate his sympathy and understanding of human behavior and feelings. He lived among the poor of Paris, as his principal model, Daumier, had done before him. Unlike Greuze, he was schooled in life rather than in an academy, studio, or fashionable salon. He worked not only from the mind but from the heart. Above all, he was an artist in his keen perception of the relationship of form and idea. Compared to Greuze's satin-costumed melodramas, Forain's father and son are poor and rough, the lines of his drawing scratchy, the design utterly simple—and appropriate.

CHAPTER 22

Coordination of Idea and Spatial Design

To be more than accidental, art must be the intended result of design. Since we judge a visual artist's intentions by what he does, design is all-important. It is crucial to expression and accounts for the difference between a dull or a vital presentation of an identical theme. Expression, however, grows out of *what* is represented as well as *how* it is treated. Form has a double role—it satisfies esthetic needs and it expresses emotional attitudes. Having considered esthetic needs, we shall discuss *how* an artist coordinates spatial design and ideas by applying the principles of design to the terms of space for emotional effects.

Communication through works of art—sometimes between artists and observers who are separated by thousands of years of time—is only possible because certain psychological responses have remained relatively constant and can be discussed with a fair chance of agreement. If this were not so, any enduring communication would be impossible. If, for instance, a brilliant red-orange color had a soothing effect upon an ancient Chinese artist instead of the highly stimulating effect it has on us today, there would be no continuing community of ideas on which we could count. But the ancient Chinese reacted to red-orange in about the same way that we do, and much as we do to such elements as line, mass, and texture. In that respect there is a universal basis for visual communication. This predictable response to the various elements in art is exemplified by many familiar works. Our main points of reference will be vitality and repose, just as order and variety were in the study of the esthetic orientation of design. However, we shall find these universals in a unique combination of energy, emotion, idea, and design in each work of art. It is thus that art achieves simultaneously both universality and exactness of meaning.

HARMONY OF ATTITUDE

Estheticians and psychologists agree on the emotional effects produced by different treatments of design. In applying harmony to the possibilities of attitude, an emphasis upon the vertical creates an air of vitality; horizontal lines induce a feeling of repose; and diagonal lines an especially dynamic effect. It is more than an accident that Winslow Homer's vigorous art is characterized by a repeated use of diagonal lines, as in his *Northeaster* (Fig. 18). The same fondness for the diagonal axis is found in the baroque art of the seventeenth and eighteenth centuries. This same dynamic pattern appears in Ribera's *Martyrdom of St. Bartholomew* (Fig. 245), in Rubens' *Rape of the Daughters of Leucippus* (Fig. 216), and in the work of the protobaroque master, Tintoretto (Fig. 254). The emphasis upon vertical members in Gothic architecture gives the feeling of vitality and spiritual aspiration (Fig. 209), whereas the more horizontal lines of a Greek temple with its long, low roof, suggest repose and classic calm.

There is abundant evidence in art criticism that these general responses and their visual causes are commonly recognized. Two examples are Jacopo della Quercia's *Tomb of Ilaria Del Caretto* (Fig. 331) and Bernini's *Saint Lodovica Albertoni* (Fig. 332). Although both these marble statues link a woman with death, the impression they make is quite different. The *Ilaria Del Caretto* is frequently said to illustrate the "sleep of death"; it is reposeful and serene. Bernini's figure, by contrast, conveys a kind of exquisite ecstasy in death—a contradictory pleasure in pain, combining the feeling of vitality and anguish. It is an exciting but disturbing work. Professor Erwin Panofsky has kindly granted me permission to quote excerpts from a letter he wrote me on November 26, 1954. They provide an excellent insight into the meaning of Bernini's statue.

The problem of the Blessed Lodovica degli Albertoni is not so simple. She was born at Rome in 1474 and married a gentleman named Giacomo de Citara, to whom she bore three children. After his death she joined the Third Order of St. Francis and spent the rest of her life as a nun, doing good works and being finally favored with visions and other marks of merit in the eyes of God. She died on January 31, 1533.... There is a short biography in the *Petits Bollandistes*... who normally condense the information contained in the A. S. [Acta Sanctorum] but in this case seem to draw from what you might call unauthorized sources. According to this brief biography, the Blessed Lodovica was stricken with an extremely painful disease in the last seven years of her life which she supported with angelic patience, and the date of her final demise was revealed to her in a vision. So she died at the proclaimed time, clutching a crucifix and saying: "Domine, in manus tuas..." The very existence of Bernini's statue bears out, to some extent, the contention that her cult *was* approved, contrary to the A. S., at about the time stated, and the

FIG. 331. Della Quercia. *Tomb of Ilaria del Caretto. ca.* 1406. Cathedral, Lucca.

FIG. 332. Bernini. *Blessed Lodovica Albertoni.* 1671-1674. Altieri Chapel.
S. Francesco a Ripa. Rome.

report of her painful disease patiently sustained and her ultimate death in spiritual bliss accounts quite nicely for the interpretation of Bernini, who, as you know, always indulged in the Baroque conflict between pleasure and pain and thus managed to endow the Blessed Lodovica with a feeling not dissimilar to that of St. Theresa, only, as it were, with an inverted sign; where St. Theresa suffers mortal pain from the angel's arrow while being transported to the bliss of ecstacy, the Blessed Lodovica experiences supreme joy while suffering the last agony of her disease.

The roles of simple, straight, horizontal lines, and complex patterns of angular, diagonal lines in creating these opposite effects is plain. The personal and historical motivations behind these methods is another matter; so is the reason why we respond to various attitudinal emphases as we do. Let us examine two other typical examples: the Scopasian *Battle of the Greeks and Amazons* in Fig. 333 and Hiroshige's *Cuckoo Flying Through a Storm* (Fig. 334). Two subjects could hardly be more unlike or their artists more widely separated by time, place, and background. Yet they are curiously similar in certain essentials of expression and design. Both subjects are dynamic in character, and this idea is in each case coordinated with an emphasis upon diagonal lines.

Both Hiroshige and the Greek sculptor utilized something fundamental in the visual effect of diagonal lines to convey a sense of intense activity, though their particular subjects differed. They partook of design attributes which are above the time and place of either a Greek or a Japanese and are universal human property. Consequently, either of these active scenes has more in common with the *Lodovica Albertoni* than with any member of the family of reposeful designs exemplified by Quercia's *Ilaria Del Caretto*.

Some of the effects created by these examples are personal and historical in origin. They derive from the personalities of Quercia and Bernini and also from the impact of their times upon them. It is not by chance that the early Renaissance work of Quercia resembles spiritually Fra Angelico's *Annunciation* (Fig. 46), while Bernini's baroque masterpiece is more akin to Tintoretto's late Renaissance *Annunciation* (Fig. 47). The baroque spirit infected both the later men, as it had late Greek sculpture. A kind of baroque spirit recurs in art, and whenever it appears it is marked stylistically by a preference for diagonal attitudes. There is, too, an inclination in the classical mind toward repose which is expressed by a wider use of horizontals. This is apparent in Giorgione's *Sleeping Venus* (Fig. 79) and allies it to the *Ilaria Del Caretto*.

Above these signs of historical fluctuation is the human response to visual stimuli which is as consistent and universal as the nature of

FIG. 333. School of Scopas. *Battle of Greeks and Amazons.* From the frieze of the Mausoleum. 353-340 B.C. Halicarnassus. British Museum, London.

FIG. 334. Hiroshige. *A Cuckoo Flying Through a Storm.* ca. 1850. Museum of Fine Arts, Boston.

perception. Like every other perceptual reaction, it is neither all sensory nor all association but a mixture of the two. The consistency of sensory reaction lies in the fact that the human mind regularly interprets intense orange color as more vital than dull blue, quite apart from any connection it may conceive between the orange color and a brilliant sunset or between blue and the quiet of night. Something of the same process occurs when we perceive lines and masses in various attitudes and shapes. To place our entire stress on either sensory or associative expression would be wrong, for the mind cannot help working synthetically. The different sensory responses of our nervous systems to color and sound and their translation into an opinion of greater or lesser vitality make music and abstract art possible. Yet association of forms and ideas is inherent in our experience with life. Most artists have accepted and exploited this dual psychological reaction by using both abstract and representational means in communicating ideas.

An artist knows that our interpretation of horizontal, diagonal, and vertical attitudes in works of art is constantly conditioned by our experience with reality. The vast plane of the earth's horizon, on land or sea, makes us associate horizontality with an immense stability. Moreover, gravity is constantly forcing every physical form to lie flat and immobile on this plane. Both Quercia's *Ilaria Del Caretto* and Giorgione's *Sleeping Venus* are in artistic accord with this world-wide conception of repose. On the other hand, we subconsciously interpret every instance of verticality as a manifestation of resistance to gravity. We speak of trees as rising and the Eiffel Tower (Fig. 211), Rockefeller Center (Fig. 212), and the vaults of Amiens (Fig. 209) as soaring. More than that, we sense the degree of energy that verticality expresses; we can measure it in the amount of power an airplane needs to ascend steeply or an elevator to reach the top of a skyscraper, and we feel the awesome force that heaved the Alps above the plains. We do not commonly talk about these things, yet they affect our thinking every time we see a horizontal line or its eternal opponent, the vertical line, in nature or in a work of art.

We derive perhaps the greatest sense of vitality from diagonal attitudes, for these suggest the dynamic, unstable movement of a falling tree, the momentum and forward drive of a warrior or a rapidly running man, the ascent or descent of a bird in flight, or a thrown spear. Here, too, the interplay between nature and art greets us at every turn. For if *Menkure and His Queen* (Fig. 160) is the epitome of upright vigor, Daumier's *Burden* (Fig. 161), Sintenis' *Runner* (Fig. 162), Bernini's *Apollo and Daphne* (Fig. 167), the ancient *Battle of Greeks and Amazons,* and Hiroshige's *Cuckoo Flying Through a*

Storm are, thanks to their many diagonal lines, even more active and vital.

There are instances which seem to contradict these principles, such as the *Flying Apsaras* which identifies rapid movement with horizontality, much like a racing car speeding over the ground. But energy is a matter of degree; and it is obvious that an airplane expends more energy ascending than it uses in level flight. So these translations of vertical, diagonal, and horizontal lines into degrees of vitality or repose are valid in most cases.

HARMONY OF MEASURE

As with attitude, our reactions to various harmonies of measure are conditioned by long-standing associations. We subconsciously attribute characteristics of power, durability, and ponderousness to that which, like an elephant, is large and heavy. Conversely, we compare a slender form with things which we know from experience to be agile, graceful, and quick, like the animals in Manship's *Dancer and Gazelles* (Fig. 302) or Renée Sintenis' *Runner* (Fig. 162).

An encyclopedia could be written on our associations with measure. We speak, for instance, of the jolly fat man, like Rubens' *Silenus* (Fig. 318), and of the "lean and hungry look" of Cassius. We insist that the associated quality be what we believe is appropriate to the appearance. There was a time when an operatic soprano could play any role so long as she could sing. But today's audiences, as Deems Taylor has pointed out, will no longer cheerfully tolerate a two-hundred pounder as the consumptive Violetta in *La Traviata*. Theatrical directors must obey the rules of common sense and cast with some respect for connotations of size; artists must paint and carve with a similar regard.

Measure and proportion, as we have seen, are closely allied. The mathematical Greeks were obsessed with the question of proportions. Having worked out pure relationships in that science and given them expression in music and poetry, they discovered the functional basis of proportions in the materials of sculpture and architecture and perfected the relationship of measure and strength. They laid the foundations of proportion which the Occident has followed ever since.

Whole styles depend on a quality of measure. In ways which give us clues to their characters, individual artists and periods choose between the lean and fat, the thick and thin, the powerful and graceful, and reveal themselves through these conceptions of scale. In their best days the Greeks preferred quality to quantity. Their temples are small. Even the Parthenon is not large. The Persian painters were content to work in miniature, aiming at delicacy rather than size. Refinement and finesse are related in our minds to a small or at least not overly assertive scale; the little illumination of a *Polo Game* (Fig. 112) is a typical example.

On the other hand, certain nations have felt compelled to assert their ambitions and will-to-power through their bigness. The Imperial Romans were essentially characterized by a love of gigantism, apparent in the Colosseum (Fig. 207), the Pantheon (Figs. 203-204), and the Pont du Gard (Fig. 206). The Cathedral builders avoided this excess by using slender members, and the early Pyramid builders by sober plainness. But when coupled with heaviness the cult of the colossal betrays vulgarity and uncertainty. Later Egypt, Rome, and the nineteenth-century baroque revivalists could not resist the temptation to impress through size, a tendency that colors our judgment of them. Historically, a people's use of measure may often serve as a measure of the people.

Another aspect of art associated with measure is *monumentality,* a term about which there is considerable disagreement. We are using the term here to mean forms which give an impression of bigness in two ways: the figures or shapes employed are generously proportioned in the relationship of width to height, and convey a sense of grandeur, dignity, and strength. Monumentality is therefore the appropriate physical manifestation of a largeness of conception. The paintings of Giotto, Masaccio, Michelangelo, and Raphael contain such figures (Figs. 133, 306, 126, and 255), for monumentality was a quality which the Renaissance mural painters understood. They worked and thought in large terms, making measure play an important part in the sense of dignity that their frescos convey. By contrast, no one would think of the Persian *Polo Game* as an example of monumentality, despite its exquisite beauty in other respects. In architecture the finest buildings in the Romanesque style exhibit a monumentality hardly inferior to Egyptian art. It is a tribute to Henry Hobson Richardson that, quite apart from accuracy in details, he captured the massiveness of Romanesque design when he revived that style in the nineteenth century. Good revivalism depends upon a perception of some fundamental quality of this sort.

Monumentality is more a matter of large, simple thinking in proportions and surface than of size in measurable feet. A small Romanesque church may be superior in this respect to a Gothic cathedral or to the Paris Opera House, a building which is large without grandeur. On the other hand it is surprising to discover how small Raphael's *School of Athens* (Fig. 104) is, for its simple dignity predisposes us to expect a large picture.

A constant test of monumentality arises from the study of works of art projected on a screen, where they are all equal in size. Separated from their scale relationships with human beings and surrounding objects, some buildings which are actually large appear insignificant, over-elaborate, and finicky. Students frequently ask those who have visited Egypt whether the Pyramids are as imposing as they seem to be in photographs. Fortunately, they are, but disappointments along this line are common. It is therefore to the great credit of Santa Sophia's designers that the actual interior is vaster than one could have ever imagined, as is the enormous nave of St. Peter's (Fig. 85c).

A vivid illustration of this point is Pollaiuolo's *Hercules Strangling Antaeus* (Fig. 64). It drew exclamations of surprise when exhibited in America for the first time, for those who had known it only through photographs and slides had always conceived it to be larger than it actually is. The energy of the struggling pair makes them seem huge. This strongly suggests that each work of art has a spiritual dimension which is more important than any that can be measured in feet or inches.

Harmony of measure is much to the point in Pollaiuolo's group. Recognizing that a struggle is only gripping if it is evenly matched and the outcome in some doubt, he made the opponents equal in size, as did Bellows in his *Stag at Sharkey's* (Fig. 77): Hercules, we remember, won as much by guile and will as he did by muscular strength. One appreciates this aptness all the more when he sees it violently disrupted by a group like Canova's *Hercules Hurling Lycas into the Sea*. Canova, a neo-classicist who forgot common sense in his attempt to outdo the Greeks, made Lycas a pigmy and Hercules a giant; the discrepancy in size and the energy expended by Hercules to throw his tiny foe off the cliff are ludicrous. Neither the neo-classicist nor any other artist can overlook common sense. This is a rather common fault among revivalists, academicians, and other book-bound artists.

One of the chief merits of any harmony is that it extends orderly emphasis throughout a design by repetition. Rubens' *Elevation of the Cross* (Fig. 335) is an admirable example of this procedure. Having decided to express the brutality of the Crucifixion in typical Counter-Reformation fashion, he made the executioners resemble a group of professional wrestlers and then extended this harmony of measure to the figure of Christ. He thus had a logical excuse for the strain exerted by the powerfully muscled soldiers. The total effect is as dynamic as it is orderly. The picture is an excellent instance of the baroque use of diagonal attitudes for vigor of expression.

FIG. 335. Rubens. *Elevation of the Cross.*
1610-1611. Cathedral, Antwerp.

FIG. 336. *Winged Deity.* Reign of
Ashur-nasir-pal II, 885-860 B.C.
Bowdoin College Museum of Fine Arts,
Brunswick, Me.

FIG. 337. *Kali.* (Karaikkal-Ammaiyar.)
Late medieval period, A.D. 850-1200.
Nelson Gallery and Atkins Museum,
Kansas City, Mo.

691

Harmony of idea and harmony of measure are similarly united in the Chinese *Sakyamuni* and *Prabhutaratna* in Fig. 172. The bodies of these two conversing holy men are as light as their agile thoughts. Every part of the design is delicate and fragile. The physical is played down here as strongly as it is stressed in Rubens' *Elevation of the Cross*. Quite different are the Egyptian *Menkure and His Queen* (Fig. 160), Daumier's *Burden* (Fig. 161), Millet's *Gleaners* (Fig. 225), and Degas' *Laundresses* (Fig. 44), all of which combine robust physiques with connotations of confidence, strength, or durability.

Harmony of measure is often a prominent expressive element in the styles of individual artists. Not all artists, of course, exhibit strong preferences of measure; Rembrandt and Van Gogh, to mention only two, were open-minded on this score. Others, however, among them Rubens, della Quercia, Bruegel, Giotto, Masaccio, Michelangelo, Tintoretto, Millet, Maillol, Renoir, and Gauguin, made effective use of this principle. The typical human figures of each of these men express a high regard for the sturdy, healthy, and strong.

The size-conscious masters seem to have leaned toward robustness, probably because of its implications of vitality. The great exception was El Greco. His primary concern with spiritual values and almost antiphysical ideas led him to create a gallery of lean and nervous religious figures. He did this consistently in the construction of every picture. His *Agony in the Garden* (Fig. 90) shows how unerring and expressive was his sense of measure relationships.

While a harmony of measure strikes us forcibly in a composition of numerous figures, it is no less effective and expressive in relating the parts of single figures. The *Winged Deity* in Fig. 336 illustrates this in several ways. Each part of the design is characterized by largeness of size and feeling, with the result that the parts "go together." It has unity of context—a harmony of measure governed by a single idea. This ponderous, muscle-bound giant expresses through its hugeness an idea which obsessed the ruthless, warlike Assyrians. Politically, socially, and militarily they worshipped brute force. In this figure they pursued that quality to the verge of caricature—which, oddly enough, is a virtue; it is a perfect expression of their coarseness.

Far more sensitively rendered, and quite opposite in character, is the small bronze figure *Kali* (Fig. 337) now in the Nelson Gallery at Kansas City and rightly acclaimed as a masterpiece of Asiatic Indian sculpture. Kali, the patron deity of the murderous Thugs, stood for evil in the Indian mind. It is therefore interesting to note how the Indians, to whom starvation was an ever-present specter, identified emaciation with moral and spiritual viciousness. Their success in making this symbol of malevolence ugly in every sense of the word negates beauty, but it also exalts artistry.

Large figures can be equated with power, very thin figures with privation, with strength and weakness, and with sturdiness and delicacy. A third corner of this triangle is occupied by the numerous figures which stand for health and vitality, if not necessarily for physical power. This is especially true when the figures are feminine. Characteristically they are full-bodied and active rather than slender or elegant. One thinks immediately of the women of Rubens and Titian. But no less representative are the female types of Maillol and Renoir, whose every limb is sturdy and full of life.

No discussion of the expressive powers of measure would be complete without some mention of architecture. Two noted and contrasting examples can speak for the field, epitomizing, as they do, the use of the consistently heavy and consistently light. They are the famous St. John's Chapel (Fig. 338) in the Tower of London and the still more famous Sainte Chapelle (Fig. 339) in Paris. The one is a beautifully consistent example of Norman Romanesque design, the other a masterpiece of Gothic architecture. Each is from the finest century of those styles. Inasmuch as the simple, massive, enclosed character of the Norman monument is as apparent as the complex, delicate, open Gothic style, with walls emphasized in one case and windows in the other, one may turn at once to the reasons behind such structural divergence. Without going into the intricate details of medieval history, one can find the answers in the contrast between the aggressive but insecure outlook of the Norman barons who had conquered England only fifteen years before the St. John's Chapel was built, and the enviable position of the French builders who knew one of those brief moments of optimism and confidence occasionally granted to man. Each of these buildings speaks eloquently of the emotional needs of its creators—the craving of the militant Normans for the reassurance of physical strength, and the urge of the Gothic peoples to express their exaltation in slender, soaring forms.

Systems of design are related in architecture to structural techniques and practical functions. Yet, while influenced by these utilitarian considerations, architectural expression is above them. It is a truism that most architectural supports are stronger than they need be; in Egyptian architecture this is the case several times over. If the Normans expanded their columns and thickened their walls while the Gothic engineers narrowed their pillars to a dangerous degree, these extra moves were dictated by expressive rather than practical motives. Though the language of architecture is abstract, it is no less ex-

FIG. 338. St. John's Chapel. *ca.* 1080-1085. Tower of London.

FIG. 339. Ste. Chapelle. Dedicated 1248. Paris.

pressive of ideas and emotions than the language of painting or sculpture.

HARMONY OF SHAPE

A harmony or emphasis of shape in design is an important means of expression. Innumerable ideas and feelings are associated with shape. We ordinarily connect curved forms with grace, flexibility, suppleness, femininity, and flowing movement. Only when combined with large-scale and heavy proportions does the round form suggest massive strength or power. By contrast, straight lines and angular forms connote harshness, austerity, strength, and masculinity. Since the straight always implies a flat plane with sharp edges it is psychologically definite, and somewhat cold. Some indication of this coldness is found in architecture. Buildings are made predominantly rectilinear for structural reasons, and architects are constantly seeking ways to relieve the severity of the straight lines and right angles of doors and windows, cross-members and supports. The long subtle curve introduced into the columns of the Greek Doric order was an inspired source of graceful beauty.

The arc of curvature and the type of angle employed with straight lines and planes are important in achieving any desired effect. The long, flat curves of the *Flying Apsaras* in Fig. 171 are ideally suited to the feeling of easy movement that it conveys, whereas the same curves in tighter arcs endow the wind-god screens of the Japanese artist Sotatsu with an air of turbulent activity, as they were intended to do. An artist who can anticipate the usual effect of right, acute, and obtuse angles commands a valuable means of controlling communication. Like a Maupassant who picks the *mot juste* unerringly, or a concert pianist who knows precisely what tones every key and chord will produce, he is exploiting something predictable in the language of the visual arts. He knows, for instance, that we normally interpret a right angle as emotionally austere, formal, and static; that the usual effect of an acute angle is harsh, active, and sharp, like the point of an arrow; and that the obtuse angle is opposite, being, like a gradation, active in a slow way.

The spectator, for his part, is conditioned to respond appropriately by life-long associations of ideas with shapes. He immediately thinks of curved or straight lines when certain types are mentioned, such as fat men, lean men, and feminine and masculine bodies. Furthermore, we associate shapes with long-time occupations. Shape, unlike attitude, develops slowly in an individual, but identifies his mode of life. The huge roundness of the professional wrestler is an example; so too is the tall angularity of the basketball player. An even better example of this specialization is found in the hunched-over, gorilla-like physiques of Meunier's returning miners (Fig. 231); occupation shaped these men's bodies with the finality of a metal mold. We also connect shapes with various stages of life when we think of the rotund bodies of babies and the spare, stringy bodies of old age. The artist can use an understanding of these facts of life to express in orderly fashion almost any idea or shade of idea that can be conveyed by shape.

Artists have frequently repeated a preferred kind of shape until it has become a personal signature. Rubens and Renoir are famous for their love of round forms, as Frank Lloyd Wright is noted for his use of right and obtuse angles, the low roofs of his early "prairie style" houses being a well-known example. Even more distinctive in this respect is Mondrian. So addicted to the rectilinear was he that he barred curved lines from his studio and living quarters, admitting clocks and phonograph records only of necessity.

Sometimes a whole period will make a shape the hallmark of its stylistic concept. This was true of the eighteenth-century rococo—a style devoted to elegance and grace. No matter how much fun Hogarth poked at the French mannerisms of his day, he unwittingly echoed them in his art and in his esthetic theories. In contradistinction to Mondrian, he decreed a long, spiraling curve to be the true "line of beauty." The Baroque period's regard for round shapes, as well as large forms and diagonal attitudes, hardly needs to be mentioned.

Occasionally a nation will manifest a recurrent or almost continuous liking for one kind of shape and employ it with remarkable consistency. The history of Japanese domestic architecture is a prominent example of loyalty to the most austere possible arrangement of straight lines and right angles. In this one aspect at least the architecture of the medieval Sanjo Palace (Fig. 322-b) is the same as the background of Hiroshige's nineteenth-century street scene in Fig. 115. The Japanese combination of fanaticism and feudal conservatism is apparent.

Few nations have excelled the Japanese in the calculated use of shape-character for esthetic and expressive purposes. Their orderliness is world-famous and their command over the emotional implications of design deserves to be, for one could easily illustrate a book on either subject with a selection of Japanese prints. Two of them will show how effectively the Japanese related form and idea. Shunsho's *Woman in a Pink Dress* (Fig. 340) is one of many that he made of reigning beauties for a Japanese public which was not less appreciative than other peoples of feminine pulchritude and ap-

FIG. 340. Shunsho. *Woman in a Pink Dress. ca.* 1775. Museum of Fine Arts, Boston.

FIG. 341. Shunsho. *Ichikawa Danjuro V as Kudo Suketsune. ca.* 1770. Museum of Fine Arts, Boston.

697

plauded such pictures. They also demanded of them a summing up of female virtues beyond facial beauty alone—charm, grace, modesty, courtesy, and social talent. In reply to this general expectation, Shunsho employed fluid curvilinear lines throughout, using design to confirm idea.

When Shunsho turned to the masculine field he was like a pianist who shifts from a nocturne to a march with equal facility. Since the Japanese ideal of manhood contrasts sharply with its ideal of femininity, Shunsho altered his means accordingly, changing from an emphasis upon sweeping curves to a drastic stressing of angularity. In the print illustrated in Fig. 341, the actor Ichikawa Danjuro V is represented as he appeared in the role of Kudo Suketsune, a medieval warrior who became legendary for the fanatical spirit he displayed in the story of the Sogo brothers' revenge. Danjuro's theatrical interpretation was noted for its fierceness; Shunsho tried to capture this quality in his print, and succeeded by his coordination of shape and idea. To our eyes such an insistent use of design approaches caricature, but Suketsune's scowl is not intentionally comical; its maniacal fanaticism had a basis in reality and is as true as it is expressive. A national favorite, the story of the Sogo brothers' revenge was dramatized every New Year's day for over three hundred years.

Shunsho's contrasting prints are a good illustration of the duality of perception; their appeal is neither entirely associational nor wholly sensory, but a combination of both. Longstanding ideals of womanhood and manhood which enjoy more or less universal validity cause us to interpret the one as an example of harmony and the other of force, and to regard the curvilinear and angular treatments as appropriate to these conceptions. But in addition, the mechanical aspects of perception influence our reactions. Our eyes do not read flowing lines in a continuous fashion or right angles along an angular path. Ocular photography reveals that they proceed, instead, in a series of fixations. Yet, as Stephen Pepper has asserted, flowing curves permit a *comparatively* smooth reading, while angular lines cause a jerkier one. The difference in the sensations is translated by the mind into different kinds of action and degrees of vitality.

On the basis of this fact, abstract artists claim that arrangements of lines and forms can express pure vitality or repose and suggest universal attributes of reality without any need for representation. Psychologically, they are perfectly correct about the direct appeal of various abstract shapes, as a glance at Mondrian's *Composition in White, Black, and Red* (Fig. 55) and Arp's *Configurations* (Fig. 229) will show; the observant viewer will not miss, either, the membership of both prints and abstractions in the two universal families of shape-character. The non-objectivists are also right in insisting upon the profound suggestiveness of common shapes; witness the living quality of Muir's *Growth* (Fig. 186).

The continuous factor in this interpretative process stems from the consistency of the human perceptual system. Since the human eye will always read, and the mind interpret, angular designs in the same way, our main impression of the Danjuro portrait must resemble our reaction to the severely angular Pyramid of Khufu (Fig. 174a). If, to put it another way, the tomb of Khufu were domical, it would bear no similarity to the Danjuro print, either physically or spiritually. In short, design governs the conception of idea and content that we derive from any work of art. This is true whether the means are purely abstract or partly representational.

The representational arts may lean more heavily on the associational character of shape meanings, while the abstract arts must rely on an appeal which appears more direct, immediate, and free. But both kinds of appeal act in concert in the long run, for the human mind will not let the Pyramid remain only a set of angles, lines, and planes, but reads innumerable connotations into its design. Artists have known this for centuries whenever they consulted their own perceptual natures, instead of an extremist theory, and have exploited these mental tendencies thoroughly and often.

HARMONY OF SURFACE

The average viewer quickly notices the pattern of angular shapes in Shunsho's *Danjuro V* and the Great Pyramid of Khufu, but observes their surfaces only secondarily. Yet the surfaces employed in the visual arts are capable of contributing greatly to their meanings. Cézanne was aware of this when he painted such pictures as his *Vase of Tulips* (Fig. 15), *Forest of Fontainebleau* (Fig. 39), and *House in Provence* (Fig. 80). By treating the surface in a uniform manner throughout the canvas, he unified the picture area; at the same time he expressed the exact nature and vitality of his temperament through the character of his vigorous, sketchy brushwork. His dynamic contemporary, Van Gogh, is even more renowned for the forceful way in which he handled the oil medium. Also significant as a general factor is the contribution of surface to harmony: while lines and forms tend to compartment and subdivide a work of art, the comprehensive nature of surface tends to unify it. If, in addition, various treatments of surface can be made to express ideas, concepts, and emotional attitudes, they become a valuable means indeed.

Some of the principal types of surface are the smooth and round mass in Arp's *Configurations*; the smooth, flat, sharp-edge plane, as in Skidmore, Owings, and Merrill's projected New York University—Bellevue Hospital Medical Center; surfaces broken in uniform contrasts, as in Bourdelle's *Beethoven*; surfaces pitted or painted with dots so as to present a soft texture, as in Seurat's *Sunday on the Island of La Grande Jatte*; and surfaces painted with a heavy impasto, as in Rouault's *Old King*. The surfaces of the last two are as different as sandpaper and roughly trowelled stucco. A painter achieves the trowelled textural effect by using a heavy bristle brush or, as Courbet frequently did, a palette knife; Van Gogh's work is a striking combination of both procedures. In addition, some surfaces are made distinctive by the linear treatment given them. The Strozzi Palace exemplifies the exploitation of functional mortar lines to create a heavy surface in keeping with the building's geometric massiveness. A similar exploitation of surface is found in the finer-grained but equally effective brickwork of Wright's Johnson Wax Company Administration Building (Fig. 86a), where surface is allied to a horizontal emphasis of the mortar lines to give a streamlined appearance. Graphic artists create the illusion of various surface textures by their manipulation of lithograph pencils and etching needles, handling them at one time smoothly and carefully, at other times vigorously.

If order alone were involved, it would not matter what type of surface a designer employed. Any texture will give unity so long as it is used consistently, but the smooth varies widely from the rough in its expressive properties. Smoothness implies repose, harmony of spirit, restraint, or vitality under control; roughness suggests a contrasting vigor, agitation, or wildness. The difference can be illustrated by a calm, mirror-like lake and the same body of water lashed by a storm; by one of Monet's lily ponds and the same artist's *Marée Montante à Pourville;* or by the suave, icy calm of the Egyptian Priest in Fig. 163 and the stormy personality of Bourdelle's *Beethoven* (Fig. 164).

Few other means of expression are capable of greater eloquence than the surface handling of the medium. It reveals precisely the personality of the artist and is as autographic as his signature. Morelli, a distinguished Italian critic of a few years ago, made a strong point of this fact when he showed how Titian and others impressed their personalities upon a composition and every detail within it by the quality of their brushwork. The detail of a head from Veronese's *Family of Darius Before Alexander* (Fig. 228) proclaims Veronese's unique personal touch in every inch of the surface. In some cases, however, autographic handling becomes an overriding factor, especially when it stems from a powerful personality like that of Vincent Van Gogh. Individuality of treatment then becomes the dominant quality in the work of art, with surface playing a prominent role.

Outstanding illustrations of harmony of surface are the smooth surfaces of the meditating *Lohan* in Fig. 3, the ancient *Governor of Lagash* in Fig. 67, and Maillol's *Female Torso* in Fig. 5. The surface character of each is exactly right for its serenity, poise, and flowing vitality. No less apt are the rougher surfaces of Rodin's *Aged Courtesan* (Fig. 6), Rouault's tensely vicious *Old King* (Fig. 227), Lautrec's rowdy, sordid *At the Moulin de la Galette* (Fig. 40), or Hogarth's effervescent *Shrimp Girl* (Fig. 301). The sketchy vigor of Hogarth's picture surface is as perfect for it as a smooth rendering is for Giorgione's *Sleeping Venus* and Van der Weyden's sedate lady (Fig. 297). Both of these examples exhibit not only esthetically valuable harmony of surface, but also harmony of form and idea. The degree of smoothness or roughness is not important, but the coordination of theme and treatment is. Another excellent demonstration of this principle is the contrast between Bellows' *Stag at Sharkeys* (Fig. 77), whose turbulent air is underscored by its dynamic brushwork, and Eakins' *Between Rounds* (Fig. 78), whose quieter mood is echoed by a smoother technique.

Yet accord between harmony of surface and idea is not to be assumed. The nineteenth-century academicians were more concerned with illusionistic representation than with either pictorial unity or expression. They repeatedly created variegated surfaces which are doubly at fault in having neither unity nor aptness. Meissonier, Bouguereau, Bonheur, and many others were insensitive on this score; even Delacroix erred when he applied a smooth brush to his onrushing *Liberty Leading the People* (Fig. 315). This inappropriate manner of painting was one of the indiscriminate traits he inherited from the statue-loving Neoclassicists and later outgrew. More appropriate for a dynamic theme is the freer, rougher, surface of Daumier's *Uprising* (Fig. 316). Goya knew when to be rough and vehement (as in the *Disasters of War*) and when to be smoothly persuasive (*The Nude Maja*), but Puvis de Chauvannes did not. That is one of the reasons why his *La Guerre* (Fig. 317) seems frozen and unconvincing.

Like the academicians who were its guide, the nineteenth-century public was often impervious to the implications of surface and misconstrued many an excellent and deliberate use of rough technique. Millet's *Gleaners* (Fig. 225) was denounced as a repulsive representation of the "Three Fates of Poverty" without any heed for

FIG. 342. *Horse*. Late archaic period, 550-480 B.C. Metropolitan Museum of Art, New York.

FIG. 343. Barye. *Prancing Horse. ca.* 1850. Metropolitan Museum of Art, New York.

FIG. 344. Ghirlandaio. *Old Man and a Boy. ca.* 1490. Louvre, Paris.

FIG. 345. Hals. *The Rommelpot Player. ca.* 1623-1625. Art Institute of Chicago.

702

the suitability of his technique to scenes of rural life. The same insensitivity to design also made Meunier's rough but accurate interpretations of industrial life misunderstood until near the end of his career. If we have recovered from this blindness, we owe a debt to the pioneers of modern art, who strove to reopen our eyes to esthetic values.

The *Horse* in Fig. 342, one of the favorite treasures in the Metropolitan Museum of Art, owes much of its popularity to its smooth surface, which together with the flowing, curvilinear lines expresses the kind of controlled vitality that the Greeks admired. It is a vivid impression of a strong but disciplined chariot horse. Now look at Barye's *Prancing Horse* (Fig. 343). Here is wild unbridled freedom, alive and bursting with energy. The difference is not only in the more agitated posture and undulating outlines, but in a consistently nervous, broken treatment of surface. The two figures are a striking contrast between the civilized and the untamed, with each a masterpiece in its unique, consistent way.

The two horses speak for the classical Greek and nineteenth-century Romanticist; equally varied are Ghirlandaio's Italian Renaissance *Old Man and a Boy* (Fig. 344) and Hals's *Rommelpot Player* (Fig. 345). One is typical of Florentine sensitivity and aristocracy prior to the ruin of Italy by invasion and religious strife; the other is characteristic of the Baroque genius for genre scenes, a field in which Frans Hals excelled. Each is an admirable spokesman for benevolent love, but in quite different ways. The old man and boy look at each other in a sensitive and dignified manner, and are imbued with a sense of peace and grace. The Rommelpot player is a diamond-in-the-rough who tramps the streets, where he amuses everyone and is loved by all. The looks of affection that the children bestow upon him are transcendent. The smooth treatment of Ghirlandaio's picture is ideal for its meaning as Hals's crisper, more vibrant brushstrokes are for his. Manners of execution are powerful factors in determining the impression a work of art makes upon us. Imagine the technique of one being exchanged for the other without radically altering its meaning.

What would happen is seen in two contrasting representations of lion hunts by Delacroix (Fig. 346) and Vernet (Fig. 347). After Delacroix had outgrown his neo-classic training under Guérin, he developed a style which expressed his forceful outlook brilliantly. Intense, broken colors, dynamic arrangements of diagonal attitudes, rapidly curving lines, and a vivacious surface went hand-in-hand with spectacular and often violent themes. Material for the latter was added to his sensational medieval lore when he journeyed to Morocco

FIG. 346. Delacroix. *Lion Hunt*. 1834. Art Institute of Chicago.

FIG. 347. Horace Vernet. *Lion Hunt*. 1838. Wallace Collection, London.

in 1832 with the French minister, Mornay. Always alert to colorful action, and a great lover of cats, Delacroix was fascinated by the combats between mounted horsemen and wild lions. Soon after, with the animal hunts of Rubens as a precedent, he launched a series of studies devoted to this theme, among which the Chicago Art Institute version is outstanding, partly because of Delacroix's reinforcement of this vital scene with a vigorous manner of execution. Treatment of surface makes it superior to any photograph of a similar scene.

It was this important factor of surface treatment that Vernet missed when he rode on the wave of Orientalism which had been started by Delacroix's African subjects. His picture, though less skilfully composed, contains the same elements and dramatic entities. Yet the result does not differ markedly from a photograph, and might easily be mistaken for one. It has the same clarity of outline and detail that the camera records but the human eye misses, and like many photographs, appears static and frozen. Expressive harmony of surface is not to be taken for granted. Delacroix sensed the importance of such factors, Vernet did not.

A difference in the treatment of textures often marks the painting of a single artist as he shifts from subject to subject, especially when he makes a preparatory sketch before completing a picture. This is particularly true of Constable, whose oil study for the *Haywain* is seen in Fig. 348 and the final version in Fig. 349. Free as is the handling in the completed picture, the sketch's surface is still more vigorous and spontaneous. An artist tends to develop a picture from a simply blocked-out study of the general composition to a more complete and detailed representation. He finally favors a more heterogeneous, individualized image over a simpler, more unified preliminary sketch.

Lionelli Venturi observed that this greater completeness is not an improvement and is probably artistically inferior. Two important aspects of art—expression and design—have been reduced in effectiveness for the sake of one—representation. The sketch in Fig. 348 is sufficiently completed; the final picture merely possesses an added "finish." The loss is greater than the gain; the sketch for the *Haywain* has a greater unity of surface, a more vital quality than the official version. What was alive and vibrant in one is quiet and tame in the other.

Constable's oil and watercolor sketches are highly prized by many connoisseurs who feel that they are frequently superior to his completed pictures. This attitude does not apply to his art alone. Collectors often prefer drawings, sketches, and studies to carefully

FIG. 348. Constable.
*Oil Study for "The
Haywain."* 1821.
Victoria and Albert
Museum, London.

FIG. 349. Constable.
The Haywain. 1821.
National Gallery, London.

FIG. 350. Courbet. *Winter.*
ca. 1860. Museum of Fine Arts,
Boston.

706

finished oil paintings because they retain the vigor and unity often lost in the final version.

An outstanding master of harmony of surface and idea was Courbet, an artist who will be more accurately appreciated in the future for his artistic ability. Much of his fame is still due to the notoriety created by his colorful and aggressive personality. Beneath his coarse antics and bragging, Courbet was an artist and had the artist's feeling for color, light, and shadow. Above all he was extremely sensitive to texture. He exploited this sensitivity, abiding by a theory which he practiced as well as preached. He painted as often as possible directly from nature, in the Forest of Fontainebleau, beside the Seine, and along the coast of Normandy. In that way, he claimed, he could set on canvas his impressions of natural qualities—the bark of a tree, the cold lushness of snow, the carpet-like verdure of grass, the hard mass and rough surface of rocks, and the sheen of water—with a maximum of intensity, directness, and clarity. He urged others, like Monet, to objectify sensations in the same way while they were still strong. Although regarded as an uncivilized boor in his own day—he recommended that museums be destroyed so that artists would be forced to see things with new eyes—his ideas undoubtedly had a strong influence on the young Impressionists who were striving for the same intensity of vision.

In addition to working out-of-doors much more than the old masters ever did, Courbet sought to convey his sensations of texture to the fullest extent by recreating the physical as well as the visual quality of matter on his canvas. His method was to use a palette knife to spread pigment on more thickly than can be done with brushes. In this way he built up layers, called *impastos,* which have the feeling of actual substance. This is something quite different from painting the appearance of a rock in a strictly visual, luministic fashion; and though today his method is widely used and taken for granted, it was an innovation in Courbet's time. He was an outstanding master in the realm of surface organization.

These qualities are borne out by his *Winter* (Fig. 350), a small but vigorously executed picture in the Museum of Fine Arts, Boston. It depicts a woodland scene in the dead of winter, probably in the Forest of Fontainebleau. The trees are bare, the colors dull, the rocks hard, and the snow deep, wet, and cold—an altogether bleak and lonely scene, but one painted with a sharp sense of appropriateness. Courbet was at his best here. Forgetting socialistic theories, he concentrated his keen senses on conveying an intense feeling of the natural matter, masses, and textures of a forest in winter. Yet his picture is much more than a fine example of representation. It expresses a profound sense of mood, an intense response of the tactile senses, an esthetically unified surface, and a harmony of rough, heavy pigmentation which is wholly appropriate to the scene. Courbet sometimes painted smoothly; it is his shrewd knowledge of *when* to paint roughly that is demonstrated in this distinguished example of the expressive use of harmony of surface.

SEQUENCE OF CONTINUITY, GRADATION, ALTERNATION

The typical plan of the Early Christian basilica illustrates a sequential arrangement in which form and purpose were closely allied. On the front of the church was a façade whose entrances were designed to attract people into the church. Within were, in order, a courtyard for the unbaptized and uninitiated, a nave and side aisles for the congregation, a transept and choir for the officiating clergy, and an apse and altar for the climactic features of the service. In other words, the architectural setting for a series of carefully graded ideas.

Sequence as an expressive means relies in several ways upon some such continuity. Both form and idea may express continuity with little or no change; this is order carried to a monotonous degree. They may express the opposite extreme, a variety in which only a slight thread of continuity gives a minimum of order. Again, they may be characterized by a slow but steady change, or gradation. Finally, they may present an alternation, or repeated change of elements. Extreme variety and alternation create an impression of marked vitality; extreme order and gradation suggest repose, stately order, or some similar condition. The principle is simple: great variety and rapid change will stand for vitality; uniformity or slow change will express repose.

Let us consider four outstanding examples of sequence which demonstrate the relationship between variety and vitality. We shall see that vitality increases with variety, but order decreases. It is a seesaw, or gain-and-loss principle.

Look first at the Byzantine mosaic of *Virgins Bearing Their Crowns to the Virgin* (Fig. 352). This procession expresses a basic belief of the collective-minded, authoritarian Byzantine clergy that order should be paramount. It is carried here to the point of monotony by the simple device of repeating a harmony of every spatial term— attitude, interval, measure, shape, and surface, and each of the terms of color. The result is dignity, stateliness, and undeviating regimentation. This type of organization is a close order or military forma-

FIG. 351. Rubens.
La Ronda. 1636-1640.
Padro, Madrid.

FIG. 352. *Virgins Bearing
Their Crowns to the
Virgin.* 6th century A.D.
S. Apollinare Nuovo,
Ravenna.

FIG. 353. Van Gogh. *Courtyard of a
Prison.* "The Round of Prisoners."
February, 1890. Museum of Modern
Art, Moscow.

tion. It is not accidental that the same air of order is found in the Mycenaen *Warrior Vase* in Fig. 230. They too are as alike as six beads on a string.

From the psychological principle of predictable response we know that similar forms produce similar reactions. Any procession which is pervaded by uniformity and a suppression of variety will resemble both the *Virgins* and the *Warriors*. As variety is increased, so also is a sense of freedom and informality. Any loose order of marching men is an example. We find an excellent one in Meunier's *Return of the Miners* (Fig. 231). His workmen are trudging toward the pit in a free and casual manner. And though their air of boredom hardly suggests vitality, it is, compared to the *Virgins* or *Warriors*, individualized and unregimented.

Somewhat higher on the scale is the frieze of the Parthenon (Figs. 268 and 321). Its renown is due in no small measure to a balance between continuity and variety and a commensurate handling of forms throughout its length. The majority of figures proceeds toward the climactic presentation with dignity and grace, but wherever monotony threatened, one or two figures were faced backwards for the sake of variety, as in Fig. 321. The Parthenon frieze earned its fame by avoiding monotony and punctuating order with variety. Quite different from the *Virgins* and *Warriors* are Michelangelo's "Bathing Soldiers Surprised" (Fig. 268) and Rubens' *La Ronda* (Fig. 351), the latter one of the most vital pictures in Western art. Michelangelo's group of bathers shows the continuity of any mass of men, but their attitudes are varied. Unlike the Mycenaean warriors or Meunier's returning miners, these soldiers are off-duty, actively exercising, and abruptly surprised. The combination of circumstances makes them spring to action in a purposeful but as yet disorganized manner—a situation which Michelangelo has represented with keen understanding and high art. Rubens' *La Ronda* is an even more vital picture because his figures are still more active. They are engaged in the wild kissing and dancing game with which the Flemish peasants celebrated the end of the harvest. With work over, they indulged in what is known as a Kermesse, probably enlivened by some well-earned alcoholic animation. It was a scene which Rubens knew well, for after he retired from Antwerp to the Château de Steen (see Fig. 83), he hired peasants like these to tend his fields. At the height of his robust powers, he was able to capture superbly the fun-loving spirit of the ronda. His method, as can easily be seen, was to introduce a great variety of attitudes and other terms into the loosely continuous circle. The result was a maximum of vitality with a semblance of order. Life, vigor, and enthusiasm are the key-notes which Rubens expressed with a master's feeling for means and ends.

The same genius was used by Van Gogh to create a picture which is, expressively, almost the opposite of Rubens' *La Ronda* (Fig. 351). Called variously the *Courtyard of a Prison* (Fig. 353) and the *Round of Prisoners*, it was suggested by one of Gustave Doré's social engravings, though deeply felt by Van Gogh himself. It depicts a circle of prison inmates getting their daily exercise. They trudge around and around an endless circle, going nowhere save to repeat their own tracks. Their bent-over bodies and dull faces are stamped with monotony and hopelessness. Their trapped, treadmill condition could not be more unlike the free, out-of-door celebration of Rubens' peasants. To emphasize that idea, Van Gogh placed his prisoners at the bottom of a well-like courtyard. Its thick, sheer walls make freedom seem remote, escape impossible; it encircles and hems them in spiritually as well as physically. Van Gogh added to the monotony of the procession by compressing the prisoners' route into a futile circle. He thereby achieved an effect of deadly, depressing social boredom. It seems superfluous to mention the aptness of his rough handling of surface texture. All in all, the picture is a powerful example of coordination of ideas and execution.

The Scopasian *Battle of Greeks and Amazons* in Fig. 333 is a good illustration of alternation for expressive purposes. It is, as we have mentioned, a vital example of a harmony of diagonal attitudes which is effective in both its orderly and expressive aspects. Alternation contributes to the idea of conflict implicit in the battle scene; this is most apparent in the alternation of directions which characterizes the design. Through repetition the vehement vigor of many face-to-face combats was built up and intensified throughout the frieze. When one dynamic means (alternation) is joined to another (diagonal attitudes), the effect of vitality is increased.

For gradation of form and idea, turn to Rodin's *Age of Bronze* (Fig. 169), a statue whose philosophical idea is not apparent on first sight. In this figure Rodin, a lover of universal themes, symbolized the slow spiritual, physical, and intellectual awakening of man during the Bronze Age. The figure appears to be emerging from a dream or trance, his body magnificently developed, but his mind still sluggishly groping. Once that idea is grasped, the propriety of Rodin's design can be appreciated. He posed the body in a slowly turning spiral which expresses the concept of an unfolding or birth from the bottom of the toes to the top of the upraised arms. Far more than comparable examples of realistic representation, Rodin's *Age of Bronze* is subtle, profound, and eloquent, a perfect instance of how gradation of form and idea can work together.

AXIAL AND OCCULT BALANCE

An artist who does not wish to resort to sequence to give vitality or repose to an idea can use balance. This method probably has no superior in the expression of vitality or repose with a minimum of means.

As a rule, an obvious balance or symmetry will excel in the expression of repose and an occult, asymmetrical balance in vitality. Similarly, an occult central balance, like the Chinese mirror (Fig. 252) in which a dragon chases its tail around a circle, will suggest a high degree of energy. These general truths are subject to qualification according to whether the figures in the design imply dynamic or static conditions, for circumstances alter cases. One example which seems to upset the rule is the bronze Chinese ritual vessel in Fig. 243. Although symmetrically balanced, its design has great vitality. This is due to the amount of contrast and variety introduced into the different measures, positions, and shapes of the formal elements. Variety is a factor which can never be discounted. Here, as elsewhere, every design must be weighed individually. Nevertheless, there are compositional arrangements which almost always produce a high degree of vitality or repose.

Every noted work of art ultimately owes its fame to the way in which it exemplifies esthetic and expressive principles; that is why it endures. The famous Harbaville Triptych (Fig. 354) in the Louvre is an example. The average visitor knows little of its history, but he can appreciate with his own eyes the perfection with which it illustrates an obvious axial balance. The symmetry could hardly be more absolute or its elements more completely static. The use of balance instead of the sequential movement of a procession gives this design an even greater stability than that of the *Virgins Bearing Their Crowns to the Virgin*. In terms of energy, it expresses complete repose.

Apart from the difference between repose and slight movement, there is an emphasis on stability running through all Byzantine and Byzantine-inspired compositions. It is prominent in the *Crucifixion* at Daphni (Fig. 87), the *Justinian and Courtiers* (Fig. 121), and Cimabue's *Madonna Enthroned* (Fig. 244). Very likely, this air of confident authority was deliberately sought by the Byzantine artists when the rest of Europe was plunging into chaos, and their apparent

FIG. 354. Harbaville Triptych. 10th century. Louvre, Paris.

FIG. 355. Botticelli. *The Last Communion of St. Jerome. ca.* 1490-1495. Metropolitan Museum of Art, New York.

FIG. 356. Studio of Phidias. *Lapith Fighting a Centaur.* Metope from the Parthenon. 447-432 B.C. British Museum, London.

rigidity was the result of sophisticated intention. In any event, their mastery of balance is unquestioned.

Vitality has been so prized in human history that its exponents have greatly outnumbered those of repose. Basically vitality comes from the use of asymmetrical balances in concert with dynamic, action-implying ideas. If great vitality is wanted, contrast, variety, and conflict will be injected into the visual elements at every opportunity. This principle can be discerned in the frantic melee of Bellows' *Stag at Sharkey's*. It also applies in a quieter way to Botticelli's *Last Communion of St. Jerome* (Fig. 355). Though far removed from a pugilistic brawl, it too is a dramatic scene in which something crucial is happening. The protagonists sense and express a crisis as they solicitously lean toward the dying saint. Botticelli makes us feel the mood of the event by the way he underscores a balance of opposing diagonals in the divergent palm branches, the slanting lines of the room, and the inward leaning figures.

Botticelli's small panel is a choice example of a coming together of human spirits, with the idea stressed by a balancing of active attitudes. The celebrated Parthenon metope of a *Lapith Fighting a Centaur* (Fig. 356) is the same idea in reverse, with struggle and conflict the dominant content. One is eagerly convergent, the other violently divergent. The means used to heighten the sense of combat are also opposite. The term *dynamic equilibrium* has been suggested to describe this stalemated struggle. The basic patterns of these designs can be found in many similar dynamic compositions. Instead of being unique with Botticelli and Phidias, they suggested themselves to many creative artists and became as universal as the game of tug of war. Secondly, the intense feeling of vitality that these works express cannot be attributed to either idea or design alone, but to a coordination of the two. Other pictures of the last communion of St. Jerome lack the vitality of this one because they also lack its design. Other Parthenon metopes of the Lapith and Centaur theme were carved by many, often less talented, studio hands. The excellent reputation of this particular metope does not lie in the subject; it lies in the quality of its design. Formal design is less effective if abstracted from its context—a trick that can be easily done. The extreme exponents of pure abstraction will not admit to any diminution of force if a representation of ideas is foresworn, but the overwhelming testimony of artists over the centuries (architects excepted) implies that representation and design together possess a power and explicitness of expression that neither possesses alone.

A balanced opposition of attitudes and directions is one of the artist's most useful methods of expressing vigorous physical activity, spiritual conflicts, and restless energy. Since these conditions have repeated themselves numberless times in human history, this means appears in many works of art. Those illustrated here enjoy well-deserved reputations for excellence in the expression of vitality. Through all three runs one noticeable characteristic—a contortion of attitudes.

This is particularly true of the dashing equestrian portrait of M. Dieudonné, or *Officer of the Imperial Guard* (Fig. 357), by Géricault. The picture is the epitome of Napoleonic military *esprit*. Dieudonné's horse rears in the air against a background of battle smoke, while he himself twists violently in the saddle. The picture contains the kind of blood-and-thunder activity that the nineteenth-century Romanticists loved and flung in the faces of the neo-classicists. The vigorous handling of oil paint which was appropriate for Géricault's active themes was also influential in returning the post-Renaissance pictorial tradition to predominance in European art, as in the work of Delacroix, who carried on after Géricault's early death. The difference created by the more vibrant treatment of surface can be grasped by comparing Géricault's bounding *Imperial Guard* with David's smoothly painted and relatively tepid *Napoleon Crossing the Alps at St. Bernard Pass*. The *Imperial Guard* caused a sensation when first shown to a classics-bred public at the Salon of 1812. Its painter was regarded as a prodigy. In that year Napoleon was still the terror of Europe, and Géricault, though only twenty-one years of age, was alert to the *élan* of his times.

Michelangelo's *Bound Slave* (Fig. 358) is a quite different subject and even more famous. Yet it is related to Géricault's painting in the similarity of certain means. It is probable that the young Frenchman inherited his penchant for contorted postures (as did Tintoretto, Rubens, and Rodin) from the great Florentine. For it was Michelangelo who made what the Italians call *contropposto* into a mighty expressive device. It is prominent in all of his works, and notably in the *Creation of Adam* (Fig. 126), *Soldiers Bathing in the Arno* (Fig. 268), and the heroic marble figures of *David* and *Moses*. But nowhere did he use it to greater effect than in the *Bound Slave*.

It is possible that Michelangelo originally intended this writhing, subtly tormented giant to imply only that the arts had been thrown into captivity by the death of Pope Julius II, for whose tomb it was designed. Yet we seem justified in sensing that Michelangelo subconsciously meant the statue to expound a more universal idea. For his far-reaching mind often dwelt on the outward signs of man's conflicts of the soul. These can make a man writhe and twist as though in the grip of a nightmare. They were torments to which

FIG. 357. Géricault. *Officer of the Imperial Guard*. M. Dieudonné. 1812. Louvre, Paris.

FIG. 358. Michelangelo. *Bound Slave*. 1514-1516. Louvre, Paris.

FIG. 359. Goya. *The Nude Maja*. 1795-1797. Prado, Madrid.

Michelangelo himself was, like Beethoven, a life-long prey and thus prepared to understand profoundly. Their universality does not require explanation; nor does their significance for all of mankind. This comprehensive interpretation seems warranted by two features of the statue. One is its strongly introspective character. The other is the strictly figurative nature of the captive's bonds—a point that is made even more significant by the actual bonds of the figure's companion piece, the (literally) *Bound Slave* also in Paris. The statue so moved Rodin when he saw it in the Louvre that he used it as the inspiration for his own great *Age of Bronze*.

That balanced contrasts of attitude and direction can be used in many ways is apparent from the widely different meanings of the *Imperial Guard,* the *Bound Slave,* and Goya's *Nude Maja* (Fig. 359), each a celebrated example of the use of *contropposto*. Quite irrelevant for our purposes is the question of whether the latter represents Goya's alleged mistress, the beautiful Duchess of Alba. So to interpret the subject is to limit its meaning. Far more than a single human being, the *Nude Maja* is a universal symbol of feminine allure. Frankly and intensely sexual in meaning, it represents physical appeal on an animal level. Yet aliveness as well as seductiveness is what accounts for its fame and that it excels in both is proof of Goya's genius. Many other men have painted the nude with a transparently sensuous interest, but only Goya knew how to pose the arms and head and twist the torso and limbs so as to capture the maximum effect of restless feminine sex-consciousness. While many rivals have come and gone, with Hollywood producing them by the hundreds, the *Nude Maja* is still in a class by itself.

This picture is one of a series of feminine nudes that established a tradition in Western painting. Beginning with Giorgione's *Sleeping Venus* and extending through Titian's *Venus of Urbino* to the present day, it underwent many changes in the course of centuries, with Goya contributing radically to them. If Manet's *Olympia* shows the final decline from a sleeping Venus to a brazenly wakeful prostitute, it was Goya who, discarding all mythological pretenses, paved the way. For whereas Titian is said to have awakened Giorgione's *Sleeping Venus,* it was Goya who made her wide awake, earthy, and alive.

The dynamic uses to which balanced diagonal attitudes and contrasting directions have been put could be multiplied many times. Illustrations of this fact can be found in the coincidence of dramatic ideas and these expressive devices in such pictures as Titian's *Entombment, Meeting of Bacchus and Ariadne,* and *Christ Crowned with Thorns;* in Tintoretto's *Annunciation* and *Adam and Eve;* in

El Greco's *Agony in the Garden;* and in Rubens' *Rape of the Daughters of Leucippus*—all powerful examples of both feeling and method.

There are, however, other ways of balance that deserve attention. If their character is less spectacular, that may be a merit in less forceful circumstances. Other means provide additional ways of expressing the complex world of ideas and the many kinetic levels between a marked repose and an emphatic vitality. The Chinese, whose Yin-Yang concept of the cosmos resembled the Greek ideal of balance, were fond of reconciling opposite ideas and expert at devising the requisite artistic means, which they handed down through the centuries. To a greater extent than in Western art, the Middle Ages excepted, their methods were preserved as conventions of formulae in a kind of systematic pictorial shorthand. Bristling pine trees, flowing clerical robes, and ragged mendicant costumes each had a standard form to which the individual artist gave only a personal touch.

Several of these distinctive but traditional shape-characters have been juxtaposed by Lin T'ing-Kuei in his *Arhats Bestowing Alms upon Beggars* (Fig. 360), one of a series of kakemono (vertical scroll) paintings in the Museum of Fine Arts, Boston. The curvilinear shapes of the well-fed holy men are typical of the treatment of such figures in Chinese art, as are the angular rags of the scrawny, bedraggled beggars. What is significant here is the way one is used to enhance and balance the other by contrast in a single picture.

A conventionalized system of pictorial shorthand has also been used more widely in the West, especially in the field of shapes, than one might suppose, despite our more realistic interests. Rembrandt consistently used a scraggly, scratchy type of line in his pen-and-ink sketches of beggars; and Claude Lorrain frequently resorted to a stylization of trees in his drawings (for example, the *Landscape with Cattle,* Fig. 117), as did Dürer, Turner, and others. But the Far Eastern artists remain the outstanding masters of contrasted stylized shapes because of their conception of art as a language of expressive, rather than imitative, forms.

Their adeptness at managing the visual vocabulary is shown by the skill with which Harunobu has used it in his color print of the *Beautiful Osen in the Kagiya Inn* (Fig. 361). Although only a typical, popular print of a Japanese beauty, it exhibits the widespread refinement made possible by a long-thought-out tradition. With regard to design, the secret of its effectiveness lies in the way Harunobu has balanced the curvilinear grace of the girl against the rectilinear character of the setting. Although her figure is not more graceful than Shunsho's similar *Woman in a Pink Dress* (Fig. 340), Osen's lithe

FIG. 360. Lin T'ing-Kuei. *Arhats Bestowing Alms upon Beggars.* 1160-1180, Sung Dynasty. Museum of Fine Arts, Boston.

FIG. 361. Harunobu. *The Beautiful Osen in the Kagiya Inn. ca.* 1768. Bowdoin College Museum of Fine Arts, Brunswick, Me.

form stands out more sharply by virtue of the angular rigidity of her background. She was, incidentally, known in her day as much for the graciousness of her character and deportment as for her comeliness, a fact that Harunobu has implied through the easy way she performs her teahouse duties.

The underlying theme of a woman in her special world has suggested a similarity between Harunobu's print and Vermeer's *Cook* (Fig. 93). A side-by-side comparison is revealing. For if Vermeer's conception is not less gracious, his methods are very different. The West's tendency toward an imitative use of the language of the visual arts and the Orient's more abstract and conventional emphasis upon expression could hardly be illustrated better. In the long run, however, each has supplied us with a treasury of skilfully coordinated ideas and spatial designs.

CHAPTER 23

Coordination of Idea
and Color Design

The skilled artist uses many means of expressing his ideas and feelings, often playing them against each other to create a kind of inner tension. He may impose a color design of great vitality on a static spatial design and a reposeful idea. The most apparent examples of such contrasts can be found in mosaics which appear dull in black-and-white, but glow when seen in color. Color is all-important to the visual impact of medieval stained glass windows, impressionist paintings, and much of modern painting. Yet color makes an even greater contribution to design when it is quiet and muted. The profound effect of subdued color with an overlay of almost imperceptible nuances is demonstrated by any of the late portraits of Rembrandt.

Lines which imply movement appeal to our motor senses, stimulating a feeling of unimpeded action or of strong muscular tensions, while massive forms and textures activate our emphatic responses. Both these reactions are, in a sense, secondary. They are associative responses related via the mind to tactile or motor phenomena. Color, however, is a more direct thing—in and of the eye itself. The result is, compared to our reading of lines and masses, both static and nonmuscular. Yet it is vivid, intense, and sometimes as shocking as a blow, or a crash of sound. The nonobjective artists are therefore correct in asserting that intense effects of vitality, or repose, and the innumerable stages in between can be expressed and appreciated through abstract, nonrepresentational means alone. The best of them have exploited color's directness and sharpness brilliantly.

This does not detract in any way from the power of color to appeal to sentiments and reveal a world of ideas and moods through associations. The intangible connotations of color that derive from its connection with such infinite attributes of reality as light and shadow, atmosphere and water, make it an excellent means of stressing spiritual values. Rembrandt recognized this characteristic of color early in life and used it fully in such pictures as his *Supper at Emmaus* (Fig. 325). Da Vinci also grasped the spiritual and psychological subtlety of color before he painted the "Mona Lisa" (Fig. 259a), for a great deal of that portrait's renown stems from the way in which he refined the treatment of light and shadow and color.

More obviously, color has enjoyed the benefit of a host of associations which are common in everyday speech. We speak, typically, of an icy blue, of red-hot, of a blue Monday, and of the shadowy "valley of death." Each of these terms has some meaning which carries beyond pure color and sensation into the world of ideas and sentiments. The medieval artists made full use of these symbolical implications in forming their own language of the visual arts. But the artists of all times have grasped these associational capacities with great adeptness.

The principal sensory and psychological responses that colors elicit are also widely and reliably known. High intensity colors and strong light create in almost everyone a feeling of vitality. Conversely, low intensity colors and dark or shadowy tones stimulate the optic senses less and are interpreted in more reposeful terms. Yet these potentialities are only the starting points of color expression. They can be intensified, increased, and altered in the direction of greater vitality or repose by the artist through a manipulation of their relationships. The expressive power of a color never comes to us out of the tube and ready to use. It must be organized on a palette and canvas if its potentiality is to be exploited. The masters whom we call great colorists merely did this better than others. And since their methods hinge upon the coordination of color designs and ideas, we must apply the principles of order to the terms of color.

HARMONY OF HUES

In most contexts, the hues on the so-called "cool" side of the circle of hues (Fig. 91a) will have a quieting, even depressing effect. Certainly, the shadows of night are more restful and suitable for sleep than the light of day. If carried far enough, an emphasis upon cool hues can express despondency. Whistler favored the merely soothing air of night when he painted his *Nocturne, Blue and Silver* (Fig. 139). Picasso, on the other hand, stressed dejection in his so-called "blue period" pictures. Blue hues and sadness are united consistently in

FIG. 362. Picasso. *The Old Guitarist*. 1903. Art Institute of Chicago.

FIG. 363. Rembrandt. *Saskia with a Red Flower*. 1641. Royal Painting Gallery, Dresden.

the output of his poverty-stricken youth in Paris. We have already noted this characteristic in his forlorn *Woman Ironing* (Fig. 45). It appears again in his gloomy *Absinthe Drinker,* and in the *Old Guitarist* in Fig. 362. In none of these does color carry the burden of expression alone. In each the blue tone merely reinforces the sadness created by hunched-over attitudes and emaciated bodies, but it supports these other expressive means effectively. The use of bluish hues therefore is only part of the expressive story. The other and greater part is contained in their harmonious organization. Harmony, like teamwork of any kind, increases effectiveness several times over.

Important, for instance, is the use of low intensities in conjunction with bluish hues, for subdued intensities add to the reposeful effect. Rembrandt shows us in his *Saskia with a Red Flower* (Fig. 363) how this reposeful property of low intensities can be used to advantage. He joined it to a set of "warm" hues to gain an over-all effect of warm-hearted social grace. He painted this portrait of his wife about a year before her premature death, when she and Rembrandt were idyllically happy. Her outgoing gesture radiates that happiness. The picture is completely unlike Picasso's mournfully introspective guitarist, and the warmth of color accounts for much of the difference.

HARMONY OF VALUES

The terms of color are as interdependent as a set of gears; when one is changed, the others are too. Consequently, the total impression made upon us by a picture which is predominantly light is different from that of a similar subject in darker values. Anyone who has made photographic prints, in which various grades of darkness can be attained, will readily appreciate this distinction.

Generally speaking, a predominance of high values will signify a high degree of vitality. This is true for two reasons. One is that the greater amount of actual light has a more stimulating effect upon the visual sense. The other reason is associational, and comes from the subconscious but universal identification of light with the sun, our greatest source of energy. Witness the persistence of sun-worship over many centuries.

Dark values, or absence of light, connote a lesser energy which is soothing and reposeful in proportion to its lesser stimulation. Ideologically, however, it may have a number of depressing, morbid, or tragic meanings, notably the suggestion of death. Evil and the so-called "powers of darkness" have been associated for centuries. Witches fly at midnight. An artist can exploit either of these reposeful or morbid possibilities. The only question is the suitability of his decision.

Whistler clearly knew what he was doing when he painted his various nocturnes, like *The Lagoon, Venice* (Fig. 139) and the *Thames at Battersea* (Fig. 154). They are among the most consistent harmonies of dark values to be found in painting. Darkly quiet, they are also among the most reposeful pictures that one can find. In these pictures dark values were linked with static scenes and connotations of peace to produce a total effect of complete serenity.

Masanobu used an opposite but equally knowledgeable system of values when he designed his *Playing Cards* (Fig. 113). Although a simple genre scene, it contains an interesting, even mildly exciting activity. When this game is presented in the full light of day, the general effect is lighthearted, cheerful, and vital. It has neither the seriousness nor moodiness of a Whistler nocturne or Sloan's *Wake of the Ferry* (Fig. 76), but its spirit is alive. The difference suggests why so many masters of the mood emotions have also been skilful exponents of shadows.

There is all the difference in the world between Perugino's *Crucifixion* in the National Gallery at Washington and Rembrandt's *Descent from the Cross* in the same museum. The Italian picture is as light as a clear morning, the Dutch painting as dark and somber as midnight. As a result, it is almost impossible to regard Perugino's painting with its lyrical atmosphere as anything other than symbolic and devotional; whereas Rembrandt's scene is dark with tragedy.

Relative lightness and darkness can make an equally telling difference in areas of more neutral content, as in Ruysdael's famous *Windmill at Wijk Bij Duurstede* and Rembrandt's great *Mill,* now in the National Gallery. While Ruysdael's masterpiece is not exceptionally light, Rembrandt's is much darker, and that darkness, combined with dull brown, low intensity colors gives the work its brooding quality.

Since lack of light causes diminution of visibility, the human mind has always associated darkness with indefiniteness and mystery. In shadows the imagination has freer play and the infinite comes to the fore. The lower range of the value scale has long appealed to the mystery-loving side of the romantic temperament. America's most poetic romanticist, Albert Ryder, was devoted to the hours of night, as in his nocturnal *Toilers of the Sea, Moonlit Cove,* and tragic *Death on a Pale Horse* (Fig. 278).

A harmonious emphasis of the darker values has been the stock in trade of all artists who wished to express an air of repose or a mood of mystery, sadness, infinity, or tragedy. Few artists have known how to use these somber tones better than Titian, who employed them with masterly effectiveness in his *Entombment* (Fig. 62) and *Christ Crowned with Thorns* (Fig. 130). Dark pictures of this sort brought a major change to painting, paving the way for Rembrandt, Ruysdael, and the later Romanticists. For this reason, among others, Titian is regarded as one of the pivotal figures of art, and his art another instance of superior control over the means of expression.

HARMONY OF INTENSITIES

Winston Churchill, a prodigious amateur painter, said that he loves the brilliant, cheerful colors and feels sorry for those that are drab and dull. In technical terms this means a preference for high intensities over low, or, when used consistently, a harmony of strong, bright colors as distinct from uniformly soft hues. The terms *high* and *low intensity* signify an emphasis of either vitality or repose in the realm of direct visual stimulation. In addition, our mental associations give intensities much the same capacity to express vitality, gaiety, and strength, and tragedy, repose, despondency, and moods as does the scale of values.

Since strong light gives high intensities their best chance to appear to full advantage, and shadows reduce their strength proportionately, high values and high intensities have been expressive teammates, while their opposites, low values and low intensities, have likewise worked together. This point, as well as the comprehensive character of expression, is clearly illustrated by Van Gogh's *Postman Roulin* (Fig. 364) and Rembrandt's *Portrait of a Woman* (Fig. 365). Offhand they are only two human beings who posed for their pictures. But the contrast between the impressions they make is sharp. More significant, it is traceable to treatment.

If Roulin, a close friend of Van Gogh during the artist's stay at Arles, seems to vibrate with excitable Gallic energy, that effect is due largely to the fact that almost every color in the picture is at the highest intensity possible at its value. The figure also enjoys the benefit of a strong light, as if in the out-of-doors. High intensities are thus reinforced by high values. In addition, the surface is a harmony of rough brush strokes, vigorously applied, and is united with a consistent angularity of shape which contributes to the man's appearance of alert awkwardness. Finally, though much of the subject's energy was his own, some of it derived from Van Gogh, who painted it during a period of feverish activity. These combined factors produce a figure which, though sitting perfectly still, radiates vitality. This ability of treatment to endow the most static subject

Fig. 364. Van Gogh. *The Postman Roulin.*
August, 1888. Museum of Fine Arts,
Boston.

Fig. 365. Rembrandt. *Portrait of a
Woman.* 1666. National Gallery,
London.

Fig. 366a. *Queen Nofretete.* Reigned
1375-1358 B.C., XVIII Dynasty.
Egyptian Museum, Berlin.

with vibrant energy is one of the attributes of design that never ceases to amaze.

Rembrandt's *Portrait of a Woman,* while perfectly still, possesses a serenity beyond the merely static. It is a spiritual poise and peace of mind to which the calm pose only gives outward expression. This peacefulness is due, as was Roulin's appearance of vigor, largely to the manner of treatment employed. The colors are low in intensity, though warm in hue, and the values primarily dark. Soft, curvilinear forms have been generally favored, and the brush strokes made to blend in a thousand tonal nuances. The background is alive with color, but of the subtlest, most infinite kind. The woman seems, by contrast with Roulin, to look at us from a shadowy room. In total effect she is the essence of feminine harmony, while Roulin is a symbol of rugged masculine force.

Some of this profound serenity may have been inherent in the woman herself, but history suggests that most of it came from Rembrandt. During his final years the bitterness of earlier disappointments faded and he attained a peaceful resignation such as few men have known. More important for us, he imbued his last pictures with a spiritual repose that radiates on air of wisdom, tolerance, and quietude. Less aristocratic than the "Mona Lisa," whose pose hers resembles, this Dutch woman is a symbol of human warmth and understanding, as Rembrandt was himself. Artistically, she is proof of the merits of a harmony of low intensities.

Over the centuries, artists of many persuasions have availed themselves of the assets of high and low intensities, some seconding the ringing choice of Churchill, others the softer voice of Rembrandt. Great works of both types abound because these artists have respected the rule of harmony or consistency and, equally, the relationship of color intensity and theme.

The following are outstanding for the suitability of color intensity to the ideas they express. Delacroix's *Lion Hunt* (Fig. 346) is extremely vital in content and spatial design and also in color intensity. How much more skilfully Delacroix exploited the latter resource can be appreciated by contrasting his brilliant hues with the realistic but tamer colors of Vernet's *Lion Hunt* (Fig. 347).

Rouault's *Old King* (Fig. 227) depicts a taut and cruel personality. Part of this impression is conveyed by the scowling facial expression and tightly clutched hand, and part by the heavy lines, angular shapes, rough surface, and the intense colors. In these two paintings by Rouault and Delacroix color stimulation is deliberately used as an irritant, a typical method of artists who aim as much at powerful expression as at esthetic pleasure.

Yet intense colors can express gaiety or a love of life, even the highest spiritual exaltation. Although Fra Angelico's *Madonna of Humility* is an excellent example of modesty, its brilliant colors communicate a singing, lighthearted spirit. Van Gogh's pictures carry this optimism to an even higher pitch, the color intensity of his *Mountainous Landscape* and *Sunset over a Plowed Field* proclaiming an almost cosmic joy in the energy of the universe. There is a gaiety, too, in the paintings of Matisse, who favored strong colors whenever possible. But the outstanding case of spiritual exhilaration expressed through vivid hues is still the stained glass windows of the Gothic cathedral-builders. It was their optimism and color sense that Fra Angelico inherited.

But since vitality and enthusiasm can turn to frustrated bitterness, a harmony of high intensities may sometimes express tension, anger, or violence. This was the case with Rouault, and it has been repeated often by contemporary artists who feel that life has gone sour and the times are out of joint. High intensities have been used by some of them to give vent to a high-pitched scream of anguish, "loud" colors being their means of showing the intensity of their dismay. Picasso's *Crucifixion* of 1930 and Abraham Rattner's *There Was Darkness over All the Land* are powerful examples.

On the whole, however, brilliant hues have signified a general youthfulness of outlook. Children and primitive artists have always loved them, as have those simple or prosperous societies which retained a confident outlook toward life. It can be said without criticism that their attitude is relatively openhanded and naive. If a society grows older and wiser without becoming cynical, its color preferences are likely to show a trend toward harmonies of lower intensities; the history of Chinese painting from primitive times to the end of the Sung Dynasty illustrates this tendency.

Low intensity colors may not always express repose. Like deep shadows, they may connote overtones of deepest tragedy. This is true of Daumier's powerful *Uprising* (Fig. 316), a picture composed mainly of dark, low intensity brownish hues. Subdued intensities are also capable of conveying an atmosphere of great spiritual depth, a fact that Rembrandt relied on when he conceived his *Supper at Emmaus* (Fig. 325). They can likewise cast a mood of sadness over the whole of a countryside, as Charles Burchfield shows in his *November Evening* (Fig. 27). And when coupled with cold gray and dull brown, they can add greatly to the icy dreariness of a scene in the dead of winter. Courbet proved this in his little canvas *Winter* (Fig. 350) no less effectively than Bruegel in his great *Hunters Returning in the Snow*.

All in all, low intensity colors express greater sobriety and restraint
of outlook, if not necessarily greater maturity, than those of high
intensity. No one would take them to mean joy and optimism. The
intensities of colors, when skilfully harmonized and controlled, are
capable of contributing as much to the feeling or mood of a work of
art as any means in the artistic repertory. They can express the
lyrical spirit of a Fra Angelico, Monet, or Renoir, the seriousness
of a Picasso, or the serenity of a Corot. More than that, they add
importantly to the means of whole period and national styles. Their
significance for the language of arts is universal.

SEQUENCE OF COLOR: ALTERNATION
AND GRADATION

Two characteristics stand out when sequences of color are considered in relation to expression. One is the power of gradation to
suggest subtlety, sophistication, control, and the sense of repose that
attends these qualities. The other is the contrasting vitality of alternation, a method of design which bombards the eye with a series of
abruptly repeated changes.

A checkerboard illustrates the potency of such effects. The direct
stimulation is strong, quite apart from any associational impetus.
Few other means have a greater ability to heighten vitality of sensation than the commonplace examples of alternation—stripes, checker-
boards, polka dots, plaids. However, alternations vary in their implications of energy content according to a simple rule. Color vibrations, as they are called, can be intensified up to a certain point by
increasing the number of contrasting factors—that is, by striking the
eye with an accelerated variation of hues, values, and intensities, and
a larger number of units, as in Figs. 366b, c, d, and e. But if this
subdividing process is carried too far, a turning point in effectiveness
is passed. A surface dotted with minute colors (Fig. 366f) misses the
maximum of visual impact; it simply tickles the eye.

A sensitive artist will avoid this extreme or use it deliberately,
according to his purposes. This principle is illustrated by the methods
of Monet, Van Gogh, and Seurat, who used the broken-color technique of Impressionism for quite different ends. Monet's alternations of high intensity hues and vigorous brush strokes make the
surface of his pictures seem alive, as though in actual motion, a
characteristic that is eminently suitable for such dynamic scenes as
the *Marée Montante à Pourville* (Fig. 137). Van Gogh carried this
device still further in his *Sunset over a Plowed Field* (Fig. 140). By
reducing the blending of strokes, he made each touch of the brush

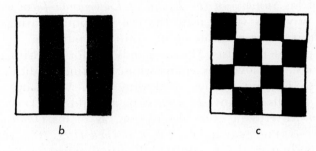

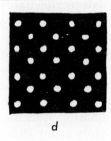

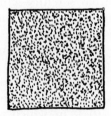

FIG. 366b–f. Diagrammatic illustrations of alternations of color ("color vibration").

stand out sharply. In his painting alternation was carried to a high pitch. Seurat, on the other hand, was of a more deliberate temperament. Aiming at a feeling of almost classic repose, he covered the surface of his *Sunday on the Island of La Grande Jatte* with innumerable tiny dots which tease the eye without agitating it. Each technique is a fine example of suitability to purpose.

Among modern artists, Matisse stands out for his brilliant use of alternations. He loves gay colors whose exciting qualities he combines with pleasant themes. Following both Van Gogh and the Persians, he fills his canvases with striped, plaid, checkerboard, and polka dot patterns of every description, as in his *Odalisque with Raised Arms* (Fig. 123) and *Girl in a Striped Dress* (Fig. 261). The effect is decorative, lively, and exhilarating, expressing one of the truly youthful spirits of our times. Few artists have made alternations of color a more prominent or successful part of their style.

The exciting qualities of alternation carry with them, however, one disadvantage. Their power to stimulate is inevitably attended by a certain obviousness. It is one of the most vital of an artist's resources, but by no means his most refined or mature. Children and primitive peoples, for example, love to enliven their simple line and local color paintings with brilliantly colored stripes and other kinds of alternation. But the potency of these characteristics makes alternation nearly opposite to gradation in its expressive effect. Therefore, an artist who wishes to emphasize a feeling of calm strength or subtlety of personality will usually avoid alternation but utilize gradation.

A striking instance of sophistication, tranquility, and poise expressed through a gradation of values is the portrait head of *Queen Nofretete* (Fig. 366a) in the famous Egyptian collection at Berlin. This queen shows a spiritual serenity which unites her with Rembrandt's *Portrait of a Woman* (Fig. 365) and Da Vinci's "Mona Lisa" (Fig. 259a). In all three this quality is achieved by an impeccable rendering of gradations. They set the tone of the three women, for while we have no proof that they were as calm as they appear, it is impossible to imagine them being wild or brusque. Any of these figures therefore presents a dramatic contrast to Bourdelle's stormy head of *Beethoven* (Fig. 164), in which an alternation of broken, plastic surface has been emphatically used.

The different effects of gradation and alternation create a similar contrast between the interiors of Saint John's Chapel (Fig. 338) and the Sainte Chapelle (Fig. 339) in Paris. The Norman building in London is sturdy, massive, and solid; the Gothic light, airy, and spindly, multi-lined piers and delicate windows making shadows and colors dance before our eyes. They exemplify outstandingly the reposeful quality of gradation and the vital qualities of alternation.

BALANCE OF COLOR

Balance, whether used for spatial or color organization, is an extraordinarily versatile means of expression. The utmost feeling of repose and dignity can be achieved by superimposing an obvious balance of color upon a symmetrical axial design, as exemplified by Cimabue's perfectly static *Madonna Enthroned* (Fig. 244). On the other hand, balance of color can preserve in a work of art an intense feeling of life while spanning a wide range of ideas and moods, thanks to its capacity for reconciling many conflicting elements. It can thus exploit both the orderliness of balance and the energy inherent in conflict.

The use of color in an obvious axial balance is relatively easy to understand. Our principal discussion will therefore be devoted to color's infinitely rich expressive uses in asymmetrical balances. Although only the principal methods can be covered, a few outstanding examples should indicate the other possibilities.

A high pitch of emotional expression can be gained through balance of colors in several ingenious ways. For example, two contrasting types of color attraction—value contrast attraction and color intensity attraction—can be opposed to each other and then balanced to produce a kind of double-barreled explosion. A consummate illustration of this method is El Greco's *View of Toledo* (Fig. 367), a picture noted for its extraordinary vitality. A prominent reason for this air of vigor is the organization of its colors. Like the spatial design, it is full of balanced contrasts—deep shadows alternating rhythmically and vibrantly with flashing lights. These conflicting elements are reconciled by the over-all balance between the sharp value contrasts in the ominous sky and the intense green and yellow hues in the violently undulating earth below. Such a dynamic treatment of the upper and lower halves of the composition expresses powerfully the tense spirit of Counter-Reformation Toledo during El Grecos's residence there. Idea and execution are perfectly coordinated.

Ideas and design are also brilliantly coordinated in Burchfield's *House of Mystery* (Fig. 368). In it two opposing characteristics—the somberness of shadow and the stark obviousness of brilliant light—are balanced with vivid effect. They are played against each other to express a theme that runs through much of Burchfield's work, a Turnerian fascination with the decay of once-respectable buildings

FIG. 367. El Greco.
A View of Toledo.
1604-1619. Metropolitan
Museum of Art,
New York.

FIG. 368. Burchfield.
House of Mystery. 1924.
Art Institute of Chicago.

and all that their decline implies of the course of human life. This Victorian house probably sheltered a thriving family in better days, but it suffered a common fate. As neighborhoods changed, it became part of a slum, most likely a house of prostitution. An evil-looking red light gleams from the darkened porch; the building is dirty, ill-repaired, and dismal. Burchfield has expressed this condition by combining spatial and color designs of the harshest kind. The building lines are hard, straight, and angular; the color scheme is composed of the sharpest possible contrast of raw light and deep shadows. The intensities are dull and drab. If the effect of both form and content approaches pure ugliness, this was artfully sought. Like John Sloan's *Wake of the Ferry*, it epitomizes hauntingly a broad and significant aspect of American city life. It is a picture rich in mood.

The proof of the greatness of Turner's *Fighting Téméraire* (Fig. 258a) lies in the number of times one returns to it to illustrate an important principle. It excels, for instance, in the use of color balance to express an idea—the last day of a great ship. Like El Greco's *View of Toledo,* the method used is a balance of intensity attraction (the glowing sunset) and value contrast (the small dark tug and the luminous ship of the line), though employed more nostalgically than in El Greco's turbulent picture. Its strength lies in the skill with which Turner has simultaneously balanced his design, created an air of sad serenity (through the horizontal sea and placid water), and expressed his ideas. The sunset serves a symbolic as well as an esthetic purpose, as does the juxtaposition of the brightly lighted old ship and the dark tug. Turner, who loved the old sailing vessels, leaves no doubt where his sympathies lie; the whole picture expresses his quiet regret over the passing of an era. Philosophical resignation is the keynote of its message. It, too, is a picture rich in mood.

The versatility of a balance of value contrasts and intensity attractions for both esthetic and ideological purposes is shown by its equally apt use in Rogier van der Weyden's *Portrait of a Lady* (Fig. 297). It exemplifies a kind of artistic reasoning that is typical of this method. Confronted with a young woman who was staid, reticent, and modest, Van der Weyden posed her in an appropriately calm, dignified position, and kept the intensities of his colors low and the gradations extremely subtle. One cannot help feeling, however, that he regarded the young lady as slightly dull. Not wishing to do violence to her personality or turn her into a Hogarthian *Shrimp Girl,* he gave the picture life and sharpness by artistic means. His method of rescue was to create an abrupt value contrast between headdress and black background, and balance it with the intensity attraction of a brilliant red belt. The latter device gives vitality to the picture without disrupting its essential calm, much as an accent of lipstick enlivens the appearance of a woman in a gray dress. But let us not mistakenly withhold credit from Van der Weyden by assuming that he simply painted the lady as she appeared. The inclusion of a vital passage of color in the right place happens too often in his work and in art at large to be an accident.

Indeed, that is the gist of this discussion. In fine works of art the coordination of color, design, and ideas is an essential part of control over the objectification of feeling. The many examples and methods we have considered are but various instances of this central activity.

CHAPTER 24

The Principle of Fitness

Anyone who wishes to review the methods of art in relation to the principle of fitness of means to ends implied by Konody's definition might well consider drawing. In so doing he will probably remember an allegation that one overhears constantly at museums and exhibitions. Its general purport is, "He can't draw!" If disgust is expressed, it may take the form of "My four-year-old son can draw better than that!"

These statements imply that there is some universally recognized norm of drawing whose rules the offending artist has violated. But if an artist happens to hear such criticisms directed at his own work, he should console himself with the testimony of history, for he can find much illustrious company. Taking these ideas together, let us note a few examples.

Legend tells us that when Titian looked at a few drawings like the *Study of a Statue* (Fig. 369) by a would-be disciple, Tintoretto, he dismissed the young man peremptorily from his studio. Whether this report is historically accurate or not, Titian's strong but balanced nature would certainly have made it impossible for him to appreciate anything drawn or painted by the impetuous Tintoretto. He might well have explained his abhorrence by saying, "The man obviously can't draw!" He would have meant that Tintoretto did not draw the way Titian did.

Ironically, Titian's own art was later criticized because it did not conform to the ideas of drawing held by certain critics. They said that he could paint, but not draw, and made the same statement about Velasquez. How both masters could paint magnificently on a so-called foundation of poor drawing was not explained. One can only assume that drawing was somehow conceived to be a step sep-

FIG. 369. Tintoretto. *Study of a Statue*. *ca*. 1560. Frans Koenig Collection, Haarlem.

FIG. 370. Rembrandt. *A Woman Sleeping*. *ca*. 1657. British Museum, London.

arated from painting, with the early Renaissance method an eternal criterion of how all other artists should proceed. Hence an artist could be weak in one and yet strong in another.

It took the clear mind of Bernard Berenson to expose the fallacy in this thinking. Grounded in Renaissance methods and ideas, he maintained that drawing is the central process of the visual arts. But he meant by drawing any process which gives strength and clarity to the forms and formal structure of works of art and expresses a strong, clear mind at work. Neither of these changes because a man picks up a brush instead of a crayon, for the medium is only incidental to an artist's perceptual and conceptual powers; it is they that give firmness to drawing and a soul to a work of art. Hence it would be impossible for Titian, Velasquez, or any other artist to be a great painter and a poor draftsman. His pictures, like his personality, are either weak or strong as a whole. Those who trouble to understand the meaning of Berenson, who sees art as a whole himself, will find it a ray of light; it illuminates one of the most persistent fallacies in art.

During modern times accusations of bad drawing have come thick and fast. Couture, an academician to whom Manet turned for instruction, dismissed that master from his studio with the denunciation that he would never be anything but another Daumier. Little did he realize what praise he was bestowing, for his mind was not large enough to comprehend a simple fact: fine drawing is where you find it, in an oil painting as well as in pen-and-ink sketches, in a cartoon of daily life as well as in a formal representation of Venus. If told that Daumier would some day be ranked among the most incisive draughtsmen of all time, he would have thought his informant insane.

The same egotistical mistake was made by Ingres, who not only declared, "Drawing is the probity of art," but appointed himself guardian of its standards. As such, he could see nothing but inexcusable violence in drawings like Delacroix's *Combat* (Fig. 153), and blocked the great romanticist from membership in the Institute until he was fifty-nine years of age. Delacroix was an artist who drew as vigorously as he painted, and he never painted to suit Monsieur Ingres.

As fortune would have it, Ingres himself was soon afterward caught in the same dogmatic trap. When, about seventy years ago, a group of his now priceless pencil drawings was offered to a great American museum at a nominal sum, the purchase was opposed by one trustee who said, "The man obviously can't draw!" In view of Ingres' exalted reputation in that field today, the statement seems incredible, but such are the ironies of history when men invoke a narrow criterion, and rule out whatever does not meet it.

Later in the nineteenth century the tempestuous character of Van Gogh's paintings and drawings, like the pen-and-ink study of cypresses in Fig. 155, caused people to say that he was mad, and smile knowingly when his suicide seemed to confirm that opinion. Even forty-six years after his death the Van Gogh exhibition of 1936 brought more howls of laughter than murmurs of praise, and the remark was common that "If my son couldn't draw better than that, I'd spank him." Only slowly do we yield our prejudices about the nature of painting and drawing.

Today some enlightened people still say that Cézanne could paint but not draw. They are but repeating the bias that a drawing of a form should be judged by some set of idealistic or realistic proportions and thereby miss the strength of modeling that Cézanne achieved. At the same time, they have overlooked his tremendously effective use of color in modeling forms, because it departed from traditional methods. These examples, which could be multiplied many times, illustrate why we say that the artist who is accused of drawing badly has excellent company.

At the root of these errors which history has had to amend lies one villain with a hundred lives. It is the *fixed idea* in art, the belief that there is one and only one correct way of doing something, namely, the way which coincides with the comfortably established beliefs of the beholder.

If we seek to find out what examples among actual works of art represent the drawing from which the man who "can't draw" departs, we find that there are actually two types. One type is submitted by the layman who wants his art to look "real." He maintains that Eakins' *Masked Nude Woman* (Fig. 150) is the way drawings ought to look, and that Van Gogh's utterly different art must therefore be crazy. Equally self-assured is the academic dogmatist who scorns the layman's realism and would have none of Eakins' vulgarity. More to his taste is the idealistic, classically based drawing of Michelangelo (Fig. 58) and Raphael. Ingres placed Raphael's drawings at the very summit of Western artistic achievement.

Plainly, one of these groups must be wrong, for an artist cannot draw like Eakins and Raphael at the same time. As a matter of fact, both views are at fault because they put the cart before the horse. Including and excluding drawings according to their resemblance to Eakins' or Michelangelo's style, they have neglected to view each drawing on its merits. They have ignored, for instance, the fact that Eakins' drawing would be useless for the Sistine ceiling, and that

Michelangelo's would be equally unsuitable for the purpose that
Eakins had in mind. "To each his own" and "live and let live" are
principles of tolerance that win only slow recognition.

The time has come, then, to substitute a flexible and universally
applicable principle—the *principle of fitness*—for any and all fixed
ideas about drawing, and to muster as much evidence and common
sense as possible to reinforce it.

The first fact that should strike a student of the history of drawings is that the acknowledged masterpieces of drawing, instead of
being alike, are widely different, a manifest contradiction if either
realism or sculpturesque idealism were the only acceptable standard.
There is room for greatness amid this rich variety because the principle of fitness demands only that the form of each picture be suited
to its content.

Since content may take a hundred directions and vary infinitely
in its subtleties, so, too, may form. This principle therefore accepts
each work of art according to its own message, instead of some other
idea. By the same token, it imposes much greater burdens of understanding on us than the fixed idea, for it requires new, fresh, and
open-minded thought about the meaning of every work of art we
approach, and a judgment of the coordination of means and ends that
is free of preconceived opinions.

To take an illustration, the author has often noted the haste with
which most students dismiss two famous drawings that do not happen
to meet their ideas of drawing. Typical remarks elicited by Tintoretto's *Study of a Statue* and Rembrandt's *Woman Sleeping* (Fig.
370) are, "Titian was right; Tintoretto was a wild man!" "The figure
is out of proportion!" (an oft-repeated but meaningless statement);
and "What's so great about the Rembrandt? It's nothing but a
sketch."

These observations of a sophisticated civilization—"What's so great
about the Rembrandt?" and "It's nothing but a sketch."—are the
nub of the problem, for they blindly miss the importance of appropriateness. They miss the fact that, though this is only one way of expressing the idea of repose, it is nevertheless an excellent way; and
that the simplicity of Rembrandt's means is an asset, not a liability,
in this subject. They miss, too, the fact that an artist must strive all
his life to say so much with so little, and that he never deliberately
aims over the years at complexity.

These remarks also miss the wonderful aptness of posture and
rapid-fire execution for the idea of vehement vitality that Tintoretto
sought to express, for there is no more powerful example of tension
and strain among old master drawings. It is as telling an expression

of force as Rembrandt's is of sleep. Each is unlike the other; each is, in fact, unique. But both are great drawings because treatment and idea are in complete accord. No one could exchange the style of the one for that of the other without also interchanging their ideas, which would be like asking Rembrandt to change personalities with Tintoretto.

Expression, as we have said, is the result of what is depicted and how it is presented, and the coordination of one with the other. What is hard to understand is that this process must be undertaken anew in every case, a necessity which imposes a burden upon both creative and appreciative minds, but adds endlessly to the enrichment of art. In any event, it cannot be judged in advance or appreciated with a ready-made or fixed idea.

Behind the infinite variation of this central principle—appropriateness of means to a given end—lies another fact of history: the multiple purposes of drawing. There is, for instance, the preparatory drawing, such as David made for the *Oath of the Horatii* (Fig. 88), and the drawing which is an end-in-itself, like Hogarth's *Enraged Musician* (Fig. 72). Common sense tells us that the function of Hogarth's engraving would normally make it more complete than David's sketch.

The multiple purposes which gave rise to the several modes of drawing also defy any fixed idea. The literal realism Nanteuil employed in his *Louis XIV* (Fig. 149) is excellent for that portrait, but would not be suitable for the more spiritual idea contained in Rembrandt's *Christ Healing the Sick* (Fig. 151). Nor could one exchange the style which Marsden Hartley used to stress the finite massiveness of the Alps for the manner Turner relied on to present the infinite movement of clouds, wind, and rain in the mezzotint of *Solway Moss*.

We find, therefore, not one but several principal ways of drawing, each with hundreds of variations that grew out of particular circumstances. Thus it was insured that while Turner's *Solway Moss* and Rembrandt's *Three Trees* (Fig. 200) would admirably represent the dynamic, infinite world, each would have an individuality of its own. When either idea or form is altered, the result is not necessarily a better picture, but it is always a different one. The fixed idea is the enemy of such differences.

Each mode of representation is likewise different from the others rather than superior to them, for each possesses assets and liabilities which obey a gain-and-loss principle. Thurber's humorous "*Touché!*" (Fig. 143) is not inferior to Michelangelo's noble study for the *Creation of Adam* (Fig. 58), at least in the realm of technique. If Michelangelo's manner were imposed upon it, Thurber's drawing would lose rather than gain in effectiveness, for its incisive wit is as bound to its simple linear treatment as Michelangelo's greater impressiveness is due to a fuller modeling of forms.

If artists drew for representational purposes alone, a few modes, if not a single standard, might serve to guide us. But artists confound our generalizations by satisfying our needs for orderly design in many ways. They offer us, on the one hand, the cleanly simple drawings on Greek vases and, on the other, the softly modeled drawings of Seurat. Though poles apart, each is beautiful. So common sense tells us to find theories that make room for both.

The principle of fitness is such a theory. It respects and underscores the integrity of each work of art. The fixed idea is the converse because it excludes all that does not conform to its narrow limits, as Ingres excluded the drawings of Delacroix and many derided the paintings of Van Gogh until very recent times.

The multiple purposes of drawings must also permit an emphasis upon emotional expression that may be at variance with conservative notions of beauty and allow the means to be used to achieve that end. The spiritual qualities of vitality and repose were as precious to Delacroix and Van Gogh as the representation of physical appearances or a feeling of beauty and order, and to achieve these ends they distorted and exaggerated freely.

Distortions of one sort or another—of form, light, color, and so on —have been the legitimate stock-in-trade of "expressionists" for many centuries. Yet when freely used they give rise to more protestation of "He can't draw" than any other artistic license, with assertions like "The figure is out of proportion" outnumbering all other explanations.

We are, however, caught in a vicious circle by phrases of this kind, for the flat generalization, "out of proportion," throws us back into the clutches of another fixed idea—that there is some one sacred kind of proportion which holds sway over all others, and that to depart from this abstraction is to be at fault.

To resolve this question, let us ask how Tintoretto's *Study of a Statue* would be improved if it were given the proportions of Michelangelo's study for the *Creation of Adam*. It would become heavier, calmer, and perhaps nobler, but it would lose its feeling of vibrant nervous energy and wiry strength. In short, it would express Michelangelo's ideas, but cease to be what Tintoretto had in mind. And that, appreciatively, is the heart of the problem—to find out what an artist is trying to say and respect his way of saying it, instead of trying to force our own views upon him. Never an easy thing to do, always demanding infinite patience, sympathy, knowledge, and respect, and never subject to absolute fulfillment, it is the only way to art that does justice to both us and it.

What we have been saying is meant to bolster beyond any doubt the profound wisdom of the final words of Konody's definition of art, that an artist imposes on his work a rhythm of his own creation *according to his own sense of fitness.* That sense of fitness is the principle of appropriateness in action. It is an artist's most precious possession, the key to his organizing intelligence, and the source of the signs we look for throughout the world of artistic expression.

Let me say, in conclusion, that most of our faults of understanding arise from seeing art piecemeal, and thus becoming sidetracked before we cross the goal. We utter such pat and fragmentary statements as "He can't draw!" "The figure is out of proportion," and "The perspective is off," and think we have rendered a considered criticism. In so doing we have been about as helpful as the art school instructor who tells a student to "do something about the nose."

We would do better to follow the practice of an automotive engineer. He does not merely design a brake, spring, or carburetor; he aims at a complete, efficient machine with its total performance in mind.

In a similar way an artist aims at the total visual expression of feeling, and each part of his result should be judged in relation to its contribution to that objective. Seen in that light, there is no such thing as poor drawing, proportions, and perspective in isolation or in the abstract. They are always good or bad in their relation to an expressive purpose.

For the most part an artist can control and coordinate the elements of total visual expression. But there are some influences which affect his actions above individual choice. They are the historical factors which envelop him as pervasively as the atmosphere he breathes and account for much of what he does. In Part III we turn to the broad outlines of these far-reaching factors and their visible signs in art.

PART III

The Historical Factors
in Art

CHAPTER 25

An Introduction to the Historical Factors in Art

An acquaintance with the historical factors in art will give us a broad view of the subject, and aid in our understanding of the many social and political influences on the changes and developments in technique and viewpoint in relation to the times in which they occurred.

Books on the history of art fall into five main groups. One is distinguished by a division along hemispheric or global lines. Books in that group treat either the Oriental tradition in art or the Western. Recognizing the existence of two great cultural traditions in the world which have emanated from Asia and Europe, they bear such titles as *The Way of Western Art* or *The Spirit of Man in Asian Art*. Their approach is sweeping and comprehensive, which inevitably leads to a good deal of generalization.

A second group, though less comprehensive, divides whole continents along regional lines in order to concentrate investigation on a limited area. *North European Painting* or the *Culture of the Mediterranean Basin* would be examples. This division pays special attention to the influence of geography and climate on the formation of traditions. Like the first group it attempts to explain the continuous or traditional elements in the history of art.

A third group also stresses continuous elements, but along different and more limited lines, working within the framework of nationality. Typical titles are *A History of French Painting, Italian Painting,* and *The American Spirit in Architecture*. Although these studies may consider the elements of geography, climate, and time, their special aim is to relate them to the cultural traditions which have grown up within political boundaries.

A fourth group of books, oriented along the time axis of history, explains the signs of change within different periods. Any book on the art of the Renaissance or the Baroque period illustrates this approach; a study of the successive periods of Egyptian sculpture does the same, as would a history of Greek sculpture in the Hellenistic period. This approach may be broad, embracing the whole of modern painting or limited to recent architecture in Sweden, but it deals in each instance with the changes wrought by time.

There are, of course, subdivisions within these groupings. There are numerous books on styles, like those on the neo-classic style in architecture. Similarly, there are books on movements, such as *The Impressionist Movement in Painting* and *Pioneers of the Modern Movement in Architecture*. But in the main the best known books on the history of art fall into the categories which we are describing in the hope of orienting the beginning student.

There is, finally, one large body of books which emphasizes the factor of individuality. These books, known universally as biographies, try to account for those characteristics of style which distinguish one Italian artist of the Renaissance from another, though they be master and pupil or the nearest of neighbors. It employs the closest approach, the ultimate refinement, the finest distinctions of any in the history of art.

If we consider these five divisions together, we can discern three guiding principles. In the first place, they lead us from the universal to the particular or individual, from the largest conceptions of time and place to the smallest source of creative action—the single personality. It is as though we first stand off from our work at some vantage point in the stratosphere from which we survey the whole of Asia; then we move closer where we can see the band of mountains that divides Europe into its Northern and Southern regions; finally, we look over the shoulder of Rubens or Van Dyck. From each of these perspectives we gain a special understanding. So, to introduce ourselves to the history of art comprehensively, and then refine our knowledge, we might well arrange our study in the same order.

These divisions suggest strongly why we should avoid the temptation to slight the history of ancient art in favor of modern, or the history of strange and distant Asiatic art in favor of the more familiar European. The purpose of studying the history of art is not to confirm what we can easily appreciate, but to extend our understanding to world-wide and historical proportions. Notwithstanding our bewilderment before Picasso's *Guernica* (Fig. 1) we generally find it easy or difficult to appreciate art in proportion to its proximity to, or remoteness from, us in time and place, art that is too close to us being the exception. We can easily enjoy Thomas Eakins' American paintings of fifty years ago, but we must normally make great adjustments to the ancient art of eastern Asia. This is the logical reason for beginning our historical study with the art of ancient, vast, and distant Asia.

Another guiding principle which these divisions suggest is that no work of art is entirely a product of any one of the factors mentioned. Rather, it is a culminating result of at least five distinguishable historical factors. A portrait by Augustus John, for example, may express his individual touch so strongly that it makes us forget the outside influences upon its conception. But it is also a portrait by an artist who is simultaneously a Northerner, Englishman, European, and Occidental of the twentieth century and whose ideas were shaped and formed by all of these facts. We tend to overlook the force of these other differentiating factors in our current emphasis upon "self-expression," but we would quickly be reminded of them if we were to hang Augustus John's painting beside a Chinese portrait from the Ming dynasty. Every work of art is thus a cross-product of many influences.

The result of these many influences is not an additive process, but a blend or mental synthesis. Their effects are so interwoven that the final result is much more than the sum of all the influences working separately. We must therefore make a conscious effort to perceive these controlling elements as separate factors for the purpose of analytical consideration. The divisions that we shall use—hemisphere, region, nationality, period, and individuality—are not sacred. Arnold Toynbee, for example, has protested against the national approach and set a persuasive precedent for a grouping by civilizations. We are merely following in our particular division the established approach along national lines because our intention here is to delineate the factors underlying the history of art, not to rewrite it.

THE WORLDS OF EAST AND WEST

When Occidentals and Orientals meet they do not see things in the same way. There have been exceptions—Western artists adopted Japanese prints at the same time that the Japanese adopted Western industrialism—but on the whole the statement is true. Typical is the case of Alexander the Great. Pushing into India he was fascinated by the doctrines of the native ascetics and tried in vain to understand them. They were unimpressed by his conquests; he was both awed and puzzled by their indifference to worldly achievements.

We may fare no better. But there are good reasons why we should examine the art of the Orient, even if briefly. Its inherent qualities make it well worth any study and rarely disappoint those who try to appreciate them. Another reason is that Oriental art speaks for two-thirds of the people on earth, India and China between them containing over eight hundred and fifty million inhabitants. To ignore Asiatic art is to distort the role of Western art in any global history. A third and practical reason is that their art is so different in style and spirit from Western art that it provides an excellent foil for the study of our own artistic heritage. It shows by contrast where we have been strong and where we have been limited. It gives us a better perspective of our own achievements while renewing our respect and tolerance for other points of view.

There is not space here to consider Asian art country by country or period by period, or to describe more than a few of the possible differences. But we can obtain an over-all view of the main differences in outlook by comparing a few typical Eastern and Western masterpieces. And we can do this with some system by contrasting their attitudes toward certain of our previously established points of reference, such as representation, design, and their resulting expression and the universal orientations of perception—naturalistic, religious, humanistic, introspective, social, abstract, architectural, and artistic.

Several of our previous illustrations are worth a second look in this connection. Fig. 2 is an Egyptian statue of Khum-Ba-F posed as a seated scribe. Fig. 3 is a statue of a Chinese *lohan*. The poses of the two men are similar, but they differ in almost every other respect. The Egyptian statue is glyptic, round, massive, appealing to our sense of finite weight and matter. This treatment brings the figure spiritually close to us. In fact, Khum-Ba-F seems to be leaning toward us and looking at us. The Chinese figure is linear, making it appear light in weight. The drapery rather than the body is stressed. The facial expression is austere and withdrawn. The effect is to make the figure seem remote. Both treatments are appropriate, for Khum-Ba-F's attitude is alert and outward looking. He is poised to write, ready for a specific act. The lohan is contrastingly introspective, lost in limitless thought.

Two worlds confront each other here—the one valuing practical awareness and materiality, the other not indifferent toward materiality but valuing meditation more, both as a method of self-realization and as a means of understanding external reality. Looking at these two statues we are reminded of a dynamic Western globe-trotter who raced up to Northern India to visit Gandhi during a hurried trip around the world. When a friend asked him afterward what he found Gandhi doing, he replied, "He wasn't *doing* anything! He was just sitting there thinking!" This was Alexander and the ascetics all over again.

The figures of *Sakyamuni and Prabhutaratna* in Fig. 172 are, similarly, just thinking and conversing; and the sculptural treatment is again linear, as weightless as thought. *Menkure and His Queen* (Fig. 160) is, on the other hand, wide-awake, down-to-earth monarchs, conscious of their surroundings and their temporal power; and their figures are appropriately massive and strong. The differences between the Chinese and Egyptian figures are consistent in each case.

The West has not been without its pride in thought. It can point to Michelangelo's "Il Penseroso" (Fig. 271), Rodin's *Thinker* and the many thoughtful men and women in Rembrandt's portraits. There is, however, a perceptible inclination in the West to want thought to concern itself with immediately practical ends. Meditation is not our forte, and mysticism leaves us cold. As a consequence, the West has excelled the East in the conquest of the natural forces through applied science. It has made thousands of practical improvements in the fields of health, agriculture, and physical comfort, bettering man's lot in all of these realms.

The Orient has concerned itself more with the welfare of man's soul. Its chief contribution has been religious. All of the major spiritual creeds, including Christianity, originated east of Suez, their main ideas coming almost invariably from India. The effect upon art in the East is plain to see; whereas many Western masterpieces are secular, the majority of Oriental masterpieces are religious. Even Western medieval art was created under the spell of an Orient-derived Christianity.

The differences between the Eastern and Western approaches to reality are thus fundamental. Even a beginner can recognize this fact. Let us see if we can explain them somewhat further by observing their effects upon the modes of representation and projection that each hemisphere has favored. We have already seen that the prominent examples of the glyptic mode in sculpture are most likely to be found in the West, whereas the Orientals have been masters of the linear mode.

A comparable difference can be found in painting. No one would mistake Vermeer's *Cook* (Fig. 93) for an Eastern painting or Harunobu's woodblock print of the *Beautiful Osen* for a Western. One reason is that Vermeer shared an interest in realism that has been latent in the West from the earliest periods of Egyptian art. He carried that realism as far as it can be carried, employing an all-inclusive artistic vision. Since he spoke our language, we understand him. However, he leaves Oriental critics unimpressed; they prefer the linear art of Botticelli. Better still, they prefer their own Harunobu who used the mode of line and local color which Eastern artists have favored for centuries on end. And it, by contrast with Vermeer's complex inclusiveness, is simple, the most selective of all the modes of painting.

The same difference appears in the field of spatial representation when one compares Perugino's *Christ Delivering the Keys of Heaven to St. Peter* (Fig. 102a) with Hiroshige's *A Traveller Buying an Otsu-E Picture* (Fig. 115). Typically, Perugino used a complex system for carrying spatial relationships to their logical conclusion. He shared a tradition which paved the way for the realism of Vermeer.

Hiroshige, on the other hand, felt no urge to push representation toward its limits. He employed the same mode of line and local color that Harunobu had used before him and the same diagonal projection that Oriental artists had used for untold generations. We should, however, be mistaken in thinking that this simplicity and conservatism were signs of ignorance. By Hiroshige's time Japanese artists were familiar with the perspective projection and realistic painting of the West. They retained traditional modes because they preferred them.

The same division of preferences appears in Oriental criticism. Baron Ino Dan and Professor Yukio Yashiro, two critics well-versed in the history of Western art, asserted to the author that they did not understand our penchant for realism. To them it seemed to favor transitory, superficial, and accidental aspects of reality at the expense of the long-range and essential. Their puzzlement over our realistic practice of recording fleeting phenomena of light and shadow is typical. This means simply that Europeans and Asiatics view reality regularly from two contrasting logical standpoints. As a result, realism has been a major tradition in the West, exceptional in the East.

The cleavage between Western practicality and Eastern mysticism can be seen repeatedly. For instance, Myron's masterpiece of athletic sculpture, *Discus Thrower* (Fig. 371), has been a favorite in the West, not only because it illustrates an athletic activity, but because it reflects a kind of thinking which we like. Typical of Greek thought at its best, it sheds light on a specific and limited problem by depicting an exact moment in time—the instant of poise between the upward and downward swing of the thrower's arm. It could not be more finite. The figure is designed as an ensemble of parts, each of which has a definite role. The dynamic meaning of the statue lies in the interrelationship which Faure referred to as "the life of the muscles" in Greek scuplture. Professor Wilhelm Koehler has perhaps come nearer the mark with his *principle of ponderation*. This means the

FIG. 371. Style of Myron. *Discus Thrower.* After Myron's statue of about 450 B.C. National Museum (Terme), Rome.

FIG. 372. *Siva as Nataraja, Lord of the Dance.* Late medieval period, 850-1200. Museum of Fine Arts, Boston.

principle by which Greek sculptors in general revealed the distribution of weight and muscular tension in a moving human figure by an exact portrayal of the muscles. Observe, for example, how perfectly Myron has revealed the tension in the upraised arm and supporting leg and the relaxation in the lower arm and leg. Every portion of the figure was studied part by part, resulting in a specific treatment of the problem of equlibrium.

This was the kind of definite and practical problem which the Greek mind loved and analyzed well. It illustrates how and why they were able to lay the foundations of Western philosophy and logic. It also defines their limitations. At their best with the finite, they fared less well with the infinite. Religious mysticism was not their forte.

Myron's secular masterpiece makes an Eastern example, the Indian *Siva as Nataraja, Lord of the Dance* (Fig. 327), seem strange indeed. The Indian figure is a deity unlike any in the Hellenic pantheon. Its spare arms not only set it apart from earthly creatures immediately, but farther than the Greek mind would ever go. So too does its sexless character, for Siva, a divine force and carrier of ideas, is not to be confused with any mortal man or woman. The rubbery litheness of the body, which radiates energy but has no human muscles, also sets it apart from the kind of figures that the Greeks and Occidentals in general have preferred.

Siva is only intelligible as a symbolical figure. The forearms and hands have the following meanings—in the upper right hand Siva holds the drum of creation, in the upper left the flame of destruction; the lower right hand is the gesture of preservation, saying "Do not fear!" while the lower left points to the raised foot signifying release. The right foot crushes the evil dwarf Mola. The sum of these symbols makes *Siva* in the role of Nataraja, the Cosmic Dancer, a composite of Creator, Destroyer, and Preserver. A summation of universal reality, the figure carries a heavy burden of meaning, heavier than any single Western statue. It is a typical product of Eastern mysticism, which has tried to see the universe as a whole.

However, we do not have here an interest in reality as opposed to indifference toward it, but only a difference in approach and scope. The Greek artist perceived universals through an exact analysis of particulars and limited himself mainly to what can be perceived sensorily and consciously. The Indian sculptor, conversely, did not hesitate to intuit a cosmic view of reality and express universal attributes in general terms. The most prominent characteristics of this dancing figure is a pervasive rhythm. But it is not the rhythm of any single human dancer or athlete. It is nothing less than the rhythm which characterizes natural phenomena globally and astronomically. It is evident in the rhythmic progression of waves, of day and night, and the seasons of the year. It is manifest in the fertilizing power of wood which has been reduced to ashes by fire. This transfer of energy in changed form we of the West formulate into the principle of the conservation of energy. The Asiatic perceives it more intuitively and is content to let it remain a natural principle without putting it to work; understanding is to him an end in itself, a source of awe and wonder. Having perceived a universal truth in its most comprehensive context, the Indian sculptor had to conceive his statue symbolically.

The East and West have both sought in their different ways to understand reality. They differ, however, in their attitudes toward the uses to which knowledge should be put. The West has placed its stress upon harnessing and controlling the powers of nature by putting its scientific understanding to work. The Orient has been relatively indifferent toward the conquest of nature and has emphasized human self-control. This has been especially true in India. In view of these different conceptions of what parts of reality should be mastered, it is not strange that the Western triumphs inherent in Myron's sculpture have been practical and scientific, the Eastern triumphs philosophical and religious.

The Orient's mystical and intuitive tendencies have not permeated its sculpture alone; they long ago created a different concept of landscape painting from that of the West. This difference can be seen concretely by comparing two landscapes in which the representation of deep space has been treated with marked success, Constable's *Weymouth Bay* (Fig. 373) and a detail of Tung Yuan's *Clear Weather in the Valley* (Fig. 374).

Considering first the similarities, let us note that both pictures present extremely panoramic points of view. Nature is large in both, the human element small. One would search far among Western landscapes to find one which conveys a greater sense of space and distance. Yet—and here we meet our point of departure—Constable's space is not without its limits. He carries us in a fashion typical of the Western mind to the limits of physical atmosphere, to the limit that the human eye can see. It may be five or twenty miles, but it is not great in global terms. Above all, it is finite, physically measurable space. Beyond that Constable would not go. He would not use the horizon as a springboard for an imaginative journey into unlimited space.

Constable's painting, a favorite in the Museum of Fine Arts, Boston, has often elicited praise for its spaciousness. It is a picture

FIG. 373. Constable. *Weymouth Bay*. *ca*. 1819. Museum of Fine Arts, Boston.

FIG. 374. Tung Yuan. Detail. *Clear Weather in the Valley*. Late 10th century, Sung Dynasty. Museum of Fine Arts, Boston.

with which we can feel at home.   Typical of the West's finest achievements in the representation of deep but finite space, it shows what can be done with Western methods of oil painting.   Tung Yuan's landscape presents another approach, with which we may or may not feel at home on first acquaintance.   In it the human figures are reduced to minute proportions.   A sense of vastness is implied.   However, his mountains are large and closer than the contours of Constable's horizon.   Why, then, do critics say that there is a greater sense of space in Tung Yuan's picture?   One reason is that his painting has no real horizon, no line of demarcation between solid earth and infinite space.   The edges of the mountains fade into nothingness. Another reason lies in a difference in medium.   Whereas Constable employed an oil pigment whose physical tangibility is felt even in the distant passages, Tung Yuan used washes of India ink, a medium as light and tenuous as air itself.   Washing over many areas just enough to give them the suggestion of atmosphere, he exploited what Chinese connoisseurs call "eloquent emptiness."   By deftness of method, suppression of outlines and economy of means, Tung Yuan created an effect which sets no earthly limits and invites us imaginatively into infinity.

The difference between these paintings is therefore not between depth and shallowness, but between a limited and a truly infinite point of view.   Among Western artists Turner, Monet, and Whistler approached the latter view, but their attitudes were exceptional.   By and large the Chinese landscapists of the Sung dynasty have never been excelled in this kind of painting.

The East and West have shared the naturalistic orientation, but have consistently produced different results.   We can see this by comparing Constable's small but masterly *Trunk of an Elm Tree* (Fig. 376) with another Sung painting, *Bamboo in the Wind* (Fig. 375) by Wu Chen.   Here we see the occidental and Oriental version of how nature should be depicted close up.   Offhand, Constable's painting looks like a photograph.   Following the Western realistic tradition, it explores every crack and cranny of the trunk, every leaf on every bough, the exact play of light on tree and grass.   No detail was too small to be observed and, if not recorded, at least suggested. Painstaking exactness is this picture's outstanding merit; it is a portrait of a particular tree.   Granted that Constable has also implied universal woodland properties in the massive trunk, rough bark, and luxuriant foliage, his treatment is limited, specific, individual.

On the other hand, universality is the keynote of the Wu Chen's *Bamboo in the Wind*.   We do not seem to be looking at a particular bamboo tree, but at a type which sums up the properties of all bam-

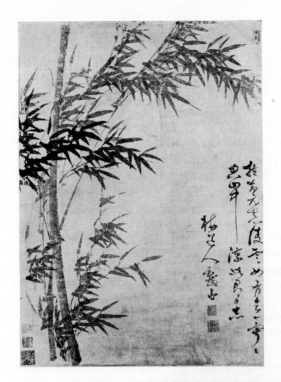

FIG. 375. Wu Chen. *Bamboo in the Wind*. Sung Dynasty, 960-1279. Museum of Fine Arts, Boston.

FIG. 376. Constable. *Trunk of an Elm Tree*. *ca.* 1820. Victoria and Albert Museum, London.

758

boo trees. Uniqueness is avoided, general character stressed. There is some variety in the leaves, yet their similarity is the quality that is stressed, as if they were made by a single kind of highly disciplined stroke. Indeed, that was the way the Chinese artists painted every kind of natural form, aiming at typical characteristics, handing their knowledge down from generation to generation. Always they aimed at what was essential—in this case the bamboo's ability to bend with the wind without breaking—instead of its surface covering or bark. The bamboo's popularity among Chinese artists was not accidental; its flexibility and lithe strength appealed to similar qualities in the Chinese mind. Thus, far from being a portrait of *a* tree, Wu Chen's bamboo stands free of any particular setting; it is all bamboos of the Orient in one.

Judging by their art, the Oriental peoples have favored the universal attributes of nature and the Western peoples the individual. The same detachment appears in the Asiatic conceptions of man's relation to nature. In the East human life is cheap. The result, to our eyes, is callousness, a retreat into introspection, and a resignation before natural laws. Especially noticeable is the absence of social sympathy. In the West, thanks to a grafting of Christianity upon the Greek humanistic tradition, human needs take precedence over any subservience to nature and the individual soul is important. Consequently, in spite of all our faults, injustice and brutality shock the Western conscience whereas they bring only a shrug in the East. This humanitarian ideal has colored occidental art, making human fate assume greater importance in it than in Asiatic art.

Let us take for observation two well-known renderings of the theme of man against the sea, Hokusai's *Great Wave* (Fig. 377) and an oil study for Géricault's *Raft of the Medusa* (Fig. 378). Looking at Hokusai's picture we are struck at once by the size of the wave; it is the leading character in the drama. Towering over the boatmen, it reduces them to minute scale. We wonder how the boatmen can survive this wall of water; we feel pity for them. But on second thought we fail to find any suggestion of fear. The boatmen race headlong into the trough as though they had survived a thousand such encounters and will survive this one by riding with the waves as a bamboo bends with the wind. Lacking any real signs of danger, we can enjoy the racy sense of movement that Hokusai conveys. Action, not fear or tragic emotion, is his message. In fact, while accepting the ocean's power, he maintained an Oriental detachment toward its effect on human life. Nothing about the picture asks for sympathy. We cannot identify ourselves intimately with these men; if we try, we encounter Hokusai's own impersonal treatment of the

FIG. 377. Hokusai. *The Great Wave*. From "Thirty-six Views of Fuji." *ca.* 1825. Museum of Fine Arts, Boston.

FIG. 378. Géricault. Oil study for *"The Raft of the Medusa."* *ca.* 1817-1818. Louvre, Paris.

boatmen. They are incredibly skilful little men who function with perfect teamwork, but not one of them is individual. Hokusai was not concerned with these boatmen as specific human beings. His interest was only in expressing his feeling for the surging power of the waves. Consequently, there is no particular story here, only a commentary on the universal relationship of the ocean with all men who travel upon it.

Nothing could have been farther from Hokusai's mind than a literal transcription of natural appearances. He used the age-old mode of line and local color favored by the Orientals and exploited its capacity for giving a sense of movement. The boatmen are treated conventionally, and so too are the waves, stressing Hokusai's interest in universal rather than particular characteristics. He has also taken liberties with normal proportions, distorting the contrast between waves and men. This, he is telling us, is not what a great wave looks like to the ordinary eye, but what it looks like to a fisherman in a tiny craft. This is the kind of painting we have come to expect of an Oriental artist and the kind of interpretation we expect from an islander who has seen tidal waves and typhoons.

Géricault's picture is totally different from Hokusai's. Typically Western, it tells the story of a particular episode and can only be fully understood in terms of that event's details. The story, briefly, is as follows: on June 17, 1816, the 44-gun frigate *Medusa* sailed from Rochefort carrying a new governor to Senegal with a crew and passengers numbering 400. Owing to inept navigation she ran aground on a well-charted shoal off Cape Blanca on July 2 and lost her convoy. Her six boats could hold only 250 of the 400 people aboard. The captain and governor took two of the boats, abandoning their charges to shift for themselves. Those who could not crowd into the four remaining boats built a large but makeshift raft from the ship's wreckage, and 147 people mounted it. The plan called for the boats to tow the raft 60 miles to land, but the rowers soon cut the ropes and left those on the raft to a nightmarish fate.

By morning of July 6, the raft bore only 127 occupants. These were being driven mad by fear and privation. That night half of them staged a senseless mutiny. The dawn rose on 60 dead. During the day of July 8 some of the men were driven to cannibalism, gnawing at dead limbs like wolves. Nightfall brought another mutiny in which 18 more were killed; the 30 left were nearly all wounded. On July 9 only 27 remained; 12 were dying: They were thrown into the sea as a necessity, leaving 15. These were saved seven days later, on July 16, by the brig *Argus*. Five of them died soon afterward, leaving only 10 survivors of the fourteen-day ordeal. The colonial authorities tried to suppress the news by coercion and, in one instance, murder; but the story which spread to scandalous proportions was still alive when Géricault painted it two years later.

Géricault's method of proceeding is significant. Like a detective gathering evidence about a crime, he consulted every survivor he could find and on the basis of their reports made a long series of studies which shows his desire to report every detail exactly. This oil sketch (Fig. 378) in the Louvre is one of the final studies which crystallized his ideas. Like the large final version, it represents the moment that the survivors sighted the *Argus*. The scene is individualized fully. A careful reporter, Géricault included only the 15 survivors who, according to the record, were on the raft at the time, and informs us correctly that one of the men who figured prominently in the saga was a Negro. He strove, moreover, to achieve portraits of their individual appearances and reactions. No two of them look or act alike. There are also subdivisions along emotional lines, some of them shouting strongly, others too weak to care, still others oblivious of the distant ship.

The raft of the *Medusa* was not just any raft. The disaster has since been called "history's most horrible shipwreck." Géricault underscored that distinction, eliciting by individualization of the scene our sympathy for the victims and our shock and anger at the captain. This concern and indignation are Western attitudes, both on our part and Géricault's. Yet they are presented skilfully. Géricault was more than a recorder of fact; he was a storyteller with an eye for the most dramatic moment in a powerful drama. He also brought considerable artistic ability to his task. Employing realism and pictorialism in exactly the proportions needed for the tragic mood, he composed with light and shadow, color, and atmosphere in a manner as characteristic of the Western tradition as Hokusai's linearism is of the Eastern.

Having considered the occidental and Oriental conceptions of man's relation to nature, what can we say finally about their respective humanistic ideals? What kind of man has each admired? For the start of an answer let us turn to two mounted figures which were cast in bronze, but are otherwise worlds apart. One represents *Lao-Tze on a Water Buffalo* (Fig. 379), the other is Andrea Verrocchio's noted *Equestrian Portrait of Bartolommeo Colleoni* (Fig. 380).

If, as it is said, societies show themselves through their heroes, Chinese culture appears at its best in *Lao-Tze*. Before the recent advent of Communism, he was one of China's most revered figures. In fact, since the bronze figure before us was cast at least two thousand years after his death, he seems to have introduced something

FIG. 379. *Lao-Tze on a Water Buffalo.* Sung Dynasty, 960-1279.
Worcester Art Museum.

FIG. 380. Verrocchio.
*Equestrian Portrait of
Bartolommeo Colleoni.
ca.* 1481-1488. Piazza
of SS. Giovanni e
Paolo, Venice.

enduring into Chinese thought. His name is a household word in the East but not in the West, so a brief description of what he signified so persistently may help us to understand the representation of him in Fig. 379.

Lao-Tze means "Old Philosopher." He is supposed to have been carried in his mother's womb for over sixty years after a supernatural conception, so that he was born white-haired, old, and wise. The legend is the sort which peoples project upon ancient heroes when they know little about their actual lives. So far as we know now, he was born about 609 B.C. and lived, the Chinese like to think, to an advanced age. His life overlapped that of his only peer in Chinese thought, Confucius, and the two reputedly met in 517 B.C., when Confucius was thirty-five.

More important than these few, uncertain data are Lao-Tze's doctrines; like most of China's heroes, he was a leader of thought. His precepts are contained in the *Tao-te-ling—Classic of Reason and Virtue*—a small book of about five thousand characters. Avoiding dogmatism and relying on the reader's intuition, he expressed himself with the utmost diffidence. His style is at once condensed, mystical, and poetic. As a result, Lao-Tze's philosophy seems vague to the average Westerner and is difficult even for scholars.

The chief difficulty is the meaning of the *Tao*. *Te*, the result of *Tao*, is correctly interpreted as virtue. The preferred meaning of *Tao* is that of the Confucians, the *way*, which means the method, means, or way through which one seeks virtue. On the face of it this would seem to resemble Platonism, but Lao-Tze's "way" differs from Plato's in one essential as much as China differs from Greece. To Lao-Tze that essential was the *quality* of one's means. The best translation of this quality seems to be spontaneous simplicity as distinct from conscious logic or reason. This set it on a different course from the Greek approach to virtue in which reason is a primary means.

According to Lao-Tze this spontaneous simplicity is exemplified best by the phenomena of the material world, whose actions are free from conscious self-seeking. They are instinctive and uncontrived, aiming at nothing but their own accomplishment. In this admiration for the natural world as a pattern for human behavior Lao-Tze differed markedly from Plato or any humanistic Greek.

The natural world passes through its processes, Lao-Tze pointed out, without assumptions, with a minimum of pride or display and a maximum of ease and grace. Therein lies its beauty. Society could have the same beauty, he believed, if it followed nature's example. His admiration for natural spontaneity was itself spontaneous. He loved it without trying to explain it. A cardinal point in

Lao-Tze's philosophy was humility, the opposite of presumption and ambition. He borrowed the example, he said, from nature and recommended it as the surest way to peace and happiness. He was, so far as is known, the first philosopher in history to advocate mercy, compassion, and gentleness. It was a bold idea, centuries ahead of his time.

Although Lao-Tze himself lived in a war-torn time which paid little attention to his advice, his teachings eventually struck a responsive chord among his countrymen and influenced Chinese philosophy and art deeply for over two thousand years. The figure of him on a water buffalo shows how well they understood what he symbolized centuries after his death. Significantly, it is a small figure, as modest in scale as it is in meaning. Lao-Tze himself could not have wished for a better characterization. He is depicted as genial and ingratiating, a man of good will and natural modesty, and, by the same token, a symbol of China's veneration for an old age that is both gracious and wise.

The contours of the statuette are modelled softly, without a hint of muscular strain, giving both man and mount an air of ease. While the buffalo ambles along, Lao-Tze perches on his back as naturally as a frog on a log and appears not to have a care in the world. The character of both is gentle and serene, the harmony between them complete. This is as Lao-Tze would have had it. His teachings show his feeling for harmony with all nature, his friendliness toward all animals. He made no distinction between them and men, since both possessed the all-important gift of life. As he saw it, vitality is the unifying property of the universe, not the monopoly of man. The whole spectacle of reality awed Lao-Tze. Although he had difficulty putting his reverence into words, his feeling for nature inspired artists and permeated the Sung landscape painting of Tung Yuan (Fig. 374) and others centuries later. It is therefore fitting that this little man should ride a water buffalo, China's infinitely patient domestic beast. A modest, civilized man himself, he would have sat ill on a war horse or other mount.

The *Equestrian Portrait of Bartolommeo Colleoni* (Fig. 380) was conceived in a different spirit. Colleoni was a fifteenth-century Italian mercenary. An opportunist and professional soldier in the most literal sense, he fought for whichever side paid him best. He changed his allegiance back and forth between the warring rivals, Venice and Milan, four times, until Venice made him a general. After his death in 1475 the grateful Venetian Republic commissioned the famous Florentine sculptor Verrocchio to immortalize him in bronze. The resulting statue, which is considered to be the finest

of all equestrian portraits, became the prototype for scores of others
in Europe and America. Large in size, it was set ostentatiously on a
high pedestal, from which Colleoni, confident that might makes right,
glowers down on weaker mortals. His hawklike, predatory face
makes him an individual, but he is also a type. The perennial "man
on horseback," he exemplifies physical power and intellectual arrogance, his chief claim to fame lying in his ability to ride roughshod
over other people. Apart from this, he is rather common; his lineage
extends back to men like the *Unknown Roman* (Fig. 307) and forward to the Prussian Junkers of our own day. Hardly a model of life,
any society which glorifies him tells us much about itself. The *Colleoni*'s quality as a work of art is another matter. The Italians did
not call the sculptor Verrocchio "true-eye" in vain. His realistic
rendering supports Colleoni's qualities perfectly, and the power with
which he imbues both man and horse makes it a masterpiece.

The Orient has not escaped its share of warlords; it has known
them all too well. But it has regarded them as evils, not as heroes.
While they appear in the Mughal art of India, in the brief Mongolian
period of Chinese art, and prominently in the Kamakura art of
Japan (Figs. 322a–c), there are few public monuments to them and
none that enjoys high favor. In the West nearly every large city has
its Colleoni-type monument, but there are no comparable monuments in Venice to Titian, Tintoretto, Veronese, Bellini, or Giorgione—who were her real glory. The West has tended more to idolize
its men of action, the East its men of thought.

If these facts seem to put the West in a bad light, let us remember
others to its credit. Although Christianity's ideals of brotherhood
and charity came from the East, it was the West which grasped their
possibilities for human progress and inspiration. The spiritual effect
upon art which can be observed in the Gothic cathedrals and in the
religious painting of the Renaissance was greatly to the credit of the
Western world. So if there is nothing in our art like the landscapes
of Tung Yuan, neither is there anything in the East comparable to
the depth of feeling in Titian's *Entombment* or Rembrandt's second
Supper at Emmaus.

Furthermore, it was the West which added to the Christian means
of spiritual growth another master key to the development of the
human potential. That was the belief in individual development in
a free society. The two together are the heart of Western liberalism.
Without that liberalism the art of the West would have been a different story—a story with many feudal castles and monastic sanctu-
aries, but few Da Vincis, Hogarths, Goyas, or Daumiers. As it was,
the artists of the West explored the whole secular world, extending

the range of artistic subject matter far beyond anything to be found in the East.

The Orient has rarely understood the Western urge for freedom, and the effect of its acceptance of autocracy upon the arts has been repressive. Compared to Western art, Eastern art as a whole has the unity and continuity of conservative effort but less variety. Its overall achievement is massive and on a high plane of spiritual and artistic refinement. Its subtlety and sophistication often make Western art seem crude. But it appears, at least to our eyes, constrained, its individuality hesitant, played down, afraid to show itself freely. Owing to political repression and practical backwardness, life in the East has been hard for most of its people, causing them to retreat, like the lohan in Fig. 3, into detachment and introspection, making them inwardly sensitive but fearful of letting themselves go. Hence, their merits have lain in extreme sensibility of feeling and design, and almost never in passionate expression. There is nothing among them like the gusto of Bruegel's *Wedding Dance*, Rubens' *Triumph of Silenus*, or Daumier's *Drinking Song*.

In another field, that of architectural conceptions, the East and West have differed widely. Owing to its practical genius, the West's architectural achievements have outstripped the East's. The most practical of the Orientals, the Japanese, employed and appreciated Frank Lloyd Wright, but they could never have designed his Imperial Hotel at Tokyo. In architectural engineering and expression the West has been in a class by itself.

These generalizations, which sweep over two hemispheres, are subject to numerous exceptions. Yet they will have served their purpose, if, being generally true, they define the Eastern and Western traditions for us in some small way or show us the strengths and weaknesses of each from a global point of view.

REGION

In the 1880s Hippolyte Taine, a French professor of art, delivered a series of lectures on the influence of *milieu*, environment, upon artistic expression. Among the influences he described, not the least were the geographical factors of climate and terrain. Today one hears little of these influences in critical discussion. Because Taine asked his theory to account for too much while neglecting the force of individuality, a reaction set in which eventually carried to the opposite extreme. Today the historical approach favors various artistic orientations and economic, social, and political factors and neglects the natural. This is an understandable bias of our urban culture, but it leaves unexplained some of the primary characteristics of art. The purpose of this discussion is to strike a balance between these two extremes and give nature its due without overemphasizing it.

There are obvious reasons for studying the role of natural environment. It is around us so much of the time that we take it for granted, yet it directs the talk of the most sophisticated city-dwellers daily toward the weather. We recognize it as a striking fact when we travel quickly from one region to another, as in an airplane flight from New York to Florida or Switzerland to Italy. It persists for centuries while racial customs and artistic fashions change and die. So it is unthinkable that it would not influence artistic expression as much as it does every other form of human life and thought, although subtly and subconsciously.

An illustration can be found in the effect that the geographical character of Egypt had upon its art in ancient times. Each year, with the melting of snow in the Abyssinian highlands, the Nile overflowed and then receded, leaving behind it a rich layer of silt. It did this with monotonous regularity year after year, century after century, bringing food to the Egyptians as a matter of course. To the east and west of this fertile ribbon there were mountain walls and limitless wastelands, minimizing invasions. If this minimizing of contact with other peoples and new ideas kept the Egyptians provincial, it also kept them safe. Safe and well-fed, they saw no reason to change their politics or customs for centuries upon end. Contributing daily to this preservation of the status quo was an environment of unusual regularity. Every day the sun crossed a cloudless sky, the great flat Nile flowed steadily toward the sea, and the desert around, devoid of life, seemed hardly to change from generation to generation.

The Great Pyramids (Fig. 381) at Gizeh, outside Cairo, eloquently reflect the character of this land. They were constructed during the Fourth Dynasty of the Old Kingdom, Egypt's greatest period of building. If, turning aside from them briefly, a visitor wanders over the nearby desert, he will notice certain characteristics of the arid countryside. The wind blows its sandy surface into mounds and natural pyramids. They are irregular in form, but smooth, planear, and sharp-edged. In the stillness after the wind, they look as though they have held their shapes forever.

Some writers have sought to explain the form of the Pyramids as tribal memories of a mountainous country from which the earliest Egyptians were driven by the drying up of the Sahara. A more likely source is the desert country immediately around. Little imagination would have been needed to give the irregular dunes the more regular permanence of art, especially if their inhabitants were inspired re-

FIG. 381. The Great Pyramids. *ca*. 2900-2771 B.C., IV Dynasty. Gizeh.

ligiously, as the Egyptians were, to create symbols of durability. Whatever the explanation of the Pyramids' origins, they are perfect man-made extensions of their environment. Borrowing their forms from the desert, they give a permanent order to its shifting sands and yet live perfectly among them. The harmony of building and environment is too complementary for one not to have influenced the other. It is hard to imagine the Pyramids of Egypt in any other setting.

In the history of art the pyramidal shape has been universal property. It seems to have occurred to men everywhere as a joint result of abstract conception and natural suggestion. But when pyramids arose in some land far different from the desert of Egypt, they were altered to reflect the new locale. For instance, the pyramidal temples which were built in the Indian region of Asia at Borobudur and Angkor Wat differ greatly from the austere Pyramids along the Nile. Intricately carved, they carry on their surfaces a tremendously complex array of sculpture. Some of this complexity is undoubtedly due to the Indian temperament and the intricacy of Indian customs and religious life. But these themselves are due partly to the character of the land, for India is as much a land of contrasts as Egypt is of uniformity. One cannot prove these influences upon the mind, for they operate on a far-flung and subconscious plane. That is one reason why Taine's theories have been discarded. Yet common sense tells us that the effects of climate and terrain upon architecture must be extensive.

Two other illustrations that suggest this are the Malwiyah Minaret in Iraq (Fig. 234) and the Great Temple (Fig. 240) at Tikal. The Minaret, a spiral variation of the pyramidal shape, is located in the arid belt that stretches from Suez to Afghanistan. And, like the Pyramids which rise from the Egyptian Desert, it is severely plain. One might take exception to this rule by pointing out the intricacy of Arabic decorations in a similar terrain. These represent a reaction against the plainness of nature, and yet they cannot escape the desert's effect. Like it, they are static, sharp-edged, linear, and finite in character.

The Great Temple at Tikal, Yucatan, is more consistent in its reflection of environment. A type of stepped pyramid, it exhibits a complexity of design reminiscent of Borobudur and Angkor Wat; like those monuments it arises from a country of contrasting weather and terrain. Its setting differs, however, from Indian environment in certain respects. Where India is vast, Yucatan is small and broken up by mountains and steep-faced valleys. Its limestone cliffs, washed bare by tropical rains in some places and overgrown with jungle in others, may not have suggested the blocky character of the stepped pyramid directly, but the fact remains that temple and terrain fit perfectly together.

The existence of stepped pyramids in desert countries, notably at Sakkarra in Egypt, does not necessarily refute this point. Their shapes derived, as do many architectural forms, from structural developments, but they differ in the decoration which men applied from choice. The pyramids of Egypt are bare, those of India and Yucatan ornate. Asiatic and Central American pyramids differ, too, in the character of their elaborateness. The Indian sculptural decorations are typically curvilinear, rounded, and sensuously soft, like the rubber-legged *Dancing Siva*. A lithe and rhythmic movement is one of their usual characteristics, along with a dreamy mysticism. The usual Mayan carvings are opposite in style and feeling, resembling more the Totonac ceremonial axe-head in Fig. 275. Harshly angular and sharp-edged, like the Great Temple itself, they reflect a different kind of country and culture. Yucatan imposed a cruel existence upon the Mayan settlers which had in turn a brutalizing effect upon their art.

No theory, of course, should be pushed to the extreme of an explain-all. Influences other than climatic and geographical entered into the Egyptian, Indian, and Mayan pyramids. Religious, cultural, economic, social, technical, and individual factors all played their parts. Nevertheless, the geography which lies behind all these should never be discounted.

The peoples of a given land may react, as the Arabic decorative artists did, against their physical milieu, especially in the harder regions of the world. We must be alert for these reactions. But a plausible theory holds that great architecture has arisen most often from a positive and harmonious union of nature and human thought, and secondly that the thought will vary in a fairly consistent fashion according to its natural inspiration.

If these ideas are true, we should find one tradition of architecture arising and persisting in the Mediterranean and another in the northern regions of Europe. That this has been the case is shown by the classical tradition which arose in the Mediterranean basin during ancient times and the contrasting romantic tradition that developed during the Gothic period in northern Europe. If the Treasury of the Athenians at Delphi (Fig. 382) and the Cathedral of Chartres (Fig. 385) appear fundamentally different, even at a glance, it is not difficult to understand why. The Treasury of the Athenians is an artistic extension of its setting. Typical of the European shores of the Mediterranean, that setting has the special character of the

FIG. 382. Treasury of the Athenians. *ca.* 515 B.C. Delphi.

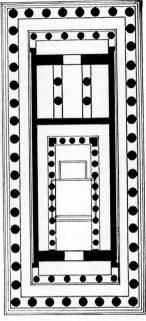

FIG. 383. Ictinus and Callicrates. Plan. The Parthenon.
447-432 B.C. Athens.

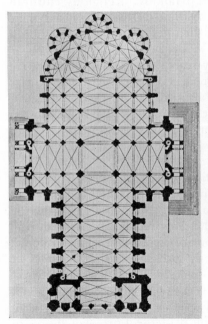

FIG. 384. Plan. Cathedral of Notre
Dame. 1194-1512. Chartres.

FIG. 385. Cathedral of Notre Dame.
1194-1512. Chartres.

Aegean islands rather than the massive hugeness of Egypt. A rugged and varied country of finite solids, its most prominent features are its hills and rocks. In the dry air and brilliant sunlight these stand out sharp and clear. Compared to Egypt's monumental harshness, it is a land of modest proportions and temperate climate which encourages balance and moderation.

Taking their cues from nature, the Greek architects designed a system of columns and porches that was suited to their temperate, sunlit climate. An architecture of balanced verticals and horizontals, it has an outstanding clarity of parts. A feature worth noting in this respect is the harmony between the gentle slope of the roof and the background mountains. The restraint of art reflects the moderate example of nature.

It was in this region that the balanced ensemble of parts basic to classic art was perfected by the Greeks. Thence it was carried along the European shores of the Mediterranean by the Hellenic colonists and conquering Romans. But it was adopted by other peoples for two good reasons: though no guarantee of beautiful art, it demonstrated its possibilities through many beautiful examples. In addition, it was "right" for the Mediterranean climate and terrain.

Far to the west and north of Greece the peoples of Gothic France lived in a different climate and terrain. They held different social, religious, economic, and political views, and had different physical needs. Nevertheless, they had lived throughout much of the Middle Ages under the spell of an alien architecture, a holdover from France's Roman days which made her architecture of the eleventh and twelfth centuries neither wholly French nor Roman but Romanesque, as one can observe in the beautiful but hybrid composition of St. Trophîme at Arles (Fig. 242). It was not until the final quarter of the twelfth century that they were ready and able to speak out for themselves. But when they did, they created a style perfectly adapted to their needs and land and, consequently, one of the most genuinely eloquent in history. A magnificent instance is the Cathedral of Chartres (Fig. 385).

It is hard to dissect such a noble monument objectively, but some analysis is necessary to bring out the contrasts we are stressing. The central fact in its existence is its location in a northern climate, with all of the infinite characteristics that the term implies—cloudy skies, changing lights and shadows, and soft outlines. A more weather-ridden land than any in the Mediterranean area, it is also more dynamic and alive. Compared to this the climate of Greece is as static and fixed as the Treasury of the Athenians.

In the North foliage grows luxuriantly. Pines, elms, and oaks rise toward the sky in intricate patterns, conveying a sense of growth along predominantly vertical lines. Trees and clouds create a different pattern in the human mind than any developed in the South. Suggesting that the most prominent features of reality are infinite, they play upon the imagination, the mood emotions, and any tendencies toward mysticism. Romantic in their effect, they prepared the northern builders psychologically for the creation of the perfect Christian church. The trees and clouds of the North do two other things. They cause men to be less conscious of the solid earth and more conscious of its vegetation and atmosphere. They set a precedent for light, airy, complex forms which reach upward to mingle with space and air along a broken skyline. They inspire, too, a fusion of structural parts into a continuous plastic whole, as different in design from the geometric Greek building as a tree is from a rock.

The character of trees permeates the Cathedral of Chartres' spires and towers, its pointed roofs and branchlike ribs. Like a tree, the whole building seems to grow from the ground instead of resting upon it like a rock. A tree has a harmonious connection with the earth that was not lost upon the Gothic builders. As for the clouds, they make men as conscious of the atmosphere above as they are of the ground beneath and induce a greater appreciation of light and shadow. Greek architecture is an architecture of solids; Gothic architecture, thanks to the trees and clouds, is an architecture of lighter and more open forms that have the power to suggest infinity.

The influence of these natural precedents is more than guesswork; it is plain to see in the character of the Cathedral of Chartres. Like the Grecian marble Treasury of the Athenians, that edifice was shaped from local materials, the limestone of the Île de France. In the course of time its surface has taken on a weather-beaten look which blends with the gray clouds overhead and bespeaks its northern location. But there is more to the eloquence of the Gothic style than material similarity. Like the wings of a gull, the impression it creates is due to a total "rightness of form."

Consistent with their superstructures are the plans of the Greek temple (Fig. 383) and the Cathedral of Chartres (Fig. 384). These give proof of separately integrated styles. The typical Greek plan is a geometric, self-sufficient rectangle, a single closed contour in which every part is separate and distinct. The equally characteristic Cathedral has a complex open-contour plan whose parts are continuously interrelated like a jigsaw puzzle and whose walls flow in and out to mingle with space and admit a maximum of light. The two plans could hardly be interchanged. It was therefore in Gothic France that the type of composition based on a fusion of parts was first perfected. Later employed brilliantly by the baroque artists of the seventeenth century, it created the second great tradition of Western art.

The aptness of classic and romantic design for their respective regions is shown by their later histories. If the former had spread mainly northward and the latter southward, our thesis of regional appropriateness would be upside down. History shows, however, that they spread consistently. The peoples of the North subconsciously recognized the propriety of the Gothic essentials for their climatic needs and kept them in their natural paths. The result was a band of buildings in the northern style which stretched from the Baltic plains to Puget Sound.

The essentials of the Mediterranean style spread south and westward in crossing the Atlantic and took root in regions similar to their European birthplace. There were, of course, exceptions, many of them quite beautiful, when cultural forces overrode the regional. The Georgian architecture of Old and New England and the Gothic buildings of the South (like the old State House at Baton Rouge) are prominent examples. But wherever natural guidance was respected the classic and romantic styles spread in parallel but separate latitudes. There is, for instance, the German town of Rothenburg, built mainly in the fourteenth century when German Gothic design was at its best. Due to its situation off the beaten path, it has retained a medieval flavor. Fig. 386 illustrates one of its streets today. Prominent are the steep roofs, harmony of shape, and continuity of design that characterize Gothic architecture. These buildings are to Gothic domestic architecture what the Cathedral of Chartres is to the ecclesiastical. The difference in quality is marked but each is representative of a common northern style.

In time that style crossed the Atlantic. In Fig. 387 we find a similarity in design that is not accidental. The Turner House at Salem, Massachusetts, is typical of those that the colonists erected during their first century on these shores. Being new in a rugged land, they were more mindful of practical than cultural requirements and built against the New England climate. Consequently, without there being any direct connection between Teutons and English colonists, the latter built as the former had. The similarities between Figs. 386 and 387 are more than coincidental. People who live close to nature in similar regions will not only build honestly and well, but they will build alike.

More than a coincidence, too, is the kinship of both Fig. 386 and Fig. 387 with the Fairbanks House at Dedham, Massachusetts (Fig. 388). All three illustrate the genius of the northern builders for har-

Fig. 386. Street in Rothenburg. Mainly 14th century.

Fig. 387. Turner House. "House of Seven Gables." 1670-1690. Salem.

FIG. 388. Fairbanks House. 1636. Dedham, Mass.

FIG. 389. Governor's Palace. *ca.* 1605; rebuilt 1744 and 1913. Santa Fe, N.M.

777

monizing buildings with their natural settings. The Fairbanks House is unusually fine in this respect. Bracing itself against the cold on its hilltop site, it seems both to hug the ground and grow from it like the Gothic cathedrals. Extremely harmonious is the way the rustic house blends with its setting of giant trees, and eloquent of its latitude are the small windows, large chimneys, and steep roofs. No one could imagine it anywhere else.

In reverse fashion the Governor's Palace at Santa Fé (Fig. 389) is perfect for its location. It would be as out of place in New England as a palm tree. First erected in 1605, it exemplifies the kind of architecture which the colonizers of the Southwest built in their early days as aptly as the Fairbanks House represents the northern colonial beginnings. The former were of Mediterranean stock, whereas the latter were English or northern. One may be sure, however, that they would not have built as they did if their positions had been exchanged. Nature demanded protection from the cold as a first requirement in the North, protection against the heat in the South. The builders who met these demands only used common sense in following traditions that had long ago taken heat and cold into account. Hence the Governor's Palace was modeled after the flat-roofed, adobe puebloes of the local Indians. These in turn resembled the international geometric, columnar architecture of the Mediterranean which had arisen in a similarly dry and sunlit climate.

In keeping with these beginnings, southern architects adhered to the classical styles of Italy, Greece, and Spain regardless of site as long as they allowed nature to guide their hands. Two examples are Figs. 390 and 391. Though separated by the width of the continent, one located in the Tidewater region of Virginia, the other on the Pacific Coast, they show how consistently the classical style kept its basic characteristics during its westward march. The Lee Mansion (Fig. 390), one of the most famous of American houses, is typical of the mansions erected all over the South during the height of the ante-bellum plantation era. Its large and shady portico is almost a symbol of that era's way of life. At the same time it is thoroughly classical. Its white façade was meant to gleam in the sun, and it sits on its hill like an ancient temple, dignifying and needing the spacious lawns around it. As if to stress its heritage, its proportions are nearly identical with those of a temple built by the ancient Greek colonists at Segesta in Sicily. It is not, however, more classical in its essentials than the Mission at Santa Barbara (Fig. 391) which was constructed by missionaries from Mexico and Spain. Both are of the great family of buildings which speak so eloquently of southern tradition.

FIG. 390. Hadfield. Lee Mansion. 1826. Arlington, Va.

FIG. 391. Mission.
1786-1800. Santa
Barbara, Calif.

779

It has been said that primitive or early architecture is seldom great but rarely bad. This is plain from the above examples. People who are attuned to nature can follow their intuitions safely and almost never build anything that is unsuited to its environment. Highly cultivated peoples, by contrast, often employ their greater knowledge inappropriately, a well-known example being the indiscriminate adoption of the neo-classic style of architecture all over Europe and America. Brogniart's Bourse in Paris is a specific illustration of the resulting violation of aptness and common sense. It is surrounded by a colonnade which is as classical as anything in Rome, but a forest of dirty chimneys rises from the roof to create a ridiculous effect. Smirke, in designing the British Museum, hid his chimneys better; yet his vast colonnade looks no less out of place in the gray dirt and fog of London. It needs the warmth and sunlight of the South. The British were truer to their instincts when they rebuilt the Houses of Parliament in the Gothic style.

A survey of the world's finest buildings shows that in general the great examples of architecture adhere to the traditions of their region; most of the bad examples conflict with their environments. It is not an accident that the Parthenon arose in the South and the Cathedral of Chartres in the North.

THE REGIONAL FACTOR IN PAINTING, DRAWING, AND SCULPTURE. Because of the practical function of architecture, architects cannot ignore the influences of climate and terrain, and at their best are extremely sensitive to them. Painters and sculptors, who work indoors and create objects which are protected from the elements, would seem to be freer from the effects of nature, but such is not the case. The history of painting and sculpture contains as much evidence of sensitivity to environment as does architecture, the principal difference being that expression is representational in the former and abstract in the latter. Otherwise, painting, sculpture, and architecture follow the same traditions in North and South.

For example, the painters of the Italian Renaissance were as classical-minded as any of its architects. Their favorite mode of representation was sculpturesque and their pictorial content primarily humanistic. From first to last the Florentine masters who inaugurated the Renaissance in Central Italy considered nature to be only a setting for the activities of man. In the pioneer efforts of Giotto, such as the *Flight into Egypt* (Fig. 224), the background is secondary in quality and dry and arid in form. It plainly interested Giotto little. It did not interest Michelangelo any more, two hundred years later. The whole world of the Sistine ceiling is a human-dominated world. During the fifteenth century, scores of Florentine artists, notably Leonardo da Vinci, took their sketch books into the midst of nature and filled their pictures with natural forms. Their designs are always composed, however, of static, finite forms in the age-old classical style. There is such a noteworthy absence of anything resembling weather among them that the exceptional sketches of storms by Leonardo are striking. In the Piccolomini Library in Siena there is a series of frescos by Pintoricchio, one of which contains a rainbow and thunderstorm. Even here the meaning was intended to be symbolical of storms and triumphs that lay ahead of Aeneas Silvius Piccolomini. As a representation of a tempest it leaves much to be desired.

The leadership in landscape painting came, significantly, from the North of Italy when Venice rose to her full heights in the sixteenth century. And the two men who effected the greatest change were born in the foothills of the Alps. They were Giorgione of Castelefranco and Titian of Cadore. Throughout their lives the luxuriant countryside from which they came appeared and reappeared in the backgrounds of their pictures. As a result, the contrast between Giorgione's *Pastoral Concert* (Fig. 392) and Giotto's *Flight into Egypt* (Fig. 224) is extreme. Whereas Giotto's background is barren, Giorgione's is green and fertile. The human element is no less prominent in the Venetian painting, but it is enveloped in a more romantic mood. Colors and outlines are soft, the backgrounds atmospheric and luminous. To show that this interest in a more dynamic and infinite nature was not exceptional, Giorgine executed one of the most beautiful of all landscape settings for his *Sleeping Venus* (Fig. 79) and painted another picture, called *The Tempest,* in which nature plays a leading role. Titian, who outlived Giorgione by sixty-six years, developed this beginning to such a degree that he anticipated the impressionist landscapes of the nineteenth century.

If our thesis is correct, the farther north we go, the more conscious of luminosity, atmosphere, blended colors, vegetation, and weather artists will be. History bears this out. When the northern schools of Holland, Flanders, France, and England came into their own after the decline of the Italian Renaissance, the great period of landscape painting followed. Rembrandt, Rubens, Ruysdael, Claude Lorrain, Constable, Turner, and Monet were conditioned throughout their lives to be aware of nature and to paint it with understanding.

In the history of art there are several examples of remarkable sensitivity to a change in environment. The most famous is the change that occurred abruptly in the painting of Van Gogh when he moved from Holland to Paris and then to Arles in the south of

FIG. 392. Giorgione. *Pastoral Concert.* *ca.* 1505. Louvre, Paris.

France. His colors altered from the drabbest of grays and browns to the most brilliant hues in nineteenth-century painting. A similar, though somewhat more restrained, transformation occurred in the palette of Winslow Homer. Born in New England, he spent most of his life in the region stretching from New York to Canada. But in 1883 he took the first of several trips to the Caribbean, with invigorating effects upon his colors that are plain to see. Corot, on the other hand, proved the point by traveling in the opposite direction. Although born in France, he elected to travel during his early years in Italy. There, under the influence of the Mediterranean sun, he painted masterly examples of blocky, clean-cut, sunlit architecture. Then, upon his return home, he shifted his attention from form to atmosphere and developed his famous method of painting feathery trees in silvery green tones.

The honors of art have been divided consistently between North and South in several other ways. By and large the South has proved its mastery over geometric form in architecture and no less in painting and sculpture, while the North has excelled in the plastic. The strength of the plastic was not confined to the builders of the Gothic cathedrals. It persisted in the Dutch Van Gogh, no matter what his addiction to the color of the South, making his landscapes, like the *Mountainous Landscape* at Copenhagen (Fig. 65), combinations of southern color and northern plastic form. Conversely, the strength of the classic tradition, with its love of finite solids in geometric shapes, never deserted Cézanne. Born within a few miles of the Mediterranean, he had the classical way of thinking in his blood.

Coexistent with these separate concepts of form were two divergent concepts of beauty, one predominantly idealistic, the other realistic. The southern artists who followed the Greeks were bent upon improving nature and making it as pleasing as possible. The results can be seen in a detail of Da Vinci's *Virgin of the Rocks* (Fig. 57). The smooth, regular features of his young angel make her an outstanding but typical representative of the southern point of view. The northern artists were not indifferent to felicities of proportion, but they valued truth to nature more. Albrecht Dürer, the greatest German artist of the Renaissance, exemplified their views. Called the Leonardo of the North, he journeyed to Italy at the height of the Renaissance and earned the respect of the Italian masters on their own ground. There is also evidence that he tried his best to emulate the Italian manner. In spite of this, he remained a northerner to the end. When he drew his own *Mother* (Fig. 395) in 1514 he presumably saw her affectionately; yet he spared none of the dried-up angularity that made her old and physically ugly. Like

FIG. 394. Raphael. *Three Graces. ca.* 1502. Condé Museum, Chantilly.

FIG. 393. Rubens. *Three Graces. ca.* 1638-1640. Prado, Madrid.

FIG. 395. Dürer. *The Artist's Mother.* 1514. Kupferstichkabinett, State Museum. Berlin.

FIG. 396. Da Vinci. Detail. *Virgin of the Rocks. ca.* 1483-1486. National Gallery, London.

northern artists in general, he believed that her real beauty was more a matter of character than of appearance. His drawing is not beautiful because of its content, but because of the flowing, plastic quality of its lines. A little later in history Rembrandt was to confirm Dürer's esthetic views when he too made old men and women seem beautiful because of the richness of their characters and the warmth of his light. He and Dürer were both northerners in their attitude toward beauty.

Thus, in comparing a southern master with a northern, we do not honor youth and beauty as opposed to age and ugliness, but different notions of where beauty lies and how it may be expressed artistically. To an idealistic Da Vinci, physical beauty was true and good; to a realistic Dürer, physical truth was beautiful and beauty of soul was good—a division of premises which persisted for centuries north and south of the Alps. True to form, Dürer did his finest work when he followed his Gothic heritage, his least convincing when he tried to follow the Italians. Not even beginners would mistake his apple-cheeked *hausfraus* for Raphael's classic-profiled Madonnas.

We can divide up the achievements of North and South a little more by observing their respective treatments of the nude. Almost as soon as the Mediterranean artists could draw and paint, they began to represent the unclad human form. In the classic art of Greece it became a common denominator, a major attribute of their humanistic orientation. The conception of the nude which they established was idealistic, emphasizing youth, grace, and felicity of proportions. When the Italians of the Renaissance revived the precedents of ancient classical art, the nude became a prominent feature of the revival. Nothing could have been more natural. Like the Greeks they lived in a warmly temperate climate where knowledge of the nude is as common as prudishness is rare. It took only a minor breakdown in medieval taboos for the Italians to reassert their frankly sensuous pagan love of the undraped human body. Michelangelo made it the subject of his whole career and Raphael represented it repeatedly. Raphael's *Three Graces* (Fig. 394) at Chantilly shows the typically southern attitude of the Renaissance mind. Painted early in his life, it was based on a Praxitelean sculptural group which he saw as a young man in the Piccolomini Library at Siena when he was assisting Pintoricchio with a cycle of frescos. Being attracted to and copying an example of Praxitelean grace was as normal to him as drinking Chianti; what is more to the point is that he did it easily and well. For him to work within the major tradition of his region was as natural as breathing its air.

What happens when an artist departs from the basic tenets of his region we saw in the art of Dürer. In a similar fashion Rubens' art provides us with a means of comparing the northern and classical conceptions of the nude. In almost every way a supreme and universal genius, Rubens went to Italy as a youthful student and absorbed the prevailing spirit of the Italian Baroque style without the slightest trouble. Not only had much of that spirit come from the North, but its expansive vitality was in harmony with his own nature. A red-blooded, sensuous man himself, he had a good deal of the pagan in him and loved the nude spontaneously. Furthermore, he equipped himself intellectually to represent classical themes by learning Latin and reading ancient mythology, history, and literature widely. If any northerner was ever to understand the classical tradition, he should have been the one. In spite of all this, he could not overcome his background. His art tells us this beyond a doubt, his own conception of the *Three Graces* (Fig. 393) being a typical example. It has vitality, and a curvilinear rhythmic unity. But grace is lacking. What Raphael attained with ease, Rubens strained for and missed. A contradictory grossness emanates from his realistic treatment of the three heavy-limbed and all-too-real models, who were probably three versions of his wife. This gross realism destroys any semblance of the idealistic symbolism requisite to any conception of the graces. Rubens himself could not resist a jest at his own misplaced realism and had one of the graces pinch the flabby arm of another.

Rubens was suited to portray the more rollicking classical themes, but he makes us love pictures like the *Three Graces* in spite of, rather than because of his buoyant, earthy spirit. The explanation for this is not hard to find. Although distinctive, as the work of genius always is, Rubens' art was not atypical. Rather it was of a piece with his inheritance. Behind him lay the materialistic realism of Van Eyck and the earthy gusto of Pieter Bruegel. He merely carried them to new heights.

More comprehensive still was another northern attitude toward the nude. Compounded of ignorance, lingering medieval taboos, and a tradition in which realism was stronger than idealism, it manifested itself in a continuous Puritanism. The northerner views the nude with different eyes from the southerner and has for many centuries. Instead of enjoying and idealizing nudity easily and naturally, the ill-at-ease and more moralistic northerner seems to be fascinated by the ugly, flabby, gross aspects of human nakedness. This attitude is apparent in the self-consciously naked farm hands whom the Van Eycks posed as Adam and Eve for the Ghent Altarpiece; and it persists through the art of Rembrandt and on into the

nineteenth century. Eakins' *Masked Nude Woman* (Fig. 150) is a
lineal descendant of this gallery of nudes whose every wrinkle and
flabby contour is not only represented, but stressed. It was this
tradition which Rubens could not escape.

If the principal laurels have gone to southern artists for masterpieces of the nude, the North can lay claim to a compensating mastery
over the representation of drapery. In the hands of their finest
artists it became a major means of expression. Let us begin, however, by recognizing that the South was not without its genius in this
field; its interest merely lay in a different direction. An excellent
representative of the Mediterranan point of view is the *Birth of
Aphrodite,* or principal relief on the Ludovisi throne at Rome (Fig.
397). An original Greek carving, it speaks in every detail for the
classical love of graceful, young, and well-proportioned human bodies.
So strong, in fact, was that love of nude bodies that the Greeks were
reluctant to hide them. When drapery was required for the representation of the female form in the centuries before unclad women
were freely shown, the sculptors devised a system which represented
both body and clothing so well that it gained lasting acceptance.
Their system was to make the drapery folds simultaneously describe
the contours of the body. Instead of clothing it to obscurity, they
enhance its forms. Rarely is their drapery thick and concealing;
more often it is diaphanous and revealing. In this way the humanistic Greeks kept the human body their principal vehicle of expression. The *Three Fates* from the Parthenon will occur to anyone as
a famous example of this system, and the *Birth of Aphrodite,* in which
it can be clearly seen, is equally effective.

The artists of the Gothic North handled drapery in a nearly opposite way. Lacking the southerner's understanding of the body, they
were content to stop with its clothing. Since that clothing meant
warmth to them, they saw it in a different light than did the south-
erners and studied it with love and care. The realistic representation of drapery became their forte until Van Eyck, Holbein, and
many other artists were the equals, if not necessarily the superiors,
of any southern masters in this field. Going beyond that, the Gothic
artists did something that the Mediterranean masters rarely did; they
made the lines and folds of drapery carriers of emotional expression.
They did this, moreover, with a greater degree of abstract design and
freedom from explicit bodily contours and movement. Instead of
making drapery cling to the body, as in the *Birth of Aphrodite,* they
declared its independence and made it an equal partner in the expression of human feeling.

The German sculptors, graphic artists, and painters of the Gothic

FIG. 397. *Birth of Aphrodite*. Central panel of the "Ludovisi Throne." Transitional period, 480-450 B.C. National Museum (Terme), Rome.

FIG. 398. *Tomb of Philippe Pot*. Late 15th century. From the Abbey of Cîteaux. Louvre, Paris.

period and the Renaissance were especially adept at this kind of emotional expression, as one can easily see by studying the art of Riemenschneider, Veit Stoss, Schoengauer, or Dürer. No small part of the fame of Dürer's woodcut of the *Four Horsemen of the Apocalypse,* for instance, is due to a mastery of expressive drapery. This abstract treatment of drapery in angular or curvilinear designs was general throughout the North. An essential characteristic of Gothic sculpture, both early and late, it is exemplified by the noted *Tomb of Philippe Pot* in the Louvre (Fig. 398). The mourning figures which support the bier are so swathed in drapery that their human character is almost lost. Their forms have become, in a sense, hangers for the all-important clothing. This is the exact reverse of what any Mediterranean master would normally do, yet it proves its worth in Gothic hands. Indeed, it expresses the tragic mood of the *Tomb* with sober power.

The artists of the northern and southern regions have thus shown equal mastery, but in divergent, and often opposite, ways. Different climates cannot account by any means for the whole of this divergence in the face of the constant countereffects of cultural exchanges, but they were still powerful factors. In almost every instance they have had a transforming effect upon all cultural importations, as in the half-Gothic, half-classical character of Georgian church steeples. This has been especially true in Europe because of the subdividing effect of the Pyrenean-Alpine-Carpathian chain. But it applies no less to Asia with its mighty Himalayan barrier. And it applies equally to any continents, like the Americas, whose expanse carries from tropical to arctic latitudes.

Art is therefore a cross-product of many factors. It is never exclusively regional, but seldom wholly nonregional. It can never be truly universal or entirely free of its geographical ties. On the contrary, it should not attempt to be, for it has most often been at its best when it has given them their due.

NATIONALITY

One day in 1903 the English author Arnold Bennett attended an exhibition of American paintings in London. Finding only galleries full of imitation Bouguereaus, Gérômes, Cabanels, and Meissoniers, he stopped before a painting by Winslow Homer and exclaimed, "That is the only truly American painting in the Exhibition." [1] To ask what he meant is easier than to answer, for when historians

[1] Related to the author by Booth Tarkington, who had attended the exhibition with Arnold Bennett.

of art began to write along national lines they raised more problems than they have solved. Recording French or German history is one thing, describing what distinguishes it as French or German is another.

All of us agree on the existence of national characteristics, but few of us can define them. The signs of nationality are nevertheless all around us. They are especially evident in languages—in the guttural masculinity of German, the melodious fluidity of Italian, the crisp vivacity of French. An amusing difference was noted by Clarence Day when he had to learn French as a boy: whereas his English Bible read, "Jehovah was wroth," the Gallic equivalent was "Le Dieu était irrité."

Musical nationalism is hardly less distinctive. A person who knows no other language in the world except his own can instantly tell French music from Hungarian or Spanish from Norwegian by fundamental differences in tempo and rhythm. Mozart's *Don Giovanni,* which is more Italian than the Italians, is a rare exception created by genius.

The most obvious illustrations of nationality can be found along boundary lines. There is a street in Europe which demonstrates this vividly. The people who live on one side speak French, those on the other side speak German. Furthermore, the Gallic minds are oriented toward Paris, while the Teutonic minds are turned in the opposite direction, toward Bonn and Berlin. Though physically only a few yards apart, the two groups are hundreds of miles apart mentally and culturally. This contrasting juxtaposition is typical of scores of European customs houses and border stations.

Because of this and similar examples, nationality has been described as a state of mind based on a geographical entity. The geographical factor, being relatively fixed, is the most continuous influence. But national attitudes can also display remarkable persistence in spite of transportation across continents and oceans. The Englishman carries his social customs with him around the world, reportedly dressing for dinner even in the jungle. An American is equally recognizable anywhere because of his American clothes, behavior, language, and manner of speaking.

Moreover, it is likely that the differences which distinguished Frenchmen from Englishmen and Chinese from Italians a hundred years ago were similar to those which differentiate them today. The national traits which Casanova shrewdly noted in his travels in the eighteenth century read as though they had been written yesterday. Truly national characteristics are therefore more than momentary; they survive both transportation and the passage of time. They seem, indeed, to be reborn perenially out of the soil of the land or the atmosphere that people breathe. So, in seeking in art the signs which stem mainly from nationality and not from something else, let us turn first to the powerful and continuous influence of geography.

In discussing region, we saw that geography overrides national boundaries. It united the Mediterranean world artistically, producing a southern architectural, sculptural, and pictorial tradition which is recognizably distinct from its counterpart to the north. This demarcation is especially apparent wherever a continent is divided by a barrier of mountains, as the Alps divide Europe and the Himalayas Asia.

Within a region geography can play two opposite roles, aiding national unity in one area and impeding it in another. Wherever geography takes the form of plains and rivers which encourage travel, it will promote the fusion of different people into nations. Wherever it takes the form of mountain chains and pockets, it will make fusion difficult if not impossible. The cohesion and continuity of Egyptian civilization illustrates geographical unification. Geographical diversification is exemplified all too clearly by the tragic disunity of the ancient Greek city states and the Italian republics of the Renaissance, both of which were subdivided by mountain ranges. As a result their art varied considerably from city to city. Neither ancient Greek nor Italian Renaissance art was national in any modern sense; each was an agglomeration of local schools.

Thus the regional factor will not explain everything when the region is physically broken up. On the contrary, diversification then becomes an outstanding characteristic. The most obvious instance of diversification along these lines occurred in the history of Gothic architecture. That style became international when it was adopted by a church which was Catholic or universal in the sense that it presided over the whole of Western medieval Christendom. When the style spread from France to the region south of the Alps and the Pyrenees, it was altered along regional lines, resulting in a Gothic style in Spain and Italy which is Mediterranean, if not wholly classical, in character, and is different from the northern Gothic style shared by England, France, and Germany.

Yet anyone can distinguish between English and French Gothic to the north and Italian and Spanish Gothic to the south, the Moorish ingredients in the Spanish being only one of several special marks. These subdivisions we can fairly call national. Such a subdivision is found in the engineering of the French cathedrals at Reims, Paris, and Beauvais, for it is more progressive, daring, and inventive than anything to be found at Gloucester, London, or York. Nothing in

England is structurally comparable to the flying buttresses of Notre Dame in Paris or the soaring vaults of Beauvais Cathedral. On the one hand we have the Gallic combination of logic and audacity, on the other British conservatism and reticence. In addition, the designs of the French cathedrals with their towers and splayed portals, stress the façade, while the English designs favor a lantern or spire over the crossing, de-emphasizing the façade proportionately. And where the French cathedrals, rising from the midsts of towns, express the Gallic social sense, the English cathedrals are often set in parks, denoting their preference for the countryside with its rural beauty and greater privacy. In only one respect did the English imagination run riot, perhaps as a compensation for its normal reserve. That was in the field of ornamentation. Lacking the French concern for structural logic, the English decorated their churches profusely from the middle period of Gothic on. Thus two different national temperaments gave rise to the differences which we can observe today between the Cathedral of Salisbury and the Cathedral of Chartres.

In a similar fashion, the Gothic style was transformed by the Mediterranean tradition when it crossed the Pyrenees and the Alps. And, what is to the point for our study, it was also reshaped by predilections which are national as well as regional. In Spain the Moorish influence modified the Gothic, especially in decoration. In Italy that influence was weak, but another, the ancient classical tradition, was growing stronger with the approach of the Renaissance.

This classical tradition was, as we saw in the previous chapter, almost diametrically opposed to Gothic architecture in every facet of spirit and design. What happened when the Gothic style from the North met head on with the resurgent classical mode can be seen today in the Cathedral of Milan. Although the luxuriant decoration of the exterior creates a Gothic impression, the proportions of the style have been radically altered from a vertical emphasis to a balance between height and width. Also, there is apparent in the nave the effect of the Italian desire for shade rather than the northern "hunger for light"; the windows are small, the interior dark as Gothic buildings go—a far cry from the openness and luminosity of Chartres.

A better example still is the Church of St. Francis at Assisi (Fig. 399). Here the young Giotto painted the first great cycle of frescos that clearly anticipated the Renaissance; classicism was in the air. The builders were caught between it and the reigning Gothic fashion. Although unable to resist the northern style, they could do little more than borrow from it superficially. Fundamentally they never understood it. The telltale flying buttresses would make a northerner smile, while he would have to hunt for the pointed arches. In

FIG. 399. S. Francesco. 1228-1253. Assisi.

FIG. 400. S. Maria Novella.
1278-1350. Florence.

form and spirit the massive geometric, static, finite building is nearly as un-Gothic as anything designed by the Greeks.

A typical Italian Gothic interior, like that of the Church of Santa Maria Novella at Florence (Fig. 400), presents a slightly different problem. Here the stylistic hallmark of Gothic, the pointed arch, stands out so strongly on first inspection that it would seem far-fetched to call the building classical. Yet if the clearly delineated parts, small windows, and heavy walls are not entirely classical, neither are they Gothic by any northern standards. Certainly they show how the Gothic style was tempered by the classical tradition whenever it entered the latter's domain.

The position of Florence in that domain suggests a further rule which might be called the principle of proximity. It is not by accident that the relatively northern Cathedral of Milan has the most Gothic character of all the major Italian churches and the central Italian Church of St. Francis at Assisi very little, for that influence increased in Italian buildings of the Gothic period in proportion to their proximity to the Alps and decreased in proportion to their nearness to the Italian center of classicism—Rome. Added to this was the important factor of communication: Milan was located on one of the busiest routes between Italy and the North, while Assisi was in the less accessible hills—a physical situation which worked against any genuine understanding of Gothic engineering and design. The validity of this general rule—proximity equated with communi-cation—has been agreed upon by scholars of the international hybrid Romanesque, but it applies no less to the transformation of the Gothic style by a tradition in which Italian and Roman classical are virtually synonymous. It is a good illustration of the national leavens at work.

We have used architecture to demonstrate nationality because, being the most collective of arts, it exemplifies group expression best. We are on less certain ground when we turn to the less collective arts of painting and sculpture in the relatively individualistic cen-turies that followed the dawn of the Renaissance. That national traits exist and can be discerned is, however, a safe assumption even here. Some of the better known examples can be found in French painting and sculpture, in the sculpture of the ancient Assyrians and Egyptians, in Dutch painting of the seventeenth century, and in American painting since the birth of our nation. There are many others.

The transforming power of national attitudes is probably most evident when a style of painting or sculpture enjoys international popularity, as Impressionism did at the end of the nineteenth century. After Monet and his group made the movement famous in France, Childe Hassam and many other Americans followed in their train. Each group painted its share of handsome pictures, but no one would mistake the one for the other. In almost every comparable instance Monet was more audacious and vivacious in color and execution. The Americans, by contrast, tended to keep their feet on the ground and paint more cautiously. Our poetic visionaries, like Ryder and Thomas Cole, have been few. Far greater in number have been our men of practical vision and rugged strength, like Eakins, Homer, and Bellows. It was undoubtedly some kind of New World virility in Homer's painting that made Arnold Bennett call it "American." It is apparent in the raw vigor of his *Northeaster* (Fig. 18) and no less in his *Coming Storm* (Fig. 119). In any case, Homer's Impressionism is very different from Monet's.

A noted change occurred in the art of Greece when it was adopted bodily by the Romans, the conquerors literally carrying off hundreds of statues to the imperial capital. They imported Greek sculptors in whole schools, or went to Athens themselves to study. Their admiration could not have been more complete. But in every case where the native Roman sculptors tried to copy the Greek originals or work in a similar vein, a transparent coarsening in style ensued. No amount of admiration or diligence could conceal the fact that the Romans were better soldiers and empire builders than the Greeks, but poorer philosophers, poets, dramatists, and artists. A comparison of the *Zeus from Artemisium* (Fig. 50) with any pseudo-Greek statue carved in Rome will make this plain.

A similar transformation occurred in the Orient in later times. The Japanese, as everyone knows, have admired the culture of China for centuries with the mixture of envy and respect that the Romans had for the Greeks. They adopted the Buddhist religion with all that it meant for the spirit and form of art; and when the Chinese turned to landscape the Japanese did the same. Not content with distant influences, their leading masters visited China to study the Chinese manner at first hand. Sesshu, to name one, journeyed on the continent from 1467 to 1469. The result was a general harmony between the styles of the Sung landscapists on the mainland and the Ashikaga idealistic school in Japan. It is illustrated by Tung Yuan's *Clear Weather in the Valley* (Fig. 374) and Sesson's *Fishing Boat Returning in a Storm* (Fig. 401). But despite the best of wills, Sesson's national consciousness of his own island home and its tradition of the sea created a major difference in outlook and subject between his work and Tung Yüan's vision of a vast, continental expanse. There is also a difference in treatment that applies generally to any

FIG. 401. Sesson. *Boat Returning in a Storm*. 16th century, Ashikaga period. Collection of Mr. Fumihide Nomura, Osaka.

FIG. 402. Goujon. *Water Nymphs*. From the "Fountain of Innocents." 1547-1549. Place des Innocents, Paris.

796

two representative masterpieces of Chinese and Japanese art. No matter how subtle Japanese art appears to Western eyes, it is relatively coarse compared to the art of China. Harunobu's *Beautiful Osen* (Fig. 361), to take an illustration, may seem like a model of grace on first acquaintance, but she is not in a class with the beauties of Ku K'ai-Chih. As in the relationship of the Romans and Greeks, the Japanese were the better warriors, but the Chinese were the finer artists, philosophers, and poets.

These adverse comparisons are, of course, one-sided on our part. No Japanese artist compares the art of his native land unfavorably with that of a foreign country. Rather, he is prone to feel that for better or worse there is "no place like home." Sesshu, as we have said, visited China; returning, he said that he had seen famous mountains and great rivers, and had sought for masters in many provinces but he had journeyed in vain, for he found that there was none to match Shubun and Josetsu. In the end he expressed the natural affinity of almost every man for the artistic language of his own country. This preference, bias, prejudice, or what you will, is one of the strongest forces behind the nationalization of art. It is constantly at work; and the reason for it is not strange.

As we noted in the beginning, the human mind is continuously attempting to bring a vast reality within the limitations of its own attention span. It tries to reduce every aspect of its experience to some manageable entity. In that endeavor the nation is, politically, socially, and culturally, the largest entity that the majority of men can master. They thus make it the focus of their loyalties to such an extent that to be a "man without a country" is to be lost.

The few exceptions to this rule only emphasize it. Generally called "expatriates," they are those few artists who are repelled by some crudeness or other quality in their homelands and seek permanent escape in a more cultured and congenial environment abroad. Henry James was an outstanding example among nineteenth-century authors; painting provided others in the persons of Whistler, Sargent, and Mary Cassatt. Without taking anything from their undoubted accomplishments, one can say that each was an artist without a country. Never quite so good as the best of the foreign masters they imitated, they were caught in the middle without anything deeply rooted to express. Having cut their ties with their homelands, Sargent ended his life a disappointed man without quite knowing what had gone wrong, and Henry James appeared both great and pathetic to the Britishers whom he copied in vain. Life in the international set never produced the results these men had hoped for. We can only conclude that there must be a sound instinct that makes most artists who study abroad return gladly, like Sesshu, to their native lands. There are only a few masters of all the arts in history who have not been closely identified artistically with their own countries.

The most famous example of diversification of an international style along national lines brings us closer to home. It is found in the history of the Renaissance. When the momentum of that movement carried it north of the Alps into Germany, France, the Netherlands, England, and westward into Spain, it was adopted with much enthusiasm but with varying degrees of success. The farther north it went, the less chance it had of meeting with genuine comprehension; it was out of its regional milieu, and it ran counter to the weakened but entrenched Gothic tradition. That tradition, which had sprung from the deepest roots of northern thinking, could not withstand the Renaissance style, but it colored or distorted it unmistakably. It acted upon the best intentions of Dürer. Its worse effects, however, are to be found where we should expect to find them, in the country which is farthest from Italy in both distance and culture. The Netherlandish artists, and especially the Antwerp Romanists of the sixteenth century, made monstrosities out of the models of Raphael. Their only claim to fame is a negative one. They demonstrated by contrast the wisdom of Bruegel who, after visiting Italy in 1551, remained true to his national heritage.

If our rule is correct, we should find the most intelligent adaptations of the Renaissance style in a country which borders on Italy and has cultural and historic ties with her. On the other hand, we should find that national evolution created a difference even here. France illustrates this principle in both respects. Early in the sixteenth century, when the Italian Renaissance was at its peak, Francis the First imported Benvenuto Cellini, Leonardo da Vinci, Andrea del Sarto, and several pupils of Raphael to his court at Fountainebleau in the hope that they would inspire a renaissance in French painting and sculpture that would rival the Italian achievement. His hopes were partially fulfilled because they were realistic. That is, he wanted a French, not a pseudo-Italian, Renaissance. And he had a right to expect that his native artists could cope with a classical Mediterranean tradition on which the Antwerp Romanists had foundered. For France not only borders on the Mediterranean and is climatically and geographically half-southern, but her southern provinces were the most completely Romanized colonies of the ancient Empire. There still stand at Arles and Nîmes examples of Roman architecture which nearly equal the monuments at Rome itself.

The artist who justified the hopes of Francis the First most fully was a sculptor, Jean Goujon. He had the requisite natural ability to learn from the Italians while creating something both excellent and French. His finest and best-known work is the sculptural decoration of a fountain in Paris (Fig. 402). For it he carved four figures of nymphs carrying urns from which flow streams of water. Each is clad in a garment which is treated in the classical rather than the Gothic manner; it curves around the body, clinging to its forms, enhancing and revealing them. In these respects his drapery is as southern as the Greek *Ludovisi Throne* (Fig. 397). Yet he also made his nymphs unmistakably Gallic. By twisting and turning their bodies he gave them that vitality and vivacity which have characterized French art for centuries.

The female type that Goujon used entered into the main stream of the French tradition. Short of waist but long of limb, it is a graceful and comparatively slender type—refined, chic, petite, and highly feminine. It is met two centuries later in the figures of Boucher, Watteau, Fragonard, Falconet, and Clodion, and again in those of Renoir and Carpeaux. No one would mistake it for Flemish, Dutch, or German however much Renoir may seem to resemble Rubens. These qualities of form and spirit—sprightliness, delicacy, clarity of design, and an eternal appreciation of femininity—have been central in French art ever since the Renaissance and probably long before it.

The signs of nationality can be seen, lastly, in human types which have affected the character of art for centuries, even when represented by foreign artists. Holbein's *Sir John Chambers* lives again in the person of Reynolds' *Lord Heathfield* and once more in Sargent's *Lord Ribblesdale*. Heavy-jowled, sober-eyed, and masculine, their stolid expressions are typical of Britain's aristocracy. They are quite different from the coldly austere Spanish grandees painted by El Greco, Velasquez, and Goya over a span of two hundred years. And both stand apart from the merry-eyed *Francis I* painted by Clouet in the sixteenth century and the equally witty-looking eighteenth-century *D'Alembert* of La Tour. Each of these groups denotes the persistence of national physical characteristics, mental traits, and concepts of behavior which, though hard to define precisely, are manifest to the eye.

An equally remarkable continuity exists in the portraits of women executed by French artists over a period of 500 years. It can be traced from François Clouet's sixteenth-century paintings through Nattier's of the eighteenth, Renoir's of the nineteenth, and Matisse's of our own time. No matter how much they seem to differ because of period styles, all are the quintessence of a special kind of femininity which is not American, English, or German, but Gallic. It is no wonder that the French were angered by Cézanne's stolid, bovine women, and overlooked the classical qualities in his art.

National continuity is also observable to a high degree in German art. The serious, hardworking, raw-boned woman who was Holbein's wife (Fig. 293) could not be imagined in the house of Goya, but she was of a type with Dürer's *Mother* (Fig. 395); and both are prototypes of two twentieth-century German portraits: Otto Dix's portrait of his parents and George Grosz's portrait of *Dr. Hermann Neisse*. The good doctor's dwarfish body was as deformed as the famous arthritic *Praying Hands* drawn by Dürer, but like Dürer's hands his figure radiates strength of character. That love of truth at the expense of physical beauty has been a German trait for many centuries. One cannot escape the feeling that it stems from a morbidity and extremism which run through the whole history of German religious, philosophical, and political thought. Always latent, if not to the forefront, it is the other side of the good nature which beams from Dürer's apple-cheeked Madonnas, and shows itself in a continuous fascination with *Tod* (Death). Hitler's speeches were full of it. But it appeared long before him in Holbein's engravings of the *Dance of Death*, in Dürer's *Four Horsemen of the Apocalypse*, in Grien's *Kiss of Death*, only to be repeated four hundred years later in Käthe Kollwitz' own *Kiss of Death*, with Wagner's "Love Death" music echoing in the background. Where this obsession comes from would be hard to say, but it is an outstanding attribute of the German genius.

Each nation expresses traditional attitudes which derive from its geographical characteristics, its climate, and its economic, social, and political history. It shows in this way what has happened to its people in the course of time. In addition, it expresses its ideals, preferences, perennial interests, and obsessions. In human history the nationalism which art reflects has caused wars and misery. In art it seems to have done no harm; instead, it has given painting, sculpture, and architecture those broad but local characteristics which account for much of their clarity, flavor, and expressiveness.

CHAPTER *26*

Period

All things change with time. This dominant, inescapable fact is recorded in all historical studies. A second and almost equally important fact is this: we cannot see historical changes from day to day, and so we divide history into perceptible but arbitrary units called periods.

Historians employ a number of words to denote different divisions of time, using *epoch* to mean a long span of many centuries and *movement* for a short one of a few years' duration. *Period,* which means a span between the two extremes, is popular with historians because it serves the double function of denoting both a temporal reign and a particular style of art. When they speak of the Renaissance period they imply not only an accepted span from about 1400 to 1550 but also the style which characterized those years.

As for the names of the various periods, the most famous have been invented long after their time. Since ancient art is ancient only in relation to the present, no Greek or Roman artist ever thought of himself as a member of antiquity. He would more likely have thought of himself as modern in comparison to the early Egyptians, who would have been his ancients. All past ages have thought of themselves as modern when they have thought of historical designations at all, but none has ever earned the title permanently. What they are eventually called is decided afterwards when their particular characteristics have been assessed in the light of a later perspective. Then, if they are fortunate—for the invention of names is an art in itself—they will be called by some such rolling phrase as the Renaissance or the Baroque period. Certainly the artists of the fifteenth century in Italy did not greet each other with, "Good Morning! How is the Renaissance progressing today?" Even a man like Francis the

801

First, who tried consciously to promote a renaissance, had no idea what to call his time and certainly no idea what it would be called eventually. If a period does not have the colorfulness that suggests a picturesque title, it will usually be named according to its politics, like the Queen Anne style of English furniture, the art of the T'ang Dynasty in China, or the sculpture of Republican Rome.

To a historian of art whose task is to record and explain the march of events along the temporal axis of history, there are two crucial aspects of time—one is the succession of periods of art, the other their rates of change. If the periods in a long epoch show only moderate changes, all signs point to a culture which is comparatively conservative, unified, and simple, and probably authoritarian. Its most prominent characteristic is continuity. If, by contrast, periods of short duration follow each other rapidly and bring frequent changes in style, all signs will point to a culture which is relatively varied, complex, free, individualistic, and experimental. It will be called dynamic. If, furthermore, changes can be shown to have been for better or worse, the historian will apply the descriptions progressive or declining, as Gibbon did in his classic *Decline and Fall of the Roman Empire.*

The history of art supplies abundant examples of massive continuity and accelerated change. The history of Western civilization since the Renaissance has been a noted example of rapid change, the art of France alone having altered course almost as often as its politics. But the most perfect illustrations of the two contrasting types are the art of the ancient Egyptians and Greeks. If, for instance, we place side by side the Egyptian portraits in Figs. 160, 366a, and 163, it is hard to believe that they date respectively from the Old Kingdom, the Empire period, and the Saite Renaissance. Though separated in time by over two thousand years, they are essentially alike in expression and design. Owing partly to the geographical influences described in Chapter 25, they exhibit a continuity of style which is unmatched anywhere else in history, surpassing even the persistence of the Byzantine style fostered by the Greek Orthodox Church in Eastern Europe from the fifth century to the present day. Behind this stable Egyptian culture was a regional environment which virtually imposed monotony upon art.

In Greece the story was almost the reverse. If we juxtapose examples of its art which were created only a few centuries apart, we are struck far more by change in style and spirit than by continuity. For example, two statues of women could hardly be more unlike than Figs. 403 and 404. The *Hera of Samos,* the earlier of the two, depicts a young woman standing proudly erect. But such skill as the

FIG. 403. *The Hera of Samos*. From the Temple of Hera on the Island of Samos. Early archaic period, 625-550 B.C. Louvre, Paris.

FIG. 404. *An Old Woman Going to Market*. Hellenistic period, 323-146 B.C. Metropolitan Museum of Art, New York.

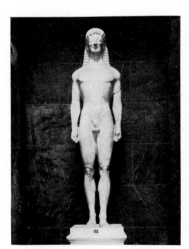

FIG. 405. *The Apollo Tenea*. Early archaic period, 625-550 B.C. Glyptothek, Munich.

FIG. 406. Agesander, Polydorus, and Athenodorus of Rhodes. *Laocoön Group*. Greco-Roman period, 146-27 B.C. Vatican Museum, Rome.

sculptor had in carving a figure which strongly suggests a precedent of tree-trunk carving went into design rather than into representation. Though the folds of drapery are handsomely arranged, the treatment of human proportions and movable limbs left a great deal more to be done. The representation of an *Old Woman Going to Market* is, conversely, skilfully realistic. Her figure sags with fatigue and age.

The same degree of contrast is found in the presentation of the male figure by sculptors of the early and later periods. Like the *Hera of Samos*, the *Apollo Tenea* (Fig. 405) is youthful and erect. His slender, masculine figure seems almost poised on tiptoe. Social customs permitted the artists of the early periods to study and represent the male nude more freely than the female, so the rendering of muscles is more advanced than the drapery of the *Hera of Samos*. Nevertheless, the artist's sense of design and inner life was far ahead of his representational ability in both of these early statues. By the time Agesander, Polydorus, and Athenodorus carved the *Laocoön Group* (Fig. 406) the sculptors of Greece had mastered human anatomy and every technical problem of realistic representation. A spiritual change had also occurred, for Laocoön and his sons are torn emotionally. Thus the great differences between early and late Greek art have come about in only a few hundred years. Such rapid improvement and change could only have occurred within a dynamic and rapidly changing society.

There are good reasons why we should trace the history which lies behind these changes. First, if we have time only for one nation's history, no other nation has a greater claim on our attention. Our Western civilization may have been cradled in Egypt, but it went to school in Greece. Yet it is remote enough in time to be viewed objectively, and known thoroughly enough to be studied accurately. Moreover, it provides us with an object lesson in the development that a dynamic society is likely to follow. Finally, its art was great enough to provide classic standards for every subsequent age.

There are also good reasons why Greek sculpture should illustrate change so clearly. One is the kind of men who produced it; a second is geography and climate. The original Greeks who poured down from Asia during Homeric times and overran the dying Cretan and Mycenaean civilizations were fair-skinned, Aryan, and highly energetic—quite different from the slower-moving, negroid Egyptians. They found themselves in a land that was conducive to variety on every hand. Physically beautiful but agriculturally niggardly, it gave them, with hard work, enough food to make them strong but not fat. A land which was neither extremely cold nor hot, it was mentally and physically stimulating. A land of many mountains, valleys, and bays, it divided the people into small and fiercely independent city-states and made them externally sea-going, sophisticated, and adventurous. It fostered nationalism only to the extent of a common Hellenic language, common gods, and the Olympic games. Between games the Greeks kept sharp and virile by fighting among themselves. It was such a people in such a land that produced the varied and beautiful sculpture of Greece.

Before tracing the course of its changes we must note certain threads which run from its beginning to its ending and give continuity to an otherwise varied art. One is the medium of sculpture, which the Greeks carried to a much higher level than painting. Another is the material of marble, of which they were excellent carvers. A third is the humanistic orientation of their perceptions. An attendant factor is their mastery of human anatomy. Regardless of other differences, Figs. 405 and 406 are all Greek in their sharing of these common features.

One of the advantages of studying the periods of Greek art is that their names, dates, and historical backgrounds have been quite generally agreed upon. In chronological order they were:

The Early Archaic Period, from 625 to 550 B.C.
The Late Archaic Period, from 550 to 480 B.C.
The Transitional Period, from 480 to 450 B.C.
The first half of the Great Period, from 450 to 400 B.C.
The second half of the Great Period, from 400 to 323 B.C.
The Hellenistic Period, from 323 to 146 B.C.
The Greco-Roman Period, from 146 to 27 B.C.

During the first of these periods the Greeks were primarily a society of farmers, sailors, and merchants who lived in tiny city-states. Their outlook was youthful, confident, and healthy, and comparatively simple and naive. Without being mystical dreamers, they were religious, especially in their sense of spiritual and mental dignity. Technically they were undeveloped for a people destined to make rapid progress in their artistic and intellectual life. These qualities are expressed in exactly the right degree by the *Hera of Samos* and the *Apollo Tenea,* and no less in the Late Archaic *Horse* (Fig. 342).

The third of their periods developed from one of the most dramatic turning points in history—the Persian Wars. During that ten-year strife the comparatively tiny free Hellenic city-states faced and repelled the massive slave forces of two Oriental tyrants at Marathon, Thermopylae, and Salamis with a valor and skill that still echoes. It was the first demonstration in history of what a few determined men could do to save their homes and freedom against incalculable odds. The stimulus to the Greeks was tremendous. During the following fifty years their confidence was at its peak; they were riding the crest of the wave. Art profited greatly by the outburst of activity inspired by the defeat of the Persians. Cities vied with each other to erect temples and sculptural offerings to the deities who had answered their prayers for salvation. Sculptors had sufficient work and encouragement and responded by developing their art to a point just short of perfection. A careful inspection of the *Ludovisi Throne* (Fig. 397) will show that some of the signs of representational awkwardness still remained, like the frontal eyes in the profile of Aphrodite. But such criticisms seem like quibbling in the presence of a figure like the *Zeus from Artemisium*. Its graceful balance and harmonious proportions represent a long stride beyond the days when the sculptor of the *Apollo Tenea* did not dare project the arms from a stiffly erect figure.

There is a widely held belief that the sculpture of the Transitional Period is the most satisfying that the Greeks ever created. Still youthful and energetic, it is more mature in its human types than the Archaic Apollos and sufficiently accomplished in technique and design, but it avoids the dangers of perfection or over-refinement. It is a simple, powerful, and impressive art. One can easily be persuaded to this belief by the sculptural decorations of the temple dedicated to Zeus by the people of Olympia, and in particular by the relief of *Heracles and the Cretan Bull* in Fig. 407. It illustrates to perfection the frame of mind and state of artistry existing at the time.

The Great Period of Greek civilization was ushered in by the appearance of a number of outstanding men who had grown to maturity in the afterglow of the Persian victories. The greatest of them was Pericles, whose name has become synonymous with this Golden Age. He gave the city of Athens an enlightened leadership which has hardly ever been surpassed, but he could not have built the Parthenon without the help of a corps of artists. During these years between 450 and 430 B.C. Greece knew her finest moment. Her leader, Athens, while prosperous and energetic, was devoted to the arts of peace without any loss of manliness. Her vigorous intellectual life showed no signs of effeteness or overcultivation. It was virile and strong, simple and balanced.

The artist who, better than any other, summed up this moment was Phidias. As the head of an extensive studio he did not, of course, personally carve the scores of statues and reliefs which Pericles ordered for Greece's finest temple, the Parthenon; and admittedly the many figures vary greatly in quality. But he is rightly given credit

FIG. 408. Studio of Phidias. *Ilissos.* From the west pediment of the Parthenon. 447-432 B.C. British Museum, London.

for the supervision of the over-all design, the finest pieces of which rank among the masterpieces of all sculpture. That status is freely granted to *Ilissos* (Fig. 408) from the eastern gable or pediment. Its outstanding qualities are the fluidity of the body and the mastery shown over a difficult horizontal position. These may be interpreted not only in the specific context of the Parthenon's decorations, but also more comprehensively. They show the progress that sculptors had made since the days of the *Apollo Tenea*, and why Phidias' time represents an optimum period in the development of Greek sculpture. The *Ilissos* stands at a point of balance between the deficiencies of the *Apollo Tenea* and the excesses of the *Laocoön Group*. All of the means of art have been brought to full development, but they are used to express the figure's inner life, not as ends in themselves.

Some critics attribute this result to Phidias' genius for balanced judgments, others to the system of idealization which most of the Greek sculptors employed during the Great Period. But neither can be divorced from the environment in which Phidias was privileged to work. Coming with the long period of peace and prosperity which followed the inspiring defeat of the Persians, it reaped the fruits of two centuries of artistic progress. Not only did Phidias have at his disposal all the technical knowledge he needed, but he worked in an atmosphere of mature confidence and enlightenment.

The importance of that atmosphere is shown by what happened after it was destroyed. During the last three decades of the fifth century before Christ, Athens and Sparta fought to the death in the disastrous and enervating Peloponnesian War. Thucydides, its great historian, tells us how Athens lost her leader Pericles in the early days of the struggle and how her arts of peace languished while she poured her money, energy, and blood into the struggle. In the end Athens, the cultural leader of Greece, was defeated and her countryside devastated, while Sparta, the Prussia of antiquity, assumed control. Athens, indeed Greece itself, never recovered from the blow. The Peloponnesian War was as disastrous for Hellenism as the Persian Wars had been inspiring. The beginning of Athens' decline dated undeniably from it. In a larger perspective it offers us unmistakable proof of the crippling role that a long war plays in the life of any society.

Fortunately for civilization, the Parthenon had been finished before the Peloponnesian War began. It would never have been conceived, much less completed, in the atmosphere of the fourth-century period which followed. The flexible unity which the Hellenic world had known when Athenians and Spartans fought side by side against the Persians was replaced by doubt, distrust, and fear. The old religious faith was weakened, while philosophical skepticism increased.

Although the fourth century that followed has been called the second half of the Great Period, it was only an echo of the Periclean decades. As often happens, one of the effects of war was a redistribution of wealth and power, and a decline in social responsibility. Ambitious, self-seeking men had grown rich with wartime trade while Athens' finest men and youths died in battle. There was a marked deterioration in leadership when the war profiteers, newly rich and eager for luxury and culture, rose to power. A creative minority changed to a simply dominant minority. Since these men were more self-centered than civic-minded, the enthusiasm for the great projects which had created the Temple of Zeus at Olympia and made the Acropolis the Glory of Greece was abandoned for individual aggrandizement. The orientation of the new patrons of art was toward personal comfort, luxury, and power, with a consequent narrowing of the aims of art. It was in this atmosphere that Plato cried out in his *Republic* for the return of the philosopher kings.

Whether smart and grasping men took the situation into their own hands because of Athens' failure, or Athens languished because of them, her history pointed out certain timeless lessons for the future of art. The period between the Persian and Peloponnesian Wars showed the conditions under which the human equation is at its best while those which followed showed the disastrous effects of military defeat. From the point of view of history the Golden Age of Pericles was but a brief and fragile moment of fifty years at most; the majority of artists in the world have had to do their best in spite of "times of troubles" and without benefit of golden opportunities.

In the disintegrating environment of the fourth century B.C., Greek sculpture split along divergent paths while expressing the signs of the times. One path is exemplified by the art of Praxiteles. His *Hermes and Dionysus* (Fig. 409) shows both the technical perfection which Greek sculpture had acquired and its use for an increasing stress upon surface realism. The figure's gracefulness is far removed from the rigid verticality of the *Apollo Tenea*, yet its languorous serenity denotes a lessening of vitality. Clearly, there is expressed here the materialistic, luxury-loving, and sensuous culture of the *nouveaux riches* of Greece. A turning point was reached in Praxiteles' art, because technical perfection, once attained, tends increasingly to become an end-in-itself as more and more minor artists acquire it.

Another and probably larger section of the artistic population was in a frame of mind which was at variance with that of Praxiteles.

FIG. 409. Praxiteles. *Hermes and Dionysus*. Great period, second half, 400-323 B.C. Museum, Olympia.

FIG. 410. Style of Scopas. *Niobe and Her Daughter*. Great period, second half, 400-323 B.C. Uffizi Gallery, Florence.

More sensitive to the disruptions of Greece's social health, it swung to the opposite spiritual pole and showed its anxieties clearly. The chief spokesman for the new wing was the sculptor Scopas, whose emotions were as strong as Praxiteles' feeling for physical grace and beauty. Most of his art must be studied through later copies, but enough of his powerful spirit remains to show why he was the great proto-baroque master of his day.

His famous group of *Niobe and Her Daughter* (Fig. 410) may seem at first only to represent one of the more tragic ancient myths, telling the story of the woman who boasted about her children until the gods angrily doomed them to be killed by arrows from the bows of Apollo and Artemis. In this pair of figures from a series, Niobe vainly shields her daughter while turning her own eyes upward in despair. The technical skill typical of Greek art at this time is shown brilliantly by the transparency of the drapery which clings to the daughter's body. And there is a command over facial expressions which had eluded the Greek masters as late as the time of Phidias. But all of this skill is now used to express the endemic fears which were infecting Greek society. In that sense the Niobe group is more than a mere myth; it symbolizes the latent social unrest to which Scopas was prophetically and keenly attuned. Its conflicting and restless spirit pervades the whole of his work, as it came in time to characterize Greek art at large. Scopas was, with Praxiteles, the co-prophet of the two major trends that followed.

The counterpart of Scopas in the field of political thought was the orator Demosthenes. A man of serious and worried mien, his features are represented for us by one of several portrait statues of famous contemporaries (Fig. 411). The appearance of these superbly rendered portraits is itself a sign of the change from religious idealism to realistic individualism. The wrinkled brow of the *Demosthenes* is not a happy one, nor was it a happy time for a man of Periclean political foresight and convictions. Finding himself surrounded by opportunists rather than patriots, he "viewed with alarm" the rise of Philip of Macedon to the north. In a series of immortal speeches, the *Philippics,* he tried to warn his fellow Athenians against the divide-and-conquer stratagems of Philip. But the patriotism of Marathon had long since given way to expediency. He lost out in one of the classic cases of fatal appeasement, and Athens never knew freedom again in ancient times.

The sixth period of Greek art is called Hellenistic because it was no longer genuinely Greek, but an international style in which Hellenism merely predominated. It followed hard upon the death of Alexander and was determined by his conquests. In the course of a

FIG. 411. Detail. *Portrait of Demosthenes.* Great period, second half, 400-323 B.C.; or early Hellenistic period, *ca.* 300 B.C. Vatican Museum, Rome.

FIG. 412. *The Victory of Samothrace. ca.* 300 B.C., early Hellenistic period. Louvre, Paris.

few years this brilliant and almost insanely violent son of Philip had conquered the whole of Asia Minor as far as the boundaries of India. A Macedonian himself rather than a Dorian Greek, he had an intense but superficial love of Athenian culture which he spread vigorously in a diluted, second-hand form wherever he went. Ironically, the conquerors were also influenced by the conquered and a typical hybrid internationalism ensued. Among other things, non-Greek types of men began to intrude in sculpture among the classic profiles of the gods. But these changes were minor compared to other effects of Alexander's life. His restless, adventurous spirit infected the tight little Hellenic world. He showed it a far larger and materially richer world which could be conquered by force of arms, but was vast, far-reaching, and complex. With one stroke he made the Greeks both more ambitious and more confused. After he died men had to cope with an infinitely greater heterogeneity of ideas than they had ever faced in their little city-states. Overnight the Hellenic world became an international complex of sophisticated and teeming foreign metropolises, and a world of industrialists and merchants to whom farmers, the once-solid citizens of Greece, were nothing but country bumpkins. It was a profoundly stirred-up world that Alexander left behind him.[1] His sudden death in 323 B.C. shattered what was left of Greek unity. His generals divided the Empire into seven parts, each with a ruling center far from Athens. Pergamum and Rhodes in Asia Minor and Alexandria in Egypt became the fountainheads of pseudo-Greek or Hellenistic culture.

With the world thus opened up and changed, art was forced to follow suit in subject matter, spirit, and form. Some of its products were great and all were various. Among the fine works is the *Venus of Melos,* which recaptured some of the qualities of the Periclean years. Another celebrated example is the *Apollo Belvedere* which was once thought to be the most beautiful statue in the world, but now seems only to have reduced Praxitelean grace to effeminate theatricality. It was the troubled spirit of Scopas which was most congenial to the time. It nearly bursts the forms of the *Victory of Samothrace* (Fig. 412), a superb work of art which expresses perfectly the driving, dynamic power of the period. Only a figure imbued with great vitality could surmount the tortured realism of the drapery, but the *Victory* does so magnificently. How much Greek art

[1] For a brilliant study of the background of Hellenistic art and culture see William Woodthorpe Tarn's *Hellenistic Civilization* (London: Edward Arnold, Ltd., 1927). A model of its kind, Tarn's book is a searching analysis of a society in a highly cultivated state of development. His conclusions shed a good deal of light on the characteristics of such societies in general.

had changed, and how exactly the *Victory* epitomized that change, can be seen by comparing it with the Early Archaic *Hera of Samos*.

No one statue, however, can speak for so diversified a period as the Hellenistic. The conflicts and contrasts of the time are shown by other statues equally representative of important trends. The *Dying Gaul* (Fig. 413) is a renowned example of one of the non-Greek models employed at far-flung centers like Pergamum. Formerly thought to be a Roman statue of a gladiator, it is now known to represent one of the Gauls who migrated from Asia westward into Europe and tried vainly to settle in the south before they found their permanent home in France. Turned aside by the Pergameans in a series of bloody battles, their defeat was commemorated in a set of statues. Though defeated in field, the Gauls' fierce appearance, stalwart physiques, and bearing made a deep impression on the Greeks. They would, as we saw in the *Death of a Gaul and his Wife* (Fig. 305), commit suicide rather than submit to captivity, and when mortally wounded they died heroically. The *Dying Gaul* depicts one of their warriors who struggles against death while his life's blood flows from a wound in his side. His dauntless spirit is reminiscent of the Assyrian *Wounded Lioness* (Fig. 286).

Another eminent statue, of a *Slave Sharpening a Knife* from the School of Pergamum, shows kindred stylistic characteristics. Like the *Dying Gaul*, it depicts a scene of death and represents a foreign type with searching realism. The thick-lipped, flat-faced slave is a brutally muscular man who prepares to flay Marsyas alive with callous unconcern. Ostensibly a representation of an ancient myth, it tells us, when coupled with a large group of similar themes, that the Greeks themselves had become brutalized by two centuries of continuous strife. In work after work they express a new and morbid fascination with cruelty, pain, and death.

Compared with the healthy balance of earlier periods, the Hellenistic mind was extremist. At one pole was a pronounced morbidity, at the other a penchant, perhaps by way of escape, for triviality. Genre subjects from everyday life came into unprecedented popularity. One of many well-known examples is Boethos' popular, much-copied *Boy and Goose* (Fig. 414). Although commonplace in theme it possesses an ingratiating carefree spirit and truth to life, and its appropriate realistic treatment could hardly be excelled. To look at it one would never know that the Greeks had a care in the world. From our vantage point we can see that it was only a carefree moment in a generally troubled time.

More typical of the genre scenes which the Hellenistic sculptors produced in quantity to satisfy a large demand is the *Peasant Going*

FIG. 413. *The Dying Gaul.* First school of Pergamum, 241-197 B.C., Hellenistic period. Capitoline Museum, Rome.

FIG. 414. Boethos. *Boy and Goose*. Hellenistic period, 323-146 B.C. Capitoline Museum, Rome.

to Market in Fig. 415. Though rendered with laudable realistic skill, it suffers from pettiness in conception. For, granted that the background or setting is true to life, it is also burdened with minor details. More important, however, is the spiritual lethargy which fills the scene. A comparison of this relief with the *Heracles and the Cretan Bull* from Olympia (Fig. 407) will show how much the Greeks had improved in technical knowledge and declined in gusto and grandeur of conception.

Taken together, the *Dying Gaul, Slave Sharpening a Knife, Boy and Goose, Peasant Going to Market,* and the *Old Woman Going to Market* reveal the extent to which the Greek mind now dwelt on the morbidly negative or commonplace side of life. Senility, decrepitude, ugliness, drunkenness, and blindness were joined with various forms of spiritual anguish as the favorite subjects of the day, the *Blind Homer* being one of their special obsessions. The Hellenic world had lost its hold on the conditions of life which had made it healthy and strong, but the worst was yet to come. The next period of Greek history was the last of its ancient life, and was only partly Greek. It began with the initial invasion of Greece by Rome in 146 B.C., and ended in 27 B.C. with the conquest and destruction of the last free city-state. The relatively small cities of Greece which had set the world an example of freedom, but seldom of cooperation, were helpless against the massive organization of Rome, and were quickly enslaved as a minor province of the Empire.

While the city-states were being conquered relentlessly, the mental climate of Greece must have resembled that of Hitlerian Europe. Nothing high-minded or serene could possibly have come out of it. The best that we can expect is great technical facility devoted to anguished or lifeless expression. The division along these lines is amply illustrated by the famous *Seated Boxer* at Rome and the *Farnese Heracles* at Naples, both of which are far superior to the *Apollo Tenea* in the rendering of anatomy, but utterly weary and resigned in spirit; and by the unbearably tormented *Laocoön Group* (Fig. 406). In representing the Trojan priest and his sons who were crushed to death by a snake, Agesander and his colleagues probably meant only to illustrate a story from Homer's *Iliad,* but they subconsciously spoke for the period in which Greece was being strangled by Rome.

During the period of her death throes the Greek sculptors gave one final proof that they had run their course. Those who were unwilling to express their times for better or worse, as the creators of the *Laocoön* had done, adopted an ostrich attitude toward the present and turned to the past. A large group of artists oriented them-

FIG. 415. *Peasant Going to Market*. Hellenistic period. 323-146 B.C. Glyptothek, Munich.

FIG. 416. Agesander, Polydorus, and Athenodorus of Rhodes. Detail. *Laocoön Group*. Greco-Roman period, 146-27 B.C. Vatican Museum, Rome.

FIG. 417. *Athena Promachos*. Greco-Roman period. National Museum, Naples.

selves toward the art of Greece's earlier and happier days. They only succeeded in proving that one can never turn back the clock. The *Athena Promachas* in Fig. 417 is neither original nor old, in the sense that it is technically superior to a truly Archaic statue but far less vital. Not by any such tricks of manner could the harassed later Greeks recapture the spirit of earlier times or elude their own. Their work is branded "Archaistic" and fools no one who is familiar with the genuine but vital awkwardness of primitive art. Yet we should thank the Archaistic School for giving us an object lesson in the consequences of using an artistic orientation as a historical escape. No one can prove that such an escape will never work, but it did not work for the Greeks. Archaism for them was a swan song. There was a parallel retreat from the world in philosophical thought through "philosophies of escape." Hedonism, Stoicism, and Epicureanism were in their heyday during the Greco-Roman period. They did not work any better.

Our purpose in studying the sculpture of a dynamic society was to draw conclusions from the evidence of drastic change which might have a general application for the history of art. One of these conclusions is that changes in the historical conditions of Greek life were followed by corresponding changes in sculpture. More specifically, Greek sculpture changed in form from a finite, geometric, glyptic mode of representation to a highly realistic and somewhat more plastic conception, with realism predominating. In the course of time there were marked advances in technical ability and in the anatomical knowledge important to a humanistic orientation of perception. But there was a concurrent decline in the sense of decorative design as realism increased; the bristling hair of the *Dying Gaul* is more real but less orderly than the stylized locks of the *Apollo Tenea*. A similar change occurred in the treatment of drapery. In short, the Greeks traded esthetic appeal for truth to actuality as the centuries passed.

Most critics believe that these changes followed a downhill course. Our opinion is that a gain-and-loss principle applies to some extent. The early periods were not without their deficiences; the later periods could point to certain gains. Consider, for example, the history of composition. The early sculptors had difficulty executing single figures like the *Hera of Samos*. The important decoration of temples, however, required them to relate many figures in such difficult spaces as pediments, metopes, and friezes. The progress they made can easily be traced through a series of temple decorations. It shows an initial awkwardness followed by increasing facility which reached a climax in the decoration of the Parthenon. By the time of its building the sculptors had mastered the most troublesome problems. Yet in a strictly esthetic sense they progressed still further in the organization of the *Laocoön*. That group is, many critics assert, spiritually repulsive and vacuous, but it is a masterpiece of fluent interrelationships of form. Michelangelo learned much from its composition, which still stands comparison with the best of the Baroque—the historical high point of compositional integration. It marked a tremendous advance over anything the Archaic sculptors accomplished in multi-figured design.

More important still are the expressive changes in Greek sculpture. There is something to be said for the so-called decadent Hellenistic period. Compared to it, the Archaic statues are pleasant to look at, but spiritually naive and immature. They would receive our entire approval only if we believe that youth, beauty, and freedom from care are the whole of life. The Hellenistic period discovered that they are not, and presented the facts of old age, weariness, drunkenness, discouragement, and death eloquently, to the greater enrichment of the spiritual side of art. During this "time of troubles" the Hellenistic Greeks learned about life through hard and trying experience and portrayed it with unprecedented sympathy in such figures as the *Old Woman Going to Market*. At least they were true to their times and skilful beyond any question. Whether or not they were pretty or pleasant is a secondary matter. Viewed as a whole, then, the spirit of Greek art was young and simple in its early days, calmly mature during the period of Phidias, wise and worried from the time of Scopas on. In form it changed, like its producing civilization, from the simple to the complex.

Many Grecophiles believe that the Hellenes discovered every really important principle of human thought and expression. This, plainly, is not so. In the field of sculptured form, for instance, the Greeks elected to follow the path of realism in their later days and left for future periods the exploitation of plastic form. Yet this neglect is insignificant compared to their spiritual shortcomings, for it was because of these that Greek civilization declined politically long before it was enslaved by Rome. Greece's great culture languished because, in the final analysis, it failed to provide a satisfactory way of life. At its best only during prosperity, it was deficient during a time of troubles.

Ironically, its time of troubles was brought on by the principal shortcoming in the Greek attitude toward life—a lack of social sympathy. The sympathy expressed in the Hellenistic statues came as a consequence of protracted strife, and it came too late—after Greece had ruined herself by wars. When she was on the top of the world, she showed little sympathy for anyone. There is no trace of human compassion in any of her sculpture prior to the time of Scopas. There is nothing in the finest speeches of Pericles comparable to Lincoln's "with malice toward none, with charity for all." Instead, her early history is a story of dog-eat-dog internecine strife in which no quarter was asked or given. The Greeks never understood the idea of "a helping hand." Customarily, they killed captives of war or sold them into slavery. Their society included hordes of slaves, while one of their greatest thinkers, Aristotle, believed that some men are slaves by nature and hence subject to exploitation.

When Greece was overrun by Rome few tears were shed over her. She herself had believed that "might makes right." One of her disastrous weaknesses epitomized by Alexander was *Archê,* or the lust for power. The freedom she fought for at Marathon was never extended to any brotherhood of men. It was a self-centered concept of freedom for Greeks alone. All other men were barbarians, fit only for conquest. So when Alexander conquered Asia Minor he could only offer its citizens Greece's cultural and intellectual gifts, and these, as history proved, left a vacuum in the soul. When Rome, following in the path of Greece, did no better, the Western world had to turn to an Oriental religion, Christianity, for a tolerable way of life. The Greeks at their best had never been able to invent a way that had universal appeal.

The far-reaching effects of Grecian lack of sympathy for human beings at large have been dwelt on because they are the key to the limitations of Greek sculpture from any long-range point of view. In these and other respects the Greeks left a great deal of work to be done. Their greatness is relative. In a predominantly predatory antiquity they were at least outstanding artistically and intellectually. Indeed, few peoples have ever accomplished so much in so short a time.

That Greece collapsed is an obvious fact. That the causes of her fall are pertinent to other historical declines is highly probable. Hence the attention that has been given to her history. It is easy to trace the pattern of Greece's breakdown, but harder to interpret it. One school of thought attributed her ruin to a loss of physical vitality, reminding one of a similar belief that the Romans lost their vigor and needed new blood from the barbarians. There is no support for this contention in the sculpture of the Hellenistic or Greco-Roman periods. On the contrary, Agesander and his contemporaries in a highly cultivated, complex period had to spend more nervous energy to solve the increasing problems of life than any of their predecessors. His *Laocoön Group* does not lack vitality; its defect is a vitality in torment. Thus the difference between the artistic expression of earlier and later periods does not lie in enervation, but in the psychosomatic corrosion of vitality by a souring of social life. A second school of thought therefore explains decline in terms of spiritual corrosion.

The causes of this corrosion are manifold. But the worst in the case of the Greeks was the cumulative effect of war. It disrupted, broke down, and disintegrated the moral fibers of Greece in an inexorable progression.[2] One of its side effects was a progressive brutalization of the mind which showed itself in a lack of sympathy and magnanimity towards others, making it impossible for her citizens to live with each other or the rest of the world. The *Seated Boxer* is an example: he represents the kind of battered professional gladiator who appeased the urban crowds of latter-day Greece when gory spectator sports replaced the old ideal of amateur athletics for all. At the same time, neither the Greek artists nor philosophers ever understood the cravings and hungers of the human soul that this brutalization was engendering with a tenth of the insight of the Hebrew prophets and Christ. Lack of any concept of unselfish mercy was a blind spot which they could not overcome.

There were other causes of corrosion which neither the Greeks nor any other society could avoid. If, in the course of time, a dynamic society changes from an agrarian to an industrial and commercial economy and its population moves from farms to cities, it cannot escape the consequences of complexity. Its people will become more sophisticated, though not necessarily better people; they will know more but believe in less. One cause of political and social complexity is inevitable: the population increases. Another is equally unavoidable: knowledge also increases. There is more to know—about one's self, one's fellow men, and the world at large. Unfortunately, values becomes proportionately difficult to assess. Somewhere along the line of change through primitive, mature, and highly cultivated states a point of balance is reached and passed as the attention span of men is overtaxed. They live in a world of ideas and impressions that is larger than they can control or understand. The usual result is confusion followed by a lack of faith and discouragement. If these conditions manifest themselves in depressed vitality or poisoned human energies, as in the *Old Woman Going to*

---

[2] The causes of social distintegration are penetratingly examined in Pitirim Aleksandrovich Sorokin's *Man and Society in Calamity* (New York: E. P. Dutton & Co., Inc., 1942). The subtitle is *the effects of war, revolution, famine, pestilence, upon human mind, social behavior and cultural life.* War, in Sorokin's opinion, is the foremost and most monstrous of all causes of calamity.

Market and the *Laocoön Group,* the basic illnesses of decline are nonetheless psychological.

A declining society is a society of weakening beliefs. This showed itself in Greece in an overextension of loyalties into unmanageable complexity. The sculptors of the Early Archaic period could represent blissful smiles because their world was simple, their faith unbroken, their loyalties few. Any of them could easily cope with, believe strongly in, and fight fiercely for a small city-state or town, life-long friends and acquaintances, closely knit families and clans, and a pantheon of well-known gods. About the vast world outside they knew little and troubled less. Primarily concerned with the finite world that they could actually see, they had no interest in a soul-troubling infinity and no affinity whatever for mysticism.

Far different was the situation of the later Greeks. After Alexander, their loyalties were pulled in a hundred directions by the increasing complications of urban and international life. Loyalty was demanded simultaneously by their friends, families, political parties, social classes, schools, clubs, cities, states, countries, and empires, and by a host of Asiatic and African deities that no Early Archaic sculptor ever heard of. They were like a man who is forced to answer nine telephones at once. At the same time that human loyalties were being cut into little pieces, such beliefs as men had left were being questioned and undermined by the rapid dissemination of knowledge. Add to this the threat of annihilation by Rome and it is small wonder that Agesander's *Laocoön* resembles a man in the grasp of a kind of cultural octopus which is crushing his mind and spirit. In similar circumstances the sculptor of the *Apollo Tenea* would also have become a nervous wreck. As Arnold Toynbee has pointed out, neither the Greek nor any other society has been conquered from without unless it has first become bewildered and corroded from within by a breakdown in understanding, loyalties, and faith.[3]

This is the story of Greek sculpture in brief. We should be naive to suppose that all dynamic societies merely repeat its history. Neither, however, has it been without parallel. Others have advanced from simplicity to complexity in both the formal and spiritual realms and never the other way around: the conditions of life

[3] For a detailed study of the multiple causes of breakdown, disintegration, and collapse in civilizations and their component societies the reader may consult Arnold Toynbee's *A Study of History.* Professor Toynbee presents the reasons for decline from a different point of view from that of Gibbon, Spengler, or Sorokin. The beginning student is advised to commence with the abridgement by David Churchill Somervell of Vols. I-VI (1947), and of Vols. VII-X (New York & London: Oxford University Press, 1954).

which promote maturity or cause decline are fundamentally similar in all societies.

The history of Gothic sculpture in France offers an excellent test because it too was produced by a society which was undergoing rapid change. The last of the great medieval styles, it also stood on the threshold of the Renaissance period and modern era. At its best it was the glory of the Middle Ages; in its final steps it saw their end. The high lights of the sculpture we can trace in a series of statues, Figs. 418 through 421, which date respectively from the twelfth, thirteenth, fourteenth, and fifteenth centuries and thus coincide with the four principal stages of Gothic sculpture's rise and fall.

The *Saints* (Fig. 418) on the West Portals of the Cathedral of the Chartres are carved in the geometric sculptural mode, with a highly linear treatment of the drapery. Tall, thin, and as columnar as they are human, they approach the abstract. This increases their effectiveness as architectural decoration. Very much a part of the building's design, they partake of Gothic verticality and join in the collective unity of the building. Part of their character is due to technical deficiencies. The later Romanesque or proto-Gothic sculptors had not yet mastered human facial expressions, anatomy, or postures. The figures seem rather to hang on hooks than to rest firmly on their feet. On the other hand, the artists compensated for their representational deficiencies by their decorative treatment of hair and drapery; their esthetic sense was strong.

The late fifteenth-century *Virgin* (Fig. 421) stands at the far pole from this conception. Her figure is treated realistically and plastically. Spiritually she is resigned, weary, depressed. She looks downward, with head bowed and shoulders hunched forward. Whereas the *Saints* are calmly confident, she is morbidly serious and introspective, as though mourning beside a grave. The folds of her drapery droop and sag in angular patterns which express her mood of sadness. She is, finally, a free-standing and highly individualized figure, rather than part of a large ensemble. Thus did the Gothic sculptors approach the end of their particular line of expression.

The stages between the *Saints* and the mourning *Virgin* are illustrated by Figs. 419 and 420. Among other things they prove that the Gothic sculptors, with a greater precedent of history behind them, advanced even more rapidly than the Greeks. Within a century after the carving of the *Saints* they reached their peak in such figures as the *Madonna and Child* (Fig. 419) on the North Portal of Notre Dame at Paris. Here, in the thirteenth century, the golden moment of balance between knowledge and the finest kind of feeling was attained. This *Madonna*, in contrast to the slightly wooden *Saints*,

FIG. 418. *Saints.* Late 12th century.
Early Gothic period. West portal.
Cathedral of Notre Dame, Chartres.

FIG. 419. *Madonna and Child. ca.* 1260.
High Gothic period, first half. North
portal trumeau. Cathedral of Notre Dame,
Paris.

FIG. 420. *Madonna and Child.* 14th
century. High Gothic period, second
half. Walters Art Gallery, Baltimore.

FIG. 421. *Virgin.* Late 15th century. Late
Gothic period. Cleveland Museum of Art.

is a living, breathing, free-moving woman in the full bloom of matronly strength. Neither naively young nor wearily old, she is confident, mature, alert, with head high and shoulders back. The folds of the drapery sweep grandly upward, echoing the lines of the building. Her figure stands somewhere in between the collective statues of the *Saints* and the lonely, free-standing position of the *Virgin*. This *Madonna* is both part of a larger design and a grand lady in her own right. In her figure all signs of awkwardness have vanished. Her sculptor was in command of his medium, but used his knowledge to express an inner buoyancy and life. Nothing finer ever came from Gothic hands.

The period that followed was transitional between the crowning achievements of the thirteenth century and the period of decline. While it basked in the afterglow of the Golden Age, it created no new greatness of its own. It is illustrated well by the fourteenth-century *Madonna and Child* of Fig. 420. This figure lacks the robustness of the *Madonna* of Notre Dame, but avoids the dejection of the mourning *Virgin* of the fifteenth century. It is petite rather than strong, cheerful instead of inspired. The lines of the drapery neither sag nor sweep upward, but maintain a discreet and well-bred balance. There is skill in abundance here, but it is devoted to a gracefulness that is delicate to the verge of mannerism and effeteness; refinement has passed the point of diminishing returns. Taken by itself, this small statue is charming, but viewed in historical comparison it contains the seeds of decline.

The similarities between Greek and Gothic trends in sculpture are sufficiently clear. Just as the *Hera of Samos* and the *Old Woman Going to Market* could not possibly have expressed each other's historical periods, neither could the *Saints* and the *Virgin* be exchanged in time. Moreover, early, middle, and late works bear in each case certain strong similarities. The columnar geometricity of the early *Saints* is comparable to qualities in the early *Hera of Samos*, while the bowed and realistic figure of the late *Virgin* is similar to the bowed and realistic *Old Woman Going to Market* from the Hellenistic Period. But coincidence does not end with attributes of form. The childlike smile of the female saint in Fig. 418 echoes the Archaic smile of the *Apollo Tenea*, and the haggard expression of the *Old Woman Going to Market* is akin to the downcast stare of the fifteenth-century *Virgin*.

The parallelism between Gothic and Greek statues of comparable periods is apparent in Figs. 419 and 420. The thirteenth-century *Madonna*'s maturity and robustness remind one strongly of Phidias' art; the fourteenth-century *Madonna*'s refinement and grace suggest

Praxiteles. The hour of balanced strength in each cultural development came before the hour of more leisurely refinement and the final period of anxiety, turbulence, and weariness. In both Greek and Gothic cycles the time of maximum opportunity was brief. It lasted no longer than the first seventy-five years of the fifth century before Christ in antiquity and for about an equal time in the thirteenth century. A fragile moment at best, it coincided in ancient Greece with the period of civic enthusiasm that produced the major temples, and in Gothic France with the years of religious fervor which created the principal portions of the cathedrals.

Other similarities are no less striking. The finest Greek sculpture was produced in an environment of optimistic peacefulness by citizens who balanced freedom against civic responsibility. They lived in relatively small city-states and benefited from the leadership of vigorous, high-minded, dedicated men. The best of the Gothic sculpture was likewise carved in an atmosphere of hope by citizens who were devoted to small cities like Chartres, Amiens, and Reims. They were guided by bishops who are less known than Pericles but not unworthy of comparison.

The breakdown and disintegration of these conditions came from remarkably similar causes. One was the shift of political loyalties from small towns to sprawling countries and empires. In France this occurred with the rise to power of the central monarchy. A second cause attended this shift—the decline in faith which followed the strengthening of the secular and temporal authorities. When the king replaced the bishops as the focus of national sentiments, material luxury and power became increasingly prominent in the pattern of human thought, and new attitudes toward those signs of a weakening faith—portraiture and the genre scene—followed in their train. These signs, however, were but symptomatic of an over-all psychological change from optimism to morbid pessimism. The late medieval sculptors carved tomb after tomb and pietàs, entombments, crucifixions, and mourners by the score; their obsession with death was as great as that of the Hellenistic Greeks.

Behind this breakdown in hope, this evidence of a souring of life, lay the same cause that poisoned Greece—war. The names differed but the effects were the same. In Greece the turning point was the Peloponnesian War. In France the destruction of the civic unity which created the cathedrals was due to the exhausting and demoralizing Hundred Years War with England.

Parallelisms of the sort we have just described have occurred so often in history that Sorokin has used them as the basis for an inclusive historical principle. Seeking to discover the conditions under which the human equation functions at its best in every walk of life, he deduced that social history evolves rhythmically through three stages which are repeated endlessly; he called them ideational, idealistic, and sensate. In our study these would be illustrated by the Greek *Hera of Samos*, the Phidian *Ilissos*, and the *Laocoön Group;* or by the Gothic *Saints*, *Madonna and Child* of Notre Dame, and the late fifteenth-century *Virgin*.

Professor Sorokin's evidence, the description of his stages, and the order of their succession seem fundamentally valid, and a study of his findings will be extremely helpful to any student of human history.[4] But since the interpretation of data is bound to be somewhat personal, one may be permitted to qualify two of his conclusions insofar as they apply to the history of art. He appears to regard the ideational phase of any cultural cycle as its finest stage, the idealistic as on a slightly lower and downward plane, and the sensate cultural period as at the bottom of the pit. This would be tantamount to ranking the *Apollo Tenea* above the *Old Woman Going to Market*. Few critics would agree to such a qualitative ranking. Each statue is superb in its own way.

Secondly, Sorokin seems to have few good words for sensate culture. In his opinion it is at the bottom of the decline from the ideational cultural peak, almost hopelessly decadent, and redeemable only by a reaction, a swing of the pendulum back to its polar opposite, ideational culture. Such a picture of the sensate Hellenistic period, for example, is painted too black. We have therefore suggested a gain-and-loss principle for periodic changes in artistic expression which seems to coincide with actual evidence. We illustrated this principle by asserting that what the late Greek sculptor of the *Old Woman Going to Market* had lost in decorative design and spiritual repose, as compared to the creator of the *Hera of Samos*, he gained in plastic fluidity and a more sympathetic insight into human life. Objectively viewed, each of these statues expresses its own period eloquently; qualitatively speaking, only a rash critic would brand the sensate *Old Woman Going to Market* as wholly decadent and without merit. Most critics find it to be a deeply moving work of art. No period of art is all black or all white; the darkest of the Dark Ages had their cakes and ale and saints, the brightest Golden Ages some blemishes on their record. The best is only comparatively great. It is more likely to be found nearer the idealistic middle than at either ideational or sensate extremes.

These remarks are intended to qualify but by no means disparage

[4] This thesis is developed fully in *The Crisis of Our Age* (New York: E. P. Dutton & Co., Inc., 1941).

the light that Professor Sorokin has shed on periodic cultural changes or, as he calls them, social dynamics. They are also meant to point out an important underlying fact of all interpretation of the language of the visual arts—that any work of art may be appreciated from two quite separate points of view. In terms of historical expressiveness the *Saints* at Chartres are exactly right for their time and place. They could not have been created earlier or later or anywhere else; neither could they be exchanged with the mourning *Virgin*. History, in this sense, has an inexorable effect upon artistic expression and reduces analysis to a question of rightness of expression more than of good or bad. But this does not refute the plain fact that human beings have worked better under certain historical conditions than under others, or deny that historical periods have varied greatly in providing these conditions. The question of what constitutes good or bad art in the long view should not, therefore, always be avoided in favor of scientific impartiality.

In this connection we are reminded of the theory that art does not progress, but only changes. Kenneth J. Conant has indirectly refuted this theory with illustrations from the field of architecture. These show that architectural styles have progressed as well as changed through a sequence of periods before passing into decline. The sequence of what we shall call the Conant thesis is based on a cycle of three periods: engineering, design, and decoration

During the first of these stages architects must devote the major portion of their energies to the solution of the most troublesome structural problems. They must concentrate on the practical function of the building art before they can achieve any higher esthetic values. Since the practical problems of architecture are well known for their difficulty, that art lends itself well to a demonstration of the esthetic gains that can be made when they are solved.

By the period of *design* Professor Conant means that time which follows the solution of most of the structural aspects of a given style. During this period architects, benefiting by inherited technical progress, can devote the major portion of their energies to the refinement of construction and the perfection of design for the sake of greater eye appeal. This period is therefore marked by a shift of emphasis in architectural effort which takes advantage of, and is made possible by, previous accomplishments. In this respect progress is deemed by critics to be real. Most of the world's buildings which they rank as crowning masterpieces fall in this middle period of evolution when a mastery of engineering and design coincide.

One of the most important signs of this coincidence is a harmony between structure and architectural composition in which major masses rather than decorative details are emphasized. Such details as are added enhance both structural lines and esthetic groupings and never obscure them. It goes without saying that such a stressing of masses will usually favor a geometric mode of organization, since plastic architecture is constantly threatened by a tendency to employ decoration as an end-in-itself.

An emphasis of decoration is the major characteristic of the third, or decorative, phase of an architectural style. It occurs historically, with a kind of blameless inevitability, when all of the hardest structural problems and most of the challenging aspects of composition have been mastered for a particular style. Architects, like other artists, are seldom content with repetition; they turn to the only field remaining for exploitation—the field of decoration. That this is the least of architectural fields is not their fault any more than is the fall of an object after its ascent. A kind of historical gravity seems to take command during the later phases of architectural evolution and pull all efforts toward greater and greater decorative embellishment.

As this occurs, so, according to Professor Conant, does decline, for the only possible direction of such a trend is downward. He has pointed this out in stronger terms by saying aptly that "the decorators take over" during this final period of change, meaning that they become the controlling figures in the building field. When this happens, the men in charge of architecture are highly trained in past styles of decoration, for the decorative stage is always backward-looking, but superficially trained in engineering. Consequently, while preoccupied with surface embellishment, they not only neglect the development of engineering, but lose the ground that has already been won. The three commonest signs that the decorators have taken over are awkward or senseless structural systems beneath sophisticated exteriors, widespread faking, cheating, or laziness in construction, and the reduction of formerly functional members, like columns, to merely decorative pilasters.

Not all highly ornate buildings automatically identify themselves as decadent. Like the frosting on a cake, they have attractions which are enticing enough to allow certain of their members to be counted among the world's popular favorites, as we shall presently see. Yet it is fair to say that the decorative stage produces the highest percentage of buildings which leave us unsatisfied when we seek something more substantial than decorative frosting and structural evasions.

The Conant thesis can be illustrated by innumerable periods in the history of architecture. The Greeks were as gifted in architecture as they were in sculpture, and combined the two brilliantly. They were not, however, gifted in the same ways at all times. This is the gist of the theory of cyclical progress and decline in the building arts.   In the course of time the Greeks originated three of the most popular orders or columnar systems in Western architecture—the Doric, Ionic, and Corinthian.   At the same time they gave proof of a change in emphasis from the engineer's to the designer's and finally to the decorator's point of view.

The engineer's phase is illustrated by the Doric-style Temple of Ceres at Paestum in southern Italy (Fig. 422).   The engineering problems connected with the Doric style were not difficult, for its basic post-and-lintel system already had a long history.   They consisted of translating the wooden members of the early temples, like the Heraeum at Olympia, into a logical system of more permanent stone construction.   The engineering of the Temple of Ceres is perfectly satisfactory.   Its design, however, leaves a good deal to be desired. We know now that the Greeks were working toward a balanced ensemble of parts in which no one member would appear excessively prominent.   Their criterion of balance seems, moreover, to have been a kind of functional rightness.   That is, each part was to appear neither stronger nor weaker than its structural role demanded and thus in harmony with the whole.   The Temple of Ceres did not fulfil these requirements.   The capitals turned out to be unduly large for their columns, while the columns were too small for the entablature above.   The result of this distortion of proportions was an awkwardness of appearance which the Greeks themselves recognized.

A remarkable thing about these artists is that, having set themselves a problem, even subconsciously, they moved rapidly toward a solution which the world still applauds.   Much of the greatness of the Parthenon (Fig. 423) rests on the ultimate refinement of this kind of organization.   It brings us to the period of design, during which architects, freed from the major problems of structure, could concentrate their attention upon esthetic appeal.   How well they succeeded will be shown by a comparison of the Temple of Ceres and the Parthenon.   Every part of the Parthenon fits into the over-all design; the former awkwardness is gone.   No member "jumps" out of place; each is a part of a perfect architectural team.

The Parthenon is a masterpiece because it was built at a time when control over engineering coincided with mastery of the kind of design at which the Greeks had aimed.   It crowned the efforts of three centuries of designers and brought them, in the persons of Ictinus and Callicrates, into the foremost ranks of architecture.   A few specific examples will show how the Parthenon earned its reputation by uniting the finest Greek engineering with the finest of all classical compositions.

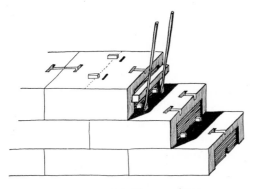

FIG. 424. Ictinus and Callicrates. Wall construction. As in the Parthenon. 447-432 B.C. Athens.

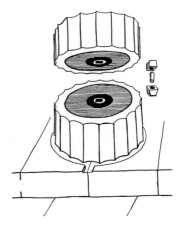

FIG. 425. Ictinus and Callicrates. System for joining the drums of a column. As in the Parthenon. 447-432 B.C. Athens.

FIG. 426. North Porch. The Erechtheum. 420-409 B.C. Athens.

FIG. 427. Style of Callimachus. Corinthian capital. From the Tholos, Epidaurus. ca. 350 B.C. National Museum, Athens.

decorative details exquisite, and its dimensions relatively small. Later on the Greeks built larger buildings, but never any finer.

The final decorative phase started with the appearance of the Corinthian order whose principal contribution was a new and more lavish capital. Although no one knows exactly when it came into being, its invention is attributed to one Callimachus, who was, significantly, a sculptor by training rather than an engineer or architect. In any event, its cluster of naturalistic and picturesque acanthus leaves clearly reveals the trend toward nonfunctional embellishment. Behind that trend was the growing desire for luxury which followed the Peloponnesian War. More sensuous than logical, it preferred variety to simplicity and the play of light and shadow to the hard, clean lines and massive stability of the Doric. A soft style, the Corinthian heralded the decline of the Greek effort and was the undoing of the luxury-loving Romans. The latter completed the cycle by adopting it avidly and smothering their great engineering under it.

Further support for the Conant thesis can be found in the evolution of Byzantine architecture. It passed successively through predominantly engineering, design, and decorative phases; and, as in the Greek cycle, produced its masterpiece, Santa Sophia, during the middle stage. The engineering period of Byzantine architecture was devoted to the perfection of an ingenious but difficult domical mode of construction—the system of space coverage now known as a dome on pendentives. We told in Chapter 14 how this dome originated in the new need of Christian congregations for a square or rectangular room, but we did not discuss the time element in its development. It took the Byzantines a long time to learn how to build a dome over a cubical space. All future success hinged on their first solving this engineering problem.

We can observe in a series of experimental squinches (Fig. 428) their initial fumbling attempts to transform stone walls from a square to a circular plan upon which a dome's base might rest. Not until they abandoned the extended course method in favor of curved pendentives were they able to refine this system into something beautifully expressive. Only then were they ready to enter their period of design. Two purposes seem to have motivated them further. One was the desire to create a feeling of spaciousness in the interior, and this they did by developing a system of subsidiary domes or semidomes. Insofar as these inward-facing domes added support for the central dome, they permitted the attainment of the second aim, which was to build a shell-thin masonry dome high in the air and pierce its base with windows so that it seemed to float above a halo of light.

The crowning of all these urges and efforts took place in the build-

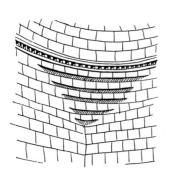

FIG. 428. Examples of
Early Byzantine
squinches.
ca. A.D. 400-500.

FIG. 429. Anthemius of Tralles and Isidorus of Miletus. Cross-section. Santa Sophia.
A.D. 532-562. Istanbul.

FIG. 430. Cross-section.
St. Mark's. 1042-1071.
Venice.

ing of Santa Sophia (Fig. 429) during the Golden Age of Justinian.
The success of its great dome and vast interior in inspiring awe and
a kind of spiritual elation was attested by many a medieval visitor.
Today, however, critics are more inclined to point to an outstanding feature which makes awe and elation possible: the articulation of
the forms. By this an architect means that they flow continuously
from one to another, integrating the huge building with apparent
ease and leading the eye upward to a grand climax in the dome. This
quality in Santa Sophia makes it a masterpiece of design.

Santa Sophia represents an emotional climax which the later Byzantine builders could not sustain. Indeed, as their feelings and
urges lost their strength, their engineering skill fell off too, showing
the relationship between the two in a historic instance that has been
repeated many times. The best the later Byzantine architects could
do was repeat the old forms in new and complex ways. The style
was sufficiently colorful and picturesque to last for another fifteen
centuries over wide areas of Eastern Europe and Asia Minor. But
picturesqueness is not a substitute for greatness. This can be seen
by comparing the cross-section of Santa Sophia in Fig. 429, with the
cross-section of St. Mark's in Venice in Fig. 430. The false domes
thrown up over wooden frames in St. Mark's neither hide nor save
the relatively pedestrian articulation of the masonry walls. Nor does
the mass of filigree on the exterior make up for the less daring conception of engineering and design. Typically, the most frequently
praised elements of St. Mark's design are its superficialities—the
colorful mosaics and exquisitely carved capitals. It is an example of
architecture in its final, decorator stage. Yet it is undeniably picturesque in its Venetian setting. No group of artists could sustain
forever the level of inspiration that went into the building of Santa
Sophia, even if the best of historical conditions were to continue—
one more reason why the arts fall into periodic declines.

A third demonstration of the Conant thesis can be found in the
history of the Gothic style. For although later in time than the Byzantine, it followed its general pattern. Only one qualification is
necessary. The engineering groundwork was laid during the preceding Romanesque period rather than within the Gothic cycle itself.
By the third quarter of the twelfth century the Romanesque master
masons of Lombardy, Normandy, and Burgundy had experimented
widely with the ribbed vault and buttress system which was to make
Gothic structural audacity possible. It remained only for the elements to be put together on the vastly daring scale of the cathedrals.
The huge third monastic church at Cluny, in Burgundy, with its

FIG. 431. St. Mark's. 1042-1071. Venice.

FIG. 432. Vault. Chapel of Henry VII. 1500-1512. Westminster Abbey, London.

forest of towers, 110-foot high nave, and open-air flying buttresses, came near to doing that.

Thereafter the Gothic evolved typically. The early cathedrals, such as Chartres and Notre Dame at Paris, were conceived in a simple style which retained something of the mural heaviness of the Romanesque. The later cathedrals at Reims and Amiens shed this massiveness for the lightness and openness of High Gothic. They were the culminating masterpieces of the Gothic trend in which engineering, composition, and decoration were perfectly blended. But so rapid were the changes in the dynamic Gothic cycle that the stage in which decoration predominated was not long in coming. It was called by a name implying ornateness—the *flamboyant* style. Signs of this flamboyance can be seen in Reims itself, but they are clearly evident in the church of St. Maclou and the Cathedral at Rouen (Fig. 433). Despite a lacelike intricacy of carving which elicits some admiration, the façade resembles an overdecorated Christmas tree. The point of balance between decoration and underlying forms had been reached and passed.

Nowhere is this trend from richness to excessive complexity better seen than in the development of Gothic towers and spires. They are to Gothic expression what the column is to the classical Greek, and the medieval builders designed them brilliantly until they lost their touch during the decline into decorative profusion. A famous example of this change can be found in the towers of the Cathedral of Chartres (Fig. 385). The southern tower, which is on the right in the illustration, is the earlier of the two. Its simple, clear-cut lines lead the eye upward from form to form in a logical progression. Its articulation is worthy of comparison with Santa Sophia's (Fig. 429). As a result, it has been called one of the finest examples of control over architectural design in the world. The north, or left-hand tower, is another matter. Built much later (about 1507—1512) it shows that the Gothic peoples and the artists who worked for them had lost their grasp of fundamentals and succumbed to the seduction of decoration. The outlines of this tower seem suffocated by details, the more so because it must stand eternal comparison with the southern tower.

The bearing that timing has on a tower's design can be seen by looking again at Fig. 433, which contains the famous Butter Tower of the Cathedral of Rouen. The Tower was so named because it was built from a tax on butter. The Conant thesis would collapse if this tower dated from an early stage in the Gothic cycle. But such is not the case. It corresponds historically with the North Tower of Chartres and presents the same relationship of form and decoration.

FIG. 433. West façade (1507) and "Butter Tower" (1497-1509). Cathedral, Rouen.

FIG. 434. Brunelleschi. Pazzi Chapel. 1429. Cloister of Santa Croce. Florence.

In England the Gothic style followed a parallel course so patently that the names *early English, perpendicular,* and *decorated* have been given to the three principal stages, the last-named being equivalent to the *flamboyant* style in France. The extent to which corruptions of design occurred during the late medieval periods may be seen by comparing the austerely simple Romanesque Chapel of St. John (Fig. 338) in the Tower of London with the Chapel of Henry VII in Westminster Abbey (Fig. 432). The latter exemplifies the so-called decorated style. It could hardly be more ornate. Moreover, despite its fascinating delicacy and undoubted skill in decorative carving, it shows a decline in engineering skill. In this fan vaulting the overzealous decorators finally went beyond their building abilities and had to hold the various vaults and stalactite pendants together with metal tie rods. Such tricks are always a sign that a style has, so to speak, reached the end of the line; its practitioners have either forgotten or exceeded its original engineering system.

History has repeated the Conant thesis down to the present day. When the architects of the Italian Renaissance got their chance to regain the cultural leadership of Europe for the Mediterranean area, they reacted against the medieval style, calling it wild or "Gothic," and returned to their classical heritage. What is more significant, they returned first to the earlier and simpler type of classical architecture instead of picking up where the late, ornament-loving Romans had left off. These points can be easily seen by comparing the early Renaissance Pazzi Chapel of Brunelleschi (Fig. 434) with the late Gothic Cathedral of Rouen (Fig. 433). Though no one would mistake the Italian building for anything Greek, it has the same slender refinement as the North Porch of the Erechtheum (Fig. 426). Decoration once again lives for the geometric composition instead of the other way around.

The Italians, however, made one mistake in their hurry to recapture cultural supremacy. They leaped over the whole period of experimental engineering which alone can give a style a firm foundation. Hence the similarity of the Pazzi Chapel to fully developed Ionic design rather than to the early awkwardness of the Temple of Ceres at Paestum. In fact, Brunelleschi, a superior designer, was a poor engineer. He willingly held his vaults together with tie rods, thus practicing at the beginning of a style what should come only in the period of decline. Unfortunately, he had plenty of company. Michelozzo used tie rods in the cloister of San Marco, as can be seen in Fra Angelico's *Annunciation*. And within a few decades Bramante gained an appearance of interior depth cheaply by resorting

to painted optical illusions. Michelangelo also accused him of cheap-
ening and weakening the piers of St. Peter's. These are engineering
shams which bode ill for the life of any architectural style. Indeed,
having evaded the hard problems of engineering, the Renaissance
architects seemed to hasten toward the decorative stage. It came
within a century with the arrival of the baroque. A comparison of
St. Peter's or Vierzehnheiligen with the Pazzi Chapel will show the
way architecture was tending.

In the course of time a reaction set in against the baroque or its
late-born sister, the rococo, when the neo-classicists of the late eighteenth century preached a return to Greek simplicity. But the ways
of decoration were adopted again in the nineteenth century with the
Romantic revival and followed during Victorian times by the worst
plunge into decorative excesses that history has ever seen. The
reason for this is twofold: first, for five centuries—from the time of
Brunelleschi to the Chicago Fair of 1893—architects evaded the
initial engineering phase of the Conant cycle and therefore oscillated
back and forth between the remaining two phases, design and decoration, with each oscillation getting worse. Not once during that
five-hundred-year span did architects pause long enough to train
themselves thoroughly in engineering. Consequently, whatever impressiveness the Renaissance, baroque, and later buildings possess is
almost always described in compositional and decorative terms.
Contributing nothing greatly new to the history of engineering, they
will not stand comparison in that fundamental respect with the best
architecture of the ancient and medieval periods. In architecture
there is no short cut to deeply satisfying forms.

Secondly, the oscillations went from bad to worse because of the
revivalist predilections of all Renaissance and post-Renaissance architecture. Unable to develop an engineering of their own and an
integrated style of design, architects borrowed repeatedly from the
past in a series of neo-this and neo-that movements. While not disastrous in itself, revivalism ruined them when they copied the
decadent stage of any given style. Their lack of a fundamental
understanding of architecture—the relationship between engineering, design, and decoration—made them gravitate all too often toward the ornamentation. For instance, whenever nineteenth- and
twentieth-century architects copied the Gothic style and funds permitted them to do so, they emulated examples of the decorative
rather than the design stages. As a consequence they came closer
to the Butter Tower at Rouen than they ever did to the South Tower
at Chartres. The copying of poor practices rarely has any other
result.

Fortunately, though slow in being learned, these lessons were not lost on the pioneers of the modern movement. While others were being applauded for their pseudo-Gothic museums and baroquish opera houses, they set out in the early nineteenth century to give modern architecture the only kind of foundation on which it could hope to last. Instead of evading the engineering problems raised by unprecedented needs, materials, and techniques, they slowly conquered them behind the scenes—in factories, bridges, office buildings, and lighthouses. The information thus accumulated allowed men like Gropius, Wright, Mendelssohn, and Van der Rohe to create a modern design which was firmly based on a modern engineering. In that far-reaching sense it was the first modern architectural style since Gothic times. Also, by starting at the true beginning the pioneers of the modern movement proved once more the validity of the Conant thesis.

At the beginning of this chapter we set out to show that art changes through successive historical periods, and how and why it is most likely to change. We have seen how the artist's individuality is affected by the conditions under which he works; and we have perceived something of the conditions which, in the opinion of most students of history, allow human beings to do their best work. This is an interesting and valuable subject, virtually synonymous with the history of art.

CHAPTER 27

Individuality

By individuality we mean the sum of the ways in which anything *differs* and *stands out* from its normal group. Early in history the West placed a considerable importance on that quality. It has continued to do so to the present day. Since the Orient has favored a different point of view, we like to believe that our stress upon individuality has been warranted. We shall examine its history from the occidental point of view, but first we must define individuality somewhat more carefully to avoid confusing it with mere novelty. Novelty is short-lived, individuality is persistent.

We can best define individuality and its relative importance by asking: What is it in general? What are its specific signs or proof? How can we test these proofs? What do they signify for the history of art?

THE NATURE OF INDIVIDUALITY

In the sense intended here, the nature of individuality is not to be found in the individuality of any nation or social group, but in a human being or the art in which he expresses himself. However, we always measure anything by comparison. When the unit is played against the group certain rules emerge. One is that since no two people perceive the world in exactly the same fashion, no two people are themselves alike. The other rule is that the overt signs of individuality vary greatly according to the pressure to conform that the group places upon its members. Thus individuality always has a group context, just as the group always has a historical context. The signs of individuality are therefore interwoven with the history of human freedom and conformity. Freedom is plainly visible in

843

ancient Greek art and in modern art from the Renaissance on, conformity in the art of Egypt and Byzantium.

THE UNIVERSAL SIGNS OF INDIVIDUALITY

Despite its close connection with history, individuality has certain universal signs. It is the residual expression which remains after we have accounted for the influences of hemisphere, region, nationality, and period. These speak for the effect of external reality upon the artist; individuality speaks for the reality that is centered within him and pushes outward. It is manifest in an attitude of mind which survives a lifetime of outside influences, compulsions, and rewards. It is expressed through temperaments—stable or flighty, good natured or testy. It shows itself in each human being's reaction to reality, whether it be optimistic or pessimistic, strong or weak, malicious or magnanimous.

For our purposes the paramount variations in individuals express themselves most clearly through two major aspects of style—idea and design. For instance, marked individuality has been expressed through pictures which are unusual in subject. Raphael's *School of Athens,* Picasso's *Guernica,* and Velasquez's *Maids of Honor* stand out to the quickest glance because of the singularity of their subjects. Pieter Bruegel is another who is outstanding for the individuality of his ideas; many of his subjects, like the *Contest of Carnival and Lent* and the *Flemish Proverbs,* are not only unusual, but unique. Others that he treated, such as his *Blind Leading the Blind,* are, if not unique, unusual for their rarity. Bruegel had a quick eye for the significant but exceptional theme. So, too, did Turner when he painted the *Fighting Téméraire.*

Individuality can also be expressed by an artist's treatment of any theme. By his selection and combination of the formal elements he can stamp his personality upon anything he designs, as Raphael did in his representations of the Madonna and Child or other subjects drawn from the Bible or classical mythology. The most hackneyed or time-honored subjects became worth looking at under his hands. The opposite of novelty-seeking, this kind of individuality permits an artist to treat a subject of recognized importance which may already have been depicted countless times. As long as he can present the subject in a distinctive way, he does not need to have a Bruegelian turn of mind. Many artists had painted apples and fruit before Cézanne, leaving presumably nothing else to be said about them. Yet we go out of our way to see a still life by Cézanne because it has something new about it. That something is its design. As a result of such experiences we come to feel that design can make the most ordinary subject inexhaustible.

Even in the freest society an artist generally works in the mode of representation common to his time, whether it be medieval, Renaissance, or modern. He will, however, develop a style which distinguishes his work in some degree from that of his contemporaries, as Raphael's is distinguishable from his master's and his pupils'. If he turns his back on the prevailing mode he will be out of place, and if he imitates slavishly, he will be lost in the crowd. Individuality is therefore always a kind of compromise.

When an artist has evolved a style of his own, it will identify every picture he composes, even when he is painting replicas of his own work. To a creative artist every composition is a new problem in organization if not in idea. There are pictures of haystacks which Monet executed within a single week, yet each is distinguishable and each has its own unique unity. The same is true of Cézanne's still-life paintings. Although all are unmistakably his, no two are exactly alike. A creative artist is always starting afresh. He cannot paint two identical pictures. Thus the flow of individuality in art is everywhere continuous yet inexhaustibly various.

THE SPECIFIC SIGNS OF INDIVIDUALITY

Since individuality is a matter of degree, it can be perceived most exactly in departures from a norm. Such departures can be found in the portraits of a single person by several artists. Thomas Jefferson, for example, was portrayed by both Gilbert Stuart and Charles Wilson Peale. Jefferson's actual appearance presumably remained the same, but the pictures of him are noticeably different. This allows us to perceive precisely the differences in interpretation that are due to artistic individuality. Similarly, a visit to Cézanne's studio at Aix will show that the vases, draperies, and tables he used repeatedly in his still-life paintings remained constant; it was his rearrangement of them that was infinitely individual.

Whenever one artist copies a painting by another, individuality emerges in specifically visible ways. Because the artistic orientation of perception is a part of the history of art, examples of this relationship abound. An excellent one concerns Hiroshige's *Shower on Ohashi Bridge* (Fig. 68), for Van Gogh proved his interest in Japanese prints by making a direct copy of it. Direct, that is, except for every element that transformed it unmistakably into a Van Gogh. The same phenomenon is discernible in Rubens' copies after Caravaggio and Michelangelo. Rubens' personal vision transformed each copy into a compound of precedent and individual interpretation. The same personal vision safeguards artistic orginality during the period of learning. Without it the artistic orientation would have been a threat to the growth of art instead of an assurance of progress. Individuality is a safeguard even in the close relationship of a living master and his pupils within a single studio. The Renaissance provides us with some pertinent illustrations. During that period there were no schools of art. Teachers were the masters of busy shops; pupils were apprenticed assistants who did their bidding. Their lessons consisted of helping with the execution of pictures and copying examples of the master's work. Discipline was the aim and rule, the style of the studio the prevailing mode. Individuality was not encouraged among the young. And yet there is a classic example of a brilliant pupil blossoming within this system. This occurred under the eye of a master and presumably with his encouragement. When Verrocchio allowed the young Leonardo da Vinci to paint the whole of an angel in his famous *Baptism of Christ,* the small figure to the left showed then, as it still does, the unmistakable touch of Leonardo. An even better point of departure than the master–pupil tie is the bond of blood. Here too we find differences between the generally similar styles of Hubert and Jan Van Eyck, the elder and younger Bruegel, Cranach, and Holbein. Yet these examples do not exhaust the yardsticks of individuality.

The history of art contains numerous instances of natural groups or schools, for a society which has had the vitality to produce one outstanding artist has usually nurtured at least three. We naturally link together Michelangelo, Da Vinci, and Raphael; Titian, Tintoretto, and Veronese; Myron, Polyclitus, and Phidias; Praxiteles, Scopas, and Lysippus; Reynolds, Gainsborough, and Romney; Monet, Sisley, and Pissarro; Cézanne, Gauguin, and Van Gogh; and Homer, Eakins, and Ryder. These associations sum up in our minds movements and trends with basic similarities and common historical backgrounds, such as the Italian High Renaissance, the Venetian school, the Golden Age of Greek sculpture, the English portrait school, and the French impressionist and post-impressionist movements. Sometimes these artists worked closely together, as did Monet, Sisley, and Pissarro. In many cases, however, they did not know each other, and the association is largely of critical making. But no matter how much these artists had in common because of shared environments, no one could mistake Eakins' work for Homer's, or Raphael's for Michelangelo's. In every instance the common style is only half the story, the other half is Gainsborough's or Tintoretto's unique and personal contribution to it.

THE MEASURE OF INDIVIDUALITY

The proofs of individuality are abundant. Yet they should not be seen in isolation, for the full meaning of individuality lies in the course of its development within a social milieu. Its most impressive proof is a resistance to conformity, a resistance which is strongest when the odds against it are great. A simple but universal example is found wherever a strong-willed parent tries to dissuade or force a son away from the pursuit of art. Vasari says that Michelangelo's father and brothers beat him repeatedly because of his interest in art. He became an artist in spite of them—a story that has been repeated in every generation.

A prominent actress of our time, Ruth Gordon, deliberately discouraged every youthful actress who came to her for advice. If, in spite of that, they persisted, she knew they had the requisite urge to act. This impulse to express oneself which reverberates in Strickland's "I've got to paint!" allies individuality with the factor of wilful purpose in the human personality.

The desire to do things in their own way has made men of strong individuality refuse to stay in the shadows of other men when all around them were willing to accept reflected glory. Van Dyck was the one artist in Rubens' studio who felt impelled to strike out on his own. As a consequence he became the most famous of the master's many pupils, the protégé with the most distinguishable personal style. In order to paint in his own way Van Dyck had to get out from under Rubens' wing and take his chances in a foreign country. The willingness, even eagerness, to do that was evident in him as a young man. By the time he was twenty he was Rubens' first assistant, with a secure, lifetime position assured him. Yet he abandoned it a year later for the chance to have a studio of his own.

Gauguin gave a similar demonstration of that urge to freedom which makes some men want passionately to do things in their own way, though he did not break his ties so young as Van Dyck. A versatile and worldly-wise man, he had sailed with the French navy and became shrewd and tough. After he married and settled down, he worked for a number of years in a Parisian financial house, establishing himself as a respectable and successful citizen. Then, in early middle life, he threw over everything he had gained in order to be an artist. His conservative family and friends thought him mad, but he pursued his aim without any assurance of future fame to a bitter and lonely end in the South Seas. Both the initial and sustaining desire to follow his own bent was strong in him. His example, like Van Dyck's break with Rubens and Michelangelo's running fight with Pope Julius II throughout the painting of the Sistine ceiling, suggests that individuality divides the world's artists into two groups. One group includes tens of thousands of artists who remained students and assistants throughout their lives. Lacking confidence on the one hand and desire on the other, they were never able to cut loose from their masters; they are the Luinis of Da Vinci's day and the Snyders of Rubens' who figure faithfully but incidentally in the history of art. Individuality they have, but only moderately. The other group is comprised of the truly creative minority who break with the group because they must. Often driven and lonely men, they are nevertheless the great ones.

The impulse to cut the artistic apron strings is only the first sign of an urge to act on one's own as a free and individual artist. A more important proof lies in development. The direction of that development we have hinted at, but not explored. It is worth a moment's notice, for it follows a significant route. Oddly enough, the route is almost the reverse of a society's cultural evolution as we traced that evolution in the previous chapter. We saw there that the progression of a dynamic society is almost invariably from the simple to the complex. A point may well be reached where complexity creates confusion, signifying the cultural anarchy of decadence. A single artist develops, contrariwise, from complexity to unity. His later work is not necessarily simple, indeed it is usually more subtle and sophisticated. But it appears simple because of its greater integration. Described in the language of design, his manner of composing progresses from an ensemble of parts to a fusion of parts, or at least in that direction.

Three prominent examples of this progression can be found in the careers of Titian and Rembrandt in painting and Beethoven in musical composition. A comparison of Titian's *Madonna of the Cherries* (Fig. 129), *Meeting of Bacchus and Ariadne* (Fig. 89), and *Christ Crowned with Thorns* (Fig. 130) will bear this out. They were painted in that order, when he was young, middle-aged, and old, the first separated from the last by some fifty-five years. Where the first is close to the Renaissance classical style from which it evolved, the last points the way to the baroque.

In Rembrandt's art, as in Titian's, spiritual maturity was accompanied by parallel changes in style. One can see this by comparing his early portrait of *Saskia with a Red Flower* (Fig. 363), which is psychologically optimistic, social, extroverted, and dynamic, with his late *Portrait of a Woman* (Fig. 365), which is spiritually subdued and retiring, but mellow, wise and serene. Stylistically, the colors of the later picture are far more subtly organized. The same type of change may be seen in three versions of the *Supper at Emmaus* which Rembrandt painted during the early, middle, and late years of his life. The version we have illustrated in Fig. 325 was painted in the middle period. When it is compared with the other representations, the youthful picture appears almost violently melodramatic, while the late version seems subdued to a whisper. The first is full of tricks, the last an expression of pure emotion.

Beethoven's development as a composer followed a similar line. In his early work every note and melody has a Mozartian clarity. By contrast, the string quartets which he composed during his last years are so formed that passages blend in a continuous flow of sound. They are as un-Mozartian as they are prophetic of the future of nineteenth-century music. Like Rembrandt's last work, they have no need for tricks, but show, rather, the final mastery of a means of transmitting feeling.

In their several but similar ways Titian, Rembrandt, and Beethoven progressed from youthful naiveté to mature profundity in the realm of feeling and from half-integrated complexity to perfect integration in the realm of design. Taken together these were the final marks of their individuality. Resolving early in their lives to depart from the group and to seek continuous development of their powers, each was soon set apart by his individuality. As the years passed their growth set them further and further apart from the crowd. Rembrandt's last years in Amsterdam were spent in isolation. The populace which had once applauded him for reflecting its own ideas, but understood him not at all at the end, deserted him completely. The last of his three paintings of the *Supper at Emmaus* must have been wholly unintelligible to them. Beethoven suffered the same fate during his life. As he became great, he left ordinary men behind. One of his last quartets was so strange to one patron that he asked, "Do you call this music?" "Yes," Beethoven replied, "but for a future generation." This temporary incomprehensibility is likely to be the lot of every creative artist who exploits his capacity for growth. The pioneer travels a lonely road; it is the price he pays for his individuality.

From these illustrations we can see that individuals and societies follow different patterns of historical development. The single artist's path is upward toward progressively greater unity; a society's path declines after an optimum period into ruinous diversity. This is not to disparage societies, for their problems are greater. Inherently heterogeneous, they become increasingly so as their populations multiply. No artist, faced with the task of unifying a single work of art, was ever so harassed as the rulers of Rome in the days of its decline.

While growth is a measure of individuality, it also divides artists into three groups. First, there are those naturally endowed geniuses whose capacities for development carried them to the lonely heights of artistic achievement. On the rungs far below are those who achieved some small measure of individuality and then grew no more. Rosa Bonheur is typical of this large group. Characteristically, she never outgrew her obsession with details. Her last paintings are little different from her first, and none ever exhibited that unity of the whole which distinguishes the final work of Beethoven, Rembrandt, and Titian.

Between these two is that large group which was destined for growth to greatness but not to superlativeness. An excellent case is the career of Winslow Homer. His youthful work is not noticeably superior to a large quantity of American art of the 1850s and 1860s. His engraving of *A Cadet Hop at West Point* (1858) is vigorous, gay, and competent, but little more; and his numerous Civil War drawings for *Harper's Weekly* are more typical of its illustrations than outstanding. Indeed, Homer continued for some fifteen years after the Civil War to draw and paint pictures of small boys, handsome men, and pretty girls that were merely fresh in technique and pleasant in content. If he had died before 1880, he would hardly be heard of today. It was at that time, when he was forty-four, that he first visited the fishing port of Tynemouth, England, and then settled at Prout's Neck on the coast of Maine. For the first time his eyes were opened to some of the deeper realities of life, and he began to paint such suspense-laden pictures as the *Fog Warning* of 1885 (Fig. 61). Furthermore, he continued to grow, so that his development from that time divided his pre-Tynemouth and post-Tynemouth work into two markedly different chapters, the work of his last years standing in powerful contrast to his ordinary beginnings. If his art is not the equal of Rembrandt's, it is at least representative of those men who developed their talents to the limit.

Although its locus is always a singular human equation, the growth of indivduality takes place almost exclusively within the spiritual faculties of that equation. Taking Homer again as an illustration, there is evidence that, like artists generally, he achieved technical competence at a rather early age. Conversely, his hand presumably grew less steady and his eyes less clear in old age. The growth of his art must therefore have been a mental, not a physical growth. There is evidence to confirm this. Homer saw tragedy at the Civil War front; but he was not ready to understand it until his character had matured. If, therefore, individuality is related to the development of perception, there is no doubt about which half of that phenomenon, seeing or knowing, contributes most to the improvement in art.

THE HISTORICAL PROOFS OF INDIVIDUALITY

Oddly enough, the strength of individuality can best be proved on the grounds where we are likely to assume that it did not exist, that is, in the great collective societies of Egypt, Byzantium, and medieval Christendom. Authoritarian as they were, they were never able to suppress individuality entirely. The signs are hard to find in much medieval art, but they are present. This is especially true in the field of portraiture, which normally thrives during individualistic eras and declines during periods when the human ego is supposed to be subordinate to higher ideals. A transparent example of defection from this anonymity is the Byzantine mosaic of *Justinian and Courtiers* (Fig. 121). Through that picture, Maximianus, the Bishop of Ravenna, guaranteed that his name would not die by having it written large above his image. By similar subterfuges of many kinds, artists and patrons contrived to insert portraits into the body of art despite church censorship throughout the Middle Ages. Individuality had its difficulties, but it never died.

We may be glad of this fact when we admire the Gothic cathedrals which arose at the end of the Middle Ages, for one of their most admirable qualities, variety within an impressive unity, contributed to a balance between the claims of freedom and authority. Although discouraged from seeking personal fame, the hundreds of sculptors who worked on the decoration of the cathedrals were apparently given a good deal of latitude. With the craving for self-expression encouraged in this way, some outstanding results were achieved. Notable among those which illustrate this point are four figures on the west façade of the Cathedral at Reims. Two of them represent the *Annunciation;* the other two the *Visitation* (Fig. 435). They stand side by side and were executed at about the same time in the fourteenth century. Yet it is perfectly clear that they were created by two different sculptors who worked as freely as they wished. The designer of the *Annunciation* was a master of the Gothic style in its simplest grace; the sculptor of the *Visitation* had somewhere seen

FIG. 435. *Annunciation and Visitation.* *ca.* 1250-1270. Main portal. West façade.
Cathedral, Amiens.

and become enamoured of examples of classical art. We do not know the names of these two sculptors, but we should search far to find better proof of the urge to individuality.

During the Renaissance period which followed Gothic times individuality was allowed such freedom that it was taken for granted. Portraiture, for example, increased with every decade. As medieval strictness relaxed, patrons and artists who had included themselves timidly in devotional pictures increased the size and prominence of their portraits in panel after panel. By the middle of the fifteenth century, the positions of sacred and secular figures were largely reversed. The most striking example of this new order is contained in a painting by Piero della Francesca. In it the patron, Sigismondo Malatesta, occupies the center of the frame; St. Sigismondo has been pushed to the side. In another hundred years, Veronese thought nothing of filling his *Supper at Emmaus* (Fig. 326) with secular figures until they nearly crowded the religious figures out of the picture. Thereafter the free expression of artistic individuality was never stopped. It finally reached a point so far removed from medieval service to the church that many artists assumed self-expression to be the primary and only purpose of art.

Nevertheless, the artists of the post-Renaissance and modern periods have known their "times of troubles." One of them was the century of the Counter-Reformation and its ruthless Inquisition, when it was worth a man's life to cross the authorities. Another was the period of the Revolution in France when David painted what he was bid under fear of the guillotine. There have been others which cast their shadows over freedom of action.

During these periods of reaction, individuality showed itself by the response of different temperaments to the challenge of difficulties and restrictions, some men succumbing to gloom, others showing extraordinary courage and faith. One might assume that Bruegel's *Wedding Dance* (Fig. 232) and Rubens' *La Ronda* (Fig. 351) reflect social conditions of the pleasantest possible sort, or that neither artist, the successful Rubens especially, had a care in the world. Nothing could be farther from the truth. Bruegel lived in a Flanders under the yoke of Spain; and Rubens lived when Europe was rent by the Counter-Reformation. Both men were acquainted with tragedy, but they reacted to it strongly and optimistically.

At the opposite pole from them is Picasso. Having lived through two world wars, he has been depressed by the magnitude of evil in the world, a condition against which he has protested vehemently in *Guernica* (Fig. 1). Yet we cannot overlook the fact that he has been disposed to view life grimly from his earliest years, as we saw in his *Woman Ironing* of 1904 (Fig. 45). The *Guernica* is therefore not to be taken as a direct reflection of history, nor as something apart from it, but as history seen through the individual eyes of Picasso.

This is a lesson that should not be forgotten when we read history through the eyes of artists. Taken alone, any one artist's view of history can be misleading. For instance, should the future judge our times by the opinion of Picasso, or should it favor the outlook of Matisse? If the latter, we shall go down as a happy period indeed, for Matisse's reaction to a life by no means free of privation has been strong and optimistic. Which man, then, gives a true picture of our times? Common sense tells us that the answer is neither and both, because no one man can speak for a time that is spiritually compounded of gloom and cheer, good and evil. Looking at the individual artist's work for the signs of any time, we must always allow for the effect of individuality. If an interpretation of history rather than individual merit is our aim, the only safe procedure is to view a society and its times as an aggregate of individualities. Then the balance sheet can be truly said to show more weakness than strength, more confusion than clarity, more subservience than freedom, or the other way around.

THE JUSTIFICATION OF INDIVIDUALITY

There are many who feel that the freedom of expression which appeared in Gothic times and carried the day in the Renaissance has degenerated into anarchy in our times. William Morris and Pugin are among those nineteenth-century critics who would have had us return to the medieval way of life. In the present day the advocates of collectivism are legion.

Certainly the merit of individuality is not licentiousness or self-indulgence. If freedom is man's greatest good, it is not freedom to be a lotus-eater or a law unto himself; the value of freedom lies in its fruits. What have these been in the comparatively free societies? One fruit was the philosophical thought of the Athenian Republic; the dictatorship of neighboring Sparta significantly produced none. Another has been modern science. Both required freedom to pursue truth, and both justified that freedom. But what of the fruits of individual liberty in the visual arts? When it was free, Greece produced sculpture that is considered beautiful and enriching to view, even after two thousand years. Western Europe, beginning with the Renaissance, followed with an unprecedented output of pictorial masterpieces. That outburst of activity in painting was unmistakably connected with a new faith in individuality. Believing that progress in painting would follow the development of talented individuals, Renaissance patrons encouraged artists to develop their abilities to the utmost. They encouraged them with money and prestige, making them feel that they were valuable members of society. They did not ignore the ego; calculating its role shrewdly, they encouraged personal effort with the incentive of fame, even exalting Raphael to the "divine." But they also encouraged every artist to put his talents at the service of something beyond himself—his republic, his patron, his church. They gave him a purpose for developing his capacities which united him with society. They set a pattern for individual freedom within a limitation of responsibility which later centuries have followed to their profit.

The results of the six centuries of free inquiry and effort set in motion by the Renaissance can now be assessed. They consist of a body of masterpieces which are in variety, originality, vitality, and profundity a complete justification of individuality. It makes the painting of the Middle Ages seem comparatively static or retarded. The world had to wait a thousand years for Giotto; but once freedom had been won by the leaders of the Renaissance, outstanding masters followed with every generation.

The best proof of individuality's worth lies, however, on the home ground of the collectivists—the authoritarian societies of antiquity and the Middle Ages. These societies were able to complete huge architectural projects with vast contributions of time, money, and energy from masses of men. Many of these men were slaves, others were emotionally inspired Christians. But in neither case would labor alone have created these monuments. A closer look at these societies will almost always show that behind every one of their endeavors were a few clear-headed and purposeful men who, being at the head of their societies, enjoyed a freedom unknown to the subservient lower classes. The Great Pyramid owes its existence to the will of a Khufu, without which it never would have been built. The Pantheon owes its existence to Hadrian, Santa Sophia to Justinian, the monastic church of Cluny to Abbott Hugh, the Cathedral of Reims to a few bishops and master masons like Jean-le-Loup and Bernard of Soissons. Masses of men do not erect cathedrals without leadership. And that leadership has always been provided by the determined intelligence of a few men of highly developed individuality.

The only real difference between the artistic performance of individuality in the collective and free societies has been in type and scope of opportunity. When freedom of action has been limited to those in authority, progress has been slow; when granted to citizens freely, progress has been rapid and widespread. The over-all accomplishments of the thousand years of the Middle Ages are overshadowed by those of the past five hundred.

In the art of every country and every time we find individual enterprise proving its right to freedom by the abundance and excellence of its results. If our examination of the visual arts has led us to no other conclusion, that study is justified, for it confirms what we as a people believe to be true of every field of human endeavor.

Appendix

An Outline of Art History

This outline will be useful in placing the periods, artists, and examples discussed in the text in their proper chronological contexts and in their historical relation to other masterpieces of the history of art. No attempt has been made to develop the outline beyond the introductory level. For convenience the figure number has been placed after each example which is illustrated in this book. Most of the other examples can be found in the University Prints or in Roos's *Illustrated Handbook of Art History*. The outline will also be a valuable factual aid to have at one's elbow for general reference purposes.

One of the problems confronting the beginning student of the arts who wishes to gain a historical perspective is that of ascertaining the senses in which the main terms denoting period-styles in the visual arts are used most commonly; the term *baroque,* for instance, is likely to mean different centuries to a musicologist and an art historian. Therefore an attempt will be made to clarify the meanings of the commonly used terms, at least in their positions in time. The best way to begin is to approach history first in terms of its largest time units, and then to observe the subdivisions within these temporal blocks.

Broadly viewed, the history of art presents four epochs or eras embracing many centuries of time, and unfolding in order: the prehistoric, ancient, medieval, and modern. These epochs extend, respectively, from the dawn of man to about 3400 B.C.; from approximately 3400 B.C. to A.D. 350; from A.D. 350 to the end of the fourteenth century (in Northern Europe) : and from the fourteenth century to the present day. The modern epoch encompasses the smallest span of time, but includes the largest number of famous works of art. Indeed, there is a progressive compression of centuries in each successive epoch from the incredibly long prehistoric to the short but dynamic modern epoch.

The increase in apparent productivity in the modern epoch is explained by two factors. First, we know far more about the centuries nearest us, due in part to the invention of the printing press, which made possible the recording and dissemination of activities in great detail. The other factor is the social, political, and artistic preferences that predominated in the various epochs. During the ancient and medieval epochs collective societies prevailed over most of the earth, and the people who lived under those systems expressed themselves most notably in architecture and sculpture, with painting running a poor third among their masterpieces. During the modern epoch the situation was nearly reversed; painting surged to the forefront until a large portion of the masterpieces produced fell within that medium. This phenomenon was closely connected with the rise of individual freedom as an artistic philosophy; the floodgates of talent were literally burst open by the concepts of political and social liberty that appeared with the modern epoch. Another source of inspiration, at least during the opening centuries of the modern epoch, was the chance to embrace the religious message of Christianity with enthusiasm instead of fear. This was a rare privilege in human history, and it paid abundant dividends in the exalted quality of Renaissance art in Italy. Thus the advent of the modern epoch was a major turning point in both the arts and human history.

THE PREHISTORIC EPOCH
(Prior to 15,000 B.C.)

The complexities of the remote and shadowy prehistoric epoch are not usually imposed upon the beginning student. He is asked only to be aware of the general character of such examples as the following:

ARCHITECTURE

The circular Druid temple called Stonehenge on Salisbury Plain, England.

SCULPTURE

The "Willendorf Venus," from Willendorf, Austria

PAINTING

Cave paintings and incised drawings at:
  Combarelles, France (Fig. 142)
  Lascaux, near Montignac, France
  Font-de-Gaume, France
  Alpera, Spain
  Altamira, Spain (Fig. 33)

There is a long gap (from *ca.* 15,000 B.C. to *ca.* 3400 B.C.) from which we have few remaining art works of outstanding quality.

THE ANCIENT EPOCH

(ca. 3400 B.C.–ca. A.D. 350)

The prestige of Greco-Roman, or Hellenic, culture has led classical scholars to establish it as an independent civilized entity and classify all previous societies as pre-Greek. The pre-Greek portion of the Ancient epoch includes the art of Egypt, Mesopotamia, and the Aegean lands. All lie within the eastern region of the Mediterranean Basin. The credit for cradling Western civilization in the area is given by some scholars to Egypt and by others, with equally good arguments, to Mesopotamia. Egypt is favored here because of the massiveness, impressiveness, and durability of its achievement.

EGYPT

Periods

Old Kingdom. Dynasties III-VI *(ca.* 2980–2475 B.C.)
Capital at Memphis
Middle Kingdom. Dynasties XI, XII *(ca.* 2160–1788
B.C.) Capital at Thebes
The Empire. Dynasties XVIII-XX *(ca.* 1580–1090 B.C.)
Capital at Thebes
Saïte period. Dynasty XXVI (663–525 B.C.) Capital
at Saïs

ARCHITECTURE

Tombs:
Old Kingdom:
Mastabas
Pyramids:
Zoser (at Sakkara)
Khufu (at Gizeh) (Figs. 174a and 381)
Khafre (at Gizeh)
Menkure (at Gizeh)
Middle Kingdom:
Pyramid-Mastabas (Abydos)
Shallow Rock-cut (Beni-Hasan)
The Empire:
Deep rock-cut (Valley of the Kings)

SCULPTURE

In the round:
Old Kingdom:
The Sphinx
Kaaper, the Sheikh-el-Beled
Seated Scribe (Louvre)
Khum-Ba-F (Fig. 2)
Ranefer
Rahotep and Nefret
Menkure and his Queen (Fig. 160)
Ankh-Haef
Khafre (Fig. 296)
The Empire:
Rameses II (Turin)

Queen Hatshepsut
School of Tell el-Amarna:
  Ikhnaton (Louvre)
  Nofretete (Fig. 366a)
Saïte and Ptolemaic periods:
  Portrait Head of a priest (Fig. 163)
  Bronze Cat (Fig. 313)
In relief:
  Reliefs from the tomb of Hesire (Old Kingdom)
  Reliefs of Ikhnaton and his Family (Empire)
  Reliefs of Seti at Abydos (Empire)

PAINTING

Wall paintings from the Tomb of Nakht, Thebes, Empire period (Fig. 120)
Mummy portrait of a Boy, from Fayum, 2nd century A.D. (Fig. 124)

MESOPOTAMIA

Unlike the civilization of ancient Egypt, that of ancient Mesopotamia has vanished from its original site, owing to the use of impermanent building material and to various historical vicissitudes. Archeologists have reconstructed the Mesopotamian culture of antiquity along these lines:

Periods

Early Babylonian (Chaldaean, Sumerian) (*ca.* 3000–1275 B.C.)
Assyrian Ascendancy (*ca.* 1275–606 B.C.)
Later Babylonian (*ca.* 625–538 B.C.)

ARCHITECTURE

Temples:
  The ziggurat
Palaces:
  Palace of Sargon II at Khorsabad (722–705 B.C.)

SCULPTURE

Early Babylonian:
  In the round:
    Statues of Gudea (*ca.* 2450)
    Heads from Tellô (Lagash)
    A Governor of Lagash, Sumerian (Fig. 67)
  In relief:
    Stele of Narâm-Sin (*ca.* 2650 B.C.)
    Stele of Khammurabi (*ca.* 1900 B.C.)
Assyrian:
  In the round:
    Statue of Ashur-nasir-pal II (885–860 B.C.)
  In relief:
    Palace reliefs of Ashur-nasir-pal II (Fig. 336)
      Sennacherib (705–681 B.C.) (Fig. 111)
      Ashur-bani-pal (668–626 B.C.) (Fig. 286)
Later Babylonian:
  In relief:
    Animals on Gate of Ishtar

PREHISTORIC GREECE

(ca. 3400–ca. 700 B.C.)

It must be emphasized that the art of prehistoric Greece is Greek only in geographical origin. The peoples of Crete, Mycenae, and Tiryns were ethnically and culturally quite different from the citizens of classical Greece who lived long after them. It is probably more correct to refer to this earlier civilization as the Aegean Age, and that term is commonly employed. Its two principal centers were on the island of Crete and at Mycenae on the Greek mainland, with the former reaching its peak at an earlier time. Crete, however, was one of the few countries in history which, like Assyria and Carthage, was abruptly destroyed after a military disaster, and never rose again. Mycenae was slowly but no less thoroughly ruined by the invasion of the Greek tribes. The two civilizations were dramatically rediscovered, along with Troy, by the archaeologists Sir Arthur Evans and Heinrich Schliemann.

CRETAN CIVILIZATION

Periods

Early Minoan (3400–2100 B.C.)
Middle Minoan (2100–1580 B.C.)
Late Minoan (1580-1200 B.C.)

Principal Sites

Knossos, Phaistos, Hagia Triada

ARCHITECTURE

Palace of Minos, Knossos

SCULPTURE

Ivory Diver
Faïence Cow and Calf
Chryselphantine Snake Goddess (Boston) *(ca. 1500 B.C.)*

PAINTING

Frescoes from the Palace of Minos *(ca. 1500 B.C.)*
Dolphin fresco
Cup-bearer
Chariot Scene
Scene from a Circus—Bull-Leaping
Flying Fish, from Melos

MINOR ARTS

Harvester Vase
Boxer Vase
Octopus Vase (Fig. 219)

Other Islands

Idols from the Cycladic Islands *(ca. 2500–2000 B.C.)* (Fig. 157)

MYCENAEN CIVILIZATION

Principal Periods

Early Helladic (2500–2000 B.C.)
Middle Helladic (2000–1600 B.C.)
Late Helladic I (1600–1500 B.C.)
Late Helladic II (1500–1400 B.C.)
Late Helladic III (1400–1100 B.C.)

The last-named period was the acme of Mycenaean civilization, but its predecessors show the antiquity of its history.

Principal Sites

Mycenae, Tiryns, Troy

ARCHITECTURE

The Citadel, Mycenae:
Treasury (Tholos) of Atreus (1185 B.C.)
The Citadel, Tiryns:
Cyclopean Walls, galleries (*ca.* 1500 B.C.)

SCULPTURE

Tombstones from Mycenae
Lioness Gate, Mycenae (*ca.* 1400 B.C.)

PAINTING

Priestess Carrying a Casket, fresco from Tiryns (*ca.* 1450 B.C.)
Warrior Vase (Fig. 230)

MINOR ARTS

Work in gold and silver:
Gold masks
Inlaid bronze daggers
The Vaphio Cups (*ca.* 1600–150 B.C.)

THE DARK AGES

(*ca.* 1100–700 B.C.)

The Dark Ages began with a mass migration of warlike, nomadic Dorian tribes into the Greek peninsula, causing the downfall of the Mycenaean civilization. The Greek tribes eventually split into two divisions, the Dorians settling on the mainland and the Ionians in Asia Minor and among the Aegean Islands. The low state of art in this unsettled time is seen in the vases in the so-called Geometric Style. During this period Homer composed his nostalgic poems about the heroic and happier days of the Mycenaean period.

HISTORIC GREECE

(*ca.* 675–27 B.C.)

One of the remarkable features of Greek classical civilization is the rapidity of its development compared to the slow movement of the massive authoritarian societies of antiquity. The lapse of time between its emergence from a semi-barbaric state and its final decline covers a mere six hundred years, during which it laid many of the strongest foundation posts of Western thought.   Another outstanding feature is the appearance of artists who were conscious of their individuality. The "name artist" appears for the first time in history on a wide scale amid the relatively democratic Greek city-states.

Periods

Early Archaic (*ca.* 625–550 B.C.)
Later Archaic (*ca.* 550–480 B.C.)
Great Period, first half (450–400 B.C.) : the Age of Pericles, the 5th century B.C.
Great Period, second half (400–323 B.C.) : the 4th century B.C.
Hellenistic Period (323–146 B.C.)
Greco-Roman Period (146–27 B.C.)

EARLY ARCHAIC PERIOD

(ca. 625–ca. 550 B.C.)

SCULPTURE

Chares of Branchidae
Victory (Nike) of Delos, by Mikkiades and Archermos
"Apollo" of Tenea (Fig. 405)
Hera of Samos (Fig. 403)
The Calfbearer

LATER ARCHAIC PERIOD

(ca. 550–ca. 480 B.C.)

IONIAN SCHOOLS

Reliefs from Thasos and Pharsalus
The Stele of Alexnor
The Treasury of the Siphnians at Delphi

DORIAN SCHOOLS

Argos:
   Agelaïdes, Statuette from Ligurio
Sicyon:
   Kanachos:
      The Payne-Knight Apollo
      The Apollo Piombino
Aegina: Onatas, sculptures from the Temple of Aphaia

ATTIC SCHOOL

Female figures from the Acropolis
The Hirsch Athena (Berlin)
Rampin head (Louvre)
Man Mounting a Chariot
Bronze Horse (Fig. 342)

ARCHITECTURE

The Development of the Doric order:
Heraeum at Olympia (*ca.* 700 B.C.)
Temple of Apollo, Corinth, 6th century B.C.
Treasury of the Siphnians, Delphi (*ca.* 525 B.C.)
Temple of Ceres, Paestum (*ca.* 520 B.C.) (Fig. 422)
Treasury of the Athenians, Delphi (*ca.* 515 B.C.) (Fig. 382)

TRANSITIONAL PERIOD

(*ca.* 480–*ca.* 450)

ARCHITECTURE

Temple of Zeus, Olympia (*ca.* 465 B.C.)
Temple of Poseidon, Paestum (*ca.* 460 B.C.)

SCULPTURE

Pediments of the Temple of Zeus at Olympia:
East Pediment:
Chariot race of Pelops and Oenomaus; with Zeus, Sterope, Hippodamia,
Cladeus, and Alphaeios
West Pediment:
Struggle of Lapiths and Centaurs; with Pirithous, Apollo, and Heracles
Metopes:
Labors of Heracles:
Heracles and Atlas
The Augean Stables
Heracles and the Cretan Bull (Fig. 407)
The Charioteer from Delphi
Critius and Nesiotes: the Tyrannicides (Harmodius and Aristogeiton)
Zeus from Artemisium (Fig. 50)
The Boston relief and "Ludovisi Throne" (Fig. 397)
Myron:
Athena and Marsyas
The Discus Thrower (Fig. 371)

THE GREAT PERIOD—FIRST HALF

(*ca* 450–*ca.* 400 B.C.)

The "Golden Age of Pericles"

ATHENS AND THE ATTIC SCHOOL. The Development of the Acropolis

The Parthenon (447–432 B.C.) :
Conceived by Pericles
Designed by Ictinus and Callicrates (Figs. 383, 423, 424, 425)
Supervised by Phidias
Sculpture, under Phidias:
Metopes, Centaurs and Lapiths Fighting (Fig. 356)
Frieze, Panathenaic procession (Figs. 267 and 321)

Pediments:
>West pediment, Contest of Athena and Poseidon for Attica: Ilissos
>(Fig. 408)
>East Pediment, Birth of Athena: Helios, Theseus(?), Ceres, Proserpina,
>Iris, Nike, The Three Fates, Selene

Later history:
A Christian church (*ca.* A.D. 450)
A Turkish mosque (A.D. 1460)
Visit of de Nointel; the Carrey drawings (A.D. 1674)
Damage by Admiral Morosini (A.D. 1687)
Stuart and Revett drawings (A.D. 1751–54)
Fauvel (A.D. 1787)
Lord Elgin (A.D. 1800–1810)

Phidias; other works:
Athena Promachos
Athena Lemnia
Athena Parthenos: Varvakeion statue, Lenormant statuette, Strangford shield
Olympian Zeus

The propylaea of Mnesicles (437–432 B.C.)
The "Theseum" (Temple of Hephaistos)
The Ionic order:
The Erechtheum (Fig. 426)
The Temple of Athena Nike (Wingless Victory) by Callicrates
>Balustrade figure of Nike Fastening Her Sandal

THE ARGIVE SCHOOL

Polyclitus:
The Spear-Bearer, or Doryphoros
The Diadem-Binder, or Diadumenos (Fig. 217)
Amazons

THE GREAT PERIOD—SECOND HALF

(*ca.* 400–*ca.* 323 B.C.)

Historians have divided the Great Period into two parts. The second half of the period was made quite different in character from the first by the Peloponnesian war (431–404 B.C.) which brought disaster to Athens. Owing, however, to the momentum generated prior to the war, the succeeding decades were still worthy of being called great. A noticeable difference, though, was a shift in emphasis from the glorification of cities to the applauding of personal genius.

ARCHITECTURE

The development of the Corinthian order:
The Tholos, Epidaurus (*ca.* 350 B.C.) (Fig. 427)
Choregic monument of Lysicrates (335–334 B.C.)
Temple of Olympian Zeus, Athens (174 B.C.–A.D. 117)

SCULPTURE

Attic grave monuments: Stelai of Agathokles, Dexileos, Hegeso, Korallion, and Damasistrate
Cephisodotus: Eirene and Ploutos, or Peace and Prosperity

Praxiteles:
  Hermes and Dionysus (Fig. 409)
  Satyr, or Marble Faun
  Apollo Sauroktonos, or Lizard-slayer
  Aphrodite of Cnidus
  Hermes of Andros
  Belvedere Hermes
  Diana of Gabii
Scopas and his school:
  Sculptures from the Temple of Athena Alea at Tegea
  Meleager
  Niobe group (Fig. 410)
Lysippus and his school:
  Apoxyomenos
  Agias
  Alexander
  Hermes
  Wrestlers
  Praying Boy
The Mausoleum, Hallicarnassus:
  Sculpture by Scopas and others (Fig. 333)
  Portraits of Maussollus and Artemisia
Portraits: Actually Hellenistic, but probably based on 4th century models:
  Demosthenes (Fig. 411)
  Poseidippos
  Sophocles
Other statues:
  Demeter of Cnidus
  Aphrodite from Cyrene
  Bartlett Aphrodite

HELLENISTIC PERIOD

(ca. 323–ca. 146 B.C.)

SCULPTURE

  The Victory of Samothrace (Fig. 412)
  The First School of Pergamum:
    Dedications of Attalus I (241–197 B.C.)
    Marsyas and the Slave, or "Arrotino"
    Death of a Gaul and His Wife, or "Arria and Paetus" group (Fig. 305)
    Dying Gaul (Fig. 413)
  The Second School of Pergamum:
    The great Altar of Eumenes II (197–159 B.C.)
  Pictorial reliefs:
    Peasant Going to Market (Fig. 415)
  Genre Figures:
    Boethos: Boy and Goose (Fig. 414)
    Drunken Old Woman
    Blind Fisherman
    Old Woman Going to Market (Fig. 404)
    Aged Shepherdess

Statues of the gods:
 Apollo Belvedere
 Artemis of Versailles
 Aphrodite of Melos

GRECO-ROMAN PERIOD

(ca. 146–*ca.* 27 B.C.)

SCULPTURE

Works under Pergamenian influence:
 Laocoön group by Agesander, Polydoros, and Athenodorus of Rhodes (Figs.
  406 and 416)
 Borghese Warrior by Agasias of Ephesus
 Farnese Bull by Apollonios and Tauriscus of Tralles
The Neo-Attic School:
 Glycon: Farnese Heracles
 Apollonius:
  Belvedere Torso
  Seated Boxer
 Archaistic works:
  Athena Promachos (Fig. 417)

GREEK PAINTING

At least three Greek painters, Zeuxis, Apelles, and Polygnotus, were as
famous in ancient times as are the contemporary sculptors; unfortunately, little
of their work has survived. The Greek talent for painting must be appreciated
today mainly through the decorations on vases; these have endured in large
quantities and are deservedly prized for the clarity, sensitivity, and vitality of
their designs. Attica was a center of this art whose golden age came between
550 and 450 B.C.

PRINCIPAL STYLES

Black-figured, mainly 7th and 6th centuries B.C.
Red-figured, mainly 6th and 5th centuries B.C. (Fig. 69)
White-figured, mainly 5th century B.C. and later (Fig. 144)

OUTSTANDING MASTERS (mostly red-figured)
Amasis, Exekios, Epiktetos, Euthymides, Euphonios, and Brygos

THE ROMAN PERIOD

(ca. 100 B.C.–A.D. 350)

Etruscan art has recently received much attention, especially in the fields of
painting and sculpture. But Rome is still considered to have been the principal
center of artistic activity in ancient Italy. It has been customary to belittle the
Roman contribution to art as a second-rate copy of Greek art, long on size and
gaudiness, but short on sensitivity. The Romans were prosaic and practical
where the Greeks were poetic and philosophical; their genius lay chiefly in
organization in the fields of politics, law, commerce, and military procedure.
But they faced and solved problems that had never confronted the Greeks.

Without the Roman contribution, Western history would lack many of its highest achievements. Their greatest contribution to art was in the field of utilitarian buildings and in the realm of architectural engineering. In these areas they were far ahead of their times and profoundly influenced later peoples down to the present.

ARCHITECTURE

Tuscan and Composite orders added to the Greek Doric, Ionic, and Corinthian orders (Fig. 241)

Temples:
  Maison Carrée at Nîmes, 1st or 2nd century A.D.
  Temple of the Sibyl, Tivoli (27 B.C.–A.D. 14)
  Temple of Fortuna Virilis
  The Pantheon (A.D. 120–124), Portico added in A.D. 202 (Figs. 176, 203, and 204)

Baths:
  Baths of Caracalla
  Baths of Diocletian

Basilicas:
  Basilica of Julia (51 B.C.)
  Basilica of Maxentius or Constantine (A.D. 306–312)

Amphitheatres:
  Circus Maximus, 1st century A.D.
  The Colosseum (A.D. 70–82) (Fig. 207)
  Amphitheatres at Nîmes, Verona, and Arles

Arches:
  Arch of Titus (A.D. 81)
  Arch of Septimius Severus (A.D. 204)
  Arch of Constantine (A.D. 312)

Tombs:
  Tomb of Hadrian (A.D. 135)

Aqueducts:
  Claudian Aqueduct, Rome
  Aqueduct, Segovia, 1st and 2nd centuries A.D.
  Pont du Gard, Nîmes (27 B.C.–A.D. 14) (Fig. 206)

SCULPTURE

Historical reliefs:
  The Ara Pacis Augustae (13 B.C.)
  Arch of Titus (A.D. 81)
  Column of Trajan (A.D. 113)

Portraits:
  Augustus from Prima Porta
  Julius Caesar
  Vespasian
  Cicero
  Marcus Aurelius
  Unknown subjects (Fig. 307)

PAINTING

Wall paintings from Pompeii and Rome
  Incrustation style (200–80 B.C.)

Architectural style (80–1 B.C.)
Ornate style (A.D. 1–50)
Intricate style (A.D. 50–79)
Examples:
Battle of Issus, mosaic from Pompeii (*ca.* 100 B.C.)
Hercules Discovering His Son Telephos, from Pompeii
Cupid Riding a Crab, from the House of Vettii, Pompeii
Portrait of Paquius Proculus and His Wife
Aldobrandini Marriage
Hercules with the Serpents, House of Vettii
Three Graces, from Pompeii

THE MEDIEVAL EPOCH

(*ca.* A.D. 350 to *ca.* A.D. 1400)

The medieval epoch is often misunderstood as being synonymous with the "Dark Ages," a term which can be applied only to the first centuries of the epoch between A.D. 350 and 1400. The Dark Ages are not to be interpreted as centuries of general unenlightenment throughout Europe. They were centuries in which parts of Europe lay dormant in varying degrees before the rise of the West. For example, in the sixth century, while Byzantine culture in the Eastern Mediterranean was enjoying its golden age, Northern Europe lay culturally inert. By the eighth or ninth century Western culture was beginning to spread and a period, which is called the "Middle Ages" (as opposed to the Dark Ages), was beginning. A fair appraisal of the medieval epoch as a whole, therefore, can be made by the following considerations.

Early Christian art, mainly 5th and 6th centuries A.D.
Byzantine art, mainly 6th, 11th and 12th, and 14th and 15th centuries A.D.
Romanesque art, mainly 11th and 12th centuries A.D.
Gothic art, mainly 13th, 14th, and 15th centuries A.D.

The first two of these cultures had their centers in Rome and Constantinople, respectively, and represented the Roman Catholic and Greek Orthodox subdivisions of the early church. They were primarily Mediterranean phenomena. The second two cultures had their efflorescence north of the Alps and manifested the emergence of France as a cultural leader, but both styles became international. In all of these styles architecture was the dominant art.

EARLY CHRISTIAN ART

(Mainly 5th and 6th centuries A.D.)

The outburst of Early Christian art in the vicinity of Rome followed hard on the recognition of Christianity as the official religion of the state. Since the principal need of the Christian congregations was for edifices in which to meet and worship, building absorbed most of their energy. The majority of the churches were erected in an outburst of activity from the fourth to the sixth centuries A.D.

ARCHITECTURE

Churches at Rome:
San Paolo Fuori-le-Mura (Outside-the-Walls) (386)

San Clemente, 4th century
Santa Maria Maggiore (440)
San Pietro, 5th century
San Lorenzo (579)
Central type tombs and baptistries:
Rome:
Santa Costanza (337)
Santo Stefano Rotondo (468–482)
Ravenna:
Orthodox Baptistry (449)
Tomb of Galla Placidia (ca. 450)
Tomb of Theodoric (526)

SCULPTURE

The Early Christians as a group came largely from the least privileged classes of Roman society. Lacking education, cultural background, and technical skill, they produced no great masterpieces of sculpture or painting; sincerity was not enough to overcome lack of training. On the other hand, with the architectural example and challenge of Rome all around them, and from which they borrowed freely, they soon erected churches which are still impressive. Saint Paul's Outside-the-Walls remains an imposing edifice by any standards.

The Good Shepherd of the Lateran, 3rd century
Sarcophagus of Junius Bassus (350)

PAINTING AND MOSAIC

The pictorial efforts of the Early Christians were first directed toward the painting of the catacombs. After the recognition of Christianity they were centered in manuscript illuminations and mosaics and gave those media an unprecedented prominence.

Catacombs of Saints Peter and Marcellinus, Saint Domitilla, and Saint Priscilla
The Vienna Genesis, 5th century
Santa Costanza (337)
Santa Pudenziana, 4th century
Santa Maria Maggiore (440)
Tomb of Galla Placidia, Ravenna (ca. 450)

BYZANTINE ART
(Mainly 5th, 11th and 12th, and 14th and 15th centuries A.D.)

Medieval Byzantine art was far from barbaric. Ultrarefined, it was essentially a continuation of Greek logic to its final stage; both the joint architects of Santa Sophia were Greek. Lacking the supple grace of classical Greek art, Byzantine art is mainly imposing in its hieratic orderliness. Centered in Constantinople, the style was carried throughout the Western Mediterranean and into the Balkans and Russia by the energetic Byzantine merchants. Its influence was widespread and persistent. The principal periods were:

First Golden Age: 6th century, the reign of Justinian
Second Golden Age: 11th and 12th centuries
Byzantine Renaissance: 14th and 15th centuries

ARCHITECTURE

Byzantine architecture was primarily ecclesiastical. Today its many churches seem alien to our eyes, but one of them, Santa Sophia, is recognized as a triumph of architecture, a Himalayan peak among buildings. The dome on pendentives system which it exemplifies is both ingenious and beautifully designed.

First Golden Age: 6th century
    Santa Sophia, Istanbul (532–537) Anthemius of Tralles and Isidorus of
        Miletus (Figs. 208 and 429)
    San Vitale, Ravenna (526–547)
    Sant' Apollinare Nuovo, Ravenna (549)
Second Golden Age: 11th and 12th centuries
    Church, Daphni, 11th century
    S. Panteleëmon, Salonica, 12th century
    St. Luke's, Phocis, 12th century
    Church of the Metropolis, Athens, 12th century
    St. Mark's, Venice (1042–1071) (Figs. 430 and 431)
Byzantine Renaissance: Age of the Palaeologi, 14th and 15th centuries
    Ravanitsa, Serbia, XIV century
    Manassia, Serbia (1407)

MOSAICS AND PAINTINGS

The Byzantine mind was especially suited to excel in the creation of pictures in mosaic and sculpture in ivory, but the results in both fields have long appeared cold, rigid, and autocratic to most Americans, who have rarely seen the originals. The recent publication by the Skira Company of Byzantine pictorial masterpieces in full color has demonstrated again the power of color and shown the Byzantine mosaics and illuminated manuscripts to be among the most exciting works of art ever created.

    San Vitale, Ravenna (*ca.* 547) (Figs. 121, 188)
    Sant' Apollinare Nuovo, Ravenna (*ca.* 560) (Fig. 352)
    Sant' Agnese, Rome, 7th century
    The Joshua Roll, Vatican, 5th-6th century
    The Paris Psalter, 10th century
    Church, Daphni, 11th century (Fig. 87)
    Royal Chapel, Palermo, 12th century
    Cathedral, Monreale, 12th century
    St. Mark's, Venice, 12th and 13th centuries
    Kilisse-djami, Istanbul, 14th century

SCULPTURE

    Archangel Michael, British Museum, 5th-6th century
    Doors of S. Sabina, Rome, 5th century
    Sarcophagus of Archbishop Theodore of Ravenna, 5th century
    Diptych of Consul Anastasius (517)
    Throne of Maximian, Bishop of Ravenna (*ca.* 550)
    Harbaville Triptych, 10th century (Fig. 354)

PRE-ROMANESQUE ART

Beginning with the time of Charlemagne, A.D. 768–814, Western Europe showed sporadic signs of emerging from the Dark Ages, as in the following examples.

ARCHITECTURE

Chapel of Charlemagne at Aachen (Aix-la-Chapelle), 796–804
Basse-Oeuvre, Beauvais, 10th century
St. Gall, 8th century
Lorsch, 8th century
St. Riquier (ca. 800)
Germigny-des-Près (806)
Earl's Barton, 11th century

PAINTING

The Book of Darrow, 7th century
The Book of Lindesfarne, 8th century
The Book of Kells, 9th century
The Bible of Charles the Bald, 9th century
Frescos at St. Savin (1080)
Archangel Michael, Winchester School, 11th century

SCULPTURE

Bewcastle Cross, ca. 7th century
Bronze doors, Hildesheim (993–1022)

ROMANESQUE ART
(Mainly 11th and 12th centuries A.D.)

The Romanesque period (not to be confused with the Roman) was one of intense activity in building, especially of churches for the flourishing monasteries of the time. Its peak, the eleventh and twelfth centuries, was marked by extensive travel along the pilgrimage routes between the great monasteries and shrines, and by an interchange of ideas which was accelerated and internationalized by the Crusades. Artistically it was a time of flux, of a vigorous blending of classical remnants and barbarian motifs from which emerged the new and distinctive Romanesque style. More than a mere prelude to Gothic art, it was powerful in its own right. Although international, Romanesque art was sharply divided into provincial schools, with classical elements and balance predominating, as we should expect, in Central Italy, and barbarian vigor more prominent in Northern Europe.

ARCHITECTURE

Lombard Romanesque:
    Sant' Ambrogio, Milan, 11th and 12th centuries
    San Michele, Pavia, 12th century
    San Zeno, Verona, 12th century
Tuscan Romanesque:
    Cathedral, Pisa (1063–92)
    Campanile (Leaning Tower), Pisa (begun 1174)

San Miniato, Florence (begun 1013)
Baptistry, Florence. Remodelled 12th century
San Michele, Lucca, 12th century.
Sicilian Romanesque:
  Cathedral, Cefalù, 12th century
  Cappella Palatina, Palermo (1140)
  Cathedral, Monreale (1174–89)
Spanish Romanesque:
  Santiago, Compostela, 11th and 12th centuries
  San Isidoro, León (1063)
  San Vicente, Avila (1089)
  San Pedro, Avila (*ca.* 1250)
German Romanesque:
  St. Michael, Hildesheim, 11th and 12th centuries
  Cathedral, Speier, 11th and 12th centuries
  Cathedral, Worms, 11th and 12th centuries
  Cathedral, Mainz, 12th century
French Romanesque:
  Aquitaine:
    St. Front, Périgueux, 12th century
    Cathedral, Angoulême, 12th century
  Central and Southern France:
    Benedictine Abbey, Cluny III (Burgundy) (1088–1130; destroyed *ca.* 1790)
    St. Sernin, Toulouse (Languedoc) (*ca.* 1080)
    St. Gilles, near Arles (Provence), 11th century
    Benedictine Abbey Church, La Madeleine Vézelay (Burgundy) (*ca.* 1120–40)
    St. Trophîme, Arles (Provence), 12th century (Fig. 242)
  Normandy and England:
    Holy Trinity (Abbey-aux-dames), Caen (begun 1062), vaults 12th century (Fig. 180)
    St. Étienne (Abbaye-aux-hommes), Caen (begun 1064), vaults 12th century
    Mont Saint Michel, 11th and 12th centuries
    St. John's Chapel, Tower of London (1080) (Fig. 338)
    Cathedral, Ely, late 11th and 12th centuries (Fig. 248*a*)
    Cathedral, Durham, late 11th and 12th centuries
    Church, Iffley, late 12th century

PAINTING

Liber Vitae, British Museum, 11th century
Bayeaux Tapestry, Bayeux Library, 12th century
Limoges manuscript, Life of Christ, Morgan Library, New York, 12th century
Virgin Enthroned, Morgan Library, 12th century (Fig. 49)
Huntingfield Psalter, Morgan Library, 12th century
Catalonian fresco from Santa Maria de Mura, 12th century, Museum of Fine Arts, Boston

SCULPTURE

French Romanesque architectural sculptures:
  St. Trophîme, Arles, 12th century (Fig. 242)

La Madeleine, Vézelay (*ca.* 1120–32)
St. Pierre, Moissae (*ca.* 1110)
St. Lazare, Autun, 12th century
Moutier St. Jean, 12th century
Abbey Church, Souillac (*ca.* 1110)

GOTHIC ART

(Mainly 13th through 15th centuries)

The term "Gothic" originated among the classical Renaissance Italians as a description of the—to them—wild and barbaric art of the late medieval Northern Europeans, but it has long since lost that connotation.

The Gothic artists continued the medieval stress upon building for religious purposes and brought that practice to a magnificent climax in the cathedrals of the French towns which supplanted the Romanesque monasteries as vital cultural centers. At the same time they developed sculpture, painting, and the minor arts to a high level. Used chiefly for religious purposes, these media were employed in close association with architecture. The powerful guilds of the time encouraged and even demanded excellent craftsmanship.

Though a part of the medieval epoch, the Gothic period was far from the concept of a dark age. Many students of civilization maintain that it produced one of the most balanced, creative, and inspired societies that man has attained, and that its art is one of the glories of Western civilization. This balance was ruined in France, the most inspired leader of the period, by the Hundred Years War (1339–1453), much as Athens had been undermined by the Peloponnesian War.

Benefitting much from the experiments and achievements of the Romanesque, especially in architectural engineering, the Gothic masters reached a superb peak in the building arts and in their brilliant stained glass windows early in their cycle; the golden age of the latter arrived after the briefest of preparations.

ECCLESIASTICAL ARCHITECTURE

France

The leader among nations in the development of Gothic architecture was France, whose achievements fall in three principal periods:

Early Gothic, late 12th century
High Gothic, the Golden Age of the 13th century; Second
    Half of Golden Age, 14th century
Late Gothic, 15th and 16th centuries; the "flamboyant" style

Morienval, 12th century
St. Denis (begun 1137)
Senlis (1155–91)
Laon, 12th and 13th centuries
Paris (begun 1163), façade begun 1210
Chartres (rebuilding begun 1194), mainly 13th century (Figs. 384, 385)
Amiens (begun 1220) (Fig. 209)
Reims (begun 1212) (Fig. 179)
Beauvais (begun 1225); choir finished 1272; vaults fell in 1284 and rebuilding
    begun; transept finished in 1548 (Fig. 210)

Ste. Chapelle, Paris (1245–48) (Fig. 339)
Bourges, 13th and 14th centuries
Rouen (begun 1280), mainly 14th century (Figs. 182, 260, 433)
St. Wulfram, Abbeville (begun 1480)
St. Maclou, Rouen, 15th century

England

English Gothic architecture, which ranks second only to the French in quantity and quality, is usually divided into the following periods:

Early English, late 12th and 13th centuries
Perpendicular, 14th century
Decorated, 15th and 16th centuries

Canterbury Cathedral, Gothic portions begun 1174
Lincoln Cathedral (begun 1192); Angel Chair (1255–80)
Wells Cathedral (1206–42)
Salisbury Cathedral (begun 1220)
Westminster Abbey (1245–80)
Peterborough Cathedral, 13th century (Fig. 222)
Lichfield Cathedral, 13th and 14th centuries
Exeter Cathedral, 14th century
Gloucester Cathedral (1327); cloisters (1351–1412)
Henry VII's Chapel, Westminster (1500–1512) (Fig. 432)

Germany

Freiburg (1260)
Cologne Cathedral (1270), finished 19th century

Italy

St. Francis, Assisi (begun 1228) (Fig. 399)
Siena Cathedral (begun 1285)
Orvieto Cathedral, 13th and 14th centuries
Florence Cathedral (1296 and 1387); Campanile, 1334
Santa Croce, Florence (1284)
Santa Maria Novella, Florence (1278–1350) (Fig. 400)
Milan Cathedral (begun 1386)

Spain

Burgos Cathedral (1221)
Toledo Cathedral (ca. 1227)
Leon Cathedral (ca. 1280)
Seville Cathedral (begun 1401); Giralda Tower, finished 1568

CIVIL AND DOMESTIC ARCHITECTURE

Owing to the emphasis upon religion during the Middle Ages, the chief contribution to architecture was in ecclesiastical buildings, but some outstanding examples of civil and domestic architecture were also produced. For the feudal system, mercantile houses, guilds, and township governments played important parts in the life of the times.

Northern Europe

Castle, Carcassonne, 12th and 13th centuries
Castle, Coucy, 13th century
Castle, Pierrefonds (ca. 1390)
Cloth Hall, Ypres 13th century
Hôtel Jacques Coeur, Bourges, 14th century
Hôtel de Cluny, Paris (1490)
Town of Rothenburg, Germany, 14th century (Fig. 386)

Italy

Palazzo Vecchio, Florence (1298–1314)
Palazzo Pubblico, Siena (1289–1309)
Palazzo Ducale, Venice, 14th and 15th centuries
Palazzo Ca d'Oro, Venice (1289–1305)

France

ARCHITECTURAL DECORATIONS

Chartres, 12th and 13th centuries (Fig. 418)
Amiens, 13th century
Paris, 13th century (Fig. 419)
Reims, 13th century (Fig. 435)
Well of Moses, by Claus Slutter (d. 1406), Champmol at Dijon, Burgundian
    School

FREE-STANDING FIGURES

Notre Dame de Paris, 14th century
Madonna and Child, Walters Gallery, 14th century (Fig. 420)
Virgin, Cleveland, late 15th century (Fig. 421)
Tomb of Phillipe Pot, Louvre, late 15th century (Fig. 398)

Italy

Nicola Pisano, 1206 (?) –1278
Giovanni Pisano, 1250 (?) –1328
Andrea Pisano, 1273 (?) –1348
Giotto, 1276 (?) –1336
Andrea Orcagna, 1329 (?) –1368 (?)

PAINTING

Northern Europe

St. Louis Psalter, Morgan Library, 13th century
Breviary by Jean Purcelle, Bibliothèque Nationale, 14th century
Stained glass windows of the 13th century, especially at Chartres and Le Mans
    (Fig. 190)
French and Flemish Tapestries of the 14th, 15th, and 16th centuries (Fig. 189)

Italy

ROME

Cavallini, late 13th century

THE MODERN EPOCH

(ca. 1400 to the present)

    The modern epoch began with the appearance of numerous attitudes which departed from the medieval concepts of life, and created a new outlook among the peoples of Western Europe. As a consequence, we today feel more at home with the products of the modern epoch than with those of the Middle Ages, regardless of how much we may admire the latter.

    The modern epoch has been divided into a succession of periods, each of which has a distinctive character of its own, in order to indicate the evolutionary changes that have taken place between the decline of the Middle Ages and our own time. Moreover, the term *modern period* has been used in several senses, and these must be defined if confusion is to be avoided. Fortunately, scholars have generally agreed on the following subdivision of the modern epoch at large; the more special meanings of the terms *modern period* and *modern art* will be noted later.

Principal Periods

Renaissance period; mainly the 15th and 16th centuries
Post-Renaissance period; mainly the 17th and 18th centuries
Modern period; mainly the 19th and 20th centuries

THE RENAISSANCE PERIOD

(ca. 1400–*ca.* 1550)

The Renaissance, or "re-birth," began the modern epoch. Clearly discernible as a movement by 1400, it lasted at full strength until about 1550. The term *Renaissance* is a biased one which favors the Italian cultural resurgence of the time over its northern medieval rivals and implies that the Middle Ages were dark ages requiring a re-birth of civilization. The only true fact is that the Renaissance was a new and different period. It brought a new attitude toward individual effort into European life, and with it a complexity which still persists. The concept of the man of versatile genius and the name-artist centered artistic creativity in the individual and began the period of the old masters.

The Renaissance had a dual character. It looked backward for its revival of antiquity, especially of Roman civilization, and, at the same time, it looked forward to reality which inaugurated the ideals of close observation of nature espoused by modern science. Consequently, the period presents antiquarians (called humanists), realists, traditionalists, experimentalists, and other specialists working side by side. Free versatility and specialization were, in fact, prominent signs that a new era was being speedily encouraged into existence.

Italy was the leader and fountainhead of this movement which saw cultural primacy return to the Mediterranean, as in ancient times, while imitation forced upon the northern countries of Europe a reversal of the situation in medieval times. Within the Italian peninsula there was not a national government, but a group of competing city-states, a subdivision which eventually made them prey to the slowly uniting northern kingdoms and terminated the Renaissance, much as the Greek cities fell before Roman organization. The chief cities were Florence, Siena, Padua, Milan, Rome, and Venice. Florence, the most progressive, dominated the art of the fifteenth century, and was called the Athens of the Renaissance. Rome and Venice dominated the sixteenth century, with Rome the center of the High Renaissance and Venice leading painting into new fields that even anticipated Impressionism.

The Renaissance is conveniently divided into two main periods; the Early Renaissance and the High Renaissance. They coincide mainly with the fifteenth and the sixteenth centuries respectively.

The Early Renaissance in Italy

The Fifteenth Century

ARCHITECTURE

Brunelleschi, 1379–1446
  Cathedral Dome, Florence (1418–46)
  San Lorenzo, Florence (1425)
  Pazzi Chapel, Florence (1429) (Figs. 273 and 434)

Michelozzo, 1396–1472
  Palazzo Mediceo-Riccardi (1444)
Alberti, 1404–72
  Palazzo Ruccellai, Florence (1451–54)
  San Francesco, Rimini (1447)
  Sant' Andrea, Mantua (1472)
Giuliano da Sangallo, 1445–1516, and Il Cronaca, 1457–1508
  Palazzo Strozzi, Florence (Figs. 175 and 181)

SCULPTURE

Jacopo della Quercia, 1374–1438 (Figs. 214 and 331)
Lorenzo Ghiberti, 1378–1455
Luca della Robbia, 1399–1482
Donatello, 1386–1466
Francesco Laurana, *ca.* 1425–*ca.* 1502 (Fig. 158)
Antonio Pollaiuolo, 1429–96 (Fig. 64)
Andrea Verrocchio, 1435–88 (Fig. 380)
Andrea della Robbia, 1435–1525 (Fig. 295)

PAINTING

Fra Angelico, 1387–1455 (Figs. 46 and 191)
Paolo Uccello, 1397–1475
Masaccio, 1401–28 (Fig. 306)
Andrea Castagno, 1401–57
Fra Filippo Lippi, *ca.* 1406–69
Piero della Francesca, 1416–92
Andrea Mantegna, 1431–1506 (Figs. 105, 106, and 108)
Andrea Verrocchio, 1435–88
Cosimo Rosselli, 1439–1507 (Fig. 324)
Luca Signorelli, 1441–1523
Botticelli, 1444–1510 (Figs. 263 and 355)
Perugino, 1445–1523 (Fig. 102)
Ghirlandaio, 1449–1594 (Fig. 344)
Filippino Lippi, *ca.* 1457–1504 (Fig. 125)

The High Renaissance in Italy

The Sixteenth Century

ARCHITECTURE

Bramante, 1444–1514
  Il Tempietto, Rome (1501–2)
  Santa Maria della Consolazione, Todi, with Cola da Caprarola (1508)
    (Fig. 175)

SCULPTURE, PAINTING, AND DRAWING

Leonardo da Vinci, 1452–1519 (Figs. 57, 259a, 323, and 396)
Michelangelo, 1475–1564 (Figs. 58, 66, 126, 147, 268, 271, and 358)
Raphael, 1483–1520 (Figs. 59, 104, 253, and 394)
Correggio, 1494–1534 (Figs. 58, 66, 126, 147, 268, 271, and 358)

Venetian Renaissance Painting

THE FIFTEENTH CENTURY

Jacopo Bellini, fl. 1430–70
Gentile Bellini, 1429–1507
Carlo Crivelli, *ca.* 1435–*ca.* 1495
Antonello da Messina, *ca.* 1444–79
Giovanni Bellini, 1430 (?) –1516

THE SIXTEENTH CENTURY

Giorgione, 1478–1510 (Figs. 79 and 392)
Titian, 1477–1576 (Figs. 61, 89, 129, 130, 131, 132, and 195)
Tintoretto, 1518–92 (Figs. 47, 128, 194, 254, 256, 257, 264, and 369)
Veronese, 1528–88 (Figs. 228, 320, and 326)

German Renaissance Painting and Drawing

Germany, which has been prolific in musicians and graphic artists, has produced relatively few outstanding painters, and these have appeared in two historical clusters; the first in the sixteenth century and the second in the twentieth century, with a barren period in between. The former was the time of her old masters, a period which was cut short by the wars of the Reformation.

THE SIXTEENTH CENTURY

Albrecht Dürer, 1471–1528 (Figs. 148, 198, 199, and 395)
Matthias Grünewald, *ca.* 1470–*ca.* 1531
Lucas Cranach, the Elder, 1472–1553
Hans Holbein, the Younger, 1497–1543 (Figs. 246 and 293)
Augustin Hirschvogel, 1503–53 (Fig. 118)

The Renaissance in France

France, during the Renaissance, finally turned her back on the declining medieval style which had given her artistic supremacy in Europe, and attempted to adopt a more modern outlook by following the lead of Italy. She produced much stylish and elegant work, but little that was outstanding. During this period in history her medieval greatness lay behind her and her modern greatness lay in the future. Following are the exceptions:

The Sixteenth Century

ARCHITECTURE

The Châteaux of the Loire Valley:
Blois (1503–15)
Chambord (1526–44)
Azay le Rideau (1521)
Chenonceaux (*ca.* 1520)
Fontainebleau, reign of Francis I (1515–47)
Ussé, 16th century (Fig. 23)
Lescot (*ca.* 1510–78), Court of the Louvre, with Jean Goujon (1546–76)

Michel Colombe, 1432–1515
Jean Goujon, 1520–66 (?) (Fig. 402)

PAINTING IN THE 15TH AND 16TH CENTURIES

Jean Fouquet, 1415–81
Jean Clouet, fl. 1518–ca. 1540
François Clouet, fl. 1541–ca. 1572

THE BAROQUE PERIOD
(Mainly 17th century)

The term *baroque* was first used by the theorists of the nineteenth-century Neoclassic school as a term of opprobrium, much as the Italian Renaissance artists had applied the term Gothic (wild or barbaric) to northern medieval art which they neither understood nor liked. Literally, the word "baroque" may come from the Portuguese *barroco,* an irregular pearl, and was used because of the admittedly theatrical aspects of some phases of seventeenth-century art, like the rock gardens of the day. But the Baroque century, as we now see it, was one of the greatest in all art, and produced a high percentage of the old masters, especially in the field of oil painting where its greatest strength lay.

Experiments with elements which were to characterize the baroque style started in Italy in the sixteenth century, but they reached their widest and fullest development after 1600; so the style is mainly associated with the art of the seventeenth century. Italy played a vital role in forming the new style, but was soon matched by the countries to her west and north. The artists of Spain, Flanders, Holland, and France rose to new heights, with France gaining a position of leadership which she has held almost to the present day. One of the important consequences of northern prominence in the movement was the elevation of true landscape to a significant place in the subject matter of art. A discernible reason for this is that the baroque artists had a genius for the unification of complex designs in deep space, whether in painting, sculpture, or architecture. In the latter art they related ensembles of buildings with their surroundings with a mastery that has hardly ever been surpassed.

The baroque style was contradictory and complex. Like the Renaissance, it was compounded of opposite tendencies—the theatrical, melodramatic, introspective, and overwrought, and the objective and realistic, with mystics and scientists both contributing to the movement. A central urge of the time was to reconcile and balance the finite and infinite, the subjective and objective, and the material and spiritual areas of reality. The resulting art could not help being, when viewed broadly, full of dynamic tensions and frequently powerful. The great productivity of this forceful, virile period was probably increased rather than harmed by the conflicts of the Counter Reformation which reached a peak of intensity at the time.

The Baroque Style in Italy

ARCHITECTURE

The 16th century
Michelangelo, 1475–1564
Palazzo Farnese, Rome (1530–80), with Giuliano da Sangallo, the Younger

Laurentian Library, Florence (1524–71)
Buildings on the Capitoline Hill, Rome (1546 and later)
Palladio, 1512–80
Basilica, Vicenza, (1549)
San Giorgio Maggiore, Venice (1565)
Villa Rotonda, Vicenza (1570–89)
Pietro Ligorio, d. 1580
Villa d'Este, Tivoli (1549)
Giacomo della Porta, 1541–1605
Façade, Church of the Gesù, Rome (1568–75)
The 17th century
St. Peter's, Rome:
Bramante, Raphael, Peruzzi, early designs, 1506–14
Michelangelo, later plan and dome, 1546–64
Carlo Maderna, nave and façade, 1606–26
Bernini, baldacchino and colonnades, 1624–56 (Figs. 85a, 85b, and 85c)
Borromini, 1549–1667
San Carlo alle Quattro Fontane, Rome (1638–65)
Longhena, 1604–82
Santa Maria della Salute, Venice (1631–82)

SCULPTURE

Lorenzo Bernini, 1598–1680 (Figs. 167, 270, 272, and 332)

PAINTING

Domenichino, 1581–1641
Caravaggio, 1573–1610 (Figs. 134 and 327)
Salvator Rosa, 1615–73
Andrea Pozzo, 1642–1709 (Fig. 110)

The Baroque Style in Spain

The Seventeenth Century

ARCHITECTURE

Dr. José Churriguera, 1650–1773
Town Hall, Salamanca
Catafalque for Queen Maria Luisa (1689)
Church of El Salvador, Seville

PAINTING

Morales, 1509–1586
Ribera, 1588–1652 (Fig. 245)
Zubarán, 1548–1663
El Greco, 1548 (?) –1625 (Figs. 52, 90 and 367)
Velasquez, 1599–1660 (Figs. 94 and 99)
Murillo, 1617–82

The Baroque Style in Germany

ARCHITECTURE

Balthasar Neumann, 1687–1753
    Wallfahrtkirche, Vierzehnheiligen (*ca.* 1750) (Fig. 184)
Matthaus Pöppelmann, 1662–1736
    The Zwinger, Dresden (1711–22)
Georg von Knobelsdorff, 1699–1753
    Sansouci, Potsdam (1745)

Flemish Baroque Painting

The Seventeenth Century

Rubens, 1577–1640 (Figs. 83, 216, 233, 318, 335, 351, and 393)
Van Dyck, 1599–1641
Jordaens, 1593–1678
Brouwer, 1605–41

Dutch Painting and Drawing

The Seventeenth Century

Hals, 1584 (?) –1666 (Figs. 196, 299, and 345)
Rembrandt, 1606–69 (Figs. 135, 151, 200, 304, 325, 363, 365, and 370)
Terborch, 1617–81
Cuyp, 1620–91
Potter, 1625–54
Steen, 1626–79
De Hooch, 1632–81 (Fig. 98)
Vermeer, 1632–75 (Figs. 93 and 100)
Jacob Ruysdael, 1630 (?) –81 (Fig. 116)
Hobbema, 1638–1709

France in the Seventeenth Century

The first half of the century

PAINTING AND DRAWING
  Simon Vouet, 1590–1649
  Jacques Callot, 1592–1635
  Louis Le Nain, 1593 (?) –1668
  Georges de la Tour, 1593–1652
  Nicolas Poussin, 1593–1665
  Claude Lorrain, 1600–82 (Fig. 117)
  Philippe de Champaigne, 1602–74
  Eustache Le Sueur, 1616–55

The Reign of Louis XIV, 1661–1715

ARCHITECTURE

Perrault, 1613–1688; East Colonnade of the Louvre (1668) (Fig. 239)
Versailles
  Le Vau, first enlargement, 1668

J. H. Mansart, further remodeling, 1678
Charles Le Brun, interior designs and general supervision
Charles Le Nôtre, the gardens, 1661 and later

SCULPTURE

Puget, 1622–94
Coysevox, 1640–1720

PAINTING AND DRAWING

Nanteuil, 1623–78 (Fig. 149)
Rigaud, 1659–1743

THE ROCOCO PERIOD

(Mainly 18th century)

The rococo style is the name associated with European art of the eighteenth century. To the Neoclassicists the term connoted something of the same lack of restraint as the baroque. But a close inspection of rococo art will show that it differed in distinctive aspects of form and content from its kindred style and predecessor. Both are marked by a love of curvilinear lines and activity. But where the baroque is heavy, the rococo is delicate; where the baroque is masculine, the rococo is feminine; and where the baroque is passionate and serious, the rococo is frivolous and lighthearted.

France, with Paris at its center, dominated the period as definitely as Florence had ruled the Early Renaissance, but England came to the fore with a noted school of portrait painters and one artist, Hogarth, of universal breadth. America likewise entered the picture for the first time with a school of portraiture. While something less than exalted, all of these schools were permeated by an unusual sense of taste and good manners that was perhaps the distinguishing feature of the century.

France in the Eighteenth Century

ARCHITECTURE

Louis XV and the rococo style
  Apartments at Versailles
Gabriel, 1698–1782
  Petit Trianon (1763)
Héré de Corny, 1705–63
  Work at Nancy (1752–55)
Soufflot, 1713–80
  Panthéon, Paris (1764)

SCULPTURE

Pigalle, 1714–85
Falconet, 1716–91
Clodion, 1738–1814
Houdon, 1741–1828 (Fig. 285)

PAINTING

Watteau, 1684–1721 (Fig. 319)
Nattier, 1685–1766
Boucher, 1703–70

Fragonard, 1732–1806 (Fig. 290)
Greuze, 1725–1805 (Fig. 329)
Chardin, 1699–1779 (Fig. 287)
La Tour, 1704–88 (Fig. 298)

England in the Seventeenth and Eighteenth Centuries

ARCHITECTURE

The 17th century
  Inigo Jones, 1572–1652
    Queen's House, Greenwich (1617)
    Banqueting Hall, Whitehall (1619)
  Sir Christopher Wren, 1632–1723
    St. Paul's, London (1675–1710)
    Later buildings at Hampton Court (1689–1703)
    Plan of the City of London (1666)
The 18th century
  Sir John Vanbrugh, 1666–1726
    Blenheim Palace (1705–24)
  James Gibbs, 1682–1754
    St. Martin's-in-the-Fields, London (1721–26)
  John Wood, 1704–54
    Work at Bath (1724–54)
  James Paine, 1725–89
    Remodeling of Kedleston (1761)
  Robert Adam, 1728–92
    The Adelphi (1772)

PAINTING AND DRAWING

The 18th century
  Hogarth, 1697–1764 (Figs. 72 and 301)
  Reynolds, 1723–92
  Gainsborough, 1727–88
  Romney, 1734–1802
  Raeburn, 1756-1823
  Lawrence, 1769–1830

American Colonial Art
(Mainly 17th and 18th centuries)

Those citizens of the United States who live in or near New England are
likely to think that the art of our country derived exclusively from the English
tradition, forgetting that the settlers of Canada came from France, the settlers
of New York and Pennsylvania largely from Holland and Germany, and the
settlers of Latin America from Portugal and Spain. All brought their own
artistic traditions. In addition the Spaniards were also influenced by the art
of the southwest Indians. Any true picture of early American art will take this
rich provincialism into account.

ARCHITECTURE

Cathedral and Sagraria, Mexico City (1573–1739)
Cathedral, Taxco (1751–58)

Alamo, San Antonio, Texas (1774)
Governor's Palace, Santa Fé, New Mexico (1605 and later) (Fig. 389)
Mission, Santa Barbara, California (1787–1800) (Fig. 391)
Fairbanks House, Dedham, Massachusetts (ca. 1636) (Fig. 388)
Capen House, Topsfield, Massachusetts (1683)
Turner House, "House of Seven Gables," Salem, Massachusetts (ca. 1690)
(Fig. 387)
Royall House, Medford, Massachusetts (1733–37)
"Westover," the Byrd Mansion, Charles City County, Virginia (1726)
Old State House, "Independence Hall," Philadelphia (1732–52)
"Cliveden," Germantown, Pennsylvania (1763)
"Mount Vernon," Virginia (1758–72)
The Cabildo, New Orleans (1795)

PAINTING

Smibert, ca. 1684–1751
Feke, fl. ca. 1748–50
West, 1738–1820
Copley, 1737–1815
Stuart, 1755–1828
Trumbull, 1756–1843

Spanish Painting and Drawing

After a century of quiescence, Spanish painting was brought to a brilliant climax by Goya (Francisco Goya y Lucientes, 1746–1828). His immense, varied art was a school in itself. More than any other single artist he was the pivotal figure in the transition from the rococo to the nineteenth century and the modern period. (See Figs. 4, 136, 197, 280, 281, and 359.)

THE MODERN PERIOD
(19th and 20th centuries)

The term *modern* is applied to at least three different spans of time in the history of art, but confusion need not arise if these are defined. The name modern is applied to the epoch which began with the Renaissance and produced the most recent major subdivision of history, i.e., the ancient, medieval, and modern epochs. Modern is also used for the period embraced by the nineteenth and twentieth centuries, giving us, within the modern epoch, the Renaissance, post-Renaissance, and modern periods. Finally, modern is commonly employed in the term *modern art,* which has come to refer by general agreement to the movement that has flourished from about 1890 to the present day. It is to the modern period of the nineteenth and twentieth centuries that we are referring at this point.

However, the subdivisions do not stop here. The complexity of the Modern Period has caused historians to divide it into a series of styles, the most accepted pattern in architecture being the following:

Neoclassicism, ca. 1775 to 1850
Romanticism, ca. 1790 to 1860
Eclecticism, ca. 1850 to the present
Modern, ca. 1890 to date

In painting and sculpture there have been Neoclassic, Romantic, Impressionist, and Modern movements which paralleled the architectural styles and flourished at the same time. But the term *Impressionism* may be substituted for Eclecticism, and *Post-Impressionism*, for the early decades of modern painting and sculpture (from about 1890 to the First World War).

The modern period was ushered into history by a series of revolutions which virtually destroyed the old regime and its way of life. The political revolutions were often violent; no less far-reaching were the bloodless revolutions in social life, industry, science, and, eventually, education. Among the consequences were the substitution of a predominantly bourgeois patronage for the old aristocratic and ecclesiastical sponsorship of art, and the radical effects this shift had upon the place of art and the position of artists in society. As these changes occurred, art altered to reflect the new conditions, bringing a radical departure from the art of the eighteenth century. Paradoxically, the cautious bourgeois mind answered the new needs in architecture with a retreat into extreme conservatism. Whether the reigning style was Neoclassic, romantic, or eclectic, it was a century of revivalist buildings. The same attitude prevailed in painting and sculpture under another guise—the pursuit of realism with a strongly materialistic emphasis. The movement called "modern art" which began sometime between 1875 and 1890 was initially a reaction against these two guiding biases—revivalism and materialistic realism. Within the period of modern art, the First World War was the major disruptive factor. Spiritually the nineteenth century ended in 1914.

NEOCLASSICISM

(*ca.* 1775–*ca.* 1850)

Neoclassicism, the first stylistic movement of the modern period, was new only in the sense that it broke with the rococo; in every other respect it was reactionary, academic, and theory-ridden. The conservatism was deepest in architecture, aided by the plenitude of ancient models. In painting the style marked a lamentable hiatus in the continuity and development of post-Renaissance pictorial methods. Spiritually Neoclassicism expressed the security-hunger of a people surrounded by revolution, uncertainty, and rapid changes.

ARCHITECTURE

France:
  Vignon, 1762–1829
    Church of the Madeleine, Paris (1807)
  Chalgrin, 1739–1811
    Arc de Triomphe de l'Étoile, Paris (1806)
England:
  Sir John Soane, 1753–1837
    Bank of England, London (1788–1835)
  Smirke, 1800–47
    British Museum (1825–47)
Germany:
  Langhans, 1733–1808
    Brandenburg Gate, Berlin (1788–91)
  von Klenze, 1784–1864
    Walhalla, Regensburg (1830–42)

America:
  Thomas Jefferson, 1743–1826
    Capitol, Richmond (1785–98)
    Monticello, Charlottesville (1795–1808)
    Quadrangle, University of Virginia, Charlottesville (1817–26)
  Charles Bulfinch, 1763–1844
    State House, Boston (1790–98)
    University Hall, Harvard University (1815)
  L'Enfant, 1754–1825
    Plan for the City of Washington (1791)
  Hoban, 1762 (?) –1831
    Executive Mansion, "The White House," Washington (1795)
  United States Capitol Building, Washington, D. C.
    Dr. Thornton, 1792–1802
    Hallet, 1792–94
    Hadfield, 1792–1803
    Latrobe, 1803–17
    Bulfinch, 1818–30, completion of the original plan
    Walter, 1851–63, addition of wings and larger dome
  Robert Mills, 1781–1855
    Washington Monument, Washington (1836–77)
  Hadfield, *ca.* 1764–1826
    Lee Mansion, Arlington (1826) (Fig. 390)

SCULPTURE

  Italy:
    Antonio Canova, 1757–1822

PAINTING

  Jacques Louis David, 1748–1825 (Figs. 88 and 292)
  Ingres, 1780–1867 (Figs. 274a, 274b, and 312)
  The Academy:
    Delaroche, 1797–1850
    Couture, 1815–79
    Meissonier, 1815–91 (Fig. 28)
    Bonheur, 1822–99 (Fig. 30)
    Cabanel, 1823–84
    Gérôme, 1824–1904 (Fig. 34)
    Puvis de Chavannes, 1824–98 (Fig. 317)
    Bouguereau, 1825–1905 (Fig. 310)

Romanticism

(*ca.* 1790–*ca.* 1860)

Romanticism in architecture was as retrospective as Neoclassicism, merely borrowing its models from the Middle Ages instead of from antiquity. The achievements of its painters were much more notable; they continued the Venetian and post-Renaissance pictorial method which the Neoclassic artists had suppressed and paved the way for impressionism. On the personal side, the romantic masters placed a new stress on individual inspiration and vitality, in opposition to the collective discipline of the Neoclassicists, and exalted color and vibrant brushwork above smooth sculpturesque forms.

ARCHITECTURE

England:
   Sir Charles Barry, 1795–1860, and Augustus Pugin, 1813–52
      Houses of Parliament (1840–60) (Fig. 56)
France:
   François Gau, 1790–1854, and Théodore Ballu, 1817–85
      Ste. Clothilde, Paris (1846–59)
   Eugène Viollet-le-Duc, 1814–79
      Archaeological restorations:
         Notre Dame, Paris (1857)
         Castle of Pierrefonds (ca. 1860)
America:
   Richard Upjohn, 1802–78
      Trinity Church, New York (1839)
   James Renwick, 1818–95
      Smithsonian Institution, Washington, D. C. (1847)
      Grace Church, New York (1843–46)
      St. Patrick's Cathedral, New York (1850–79)

SCULPTURE

France:
   Rude, 1784–1855
   Barye, 1796–1875 (Figs. 31, 314, and 343)

PAINTING AND DRAWING

England:
   Blake, 1757–1827
   Turner, 1775–1851 (Figs. 11, 25, 48, 82, 146, and 258a)
   Constable, 1776–1837 (Figs. 348, 349, 373, and 376)
   The Brotherhood of the Pre-Raphaelites
   The Royal Academy
France:
   Baron Gros, 1771–1835
   Horace Vernet, 1789–1863 (Fig. 347)
   Géricault, 1791–1824 (Figs. 357 and 378)
   Corot, 1796–1875
   Delacroix, 1798–1863 (Figs. 153, 315, and 346)
   Théodore Rousseau, 1812–43 (Fig. 38)

The Second Half of the Nineteenth Century

ARCHITECTURE

France:
   Hittorff, 1793–1867
      Gare du Nord, Paris (1862–64)

Labrouste, 1799–1875
  Bibliothèque Ste. Geneviève, Paris (1850)
Garnier, 1825-98
  Opera House, Paris (1861–74)
Baron Haussmann, 1809–91
  Replanning of Paris (1853–70)
Abadie, 1812–84
  Sacré Coeur, Paris (1874–1919)
Germany:
  Wallot, 1841–1912
    Reichstag Building, Berlin (1882)
America:
  Mullett, 1834–90
    Old General Post Office, New York (1869)
  MacArthur, 1823–90
    City Hall, Philadelphia (1871–1901)
    Centennial International Exposition, Philadelphia (1876)
  Flagg, 1857–1947
    United States Naval Academy, Annapolis (1899)
  Chedanne and Murchison
    Clark Mansion, New York (1901–3)
  Richard Morris Hunt, 1827–95
    William K. Vanderbilt Mansion, New York (1883)
    "Biltmore," Asheville, North Carolina (1890–95)
  Henry Hobson Richardson, 1838–86
    Trinity Church, Boston (1872–77)
    Sever Hall, Harvard University (1880)
    Allegheny County Buildings, Pittsburgh (1884)
    Field Warehouse, Chicago (1885)
  McKim, Mead, and White
    Public Library, Boston (1888-98)
    World's Columbian Exposition, Chicago (1893), with Hunt, Atwood, Burnham, and others
    Library, Columbia University, New York (1893)
    Pennsylvania Station, New York (1910)
  Ralph Adams Cram, 1863–1942, and Bertram Grosvenor Goodhue, 1869–1924
    Post Headquarters, West Point, New York (1903)
    St. Thomas', New York (1906) (Goodhue)
    California Building, San Diego (1915) (Goodhue)
    State Capitol, Lincoln, Nebraska (1922–32) (Goodhue)
    Cathedral of St. John the Divine, New York (1911 and later) (Cram)
  Carrere and Hastings
    New York Public Library (1911)
  Warren and Wetmore
    Grand Central Station, New York (1903-13)
  Bacon, 1866–1924
    Lincoln Memorial, Washington, D. C. (1915–23)
  Rogers, 1867–1947
    Harkness Memorial Quadrangle, Yale University (1915–21)
  Coolidge, Shepley, Bulfinch, and Abbott
    New Houses, Harvard University (1930–33)

SCULPTURE

France:
   Carpeaux, 1827–75 (Fig. 300)
   Rodin, 1840–1917 (Figs. 6, 169, and 291)
Belgium:
   Meunier, 1831–1905 (Fig. 231)
Italy:
   Vincenzo Gemito, 1852–1905 (Fig. 168)
   Medardo Rosso, 1858–1928 (Fig. 170)
America:
   Augustus Saint-Gaudens, 1848–1907
   Daniel Chester French, 1850–1937 (Fig. 277)

PAINTING AND DRAWING

France:
   Precursors of "Realism:"
     Millet, 1814–75 (Fig. 225)
     Daumier, 1808–79 (Figs. 63, 70, 152, 161, 303, 312, and 316)
   "Realism:"
     Courbet, 1819–77 (Fig. 350)
   Impressionism:
     Manet, 1832–83 (Fig. 262)
     Monet, 1840–1926 (Fig. 137)
     Pissarro, 1830–1903
     Sisley, 1839–99
     Degas, 1834–1917 (Figs. 44, 107, 247, 266, and 311)
     Renoir, 1841–1919 (Figs. 41, 43, and 138)
     Toulouse-Lautrec, 1864–1901 (Figs. 40, 42, 122, and 383)
     Forain, 1852–1931 (Fig. 330)
America:
   Inness, 1825–94
   Whistler, 1834–1903 (Figs. 139, 154)
   Winslow Homer, 1836–1910 (Figs. 18, 20, 36, 60, 61, and 119)
   Eakins, 1844–1916 (Figs. 78, 150)
   Ryder, 1847–1917 (Fig. 278)
   Sargent, 1856–1925

Modern Art

The art of our time appears bewilderingly complex even to the diligent student. Only the main outlines are indicated here, but something of its intricacy can be discerned from the plethora of pictorial movements which demand attention, such as Fauvism, Modern Primitivism, Expressionism, the Blaue Reiter, Dadism, Surrealism, Orphism, Neue Sachlichkeit, Futurism, Analytical Cubism, Synthetic Cubism, and Abstractionism. The outlines of the Modern Movement in architecture are perhaps clearer. It was partly a reaction against nineteenth-century revivalism, and partly a concerted effort to meet needs which arose for the first time in the modern period—for factories, railroad stations, exposition halls, office buildings, and the like. Its chief triumphs have been in these utilitarian fields rather than in religious, governmental, or educational structures where traditionalism is strong. In meeting the new needs of an industrialized and vastly increased society the Modernists sought to exploit materials and structural systems for their utmost practical value and to allow function to play an important role in planning. It is hard to deny that many of their successes have been spectacular.

ARCHITECTURE

England:
    Paxton, 1803–65
        Crystal Palace, London (1851)
France:
    Eiffel, 1832–1923
        Eiffel Tower, Paris (1889) (Fig. 211)
    Freyssinet, b. 1879
        Hanger at Orly (1916)
    Perret, b. 1874
        Notre Dame, Le Raincy (1923–25)
    Sicilis, 1889–1942
        Théâtre St. Georges, Paris (1928–29)
    LeCorbusier, b. 1887
        League of Nations Building Project, Geneva (1927)
        Savoye House, Poissey-sur-Seine (1925)
Germany:
    Wagner, 1841–1918
        Postal Savings Bank, Vienna (1905)
    Hoffmann, b. 1870
        Stoclet House, Brussels (1905–11)
    Behrens, 1868–1938
        A. E. G. Turbine Factory, Berlin (1909)
    Berg, 1870–1947
        Centennial Hall, Breslau (1913) (Fig. 205)
    Bonatz and Scholer
        Railway Station, Stuttgart (1913–27)
    Boehm, b. 1880
        Roman Catholic Church, Bischofsheim-bei-Mainz (1926)
    Gropius, b. 1883
        Bauhaus, Dessau (1926)
    Mendelssohn, 1887–1953
        Schocken Building, Stuttgart (1927)
    May, Boehm, and Rudloff
        Burchfeldstrasse Housing Group, Frankfort-am-Main (1926)
    Mies Van der Rohe, b. 1886
        Tugendhat House, Brno, Czechoslovakia (1930)
        Plan for a brick country house (1923) (Fig. 250)
Holland:
    Dudok, b. 1884
        School, Hilversum (1922) (Fig. 223)
    Oud, b. 1890
        Houses, Hook of Holland (1926–27)
America:
    Kellum, 1809–71
        A. T. Stewart Store, New York (1862–63)

Buffington, 1848–1931
   28-storey Building Project, Minneapolis (1882)
Holabird, Roche
   Tacoma Building, Chicago (1887–89)
Louis Sullivan, 1856–1924
   Wainwright Building, St. Louis (1890–91)
   Transportation Building, World's Columbian Exposition, Chicago (1893)
   Guaranty-Prudential Building, Buffalo (1895)
   Schlesinger-Mayer Building, now the Carson, Pirie, Scott Store, Chicago
      (1899)
Flagg, 1857–1947
   Singer Building, New York (1906)
Cass Gilbert, 1859–1934
   Woolworth Building, New York (1911–13)
New York Zoning Law, 1916
Hugh Ferriss, b. 1889
   Projects of skyscrapers (1915 and later)
Chicago Tribune Building Competition, 1922
   Designs by Hood and Howells, Goodhue, Gropius, Saarinen, and others
A. L. Harmon, b. 1878
   Shelton Hotel, New York (1924)
Klauder, 1872–1938
   University Building, Pittsburgh (1924)
Van Alen, 1882–1954
   Chrysler Building, New York (1929)
Shreve, Lamb, and Harmon.
   Empire State Building, New York (1930)
Raymond Hood, 1881–1934
   Daily News Building, New York (1930)
   McGraw-Hill Building, New York (1931)
   Rockefeller Center, New York, with Corbett, Reinhart, Hofmeister, and
      others (1930) (Fig. 212)
Skidmore, Owings, and Merrill
   New York University–Bellevue Hospital Medical Center, New York (1949–
      56) (Figs. 71, 178 and 251)
Frank Lloyd Wright, b. 1869. Wright's pre-eminence in achitecture can be
illustrated simply: he is the first American in history to be the world's lead-
ing master of one of the visual arts.
   Larkin Building, Buffalo (1903–4)
   Coonley House, Chicago (1907)
   Baker House, Wilmette, Ill. (1909) (Fig. 249)
   Robie House, Chicago (1909–10)
   Imperial Hotel, Tokyo (1916)
   Millard House, "La Miniatura," Pasadena (1921)
   Johnson Wax Company Building, Racine (1938) (Figs. 86a and 86b)
   Kaufmann House, "Fallingwater," Bear Run, Pa. (1937) (Fig. 213)
   Taliesen III, Spring Green, Wis. (begun 1925)
   Taliesen West, Paradise Valley, Ariz. (begun 1938)

The skyscraper is emphasized in the preceding list because it has been
America's unique and distinctive contribution to the advancement of archi-

tecture. Although seldom a thing of unusual esthetic or spiritual import, the skyscraper does represent man's triumph over two structural obstacles which had limited the attainment of free space and great height for centuries.

SCULPTURE

Germany:
    Hildebrand, 1847–1921
    Barlach, 1870–1938
    Metzner, 1870–1919
    Lehmbruck, 1881–1914
    Sintenis, b. 1888 (Fig. 162)
England:
    Epstein, b. 1880
    Moore, b. 1898
Rumania:
    Brancusi, b. 1876 (Fig. 159)
Jugoslavia:
    Mёstrovič, b. 1883
Sweden:
    Milles, b. 1875
Russia:
    Archipenko, b. 1887
France:
    Bourdelle, 1861–1929 (Fig. 164)
    Maillol, 1861–1944 (Figs. 5, 269, and 289)
    Despiau, b. 1874
    Lipchitz, b. 1891
    Arp, b. 1887 (Fig. 229)
America:
    Manship, b. 1885 (Fig. 302)
    Zorach, b. 1887 (Figs. 84a–d)
    Calder, b. 1898 (Fig. 173)
    Muir, b. 1906 (Figs. 185 and 186)

PAINTING AND DRAWING

Europe:
    Cézanne, 1839–1906 (Figs. 15, 39, 80, and 127)
    Henri Rousseau, 1844–1910 (Fig. 13)
    Gauguin, 1848–1906 (Fig. 141)
    Van Gogh, 1853–90 (Figs. 65, 140, 155, 328, 353, and 364)
    Seurat, 1859–91 (Fig. 226)
    Munch, 1863–1944
    Kandinsky, 1866–1944
    Bonnard, 1867–1947
    Kollwitz, 1867–1945 (Figs. 294 and 309)
    Vuillard, 1868–1940
    Matisse, 1869–1954 (Figs. 123 and 261)
    Rouault, 1871–1958 (Fig. 227)
    Mondrian, 1872–1944 (Fig. 55)
    Klee, 1879–1940
    Picasso, b. 1881 (Figs. 1, 45, and 362)

Braque, b. 1882
Marc, 1880–1916 (Fig. 32)
Utrillo, 1883–1955 (Fig. 22)
Modigliani, 1884–1920
Kokoschka, b. 1886 (Fig. 9)
Chagall, b. 1887
Chirico, b. 1888
Dix, b. 1891
Miro, b. 1893
Grosz, b. 1893
Dali, b. 1904 (Fig. 53)
America:
Hassam, 1859–1935
Prendergast, 1859–1924
Waugh, 1861–1940 (Fig. 17)
Kane, 1860–1934
Davies, 1862–1928
Luks, 1867–1933
Marin, 1870–1953
Sloan, 1871–1951 (Fig. 76)
Feininger, 1871–1955
Hartley, 1877–1943
Kuhn, 1880–1944
Weber, b. 1881
Hopper, b. 1882
Bellows, 1882–1925 (Fig. 77)
Orozco, 1883–1949 (Fig. 29)
Sheeler, b. 1883 (Fig. 54)
Rivera, 1886–1957
O'Keeffe, b. 1887
Benton, b. 1889
Burchfield, b. 1893 (Figs. 27 and 368)
Davis, b. 1894
Thurber, b. 1894 (Fig. 143)
Fiene, b. 1894
Wood, 1892–1942 (Fig. 96)
Rattner, b. 1895
Curry, 1897–1946
Shahn, b. 1898
Marsh, 1898–1954
Kunyoshi, 1893–1953
Etnier, b. 1903
Wyeth, b. 1907
Levine, b. 1915

ORIENTAL ART

The art of Asia has been included in this outline because it represents the artistry of at least two-thirds of the people who have
inhabited this globe and because it has intrinsic worth. Almost every-

one who gives it the attention it deserves finds it profoundly beautiful and rewarding. In this century such devotees have been aided
by improvements in the opportunities to study fine examples of
oriental art. Many scholarly, well-written, and beautifully illustrated
books on the subject have appeared, and a number of our large
cities across the country have assembled excellent collections of
original works of oriental art. Also available for practical use by
college students and others is an extensive and carefully chosen set
of reproductions published by the University Prints Company as
Series–O. Most of the examples cited in the outline can be seen in
that series. A third practical motivation of this outline was to provide the student and general reader with a concise factual outline of
the main periods, monuments, and artists of oriental art history.
Such an outline, though often needed, is difficult to find.

The present outline includes two examples of Islamic art and two
of pre-Columbian American art, but limitations of space made it
impossible to include in either the outline or the book any examples
from the vast field of primitive art, a subject which has received
increasing attention from artists and the public in recent years.
Mention of the subject is made here because these art forms are
more closely associated stylistically with the oriental tradition than
with any European school, and careful attention must ultimately be
given to this relationship in any global study of art.

If the art of Asia is viewed broadly, the art of four countries—
Persia, India, China, and Japan—stands out. Among these, India
and China are the most prominent. Like Greece, Italy, and France
in the West, they have been the fountainheads of inspiration and
productivity. But though relatively secondary to China, Japan has
nevertheless produced an impressive body of art, and Persia has compensated in quality for what she lacked in quantity. Even this lack
is comparative, for all the oriental countries have been prolific, India
particularly. Within Indian art, sculpture abounds. India's creation
of paintings has been less fertile, but the frescoes in the caves of
Ajanta and Bagh are known around the world. The Persian school
is perhaps best known and loved for its exquisite miniature paintings
and superb decorative arts. Its textiles and carpets are among the
most prized in the world, and its ceramics are nearly as revered as
those of China.

In China and Japan sculpture and painting have divided honors
almost equally, with Japan especially noted for her carving in wood.
The great triumphs in sculpture came rather early in history, those

in painting somewhat later, as in the West. The Japanese, like the Persians, have shown superior gifts for the decorative arts.

Most Asian art was religiously inspired. Natural landscapes and scenes from everyday life motivated some fine paintings in China and Japan, but at relatively late dates. Though excellent in quality and sensitive in feeling, they comprise only a minority of Asiatic paintings. The three predominant faiths represented in art were Mohammedanism in Persia, Hinduism and Buddhism in India, and Buddhism in China and Japan. These creeds gave Asiatic art most of its profound insights into life and its air of dealing with universal and timeless problems while eschewing the transitory and trivial. One senses these qualities in oriental religious art, but it is not necessary for the beginner to become involved in the extremely complex ideologies of Hinduism and Buddhism to enjoy the art of Asia, for its esthetic qualities are rich and appreciable. In the handling of lines, colors, forms, and compositions it is the equal of any other art. If it sometimes lacks the force of Western art, its grace, refinement, sensitivity, and depth of feeling are unquestioned.

Only in architecture does Asiatic art seem comparatively deficient to Western eyes. That, however, may be a biased view arising from our tendency to stress the structural and functional facets of building. Generally speaking, Indian and Chinese architecture have met with little interest and understanding in the Occident. Persian and Japanese architecture have found greater favor. Persian architecture influenced European building during the late Middle Ages through the Crusaders and the spread of Islam across Africa and into Spain. Japanese domestic architecture has elicited the praise of Frank Lloyd Wright and other modernists who found in its clean, asymmetrical balances and rectilinear shapes the same kind of simplicity and clarity that Western architects were seeking. But by and large we have not been able to fathom or enjoy the architecture of the East so well as we have its pictorial and sculptural products and its beautiful decorative arts. The Japanese print still ranks well ahead of the Japanese house in general appreciation.

PERSIAN AND ISLAMIC ART

Pre-Islamic Iranian Art: Pre-Achaemenian period (*ca.* 5th millennium–550 B.C.)
    Bronze finial from Luristan. Museum of Fine Arts, Boston
Achaemenian Period (550–331 B.C.)
    Relief of Darius with Xerxes giving an audience, Treasury, Persepolis
    Palace of Darius, Persepolis
    Man-bull capital from Tripylon, Persepolis

Relief of the royal arms, lion attacking a bull, south end, eastern stairway, Apadana, Persepolis

Sasaniar Period (A.D. 226–642)

Relief of a Bactrian tribute bearer with a camel, eastern stairway, Apadana, Persepolis

Winged ibex handle, gilded silver, Staatliche Museum, Berlin

Silver plate with Khusraw II hunting deer, Bibliothèque Nationale, Paris

Islamic Art

Umayyad Caliphate (661–750)

Architecture:

Great Mosque, Damascus

Façade in late classical style, from West entrance, Mshatta, Staatliche Museum, Berlin

Early 'Abbasid Caliphate (750–900)

Architecture:

Malwiyah Minaret, Sammara, Iraq (Fig. 234)

Mosque of ibn-Tulun, Cairo

Early medieval Persia (10th–mid-11th centuries)

Architecture:

Tomb Tower of Qabus the Ziyarid (Gumbad-i-Qabus) , Gurgan

Fatimid Caliphate (969–1171)

Decorative Arts:

Bronze Griffin, Campo Santo, Pisa

Wood Mihrab from the Mausoleum of Sayyidah Nafisah, Musée Arabe, Cairo

Saljuq period, Great Saljuqs and Atabegs (mid-11th–mid-13th centuries)

Decorative Arts:

Hawk striking a goose, stucco relief, Museum of Fine Arts, Boston

Bronze door knocker with winged dragons, Staatliche Museum, Berlin

Silk with winged lions and birds in ovals, Victoria and Albert Museum, London

Bronze cauldron, silver and copper inlaid, with inscriptions of war and revel, Hermitage, Leningrad

Book Illumination and Painting:

Woman herding camels, by Yahya b. Mahmud al-Wasiti, from a MS. of al-Hariri's "Maqamat," Bibliothèque Nationale, Paris

Ayyubid period in Egypt and Syria (1171–mid-13th century)

Decorative Arts and Paintings:

Dimnah and Lion-King, from a "Kalilah wa-Dimnah" MS., Bibliothèque Nationale, Paris

Mongol through Timurid period in Persia, Iraq, and Turkistan (1258–1507)

Architecture:

Mosque of 'Ali Shah, Tabriz

Mausoleum of Tamerlane (Gur-i-Mir) , Samarkand

Book Illumination and Painting:

Elephants, from a "Manafi 'al-Hayawan" MS., Morgan Library, New York

Serpent, from a "Manafi 'al-Hayawan" MS., Art Institute, Chicago

Ardashir defeats Ardawan, from a "Shah-namah" MS., Institute of Arts, Detroit

The duel, by Junayd, from a Khwaju Kirmani MS., Musée des Arts Décoratifs, Paris

Gulnar sees Ardashir from a palace window, from a "Shah-namah" MS., Gulistan Palace, Teheran

King Darius reproved by his herdsman, by Bihzad, from a "Bustan" MS., Royal Egyptian Library, Cairo

Sick lion catching an ass, from a "Kalilah wa-Dimnah" MS., Gulistan Palace, Teheran

Humay meets Humayun, from a Khwaju Kirmani MS., Musée des Arts Décoratifs, Paris

Moorish period in Spain (711–1492)

Architecture:

Great Mosque (La Mezquita) and Mihrab of Hakam II, Cordova

Courts of the lions, Alhambra, Granada

Mirador Da Darraxa, Hall of the Two Sisters, Alhambra, Granada (Fig. 183)

Court of the Maidens, Alcazar, Seville

Safawid period (1502–1737)

Architecture:

Royal Square (Maydan-i-Shah), Royal Mosque (Masjid-i-Shah), and Palace ('Ala Qapu), Isfahan

Mosque of Shaykh Lutfallah, Royal Square, Isfahan

Decorative Arts:

Medallion carpet from Ardebil Shrine, Victoria and Albert Museum, London

Book Illumination and Paintings:

Lady with spray of flowers, Cartier Collection, Paris

Polo game, Tabriz school, Freer Gallery of Art, Washington, D. C. (Fig. 112)

Khusraw sees Shirin bathing, from a MS. of Nizami's "Khamsah," attributed to Sultan Muhammed, School of Tabriz, British Museum, London

Dwarf of Murad II, Fogg Museum of Art, Harvard University (Fig. 145)

Ottoman Empire (*ca.* 1300–1922)

Architecture:

Mosque of Sultan Ahmad I, by Mehmed Agha, Istanbul

Decorative Arts:

Geometric tile pattern rug from Anatolia ("Holbein Rug"), City Art Museum, St. Louis

Period of the Great Mughals (1526–1707)

Architecture:

Mausoleum of I'timad-al-Dawla, Agra

Taj Mahal, Agra

Pearl Mosque, Agra

Painting:

Scene from the story of Amir Hamzah, the prophet's uncle, Metropolitan Museum of Art, New York

Sketch from life: "Inayat Khan Dying," Museum of Fine Arts, Boston

Prince Dara Shikuh and son, by Govardhan, Staatliche Museum, Berlin

PRE-COLUMBIAN ART IN AMERICA

Chimu and Inca (*ca.* 100 B.C.–*ca.* A. D. 1550)

Fortresses at Chan-Chan and Paramonga

Collaguas Terraces
Fortress, Machu Picchu
Palace, Tambo di Mora
Fortress, Sacsahuaman
Ceremonial seats, Cuzco
Palace, Cora Cora
Maya
 Chief centers: Palenque, Acanceh, Chichen Itza, Tulum, Uaxactum, Copan, Tikal
 Chief periods:
  176 B.C.–A.D. 373, Old Empire
  373–A.D. 472, Middle period
  472–A.D. 620, Great period
  980–A.D. 1200, Mayan renaissance (New Empire)
  1200–A.D. 1450, Period of Mexican influence
  1450–A.D. 1551, Modern period, conquest and decline
 Architecture:
  Great Temple Pyramid, Tikal, Mayan renaissance (Fig. 240)
 Decorative Arts:
  Ceremonial axe-head, Totonac (Vera Cruz region) (Fig. 275)

INDIAN AND INDONESIAN ART

Indus Valley (*ca.* 3300–2000 B.C.)
 Torso from Harappa, Archaeological Museum, Mohenjo-Daro
Maurya (322–185 B.C.)
 Asokan Column, Lauriya Nandangarh
Sunga (185–80 B.C.)
 Gateway and railing, Bharhut, Indian Museum, Calcutta
 Chaitya Hall, Karli
 Donors, Chaitya Hall, Karli
Early Andhra (*ca.* 70–25 B.C.)
 Great Stupa, Sanchi
 East gate of Great Stupa, Sanchi
 Yakshi, East gate of Great Stupa, Sanchi
 The great enlightenment, Walking on the water, Return to Kapilavastu, Dvarapala; East Gate, Great Stupa, Sanchi
Kushana (*ca.* A.D. 50–320)
 Seated Buddha, Curzon Museum of Archaeology, Muttra
 Yakshis on railing pillars, Indian Museum, Calcutta
Gandhara (1st–5th centuries A.D.)
 Bodhisattva from Shahbaz-Garhi, Louvre, Paris
Fifth century A.D.
 Head from northwestern India, Museum of Fine Arts, Boston
 Head from Hadda, Nelson Gallery, Kansas City
Later Andhra (*ca.* 1st–3rd centuries A.D.)
 Buddha and the elephant, Nalagiri (detail from Amaravati), Government Museum, Madras
Gupta (A.D. 320–600)
 Buddha preaching in the deer park, Archaeological Museum, Sarnath

The Great Bodhisattva, Cave I, Ajanta
Palace scene, Cave I, Ajanta
Early medieval (A.D. 600–850)
Descent of the Ganges, Mamallapuram
Ravana under Mt. Kailasa, Kailasa Temple, Ellora
Late medieval (A.D. 850–1200)
Jaina Temple, Mt. Abu
Parvati (or deified Queen), Freer Gallery of Art, Washington, D. C.
Kali, Nelson Gallery, Kansas City (Fig. 337)
Ceylon
Avalokitesvara, Jambhala, Museum of Fine Arts, Boston
Siva as Nataraja, Lord of the Dance, Museum of Fine Arts, Boston (Fig. 372)
Sundara-murti Svami from Polonnaruva, Museum, Columbo
Cambodia
Harihara, Musée Albert Sarraut, Phnom-Peonh
Head of Buddha, Fogg Museum of Art, Cambridge
Lintel from the Temple of Sla Ket, Metropolitan Museum of Art, New York
Angkor Wat, Angkor Wat
Dancing girls, or Apsarases, Angkor Wat
Java
Great Stupa, Borobudur
Reliefs of bath of the Bodhisattva, Hiru landing in Hiruka, Archery contest,
Story of Mandhatar; Great Stupa, Borobudur
Dhyani Buddha, Great Stupa, Borobudur

CHINESE ART

Yang-Shao (prehistoric, prior to 1400 B.C.)
Painted pot from Kansu, Museum, Stockholm
Shang (Yin) Dynasty (ca. 1400 B.C.–1100 B.C.), Early and Middle Chou Dynasties
(ca. 1100–ca. 600 B.C.)
Bronze ritual vessel, Type Ku, Gardner Museum, Boston (Fig. 237)
Bronze ritual vessel, Type Yu, Museum of Fine Arts, Boston (Fig. 243)
Bronze spiral finial, Nelson Gallery of Art, Kansas City (Fig. 236)
Late Chou Dynasty (ca. 600–ca. 250 B.C.)
Bronze vessel, Type Chien, Oeder Collection, Berlin
Bronze bell, Type Chung, Stoclet Collection, Brussels
Bronze ritual vessel, Type Ting, Nelson Gallery, Kansas City, (Fig. 218)
Jade disk, Type Pi, Nelson Gallery of Art, Kansas City (Fig. 220)
Bronze wrestlers, Spencer-Churchill Collection, Gloucestershire
Bronze winged dragon, Stoclet Collection, Brussels
Han Dynasty (206 B.C.–A.D. 221)
Pair of gilt-bronze bears, Gardner Museum, Boston
Jade horse's head, Eumorfopoulos Collection, Victoria and Albert Museum,
London
Sculpture:
Stone pillar of Shen, Szechwan
Painted pottery house model, Nelson Gallery, Kansas City
Painted tile: Men in conversation, Museum of Fine Arts, Boston

Wei Dynasty (A.D. 386–557)
  Sculpture:
    Stone lion of Liang, Tomb of Hsiao Hsiu, near Nanking
    Buddhist cave sculpture, Yun Kang
    Buddhist cave sculpture, Lung Men
    Head of a Bodhisattva, from Lung Men, Metropolitan Museum of Art,
      New York
    Relief of the Empress as a donor, from Lung Men, Metropolitan Museum
      of Art, New York
    The Bodhisattva Avalokitesvara, Okakura Memorial, Museum of Fine
      Arts, Boston
    Buddhist stele, ex-Gualino Collection, Villa Madama, Rome
    Buddhist stele (Wetzel Stele) (A.D. 554) , Museum of Fine Arts, Boston
    Bronze group: Two Buddhas, Sakyamuni and Prabhutaratna (A.D. 518) ,
      Musée Guimet, Paris (Fig. 172)
  Painting:
    Ku K'ai-chih, Admonitions to the ladies of the palace, British Museum, Lon-
      don
    The Azure Dragon of the East, tomb painting, Guken-ri, Korea
  Pottery:
    Tomb figurines, Museum, Toronto
North Ch'i Dynasty (A.D. 550–557) and Sui Dynasty (A.D. 581–618)
  Kuan Yin, Nelson Gallery, Kansas City
  Kuan Yin (Padmapani) , Museum of Fine Arts, Boston
  Flying Apsaras, Nelson Gallery, Kansas City (Fig. 171)
  Bronze shrine (Tuan Fang) (A.D. 593) , Museum of Fine Arts, Boston
T'ang Dynasty (A.D. 618–906)
  Sculpture:
    Relief, Horse of T'ang T'ai Tsung, University Museum, Philadelphia
    Front of a Buddhist shrine, Nelson Gallery, Kansas City
    Buddha and Bodhisattvas, T'ien Lung Shan Caves, Shansi
    Kneeling Bodhisattva from Tun Huang, Fogg Museum, Cambridge
    Six-foil bronze dragon mirror, Freer Gallery, Washington, D. C. (Fig. 252)
  Painting:
    Paradise of Amitab'ha, Stein Collection, British Museum, London
  Ceramics:
    Tomb figurines: Prancing horse, Loaded camel, Hoyt Collection, Museum of
      Fine Arts, Boston
    Three-colored glazed jar, Art Institute of Chicago
    Vases and jars, Nelson Gallery, Kansas City (Fig. 187)
Sung Dynasty (960–1279)
  Sculpture:
    Lohan, Nelson Gallery, Kansas City (Fig. 3)
    Lao-Tze on a water buffalo, Worcester Art Museum (Fig. 379)
  Painting:
    Waterfall and pine tree, Museum of Fine Arts, Boston (Fig. 215)
    Tung Yuan, Clear weather in the valley, Museum of Fine Arts, Boston (Fig.
      374)
    Mi Fei, Misty Landscape, Freer Gallery, Washington, D.C.
    Wu Chen, Bamboo in the wind, Museum of Fine Arts, Boston (Fig. 375)
    Li T'ang (?) , Man on a water buffalo, Museum of Fine Arts, Boston
    Emperor Hui Tsung, Five-colored parakeet, Museum of Fine Arts, Boston

Emperor Hui Tsung, Ladies preparing newly woven silk, Museum of Fine Arts, Boston

Lady Wen-chi's return from her captivity in Mongolia, Museum of Fine Arts, Boston

Ma Yuan, Two sages and an attendant under a plum tree, Museum of Fine Arts, Boston

Ma Yuan, Bare willows and distant mountains, Museum of Fine Arts, Boston

Hsia Kuei, Rain storm, Baron Kawasaki Collection, Kobe

Ma Lin, Ling-chao-nu standing in the snow, Museum of Fine Arts, Boston

Chao Meng-chien, Narcissus, Freer Gallery, Washington

Lin T'ing-kuei, Arhats bestowing alms upon beggars, Museum of Fine Arts, Boston (Fig. 360)

Ch'en Jung, Nine dragon scroll, Museum of Fine Arts, Boston (Fig. 276)

Ceramics:

Glazed pottery dish, Museum of Fine Arts, Boston (Fig. 221)

Vase with a dragon design, Tz'u Chou ware, Nelson Gallery, Kansas City

Ming Dynasty (1368–1644)

Painting:

Lotus flowers, Museum of Fine Arts, Boston (Fig. 288)

K'ang Hsi period (1662–1722)

Ceramics:

Oxblood porcelain vase, Museum of Fine Arts, Boston (Fig. 238)

JAPANESE ART

Archaic period (before A.D. 552)

The Great Shrine, Izumo, Shimane Prefecture

Suiko period (552–646)

Architecture:

Temple, Horyuji, Nara Prefecture

Sculpture:

Kwannon, Yumedono Hall, Horyuji Temple, Nara

"Kudara" Kwannon, Horyuji Temple, Nara

Tori Busshi, Yakushi, Golden Hall, Horyuji Temple, Nara (dated 607)

Tori Busshi, Shaka Trinity, Golden Hall, Horyuji Temple, Nara (dated 623)

Bodhisattva in meditation, Chuguji Nunnery, Horyuji Temple, Nara

Painting:

Tamamushi Shrine, Golden Hall, Horyuji Temple, Nara

Hakuho period (646–710)

Sculpture:

Lady Tachibana's Shrine, Golden Hall, Horyuji Temple, Nara

Painting:

Amida enthroned in the western paradise, Golden Hall, Horyuji Temple, Nara

Tempyo period (710–794)

Sculpture:

Shikkongojin, Hokkedo, Todaiji Temple, Nara

Heavenly musician, lantern panel, Todaiji Temple, Nara

Eleven-headed Kwannon, Shorinji Temple, Nara

Priest Ganjin, Kaizando, Toshodaiji Temple, Nara

Painting:

Kichijoten, Yakushiji Temple, Nara

Jogan period (794–897)
Sculpture:
Hachiman as priest, Yakushiji Temple, Nara
Fujiwara period (897–1185)
Sculpture:
Amida of Hoodo, Byodoin Temple, Uji, Kyoto Prefecture
Meikira, one of the twelve generals, Tokondo, Kofukuji Temple, Nara
Gigaku mask, Museum of Fine Arts, Boston
Painting:
Takayoshi (?) , Genji Monogatari Scroll, Reimeikai Foundation
Toba Sojo, Animal caricature scroll, Kozanji Temple, Kyoto
Sutra dedicated by the Taira family, Itsukushima Shrine, Hiroshima Prefecture
Kamakura period (1185–1392)
Sculpture:
Unkei, Dainichi, Enjoji Temple, Nara Prefecture
Unkei, Hosso Patriarch Muchaku, Hokuendo Kofukuji Temple, Nara
Kaikei, Miroku, Museum of Fine Arts, Boston
Koben, Demon lantern-bearer, Kofukuji Temple, Nara
Style of Unkei, Basu-Sennin, Sanjusangendo Temple, Kyoto
The Great Buddha, Kamakura (dated 1252)
Benzaiten, Tsurugaoka Hachimangu shrine, Kamakura (dated 1266)
Uesugi Shigefusa, Meigetsuin Temple, Kamakura
Koshun, Hachiman as a priest, Museum of Fine Arts, Boston (dated 1328)
Painting:
Jizo, Metropolitan Museum of Art, New York
Kobo Daishi as a child, Murayama Chokyo Collection, Mikage
Nachi Waterfall, Nezu Kaichiro Collection, Tokyo
Takanobu (?) , Minamoto No Yoritomo, Jingoji Temple, Kyoto
Makemono scroll of Kibi's adventures in China, Museum of Fine Arts, Boston
Nobuzane, scroll of the Thirty-Six Poets, ex-Marquis Satake Collection
Heiji Monogatari, Makemono scroll of the burning of the Sanjo Palace, Museum of Fine Arts, Boston (Figs. 322a, b, and c)
Imperial mounted guard, detail of a scroll, Baron Okura Collection, Tokyo (dated 1247)
Mokuan, The four sleepers, Marquis Maeda Collection, Tokyo
Ashikaga period (1392–1568)
Painting:
Cho Densu, The Master Shoichi, Tofukuji Temple, Kyoto
Josetsu, Catfish and gourd, Taizoin Temple, Kyoto
Shubun, Landscape, Museum of Fine Arts, Boston
Sesshu, Winter landscape, Imperial Household Museum, Tokyo
Shuku, Sage riding a donkey, Museum of Fine Arts, Boston
Jasoku, Summer landscape, Count Tokugawa Collection, Tokyo
Kei Shoki (Shokei) , Landscape, Nezu Kaichiro Collection, Tokyo
Soami, Chinese landscape, Metropolitan Museum of Art, New York
Kano Motonobu, Crane (sliding screen panel) , Reiunin Temple, Kyoto
Kano Motonobu, Rapids, Hara Sueko Collection, Yokohama
Sesson, Boat returning in a storm, Fumihide Nomura Collection, Osaka (Fig. 401)

Momoyama period (1568–1615)
  Painting:
    Kano Eitoku, White eagle on a pine tree (screen), Imperial Art School, Tokyo
    Sanraku (?), Uji bridge (screen), Mizoguchi Munehiko Collection, Tokyo
    Hasegawa Tohaku, Tiger, Museum of Fine Arts, Boston
    Kaihoku Yusho, Crane, Museum of Fine Arts, Boston
Tokugawa period (1615–1867)
  Architecture:
    Sanboin garden, Daigoji Temple, Kyoto Prefecture
    Castle, Nagoya
    Imperial Katsura Palace, Kyoto
    Imperial Shugaku-in Palace, Kyoto
    Rinshun-kaku, Sankei-en Park, Yokohama
    Yoko-kan, Fukei, Choshu-kaku, Sankei-en Park, Yokohama
  Painting:
    Miyagawa Niten (Musashi), Shrike on a withered limb, Nagao Kinya Collection, Tokyo
    Nonomura Sotatsu, Wind and thunder god screens, Kenninji Temple, Kyoto
    Nonomura Sotatsu, Waves at Matsushima, Freer Gallery, Washington, D.C.
    Iwasa Matabei, Lady viewing chrysanthemums, Hosaka Junji Collection, Tokyo
    Hanabusa Itcho, Cloth-drying dance, Toyama Motokazu Collection, Tokyo
    Tosa Mitsunori, Genji Monogatari Album, Freer Gallery, Washington, D. C.
    Ogata Korin, Red and white plum trees (screens), ex-Count Tsugaru Collection, Tokyo
    Maruyama Okyo, Hozu river screen, Nishimura Sozaemon Collection, Kyoto
Wood-Block Prints: The Ukiyoé School
    Hishikawa Moronobu, 1638–1714, Wakoku Shosoku Ezukushi (illustrations of various occupations)
    Iwasa Matabei, fl. 1680–1705, Dancer
    Okumura Masanobu, 1690–1768, Playing cards (Fig. 113); Playing the game of sugosuku in a restaurant (Fig. 114)
    Torii Kiyomasu, fl. 1715, The actor Matsumoto Shigemaki as a woman
    Torii Kiyonaga, fl. 1716, Coming ashore (triptych); Beauties strolling
    Suzuki Harunobu, 1725–70, The beautiful Osen in the Kagiya inn (Fig. 361)
    Isoda Koriusai, fl. 1760–80, Couple in snow under a big umbrella; two children playing with a wooden horse
    Katsukawa Shunsho, 1726–92, Woman in a pink dress (Fig. 340); Ichikawa Danjuro V as Kudo Suketsune (Fig. 341)
    Itsuhitsusai Buncho, fl. 1770–96, Girl with a parasol
    Saito Sharaku, fl. 1789–1800, Ichikawa Ebizo IV as Washizuka Kwandayu
    Kitigawa Utamaro, 1754–1806, Three geisha; Mother and child
    Kitao Shigemasu, 1739–1819, Mirror of the beauties of the greenhouse
    Katsushika Hokusai, 1760–1849, The great wave (Fig. 377); Fuijiyama in clear weather (Fig. 265)
    Utagawa Kunisada, 1786–1864, Horse in action
    Ando Hiroshige, 1797–1858, Shower on Ohashi Bridge (Fig. 68); A traveller buying an Otsu-E picture (Fig. 115); A cuckoo flying through a storm (Fig. 334)
    Utagawa Kuniyoshi, 1797–1861, Nichiren in exile

Selected Bibliography

The books listed here comprise a suggested nucleus for a library on the nature, methods, and history of art. An outgrowth of work with students in Bowdoin College, the list approaches art on a broad front, but with emphasis on books which stress principles. Anyone who wishes to push beyond a general knowledge of this field and explore some of its numerous special subjects will find a thorough and well-chosen list of books on every aspect of art in E. Louise Lucas' *Books on Art, a Foundation List* (Cambridge, Mass.; Fogg Museum of Art, 1936). In addition to the books included here and in Miss Lucas' list, several series are available which are invaluable for their numerous reproductions, many in color. Especially useful are those published by Abrams, Braun, Crown, Hoesch, Hyperion, Klassiker der Kunst, Phaidon, Propyläen-verlag, Silvano, Skira, Tel, Unesco, and the University Prints. Also outstanding is a new, extensively illustrated series called the *Pelican History of Art,* published by Penguin Books, Baltimore. Written by leading scholars, the series will eventually cover the whole history of art.

ABELL, W. *Representation and Form, a Study of Aesthetic Values in Representational Art.* New York: Charles Scribner's Sons, 1936.

ACKERMAN, P. *Tapestry, the Mirror of Civilization.* New York: Oxford University Press, 1933.

———. *Ritual Bronzes of Ancient China.* New York: The Dryden Press, Inc., 1945.

ADAMS, E. K. *The Aesthetic Experience; Its Meaning in a Functional Psychology.* Chicago: University of Chicago Press, 1907.

ADAMS, H. *Mont-Saint-Michel and Chartres.* Boston: Houghton Mifflin Co., 1905.

ADRIANI, B. *Problems of the Sculptor.* New York: Nierendorf Gallery, 1943.

ANAND, M. R. *The Hindu View of Art.* London: George Allen & Unwin, 1933.

ANDERSON, M. D. *The Medieval Carver.* Cambridge, England: Cambridge University Press, 1935.

ANDERSON, W. J., and STRATTON, A. *Architecture of the Renaissance in Italy*. London: B. T. Batsford, Ltd., 1927.

AUBERT, M. *French Cathedral Windows of the Twelfth and Thirteenth Centuries*. New York and Toronto: Oxford University Press, 1939.

BACHELDER, E. A. *Design in Theory and Practice*. New York: The Macmillan Co., 1916.

BAKER, C. H. C. *Dutch Painting of the Seventeenth Century*. London: The Studio Publications, Inc., 1926.

BARNES, A. C. *The Art in Painting*. New York: Harcourt, Brace & Co., Inc., 1928.

BARR, A. H., JR. *Cubism and Abstract Art*. New York: Museum of Modern Art, 1936.

———. *Fantastic Art, Dada, Surrealism*. New York: Museum of Modern Art, 1936.

———. *Picasso: Fifty Years of His Art*. New York: Museum of Modern Art, 1946.

———. *What Is Modern Painting?* New York: Museum of Modern Art, 1949.

BEHRENDT, W. C. *Modern Building*. New York: Harcourt, Brace & Co., Inc., 1937.

BERENSON, B. *Aesthetics and History*. New York: Pantheon Books, Inc., 1948.

———. *The Italian Painters of the Renaissance*. London: Oxford University Press, 1932.

———. *Three Essays in Method*. London: Oxford University Press, 1927.

BEST-MAUGARD, A. *A Method for Creative Design*. New York: Alfred A. Knopf, Inc., 1937.

BIEBER, M. *The Sculpture of the Hellenistic Age*. New York: Columbia University Press, 1955.

BINYON, R. L. *The Flight of the Dragon*. London: J. John Murray, Ltd.; New York: E. P. Dutton & Co., Inc., 1911.

———. *The Spirit of Man in Asian Art*. Cambridge: Harvard University Press, 1935.

BIRKHOFF, G. D. *Aesthetic Measure*. Cambridge: Harvard University Press, 1933.

BLAKE, V. *Relation in Art*. London: Oxford University Press, 1925.

BLISS, D. P. *A History of Wood-Engraving*. London: J. M. Dent & Sons, Ltd.; New York: E. P. Dutton & Co., Inc., 1928.

BLOSSFELDT, K. *Art Forms in Nature*. 2 vols.; New York: E. Weyhe Co., 1929–1932.

BLUNT, A. *Artistic Theory in Italy, 1450–1600*. London: Oxford University Press, 1940.

BOAS, G. *Wingless Pegasus, A Handbook for Critics*. Baltimore: Johns Hopkins University Press, 1950.

BOECK, W., and SABARTÉS, J. *Picasso*. New York and Amsterdam: Harry N. Abrams, Inc., 1955.

BOLLER, W. *Masterpieces of the Japanese Color Woodcut*. Boston: Boston Book & Art Shop, Inc., 1950.

BOWIE, H. P. *On the Laws of Japanese Painting*. New York: Dover Publications, Inc., 1951.

BRANDT, H. F. *The Psychology of Seeing*. New York: Philosophical Library, Inc. 1945.

BRAUN-VOGELSTEIN, J. *Art, the Image of the West*. New York: Pantheon Books, Inc., 1952.

BREASTED, J. H. *History of Egypt from the Earliest Times to the Persian Conquest*. New York: Charles Scribner's Sons, 1924.

BRIGGS, M. S. *Baroque Architecture*. New York: The McBride Co., Inc., 1914.

———. *The Architect in History*. London: Oxford University Press, 1927.

BROWN, G. B. *The Fine Arts*, New York: Charles Scribner's Sons, 1927.

BUERMEYER, L. *The Aesthetic Experience*. Merion, Pa.: Barnes Foundation, 1924.

BULFINCH, T. *The Age of Fable*. London: J. M. Dent & Sons, Ltd.; New York: E. P. Dutton & Co., Inc., 1910.

BURCKHARDT, J. *The Civilization of the Renaissance in Italy*. New York: Oxford University Press, 1944.

BUTLER, A. S. G. *The Substance of Architecture*. New York: Dial Press, Inc., 1927.

CARRINGTON, F. R. *Prints and Their Makers*. New York: Appleton-Century-Crofts, Inc., 1912.

CARRITT, E. F. *Philosophies of Beauty, from Socrates to Robert Bridges*. London and New York: Oxford University Press, 1931.

————. *The Theory of Beauty*. 4th ed.; London: Methuen & Co., Ltd., 1931.

CASSIRER, E. *Language and Myth* (trans. by S. K. Langer). New York: Harper & Bros., 1946.

CELLINI, B. *Autobiography* (trans. by J. A. Symonds). Garden City, N. Y.: Doubleday & Co., Inc., 1927.

CENNINI, C. *The Book of the Art of Cennino Cennini* (trans. by Christiana J. Herringham). London: George Allen & Unwin, 1922.

CENTANO, A. (ed.). *The Intent of the Artist*. Princeton: Princeton University Press, 1941.

CHAMBERS, F. P. *The History of Taste*. New York: Columbia University Press, 1932.

CHASE, G. H., and POST, C. R. *A History of Sculpture*. New York: Harper & Bros., 1925.

CHENEY, S. *Expressionism in Art*. New York: The Viking Press, Inc., 1934.

————. *Primer of Modern Art*. New York: Liveright Pub. Corp., 1924.

CLARK, K. *The Gothic Revival; an Essay in the History of Taste*. London: Constable & Co., Ltd., 1928.

COLLINGWOOD, R. G. *Outlines of a Philosophy of Art*. London: Oxford University Press, 1925.

————. *The Principles of Art*. London: Oxford University Press, 1938.

CONNICK, C. J. *Adventures in Light and Color*. New York: Random House, Inc., 1937.

CONSTABLE, W. G. *The Painter's Workshop*. London: Oxford University Press, 1954.

COOMARASWAMY, A. K. *The Dance of Siva*. New York: Sunwise Turn, Inc., 1924.

CROCE, B. *Aesthetic as a Science of Expression and General Linguistic* (trans. by Douglas Ainslie). 2d ed.; London: Macmillan & Co., Ltd., 1922.

————. *The Essence of Aesthetic*. London: William Heinemann, Ltd., 1921.

CUMMINGS, D. *Handbook of Lithography*. 3d ed.; London: A. & C. Black, Ltd., 1932.

DALTON, O. M. *Byzantine Art and Archaeology*. London: Oxford University Press, 1911.

DAVENPORT, C. J. H. *Mezzotints*. New York: G. P. Putnam's Sons, Inc., 1903.

DEWEY, J. *Art as Experience*. New York: G. P. Putnam's Sons, Inc., 1934.

DICKINSON, G. L. *The Greek View of Life*. 7th ed.; Garden City, N. Y.: Doubleday & Co., Inc., 1925.

DOERNER, M. *The Materials of the Artist and Their Use in Painting* (trans. by Eugen Neuhaus). New York: Harcourt, Brace & Co., Inc., 1949.

DUCASSE, C. J. *Art, the Critics, and You*. New York: Piest, 1944.

————. *The Philosophy of Art*. New York: Dial Press, Inc.; Toronto: Longmans, Green & Co., Inc., 1929.

EDMAN, I. *Arts and the Man, an Introduction to Aesthetics*. New York: W. W. Norton & Co., Inc., 1939.

ELIOT, A. *Three Hundred Years of American Painting*. New York: Time, Inc., 1957.

EVANS, J. *Art in Medieval France, 987–1489*. New York: Oxford University Press, 1948.

EVANS, R. M. *An Introduction to Color*. New York: John Wiley & Sons, Inc.; London: Chapman & Hall, Ltd., 1948.

FAULKNER, R., ZIEGFELD, E., and HILL, G. *Art Today*. 3d ed.; New York: Henry Holt & Co., Inc., 1956.

FAURE, E. *The Spirit of the Forms* (trans. by Walter Pach). New York: Harper & Bros., 1930.

FELDSTED, C. J. *Design Fundamentals*. New York: Pitman Pub. Corp., 1950.

FENOLLOSA, E. F. *Epochs of Chinese and Japanese Art*. 2 vols.; New York: Frederick A. Stokes Co., 1913; London: William Heinemann, Ltd., 1921.

FERGUSON, G. *Signs and Symbols in Christian Art*. New York: Oxford University Press, 1954.

FIEDLER, K. *On Judging Works of Visual Art* (trans. by Henry Schaefer-Simmern and Fulmer Mood) . Berkeley: University of California, 1949.

FLACCUS, L. W. *The Spirit and Substance of Art.* 3d ed.; New York: Appleton-Century-Crofts, Inc., 1947.

FLEMING, W. *Art and Ideas.* New York: Henry Holt & Co., Inc., 1955.

FLETCHER, B. *A History of Architecture on the Comparative Method.* New York: Charles Scribner's Sons, 1947.

FOCILLON, H. *The Life of Forms in Art* (trans. by Beecher Hogan and George Kubler) . New Haven: Yale University Press, 1942.

FRY, R. *Cézanne; A Study of His Development.* 2d ed.; London: Hogarth Press, Ltd., 1932.

————. *Characteristics of French Art.* London: Chatto & Windus, Ltd., 1932.

————. *Transformations.* London: Chatto & Windus, Ltd.; New York: Brentano's, 1926.

————. *Vision and Design.* London: Chatto & Windus, Ltd.; New York: Brentano's, 1924.

GARDNER, H. *Art Through the Ages.* 3d ed.; New York: Harcourt, Brace & Co., Inc., 1948.

GEDDES, P. *Cities in Evolution.* London: Williams & Norgate, Ltd., 1915.

GIEDION, S. *Space, Time, and Architecture.* Cambridge: Harvard University Press, 1941.

GLASS, F. J. *Modelling and Sculpture.* New York: Charles Scribner's Sons, 1929.

GOLDSMITH, E. E. *Sacred Symbols in Art.* 2d. ed.; New York: G. P. Putnam's Sons, Inc., 1912.

GOLDWATER, R., and TREVES, M. *Artists on Art, from the XIV to the XX Century.* New York: Pantheon Books, Inc., 1945.

GOMBRICH, E. H. *The Story of Art.* New York: Phaidon Press, Ltd., 1950.

GRAVES, M. *The Art of Color and Design.* New York: McGraw-Hill Book Co., Inc., 1951.

GREELY, W. R. *Essence of Architecture.* New York: D. Van Nostrand Co., Inc., 1927.

GREENE, T. M. *The Arts and the Art of Criticism.* Princeton: Princeton University Press, 1947.

GREENOUGH, H. *Form and Function.* Berkeley: University of California Press, 1947.

GROPIUS, W. *The New Architecture and the Bauhaus.* New York: Museum of Modern Art, 1936.

GROUSSET, R. *The Civilizations of the East* (trans. by C. A. Phillips) . 4 vols.; New York: Alfred A. Knopf, Inc., 1931–1934.

HAGEN, O. *Art Epochs and Their Leaders.* New York: Charles Scribner's Sons, 1927.

HAMLIN, T. *Architecture, An Art for All Men.* New York: Columbia University Press, 1947.

————. *Architecture Through the Ages.* New York: G. P. Putnam's Sons, Inc., 1940.

HAUSER, A. *The Social History of Art* (trans. by Stanley Godman) . 2 vols.; London: Routledge & Kegan Paul, Ltd., 1951.

HEGEL, G. W. F. *The Philosophy of Fine Art* (trans. by F. P. B. Osmaston) . 4 vols.; London: G. G. Bell & Sons, Ltd., 1920.

HEKLER, A. *Greek and Roman Portraits.* London: William Heinemann, Ltd., 1912.

HENRI, R. *The Art Spirit.* Compiled by Margery Ryerson. Philadelphia: J. B. Lippincott Co., 1923.

HILDEBRAND, A. *The Problem of Form in Painting and Sculpture* (trans. by Max Meyer and R. M. Ogden) . New York: Stechert-Hafner, Inc., 1932.

HIND, A. M. *History of Engraving and Etching.* Boston: Houghton Mifflin Co., 1923.

HIRN, Y. *The Origins of Art; a Psychological and Sociological Inquiry.* New York: The Macmillan Co., 1900.

HITCHCOCK, H.-R. *In the Nature of Materials, the Buildings of Frank Lloyd Wright.* New York: Duell, Sloan, & Pearce, Inc., 1942.

HITCHCOCK, H.-R. *Modern Architecture, Romanticism and Reintegration.* New York: Harcourt Brace & Co., Inc., 1929.

HOBHOUSE, C. *1851 and the Crystal Palace.* New York: E. P. Dutton & Co., Inc., 1937.

HOBSON, R. L. *Art of the Chinese Potter from the Han Dynasty to the End of the Ming.* London: Ernest Benn, Ltd., 1923.

HOFFMAN, M. *Sculpture Inside and Out.* New York: W. W. Norton & Co., Inc., 1936.

HOGARTH, W. *The Analysis of Beauty, Written with a View of Fixing the Fluctuating Ideas of Taste.* London: L. Reeve & Co., Ltd., 1810.

HOLMAN, L. A. *The Graphic Processes.* Boston: C. E. Goodspeed & Co., 1929.

HOLMES, C. J. *A Grammar of the Arts.* New York: The Macmillan Co., 1932.

———. *Notes on the Science of Picture-Making.* London: Chatto & Windus, Ltd., 1927.

HOLT, E. *Literary Sources of Art History.* Princeton: Princeton University Press, 1947.

HUDNUT, J. *Architecture and the Spirit of Man.* Cambridge: Harvard University Press, 1949.

———. *Modern Sculpture.* New York: W. W. Norton & Co., Inc., 1929.

HUIZINGA, J. *The Waning of the Middle Ages.* London: Edward Arnold, Ltd., 1924.

IVINS, W. M., JR. *How Prints Look.* New York: Metropolitan Museum of Art, 1943.

JACOBSON, E. *Basic Color.* Chicago: Theobald, 1948.

JAMESON, A. *Sacred and Legendary Art.* 2 vols.; Boston: Houghton Mifflin Co., 1897.

JEANNERET-GRIS, C. E. (LE CORBUSIER). *Toward a New Architecture* (trans. from the 13th French ed. by F. Etchells). London: Rodker, 1931.

KANDINSKY, W. *The Art of Spiritual Harmony* (trans. by M. T. H. Sadler). Boston: Houghton Mifflin Co.; London: Constable & Co., Ltd., 1914.

KEPES, G. *Language of Vision.* Chicago: Theobald, 1944.

KIMBALL, F., and EDGELL, G. H. *A History of Architecture.* New York: Harper & Bros., 1917.

KIMBALL, F. *The Creation of the Rococo.* Philadelphia: Philadelphia Museum of Art, 1943.

KLEE, P. *Pedagogical Sketchbook* (trans. by Sibyl Moholy-Nagy). New York: Frederick A. Praeger, Inc., 1953.

LANGER, S. *Feeling and Form.* New York: Charles Scribner's Sons, 1953.

LAURIE, A. P. *The Painter's Methods and Materials.* Philadelphia: J. B. Lippincott Co., 1926.

———. *The Pigments and Mediums of the Old Masters.* London: Macmillan & Co., Ltd., 1914.

LECOQ DE BOISBAUDRON, H. *The Training of the Memory in Art, and the Education of the Artist* (trans. by L. D. Luard). 2d. ed.; London: Macmillan & Co., Ltd., 1914.

LEDOUX, L. V. *Art of Japan.* New York: Japan Society, 1927.

LESCAZE, W. *On Being an Architect.* New York: G. P. Putnam's Sons, Ltd., 1942.

LETHABY, W. R., and SWAINSON, H. *Church of Santa Sophia, Constantinople; a Study of Byzantine Building.* London: Macmillan & Co., Ltd., 1916.

LODGE, R. *Close of the Middle Ages, 1273–1494.* 5th ed.; London: Rivington; New York: The Macmillan Co., 1923.

LORAN, E. *Cézanne's Compositions.* Berkeley: University of California Press, 1943.

LOWRIE, W. *Monuments of the Early Church.* London: The Macmillan Co., 1923.

LUCKIESCH, M. *Color and Its Application.* 3d ed.; New York: D. Van Nostrand Co., Inc., 1927.

LUMSDEN, E. S. *The Art of Etching.* London: Seeley, Service & Co., Ltd.; Philadelphia: J. B. Lippincott Co., 1925.

McANDREW, J. *What Is Modern Architecture?* New York: Museum of Modern Art, 1942.

McMAHON, A. P. *The Art of Enjoying Art.* New York: McGraw-Hill Book Co., Inc., 1938.

MALRAUX, A. *Le Musée Imaginaire de La Sculpture Mondiale.* 3 vols.; Paris: De La
Pléiade, 1952.

———. *The Psychology of Art* (trans. by Stuart Gilbert) . 3 vols.; New York: Pantheon
Books, Inc., 1949–1950.

———. *The Voices of Silence, Man and His Art* (trans. by Stuart Gilbert) . Garden City,
N. Y.: Doubleday & Co., Inc., 1953.

MARINGER, J., and BANDI, H.-G. *Art in the Ice Age.* In execution of a plan by Hugo
Obermaier. New York: Frederick A. Praeger, Inc., 1953.

MASKELL, A. *Wood Sculpture.* New York: G. P. Putnam's Sons, Inc., 1911.

MATHER, F. J., JR. *A History of Italian Painting.* New York: Henry Holt & Co., Inc.,
1923.

———. *Western European Painting of the Renaissance.* New York: Henry Holt & Co.,
Inc., 1939.

MAYER, R. *The Artist's Handbook of Materials and Techniques.* New York: The Viking
Press, Inc., 1948.

MOHOLY-NAGY, L. *The New Vision* (trans. by D. M. Hoffmann) . New York: W. W.
Norton & Co., Inc., 1938.

MOORE, C. H. *Development and Character of Gothic Architecture.* 2d ed.; New York:
The Macmillan Co., 1904.

MOREAU-VAUTHIER, C. *Technique of Painting.* New York: G. P. Putnam's Sons, Inc.,
1928.

MOREY, C. R. *Christian Art.* New York: Longmans, Green & Co., Inc., 1935.

———. *Early Christian Art.* Princeton: Princeton University Press, 1942.

———. *Mediaeval Art.* New York: W. W. Norton & Co., Inc., 1942.

MOTHERWELL, ROBERT (ed.) . *Documents of Modern Art.* (*Contemporary Sculpture,* C.
Giedion-Welcker, Vol. XII.) New York: George Wittenborn, Inc., 1955.

MUMFORD, L. *Sticks and Stones.* New York: Boni, 1942.

———. *Technics and Civilization.* New York: Harcourt, Brace & Co., Inc., 1931.

———. *The Brown Decades.* New York: Harcourt, Brace & Co., Inc., 1931.

———. *The Condition of Man.* New York: Harcourt, Brace & Co., Inc., 1944.

———. *The Culture of Cities.* New York: Harcourt, Brace & Co., Inc., 1938.

MUNRO, T. *Scientific Method in Aesthetics.* New York: W. W. Norton & Co., Inc., 1928.

MUNSELL, A. H. *A Color Notation.* 5th ed.; Boston: Munsell Color Co., 1919.

MÜNSTERBERG, H. *The Eternal Values.* Boston: Houghton Mifflin Co., 1909.

OGDEN, C. K., RICHARDS, I. A., and WOOD, J. *The Foundation of Aesthetics.* London:
George Allen & Unwin, 1922.

OKAKURA, K. *Ideals of the East.* London: J. John Murray, Ltd., 1905.

———. *The Book of Tea.* New York: Fox, Duffield, 1912.

OLMSTEAD, A. T. *History of Assyria.* New York: Charles Scribner's Sons, 1923.

OZENFANT, A. *Foundation of Art.* New York: Brewer, Warren, & Putnam, 1931.

PANOFSKY, E. *Meaning in the Visual Arts.* Garden City, N. Y.: Doubleday & Co., Inc.,
1955.

———. *Studies in Iconology.* New York: Oxford University Press, 1939.

PARKES, K. *The Art of Carved Sculpture.* 2 vols.; London: Chapman & Hall, Ltd., 1931.

PEPPER, S. C. *Principles of Art Appreciation.* New York: Harcourt, Brace & Co., Inc.,
1949.

———. *The Basis of Criticism in the Arts.* Cambridge: Harvard University Press, 1945.

PEVSNER, N. *An Outline of European Architecture.* Harmondsworth, England: Penguin
Books, Ltd., 1945.

———. *Pioneers of the Modern Movement, from William Morris to Walter Gropius.*
London: Faber & Faber, Ltd., 1936.

PEVSNER, N. *The Englishness of English Art*. New York: Frederick A. Praeger, Inc., 1956.

PFUHL, E. *Masterpieces of Greek Drawing and Painting*. New York: The Macmillan Co., 1926.

PHILLIPS, D. *The Artist Sees Differently*. 2 vols.; New York: E. Weyhe Co., 1931.

————. *The Enchantment of Art, as Part of the Enchantment of Experience*. London: John Lane, The Bodley Head, Ltd., 1914.

PHILLIPS, L. M. *Art and Environment*. New York: Henry Holt & Co., Inc., 1911.

————. *Form and Color*. London: Gerald Duckworth & Co., Ltd., 1925.

POPE, A. *The Language of Drawing and Painting*. Cambridge: Harvard University Press, 1949.

POPE, A. U. *Masterpieces of Persian Art*. New York: The Dryden Press, Inc., 1945.

PORTER, A. K. *Medieval Architecture*. 2 vols.; New Haven: Yale University Press, 1912.

POST, C. R. *A History of European and American Sculpture from the Early Christian Period to the Present Day*. 2 vols.; Cambridge: Harvard University Press; London: Oxford University Press, 1921.

PRALL, D. W. *Aesthetic Analysis*. New York: The Thomas Crowell Co., 1936.

PRENTICE, S. *The Voices of the Cathedral*. New York: William Morrow & Co., Inc., 1938.

RADER, M. *A Modern Book of Esthetics*. New York: Henry Holt & Co., Inc., 1952.

RANK, O. *Art and Artists, Creative Urge and Personality Development* (trans. by C. F. Atkinson). New York: Alfred A. Knopf, Inc., 1932.

RASMUSEN, H. N. *Art Structure*. New York: McGraw-Hill Book Co., Inc., 1950.

RATHBUN, M., and HAYES, B., JR. *A Layman's Guide to Modern Art*. New York: Oxford University Press, 1949.

READ, H. *Anatomy of Art; an Introduction to the Problems of Art and Aesthetics*. New York: Dodd, Mead & Co., Inc., 1932.

————. *Art and Society*. New York: The Macmillan Co., 1937.

————. *Art Now*. New York: Pitman Pub. Corp., 1949.

————. *The Meaning of Art*. Harmondsworth, England: Penguin Books, Ltd., 1949.

REWALD, J. *The History of Impressionism*. New York: Museum of Modern Art, 1946.

RICH, J. *The Materials and Methods of Sculpture*. New York: Oxford University Press, 1947.

RICHARDS, J. M., and MOCK, E. B. *An Introduction to Modern Architecture*. Baltimore: Penguin Books, Inc., 1947.

RICHARDSON, E. P. *The Way of Western Art*. Cambridge: Harvard University Press, 1939.

————. *Painting in America; the Story of 450 Years*. New York: The Thomas Crowell Co., 1956.

RICHTER, G. M. A. *Sculpture and Sculptors of the Greeks*. New Haven: Yale University Press, 1930.

RICHTER, I. A. *Rhythmic Form in Art; an Investigation of the Principles of Composition in the Works of the Great Masters*. London: John Lane, The Bodley Head, Ltd., 1932.

RIVOIRA, G. T. *Roman Architecture and Its Principles of Construction Under the Empire* (trans. by G. M. Rushforth). London: Oxford University Press, 1925.

ROBB, D. M. *The Harper History of Painting; the Occidental Tradition*. New York: Harper & Bros., 1951.

ROBB, D. M., and GARRISON, J. J. *Art in the Western World*. 3d ed.; New York: Harper & Bros., 1953.

RODIN, A. *Art*. Conversations collected by Paul Grell; translated by Mrs. Romely Fedden. Boston: Small, Maynard, 1917.

ROOS, F. J. JR. *An Illustrated Handbook of Art History*. 2d ed., rev.; New York: The Macmillan Co., 1954.

ROSS, D. W. *A Theory of Pure Design*. Boston: Houghton Mifflin Co., 1909.

Ross, D. W. *On Drawing and Painting*. Boston: Houghton Mifflin Co., 1912.
———. *The Painter's Palette*. Boston: Houghton Mifflin Co., 1919.
Rowland, B. *Art in East and West*. Cambridge: Harvard University Press, 1954.
Rowley, G. *Principles of Chinese Painting*. Princeton: Princeton University Press, 1947.
Ruhemann, H., and Kemp, E. M. *The Artist at Work*. Harmondsworth, England: Penguin Books, Ltd., 1951.
Ruskin, J. *Modern Painters*. New York: Merrill & Baker, 1873.
———. *The Seven Lamps of Architecture*. Orpington: Allen, 1880.
Sachs, P. J. *The Pocket Book of Great Drawings*. New York: Pocket Books, Inc., 1951.
———. *Modern Prints and Drawings*. New York: Alfred A. Knopf, Inc., 1954.
Sakanishi, S. *The Spirit of the Brush*. London: J. John Murray, Ltd., 1939.
Sansom, G. B. *Japan, A Short Cultural History*. New York: Appleton-Century-Crofts, Inc., 1943.
Santayana, G. *The Sense of Beauty*. New York: Charles Scribner's Sons, 1896.
Schmeckebier, L. E. *Modern Mexican Painting*. Minneapolis: University of Minnesota Press, 1939.
Scott, G. *The Architecture of Humanism; A Study in the History of Taste*. 2d ed.; New York: Charles Scribner's Sons, 1924.
Sewall, J. E. *A History of Western Art*. New York: Henry Holt & Co., Inc., 1953.
Sirén, O. *Chinese Painting, Leading Masters and Principles*. New York: The Ronald Press Co., 1956.
———. *Leonardo da Vinci, The Artist and the Man*. New Haven: Yale University Press, 1916.
———. *Chinese Sculpture from the Fifth to the Fourteenth Century*. 4 vols.; London: Ernest Benn, Ltd.; New York: Charles Scribner's Sons, 1925.
———. *Essentials in Art*. London: John Lane, The Bodley Head, Ltd., 1920.
Snow, B. E., and Froehlich, H. B. *The Theory and Practice of Color*. New York and Chicago: Prang, 1918.
Spearing, H. G. *The Childhood of Art*. 2 vols.; London: Ernest Benn, Ltd., 1930.
Stites, R. S. *The Arts and Man*. New York: McGraw-Hill Book Co., Inc., 1940.
Struppeck, J. *The Creation of Sculpture*. New York: Henry Holt & Co., Inc., 1952.
Sullivan, L. *Kindergarten Chats and Other Works*. New York: George Wittenborn, Inc., 1947.
———. *The Autobiography of an Idea*. New York: George Wittenborn, Inc., 1947.
Swindler, M. H. *Ancient Painting*. New Haven: Yale University Press, 1929.
Symonds, J. A. *The Life of Michelangelo Buonarroti*. 3d ed.; 2 vols.; New York: Charles Scribner's Sons, 1925.
———. *The Renaissance in Italy*. 7 vols.; London: J. John Murray, Ltd., 1898.
Taine, H. *Lectures on Art*. 2 vols.; New York: Henry Holt & Co., Inc., 1883.
Talbot Rice, D. *Byzantine Art*. New York: Oxford University Press, 1935.
Tarn, W. W. *Hellenistic Civilization*. London: Edward Arnold, Ltd., 1927.
Taylor, H. O. *The Medieval Mind; a History of the Development of Thought and Emotion in the Middle Ages*. 4th ed.; 2 vols.; London: Macmillan & Co., Ltd., 1927.
Teague, W. D. *Design This Day*. New York: Harcourt, Brace & Co., Inc., 1940.
Thompson, D. V. *The Materials of Medieval Painting*. New Haven: Yale University Press, 1936.
———. *The Practice of Tempera Painting*. New Haven: Yale University Press; London: Oxford University Press, 1936.
Thompson, J. W. *The Middle Ages, 300–1500*. 2 vols.; New York: Alfred A. Knopf, Inc., 1931.
Thornburn, J. M. *Art and the Unconscious*. London: Routledge & Kegan Paul, Ltd., 1925.

TOLSTOI, L. N. *What is Art?* (trans. by A. Maude). London: Oxford University Press, 1932.

TOYNBEE, A. J. *A Study of History*. Abridgement by D. C. Somervell. New York and London: Oxford University Press. Vols. I-VI, 1947; Vols. VII-X, 1957.

UPJOHN, E. M., WINGERT, P. S., and MAHLER, J. G. *History of World Art*. New York: Oxford University Press, 1949.

VALENTINER, W. R. *The Origins of Modern Sculpture*. New York: George Wittenborn, Inc., 1946.

VAN GOGH, V. *Vincent Van Gogh, Letters to Émile Bernard*. (ed. and trans. by Douglas Lord). New York: Museum of Modern Art, 1938.

VASARI, G. *The Lives of the Painters, Sculptors, and Architects* (trans. by A. B. Hinds). 4 vols.; London: J. M. Dent & Sons, Ltd.; New York: E. P. Dutton & Co., Inc., 1927.

VENTURI, L. *Four Steps Toward Modern Art*. New York: Columbia University Press, 1956.

———. *History of Art Criticism* (trans. by Charles Marriott). New York: E. P. Dutton & Co., Inc., 1936.

———. *Painting and Painters*. New York: Charles Scribner's Sons, 1935.

WALTERS, H. B. *The Art of the Romans*. New York: The Macmillan Co., 1921.

WARD, C. *Medieval Church Vaulting*. Princeton: Princeton University Press, 1915.

WHISTLER, J. A. McN. *"Ten O'Clock."* Portland, Me.: Mosher, 1920.

WICKISER, R. L. *An Introduction to Art Activities*. New York: Henry Holt & Co., Inc., 1947.

WILENSKI, R. H. *English Painting*. London: Faber & Faber, Ltd., 1933.

———. *French Painting*. Boston: Charles T. Branford Co., 1950.

WÖLFFLIN, H. *Classical Art* (trans. by Peter and Linda Murray). New York: Phaidon Publications, Inc., 1948.

———. *Principles of Art History* (trans. by M. D. Hottinger). 7th ed.; London: G. G. Bell & Sons, Ltd.; New York: Henry Holt & Co., Inc., 1932.

WORRINGER, W. *Form Problems of the Gothic*. New York: Stechert-Hafner, Inc., 1920.

WRIGHT, F. L. *An Autobiography*. New York: Duell, Sloan, & Pearce, 1943.

ZIGROSSER, C. *The Book of Fine Prints*. New York: Crown Publications, 1948.

ZIMMER, H. *Myths and Symbols in Indian Art and Civilization*. New York: Pantheon Books, Inc., 1946.

ZUCKER, P. *Styles in Painting*. New York: The Viking Press, Inc., 1950.

Index

(NOTE: A page number set in italic type indicates an illustration page.)